The Meaning of Freedom of Speech

Recent Titles in
Contributions in American History

Critical Studies in Antebellum Sectionalism: Essays in
American Political and Economic History
Robert R. Russel

Transportation to the Seaboard: The "Communication
Revolution" and American Foreign Policy, 1860–1900
Howard B. Schonberger

Protestants Against Poverty:
Boston's Charities, 1870–1900
Nathan Irvin Huggins

Horace White, Nineteenth Century Liberal
Joseph Logsdon

The New York Abolitionists: A Case Study of
Political Radicalism
Gerald Sorin

The Law of Treason in the United States:
Collected Essays
James Willard Hurst

Labor Organizations in the United States and
Mexico: A History of Their Relations
Harvey A. Levenstein

The Bonus March: An Episode of the Great Depression
Roger Daniels

Family Law and the Poor: Essays by Jacobus tenBroek
Joel F. Handler, Editor

The Butterfly Caste: The Social History of
Pellagra in the South
Elizabeth W. Etheridge

The Meaning of Freedom of Speech

First Amendment Freedoms from Wilson to FDR

Paul L. Murphy

Contributions in American History
Number 15

Greenwood Publishing Company
Westport, Connecticut

Library of Congress Cataloging in Publication Data

Murphy, Paul L   1923–
  The meaning of freedom of speech.

  (Contributions in American history, no. 15)
  Bibliography: p.
  1. Liberty of speech--United States.   I.   Title.
JC599.U5M83   323.44′3′0973   72-133500
ISBN 0-8371-5176-7

Library of Congress Catalog Card Number: 72-133500
ISBN: 0-8371-5176-7

First published in 1972

Greenwood Publishing Company
A Division of Greenwood Press, Inc.
51 Riverside Avenue, Westport, Connecticut 06880

Printed in the United States of America

To the memory of my parents,
Paul and Ruth W. Murphy, two gentle
conservatives dedicated to
decency and dignity in
human relations

Contents

	Acknowledgments	ix
1	Introduction	3
2	The Theory and Practice of Free Speech in American History	11
3	The Crucible Years for Freedom of Speech	23
4	Creating the Instruments of Suppression	38
5	The Attrition of the Right of Free Speech in 1919	59
6	Nadir and Recovery: Free Speech and Guilty Consciences	77
7	The New Consensus: Acceptance and Alienation	101
8	The Quest for Equality Through Free Speech	122
9	The "Firing Line" in the 1920s	133
10	The Quest for Security Through Proper Free Speech	171
11	The Counterassault Against the "Free-Speech Fakers"	184
12	The Depression and Repression of Free Speech	220
13	The Legal Community and the Meaning of Free Expression	248
14	Epilogue	273
	Notes	289
	Note on Sources	377
	Index	385

Acknowledgments

In the depersonalized confines of our frenetic society, it is always gratifying that one subculture remains a helpful, cooperative, sympathetic, and generous refuge—the community of scholars. It is heartening to find people concerned enough about scholarship to go out of their way to assist a researcher, with no thought of personal gain or ultimate recompense. Public acknowledgment is poor payment, but hopefully the opportunity to aid future laborers in the scholarly vineyard may ultimately help to balance the ledger and extend the process.

I am particularly indebted to Oscar and Mary Handlin and other Fellows of the Center for the Study of the History of Liberty in America, especially Sidney Aronson, Peter Coleman, Paul Freund, P. M. G. Harris, the late Mark DeWolfe Howe, Leonard Levy, Gerald Nash, and William Taylor. Academic friends in a dozen states assisted both in tracking down elusive materials and in perceptive criticism. I particularly want to thank George Anderson, Richard Berner, John Blum, Stanley Coben, David B. Davis, Donald Johnson, James Shideler, James M. Smith, Carl Ubbelohde, Albert Ullman, Stephen Ullman, Merle Wells, and Mary E. Young. Colleagues, former colleagues, and students are at once one's sharpest critics and best aids. I benefited in this regard from Clarke Chambers, Ed Gross, Robert Lindsay, William Lockhart, David Montgomery, Fred Morgner, and Ken Smemo. In addition, graduate students in an American Studies seminar afforded insights from which I drew with great profit. The late Norman Thomas and Roger N. Baldwin kindly granted

ix

personal interviews and otherwise answered my queries. So also did a number of correspondents who I fear may have found my questions obscure, but who, nonetheless, took the time to reply to them carefully. The staffs of Widener, Littauer, and the Harvard Law libraries were gracious with their assistance, as were library staff members at the New York Public Library, the Library of Congress, Walter Library, and the Law Library of the University of Minnesota. The John Simon Guggenheim Foundation awarded me a much appreciated fellowship, which made the later research and writing of this work possible. The University of Minnesota Graduate School also extended valuable financial aid.

Finally to my three girls, Helen, Pat, and Karen must go an inadequate accolade for putting up with both me and the project for an inordinately long period. It was they who provided the inspiration, and, in my wife's case, the skillful assistance as well, which made it all seem worth undertaking in the first place.

The Meaning of
Freedom of Speech

1

Introduction

John F. Kennedy, in a widely quoted commencement address at Yale in June 1962 laid heavy emphasis upon the responsibility of each new generation for defining the accepted clichés and value phrases of the American heritage in terms of its own needs and challenges. "As every past generation has had to disenthrall itself from an inheritance of truisms and stereotypes," argued the President, "so in our times we must move on from the reassuring repetition of stale phrases to a new, difficult but essential confrontation with reality."[1] Mr. Kennedy was echoing, in a simplified, and political, way, a familiar proposition once put forward by Alfred North Whitehead:

> The art of free society consists in the maintenance of the symbolic code; and secondly in fearlessness of revision, to secure that the code serves those purposes which satisfy an enlightened reason. Those societies which cannot combine reverence to their symbols with freedom of revision, must ultimately decay either, from anarchy or from the slow atrophy of a life stifled by useless shadow.[2]

The story of freedom of expression in the 1920s is a complex composite of the application of attitudes, premises, and assumptions concerning the liberty of the individual to freedom of speech under explicit, but constantly changing, circumstances. It is a story with many strands, a story of theory and practice, but also a story of the use of an abstract concept to elicit concrete action toward a

3

variety of ends. It calls for the analysis of the attempts of diverse groups and individuals to shape social processes. It is therefore a chapter in the history of both American reform and American resistance to reform, as well as an assessment of the particular value orientation of the American people in the 1920s.

The process of translating and utilizing a basic American shibboleth was certainly not unique to that decade but it did have its own peculiar qualities within it. In America, freedom of speech had been an operational reality largely outside the area of either legal definition or restriction from the adoption of the Bill of Rights until World War I. It was generally accepted as a tradition and a practice, although it had few public guarantees. The need for formal avenues of protection had hardly seemed essential to nineteenth-century Americans; for with the exception of isolated, war-induced crises, such as the old Federalists' move against the "seditionists" of 1798 or Lincoln's acquiescence to Civil War oath makers and loyalty probers, federal abridgment of the First Amendment was negligible. State restrictions on free speech, either directly or subtly, were rarely important enough to raise the question of the need for federal supervision. Private impairment of another's rights, although certainly susceptible to civil action, was considered totally outside the realm of public law. Thus, freedom of speech was treated as a dearly won prize, protected in a symbolic trophy case, but not used from day to day

To this pattern, World War I brought a rude shock, when the federal government restricted many forms of freedom of expression and officials launched a propaganda drive to indoctrinate Americans with the idea that a number of democratic procedures and guarantees had to be sacrificed temporarily to save their way of life. Many states followed with effective restrictions on individual expression; and when federal restraints gradually became inapplicable after the peace, even more states tried to preserve the wartime sanctions and spirit. These moves, resting upon a series of assumptions about the dangers of freedom of expression, were significant for their lack of peacetime precedent as well as for the fact that they met with general acquiescence. The first broad-scale departure from the supposedly sacrosanct American credo of freedom of speech happened with distressingly little protest and with an appalling unconcern for the implications.

Some Americans were not only disturbed by this callous shelving of a basic American value, but they also felt called to counteraction. For them, the 1920s became the crucible years in which freedom of expression had to be rescued and given new meaning and vitality.

The most advanced of this small minority felt an obligation to achieve through all possible channels some functional harmony between the nobility of the concept and its meaningful practice by all elements within American society. This objective required far more than a crusade to remove artificial restrictions or legal impediments. It also entailed an attempt to lessen the gross inequalities of the time on the logical but hard assumption that meaningful freedom accompanied power and that, until depressed individuals had some measure of personal self-determination, civil rights had little significance for them. Responding to the communist goad that "all of the so-called 'Rights' that the workers of this country are supposed to possess are lost at the first attempt to use them,"[3] but also generally accepting the view of many disillusioned Progressives that there were few safe avenues to freedom through positive government, these crusaders staked their hopes on campaigns for social justice led by aroused, articulate, private citizens. The ultimate objective was a new freedom for the individual, who could protect his own liberties from an enhanced position of economic power and status. Freedom of speech, then, became both an end and a means to an end; a meaningful objective, and a device by which to obtain that objective; a way to bring about a workable economic and social democracy; and the ultimate prize which that new democracy would award.

For these Americans, the decade of the 1920s was filled with bitter disappointments and galling frustrations; however, in certain limited and qualified ways, it was also marked by gratifying, if halting and perilous, victories. Progress was made both in convincing the public of the need to preserve certain basic American liberties and to remove concrete personal or legal barriers to the practice of these liberties. Significant in the latter area was the quiet, but steady, movement of the Supreme Court to a new and vitally important definition of First Amendment freedoms in 1931. For the first time in American history the federal government was given the right to intervene, if requested, between the states and their citizens, when governments too rigorously qualified the limits of individual expression.

This study probes the meaning of freedom of speech in the years from the World War I armistice, November 11, 1918, to the inauguration of Franklin D. Roosevelt, March 9, 1933. To determine precisely what that meaning was necessitates the asking of innumerable questions, some moot, some susceptible to answer, some obviously unanswerable, about the people and the times.

The people who callously rejected broad-scale freedom of speech as a practice generally seem to have been the established, conservative, propertied elements of society or those who fully ascribed and aspired to the same goals. Why did the ability of others to express themselves freely suddenly seem to pose a danger? Loss of faith in the power of free discussion led to the belief that free speech for the wrong men would lead to undesirable ends. Did those who accepted that conclusion fear the loss of their power and status as society altered and threatened their formerly acknowledged places? Were these rational fears, given the powerful political, economic, and social sanctions which these people possessed and which the others lacked? Furthermore, those who sought restrictions did not reject the theory of free expression and individual liberty, but, rather, displayed a new vigor in publicly affirming it. Did not the necessity to rationalize this double standard disturb them and those who hawked popularized versions of the new doctrines?

As to those who fought against the denials of free speech or sought to use it as a weapon for attaining some level of meaningful equality for depressed Americans, equally difficult questions arise. Whom did they represent? What motivated them? No doubt some remnants of the old Progressive movement carried on the tradition of social reform and responded to the most immediate challenge to liberalism at that time. Possibly there was instinctive opposition to any effort to suppress free speech. On the other hand, might not they merely have been decent, but irate, men of principle, shocked by the implications of the departure from American ideals which the actions of the repressors represented? To treat such a group monolithically would miss the key point—the divergence of their motives. For with a term as abstract and with as many meanings and images as freedom of speech did, many men might have been defining the term in their own context and seeking its preservation, extension, or redefinition largely to fit their own concepts. Each might have felt freedom of speech related to the fulfillment of his own most pressing social needs.

None of these people, no matter how diverse in motivation, was acting in a vacuum; rather, each was clearly reflecting the times of which he was a part. This raises still further questions. The identifiable trends within society in the 1920s conditioned the behavior of activists on both sides of the free-speech question. Here, the *gemeinschaft-gesellschaft* delineations of the German sociologist Ferdinand Tönnies, concerning the differing internal patterns within a social structure, have relevance in assessing the tensions between various groups in the decade; the studies on value-orientation help explain why the broad concept of freedom of speech was simultaneously worshipped and violated by some and turned into a weapon for social action by others. But how central was the social dislocation and disorganization of the decade to the production of apprehensions concerning deviant behavior?

More concretely, what explicit social tendencies seemed peculiar to the decade? How did the cynicism toward older American values relate to the long-accepted importance of man's ability to discuss his problems in order to find workable solutions? Surely the broad-scale disillusionment with democracy that was evidenced throughout the decade was pertinent. But how significant was the revulsion toward the wartime experience and the concomitant rejection on the part of many Americans of war as a meaningful device for solving the problems of society and of nations? Was the Legionnaire who urged Americanism contests in the school, supported A. Mitchell Palmer, publicly assaulted a pacifist meeting, and, at the same time, participated in a "get out the vote" campaign simply schizophrenic, or did he reflect the general confusion in the decade about "the American way"? His position was no more contradictory than that of the seemingly logical business leader who strongly supported firm governmental intervention to suppress strikes and unpopular speakers, but openly flouted authority and demanded a laissez-faire policy. Or what of the incensed liberal who crusaded for freedom from restraint while advocating an enhanced role for government agencies in guaranteeing individual liberty? The ambivalence of life and of attitudes in the decade made it impossible to pinpoint precisely consistent public values.

And finally, for the historians, there are problems of causation and general implication. Once we understand why free speech was defined in so many different ways by so many different Americans, there remains the problem of explaining the fact that the process of restriction went through several distinct phases of intensity. The issue also has to be treated situation by situation as differing stimuli brought it into focus. And if individual incidents demand analysis, what was the effect of a national incident like the depression? Did it interrupt and divert former practices, attitudes, and behavioral patterns?

The new and formal Supreme Court definition of freedom of speech and press set forth in 1931 did not suddenly open new vistas for individual expression. It was so subtle and unexpected a development as to be beyond popular comprehension and of little contemporary importance. Yet the Court went on from these rulings to build a new wall of protection around First Amendment freedom so that, by the late 1940s, a leading constitutional authority such as Robert E. Cushman could contend that, in the fifteen years prior to the

intensification of the cold war, freedom of speech had never been
so strongly protected and guaranteed at any time in American history.[4]
In fact, 1931 was a major turning point toward a new type of judicial
instrumentalism in civil liberties in which the judiciary came to take
the lead in opening up new federally guaranteed channels to assure
formerly helpless Americans a new opportunity to utilize their consti-
tutionally guaranteed rights. But if 1931 was the quiet and subtle
beachhead of a new era, why did the Supreme Court make this
move at this time? If the Supreme Court followed the election returns,
as Mr. Dooley claimed, what possible voices out of the cacophony
of the 1920s did the Court heed? Why did a Court dominated by
conservatives in a conservative era revolutionize constitutional law
in the civil liberties area?

If a broad general question might be stated which constitutes
the single statement of the problem of this study it might best be
asked in terms of the purpose of meaningful symbols. In that revealing
period piece, *The Encyclopedia of the Social Sciences,* published
in 1933, Harold Laski's essay "Liberty" stated that "the idea of liberty
depends upon the results of the social process at any given time;
and it is against that background that its essential elements require
analysis." The idea of liberty in the 1920s was cast very largely
and most frequently in terms of one of its essential elements, freedom
of expression. This aspect of liberty was one of the major instruments
for the redefinition of fundamental social relationships in the 1920s,
as the question of racial equality was to become in the 1950s and
1960s. An understanding of the reasons will tell us something about
liberty in America, about freedom of expression, and about the American people in the frenetic and contradictory years of the jazz age.

This study, while it concerns itself with a concept which is ultimately definable most precisely in legal terms, is a legal work only
in external ways. Instead of starting with the traditional constitutional
lawyer's assumption that one determines the extent of permissible
freedom of expression which a given society is prepared to tolerate
by reading the main cases of the period, and extrapolating from
them the contemporary public values, it begins from the opposite
vantage point. Assuming that the orientation of judges is a product
not solely of precedents, but also of the values and general milieu
of the times, it seeks to reconstruct that milieu by probing through
the entire spectrum of public opinion on the proper meaning of
free speech and its correct social utilization. Only then does it hold
a constitutional mirror to those values to see how they were reflected
in the behavior of bench and bar.

More specifically, the work begins with the World War I crisis in civil liberties, exploring both the pathology of that crisis and the immediate postwar and red scare periods. In the latter, it delves into the origins of liberal and repressionist antagonisms over the permissible limits of dissent and protest and the proper role of free expression within the society. As repressionist muscle and eventual overkill alarmed even conservatives and normalcy demanded a lessened role for government, and with the utilization of more subtle, informal methods of containing social discontent, it shifts attention to those methods and the leaders and groups who moved to achieve them. But since concerned libertarians were still determined to establish new levels of free expression simultaneously and sought to utilize free speech as an instrument for obtaining social justice and economic democracy, detailed attention is given to numerous representative episodes and confrontations in the decade which kept the free-speech issue before the public and elicited concrete responses to it. Yet the study also acknowledges that the 1920s was not a monolith, but went through changing patterns in which conservatives shifted their apprehensions regarding the true threat to the status quo. With such shifting apprehensions inevitably came demands to suppress differing forms of expression or the pronouncements and advocacy of different groups. Libertarians were then challenged to evolve reasons why the speech of those groups also should have protected status. Finally, the study explores the depression, viewing it as a testing period, which, while punctuated with episodes of direct suppression, nonetheless saw broadening popular acceptance of the socially valuable function of free discussion. It contends that such an acknowledgment, along with a new retrospective reassessment of the previous dozen years, generated a liberalized societal concept of speech which the Supreme Court, after much equivocation, finally embraced as a proper legal one.

The work thus proceeds on different assumptions than did Zechariah Chafee's classic treatise. Chafee, a law professor with a high sense of noblesse oblige and an active contemporary campaigner for public acceptance of Holmes's "clear and present danger" test as the best available guarantee of decency in free-speech matters, was inclined to evaluate the 1920s on a legal scale and accordingly gave the American people low marks for not accepting Holmes's delineation. Although Chafee's legal expertise did not mislead him into the smug belief that wise judicial decisions guarantee an enlightened society, ultimately he was optimistic that proper judicial handling of free speech was the key to the concept's viability.[5] Seldom, if ever, did it occur to him that the orientation of judges themselves was highly relevant to their behavior or that that behavior was a response to contemporary values and public pressures of the day or that judges belonged, accepted, and contributed to a milieu hostile to his own values. Nor could he acknowledge, viewing society from his patrician pinnacle, that a practical, operational definition of free speech could come from below—through the general public's experimentation with it as a practical instrument for achieving concrete social purposes. This study assumes that it could and did during the 1920s and that the Supreme Court, which until the mid-twentieth century was nearly always a phase behind what was going on in the society, did not play the molding role. Rather, it came ultimately to find new legal ways to validate a definition which the public had come to embrace, not out of admiration for Holmes, or even comprehension of his line-drawing, but out of pragmatic experimentation.

In following this approach, the legalities of the problem are deliberately left to one concluding chapter. This does not imply any intention to downgrade the importance of the constitutional aspects of the subject. Rather, it proceeds from the author's convictions that the constitutional historian should not confine himself to the luxury of exploring the rendering of cases and statutes, but should probe those societal factors that shape the law. He should seek to determine why courts and legislative bodies behave as they do and the ways in which they react to public concepts of the proper function and role of the law in differing periods of American history. Only then does legal history have a meaning, for law is a social phenomenon and, as Holmes once contended, is ultimately "the witness and external deposit of our moral life."

2

The Theory and
Practice of Free Speech
in American History

Freedom of speech . . . is only a human ideal and is incapable of exact expression. It is an innate instinctive desire of man for the right of self-expression and for the right to commune freely with his fellow men. This desire is a natural one and hence this freedom is a natural right. . . . It is an essential of organized society and of progress from barbarism to civilization. Without its existence, individuality of man is suppressed. Without the right to acquire and impart information, knowledge becomes static, and subsequent generations can learn nothing from their predecessors.

Giles J. Patterson, *Free
Speech and a Free Press,* 1939

The theory and practice of freedom of speech has adapted the instinctive tendency of rational man to wish to communicate freely with his fellowmen to the conditions and needs of the American situation. Because that situation was, from its inception, one in which man sought to manage his own destiny, freedom, in a functional sense, early was considered essential to the successful operation of society.

Americans slowly but steadily accepted a series of common assumptions about the inherent ability of rational man to manage his own affairs openly. Convinced by Enlightenment thought that diversity of opinion was a guarantee that eternal truths would not be obfuscated by the false authority of custom or by transient prejudice, Americans symbolically contracted with one another to conduct their affairs by free procedures and to abide by the will of the most persuasive.

11

This belief in man and faith in freedom was "the condition precedent to the existence of the American republic."[1] The fact that freedom was fought for as a right in the Revolution elevated it to the status of a "hard-won principle," a prize to be exhibited proudly by future generations as an integral part of the American tradition. In fact, partly as a result of the Revolution, "the values of liberty and equality became institutionalized within America to a greater extent than in any other nation."[2]

A series of problems, however, developed in connection with the proper preservation of the principle in practice. Few Americans at any time doubted that freedom could be restricted when it served no constructive public function; and laws of libel, defamation, conspiracy, slander, and malicious intent fenced the concept with clear legal restraints. The limits of political free speech created the problem area; here contestants found room for controversy. To the patriot concerned primarily with preservation of the state from which freedoms flowed, temporary, and at times even violent, curtailment by an aroused and militant majority was warranted as a means to a desirable end. To the champion of individual liberties, the realization of the principle came only from its consistent and uninterrupted practice, with any modification unjustified.

In its early history, the problem raised the further question of the responsibility of government. During the Revolution, Americans struggled to define their rights in a unique and direct way. The Sons of Liberty, in dealing with those who too freely expressed hostility to the American cause, did not hesitate to use spontaneous strong-armed methods—"that ultimate symbol of the sovereignty of numbers."[3] Their tactics frequently aroused protests from those who considered such methods fraught with threats to a rational society. On the other hand, even the protesters subscribed to and sponsored wartime sedition acts in the various states, feeling that such legislation forestalled speech which might induce the direct action they found distasteful.

The framers of the United States Constitution fell between the two schools. Their fear of direct democracy, the path to anarchy and destruction, led them to inveigh openly against the tyranny of the majority, but their concern was equally strong against state-prescribed programs for coercing individual behavior. Thus, George Mason, at the Constitutional Convention, although solicitous for the rights of citizens, worried about their relations to the federal government. He admitted "that we had been too democratic," but feared lest "we s[houl]d incautiously run into the opposite extreme."[4]

The answer had to lie elsewhere, as witness the omission of any freedom of speech provisions in the original document. The answer was found in a system that institutionalized and constructively channeled the conflicts among opposing interest groups in society. This in turn presupposed an open system of free discussion, but conceived of it as both a vital element for the working of the system as well as an end which the system could and should evolve. Or, as James Madison wrote in *The Federalist*, Number 51: "In a free government the security for civil rights must be the same as that for religious rights. It consists in the one case in the multiplicity of interests, and in the other in the multiplicity of sects. The degree of security in both cases will depend on the number of interests and sects."[5] The protection of freedom of speech thus rested on diffusion of the potential power to suppress opposing views through the creation of some sort of countervailing balance and certainly assumed the absence of centralized interference with the process.

A recent study has raised doubts about the sincerity of the founding fathers' devotion to the principle." The study contends that no concrete attempt was made at the Convention or in the Bill of Rights to modify explicitly the common law proscriptions on seditious libel, a standing device for curtailment of criticism of government.[7] The existence of a variety of state common law prosecutions indicated that the steady curtailment of freedom of expression was an accepted reality. Critics have raised serious questions concerning the implications drawn from this evidence.[8] There was almost certainly a wide degree of freedom of expression in colonial and early national America. Granting the existence of the narrow common law definition of seditious libel, it was nevertheless true that "the mere fact that people were willing to run the risk of prosecution for uttering unpopular opinions suggests that there was a 'popular' concept of liberty of expression, no matter how unarticulated in terms of a theoretical definition, which clashed with the legal definition."[9]

Whichever side is correct, neither denies that the First Amendment to the Constitution at least institutionalized the presumption that Americans proposed to conduct their public affairs on the basis of free discussion. Enunciation of these substantive rights gave constitutional sanction to the principle of freedom of expression and made it possible for future generations to utilize the concept when they wished to establish more explicit practices and processes. This development was not long in coming and evolved rapidly when the Alien and Sedition Act crisis produced a pressing need for it.[10]

As Americans after 1815 settled into a stable domestic world, their attitudes and actions demonstrated the value they placed upon freedom of expression. For well over a hundred years, they continued to treat the explicit First Amendment guarantee as a presumption. Their federal government made no move to enact the sort of legislation the amendment proscribed, so that court cases and legal definition were unnecessary. Their state constitutions, unlike Pennsylvania's of 1776 (which had designated freedom of speech as a "right"), generally proscribed only legislation which might limit the practice.[11] The paucity of cases which required judges to explicitly define the extent of permissible expression implied that the controlling forces over dangerous words were those mechanisms within an open society that ensured that improper concepts would fail before convincingly expressed truths.

Americans in the middle period of the 1830s and 1840s placed a high priority upon the power of sheer communication. The oratory of a Daniel Webster or a Henry Clay had the power to convince Supreme Court justices and backwoods constituents alike. Hell-fire religion or sophisticated theological theorizing was best propagated by the words of the revivalist preacher, or the lecturing transcendentalist. Oral persuasion was the medium for reform movements from temperance and women's rights to abolitionism and Fourierism. "So long as a man was confident that the truth of his own doctrines could not fail of acceptance, as soon as they won sufficient circulation, he would not fear diversity of opinion or even the freedom of others to propagate patent falsehoods."[12]

Josiah Warren, the American forerunner of Proudhon and Marx, published a weekly anarchist newspaper, the *Peaceful Revolutionist,* and held meetings in which his unorthodox ideas about everything from education to the futility of capitalist economics were discussed, drawing only occasional murmurs of public protest.[13] Robert Dale Owen, freethinking son of the patron of the New Harmony experiment, and Frances Wright, brilliant champion of a dozen unpopular causes ranging from black equality to anticlericalism, were absorbed by the tolerant spirit of their day.

Yet subtle restrictions on complete freedom of expression stemmed from the assumptions and values of the society. The theory that free discussion by free men was salutary to truth raised the question of who was a free man. In nineteenth-century America, the answer was one who was master of his own destiny, a man of some substance. As Daniel Webster once put it: "Property . . . is the fund out of which the means of protecting life and liberty are usually furnished. We have no experience that teaches us, that any other rights are safe, where property is not safe."[14] John C. Calhoun put it even more directly: "Liberty, equality and freedom are all in a sense dependent on the ownership of property." Or, as certain twentieth-century libertarians liked to remind the public, "those who have power have civil rights."

This, however, implied two basic and converse assumptions. Those who did not have power, being without its corollary, property, were to confine their activities to gaining a place within the system. For as Mark Twain remarked: "The American people enjoy three great blessings—free speech, free press and the good sense not to use either."[15] If, however, they unwisely insisted upon speaking out prematurely, they were to do so openly so that their concepts could quickly be rebutted.

Hence, even in the ebullient middle period, certain types of expression elicited censorship by either formal restraint or informal pressures. Americans drew the line when the value of freedom of expression seemed outweighed by the danger to more essential values. The fundamental sanctity of the family, of the essentially Christian establishment, and of the Union were shielded from expression which might undermine them. The story of Mormon persecution and expulsion was frequently appalling. When freedom of conscience led to the advocacy or defense of actions which a popular majority could not sanction, suppression followed.

Restrictions on those who, by speech as well as action, endangered the order found concrete expression as abolitionist strength and raucousness alarmed the South. "To retain political and economic control of the South, the slaveholders felt it necessary that no deep-seated criticism of slavery be tolerated."[16] Every southern state except Kentucky passed laws authorizing public control of speech, press, and discussion, and Andrew Jackson demanded federal censorship of abolitionist literature.

Yet even here a tolerance factor was present. The first application of any of these laws, the arrest in 1839 of Lysander Barrett on a charge of distributing "incendiary publications" in violation of a Virginia statute of 1836, led to acquittal.[17] And in subsequent cases the record of conviction was minimal.[18] Jackson's censorship law, which failed to pass, drew fire from abolitionists and southerners alike. Anti-Slavery Society leaders defiantly told the President, "We never intend to surrender the liberty of speech, or of press, or of conscience—blessings we have inherited from our fathers, and which we mean, so far as we are able, to transmit unimpaired to our children."[19] Only with the emergence of a younger generation of southern judges in the 1850s were legal restrictions formally enforced, although the compelling pressure of public disapprobation was felt early.

Anti-Mason, anti-Mormon, and anti-Catholic crusades by a variety of nativist groups sought less to curtail free expression of supposed enemies than to force them to live by the American norms of an open society. All patriotic participants were to lay their ideas open to the cleansing currents of public opinion. These groups operated in secrecy, and their leaders deluded the membership so that their capacity for weighing true doctrine was blunted. Hence, in order for truth to prevail, it was necessary to break down isolation and uniqueness and force their ideas into the forum where they could be sifted. One end, then, of such assaults on suspect autonomous groups was the preservation of liberty. Those who did not play by the accepted free-speech code surrendered the right to play by their own.

In the realm of less hortatory and more informal forms of communication, especially in relation to coexistence within a stable nineteenth-century community, certain patterns regarding the permissibility of free expression emerge. Deviation in personal beliefs and their expression was sanctioned for those orthodox in their personal life, and, conversely, deviation in personal life was possible by those orthodox as to beliefs. But deviation in both by the same individual could not be tolerated. Certainly the ideas of Ralph Waldo Emerson were startling, as were those of the freethinking agnostic, Robert Ingersoll. Yet Emerson's personal life represented the height of nineteenth-century respectability, and Ingersoll frequently partook at the tables of the rich. The Reverend Henry Ward Beecher, whose ideas were certainly orthodox, was allowed a considerable degree of deviation in his personal morals. Yet the Mormon or Shaker leader who was religiously, politically, and morally unorthodox could not be assimilated by the average community with equanimity. He was too great a threat to the existing order and to its value orientation. His freedom was the freedom to withdraw from the immediate society and either live with those of his kind in isolated communities or seek the anonymity of the city, a freedom which D. H. Lawrence once categorized as unreal:

> Men are free when they are in a living homeland, not when they are straying and breaking away. Men are free when they are obeying some deep inward voice of religious belief. Obeying from within. Men are free when they belong to a living, organic, believing community, active in fulfilling some unfulfilled, perhaps unrealized purpose. Not when they are escaping to some wild west.[20]

The inability of such deviants to attain meaningful freedom within organized society, however, must neither be judged by extreme examples, nor measured by too rigid formulas. Accommodation was possible to a point. Only beyond a certain threshold did sanctions become necessary. The mode and form of communication of the times is relevant. People of similar economic and social class status, accepting similar assumptions concerning the world, hardly found communication with others of their own kind a source of great anxiety. Communication between members of different economic and social classes was less frequent and more formal, with permissible subjects limited by fairly rigid taboos. And even when subjects of common interest were discussed, differing assumptions and language often led to incomprehensible chatter instead of ardent idea-swapping.

Such obstacles to the ability to persuade through verbal advocacy lessened the necessity for formal repression. And life in the average nineteenth-century smaller community was often sufficiently colorless so that even when ideas were unorthodox enough to startle, they frequently added some spice to the dreary daily routine. Further, informal ways of reducing the volume existed, short of enforced removal; social ostracism and economic pressure often made poor loud citizens, good quiet ones. The "fatalism of the multitude" could, with "neither legal nor moral compulsion," dispose "a minority to submit without the need of a command."[21] "Moving on" became essential when the informal pressures had not done their work, and the deviant's continued presence was too disrupting to be accommodated.

The process for implementing such an informal but firm consensus of the community in the laissez-faire society of nineteenth-century America was usually highly effective. The righteous vengeance of a free people had to be appeased and could be casually rationalized. Locally elected law enforcement officials had little trouble translating a wide variety of prohibitory statutes to apply to recalcitrants. "Disturbing the peace" was a term that encompassed a wide variety of actions and words and, if the community tacitly approved, the test of vagrancy could be left to the discretion of the enforcing official. In such instances, locally elected or sanctioned judges and jurors, bound informally by a predetermined consensus, rarely raised fine points. This often proved to be equally true when sanctions were imposed by private organizations, whether they were hastily organized vigilante groups, well-established societies, such as the American Protective Association or the Ku Klux Klan, or imported professionals such as Pinkertons of later years.[22] Hence, the good old days, to which civil libertarians of the 1920s pointed, when "the old notion of freedom of agitation as a safety valve of the public order persisted even in conservative minds," existed far more as a useful frame of reference for a later repressive day than as a functional reality.[23]

The first concerted legal effort against any identifiable minority for excess expression came at about the turn of the century against various anarchist groups. American anarchism, because of its over-riding emphasis on individuality, tended to attract more irresolute egotists than most other radical movements. Most American anarchists derived common philosophic inspiration from the peaceful theories of Kropotkin. In his writings, violence never assumed the overriding importance that it assumed in the works of Bakunin. A few American anarchists in the 1870s and 1880s, especially the German fanatic Johann Most and his followers, temporarily sidetracked the movement, unfurling "the black flag of assassination and terror."[24] The Haymarket Affair of 1886 permanently identified anarchism with bomb-throwing and violence. Ironically, however, its effect on the anarchist movement was to confine activity to peaceful agitation and persuasion. This trend interested other malcontents in the discussion and exploration of a widespread spectrum of revolutionary and radical theories.

But despite the movement's actual orientation, Haymarket and the later assassinations of President Carnot of France in 1894 and President McKinley in 1901 brought demands for formal governmental suppression in the United States. In 1902, the New York legislature passed a law imposing rigid penalties upon the advocacy of anarchistic principles and the publication and distribution of anarchistic literature. And in the following year, Congress enacted an immigration act banning alien anarchists from the United States and prohibiting their naturalization. Clearly the product of fear of radicalism, the measure blandly accepted the assumption that radicalism had a clear tie with immigrants and thus provided further fuel to smouldering nativism. Further, the legislation symbolized "a real loss of nerve and faith in the virtue of freedom," despite the fact that it applied to a minute fraction of the American population.[25]

To the middle-class, reform-minded progressive American, freedom of expression did not rank high in the hierarchy of values.[26] He was certainly not suffering from denial of freedom of speech, nor, from his vantage point, was this one of the serious defects in society. Dubious organizations, ranging from the ruthless trusts and the un-scrupulous city machines to the labor unions, destroyed men's freedom by undermining individuality and destroying the ability to attain personal fulfillment and self-determination. But a free-speech context could not be attributed to Progressive goals and idealism.

Progressive techniques for restoring economic, and hence personal, individualism lay largely in special forms of social control, not in problem-solving by the lone individual or the aroused masses. Oppression sprang from too much liberty, the tyranny of mass democracy, and the lack of firm public control. Hence positive, intelligently led group social action—the harnessing of a socially useful privilege—which, with its "mastery" could reconstruct a more open society, was the focus. Liberty was to come from inequality. The enlightened leadership of those who had the right vision would create a society from which would flow the freedoms and opportunities which a drifting, ill-constructed order had not permitted.

Thus, the Progressives may have been trying to create a system of social interaction whereby a higher degree of individual liberty could eventually be realized. Yet freedom on their terms and with their definitions was, ironically, often arrived at through censorship, quashing of dissent, the superimposing of moral, middle-class values on all, and the disapproval and virtual exclusion of the ideas or wants of the deviant who wished to operate either in his own context or seek ends mildly divergent from the approved consensus.[27] Thus, freedom of expression to the average Progressive was viewed as an eventual prize which could be enjoyed once the type of society he conceived of as good was recreated and the deserving individual placed in the right relationship to it. Excessive and critical freedom of speech bore hostile scrutiny, unless, as with the muckrakers, it served as an instrument by which people could acquaint themselves with the necessity for meeting the pressing social problems of the day. Freedom of expression to deny or reject these social plans could scarcely be tolerated. Freedom was to be restored through positive social control, which almost inevitably implied reliance on legislation and governmental intervention. These assumptions precluded the possibility that any private organization of progressive-minded citizens would focus its energies solely upon the preservation of civil liberties.

Nor would the opponents of progressivism do so. To the conservative business leader, freedom of speech was of little immediate concern. Having power, he had no problem unless it was from the Progressives themselves, who were seeking to curtail his rights. Yet there were individuals for whom freedom of speech was extremely meaningful, individuals who lacked economic power and the paternalistic motivations of the Progressives to legislate a moral order. Anarchists such as Emma Goldman, Alexander Berkman, and Benjamin Tucker, free spirits such as Margaret Sanger, Lincoln Steffens, and Floyd Dell, and legalists such as Attorney Gilbert E. Roe and the literarily verbose, but generally reclusive, Theodore Schroeder, climaxed a general campaign for uninhibited individuality by supporting the organization of a Free Speech League in 1913.[28]

Such Americans clearly considered free speech primarily as an attribute of fierce personal independence with which society had no right to tamper. The individual should be free to pursue his own special interests even if they contained antisocial manifestations.

The good society to them was one free from the strangling inhibitions which the Progressives felt essential. Theodore Schroeder, when called to testify before the Industrial Relations Committee of the Senate in 1914, candidly stated: "we have less conceded and protected freedom of speech and of the press in the United States than in any country in the world at any time in the history of the world."[29] And when asked to explain precisely what he meant by free speech, he stated categorically that "[it] means that no man should be punished for any expression of opinion on any subject so long as the consequence of that speech is nothing but the creation of a state of mind in someone else."[30]

Schroeder went on to denounce the censorship of books and plays, the closing of the mails to "questionable" material, the curtailment of discussion of planned parenthood, and the denial of the public podium to anarchists. His totally permissive view of slander and libel was curiously similar to that of Justice Black a half century later.[31] But Schroeder and the Free Speech League derived little support from the economically depressed classes to whom progressive paternalism had little appeal.

Schroeder and his cohorts were remnants of nineteenth-century liberal thought. Optimistic individualists themselves, they believed that man's basic problem was unwarranted restraint. Freeing the individual was an end in itself. Schroeder had little concept of the need for conditions of equality under which individuality could be meaningful. He saw no necessity for economically underwritten power to protect the free speech of people with dependent status. Nor did he have faith in working through organizations that subjected members to group leadership and policies.[32] Freedom of speech was, for Schroeder, a pristine concept for which few people seeking economic equality or social justice could work up much enthusiasm.

Other groups, however, quickly saw the possibility of using certain Progressive principles, goals, or techniques for their own ends. The Socialists and the Industrial Workers of the World (IWW) operated on the Progressive premise that society could be altered by properly managed group action. Their spirit was more Populist than Progressive, however. The Socialists called on the depressed to take over the instrumentalities of the state, hopefully by popular election, and looked to the subsequent restructuring of society by well-organized groups of militant workingmen. The IWW wished the workers, organized as a class, to take "possession of the earth and the machinery of production and to abolish the wage system."[33]

Both groups saw a clear utilitarian function for freedom of speech in their overall plans. For the Socialists, it was the more traditional one of affording an avenue for propagandizing and education. For the leaders of the IWW, however, it provided a useful, if somewhat devious, instrument for advancing their cause. The Wobblies began to use the "free-speech fight," which became one of their standard techniques, in a number of battles in 1908 and 1909.[34] Hampered by a variety of local ordinances and by the traditional tendency of public officials to enforce the law on their own terms, the Wobblies, much like the black militants of the 1960s, set out to defy and thereby test arbitrary restraints in the name of free speech. "The same tactics were pursued in nearly every instance—a policy of sullen non-resistance on the part of the I.W.W. and wholesale jailing by the authorities."[35] The effectiveness of the technique, however, was undeniable. Suppression had the same effect "as would an effort to smother an active volcano." The ideas got "expressed anyhow—and more bitterly, with the added circumstance that those who tried to do the smothering were burned."[36]

Thus, between 1908 and 1917, free speech became an instrument for possible martyrdom for the cause of economic justice and emancipation of the workers, with the technique used vigorously in cities from San Diego and Spokane to New Bedford, Massachusetts, and Paterson, New Jersey.[37] Wobbly leaders were clever students of the American psyche. For whether Americans adhered to the practice or not, they honored free speech as a symbolic portion of their tradition. British denial of this precious freedom was one of the ancient tyrannies against which American heroes had fought and died at Lexington, Bunker Hill, and Yorktown. Free speech was part of the Bill of Rights of the Constitution, placed there by the infinite wisdom of the founding fathers. The association of radical objectives with freedom of expression was shocking to both Progressives and conservatives. This concept of free speech was unprecedented and inherently dangerous, difficult to attack wrapped as it was in the American flag of First Amendment ideals and rhetoric. Furthermore, some naive Americans were actually nibbling at this clever bait.[38] This was hardly, to quote the editor of the Progressive magazine, *The Survey*, "playing the game respectably."[39] The general audacity of people who rejected the opportunities open to anyone willing to work within the system was outrageous ingratitude. Yet it took wartime exigencies to provide the rationale for massive national retaliation.

The story of freedom of speech during the World War I period is a dreary and depressing tale of repression, "witch-hunting," and the steady violation of individual liberties. Freedom of expression was one of the early casualties of the war. Woodrow Wilson's prediction, "once lead this people into war and they'll forget there ever was such a thing as tolerance," was clairvoyant, as the government quickly set out to turn it into official policy and succeeded frighteningly well.[40] Every element of American public opinion mobilized behind "my country, right or wrong," dissent was virtually forbidden, democracy at home was suspended so that it could be made safe abroad, while impressionable children were educated in Hun atrocities or spent their time working in liberty loan, Red Cross, war-saving stamp or YMCA campaigns. It was not difficult to channel an aroused nation's wrath against earlier dissenters—a development made easier by the fact that many IWWs and Socialists stood out boldly against the war from the start.

The Espionage Act of 1917, while ostensibly a measure to strike at illegal domestic interference with the war effort, was used to stamp out criticism of the war. Its subsequent 1918 amendment, the Sedition Act, was a less subtle device. Passed by the pressure of western senators and modeled after a Montana–IWW statute, its purpose was to undercut the performance and advocacy of undesirable activity, its clear implication being that people who utilized speech in an attempt to gain improper ends had to be restricted.[41] And with the subsequent federal prosecution of 184 members of the IWW in 1918 and 1919, to say nothing of a crackdown on Socialists, German-Americans, conscientious objectors, and Non-Partisan Leaguers, the war's end found political prisoners in a variety of American jails and prisions.[42]

In more abstract terms, however, the sharp governmental suppression of freedom of expression was an abrupt break in the assumptions that had surrounded that concept throughout American history. Federal repressive legislation, with the exception of the Alien and Sedition Act episode of 1798, had been almost nonexistent. Quickly, and with little protest, it became the instrument of a worried President and Congress for wartime social control.[43] Security eclipsed liberty, yet the rank and file of Americans accepted this massive violation of a previously unchallenged concept with equanimity.

The wartime situation created abnormal pressures and was hardly a fair test of the American people's devotion to first principles. The real test of the vitality of the concept of free speech would depend upon its postwar future. Had the wartime departure permanently undermined the age-old presumption that Americans could and should conduct their public affairs on the basis of free discussion? Could there be a restoration of the practice and the philosophical premises which had previously underpinned the concept? What, in light of prewar practice and wartime qualification, would freedom of speech mean and constitute in a postwar world? Controversy over the answers to those questions agitated many Americans in the years between the Armistice and the inauguration of Franklin D. Roosevelt.

3

The Crucible Years
for Freedom of
Speech

The members of the press were patriotic. They laid on the altar of patriotism the liberties of the press. They laid on the altar your liberties. They laid on the altar free speech and the constitutional right to speak. . . . We are going to make a very earnest endeavor to win back some of the constitutional rights of American citizenship. We hope to re-constitutionalize our courts. We hope to make our Constitution and our courts defenders, not of the special privilege and property alone, but defenders of the rights of human beings.

> Gilson Gardner,
> the Scripps Editorial Board,
> An address at the Reconstruction
> Conference of the National
> Popular Government League,
> January 11, 1919

If we as a free people are to retain unhampered our prized privilege of free speech, we must heartily encourage every reasonable effort to close the mouths of those who habitually abuse the privilege. There have been a number of people in our midst whose rantings have about convinced the people that free speech is a dangerous liberty. If the privilege is to be saved from destruction we must see to it that its sanctity is preserved.

> Editorial, *Tulsa*
> (Oklahoma) *Daily World*,
> February 16, 1919

The postwar future of freedom of speech rested largely upon the presumptions and values of the group that shaped the public policies and intellectual climate of post-Armistice America. But until the leisurely but firm ascendency of Harding normalcy in 1921, which institutionalized a conservative business-oriented consensus, there was vigorous and often vicious jockeying for control. Numerous elements saw in the war's end an opportunity for pushing through their own form of reconstruction, which they defined in terms of their own self-interest.

The war had gone far to foster such a variety of hopes and expectations, for, like the peace, it had meant many things to many people. The crisis years accelerated socioeconomic change and aroused strong passions either to capitalize upon the ruptures in a previously stable situation or to confine and restrict them. In fact, much of the wartime domestic maneuvering was aimed at establishing a better position in which to start out the inevitable postwar showdown.

But the war did not divide liberals from conservatives on the question of preservation or rejection of government controls. Conservative business groups looked forward to a further escape from a variety of Progressive restraints which had softened in the face of industry's vital role in the struggle. They also hoped to preserve and extend certain advanced wartime techniques in management, technology, and general efficiency. And they were equally anxious to preserve, if not extend, restrictions upon radicals. At the same time, they were fully as interested in undoing certain of the policies favorable to labor which wartime exigencies had demanded.

Liberals and radicals, on the other hand, were fully as anxious to terminate the restrictions on individual rights and such inhibitions as labor's wartime "no strike" pledge. Attorney Gilbert E. Roe, before the Civic Club of New York in early December 1918, took Woodrow Wilson to task for taking the harness off business with the armistice but doing nothing about "taking the halter off from free speech."[1] Yet, imbued with the American concept of inevitable progress, they looked forward to preserving and extending the same economic gains for labor that business opposed and sought to enhance programs for social justice which the war years had brought close to realization.

Certain small but well-defined groups, such as the IWW and the Socialists, sought to capitalize upon wartime tendencies to realize their objectives. They wished to cast their intensified wartime persecution as martyrdom in the name of freedom and justice for the working class, hoping, through renewed forms of civil disobedience, to gain new adherents.

Other groups responded in divergent ways. A substantial element of as yet undisillusioned devotees of the noble ideals of the Wilson administration sought to recast progressivism as democracy through social control on the world sphere, through the League of Nations, or, in the domestic area, through prohibition or woman suffrage. These people still were convinced of the viability of elevating society through continued sublimation of individuality to broad social needs.

For conservative idealists, from Nicholas Murray Butler to William Howard Taft, from Irving Babbitt to the National Association of Manufacturer's vocal counsel, James A. Emery, reconstruction meant as rapid a return as possible to laissez-faire individualism and hopefully an end to political and economic experimentation, to say nothing of the curtailment of various new, puzzling, and disturbing tendencies in thought and culture which misguided iconoclasts had deviously injected into American life.

Freedom of speech was an essential aspect of the postwar ambitions of virtually every group wishing to advance specific programs and policies, for its meaning was to be a central aspect of the direct skirmishing among antagonistic groups and for the campaign to attract supporters. Free speech, both as a concept and practice, became a shorthand symbol which each side used as an instrument to secure its goals. All contestants proclaimed strong devotion to the principle and sought its preservation. Each obviously conceived of it in a frame of reference best suited to fit its own needs. Thus, the meaning given the concept was a useful key to the ambitions of various groups struggling for immediate power and seeking to define the symbols of democracy so as to make best use of them for an indefinite future period.

Not all Americans were concerned with the future of freedom of speech following World War I. Those consciously involved with the question constituted a small minority. Yet this minority was highly cognizant of the fact that to prevail it had to rally a sizable number of otherwise impassive Americans behind its view of free speech and convince them that such policies were advantageous to both the individual and the nation.

The activist-repressionists included business leaders, employers, and entrepreneurs—in general, propertied men with a stake in society and in the preservation of its hierarchy of economic authority and social control. Translated into explicit desires, this meant rapid economic reconversion; reducing, with a minimum of public criticism, excessively high wartime wages; undermining union strength through a vigorous nationwide open-shop campaign and the revival of the labor injunction; and a return to a minimum of governmental interference in the management and use of property. The system which these people were convinced was right for America was an open one which afforded individuals the liberty to travel as fast as individual abilities permitted toward the personal ownership of property and its unhindered use.[2] Within the present system any man of talent could attain ends which, Nicholas Murray Butler told a Columbia University audience in October 1919, contained the attributes of liberty and were "an essential condition of social and political progress."[3]

People of this view were apprehensive about militant minority groups crying out at maladjustments which conservatives or progressives had failed to ameliorate. Such malcontents were simply people who did not want to play by the rules, incompetents who wanted something for nothing. It was necessary to silence this unwarranted criticism, or, at the least, to discredit its advocates by assailing their foreign philosophies and subversive activities so that they would fail in their plans. Hence, it was natural to portray past labor violence, strikes, mob action, demonstrations, free-speech fights, and clashes with authority as the fruits of the radical doctrines of revolutionary groups rather than as the upshot of grave social and economic evils. The public called for the postwar curtailment of such activities and the constant surveillance of those who advocated them. The economic and social problems of the immediate postwar period were best treated by silencing troublemakers.

Further, it was essential to warn those misguided and gullible liberals of the error of their ways, and, if they persisted in assailing the shortcomings of the system, it was necessary to discredit them by connecting them in the public mind with the radicals themselves. Indicative of proper needs and the means of attaining them was the position of the editor of the *Minnesota Banker* who told open-shop advocates that the best road to sucess was to "eliminate" the radical, closed-shop wing of the labor movement by associating it with disruptive lockouts and disastrous strikes.[4]

The need then was for the creation of a consensus so that unwarranted and raucous protest would be quietly and automatically suppressed or discredited and its purveyors checked. But this necessitated a sufficiently compelling set of rationalizations about free speech to draw a substantial element of the population behind such restraint.

Ideally, the activist-repressionists favored a restoration of the old nineteenth-century system of informal and private sanctions, whereby personal and quiet proscription took care of dissidents at the local level. Yet they no longer fully trusted such sanctions. Society was becoming more complex, and it was no longer possible to maintain surveillance over a local deviate. Formal controls were now needed to augment informal ones. Despite generally laissez-faire views about the positive role of government, the activist-repressionists were willing to acknowledge the utility of certain forms of legislation and public regulation, such as those the Wilson government had utilized on a national scale during the war years.[5] They demanded new devices to curtail freedom of expression by insisting that this was the only way to return to old-fashioned freedom of speech. Conservatives felt the need to forestall quickly and positively any renewal of the use of free speech by militant radical groups as a wedge for advanced programs of social and economic change.

The free-speech line of the activist-repressionists was then an interesting amalgam of the need to preserve democratic ideals and the need for practical restrictions on them. Every American has the privilege of free speech, but "liberty is not license," became an almost ritualistically parroted statement. James A. Emery told the Annual Convention of the NAM in 1920 that there was "danger in restricting liberty, but not in controlling license. . . . Every form of restriction exercised by government," he contended, "rests upon the necessity of protecting the public welfare and securing the equal freedom of all. Liberty without order is fire on the floor; liberty with order is fire in the hearth."[6] Drawing upon the acknowledged truism that there were clear social and ethical limits to free speech, its expounders deliberately confused nonpolitical abuse with the acknowledged right to fair political comment. They hoped thereby to curtail unpalatable or dangerous criticism. When free discussion led to the advocacy of improper social, economic, and political ends, reasonable repression of its advocates was not an unwarranted restriction on free expression. Thus President Alton B. Parker of the business-oriented National Civic Federation, an organization which had publicly stated during the war that only anarchists or traitors opposed such limitations, cautioned the membership at the 1920 annual meeting against "uninformed" and "mistaken" advocates of full free speech.[7] Referring especially to a public statement by two dozen clergymen condemning a proposed federal sedition law as "threatening the primary rights of free speech, free press, and peaceable assembly," Parker maintained that such a position was as misguided as "the notion of the 'Reds,' of the anarchists, and of the I.W.W. that they have a right to stand up and say whatever they choose, that it is their privilege to advocate on the stump the overthrow of the Government by force."[8] Parker carefully and judiciously documented this view by citing various legal opinions. But Ralph Easley probably came closer to the general attitude of the membership when shortly thereafter he issued a pamphlet, through the body's Department on the Study of Revolutionary Movements entitled, "Free Speech, a Nuisance."

There were more subtle appeals in the repressionist rationale. Their free-speech position was solicitously paternalistic and drew on ancient American fears of the demagogue. The innocent pawn, induced to strike and engage in violent activities, was not really to blame for such disturbances. Sinister advocates tricked the simple workingman into such action with deceitful talk and writings. The criminals were not the poor dupes who committed the acts, but the agitators who inspired them. Reasonable and firm repression would, in the end, be a great benefit to both honest, but misguided, workingmen and the nation at large. By joining a radical organization or a labor union, the workman sublimated himself to group leadership and policies which he could not control, and thereby surrendered his liberty and the rights of self-determination and self-expression. The misguided laborers had to be freed from the radicals if they ever were to achieve any real individuality, if they ever expected to operate within the American success ethic.

It was also frequently argued that "reasonable" suppression was necessary to provide a secure and stable society. A large proportion of people who believed in the existing economic and social order disliked attacks on established institutions and tradition. There was, therefore, calculated logic in arguing that silencing critics of the system would ease the public mind and bring renewed confidence in American institutions and the general status quo. "We ought to organize and fight, with all legitimate means in our power," responded a New York attorney in answer to a National Civic Federation questionnaire on how best to deal with the radical challenge, "all propaganda under whatsoever name, by whomsoever conducted and howsoever carried on . . . which seeks to obscure the fact that economic conditions in this country are about the best in the world and difficult to improve."[9] Finally, some nervous citizens even responded to the concept that reasonable repression would eliminate vigilantism and mob action.[10]

Although these appeals seemed to suggest that the way to preserve free speech was to end it, its advocates were sincere in their beliefs. The only freedom that was meaningful and valid to them was the freedom to acknowledge the virtues and advantages of the American way. A federal court judge, in his charge to a jury trying Emma Goldman and Alexander Berkman for incendiary statements, explained that "free speech does not mean license, nor counseling disobedience to the law. Free speech means that frank, free, full, and orderly expression which every man or woman in the land, citizen or alien, may engage in, in lawful and orderly fashion."[11] For those who held such views, the times were favorable.

The end of the war brought disruption, dislocation and, for many, intense anomie. The year 1919 especially was beset with sudden unemployment as a result of the termination of hostilities and war contracts, aggravated by the wide-scale, rapid release of military personnel who were anxious to get work quickly and who were hopeful of cashing in on high wages. This new expanded labor force enabled employers to cut back on wages, however, even though the demand for, and scarcity of, civilian goods created galloping inflation and an astronomical increase in the cost of living. To add further tension, the war's end signaled the renewal of immigration to the United States when depression was already distressing worried citizens. The result was a revival of loud protests from those living closest to economic stringency and a revivification of the Socialists, the IWW, and the Non-Partisan League. Simultaneously, a variety of Americans, intrigued by the exciting potentialities of the new experiment in Russia, took steps toward organizing an American Communist party,[12] and, like their less revolutionary counterparts, channeled part of their enthusiasm into an outpouring of literature and rhetoric on the inadequacies of the current American system and the need for erecting a new order.[13]

To the extent that the restriction of free speech seemed at least a partial remedy and a potential avenue to stability and security, the rationalizations of the activist-repressionists had considerable appeal to distraught and confused Americans.[14] As the militancy of liberal and radical criticism increased, a variety of citizens' organizations, from the American Legion and the National Security League to the Ku Klux Klan, joined in the cry to save America from internal revolution by silencing those who undermined the people's faith in their institutions.

The appeal of suppression had economic and status overtones to a great many Americans who would not themselves have actively moved to set up repressive machinery, but who could easily be shown its relevancy to their situation and the desirability of supporting it. The Immigration Commission Report of 1911 had lent scientific veneer to apprehensions that certain types of immigrants had to be carefully checked. Concluding that restriction of immigration was "demanded by economic, moral, and social considerations,"[15] the report, in calling for a literacy test, had endorsed the view that the new unassimilatable immigrants with alien views and ideologies migrated to cash in on American opportunities with no intention of fulfilling corresponding responsibilities.

Although Congress enacted a literacy test over President Wilson's veto in 1917 and postwar immigration hardly resumed the flood stage of earlier years, strangers seemed to be entering every American town and city, many with unusual accents and foreign looks, many economically depressed and aggressively seeking economic and social advancement. Some were undoubtedly Americans in the throes of wartime dislocation. Many were also undoubtedly returning servicemen no longer content to remain "down on the farm after they'd seen Paree." And many were just what entrenched Americans feared—immigrants with a different religion, ethnic background, and value orientation, searching for new economic opportunity. Such an influx came at a time of abrupt, distressing, and inexplicable changes. The strangers served as scapegoats upon whom to blame the evils of this change.

Much of the society's values had a *gemeinschaft* orientation—rural, religious, homogeneous, and characterized by status relationships and low mobility. The *gesellschaft* values of an urban, secular, heterogeneous society of contract with high mobility potential were widely acknowledged to be fraught with intensifying danger.[16] To make matters worse, the strangers demanded entry into the system on their own terms and showed very little incentive to become assimilated or to accept the exploitation and deference expected of them. A disturbingly large number of radicals, and even liberals, championed their entry and demanded that the system be altered to accelerate such entry.[17]

The most responsible approach was to subject them to a vigorous and intense campaign of Americanization, to indoctrinate them gradually with proper values and to point out the desirability of accepting the country as it stood. The less responsible and, as it turned out, popular way was through vilification and deportation. There was little question of the appeal which silencing such critics had to the insecure American who was highly conscious of accommodating any significant change so as not to endanger his basic control of the system. Those most deeply committed to preserving a *gemeinschaft* orientation saw suppression of dangerous expression as a primary means toward shaping the values which they felt should prevail in the postwar world.[18]

Activist-libertarians from the outset confronted a powerful, well-financed, and eminently respectable opposition. The general climate of opinion was conducive to suppression of dissent. The effectiveness and ruthless determination of this entrenched group was not immediately apparent since it operated on the liberal premise that everyone surely wanted a brave new world after a war. Thus, in the first few months after the Armistice, this group moved ahead with the bland assurance that its views would easily and quickly prevail. With the first wave of disillusionment, however, their position changed from naiveté to shock, and then, as the 1920s progressed, to gradual grim determination.

Among these ardent reconstructionists were Wobblies, Non-Partisan Leaguers, Marxists, middle-class Americans repelled by wartime excesses and abuses, social crusaders and humanitarians, liberals, and instinctive reformers. All were frankly convinced of the real possibilities for a "revitalization" of society.[19] Each in turn held roughly comparable views concerning the central role and function of free speech in this process, even though in some cases these views were implicit in their actions rather than explicit in their pronouncements.

Accepting realistically the ancient principle that he who has property, and hence power, has civil rights, and convinced that governmental control in this area meant only intensification of the status quo rather than liberation from unwarranted public sanctions, the activist-libertarians were prepared to crusade for the creation of economic conditions in which this could take place. They rejected the Progressive premise that once the responsible members of society had eliminated its evils through paternalistic programs of public regulation, freedom would someway flow evenly to all the deserving. Far more practical than the Free Speech Leaguers in their comparable desire to enhance human individuality, they favored active, although generally private, programs to secure economically underwritten status for those unable to protect their own civil liberties. More explicitly, they focused on the necessity for giving the worker a voice in controlling the industrial processes and the distribution of his product.

Illustrative of this latter distinction was the polite shadowboxing between Roger N. Baldwin, former professional social worker and later guiding light of the American Civil Liberties Union, and Theodore Schroeder, head of the Free Speech League. Baldwin, later jailed as a conscientious objector and unrelenting critic of the war, attempted to organize a conference of liberal groups in Washington in late 1917 with the hope of developing some common policy against wartime restraints. In the process, he approached the Socialist party, the Non-Partisan League, and a large number of pacifist and liberal labor organizations, such as the Amalgamated Clothing Workers, all of whom promised support. But Schroeder flatly rejected all advances, writing to Baldwin that he was not going to have "the issue narrowed to economic liberty with a maximum pacifist leaning. This seems to me to involve a possible neglect of the more personal liberties which are being very much involved."[20] Those personal liberties were being challenged by restrictions on Sunday concerts and plays, local regulations on beach wear, laws prohibiting doctors from practicing without a license, the suppression of free thought lectures, compulsory vaccination laws, antiliquor and antitobacco regulations, and the unwarranted use of public money for religious institutions. Baldwin replied, simply: "I don't believe that we will want to consider inviting organizations which deal only with these personal liberties. They are not an issue before the country just now, and are hardly involved in the wider political question which we are discussing."[21]

Thus, although Baldwin and Schroeder might agree that liberty could flow only from the active participation by all members of society in the open competition for personal fulfillment, this objective was apparently attainable for the latter by simply freeing the individual from artificial restraints. Baldwin insisted on positive action to insure that the rules were fair and equitable. Liberty for such activist-libertarians could flow only from equality of economic opportunity sustained by a conscious drive against the artificial restrictions with which those entrenched in the current structure sought to guarantee their own special privileges. This meant not only an end to wartime sedition laws, but forestalling the renewed use of the private, informal instruments of restraint.

Hence, when the Central Conference of American Rabbis issued its "Social Justice Program" in mid-1920, it condemned "all interference, whether by private citizens or by officials with the exercise of freedom of speech, oral or written" but also candidly acknowledged and denounced "the use of private police under the guise of and in the capacity of public administrators of the law as tyrannical and conducive to injustice and violence."[22] Similar sentiments were included in the Federal Council of Churches' statement, the "Social Ideals of the Church," enunciated in May 1919. A prominent Protestant leader, Sherwood Eddy, in seeking answers to the question "What are the principles of Jesus that have a bearing upon our present industrial problems?" included both "liberty, involving the right of each individual to self-realization, self-expression, and self-determination; obligating Christians to aid in providing these things for all men," and "justice, involving the condemnation of all forms of exploitation and oppression of the weak by the powerful." Protestant social reformer Kirby Page, in publicizing these views, asked, in summation: "Does not self-expression involve an increasing degree of self-government and democracy in industry, as in the political realm?"[23]

The famed "Bishops' Program" of the Catholic War Council's Reconstruction and After-War Activities Committee, issued on Lincoln's birthday in 1919, placed primary emphasis on the "identity of interest" between "true religion" and "economic democracy,"[24] but also explained that a living wage was minimum justice in the United States.

Thus, those who spoke for liberal theology acknowledged the necessity of liberation from arbitrary restraints on depressed individuals.[25]

Although the activist-libertarians had the difficult task of confronting both entrenched privilege and an apprehensive, insecure, and at times irrational, public in pressing their case, they were confident that the cause for which they stood had elements within it of altruism, humanitarianism, tolerance, and social progress. This, in turn, encouraged them to hope that even their die-hard opponents might eventually be reached through their consciences. One possible tack in such a campaign would be to draw upon the effective symbolism of restoring ancient principles of freedom of speech.

The immediate problem, however, was gaining general support from a sufficiently large body of everyday Americans. This meant convincing such Americans that uninhibited free expression was important and desirable as a means to a positive end, or, more explicitly, it meant selling the idea that militant dissent and criticism were beneficial in encouraging concrete action toward eliminating the shortcomings of the system. Americans had never really had full and meaningful freedom of speech. Now, by a broad program of social and economic reconstruction, it was possible to attain that end. Unlike the activist-repressionist, who argued that the only way to preserve free speech was by closing the mouths of those who abused the privilege, the activist-libertarians argued that the only way to make free speech meaningful was for more people to participate in the system and thereby gain the status that would bring weight, meaning, and influence to what they said. Then, and only then, would the process of "free trade in ideas," with the ultimate truth triumphing, be a meaningful one to all.

The activist-libertarians had to take into account a far wider variety of challenges than those of their opponents. With the initiative clearly in the hands of those who would extend and tighten patriotic wartime restrictions, it was necessary to rebut the rationalizations of the repressionists.

The appeal of logic had to override the appeal of catchy sloganeering. Certainly liberty was not license, but it was necessary to show that that was not the issue. The important question was how to define license, that is, the criteria for determining when free speech had been abused. The activist-libertarians took their stand on two grounds. They acknowledged that there were clear limits to speech which had no political or constructively educational purpose, but pointed to the fact that there were on the statute books of every state and political subdivision batteries of laws covering libel, defamation, slander, obscenity, and frequently conspiracy. They were even willing to admit that there were proper limits to speech which, in the name of political and economic change, called for irresponsible actions. They agreed with Professor Zechariah Chafee of the Harvard Law School when he wrote in 1920 that "actual violence against government, life and property is punishable everywhere. Those who do plan or counsel such violence are liable even if they do not actively participate."[26]

But there was serious danger to the democratic process in limiting speech, no matter how inflammatory, which merely explored the political and economic system of the country, even if such expression was hypercritical and called for revolutionary changes in the current structure. These spiritual heirs of Milton, Mill, and Jefferson were convinced of the ultimate triumph of truth if reason was left free to combat error, and they sincerely maintained that progress was impossible unless all ideas could be heard and discussed. As Charles T. Sprading wrote in the early 1920s: "There are no infallible rules to guide us in determining the true from the false, but with freedom to set forth all opinions, and reason to sift the evidence, the result will be as near the truth as a fallible people can reach."[27] Arbitrary restrictions on free discussion assumed that only one orthodox set of options was permissible, thereby totally undermining the ability of the American people to manage and direct their own destiny. Ways had to be guaranteed for constant comment and criticism, for correction was impossible if inquiry itself was subject to authoritarian control.

The active civil libertarians never missed an occasion to point out certain contradictions in the repressionists' position. Noting the cry for restriction of radicals who advocated inflammatory actions and theories, they also noted that repressionists deemed it permissible to advocate violent retributive action against "radicals" and "traitors." In fact, it was apparently the height of patriotism to state, as did Secretary of State Albert P. Langtry of Massachusetts in a public address on radicals in 1920: "If I had my way, I would take them out in the yard every morning and shoot them, and the next day would have a trial to see whether they were guilty"[28]; or to call for continuation of the wartime sentiments of former ambassador James W. Gerard who had maintained that "we should 'hog-tie' every disloyal German-American, feed every pacifist raw meat, and hang every traitor to a lamp-post"[29]; or for a newspaper to editorialize concerning arrested IWW members: "It would be a waste of time to have them arrested and tried. The best thing to do is to shoot them, and not wait for sunrise either. The sooner, the better, even if there is not time to permit them counsel or benefit of clergy."[30]

The activist-libertarians answered the argument that the innocent workingman had to be protected against the deviously persuasive talk of the wily agitator by contending that the way to undermine the attraction of such talk was not to silence it, but to destroy its appeal by removing the economic and social maladies on which it sought to play. Such a note was sounded by Woodrow Wilson's close advisor, Joseph Tumulty, in June 1919 in "perhaps the most penetrating memorandum of his career."[31] Demanding "vitally reconstructive" action to eliminate public tension, Tumulty urged a national industrial conference of employers and employees to recommend a national plan for the improvement of relations between capital and labor. He recommended as several agenda items: government assistance in the development of consumer cooperatives to reduce labor's cost of living, the establishment of federal home loan banks to extend credit on easy terms for the construction of workmen's homes, federal vocational training for those injured in industrial pursuits, a permanent federal employment agency, federal health insurance and old-age pensions, federal laws fixing minimum wages, establishment of an eight-hour day, and recognition of the right of collective bargaining. Only by real concessions, Tumulty declared, could America resist the radicalism sweeping Europe.[32] The same view was stated in a slightly different, but equally penetrating, form in an editorial in the liberal religious magazine *World Tomorrow*, forthrightly entitled, "There Is But One Agitator—Injustice."[33]

Other activist-libertarian arguments emphasized that the resort to group activity by the economically distressed demonstrated their determination to escape the helpless subservience in which the rigid economic structure held them. The willingness to resort freely to cooperative methods expressed their desire for economic emancipation and personal dignity.

Liberals also drew upon a variety of other sentiments which they hoped would make sense to potential supporters. The end of the war also ended the necessity for emergency restraints. With the battle for democracy won abroad, it was time to restore democratic procedures at home.[34] Federal legislation proscribing espionage and sedition was, by its wording and intent, geared to strike at those who, by word or action, interfered with the war effort. Peacetime sedition and espionage legislation was irrelevant and, in light of past American practice, unprecedented.

Patriotism and American uniqueness were also stressed. Suppression, artificial and arbitrary restraints on individual freedom, and the "tyranny" of enforced conformity were attributes of European autocracy and unwarranted departures from traditional principles of freedom and liberty characteristic of America's open society.[35] "The American people have lived for 120 years without a Sedition Law," editorialized Pulitzer's *New York World*, in early 1920, in commenting on a proposed federal statute then before Congress: "They have prospered as no other people ever prospered, and to impose this measure of European despotism upon them at this time is an insult to their patriotism and a defiance of their traditions."[36]

Conscious of the fact that many Americans were distressed about the dangers of radicalism at home and abroad and realistic enough to know that it would be futile to argue that such dangers were fanciful, the activist-libertarians traced the sources to the suppression which they opposed. "I have been asked tonight to discuss the perils as well as the value of free speech," editor Frank Cobb of the *New York World* told the New York Economic Club in early 1920. "Most of the perils lie in repression. There is likely to be far more danger in the limitations than in the free speech itself, however foolish and intemperate the speech may be."[37] Cobb argued that if there were any virtue in repression the old autocratic dynasties would still be ruling in Europe and insisted that there was also danger to society of bottling up social unrest: "It would not be difficult to maintain the thesis that the amount of violence which has resulted from incendiary speech is infinitesimal when compared with the amount of violence that has resulted from the efforts of the Government to suppress manifestations of discontent."[38]

Others emphasized that the denial of free speech not only added fuel to the flames of hostility, but it created political stagnation, social inertia, and the worst aspects of social inbreeding, which were sooner or later bound to lead to a form of social revolution mild by comparison with the present turbulence.

A redefinition of the content, meaning, and implication of freedom of speech, whether in theory or practice, emerged from this tugging and pulling. Its professed repressionist devotees were apparently convinced that the only way freedom of speech could exist was as an abstract symbol. Yet serious question arose whether it could be widely denied as a practice and retain its effective symbolism as a vital American ideal. Thus, its libertarian champions were on solid ground in fearing that if the abstract concept were used as a device to stifle its practice, many Americans would become highly cynical of, if not hostile to, the symbol.

For the libertarians, it was essential that people maintain their respect for the symbol. It was therefore vital that it be made relevant to contemporary problems. The goal was a new plateau in which, for the first time in American history, there was a realistic relationship between the ideal of free speech and its practice by all, free of the informal restraints of an earlier era.

No matter who eventually emerged victorious from this struggle, freedom of speech was bound to change in the long run. The tensions and challenges of the immediate postwar years clearly precluded the possibility of restoring it to the same status it had enjoyed, both as a symbol and as a practice in the *gemeinshaft* society of an earlier day.

4

Creating the
Instruments of
Suppression

The scope of this proposed legislation was not limited to resident
aliens. . . . Citizens were within its purpose. Like our alien deportation
laws, these more inclusive measures were cleverly drawn. While they
seemed to penalize only such opinions and such speech as were inten-
tional incitements to crime, they . . . furnished pretexts for punishing
protagonists of any kind of change in government however peaceable
the method advocated, if it were repugnant to prevailing habits of
partisan thought among the powerful.

> Louis F. Post, *The*
> *Deportations Delirium*
> *of Nineteen-Twenty,* 1923

Accurst be the cowardice hidden in laws.

> Ralph Chaplin, "Joe Hill,"
> *The IWW Songbook*

The techniques developed for keeping the lid on the nation's discontent in the immediate postwar years were the products of fear, misunderstanding, and frequently ignorance and prejudice. The easiest
way to deal with the chronic complaints of the lower classes was
to surround them with formal legal restraints. This minimized the
necessity for coping directly with their miseries. They could be
coerced into either solving their own problems or keeping quiet about
them. Unfortunately for those who sought such ends, this solution
only stirred louder protests, for what the great majority of those

unhappy with the system wanted most was to be understood. Constant rebuke only induced them to verbalize their wants and complaints more vigorously.

It was necessary, however, to frame such legislation carefully. The First Amendment to the federal constitution seemed to preclude laws directly restricting freedom of speech, press, and assembly, in peace, at least, if not in war. The standard state constitution contained comparable proscriptions on such legislation. Further, a civil liberties-minded judge might react strongly to any law curtailing individual rights unless it were sufficiently ambiguous. And laws aimed at unwarranted activity were superfluous since every state and municipality had legislation punishing everything from disturbing the peace to insurrection. The legislation could hardly state on its face that its purpose was to undermine the labor movement or admit that it was designed to intimidate malcontents or give law enforcement officials flexible tools for quiet local suppression. The legislation was thus carefully geared to a recognizable problem and so structured that, while seeming to provide needed redress for that immediate and otherwise unprovided for problem, it accomplished the broader purposes which its sponsors sought.

The Armistice had hardly been signed in November 1918 when moves began to curtail radical activities. The advocates attempted to capitalize on immediate postwar dislocation to bring pressure on Congress for extraordinary action, and congressmen, ever conscious of the political advantages of appeasing public clamor, responded quickly. The Sixty-sixth Congress of 1919–1920 established a record introducing over seventy measures designed to restrict peacetime espionage and sedition, the sending of seditious matters in the mails, the advocacy of murder, revolution and the destruction of property, the display of the red flag, immigration, criminal anarchy, and criminal syndicalism.[1]

In January 1919, a Senate committee headed by Senator Lee S. Overman, Democrat of North Carolina, decided to focus attention on a variety of radical and bolshevik activities with an eye to restrictive legislation. One of the principal witnesses was Archibald Stevenson, a young lawyer who had been an insatiable wartime spy hunter and who later led the movement in New York State which resulted in the infamous Lusk Laws. Walter Nelles, writing of the period some years later, said of Stevenson:

> To such minds as his, "un-Americanism" was the crime of crimes, and the definition of "un-American" was comprehensive. Persistence in pressure towards ideals for which Theodore Roosevelt and Woodrow

Wilson had stood before the war, had been declared "un-American" during it because not helpful in the great task of crushing Germany. It was equally "un-American" after the war because not helpful in the greater task of crushing Bolshevism.[2]

Stevenson and others of his mentality convinced the committee of the pressing necessity for a federal peacetime sedition law which was introduced at the conclusion of the hearings in February 1919 and became generally known as the Overman bill.[3] Still, the fact that such legislation would restrict free speech could not be kept out of the hearings and inevitably caused some discomfort. When Stevenson urged that American citizens who advocated revolution should be punished under a law drawn for that purpose, Chairman Overman queried: "Then you will hear somebody in the Senate talking about freedom of speech, will you not?" Stevenson replied: "Yes, but revolution is somewhat different from freedom of speech."[4]

Raymond Robins, head of the American Red Cross mission to Russia, expressed reservations to Mr. Stevenson's proposal on the ground that enforcement would be in the hands of bureaucrats, who would be highly insensitive to freedom of speech and of the press: "We have preferred in the past to take those evils that flow from this misuse of liberty as less evil than would be the restriction of the liberty and freedom of the press."[5] And Albert Rhys Williams, former Congregational clergyman, quickly branded by Stevenson as one of "several avowed agents of the bolshevik government here," questioned both this and the wartime sedition act as free speech violations and a poor way to suppress agitation. An agitator, argued Williams:

is a man who is agitated because something . . . has made him mad, because he has had low wages, or been thumped on the head, or something of that sort. . . . instead of the repression of free speech in this country, instead of the repression of newspapers that point to the dangers of this eruption or that earthquake, we should in the most open fashion call for forums and free expression and free speech in every way.[6]

The National Civil Liberties Bureau, precursor of the American Civil Liberties Union, also took up the cause of free speech and, urging Congress to reject the measure, seized the opportunity to plead for release of political prisoners.

With Congress at least temporarily interested in other matters, the measure was quietly buried in the Senate in March. There were good reasons for the lack of strong support for formal peacetime suppression by the federal government. Subtle control through local officials with ambiguous but clearly understood authority to take the proper and necessary actions against the wrong people was preferable. This same syndrome was evident during the campaigns for restrictive local laws against radicalism and for the nationwide open shop. Again the jockeying that took place was between the local representatives of national organizations from the American Legion and businessmens' and employers' organizations to state AFL and other labor and liberal groups.[7]

Once again the wartime background provided both the rationale and the pattern for peacetime restraint. Following the lead of the federal government, various states had enacted legislation against opposition to the war. These laws fell into two categories: sedition statutes to strike at those who might undermine morale, particularly among recruits, and legislation aimed at the IWW and geared to eliminate criminal syndicalism, which was generally described as "the doctrine which advocates crime, sabotage, violence or unlawful methods of terrorism as a means of accomplishing industrial or political reform."[8]

In both types of legislation there were overtones of more restrictive intentions. The Iowa sedition law of 1917, a model for other states, also punished the inciting or attempt to incite insurrection or sedition, the advocacy of subversion or destruction by force of the Iowa or the United States governments, and the attempt to incite hostility or opposition to them.[9] New York's 1917 act provided for removal of officers, civil service employees, and teachers for treasonable or seditious acts or utterances, and a 1918 addition called for the elimination of school textbooks containing seditious or disloyal matter.[10]

The atmosphere surrounding the enactment of the Idaho criminal-syndicalism law of 1917—a model for other states—revealed the intent of the framers. Idaho had long been the scene of violent struggles between mine operators and the Western Federation of Miners. With the war, the mining and lumber interests introduced six bills, all ostensibly designed to curtail IWW activities. These included an antisabotage bill, an antistrike bill, an antipicketing bill, a bill making the inciting or soliciting of crimes a misdemeanor, and a measure to redefine conspiracy in the existing state code to include two or more people organizing for the purpose of quitting work, thereby hampering, annoying, or intimidating their employer and impeding the progress of his business. When this latter measure was tabled, its sponsor introduced in its place a criminal-syndicalism bill. All five measures then passed the state senate, but the antistrike and antipicketing bills died in the house committee because of the opposition of the State Federation of Labor.[11] The solicitation bill passed the house, however, as did the antisabotage and criminal-syndicalism measures, both of which went unopposed by labor, which feared that by fighting them they would place themselves in the position of upholding such practices.

The criminal-syndicalism measure was drafted for the business interests by a Boise attorney, Benjamin W. Oppenheim, who later admitted that it was copied largely from the earlier New York criminal anarchy law of 1902. He also candidly stated that the measure was aimed not at the poor dupes who generally committed the acts of sabotage but was designed to "get the agitator." "At that particular time it was more important to shut up the agitators and keep them off the job than it was to put them [the saboteurs] in a penitentiary."[12]

Minnesota, Montana, and South Dakota also enacted criminal-syndicalism legislation during the war period. In each instance, local situations dictated the movement surrounding the laws, and, in each, a hard core of apprehensive opposition emerged, seeing at the outset seriously repressive implications from such moves.

In Minnesota, where Wobblies had been active in the lumber industry and had conducted an unsuccessful strike against twenty Mesabi mining companies from June 21 to September 17, 1917, the cry for legislation had grown. However, when a committee of the legislature set out to investigate conditions, prior to enacting controlling legislation, two IWW organizers appeared before it, demanding the privilege of examining witnesses.[13] They threw the hearings into a turmoil by testifying about the advocacy of violence against the IWW by lumber operators, the use of third-degree methods by company-intimidated law enforcement officials, and the denial of free speech and assemblage to IWW groups seeking merely to alleviate intolerable working conditions. While the majority report of the committee generally ignored such charges, a minority report submitted by a Minneapolis representative, C. E. Ryberg, deplored the denial of the constitutional rights of the IWW organizers by public officials and recommended an appropriation for an industrial relations commission to insure fair play in the future.[14] In the end, however, a revised version of the Idaho bill passed the senate 61 to 1, the lone dissenter being Senator Richard Jones, a Socialist of Duluth and president of the Duluth Federated Trades Assembly. When Socialist Representative Ernest G. Strand of Two Harbors cast a similar solitary protest vote in the house, hisses and cries of "Put him out!" were heard from fellow members.[15] A few weeks later, in June 1917, the City Council of Duluth passed an ordinance defining vagrancy as "advocating the duty, necessity, or propriety of crime or violence as a means of accomplishing industrial or political ends."[16]

Montana, partly due to its vast mining operations, was the home of the powerful Western Federation of Miners; however, it was also an agricultural state with a sizable portion of its economy dependent on farm production. With farm laborers particularly subject to discrimination and exploitation, it was thus a natural recruiting ground for organizers of the Non-Partisan League. Fear grew among the conservative property interests of the state that a dangerous rapprochement might take shape between agrarian Leaguers and the unions. The lukewarm attitude of both toward the war added the opportunity to raise charges of disloyalty and call for repressive legislation, but not before tensions had exploded in the form of mob violence against left-wingers—lynchings, beatings and general assaults—widely attributed to copper company goons.

Again, a few courageous men stood firm from the start. United States District Judge George M. Borquin and United States District Attorney Burton K. Wheeler lost no occasion to denounce mob violence. Both took the stand that the 1917 Espionage Act did not apply to unpopular expressions of opinion merely because of the tendency of such expressions to interfere with the conduct of the war.[17] Their opponents developed a rationale for repression by contending that the refusal to curb dangerous utterances was responsible for the mob outbreaks by indignant citizens who had no other recourse. A special session of the legislature was called in 1918 by company-oriented Democratic Governor Samuel V. Stewart to consider a law "to define sabotage, criminal syndicalism and industrial and political anarchy."[18]

Governor Stewart, however, apparently felt the political need for support for his programs. He agreed to address the Cooperator's Congress meeting at Great Falls, composed primarily of farmers and union men. But his pleas for restrictive legislation evoked only a strongly worded resolution:

We do not approve [the item calling for such legislation], although we do concede the existence of a vast amount of criminal syndicalism and industrial anarchy of nation-wide importance and from which the rights of the people suffer invasion and which tends to paralyze production in both state and nation, as witnessed in the activity and operations of the flour mill and grain gambling trust, the packing trust, the sugar trust, the usury trust, the political trust and some dozens of others, but we believe that even they should not be deprived of their rights to be tried before the courts in the manner provided by the federal constitution.[19]

The legislature proved more pliable, however, and promptly passed two criminal-syndicalism laws like the one in Idaho.[20] The fact that a dozen house members, primarily from industrial centers where unions were strong, abstained from voting indicated that they feared being denounced by the bill's supporters as unpatriotic. In the end, only one newspaper in the state opposed the measure. This was William F. Dunne's *Butte Daily Bulletin,* born of the 1917 copper strike, official organ of the Montana State Federation of Labor and the Central Labor Union of Silver Bow County, encompassing Butte and environs, and at that time one of the largest labor dailies in the United States.[21] This opposition was taken by the act's supporters as evidence that the measure was striking where it should, at the radicals in the state.

In South Dakota, a conservative citizens' group, the State Council of Defense, had sufficiently regimented public opinion so that there was no opposition to the passage of a strongly worded measure, although a large number of abstentions again indicated the reluctance to risk public condemnation.[22]

The other wartime movement for criminal-syndicalism legislation came in the state of Washington. Here too the IWW situation had been tense for some years. In November 1916, the IWW, in an attempt to organize lumber workers in Everett, landed 288 members by boat from Seattle with instructions to use "free-speech fight" techniques in an effort to push organization. Forewarned, over a hundred gunmen, organized by the sheriff, who apparently acted under the orders of the Everett Commercial Club, met them at the dock with rifle fire from 3 sides, killing 5 and injuring 16. Two of the attackers were killed and 16 wounded, apparently by the cross fire of their fellows, since the Wobblies were unarmed.[23] Subsequently, 294 members of the IWW were arrested and 74 charged with murder, in a trial which began the day before an Idaho-type criminal syndicalism bill, sponsored by lumber interest legislators, was up for passage in the state House of Representatives.[24] This measure had drawn fully upon public hostility to the IWW, and during its debate the Wobblies were violently castigated for their role in the Spokane free-speech fight, for street demonstrations in Seattle, and for the Everett affair, one senator candidly admitting, "I want to send such cattle to the penitentiary."[25]

The measure elicited important wartime statements on the proper meaning of freedom of speech. When the clerk called the bill the president stated: "Are there any remarks before the bill goes to a vote?" Silence reigned. Then Peter Iverson, a small-town Republican newspaper editor rose and, looking around at the body, said:

> Mr. President: Is there not one voice in this splendid assembly that is willing to be raised against this far-reaching, vital and vicious measure? This measure is not to curb crime, but to make that a crime which is not a crime. It is an infringement, pure and simple, on our right to free speech and free press. I would go to any extent to curb mob rule or lawlessness, but I can not and will not be a party to such flagrant violation of our constitutional rights as this bill would provide for. We have in this State one of the most intelligent, wide-awake and liberty-loving citizenships in the world, and a law of this kind will be a dangerous measure in more ways than one. It makes that a crime which is one of the foundation stones of a free and popular government, that is, free speech and free press.[26]

Brief debate followed, but the question was quickly moved and the measure passed 32 to 5. Six senators, three supporters and three opponents, quickly moved to insert explanations of their votes into the legislative journals.[27]

In the house a strong move to table the measure as a deprivation of free speech and assemblage was beaten down and passage followed, 83 to 12, but not before strong objections had been voiced, especially by Republican Representative D. P. Reid, president of the Spokane Central Labor Council, who, in raising the free-speech point, went on to proclaim:

> so long as we exalt property rights above human rights—so long as we tolerate a condition of society in which some heap up wealth they cannot use while others live in want—so long as the fires beneath our social structure are fed with the flames of greed and corruption and special privilege—we must not court disaster by weighing down the safety valve by the enactment of such a bill as this.[28]

Other labor leaders also read the implications of the measure, with its loose definition of syndicalism, which could easily be applied in industrial disputes to the rightful acts of workers and to the AFL as well as the IWW. Thus the Federation petitioned the governor to veto the bill, which English-born Wilsonian Democrat Ernest P. Lister did, arguing that the measure would jeopardize the liberties of many loyal citizens and give added force to the arguments of agitators.[29] The press promptly exploded. The *Seattle Post-Intelli-*

gencer stated editorially: "The fact that the Governor is moved to disapprove legislation . . . so pointedly aimed at anarchists and direct-actionists, will be hailed by the Emma Goldmans of the land with fiendish glee and the red flag unfurled in celebration of it."[30] Yet such gubernatorial disapproval stuck until postwar conditions reinvigorated the advocates of the law.

The Armistice brought renewed interest in state restriction. Emphasis shifted to suppressing dangerous words and activities. In 1919 Pennsylvania's law, for example, passed in a state which had long been the scene of intense management–labor tensions; it defined sedition as any writing, publication, printing, cut, cartoon, utterance, or conduct, either individually or in connection or combination with any other person or persons which tends to encourage any person or persons to take measures with a view of overthrowing or destroying or attempting to destroy the government by any force, or show or threat of force; to incite or encourage anyone to commit any overt act with a view to bringing the government into hatred or contempt.[31] Connecticut's law provided that no person shall, before an assemblage of ten or more persons, advocate any measure, doctrine, proposal, or propaganda intended to affect injuriously the government of the state or the United States, and it would penalize any abusive, disloyal, scurrilous language about the form of government of the United States.[32] The laws of the other states varied only in their wording. The intimidatory nature of such legislation was obvious, as was the manner in which the various provisions afforded occasion for prosecution and punishment of those whose speech society felt should be curtailed in some way.

Postwar criminal-syndicalism laws were less obviously economic in their motivations than their predecessors and tended more to appeal to public opinion by striking at bolshevism, communism, socialism, and radicalism.[33] Most of these laws were enacted in the tension-ridden year of 1919, although the momentum for passage carried into the early 1920s in some states. Again the pattern of passage, while generally similar, was marked by local difference and the opposition, when courageous enough to stand up and be counted, drew upon a variety of the free-speech clichés, then a part of the beleaguered liberal's defense arsenal.

Several measures were unfinished business from the war years. The Seattle general strike in 1919 aroused Washington repressionists to revive the earlier, vetoed criminal-syndicalism law, which was enacted over another veto by Governor Lister. During the move to override, Representative George N. Hodgdon of Seattle, a Democrat and former Populist, arose to state that he was "astounded at the audacity of anyone bringing this bill on the floor, after the wars of America had been fought for free speech."[34] His demand that the Declaration of Independence and the free-speech guarantees in the United States Constitution be read before the house was declared out of order. When he again gained the floor, Hodgdon insisted, to the discomfort of certain Republican members, that Lincoln and Greeley would have had a hard time under this law.[35]

Conservative labor's vigorous opposition to this bill apparently created apprehensions among vote conscious legislators, who introduced and rushed into law a sabotage measure which punished whoever attempted to injure property or damage machinery with intent to impair, interfere with, or obstruct enterprises employing wage earners and whoever, with the same intent, took unlawful possession or control of any property or instrumentality used in such enterprises. Senator Iverson derived little satisfaction, but a certain perverse pleasure, out of having the chairman of the Senate Judicial Committee denounce as unconstitutional a proposal making a felony of organizing in restraint of trade or for the purpose of controlling the prices of any of the necessities of life or to press money out of people for selfish gain.[36]

Furthermore, twenty Washington cities moved to plug any loopholes the legislature might have left by creating essential enforcement machinery. Municipal sedition and criminal-syndicalism ordinances, measures against littering or distributing literature on the streets, traffic rules authorizing the breaking up of public meetings, and regulations penalizing obstructions on sidewalks were used to prohibit picketing. Roger Baldwin, writing in the 1921–1922 *American Labor Year Book*, claimed that over one thousand convictions were sustained under such laws in the city of Spokane alone, many carrying sentences of sixty to ninety days.[37] "Syndicalist disloyalty" was controlled in Washington in one way or another.

A State Council of Defense, similar in many ways to the one in South Dakota, had operated in Nevada during the war years and had been sufficiently ominous to intimidate critics. The dominant mining operators of the state maintained a strong position in the legislature and moved quickly, with the Armistice, to extend the council's operations into the postwar era. Democratic Governor Emmet D. Boyle, himself a mining engineer, addressed the legislature in early 1919, calling attention to the reduced postwar position of labor, the approaching problem of unemployment, the possibility of "false philosophies" being absorbed by idle and discouraged workers, and the resultant danger of the recurrence of intense and bitter industrial disputes. That body quickly responded by enacting an

Idaho-type criminal syndicalism law, with only very cautious opposition from the state Federation of Labor.[38]

Arizona, like Idaho, had been the scene of acute tensions between mine operators and workingmen since well before statehood in 1911. But, unlike Idaho, the political parties in the state had come to align themselves with the conflicting economic interests, the Democrats and their leader, George W. P. Hunt, clearly on the side of labor and opposed to the powerful copper companies which dominated the Republican party. Hunt, first governor of the state and reelected seven times between 1911 and 1929, had sent state militia in 1915 to quell trouble arising from a Western Federation of Miners strike, but had ordered that no strikebreakers or gunmen should be admitted to the district involved and had upheld a prolabor sheriff who had deputized the strikers to protect the company's property. The outcome was a singular lack of violence and no loss of life.

However, in return for promised wage increases and better working conditions, he indirectly acquiesced in the transfer of miners' allegiance from the Western Federation to the Arizona Federation of Miners, a much weaker body. This inspired IWW leadership to step up propaganda and direct action plans until, by 1917, they were scoring singular organizational successes at Phoenix, Jerome, and Bisbee. When these miners openly opposed the war, however, and a wave of strikes broke out, the companies turned to the federal government, maintaining that copper was essential to the nation's war program. The eventual result was the sending in of federal troops in July 1917 and the famous, but then well-concealed, Jerome and Bisbee deportations. In the Jerome case, 100 miners were taken from their homes by the Loyalty League and shipped in cattle cars to the state line, where they were intercepted and held in jail three weeks before being released. At Bisbee, 1,186 striking miners and their sympathizers were rounded up, shipped into the New Mexico desert, and abandoned. They were subsequently escorted by federal troops to Columbus, New Mexico, where they were held until September.[39]

Hunt sought moderation through this crisis and eventually acted as a federal mediator in an attempt to ease the tensions. He also delivered to an extraordinary session of the Arizona legislature a stinging denunciation of the "profiteering patrioteers" who had committed the atrocities.[40] The result opened him to charges of sympathy with the Wobblies and, in 1918, he was defeated for reelection by Republican Thomas E. Campbell, who campaigned on a platform calling for stringent laws against enemy propaganda, sabotage, and the IWW. When the legislature began to consider repressive legislation, the issue was clearly drawn between loyalty and treason as epitomized by the IWW and its weak-kneed supporters. Anyone who opposed the legislation was clearly a menace to the safety and honor of the state.

Even so, certain consciences were perturbed. The legislature, although refusing to consider a proposed "act to prohibit and punish the interstate deportation of laborers and other persons," did pass a resolution expressing horror at invasions of constitutional rights and mob rule committed under the cloak of patriotism.[41] When the state Federation of Labor openly opposed strongly worded sabotage and criminal-syndicalism measures, the bills' sponsor quickly arose to give assurance that the measures sought only to repress seditious acts and utterances and certainly were not intended to interfere with freedom of speech.[42] Nonetheless a watered-down measure was enacted in 1918 with the support of Governor Campbell and the copper companies, although a move in 1919 to strengthen the measure failed.

The California law, one of the most widely used for attaining a variety of convictions, was shrouded in confusion. The labor situation there had been a powder keg for many years. In San Francisco, where unions had been strong since the 1906 fire, employers had searched in vain for ways to weaken their power. Los Angeles, by contrast, was the leading open-shop city in the United States, in large part due to the activities of General Harrison Grey Otis, owner of the *Los Angeles Times*. The dynamiting of the *Times* building in 1910 had stigmatized the cause of unionization in Los Angeles, and the Mooney-Billings case in San Francisco in 1916–1917 eased few feelings in the Bay Area.[43]

Moreover, the campaign of the IWW to organize the migratory agricultural workers, on whose labor the seasonal fruit and vegetable industries of California depended, produced violent reaction from the powerful packers and planters in the agricultural districts. Finally, tensions existed as a result of the IWW's successful efforts among lumber and construction workers and seamen. The American Federation of Labor seaman's union in San Francisco found such tactics diversionary to its own desires to gain a foothold on the waterfront.

The California criminal-syndicalism law, finally enacted in 1919, was the culmination of a two-year struggle between antiunion forces in the state, well financed with a million-dollar slush fund and labor representatives from the California Federation of Labor, the Building and Trades Council of San Francisco, and the Railroad Brotherhoods. A bill, modeled on the Idaho law, introduced in 1917, was beaten by the concerted efforts of labor legislators.[44] Two future governors of California supported the measure, however. C. C. Young, later to pardon a prominent social worker, Charlotte Anita Whitney, when she was convicted under the 1919 law, voted for the measure. William D. Stephens, former mayor of Los Angeles and president of the Los Angeles Chamber of Commerce, at that time lieutenant-governor and president of the Senate, obviously was in sympathy with it.

It took the hysteria of the postwar years to bring passage. Stories of IWW terrorism and plots, nationwide federal raids on the organization, and the highly publicized Sacramento trial of fifty-five California Wobblies in December 1918 created an atmosphere conducive to restrictive legislation.[45] Governor William D. Stephens, in his campaign for reelection in 1918, took every occasion to stress the need for curtailing the IWW, and the California legislature of 1919 was highly sympathetic. Before it was through, the legislature also enacted a red-flag law.

The criminal-syndicalism law, framed at the request of the governor, was written by the Republican state chairman, Raymond Benjamin, a onetime labor union man, who, as Chief Deputy Attorney-General, had been sent by Governor Hiram Johnson to investigate the San Diego free-speech fight in 1912. It was introduced into the legislature, at the request of the governor, by Senator William H. Kehoe of Eureka, identified as a spokesman for organized labor. Kehoe later admitted that he could not explain the provisions of the bill and was not responsible for them,[46] and after the subsequent arrest, under the measure of Miss Whitney, he publicly stated: "The purpose of the Criminal Syndicalism law was to protect the freedom of thought and action. If the operation of the law is such as to defeat this freedom of thought and action and to deny the right of free speech, then it ought to be repealed."[47]

Other legislators spotted the implications of the measure from the outset. Labor-oriented members in the assembly feared the measure as a cleverly drawn antiunion bill, and others saw it as a weapon to overthrow the party in power and as a bar to public ownership of public utilities. Yet it remained for a representative from largely agricultural Kern County, Grace S. Dorris, to cast the issue in clear free-speech terms and point out the threat of the measure to traditional and hard-won guarantees of free expression.[48] But despite protests, on April 30, 1919, the measure was signed by Governor Stephens and went into effect immediately. There is no doubt that it was a victory for employers. Lobbyists of the San Francisco Chamber of Commerce pushed it with vigor, and George P. West, writing in 1923, undoubtedly came close to the truth when he wrote:

> This was no hysterical demand on the part of a foolish herd. It was a deliberate policy conceived and executed by Los Angeles employers

as organized in the Better America Federation and the Merchants and Manufacturers Association. It was strictly an industrial policy, a belief that legal terrorism would dispose effectually of labor unrest, a belief that they had always held, a belief that they had always practiced up to the limit which public opinion would tolerate, a belief on which they found themselves able to act without restraint as a result of the anti-red hysteria of 1919.[49]

Colorado, in the years before World War I, had also been the scene of violent industrial warfare. Between 1880 and 1904 the state militia was called ten times to quell trouble, and federal troops were sent into the state in 1914 to attempt to restore order after the famous Ludlow massacres in which forty-five people—striking miners or their wives and children—were killed and many more wounded when their tent village was attacked and burned by the state militia.[50] Ludlow epitomized the ruthlessness with which Colorado employers, prominently the Rockefellers and the Guggenheims, countered labor's demands. Labor's complaints about the deportation of leaders, the use of "bull pens" and strike-breaking gunmen, the repeated proclamations of martial law, the activities of antiunion "citizens' alliances," mock trials by obedient company judges, and the general hostility of the employer-oriented press, were generally warranted. But to militant labor, the greater the persecution, the greater the challenge. The IWW worked in the state after first leading a quarry strike in 1908, staging free-speech fights in Denver and Grand Junction in 1911 and 1913, respectively, and in a Recruiting Union operated in Denver through World War I in a vigorous attempt to organize the coal mining and steel workers. The United Mine Workers, already claiming 8,000 members in 1917, also increased its campaign for greater membership in the war years.[51]

The crusade against aggressive labor in Colorado aroused predictable and typical reactions in the years immediately after the war. Two Colorado coal strikes in 1919 were stopped by court injunction, with United States Attorney General A. Mitchell Palmer actually petitioning United States District Judge A. B. Anderson to issue the former, on October 31, 1919, and Governor Oliver H. Shoup, happily supporting Palmer by calling out the National Guard to prevent picketing and protect the mines.[52] The Colorado Federation of Labor, in which the United Mine Workers played a strong role, took out its bitterness over the failure to make headway on the IWW. Growing local demands for action led to the calling of a special session of the legislature which met December 8–19, 1919.[53]

The first measure introduced was a bill "for the suppression of anarchy and sedition and to suppress conspiracies against the state and its laws." Its key sections proscribed every person who orally or in print "shall advocate, teach, incite, propose, aid, abet, encourage or advise" unlawful injury to property by physical force or violence, "either as a general principle or in particular instances, as a means of affecting governmental, industrial, social or economic conditions."[54]

Little opposition to the measure developed, virtually none on free-speech grounds, and the legislature was warmly commended for its actions by Major General Leonard Wood in an address to a joint session two days after the enactment of the bill. Coming to Colorado from Kansas City, where in a public address he had vigorously condemned all types of radicals, insisting we should "deport these so-called Americans who preach treason openly,"[55] Wood held that agitators were responsible for most of the prevailing unrest in the United States and agreed that "we must advocate radical laws to deal with radical people."[56] Coloradoans agreed. Even John Shank, secretary at Pueblo of Metal Mine Workers Industrial Union No. 800 of the IWW, wrote somewhat sardonically to the governor in approval of the legislation.[57]

The remainder of criminal-syndicalism legislation enacted in 1919 was significant primarily for the variation of local pattern. In Indiana, the framers of the law sponsored by the Daughters of the American Revolution and the Associated Employers of Indianapolis felt compelled to stress the "liberty is not license" point, and inserted in its preamble the theory that unrestrained free speech was one of the contributing causes of the Russian Revolution.[58]

In Iowa, where rural groups controlled the legislature, a 1917 sedition act was bolstered by 1919 red-flag and criminal-syndicalism laws, even though IWW action in the state had been minimal.[59] In Michigan, by contrast, the sponsors of both 1919 red-flag legislation and a criminal-syndicalism statute were employer organizations, especially the Michigan Manufacturers Association and various employer groups connected with the automobile industry. Labor fought hard against both measures, attempting to add amendments to exempt established unions.[60] In the end, fifteen representatives voted against it, eight of whom were of foreign birth or foreign parentage, predominantly German, the majority either from Detroit or from the mining counties of the upper peninsula. On the other hand, eleven foreign-born members supported the measure, five from Canada, two from Scotland, and one each from Holland, Ireland, Italy, and Wales. Unlike California, Colorado, and Washington, the press ignored the law, despite the heat of the debates surrounding it.

The free-speech issue was raised in one form or another in nine other states in 1919 or early 1920. In Nebraska, the influential *Omaha World-Herald* editorialized frequently on the need for repressive legislation during the session that eventually enacted a criminal-syndicalism law. A January 15, 1919, editorial, "The Shelter of Free Speech," charged that "the anarchistic element in the United States" was using this constitutional right to cover up crimes,[61] and, on April 4, the preaching of cooperation among farmers was decried as "the beginning of Communism."[62]

In Ohio the free-speech point was raised in legislative debate, but with little effect.[63] In Oregon, two labor-oriented legislators vainly opposed an Idaho-type law as a bill "born in fear and reared in selfishness" and "an attempt to restrain the free speech of American citizens."[64]

In Oklahoma, farmer discontent had spawned an organization known as the Working Class Union which directed its hostilities in 1917 against participation in the "rich man's war." IWW organizers were also active in the state. The resultant Green Corn Rebellion, with mass movements and at times violent demonstrations against the draft, was the immediate provocation for Oklahoma's criminal-syndicalism law.[65] The newspapers let loose a drumfire of attack on the IWW so that opponents of the bill ran the risk of being cast as supporters of both agrarian lawlessness and industrial sabotage.

The first expression of public opposition did not come until after passage was secure. Then, however, the socialist *Oklahoma Leader* felt compelled to comment. Calling attention to the fact that a similar measure was before the national Congress, the paper praised the National Civil Liberties Bureau's statement on that measure, indicating it applied equally to the Oklahoma law. The bureau had stated:

> The vice of the legislation is not so much what it purports to do, as what it will be construed to do. . . . Under the terms of the proposed legislation which penalizes the advocacy or the incitement to violent overthrow of the government of the United States, it is easy to imagine how juries will be found who will convict upon no other evidence against the defendant than his articulate protest against economic, social and political conditions. . . . An engine of tyranny of well nigh incalculable power will have been forged. The possible effect upon the legitimate strike activities of organized labor can be surmised.[66]

In Utah, the execution of IWW troubadour Joe Hill in late 1915 on flimsy trumped-up charges had produced high tensions in the state and frequent threats on the lives of the governor and members of the State Pardon Board. The fact partly explained why Utah's

Democratic Senator, William H. King, became a leading advocate
of federal legislation to curtail radicalism. Nonetheless, conservative
labor's representative boldly raised questions concerning the implication of strong state restrictive legislation, and one representative
sought to qualify a proposed criminal-syndicalism law with an amendment reading:

> There is nothing in this act to be construed to abridge the right of
> American citizens to peaceably assemble or to prohibit the right of
> free speech or freedom of the press when public questions may be
> discussed, including economic, political and industrial questions, when
> conducted in a peaceable and orderly way.[67]

Although the amendment was defeated 21 to 8, with eighteen members absent, those who voted against it felt the necessity for proclaiming that the guarantees of the state and national constitutions of
free speech and press made such further protection superfluous.[68]

In West Virginia, certain locals of the United Mine Workers sought
to turn the bolshevik argument on their enemies, calling on their
membership to oppose a combined sedition–red-flag law and a constabulary bill to create a state police force and thus "prevent our
American institutions being Russianized by a Russian law."[69] A loud
and vigorous protest march on the state capitol was staged to oppose
the enactment of the two measures, with the famed Mother Jones
joining the placard-carrying, rain-soaked mob. One militant UMW
local in Ramage went so far as to throw the gauntlet to the measures'
sponsors, warning that if such legislation were enacted:

> As a final arbiter of the rights of public assembly, free speech and
> a free and uncensored press, we will not for a single moment hesitate
> to meet our enemies upon the battlefields, and there amid the roar
> of the cannon and the groans of the crash of systems purchase again
> our birthright of blood-bought freedom.[70]

But state officials of the union hastened to condemn the statement
as "un-American."[71] In the end, the legislation was enacted and signed
into law with no dissenting votes cast.

Kansas had also experienced a variety of IWW actions. The federal
government had moved against the Wobblies in November 1917,
raiding various halls and picking up members on John Doe warrants,
apparently issued in Butler County, Kansas, "at the suggestion of
agents of the Carter Oil Company, the Sinclair Oil Company, Gypsy

Oil Company, and other oil companies doing business in this section of the country."[72] The arrested men were held until finally indicted the following June. Conviction of twenty-seven finally followed with the testimony of "ex-IWWs" prominently relied upon.[73] These actions and attempts of the Non-Partisan League to operate in the state had led to the organization of an informal local organization, the Kansas Anti-Bolshevik Campaign, which flooded the state with literature against Wobblies, Non-Partisan Leaguers, and left-wing Socialists.

The time was thus ripe for formal restrictive legislation, and the predominantly rural legislature, with the American Legion prodding it,[74] responded with a red-flag law in 1919 and was prepared to go further the following year.[75] Thus, although Republican Governor Henry J. Allen urged the legislature to "keep in mind that which every just government holds sacred—the right of free speech, of a free press and free right of assemblage," and cautioned, "if we seek to pass anti-sedition laws which deprive civilization of the benefit which comes from discussion and criticism, we lead to evils far more dangerous in their pent-up power than those which usually follow the freedom of radical expression,"[76] the legislature promptly accepted for consideration a bill which, if enacted, would have been the most stringent and restrictive measure passed in the period. Defining sabotage as "any act intended to slacken, restrict, limit or reduce production in any industry, or to slacken, limit or restrict trade or commerce or to interfere in any manner with the distribution, sale, transportation or delivery of any commodity,"[77] it branded as criminal syndicalism the doctrine that advocated any of a long series of acts as a means of accomplishing industrial or political revolution. These acts included free love, sabotage, and virtually any form of social, political, or economic change. The president of the Kansas Federation of Labor came close to the truth when he later stated: "Should the bill have passed as it was originally drawn, it could and probably would have been used to destroy every local union in the state."[78]

Opposition formed from the outset, however. The influential *Topeka Daily Capital* assailed the measure openly and frequently. In an editorial entitled "Forbidding Free Speech in Kansas," it called the bill "one of the worst examples of this sort of harmful legislation," questioned the need for legislation of this type at all, and ended on a historic note arguing: "The sedition law of 1798 . . . has stood for 120 years as a 'horrible example' of arbitrary and autocratic interference with human rights, but the sedition bill in the legislature exceeds that of 1798 in contempt of liberty of thought and speech."[79] The legislators then moved to amend and water down the provisions of the measure.

The bill was eventually passed at the height of the nationwide red hysteria of early 1920. In commenting on its final passage, the *Topeka Daily State* candidly exposed the motivation behind such laws: "There is no cause for uneasiness. These laws are intended only for political purposes. They are not designed for enforcement. Wherever there exists a genuine need to deal drastically with radicalism there are already laws in existence sufficient for that purpose."[80]

A. Mitchell Palmer himself appeared in coal-strike ridden Kentucky in early 1920 to address a joint session of the state General Assembly and to cap a statewide Americanization campaign launched by the American Legion with a plea for antiradical legislation. The assembly was in a receptive mood having begun its session by passing a resolution which demanded loyalty, belief in democracy as enunciated by the constitution, and obedience to the laws and then commended the Department of Justice for the deportation of alien radicals, the American Legion for its suppression of disloyalty, and the U.S. House of Representatives for refusing to seat Victor Berger.[81] Legislators had then vied with one another in introducing seven criminal-syndicalism and antisedition bills.

In his address, Palmer described the red menace and the lack of federal laws to meet the situation. He declared that labor now wanted too much and was the aggressor capitalism had been in 1890 and 1900.[82] Labor in the state took the cue and quickly came out against legislation motivated by such sentiments. After senate passage 21 to 14, the house agreed to hear testimony on the bill and was told eloquently by Peter Campbell, Secretary of the Kentucky Federation of Labor, that the bill would be misused to intimidate labor, that this issue would incite race and class hatred and turn men against the government.[83] Other opponents of the measure raised the free-speech point as well, but the measure passed 54 to 22, with twenty-one house members absent, two paired, and the Speaker not voting.

However, the legislature was not prepared for the response from the public. The assembly and the governor were promptly deluged with letters protesting the measure. The *Louisville Courier-Journal* branded it editorially "A Menace to Free Speech," advising the governor to seek major qualifications in the measure or veto it.[84] Republican Governor Edwin P. Morrow responded, signing the measure but proclaiming at the time that he felt at least three sections unconstitutional and promising to employ "the full power of the executive" to thwart any attempt to use section ten to prevent free speech, a statement generally interpreted to mean he would pardon all those convicted under the law.[85]

In only two states was strongly supported legislation beaten down. In North Dakota, still firmly in the hands of the Non-Partisan League, a proposed criminal-syndicalism measure died in legislative committee but not before League leaders had taken the opportunity to denounce it and similar legislation in other states as a carry over of wartime suppression. In the national platform of the body adopted at its convention in St. Paul on December 3, 1918, the League had stated that "the rights of labor surrendered for patriotic reasons must be restored and laws limiting civil rights of the people as war measures must be repealed."[86]

The same sentiment concerning the proposed 1919 North Dakota measure was widely expressed in the more than fifty League newspapers then being published in the state. Such momentum could not be overcome even by labor, which in a 1921 legislative report rather cynically wondered if such legislation might not have had some virtue, expressing curiosity "to see how their definition of criminal syndicalism would affect the profiteers and big business hogs doing business in this state."[87]

Wisconsin had enacted a criminal anarchy law as early as 1903, identical with the New York measure of the previous year, and a 1918 special session of the legislature had passed a bill against opposition to the war, and a red-flag law. In June 1919, however, a criminal-syndicalism measure ran into strong opposition from the large Socialist element in Milwaukee, the State Federation of Labor, and various farm cooperative groups. Free-speech objections were vigorously raised, but, ironically, the failure of passage was due to the inability to get a quorum in the state assembly; in the dying hours of the session, members had departed rapidly for home.[88]

The enactment of the wide range of sedition and criminal-syndicalism laws by the states in the postwar years has a variety of overtones for free speech and the tradition of free speech. The criminal-syndicalism laws "were not passed on their own intrinsic merits as necessary or desirable legislation. Rather, their passage was due to the approval of their objective which was to eliminate the existence and activities of radical groups."[89] With their passage, the conservative business community gained new and potent legal weapons with which to control any criticism of its postwar programs.

But in a broader sense, this legislation was the first open and overt legal peacetime departure from the principle of freedom of speech by the states. The departure distressed some Americans enough to call attention to the free-speech implications involved. But popular democracy and majority rule carried the day in spite of such protest and frequently seemed viciously hostile to its critics. The tradition of free speech was not sufficiently strong to prevent the enactment of laws to achieve the curtailment of its practice when public clamor deemed that practice detrimental. Such a turn gave meaning to de Tocqueville's observation: "The majority have ceased to believe what they believed before, but they still affect to believe, and this empty phantom of public opinion is strong enough to chill innovators and to keep them silent and at a respectful distance."[90]

5

The Attrition of the
Right of Free Speech
in 1919

Democracy has prevailed over autocracy. The reconstruction period is upon us. The next step is to create an intelligent public opinion and to prepare ourselves to deal with the problems of democracy.

Federal Council of Churches,
Advertisement, *The Survey*,
November 16, 1918

"So you want a permit to speak in Duquesne, do you?" he grinned.

"We do that," said I, "as American citizens demanding our constitutional rights."

He laughed aloud. "Jesus Christ himself could not hold a meeting in Duquesne!" said he.

"I have no doubt of that," said I, "not while you are mayor."

*Autobiography of
Mother Jones*, 1925

The boldness with which labor's champions expressed their views about the desirable forms of postwar reconstruction created gnawing apprehensions among employers in the United States. Late 1918 and early 1919 saw a wave of reconstruction conferences in various parts of the country. Starting with the National Municipal League, at Rochester, New York, November 20–22, 1918, in which Charles A. Beard claimed that the bolshevik government of Russia had a greater regard for efficient public expert service than the average American community,[1] these meetings ranged widely. The Conference of American Industries endorsed John D. Rockefeller, Jr.'s credo for collective relations through shop committees.[2] The Open-Forum National Council in New York concerned itself with the necessity of preserving the right of free speech and the possibility of solving problems by full public discussion.[3] An Atlantic City gathering of twenty-seven Protestant church groups,[4] the Conference on Demobilization and the Responsibilities of Organized Social Agencies,[5] and reconstruction meetings of the American Academy of Political Science and the National Popular Government League also offered sounding boards on these issues.

The meetings of the Academy, billed as a great love feast between labor and management, featured such speakers as Frank A. Vanderlip of the National City Bank, "a great captain of finance," Charles M. Schwab, of Bethlehem Steel, "the greatest captain of industry in the United States," Samuel Gompers, "the greatest labor leader in the world," William Howard Taft, "the best loved man in the country," and various lesser dignitaries.[6] Vanderlip initiated the proceedings rather jarringly by acknowledging the necessity of wartime restrictions on industry, but maintaining that it was now necessary to return to "our former individualism."[7] Schwab sought to temper the seeming finality of this business position by suggesting that "capital and labor will get closer together in the future, in better economic understanding." But Gompers frankly warned that labor would not go back to the old conditions and would not surrender what it had won.[8] John A. Fitch, in reporting the conference for *The Survey* concluded that "in spite of the call for a return to the 'old order,' . . . in spite of holding a discussion of labor problems at a four dollar dinner in the Hotel Astor ball room, the program as a whole was forward-looking and constructive."[9] He might have more candidly admitted that this was at best a civilized interim in an ancient struggle which the Armistice had clearly reactivated.

The National Popular Government League Conference, held in the Department of the Interior in early January 1919, involved cabinet members Franklin K. Lane and Josephus Daniels, Assistant Secretary of Labor, Louis F. Post, Senators Norris and Lenroot, Arthur Le Seuer of the Non-Partisan League, Basil M. Manly, Joint Chairman of the National War Labor Board, and William H. Johnson, President of the International Association of Machinists. The emphasis of the conference was largely on determining the best and most constructive steps toward a new order, "more capable of supplying the needs of the world, tending to distribute benefits more justly." The sympathies expressed seemed radical to large portions of the business community, particularly labor's insistence "that it have at home a large measure of democracy, both political and industrial."[10] Louis Post suggested specific goals, the bare minimum being the right of collective bargaining. "Neither industrial nor political democracy" could exist unless every man had equal opportunity—an equal standing in the government and on the earth.

> Unless we have some kind of adjustment that will give to every one an equal opportunity to live up to the full realization of his own powers and his own will to work, without making him subject to another man, except in the way of a contract made upon equal terms and not under advantages for one and disadvantages for the other, we shall not have industrial democracy.[11]

When working with its own membership, labor was equally insistent. A special reconstruction committee of the AFL called for immediate democracy in industry and spoke of an 8-hour day and 5½-day week. It also suggested making employer interference with the workers' right to organize a criminal offense and proposed consumers' cooperatives to curb profiteering, public ownership of utilities, wide-scale tax reforms with relief to the lower income groups, rapid demobilization, and an end to militarism. The report also emphasized the necessity for immediate removal of all restrictions upon freedom of speech, press, or association, "individuals and groups being responsible for their utterances." There was also no doubt that uninhibited freedom of expression was essential to the process of organization, the stepping up of collective bargaining, and the seeking of public converts to its cause through broad-scale propagandizing.[12]

The more aggressive state organizations went even further in boldly apprising business and the public of their postwar purposes. In November 1918 the California Federation of Labor called for an end to industry

> controlled by a jostling crowd of separate and private employers with their minds bent, not on the service of the community, but by the very law of their being, only on the utmost profiteering. We should look to scientific reorganization of the nation's industry, not deflected by individual profiteering; on the basis of a common ownership of the means of production.[13]

The Ohio State Federation called for extended governmental control of railway, telegraph, and telephone systems and governmental takeover of coal mines, oil wells, pipelines, and refineries, as well as all metallurgical mines and gas wells, at their true physical valuation. The Chicago Federation of Labor, the largest and most important of the AFL city central labor unions, called for representation in all departments of government as well as at the Peace Conference, and, following the inspiration of the British Labour party, urged an independent labor party for Illinois and the United States.[14]

The specter of labor's winning wide public support for such programs was disturbing to management. Certain employers were willing to compromise with wage demands, but on their own terms. The possibility of the extension of collective bargaining was a dangerous, and totally unwarranted, threat to their right to manage their own businesses in their own way. This view was widely enough held to break up a National Industrial Conference of representatives of industry, labor, and the public, called by President Wilson in 1919. Labor denounced company unions, but Judge Elbert H. Gary, board chairman of the United States Steel Corporation, one of the public representatives, made it clear he would have none of "dealing collectively as insisted upon by the labor union leaders."[15] To business, peace was supposed to bring freedom from coercion by "outside" forces, not an extension of it. Every demand that labor set forth reeked of extended control and the curtailment of individualism in one form or another.

Labor quickly realized that it would have to fight to retain its supporters through public persuasion. Such support would not only enhance the possibility of the success of its long-range objectives, but also add to the effectiveness of picketing and striking. In late 1918 and early 1919, such a course seemed extremely hopeful. Wartime successes and faith in the humanitarianism of the postwar democratic world encouraged labor to push the fight for "democracy in industry now!"

Business reached quickly for its carefully prepared tools to save "the old American way." The ends labor sought were disastrous. Righteous causes were never attained by foul means. But there was always the possibility that foolish dupes would be convinced. Hence it was absolutely necessary to silence agitators by casting them as immoral, irresponsible crackpots or, in the more relevant symbolism of that day, as "anarchists," "reds," and "Bolsheviks."[16]

In this situation, freedom of expression played a vital part, with labor basing much of its hopes on the ability to publicize its case, and business equally convinced that the silencing of critics was essential to the realization of its postwar goals.

Ironically, one technique for accomplishing such suppression was

that of counter-propaganda. The war had taught business the potentialities of manipulating public sentiments so well, that 1919 saw
the first market survey set up in an advertising agency and the first
independent surveying organization established.[17] The possibility of
undermining critics as "bolsheviks and anarchists" was quickly extended by such private organizations as the National Defense Society,
the American Security League, and the National Civic Federation.
Basil M. Manly had impressed, and partially amused, the National
Popular Government League conference by telling of a situation in
which:

> a little group of mill workers brought their complaints before the Na-
> tional War Labor Board. The employer's reply in that case was that
> they were a lot of I.W.W.'s, anarchists, Bolshevists, etc. We thought
> we would look into the matter, so we got access to the records of
> the Department of Justice, and we found that the leader of the so-called
> I.W.W.'s, the Bolshevists and anarchists was a detective in the pay
> of this very employer who made the charge against him.[18]

But Manly did not consider this an isolated example:

> These . . . situations, where autocratic groups have refused any means
> of settlement on the one hand, and on the other hand, where provocatory
> agents—detectives and stool pigeons—have gone in to force men out
> into the street and force them to use methods which are known perfectly
> well to destroy the organizations, are bringing us very rapidly to a
> condition which may become uncontrollable.[19]

Nonetheless, at first, labor was prepared to take on even the risk
of such devious counterattacks, feeling confidently that right would
triumph over all.

The extent of labor's determination to push its case was evident
in the strikes of the period. One of the first to make national headlines
was in Washington. On January 21, 1919, 35,000 Seattle shipyard
workers struck for higher wages and shorter hours. The militant Seattle Labor Council, led by Soviet sympathizer and AFL critic James
A. Duncan, promptly announced its intention to support the action
by a general strike. In the desire to promote labor solidarity, various
local AFL unions agreed to go along until 110 locals in all were
pledged to walk out on February 6.

Announcement of the plan plunged the city and various national
leaders into grave panic. "Intention of strike is revolution led by

extreme elements openly advocating overthrow of Government," wired
the local United States attorney to the Department of Justice,[20] and
the local press promptly deemed the whole operation a Russian-type
move, indicating the extent to which Seattle labor was riddled with
Bolsheviks. Immigration officials, now having an excuse they had
long sought, moved in quickly on local radicals, and, by the time
the strike began, thirty-six "desperate" Wobblies were on board a
"Red Special," rushing toward Ellis Island and deportation. In the
meantime, the War and Navy departments placed personnel at the
disposal of the governor of Washington, and army undercover operatives in the unions tightened up their surveillance.

The strike came off on schedule, and much incendiary literature
was distributed by both sides, but no one was arrested and no violence
occurred. The situation was ripe for exploitation by ambitious politicians, however, and the opportunity was not lost on Mayor Ole
Hanson, long an enemy of the IWW. Hanson requested federal troops
from neighboring Fort Lewis and, with a huge American flag draped
over the top of his car, personally led the soldiers into the city
and directed their deployment. He soon called on the strike committee
to surrender, assuring the general populace that "the anarchists in
this community shall not rule its affairs."[21] The strike was shortly
terminated, although far more because of the withdrawal of support
by national and local AFL leaders who were fearful that the whole
cause of organized labor was rapidly being discredited, than by the
histrionics of Ole Hanson.

The strike, however, had a galvanizing effect on the nation's press
and other organs of public opinion, propelling them almost en masse
into denunciation of Bolsheviks and their takeover of the American
labor movement.[22] Even religious organs took the opportunity to condemn labor's action: the *Homiletic Review* spoke of the "cold-blooded
criminality" of the strikers, the *Presbyterian Advance* insisted that
it was more than a strike, it was an attempted revolution, and the
New Era Magazine happily endorsed Hanson's exemplary techniques;
"no more mush and milk dealings," proclaimed the latter's editor.[23]
Congressmen and senators used the occasion for much patriotic oratory, further calls for repressive legislation, and warnings to AFL
leaders to renounce selfish and unpatriotic designs.[24]

The Seattle fiasco taught labor impressive lessons. Seeing the growing difficulty of getting its views expressed and its actions honestly
reported, it began to question the possibility of gaining concessions
through public persuasion and acknowledged realistically that the
struggle would have to be fought through direct pressures on the
parties from whom it sought concessions.

Strike figures in the months following the Seattle incident indicate the extent of the shift in attitude. In March there were 175 strikes; in April, 248; in May, 388; in June, 303; in July, 360; and in August, 373.[25] These ranged from a harbor strike in New York in January, where, amusingly, both sides tagged each other with the bolshevik label,[26] to a bloody and violent textile strike in Lawrence, Massachusetts, where eventually conscience-striken clergymen, led by the Reverend A. J. Muste, intervened and took over the strike committee, prosecuting the affair to a workers' victory,[27] to strikes of telephone operators in New England, machinists in Toledo, workers in the building trades in Dallas, and street railwaymen in Chicago. Labor also pushed for public policies which it considered basic, but which added to public concerns. Two such instances were a proposed nation-wide protest demonstration against the "frame-up" of Tom Mooney and Warren K. Billings, a cause which had rapidly come to symbolize the working class's fight for social justice, and support of the Plumb Plan for continued governmental operation of the railroads. Each move was quickly branded as bolshevik and used to discredit labor generally.

Other events also played into the hands of labor's detractors. Ole Hanson who, after his triumph in Seattle, resigned the mayor's job to begin a far more profitable nationwide anti-Bolshevik speaking tour,[28] received a homemade bomb in the mail on April 28. On the following day, a former senator from Georgia, Thomas W. Hardwick, who had earlier advocated that undesirable foreign agitators should be denied admission to the United States, received a bomb which blew the hands off the maid who opened it and burned his wife severely. Rapid searching of the mails by post-office officials then turned up thirty-four more such packages addressed to leading public figures and business leaders, all apparently designed to be delivered on May Day.[29] Public furor was expressed by self-appointed patriots and the police, making planned May Day marches and celebrations in a variety of cities objects of assault. The nation's press demanded repressive action.[30] "Free Speech has been carried to the point where it is an unrestrained menace," stated the *Salt Lake Tribune,* while the *Washington Post* called for silencing "the incendiary advocates of force. . . . Bring the law's hand down upon the violent and the inciter of violence." "Do It Now!" wrote the editor.[31]

By mid-1919, any leader who either proposed or took strong public action was virtually guaranteed broad public support. The results were further vigorous assaults on public expression. State leaders, impatient with the slowness of federal action, moved quickly to protect their local citizenry from all types of local troublemakers.[32] The situation in New York, while extreme, had parallels in a variety of other tension-ridden areas.

Archibald Stevenson, after the disappointing failure of the Overman bill's passage, focused his attention upon statewide suppression. Persuaded by his eloquence and by the growing apprehensions of such conservative bodies as the Union League Club that seditious activities were threatening "the very basis of government and the rights of its citizens,"[33] the legislature created a special committee to investigate the "scope, tendencies, and ramifications of such seditious activities."

The committee's precise function, its procedures and its long-range objectives were carefully left ambiguous from the outset. This was an invitation for it to undertake uninhibited dragnet operations. "In its day-to-day operations the committee was never clear whether it was a fact-finding body, a prosecuting agency, or a police force. Indeed, at times it seemed to regard itself more as a propaganda bureau than anything else."[34]

However, its sponsors and members were determined to broaden the base for the current drive against radicals and aggressive labor leaders by digging up evidence that would lead to their indictment, either in the courts or in the forum of public opinion. Silencing the agitator would solve all current social and economic problems. Operating on these assumptions, the committee, armed with blanket search warrants,[35] employed the raid as its chief instrument and on June 12 sent agents swooping down on the offices of the Russian Soviet Bureau in New York City. Raids of the Rand School of Social Science, of the "Russian Branch" of the IWW, and of the headquarters of the left-wing Socialists followed on June 21.

The raids produced disappointingly little incriminatory material. The committee, however, was undisturbed[36] and gained wide publicity for its charges that radicals were in control of at least one hundred trade unions and that the Rand School was cooperating with Russian agents in a deliberate plan for bolshevizing American labor.[37] The committee also moved to have the school's charter revoked. But State Supreme Court Judge John V. McAvoy threw the case out of court in late July. "So ends the spectacular raid on the inner seat of Bolshevism in New York," declared the *New York World*. "It proves to have been a raid chiefly on ordinary rights of free speech, and is thus calculated to produce quite as much Bolshevism as it suppressed."[38]

Such temporary humiliation did not dim the ardor of the committee. It finally gained the indictment of two unknown left-wing Finnish editors and set out to push for formal legislation geared to silence any public school teacher "for any act or utterance showing that he is not obedient to the constitution and laws of this state or of the United States, or that he is not in hearty accord and sympathy with the government and institutions of this State or of the United States."[39] It also sought, by law, to close the Rand School and set forth programs of Americanization for both foreign-born and certain native adults.[40]

Despite strong public support, especially from *The New York Times,* Governor Alfred E. Smith eventually vetoed these measures in May 1920. Pointing out that the avowed purpose of the legislation was to guard the institutions and traditions of America, Smith stated:

> In effect, it strikes at the very foundation of one of the most cardinal institutions of our nation—the fundamental right of the people to enjoy full liberty in the domain of idea and speech. To this fundamental right there is and can be under our system of government but one limitation, namely, that the law of the land shall not be transgressed, and there is abundant statute law prohibiting the abuse of free speech.[41]

Unfortunately, the action came after the nation's bolshevik nerves had calmed and far too late to undermine the snowballing red hysteria of 1919.

Other states moved to follow New York's lead and began to seek prosecutions under recently enacted sedition and criminal-syndicalism laws. With renewed bombings in June, especially of the Washington home of recently appointed Attorney General A. Mitchell Palmer,[42] Congress rushed to consider proposals for federal legislation.[43] So many measures were introduced with such overlapping intentions that their very profusion, plus Congress's felt obligation to consider them all, delayed any from immediate enactment. Most were ill-considered and rash. One prohibited bomb throwing or any destruction of life or property on penalty of death (one critic suggesting that this could result in the death penalty for anyone who threw a rock through a window).[44] Another closed the mails to any matter printed in the German language. Senator William H. King of Utah introduced a slightly more severe version of the earlier Overman bill, adding a provision prohibiting the display of any emblem or flag which symbolized the advocacy of revolution or the destruction of property. If it had not been for contemporary Senate interest in the peace treaty, undoubtedly more such legislation would have been proposed.

Little congressional hostility to such proposals developed, although certain small, but courageous, private organizations attempted to rally the opposition. The National Civil Liberties Bureau moved to support one Washington lobbyist for at least two days a week, a task which the energetic and redoubtable Albert DeSilver promptly turned into a full-time operation. DeSilver tried to reveal the anti–free-speech aspects of the various proposals in discussions with congressmen. To Senator Thomas Sterling, supporter of the King Bill, who maintained he did not want to interfere with freedoms of speech and press, but that a person had no right to advocate change through force or violence, DeSilver argued that whenever advocacy alone became subject to restriction, the protection of freedom of speech passed into the questionable hands of juries and law enforcement officials. He and the NCLB also opposed force, he readily admitted, but punishing its advocates was a poor way to deal with social and economic unrest.[45]

Despite overwhelming congressional support, fall 1919 still found no federal restrictive legislation on the books. It did see an important new federal agency, however, which quickly interpreted its charge as one of stepping up the war against radicals. After the bombing of his home, Palmer, with broad public acquiescence, called for the creation of a new General Intelligence or radical division within the Department of Justice. Congress responded quickly, voting a half-million dollar appropriation for the purpose. The new division was to be under the Bureau of Investigation, headed by William J. Flynn, former chief of the Treasury Department's Secret Service. Palmer had assured Congress that "Flynn is an anarchist chaser . . . the great anarchist expert in the United States. He knows all the men of that class. He can pretty nearly call them by name."[46] But despite the chief's boasted omniscience, the new head of the division, J. Edgar Hoover, promptly turned the entire efforts of the body to collecting information about radicals, seeking also to coordinate the results of its investigations with those of other governmental investigative agencies. The result was an index of over 200,000 cards on radical leaders, publications, and organizations, as well as on radical activities in various localities.

Initially, the division worked under the legal handicap of the charge in the congressional appropriation which had specified that the money was to be used for the "detection and prosecution of crimes." To expand its activities to include the detection of seditious speech and writings, it had to wait for Congress to enact appropriate peacetime legislation making certain types of utterances punishable. This obstacle gave little trouble, however. On August 12, 1919, eleven days after the creation of the division, the Bureau of Investigation solved the problem by instructing its agents to engage in the broadest detection of sedition and to secure "evidence which may be of use in prosecutions . . . under legislation . . . which may hereafter be enacted."[47] Agents lost little time in gathering information so as to have it ready when the inevitable punitive legislation would authorize its use.

Unfortunately, the men Palmer "depended upon to inform him about American radicalism and help establish anti-radical policies were extraordinarily susceptible to the fear and extravagant patriotism so prevalent in 1919. Furthermore, they were often careless about the language they used in evaluating the danger of revolution."[48] Max Lowenthal has even charged, in his hypercritical study of the FBI, that Flynn and Hoover purposely played on the Attorney General's fears and exploited the whole issue of radicalism to enhance the Bureau of Investigation's power and prestige.[49] Whatever the validity of such assessments, the bureau very cautiously shied away from specific actions through the early months of its existence, contenting itself with creating the impression that the radical menace was so large and dangerous that it would have to be approached with great care.

Two massive strikes in the nation's steel and coal industries in early and mid-autumn of 1919 proved determinative in the immediate struggle between management and labor and in the long range attitudes toward the role of free speech in the struggle for economic democracy. The steel companies' immunity from public pressures was common knowledge. Labor's problem was to create a countervailing force powerful enough to bring some sort of effective coercive pressure on the companies to gain concessions. This meant, very simply, stepped-up union organization. But organization depended upon the ability to reach employees orally and verbally. Hence, prerequisite conditions for union activity in steel were free speech, free press, and free assemblage, facts known only too well by the company officials.

The steel strike, which eventually went into effect in September 1919, had a long and stormy background. Steel was one of the last major industries which still employed the twelve-hour day, or the seventy-two-hour week, combining these with twenty-four-hour shifts in certain branches of the industry. The industry, although making feeble gestures toward improving conditions, had carried through on few of its promises and until near the end of the war remained a defiant bastion against collective bargaining. Leader of steel's procedures and policies was the United States Steel Corporation, for many years the largest and most powerful industrial domain in the world. At the time of its founding in 1901, its executive committee had laid down a firm policy: "We are unalterably opposed to any extension of Union labor and advise subsidiary companies to take a

firm position when these questions come up and say they are not
going to recognize it."[50] The ferocity with which steel clung to these
views was intense. Strikes against the industry in 1909 were quickly
put down and, from that year on, steel refused to deal with organized
labor.

During the war, the National War Labor Board championed collective bargaining, stating at one point that "this right shall not be
denied, abridged or interfered with by the employers in any manner
whatsoever."[51] Encouraged by such sympathy and by progress in
organizing the previously nonunion meat-packing industry in Chicago,
members of the Chicago Federation of Labor, with the aid of William
Z. Foster, a delegate from the Chicago local of the Brotherhood
of Railway Carmen, determined to press the national AFL into action
in steel. At the national convention in St. Paul in June 1918, they
introduced a resolution to initiate a joint organizing campaign in
the industry. Samuel Gompers, while never enthusiastic about the
proposal, agreed to a meeting in Chicago on August 1 and lent his
name to the new National Committee for Organizing the Iron and
Steel Workers. As it turned out, John Fitzpatrick, president of the
Chicago Federation of Labor, became the de facto head of the committee, since Gompers was in Europe for much of the next year,
and Foster designed the tactics of the drive, directing the organizers
and controlling the publicity.[52]

Foster planned to move rapidly while the war was still on. Extensive use was to be made of mass meetings and quickly organized local
committees. Emphasis was also to be placed on the relation of the
fight for democracy in Europe to industrial democracy at home. Organizers seldom lost an opportunity to speak of "showing the boys
abroad we have been fighting for industrial democracy at home"
or to proclaim "now is our time to build an industrial army to be
able to demand full democracy that the suffering and dying are
fighting for on the battlefields at this moment."[53] Such appeals were
particularly effective to the immigrants, who made up a sizable portion
of the labor force in the industry and who relished the ability to
demonstrate their patriotism by doing something about their depressed
conditions. This organizational campaign was responsible for drawing
a large segment of foreign laborers into the AFL and the union
movement for the first time, and was also responsible for a United
States Steel announcement that it would move quickly to a "basic
8-hour day," a promise, however, which it had no intention to fulfill.

The campaign was immediately successful in the Chicago area,
Gary, Hammond, and Joliet, so much so that alarmed steel promptly
pulled out the red flag. "As German armies marched through Belgium

in an endless stream, carrying devastation and ruin to the stricken Belgians, so the American Federation of Labor is marching its forces through Gary in the attack upon our industries,"[54] wrote the editor of the *Gary Tribune* in a feature story, which went on to characterize the activities of the steel organizers as a "violent display of anarchist Bolshevik spirit against all capital."[55]

Such criticism however, had, as yet, gained little support, and Foster and the National Committee promptly expanded their activities, scoring similar organizing successes in Youngstown, Cleveland, Buffalo, Sharon, Johnstown, and Wheeling. By the end of 1918, organization had ringed the hard core center of the steel industry, the Pittsburgh and western Pennsylvania area. In early 1919, Foster decided to challenge steel in its own lair. By this time the war was over, however, and steel, quickly sensing the resultant weakness of the lame-duck War Labor Board, girded itself for battle.

The first step in cracking the Pittsburgh district was to establish the rights of free speech and free assemblage. The steel towns of the area—McKeesport, Homestead, Monessen, Clairton, Braddock, Duquesne, and Rankin—were under a system of informal, but rigid, controls imposed through a variety of local ordinances, enforced by obedient local officials, or, if trouble arose, by state troopers (called Cossacks by the miners), whose use of violence and strong-arm methods was notorious. The press in each town was rigidly controlled also. So great was the suspicion of outside agitators that a speaker sent to Duquesne by the federal wartime Committee on Public Information to deliver a patriotic address on Abraham Lincoln had been arrested and jailed for three days, and in Homestead no labor meetings had been held for twenty-six years.[56]

Local officials acted rapidly when the Pittsburgh region became the target for further organization. The mayor of McKeesport, armed with a local regulation requiring his permission for any public meeting, rejected an AFL request to hire a hall in the city with the statement that the "A. F. of L. is a bunch of I.W.W.'s, anarchists, Bolsheviks and agitators."[57] Organizers then approached the city council, but the one labor member could not get a second to his resolution requesting the mayor to grant a permit. In Braddock, Homestead, and Monessen, local officials terrorized the owners of the halls into calling off meetings and refunding the rent money. In Rankin, where the hall proprietor refused to submit to such pressure, the Board of Health promptly closed his place of business. At Aliquippa, private detectives turned back union men at the railroad stations, and, although Pittsburgh authorities allowed meetings, they prohibited the distribution of organizational literature of any sort.

Such actions were discouraging, and even brought forth a mild protest from Gompers. Upon returning from Europe, he wrote to Mayor Lysle of McKeesport: "It is the lawful and moral right for working men to meet in McKeesport or elsewhere."[58] The national magazine, *The Survey,* explained:

> No one who ever supported the recent war on the ground that it was a war for freedom and who honestly meant a word of what he said, can fail to hope that the American Federation of Labor will push this matter vigorously and to a successful issue. American soldiers on the Rhine are guarding the fruits of the victory of democracy. Let them not be lost on the Monongahela![59]

Secretary of Labor William B. Wilson promised an investigation, and the governor of Pennsylvania agreed to exert his influence. A special convention of 400 labor representatives met in Pittsburgh in February to condemn the infringements on free speech and assembly as "un-American, illegal, and fatal to peace and progress."[60]

Labor then set out to push its case. A "Flying Squadron," under B. L. Beaghen, head of the Pittsburgh Bricklayers' Union, invaded the mill towns. It held public meetings in the streets in defiance of local authorities and, although Beaghen was jailed eight times and other leaders arrested and fined, by April the towns were succumbing. In May, Mayor Lysle made no attempt to break up a public meeting in McKeesport. By summer 1919, speech and assembly had a new and more universal meaning and application in the Pittsburgh area.

Such a condition was not to last, however. Steel was approached by representatives of the new union bodies with demands for the right of collective bargaining, the eight-hour day, one day's rest in seven, and increased wages.[61] Judge Elbert H. Gary refused even to meet representatives of the unions.[62] In the meantime, the companies stepped up their practice of discharging employees who had joined the union. Gompers then approached Woodrow Wilson. The President, at the time in the midst of his exhausting fight for the League, stated that the time had passed when any man should refuse to meet representatives of his employees. But no action was forthcoming. Labor then voted to strike the industry on September 22, and, although Wilson requested a postponement, union officials could not hold their men.

The strike began on schedule, and, before it was finally broken by the industry in January, close to 400,000 men went out. Its advent brought immediate cancellation of the earlier won rights of free speech and assembly. Sheriff Haddock of Allegheny County announced on September 20 that there would be no further outdoor meetings anywhere in Allegheny County and 5,000 "loyal" steel employees were deputized, along with various service veterans and local tradesmen to suppress union activity. The mounted "Cossacks," as the miners called them, clubbed men and women off the streets, dragged strikers from their homes and jailed them for breaching the peace, rode down public meetings, and maintained a reign of terror which continued during the 1920s. Private detective companies attempted to stir up internal dissension among the strikers, especially playing upon ethnic hostilities. Spies attempted to identify the leaders and turn them over to the legal authorities.[63] Town officials reenforced earlier restrictions and in Pittsburgh, which had been fairly open, meetings could be held only in two small, inaccessible outlying halls.[64] "Each day sees the suppression of free speech go relentlessly on. This is a case that should have been tried at the bar of public opinion, but the public has remained indifferent. Apparently the rights and liberties of citizens do not apply to the steel strikers."[65]

There was reason for public indifference. Steel, playing on public apprehensions and growing hysteria,[66] had launched a massive red-baiting campaign against the unions. Over thirty full-page advertisements appeared in the Pittsburgh papers alone between September 27 and October 8, many hinting of "red agitation," "bomb plots," and "revolution."[67] On November 11, 1919, Samuel H. Church, president of Carnegie Institute, in a flag-waving address to the World Christian Citizenship Conference, maintained:

> The abuse of unionism comes when two or more labor unions amalgamate into one society. They immediately become a menace to the happiness and welfare of the nation. The American Federation of Labor is the final exemplification of this peril. The time has now come when that organization ought to be dissolved. Not until this is done can the life and liberty of the nation be made secure.[68]

The speech was printed and widely distributed by the Employers Association of Pittsburgh. Similarly, Foster's earlier IWW connections, although long since severed, were headlined with regularity and his 1911 pamphlet on syndicalism was distributed widely by the steel companies. A United States Senate committee, called quickly in late September to investigate, left no doubt of its conviction that behind the strike there was massed a "considerable element of I.W.W.'s. anarchists, revolutionists, and Russian soviets."[69] The committee ignored the violation of the civil liberties of the strikers, even though John Fitzpatrick filled his testimony with examples of the abridgement of freedom of speech and assembly.[70] Military intelligence officers raided radical centers in Gary, informing a waiting press that they had discovered evidence linking strike leaders to a nationwide bomb plot and to representatives of Soviet Russia.[71] Such propaganda, and the fact that many strikers were immigrants, led large segments of the American public to accept all charges unquestioningly and to join in assaulting the "reds" through Citizens' Protective Leagues.

Such opinion was not universal. The Interchurch World Movement, representing the social consciousness of a large number of Protestant denominations, appointed a Commission of Inquiry whose conclusions stressed the orderliness of the strikers, the absence of foreign and radical influences, and the disgraceful and unrelenting violation of the civil liberties of workers at every turn. On October 28, a delegation of 18 persons, representing 150,000 organized workers in Pittsburgh and Allegheny County, went to Washington to protest the denial of the rights of free speech and assembly to labor. The Pennsylvania State Federation of Labor, in a special convention at Pittsburgh, voted to call a general strike unless the governor took positive action to protect civil liberties.[72] The problem was that the normal channels for expression were very nearly closed, with the nation's press firmly on the side of management and with little opportunity for oral expression through public meetings.

This latter fact was undoubtedly a factor in hastening the collapse of the strike. Steel, early and with increasing insistency, used the public press and other channels to emphasize the idea that the strike had failed. With virtually no channels to counter such propaganda, it became difficult to convince demoralized workers that this was not true; and as more and more returned to their jobs, fearing the use of imported black strikebreakers, the formerly solid front began to give way.[73] The strike leaders fought desperately to stem the tide, but internal dissension and the Gompers's caution proved fatal. On January 8, 1920, with 100,000 men still out, the National Committee decided to call off the strike, and labor's hopes collapsed without a single concession being gained. "Back to the Twelve Hour Day," wrote an editor of *The Survey*. But in response to Gary's views that the failure of the strike demonstrated that the workers were basically happy with their jobs, he added, "with no machinery by which they can protest against these conditions, and with an espionage system which effectively prevents them from letting their wants be known, it would seem to be a sweeping statement of Judge Gary's that the men are 'satisfied.' "[74]

The massive coal strike, which saw nearly 400,000 miners leave the pits on November 1, turned on hours and wages, but involved also a wartime contract which labor felt should no longer bind it. Many workers, despairing of any successful mediation with the companies, openly advocated nationalizing the industry, a position quickly interpreted as demonstrating their bolshevik tendencies. Superpatriotic groups willingly extended the charges and pressed for positive action.[75] The *Los Angeles Times* argued that "the steel strike and the coal strike were organized with all the care and strategy of a military campaign. They mark two of the offensives of the Bolshevist plotters who are trying to smash the American Republic, destroy the Constitution and set up a Soviet government on the ruins."[76] This fear no doubt accounted in part for the willingness of the government to intervene actively in the coal strike. With Woodrow Wilson virtually incapacitated after his fateful collapse on September 26 and with a Senate rebuke for his inactivity in the face of radical threats to the government,[77] A. Mitchell Palmer applied for a federal court injunction under the wartime Lever Act. The AFL executive committee denounced Indiana District Court Judge Anderson's response as "so autocratic as to stagger the human mind."[78] But the October 30 injunction was shortly made permanent, and John L. Lewis, sensing mounting public disapproval, ordered the strike call cancelled on November 11. The miners, who had defied the original injunction in going out on November 1, now refused to obey Lewis's rule, and with winter coming, more Americans became panicky. Eventually a sick President moved to suggest some minor wage concessions as a conciliatory gesture and with contempt proceedings also filed against eighty-four UMW officials, the strike finally ended December 10.

By late autumn 1919, business had learned to its gratification that by marshalling public opinion against the reds it could not only break strikes but also could weaken unions and push the open-shop movement forward significantly.[79] To certain labor leaders, like William Z. Foster, the experience proved that little could be accomplished through the cautious, existing union structure. The siren song of communism gained new appeal for them. At the other end of the spectrum, fear that red baitings would further undermine the weakened existing structure led Samuel Gompers and John L. Lewis to profess their Americanism and deny any connection with radicals bent on destroying the legitimate labor movement. Gompers, in fact, became so vehement in denouncing "Bolsheviks," "radicals," "reds," and "outlaws" that the editor of the Amalgamated Clothing Workers' newspaper, *Advance,* charged that he was "availing himself of the anti-labor vocabulary of our enemies in denouncing the discontented workers."[80]

To the rank and file, the experience was perplexing and demoralizing. Leadership had failed, and the possibility of meeting basic human wants through group action was frustrated completely. The result was a growing apathy toward unionization and a resultant decline in membership and support. Thus labor confronted the lean years of the 1920s with bitter disillusionment, which was manifested in its distrust of politics, in its hostility toward the press and other communications media, and in hopelessness about social justice, sentiments at least temporarily shared by many liberals.[81]

From the standpoint of free speech, the broken strikes were merely another step in an atrophying process. Undermining the validity of labor's objectives and raising doubts about the acceptability of its techniques reduced its will to speak out and the inclination of the public to give its view a fair forum. It remained only to silence those few agitators who still persisted in criticizing American institutions. The process almost succeeded as the mounting hysteria of late 1919 enveloped Americans. For a time it began to look as if nothing but glowing praise of the status quo would constitute free speech in the United States.

6

Nadir and Recovery:
Free Speech and
Guilty Consciences

If some or any of us, impatient for the swift confusion of the Reds, have ever questioned the alacrity, resolute will, and fruitful intelligent vigor of the Department of Justice in hunting down those enemies of the United States, the questioners and the doubters have now cause to approve and applaud.

The New York Times,
January 5, 1920

I come of a family that have been in America from the beginning of time. My people have been business people for generations. My people have been people of substance. They have made money. My family is a family that has money. I believe in property and I believe in making money, but I want my crowd to fight fair.

Zechariah Chafee, Jr., in
Felix Frankfurter Reminisces,
1960

By November 1919, many Americans who had deliberately contrived fears of revolution, bolshevik subversion, bomb plots, and destruction to quell their enemies were caught up in their own propaganda. Harmless eccentrics became dangerous enemies of the nation and unorthodox ideas became dangerous viruses, spreading "a disease of evil thinking," whose purveyors had to be either quarantined or gotten out of the country altogether.[1] Legally elected representatives of the people were refused their seats in legislative bodies lest their

77

activities destroy the American way of life. Thus, by late January 1920, liberal cartoonist Art Young, who a few months earlier had still found amusement in an aesthetic parlor Socialist reading his poem "Primeval Me" to a boiler-makers' union, drew a deadly grim "Deported," picturing a ship depositing on a rocky island not only chained people but tolerance, justice, free speech, the constitution, and the ballot.[2]

But this damaging assault on free speech proved too much and activated previously inert Americans to step in and attempt to restore public sanity and respect for democratic principles. The problem of charting a constructive road back then engaged the concern of substantial numbers and reopened the question of what constituted permissible freedom of expression.

When the United States Senate goaded A. Mitchell Palmer to action with its resolution of October 17, the Attorney General vowed to move not only against the rapidly approaching coal strike, but against a variety of undesirable seditionists as well.[3] State officials, apparently awaiting some semiformal green light, also moved in on troublemakers. Each was well armed, although in different ways, for although Palmer lacked comparable federal sedition or criminal-syndicalist laws, he had an arsenal of less formal weapons. The Justice Department, unbound by formal legislation and working closely with federal courts, could quickly obtain warrants, issue general orders which left to local officials wide discretion as to implementation, and follow pressures to the conclusions which they demanded.[4]

In addition, some legislation was available. Section 6 of the Penal Code authorized federal punishment of seditious conspiracy if actual conspiracy, and not merely irresponsible talk, could be demonstrated. More pertinent, during the war period, the government had used deportation as a weapon in its anti-Wobbly crusade, shipping IWW members, delegates, and organizers out of the country. In 1918 Congress had broadened the basis for deportation to include any alien, no matter how long or short his residence, who professed belief in the doctrines of proscribed radical organizations or held membership in them.[5] Without this act, no large-scale arrests would have been possible in 1919 and 1920, for it became the starting point for most of the massive federal activity against radicals in those years.

On November 7, 1919, then, one day before the coal strike injunction was issued, federal agents were instructed to move rapidly upon various city offices of the Union of Russian Workers, an anarchist group whose headquarters were in New York. Working with precision, under the supervision of J. Edgar Hoover, agents seized some 300 members and the records of the organization. During the previous year, federal court judges had been sensitive to the argument of IWW attorneys that the rule against self-incrimination was still in force in the United States. More and more arrested radicals invoked this right in refusing to testify about their affiliations. In order to deport them, Justice Department agents had to get incriminating records concerning the activities and policies of the organization involved. This fact helped shape the policy of whirlwind, unannounced raids, for "success lay with the sudden and surprise attack, not with a long sniper's campaign."[6] The government also made extensive preliminary arrangements to prevent bail, fearing that arrested radicals might tip off other victims. "Like a pig in a Chicago packing plant, the immigrant would be caught in a moving disassembly line, stripped of all his rights, and packaged for shipment overseas—all in one efficient and uninterrupted operation. American know-how was going to put an administrative procedure on a mass-production basis."[7]

The raid against the Russian Workers set a pattern that not only ran roughshod over the rights of its victims but also permitted considerable violence and brutality. When J. Edgar Hoover was presented with evidence by a New York attorney of assaults, beatings, and wanton and needless destruction of property, his reply was to urge that the attorney be disbarred for making such information public.[8]

Activities at the state level far exceeded those at the federal in both numbers seized and in callousness of treatment. The great battery of state sedition and criminal anarchy and syndicalism laws became the basis for action. Estimates of the number indicted varied.[9] Yet the count of the individuals and, more significantly, the nature of the activity which brought arrest gave a fairly accurate index as to what state officials considered permissible free expression by the autumn of 1919.

New York once again proved a leader with the Lusk Committee, still thirsting for concrete evidence to confirm its suspicions of imminent revolution, staging a massive raid on November 8 with the aid of 700 policemen. This action against over 70 radical centers netted the arrest of over 500 individuals and the seizure of tons of records and material. The committee quickly turned the aliens over to receptive federal authorities for expected deportation and promptly indicted the native-born under the 1902 criminal anarchy law. Of the group so indicted, five were prominent leaders of the left wing of the Socialist party—Benjamin Gitlow, Charles Ruthenberg, Isaac A. Ferguson, Harry Winitsky, and "Big Jim" Larkin, all of whom were charged with advocating the violent overthrow of the government, circulating the manifesto of the party, and being "evil-disposed and pernicious persons" with "wicked and turbulent dispositions" who tried "to excite discontent and disaffection."[10]

Gitlow was the first to be tried, the trial beginning on January 22, 1920, before a silk-stocking jury and a highly property-conscious judge, Bartow S. Weeks.[11] Clarence Darrow represented Gitlow and, from the outset, sought to turn the entire issue on freedom of speech, subjecting each potential juror to a searching examination and constantly injecting the issue into the proceedings in an attempt to show that in advocating nothing but abstract doctrine the Left-Wing Manifesto did not come under the criminal anarchy statute. However, Gitlow was convicted and sentenced to from five to ten years in Sing Sing, Judge Weeks having undercut Darrow's position by charging the jury, "You are not sitting here to determine any question of the rights of free speech,"[12] and later congratulating them: "Your verdict reflects credit on your sincerity and intelligence and is one of distinct benefit to the country and the state."[13] Subsequently, in 1921, the Appellate Division of the New York Supreme Court, in upholding the conviction, agreed that the manifesto was no direct incitement to violence, but still ruled that the Communists had to be held responsible for the potential dangers of their abstract concepts. Ultimate resolution, before the United States Supreme Court, did not come until 1925, but when it did, both the majority opinion and Holmes's eloquent dissent became milestones in the history of the permissible limits of public expression in the United States. In subsequent trials, Ruthenberg, Ferguson, and Winitsky were given similar sentences by Judge Weeks. Irish-born Jim Larkin received comparable treatment, but not before challenging Weeks as a prejudiced judge, a charge which Weeks himself decided was unfounded. The verdict in this decision had international implications: the dockers in Dublin struck in sympathy and the British House of Commons petitioned Governor Smith for pardon.[14] Neither action seemed to affect the American conscience strongly.

In Illinois, the spawning grounds for the union move against big steel, state authorities were equally active. As a result of "carefully matured plans laid by Chicago merchants, bankers, and businessmen, aided by the State Attorney's office,"[15] a large raid on January 1, 1920, netted several hundred radicals, including Rose Pastor Stokes and "Big Bill" Haywood. Thirty-nine of those jailed, mostly intellectuals, were members of the Communist Labor party, which had been formed in September 1919. Twenty were convicted for advocating the overthrow of the government by force, a charge held a violation of the Illinois Sedition Act of 1919. Eighteen appealed, among them

William Bross Lloyd, millionaire Socialist, and one of the organizers of the Communist Labor party in America. Lloyd's prominence turned the spotlight of public interest on the case. He was charged, among other things, with driving his automobile down State Street in Chicago, flying a large red flag and an American flag. When his car stopped in front of the Palmer House, a crowd soon gathered, shouting, "Take that flag down." Upon refusal, the red flag was removed by a police officer, and Lloyd was arrested. At the trial in police court, he stated that he put the American flag there as a matter of courtesy; the red flag was his most valued flag, and, if he could not fly it, he would go to Russia. He was also later charged with incendiary statements in a Milwaukee speech to several thousand workers in which he berated President Wilson, praised the IWW, and urged his "comrades" to begin gathering the weapons for revolution.[16]

The subsequent trial again found Clarence Darrow arguing for free speech and riddling the state's position even more thoroughly than he had done in the Gitlow case.[17] Darrow derived great pleasure in raising doubts about the danger of the text of the song "Red Flag," or the bolshevik yell:

> Bolshevik, bolshevik, bolshevik, bang!
> We are members of the 'Gene Debs gang.
> Are we rebels? I should smile.
> We are with the soviets all the while!

He also questioned a circular announcing a picnic to celebrate the second anniversary of the Russian Revolution,[18] and a letter from Edgar Owens, Illinois secretary of the Communist Labor party, to John Reed stating that he would like his sensitive son Arvid to grow up to be a rebel, "a musician of the revolution."[19] Darrow also openly challenged indictment under the Sedition Act for acts committed before its passage, a charge which the state answered by contending that such acts were evidence of intent to violate a law that was surely forthcoming. Apparently unsure of its case, the state brought Mayor Ole Hanson into the proceedings to testify on the dangers of bolshevism and the general strike, even though no connection had ever been shown between the Communist Labor party and the Seattle episode. Darrow challenged this action also and produced evidence to show that the Seattle general strike had been nonpolitical in origin and peaceable and disciplined in conduct, charging that if violence was created in Seattle it was by Hanson himself.[20] But with the state's attorney impugning in advance the unpatriotic nature of anything but a guilty finding, the jury's ruling was predictable.

The red hysteria also afforded Californians the opportunity to try out their stringent proscriptions against radicals. The famous Centralia, Washington, American Legion–IWW battle in November 1919[21] had a profound effect upon conservative Californians. A Los Angeles Legion post demanded that "all guilty of seditious statements or acts be immediately incarcerated or deported," and formulated plans for the immediate organization of a military branch to support the police.[22]

Such pressure resulted in the November 28 arrest of several dozen left-wingers active in the affairs of the Communist Labor party. Prominent among them was well-known philanthropist and social worker, Charlotte Anita Whitney, daughter of a distinguished California family. Her arrest in Oakland, as she was leaving a meeting of a women's club in which she had been speaking on the condition of the American Negro, came three weeks after the convention in which, ironically, she opposed violent overthrow of the existing order and urged the new state party to capture political power through the ballot. The fact that she still remained at the convention once her position was overridden was taken as proof that she acquiesced in the final position adopted. After a dubious trial, during which her attorney died but no postponement was permitted, she was sentenced to serve from one to fourteen years in the state penitentiary. The California press hailed the verdict as "another gratifying victory in the absolutely necessary program of government to scotch the communists, I.W.W., and other organizations and individuals engaged in and pledged to criminal revolution against the Republic!"[23]

The pattern of arrests and convictions in other states produced numerous revealing examples of local hysteria, but also interesting local variations. The IWW was prosecuted in Kansas, Washington, California, Idaho, and Minnesota. Usually, such prosecutions were for mere membership, although in some cases for the espousal of IWW views either orally or in print. A logger was indicted in Spokane for making out a receipt for membership, while a harvest worker was arrested when he informally expressed "radical views to the other members of a threshing crew of which he was a part."[24] A Socialist editor in Duluth, Minnesota, was indicted for various editorial positions which his paper had taken,[25] while a man was arrested in New York for having given a fellow worker a communist leaflet, even though, in reality, he was handed the leaflet and was asked to translate it by the person making the charge.[26]

In two states, actions taken during the height of the red scare were subsequently reversed by sensitive state courts. New Jersey authorities, with the aid of various agents provocateur of the Department of Justice, had arrested several members of the Communist Labor party and indicted them under the state sedition law for party membership. Walter Gabriel appealed his conviction to the state supreme court. Gabriel had been arrested without a warrant and taken before a police justice, who, after assuring him he was only seeking information, cross-examined him on the doctrines of the party and convicted him on the subsequent information he gave. The state supreme court in reviewing the conviction stated hostilely that the evidence hardly showed that the plaintiff was "advocating in public by speech" subversive doctrine and ruled section 3 of the Sedition Act as unconstitutional because it violated that portion of the state constitution guaranteeing the people "the right to freely assemble together, to consult for the common good, to make known their opinions to their representative, and to petition for redress of grievances."[27] New Mexico state authorities acted under a statute which declared unlawful any act, the purpose of which was the destruction of organized government, to convict Jack Diamond for soliciting members of the IWW.[28] But the state supreme court intervened; Justice Parker, basing his position on the Gabriel case, ruled the statute unconstitutional as a violation of freedom of speech and assembly.[29]

The only other states in which the repressive legislation was not used with consistent impugnity were Nevada and Montana. In the mining regions, it was virtually impossible to secure a convicting jury, so that the carefully prepared criminal-syndicalism statutes proved useless. The mining interests urgently called for federal intervention to gain the "quiet elimination of these men from the community" in Nevada by the Immigration Bureau and in Montana by the Department of Labor.[30] To their disappointment, federal authorities moved with extreme caution, especially after careful investigation showed that these men were nondeportable American citizens, and, that given their activities, it would be next to impossible to prove honestly that there had been either actual destruction of property or the advocacy or teaching of it.

Such exceptions were the result of unique conditions, however. Far more typical was the action of Connecticut authorities in using a law forbidding loitering by three or more persons on any bridge or highway to break up a meeting of the American Civil Liberties Union. A broad spectrum of city ordinances, from Los Angeles to Mount Vernon, New York, served to jail radicals for actions ranging from distributing pamphlets to holding street meetings without previous permission.[31]

In summarizing these various actions, the Methodist *Social Service Bulletin* raised this question for the church: "If the rights of free speech, free press and free assemblage are denied those who seek to change the present social order, what hope is there that progress can be secured by peaceful means?"[32] The answer, in the winter of 1919–1920, seemed rather bleak. In light of the obvious domination of state courts, legislatures, and law enforcement agencies by repression-oriented individuals, it might have been the better part of wisdom for liberals and radicals to resign themselves to quiet, personal action which would not run afoul of powerful interests. Temporary surrender of freedom of expression through self-imposed restraint might have cleared the air for later rebirth.

There was always the danger, however, that during such a temporary retreat the repressionists might push through such permanent restrictions as to prevent renewed activity. Such threats were sufficiently ominous at the time to forestall complete withdrawal by those seriously concerned with civil liberties. A. Mitchell Palmer's sudden manic outbursts in October and November 1919 and public distress over the autumn strikes renewed the dormant interest at the time in a peacetime federal sedition law; and the concerned leaders of the major labor unions, having been hit hard by the federal injunctions, saw the new proposals as invitations to further massive intervention in the interests of management. A number of measures were introduced at this time to simplify deportation. More important, the former Overman bill, reintroduced in October as the Sterling bill, would have gone further than its predecessors by denying the mails to any printed material that the Postmaster General labeled seditious.

Palmer publicly branded the Sterling bill as too drastic and denied the necessity for censorship; but he may have been concerned lest Postmaster General Albert Burleson take away the initiative in the snowballing red hunt. To Palmer, the real need was for legislation that would enable the Justice Department to prosecute individual American citizens who were prepared to overthrow the United States government by force and violence. The Justice Department's "radical division" had been compiling long lists of such individuals since August. Palmer's own sedition measure, introduced into the House by Democratic Representative Martin Davey of Ohio and into the Senate by Republican Senator Knute Nelson of Minnesota and shortly endorsed by President Wilson, sought to define as punishable sedition any activity designed to change the government or the laws of the United States or any action which might be interpreted as "an act of force against any person or any property, or any act of terrorism, hate, revenge, or injury against the person or property of any officer, agent, or employee of the United States."[33] The interpretation and application of various vague terms were to be left to law enforcement officials and ultimately to the Justice Department.

Labor leaders promptly denounced the measure arguing that the prohibition of the use of "force . . . against property" clearly outlawed strikes, a judgment with which the *New Republic* concurred, adding that overzealous language might also be applied to newspaper editors critical of the administration or even to voters who, by casting a ballot against patriotic public officials, might be committing "an act of revenge against the government."[34] Gompers and AFL leadership even turned to the National Civil Liberties Bureau in an attempt to rally combined support against the legislation. Liberal opinion also spoke out with the *Nation, Independent,* and the *Survey,* as well as Pulitzer's *New York World,* expressing hostility. A *Survey* author wrote in January 1920:

> What is going to be the outcome of all this legislation? Will it stop unrest? Yes! Just as shaving a dog will keep his hair from growing. . . . How can our legislators be so childish as to think they can put a stop to thoughts about the government, and even their communication from one person to another, by punishing such manifestations of these as can be discovered? Even as a matter of policy is it not better to allow people to express their discontent and their recommendations for its remedy, if only for the purely interested purpose of seeing what they are up to, that we may cope with them better? We are forgetting that we are a democracy when we let administrative officers hold a monopoly of information as to the nature and prevalence of doctrines and beliefs about the state.[35]

On December 21, the "Soviet Ark" *Buford* sailed from New York with 249 "dangerous radicals" aboard, including anarchists Emma Goldman and Alexander Berkman; on January 2, federal raids dwarfed their November predecessors in the number of people seized, the accompanying disregard for due process, and individual brutality. Government officials promptly announced that seized papers and documents clearly proved that "radical leaders planned to develop the recent steel and coal strikes into a general strike and ultimately into a revolution to overthrow the government."[36] Such action apparently shamed the Senate into action. Responding to renewed pressure by Palmer, the Senate passed the Sterling Bill on January 10, without a roll call and without a quorum present, but not until a hard core of courageous opponents, led by Senator William E. Borah of Idaho, had fought to modify the postal censorship provisions and to make a court hearing mandatory whenever the Postmaster General sought to clamp down on material he found offensive.[37] Passage of the measure threw the gauntlet to the House to demonstrate its Americanism. There, under the leadership of Republican Representative George S. Graham of Pennsylvania, a measure was prepared and unanimously agreed upon which was no disappointment. Graham, after stating that "the right of free speech and a free press will always be maintained inviolate," unveiled a measure which called for the death penalty for anyone inciting or conspiring to bring about destruction or overthrow of the government by force or violence where human life was lost as a result.[38] Aimed admittedly at the "parlor bolshevists," the measure was a composite of all of the most restrictive features urged upon Congress. Its advocates sought to speed its passage and approached the Rules Committee with a resolution asking for a special rule to provide for its immediate consideration.

But the Graham bill was never passed, and, as spring approached, it became obvious that something had punctured the inflated balloon of swelling national hysteria. The revelation of inhuman treatment of hundreds of Americans, many arrested on little more than suspicion in the sweeping nationwide dragnet, raised questions in Congress and in various public forums whether tyrannical and arbitrary methods could save democracy.[39] Prominent public figures suddenly stood out openly against the growing danger to American institutions. United States District Court Judge George W. Anderson[40] told the Harvard Liberal Club, in a widely reported and quoted speech, that 99 percent of the pro-German plots never existed and expressed doubts "whether the Red menace has any more basis in fact than the pro-German peril." Justice Oliver Wendell Holmes sent a message to the same meeting condemning suppression of radical views and avowing that "with effervescing opinion as with the not yet forgotten champagne, the quickest way to let them get flat is to let them be exposed to the air."[41]

Frank I. Cobb, editor of the *New York World,* publicly proclaimed that "nobody ever succeeded in bettering the weather by putting the thermometer in jail, and nobody will ever remove the cause of unrest and discontent by trying to suppress their manifestations."[42] Senator Joseph I. France of Maryland not only pointed out the superfluousness of laws restricting speech ("Free speech is the safety valve for abnormal times. . . . Article I. of the Constitution was written for times such as these."), but called for repeal of the wartime Espionage Act by the current session of Congress.[43] Even more revealing was the release to the press on January 12 of the uncomplimentary

circumstances surrounding the resignation from the Justice Department of the prominent Philadelphia attorney Francis Fisher Kane,
close political associate of Palmer (wrote Paul U. Kellogg to a friend
at the time: *"There's* one man in Sodom!"),[44] indicating, as it did,
that there were some high public officials who had grave doubts
regarding the extent of the claimed danger of the moment and the
tactics used to confront it.

But it a single event shocked the public into realization that repression had gotten out of hand, it was the refusal by a group of opportunistic politicians in the New York legislature to seat five duly elected
Socialist assemblymen on the lame claim that the program of the
party they represented was revolutionary, unpatriotic, and disloyal.[45]
The fact that the sixty-thousand constituents whom the Socialists
represented had elected four of them before and felt confidence in
The fact that the sixty thousand constituents whom the Socialists
party was a legally recognized party under New York election laws.
Hazy precedent for the action existed in Congress's persistent failure,
even in light of reelection by his constituents after disqualification,
to seat Milwaukee Socialist Congressman Victor Berger, but Berger,
at least, had been convicted of violating the Espionage Act for antiwar
statements, while no action of the five elected Socialist members
had in any way created plausible grounds for any movement against
them. The action, branded by *The Nation* as "the most ominous
happening of all the political events of this period of reaction,"[46]
aroused a hornet's nest of protest from even conservative newspapers
and journals. Words commonly used were "hasty," "politically un-
wise," "extraordinary," "dangerous," "legally unjust," "unwarranted,"
"reactionary," "biased," "the result of prejudice," and "unfair."[47] The
Young Republicans of New York adopted a strong resolution condemning the action and maintaining that Speaker Thaddeus C. Sweet
was blindly aiding the extreme radicals by undermining our "sacred
heritage" of "freedom of speech and of assembly and full opportunity
for the expression of ideas."[48] The Reverend Percy Stickney Grant,
who had been temporarily deprived of his pulpit in New York's
fashinoable Church of the Ascension at the time of the *Buford's*
sailing for comparing it with the *Mayflower* and mockingly suggesting
that its voyage be postponed one year so it could fall on the 300th
anniversary of the pilgrims' flight from oppression, called a public
forum on "Free Speech," to which were invited men of all shades
of opinion and which drew a packed crowd genuinely aroused over
the situation in Albany.[49] George Bernard Shaw wired from England
stating "Americans are savages still," with the action clearly confirming
that "the primitive communities prosecute opinion as a matter of

course."[50] Yet it remained for Charles Evans Hughes, former governor of New York and, at the time, titular head of the Republican party, to boldly rally responsible, conservative support against the action. Hughes wrote a strong letter to the *New York Tribune* stating: "I have sufficient confidence in our institutions to believe that they will survive all the onslaught of discussion and political controversy. But democracy can not be preserved if representation is denied."[51] He prepared to draw the state and city bar associations of New York into the fight.

Those who sought to go the final step in silencing liberal opinion had not counted on the fact that such action was a double-edged sword. For if the ballot was to become meaningless in the light of arbitrary majorities and one's legally elected representative were to be prevented from either speech or action in a legislative body, minority opinion and rights in the United States were in serious danger. The danger of creating such a precedent for frustrating the democratic process was not hard to see by even the most smug and obtuse.

Hughes and those who rallied to him aroused massive public condemnation but lost the immediate battle for seating the assemblymen. The Association of the Bar of the City of New York, a citadel of legal conservatism, condemned the suspension of the assemblymen and appointed a committee to go to Albany to "protect the principles of representative government." The committee which included among others, Ogden L. Mills, millionaire Republican publisher of the *New York Tribune* and later Secretary of the Treasury under Herbert Hoover, got a firsthand taste of legislative suppression.[52] Hughes, as spokesman, attempted to speak to the assembly but was ruled out of order. His attempt to submit a statement was also rebuffed. The action was particularly arbitrary since a great variety of nonlegislative supporters of the expulsion had been permitted to speak at great length.

The even more conservative State Bar Association was persuaded not to support the legislature by the vigorous and eloquent oratory of Hughes, Attorney Louis Marshall, John Lord O'Brian, former chief of the Justice Department's War Emergency Division in charge of prosecutions under the Espionage Act, and William Howard Taft's Attorney General George W. Wickersham.[53] Nevertheless the delegates went unseated and even when reelected the following September were still barred. More representative government in New York had to await calmer times. But a change of national temper regarding overly zealous suppression was now clearly evident. A sudden swell of hostility blocked the movement toward a federal peacetime sedition

law. Albert De Silver sent out the first encouraging letter in many
months from the National Civil Liberties Bureau:

> The Speaker of the New York Assembly, egged on by the Lusk Com-
> mittee, had suspended the five Socialist Assemblymen from New York
> City without specific charges, and in advance of a hearing. A great
> to-do had arisen about it. Voices all over the country were raised
> in protest, including those of Mr. Charles E. Hughes and the New
> York Bar Association. The statesmen in Washington up on Capitol
> Hill sat up and rubbed their eyes. They had been taking all this
> sedition business pretty much on faith but here was something new.
> They began to scratch their heads and wondered if they really knew
> where it all led to. The Rules Committee decided that they had better
> hold hearings before they granted the special rule.[54]

The hearings to which De Silver referred began on January 23
and lasted three days. They quickly took on the form of what a
New Republic writer later called "a sort of set of lectures on free
speech, its origin, nature and nurture."[55] The outcome was pre-
ordained. The Rules Committee had received so many protests about
the Graham bill that it quickly came to regret its willingness to
consider it in the first place. Previously enthusiastic congressmen
and senators were suddenly moved to public denunciation, inspired
by mail swelled with individual and group protests against the anti-
free speech aspects of the measure.[56] And, although such bitter repressionists as Representative Thomas L. Blanton of Texas tried every
parliamentary trick to prevent it,[57] many such expressions were read
on the floor of Congress. Congressman George Huddleston of Alabama
summarized much of their sentiments in a speech in which he
maintained:

> For months an extensive propaganda has been carried on in behalf
> of suppression of free speech. That is what it has really been, although
> it has been disguised, as only the ingenuity of professional propagandists
> can do, with the cloak of patriotism. It has been hidden away, but
> the real purpose of this movement is to strike at this fundamental
> right that is safeguarded to us in the first amendment to the
> Constitution.[58]

Public leaders in labor, the church, the press, and the legal profession vied with one another in pointing out the dangers of the bill,

while such a little-known organization as the National Popular Government League was suddenly hailed with popular praise for its announced intention to stop this sedition law and any others like it.[59]

Practically all of the activist-libertarian arguments and clichés, which a year before had seemed high-flown abstractions, were now seized upon by a public genuinely aroused over the threat to individual liberty. The legislation was denounced as superfluous and branded as dishonest. Cast in the pious terms of suppressing revolution, it was really designed to stifle honest criticism born of discussion and nurtured through the give-and-take of conflicting ideas and policies. Suppression was denounced as old world tyranny, even characterized as the Russian approach to dissent, necessary, at the very most, in a period of national wartime emergency, but irrelevant in peacetime. Congressman Huddleston, a strong champion of organized labor, emphasized that those without power in society needed safeguards to their freedom of speech and expression since they were poorly equipped to protect it themselves, as powerful property owners and business interest could.[60]

This rhetoric was elaborated when the hearings actually took place. Virtually no one defended the measure, which two weeks earlier had been recommended by a unanimous House. Samuel Gompers, attorney Jackson Ralston, and law professor Zechariah Chafee of the Harvard Law School assailed the measure's shortcomings and sinister overtones. Captain Swinburne Hale, formerly a member of the Military Intelligence Division of the Army General Staff, not only blasted the anti–free-speech aspects of the Graham measure, but insisted that the Justice Department had adopted the "historical Russian habit" of planting things in places where subsequently they could be victoriously "found," and had taken part in committing the crimes which it detected.[61] Francis Fisher Kane took the occasion to speak against the measure and the earlier abuses of the Justice Department and its head, whose name had now been firmly attached to the January raids. Palmer himself, who had earlier come to the chairman of the Rules Committee on the floor of the House to request an opportunity to be heard first in favor of the rule, suddenly found himself far too busy to appear and sent a courteous note stating that he had had serious misgivings about the measure from the outset.[62]

After the first day of the hearings, the *New York World* carried a story headed: "Sedition Bill Has No Chance in Face of Bitter Attacks: Palmer Repudiates It and Gompers Tells Committee It Strikes at All Freedoms."[63] In fact, its authors were now suddenly on the defensive. One of them, Republican Representative James

W. Husted of New York, admitted under questioning on the House floor that the measure was too harsh and that its earlier sections which gave to the government "the power of efficient threat" over organized labor would have to be removed.[64] The committee quickly decided to deny the application for the special rule, and the whole subject went back to the House Judiciary Committee, which met on February 4.

A. Mitchell Palmer finally appeared and informed the committee that he wished to be heard in support of his own measure, the Davey bill, and dissociated himself from the Graham measure, which he confessed made him shudder: "No man can go further than I will go in his earnestness to protect the people in the guaranty of free speech."[65] Palmer went on to discuss his concept of permissible free expression. He attempted to draw a clear line between the advocacy of abstract doctrines, which he felt was permissible, and the advocacy of force and violence. He claimed the latter was all the Davey bill sought to punish. But when Congressman Rank Reavis of Nebraska questioned his inference that this would include "organized direct economic action," Palmer assured him that that was surely the same thing as the advocacy of force and violence, especially when used by an organization such as the IWW. As to whether the same would be true of organizations other than the IWW, Palmer was evasive and reserved decision. When Reavis asked if the Davey bill would not in essence make strikes illegal, Palmer assured him it would not, unless, of course, the strike was to be used for some illegal purpose.[66]

Palmer's tendency to speak generally, frequently equivocally, and with little precision, injured his case. It also illustrated the danger of leaving to administrative officials unqualified grants of authority to implement as they saw fit. This fact was coming into hostile focus more and more as the procedures surrounding the raids were being revealed.

Another witness for sedition legislation also inadvertently undermined the repressionist position. In his desire to praise the Lusk Committee with which he had worked closely and to justify the action against the Socialists, Charles D. Newton, the Attorney General of New York, asserted that between 300,000 and 500,000 persons in New York City alone wanted to overthrow the government by force. Such claims, which a month before might well have been swallowed unquestioningly, now had the hollow ring of personal self-justification, especially when John D. Moore, former New York State Conservation Commissioner, replied to Newton, contradicting his facts and proving his exaggerated figures utterly misleading.[67]

For the other side, Gompers, Ralston, and Kane appeared again. They reiterated and elaborated upon earlier charges. So many individuals and spokesmen for various private groups ranging from farm organizations and the National Popular Government League to the Religious Society of Friends and the NAACP demanded the opportunity to be heard that the committee set rigid limits on the time for testimony, urging the submission of written statements when possible. The outcome again was to weaken the position of those demanding sedition legislation. By March it was clear that even the mildest sedition bill would muster little congressional support.

In a general way, the rapid public reversal on the free-speech issue was due to a reevaluation of national trends by many people who came to the conclusion that liberty was in jeopardy. This was of necessity a very personal process, and the cumulative reaction was the sum of individual shocks at the realization that each man's livelihood and life style might well be threatened unless events were quickly reversed.

Conservative labor was a good case in point. Smarting from the tar-brush of bolshevism applied during the steel and coal strikes, AFL leaders worried about their dwindling power. Unlike radical labor, which dug in to confront suppressive legislation head on, conservative labor still hoped to play the game both ways and frequently supported governmental suppression of Wobblies, advocates of industrial unionism, and Bolsheviks as vigorously as the most vocal of the repressionists. In fact, a *Literary Digest* poll in early 1920 showed that of 526 union officials questioned the great majority favored ridding the country of agitators and supported Palmer's deportation policies with few qualms. Only 100 officials actually objected without reservation to federal repressive policies.[68] But the Graham bill, the growing number of indictments of prolabor partisans, and the refusal to seat the Socialists at Albany suddenly revealed that the labor leaders could well become targets of the very hysteria they so blandly endorsed. Consequently, the AFL and the even more conservative railroad brotherhood took the most unequivocal position labor had taken on the free expression issue in the struggle against the Graham Measure. Gompers wrote in the *American Federationist:*

It has been widely advertised that this measure protects free speech fully, but prevents advocacy of forcible revolution, bolshevism and anarchy. In fact, it would perpetuate an autocratic censorship over the entire American Press. It can be used to kill free speech and free assembly. It strikes a deadly blow at legitimate organizations of labor or any other progressive movement for the betterment of the masses which may be opposed by the advocates of privilege and reaction.[69]

William Hard explained that the AFL perceived that "the tide to engulf the Reds in whirls of criminalized words was not likely really to do so much harm to Moscow as to the building at Ninth Street and Massachusetts Avenue, inhabited by trade-union leaders who have done their best to deserve well of the republic by being patriotic in war and staunch against revolution in peace."[70]

Numerous business leaders were also developing serious misgivings about the potential adverse effects of red baiting and of antiradical nativism. With the strikes clearly broken, they began to worry that further raiding and deportations might hasten rigid immigration restrictions and discourage foreign workers from migrating to the land of the free. A nation which brooked no dissent would lose much of its appeal to foreign workers tired of tyranny at home. Such businessmen began actively to defend the foreign-born and to assail the Justice Department for the maltreatment of immigrants. In fact, business seemed so anxious to throw oil on troubled waters that it reached the point of arguing that native Americans had caused the red scare, that it was "sheer Red hysteria, nothing more," and that "Bolshevism was conceived in America by Americans."[71] The time to call off the antiradical campaign was at hand.

The press had benefited from increased circulation as the red hysteria had mounted and had blindly supported Palmer, state raiders, and suppressionists. However, the press also came to its senses in the new, quickly relaxing climate and now saw in the Sterling and Graham bills a potential threat to its own freedom.[72] Certain newspapermen, such as Frank Cobb of the *New York World* or Gardner Gilson, Washington representative for the Scripps McRae chain's editorial board, had always been aware of the potential danger to freedom of the press and grew highly disturbed about the inadequacy of public information in the face of the government's clear intention to manipulate and suppress opinion.[73] But not until the threat of the Graham bill did the *New York Globe*, the *New York American*, the *Springfield Republican*, the *Detroit Free Press*, and the *Chicago Daily News* awake. The *St. Louis Post Dispatch* then warned that the bill "not only establishes a censorship of news, which is intolerable in time of peace and is endurable only as a military necessity in time of war, but it establishes a censorship of newspapers."[74] Even *The New York Times*, which had consistently supported the repressionist position, worried editorially that the measure's "prohibitions, however patriotic in purpose, seem to go beyond the accepted and natural limit of constitutional definition."[75]

Before the Graham bill hearings, twenty-two eminent Protestant clergymen issued an eloquent public statement denouncing further governmental interference with personal liberty. The declaration restated a similar condemnation of the King bill issued six months earlier and reflected opinions publicly proclaimed by the liberal wings of religious bodies since the war's end.[76] But it now made a firm impact on Protestantism. Conservative religious opinion had been content with denouncing atheistic communism and encouraging public control and governmental interference.[77] But now government, which in the Progressive period had seemed to ensure the hastening of God's kingdom, had become both irresponsible and immoral. The church, the guardian of the morality of the community, confronted its totally new problems and had to alter its rationale toward public control.

In many ways the problem was part of a classic controversy. The rise of the modern state and its tendency to intervene in religious controversies had been a force toward tolerance and pluralistic coexistence, with no single body in a position to proscribe the doctrines of others as heresy. As the application of this principle intermingled with the ideas of the Enlightenment, religious leaders came to accept the concept that the protection of civil rights was one of the essential duties of the state. The state would create the conditions in which morality could be sought and moral progress could best advance through intellectual and social experiment in an open society. The feeling, in fact, became so rooted during the Progressive era that the beneficiaries of the state came to worship it as a virtually infallible source of public morality, and sensitive churchmen worried about the dangers of moral arrogance which might undermine its sensitivity and responsibility.

The war confirmed their worst suspicions. At a time when the best thinking was needed to solve problems caused by dislocation and physical and social destruction, democracy lost its nerve and the state resorted to censorship and highly questionable, frequently deceitful, and immoral propaganda. What was worse, the clergy had acquiesced on the dubious rationale that the need would naturally end with the successful conclusion of the war.[78] With the war over, however, the government extended various unwarranted forms of peacetime suppression and regimentation. It was clearly time for the church to place itself in direct conflict with constituted authority. It was time to expose the moral arrogance of the state and reassert the church's role of moral leadership. Churchmen, the *New Republic* at the time pointed out, could not "challenge the state in a cause more near to their own vital interest than that of freedom of speech and opinion. For the authority of religion is not the authority of power but the authority of truth, and the truth which will set men free cannot prevail in an atmosphere of intolerance, proscription and terror."[79]

Billy Sunday undoubtedly spoke for a large segment of religious fundamentalism when he urged "standing the ornery, wild-eyed I.W.W.'s, anarchists, crazy Socialists, and other types of 'Reds' before a firing squad to save space on ships."[80] But liberal clergymen were convinced that the future strength of the church depended on the termination of governmental suppression. A strong stand on behalf of a large minority might elevate the church and possibly attract adherents from a group previously alienated from organized religion.[81]

The legal community was also aroused by the red raids, the highly irregular parliamentary maneuvering at Albany, and the flouting of constitutional guarantees by state officials and by the Justice Department. If cynical officials could warp the public law, the teaching and practice of it would become difficult. If legal certainty was undermined by the federal agency that was supposed to enforce the law, there would be no meaningful guidelines in advising clients, preparing cases, or instructing students.

At the April meeting of the National Popular Government League, lawyer Frank P. Walsh suggested appointing a committee to look into the Justice Department's activities. The committee, which included Zechariah Chafee, Felix Frankfurter, Ernst Freund, Swinburne Hale, Francis Fisher Kane, Roscoe Pound, Jackson H. Ralston, and Walsh, shortly issued a report entitled the "Illegal Practices of the United States Department of Justice." The committee noted the continued violation of the Constitution and presented a bill of particulars ranging from cruel and unusual punishment, arrests without warrant, unreasonable searches and seizures, and the compelling of persons to be witnesses against themselves to documented evidence of the use of agents by the Justice Department. These agents were introduced into radical organizations to incite members to activities that could be punished subsequently, and the creation of sentiment through questionable propaganda in support of these illegal acts. The report vigorously concluded:

It is a fallacy to suppose that, any more than in the past, any servant of the people can safely arrogate to himself unlimited authority. To proceed upon such a supposition is to deny the fundamental American theory of the consent of the governed. Here is no question of a vague and threatened menace, but a present assault upon the most sacred principles of our Constitutional liberty.[82]

Many of the same lawyers had spoken out with vigor against the proposed federal peacetime sedition legislation, Chafee especially, condemning both the Sterling bill ("It is a kindergarten measure. The assumption of the law is that our patriotism and our institutions are so weak as to crumble away at any talk of revolution")[83] and the Graham measure. He dwelled especially upon the fact that the First Amendment was clearly violated by many clauses punishing words for their *assumed* tendency to produce bad consequences in the remote future.[84] His book, *Freedom of Speech,* published later in the same year, was a masterful legal brief in popular form, surveying the whole question of suppression of dissent since the end of the war. It undermined with devastating legal logic the historical and constitutional fallacies of the entire suppressionist position.[85]

Large segments of the American bar, whose entire livelihood was concerned with private law, maintained an ultraconservative position as did politically ambitious judges. Judge Kenesaw Mountain Landis, for example, at the height of the crisis over the Graham and Davey measures, stated that "what we need is a new definition of treason. Then we can use the side of a barn for those who would destroy our government."[86] But for the constitutional lawyer, whose professional obligations were directly and clearly involved, the question was personal and meaningful.

The interest of other groups in the Graham bill illustrated two important trends regarding freedom of speech. Generally speaking, the intensity of interest varied directly with the degree of personal involvement. Only when such involvement became urgent did individuals have to state in their own words and for their own immediate welfare just what freedom of speech meant. The tendency then was to counterpose the concept against those interests which they felt it most clearly affected. Thus Gompers saw free speech as directly related to the problem of union organization, striking and picketing, and the labor injunction.[87] But Benjamin C. Marsh, secretary of the National Farmers' Council, was concerned that Congress was spending far too much time on such measures to the neglect of programs to aid agriculture. He maintained that the way to demonstrate faith in freedom was to create conditions which guaranteed economic justice to the farmer.[88]

The Religious Society of Friends, which had suffered for its pacifism, urged the government to concern itself less with the prohibition of minority gatherings and more with protecting American citizens in their lawful right of peaceful assembly.[89] Archwood H. Grimke, representing the NAACP, related the question to the dangers of fellow Negroes in the South.[90]

Yet some Americans suddenly entered the fray in the defense of free expression for reasons which were not merely professional and personal. These respectable, conservative citizens were Anglo-Saxon Protestants, products, as in the case of a Chafee, Kane, or Hughes, of distinguished families whose ancestry went well back into American history. The great majority were propertied people with power and prestige, whose own personal liberty was secure, but who were disturbed that values which they held dear were in danger of serious perversion.[91]

Their motivation can hardly be measured precisely, but there was a certain revealing consistency in their actions. Pillars of respectability and products of a culture that placed heavy emphasis upon the public responsibility of privilege, they were upset that community leadership had passed into the hands of men who were wantonly abusing it. They felt a clear sense of guilt about the situation. These latter-day mugwumps, conservative and hostile toward unseemly behavior, certainly could not endorse the crass methods of the IWW, the Socialists, or even militant labor, any more than their predecessors endorsed the Populists or the Pullman strikers. But, conversely, they could not accept the vigilantism of the Palmers and the Luskers.

Thus, Oliver Wendell Holmes, Jr., could sincerely maintain the right of a depressed member of an unpopular radical minority to agitate for his point of view, assuming, of course, it was responsible agitation and done in the right context and not falsely yelling fire in a crowded theatre and causing a panic. Or Albert J. Beveridge could address the American Bar Association Annual Convention in August 1920 and tell the elite of the law profession:[92] "If any man, or body of men feel that they have a just grievance, let them, by speaking, writing, agitating and organizing win public opinion to their side, and their wrongs will be righted in the effective way marked out by our Constitution."[93] David Starr Jordan, president of Stanford University and vigorous critic of restraint of freedom of expression said: "It is free stock that creates a free nation."[94] And alarmingly, the free stock had remained inert too long in the face of the growing destruction of individual liberty.

Many of these individuals had been foursquare in the Progressive movement. Now, like the liberal religious leaders, they realized that the state could be an instrument for evil as well as good. John Lord O'Brian dramatized the problem well. An insider, former assistant

United States Attorney General, he had appalling firsthand knowledge of how politicians had left discretionary authority in the hands of incompetent underlings and had refused to accept responsibility for the monstrous abuse of such authority.[95] Conservatives saw it as their duty to work industriously to counteract that tendency, to oppose governmental centralization, and to fight the tendency to rely upon the state.

Hostility toward improper social control hardly meant the rejection of progressivism. Most people continued to stand forthrightly for forms of control which guaranteed a moral society—prohibition, federal control of narcotics, or striking at the corrupt local political boss. But in areas where national programs had turned into devices for personal gain and selfish interest, the old Progressives advocated a return to control by responsible private individuals, who would accept the responsibility of advancing the morality of American society. Hughes, who as governor of New York or progressive Associate Justice of the Supreme Court, had supported a wide range of programs of public regulation and reform, directed his energies in the 1920s toward legal aid clinics, private welfare organizations, and private philanthropy.[96]

To that end, a restoration of informal social controls to maintain peaceful, decent, quiet order was necessary. These leaders did not advocate any new departures in freedom of expression. Few had connections with the ACLU, nor would they support that body through the 1920s. Their purpose was not that of the ACLU, to make civil liberties and free speech meaningful to all Americans through fostering the redistribution of property and power to those currently unable to personally protect their own rights. Their purpose was clearly to get society back into proper relationship; to structure it so that the nation would again be safe for dissent, with the dissenter knowing his rights and his place, and understanding clearly the responsibility of not pushing his case so far as to bring the reaction of hostile and violent public censure.

In many ways these people attained their goals in late 1920 and early 1921. Public officials who had engaged in unseemly behavior were either quietly forced out of office or gently, but firmly, persuaded to ease their tactics. At the local level, early raiding and scare mongering gave way to a far more dignified and subtle set of controls and procedures. The return of mild prosperity in 1920 and the sudden headlining of other national events and ephemeral crazes quickly drew public interest away from red-baiting.[97] Not the least of these were the colorful national presidential conventions and the subsequent campaign which the simplest American could understand.

But free-speech problems were not solved. Miners in Pennsylvania continued to live under the threat of violent retribution at any loud complaint, and in May, when anarchists Sacco and Vanzetti were arrested in Massachusetts, a bloody war broke out in the coal fields of West Virginia as the companies sought to prevent union organization.[98] ACLU representatives entered the virtually closed textile town of Passaic, New Jersey, in March to challenge local suppression and attained surprising temporary success.[99] Virtually everyone arrested under the state criminal-syndicalism and sedition laws had been indicted, and in some cases the indictments had been sustained at a higher level. In the meantime, although slackening somewhat, prosecutions continued, especially in California, and the Lusk Laws, which Al Smith vetoed in May 1920, were reenacted and signed into law by his Republican successor, Governor Nathan L. Miller, the following year. The Justice Department continued to maintain its aggressive antiradical program, and political prisoners languished in federal penitentiaries and state prisons.

Although each party in the election campaign of 1920 spoke of free speech in its platform (the Farmer-Labor party, in seeking to appeal to all malcontents promising to restore free speech in one way or another to every maligned citizen),[100] the question no longer had in November the same meaning or urgency it had had in January and February. The question now became one for private groups which tried to use it to advance special causes.

The election of Harding and Coolidge was further confirmation that properly oriented control had been officially reestablished. Harding was hardly the responsible public servant who would maintain acceptable forms of moral social control. But he could be trusted to acquiesce in such a development. His election eased the minds of business which held government in relatively low esteem. It did not seem unreasonable to keep the presidency where Wilson's illness had landed it—in virtual impotence.[101] The downgrading of government was satisfying reassurance that even should misguided advocates of strong public control continue to speak out, there would be no viable means for implementing their plans.

The "old order" had triumphed. The propaganda campaigns of the starry-eyed reconstructionists and their agitator cohorts had been defeated. As Roger Baldwin was to write a few years later, "the big job of taming the rebel spirit of labor was done."[102] The country could now easily tolerate even the wild-eyed agitator. The Sedition Act amendment to the wartime Espionage Act was repealed in March 1921, with scarcely a murmur of public interest, much less protest. As Albert De Silver wrote in May 1921: "The new Attorney General

[Harry M. Daugherty] is a nice fat man with a big cigar in his face and instead of getting excited as Palmer used to do, he grins when somebody talks about revolution and says, well, he thinks it probably best 'not to agitate the agitator' too much."[103]

Thus free speech was returned in late 1920 and early 1921 to its prewar status of a fine, generally disembodied shibboleth in which everyone believed, with its limits in practice carefully confined by private, subtle restriction. Those who still wished to utilize it as an instrument, both practical and symbolic, for societal change then had to rethink their position. The possibility did interest a diverse set of concerned Americans who were unwilling to leave things as they were. The controversy over the meaning of free expression persisted in this new setting.

7

The New Consensus: Acceptance and Alienation

In recent years we have seen random majorities, collected and directed by organized propaganda, claiming jurisdiction over personal beliefs and personal habits, overriding minorities in fields where the collective judgment has no business to go. There is a silent referendum in the hearts and minds of men against which no impertinent pronouncement by a majority can stand. For knowledge, for truth, for a valid line between right and wrong, for an appreciation of spiritual values, one does not consult the greatest number.

> Raymond B. Fosdick, *The Old Savage in the New Civilization,* 1928

The new consensus, which gained formal sanction with the inauguration of Warren G. Harding in March 1921, stood for the control of public affairs by a socioeconomic elite, utilizing pliable politicians on one hand and subtle appeals, pressures, and restraints on the other. In certain European nations, the attrition of older stratified social structures laid a basis for a strong man to provide a new order. In the United States, by contrast, there was a surprisingly consistent extension of earlier economic power, with the government working vigorously to create favorable taxing, regulatory, and international conditions for its functioning.[1]

Despite the authority with which this element shaped public policy and economic patterns, its leaders stood for no static order. This elite advocated virtually unlimited progress in improving industry, enhancing new technology, and adding to the convenience, comfort, and pleasure of daily living. No horizon was too remote for the vision of the modernizers of American life, whether it was in making motion pictures talk or in putting two cars in every garage. The same spirit developed patterns of permissiveness toward personal behavior so generally lenient that a revolution in morals, manners, and values took place. There was little concern about dissenters who advocated the overthrow of older ways, even if occasionally by force and violence. So callous, in fact, did the men in power become toward public iconoclasm that eventually private citizens, especially the older generation and certain rural types, intervened to restore controls upon unwarranted activity. Even such actions, however, seldom led to restriction. The only serious enemy worth proscribing was the radical agitator who openly and aggressively challenged the economic and power structure; and he raised his voice infrequently and with caution, in marked contrast to the ebullient direct action of the immediate postwar months.[2]

Free speech, then, lost its former role as a major bone of contention. The activist-repressionist triumph had been so complete that it left little question about the official rationale regarding permissible free speech for Americans. Yet the fact that free speech had temporarily become a personal question for some citizens led a far wider group to be concerned with the importance of keeping the symbol alive; and it led those whose consciences were more sensitive to be alert to situations in which its curtailment might be challenged in both a constructive and didactic way.

The prosperity decade progressed under the vivid memory of the Palmer days. Far more people were concerned with free speech than had been the case when it had been primarily the heart of a major controversy between reconstructionists and the advocates of the old order. Certainly no official governmental position on free speech came from the White House or the Cabinet or even the Attorney General's office. But the assumptions of both the business community and conservative leaders of American society were frequently evident.

Business leaders, like Progressives of the prewar period, considered free speech an attribute of individuality which they felt to be one of the rewards of success. To the extent that they believed in eternal progress, freedom was linked with opportunity as a valuable asset in moving ahead to new plateaus of material success. It could certainly be abused. But constructive complaining was not to be discouraged if carried on in a spirit of helpfully suggesting better steps to the world of tomorrow. Still, this was a negative freedom—from governmental restraint, from the overly aggressive labor leader, from the misguided but vocal social reformer, or from the radical who sought to overthrow the structure of power.

The business community regarded other types of restraint as salutary. There was utility in retaining the older forms of subtle restriction and pressure upon irreverent and dangerous troublemakers or overly ambitious have-nots. Concretely, this meant, for example, that one did not deal with labor directly, honoring either the letter of regulatory or welfare legislation or the letter of the private contract. One bolstered his position with open-shop techniques, business-sponsored, but citizen-advanced, Americanism campaigns, the labor injunction, the "Mohawk Valley Formula," "influence" with courts and legislatures, private detective agencies, state constabularies, and local police, armed with the usual ambiguous statute that could be used against strikers, picketers, and organizers. Business needed such added insurance against the potential power of militant labor leaders and radicals, and it was possible, through the effective use of simple symbolism, to argue that such a movement as the open shop actually liberated the workers from cynical union bosses.

Other individuals within the elite of the 1920s viewed the demands of the society with a considerably different perspective. Men like Hughes, Holmes, Ogden Mills, and a variety of other respectable professionally oriented conservatives balked at further repression when basic American values seemed in serious danger. Many were to hold high public office—Hughes as Secretary of State, Mills as Secretary of the Treasury, Holmes on the Supreme Court. Even the rapid destruction of many basic values did not diminish the devotion of this type of American to public service or the sense of responsibility to guarantee a decent community. To them, free speech had great importance as an element in the creation of sensible, responsible public policy through public discussion by responsible public leaders. These figures were far more concerned than the typical businessman about the necessity for saving the average American from his own personal and moral weaknesses. Prohibition as a viable form of morally oriented social control was not only permissible but desirable. So also were a variety of forms of public regulation, such as the Hays office to impose minimum standards of decency and respectability upon the movie industry or comparable forms of proscription of obscene literature. Such regulation was geared, however, toward eliminating or curtailing the evil forces within society which contributed to the personal degradation or erosion of the individual self-determination of the average American.

Further, freedom to these citizens had certain overtones which were positive. If Hughes expected little from the average venal American citizen, he did expect a great deal from members of his own class. Businessmen might prescribe a set of rules governing society and still feel little obligation to adhere to such rules themselves. But respectable and responsible conservatives had an obligation to play the game honestly and not cheat on other participants. Hughes's presidential address to the American Bar Association Annual Convention in September 1925, characterized by the editor of the Bar Association journal as "one of the most timely, useful, fearless, patriotic and able utterances ever made . . . by any public man of recent years in this country,"[3] bluntly charged the members of the profession with the obligation of creating a positive atmosphere for the free exchange of widely divergent ideas.[4] This approach operated on the assumption that one could let highly unorthodox opinion be aired since there was no possible chance that it could persuade or influence anyone. Nonetheless, this was a far more constructive view of divergent opinion than that held by the more apprehensive business community.

Hughes further emphasized the obligation of his colleagues to support better and more liberal education for greater numbers of Americans, presuming, of course, that spreading information would aid public discussion. This was primarily a mechanism for dispersing orthodoxy more widely, but it was a refreshing contrast to programs of indoctrinated Americanism which many businessmen felt was the only education, aside from vocational studies, applicable to the masses. Thus, Hughes ended his address on a note calculated to flatter and prod his colleagues: "Let us rise to our opportunity and as guardians of the traditions which constitute the precious possession of our democracy play our part in establishing and making secure the authority of law as the servant of liberty wisely conceived, as the expression of the righteousness which exalteth a nation."[5]

The positive obligations toward freedom of expression were still to be acted upon within the context of orthodox controls. One played the game and expected the working class to do so as well; otherwise, the various informal controls which held society on an even keel would be applied. The way to foster material progress was by rewarding those who, by vigorous effort, worked up within the system, encouraging others to do likewise, and gradually making it easier for the process to expand. To remove informal and subtle restrictions, especially when the government was in the hands of lesser politicians and had surrendered its role as an enforcer of public behavior, would put too much personal responsibility on those unprepared to accept it. The immediate obligation of freedom of speech was met by freedom from formal governmental restriction. The fact that informal controls also impinged upon the freedom of expression of powerless individuals did not occur to the elite.

Some critics, from the outset, were estranged from the power structure and found ways to protest against it; but they were not of one mind either about what was wrong with the country or about the steps to correct the situation. The most familiar of those who delighted in lampooning the American "booboisie" were H. L. Mencken and his supporters, who had viewed the jockeying of 1919 and 1920 with cynical and contemptuous detachment.[6] Their criticism, even though frequently aimed at the strictures of puritanism and philistinism, was in many respects shallow and cautious, focusing upon the foibles and frailties of human nature while never seriously questioning the economic, political, and social premises which governed American development.

The rationale of the Menckenese school included some overt, if not clearly thought out, premises concerning free speech. Mencken, himself a devotee of Nietzsche, had as early as 1908 expressed serious doubts about Progressive tendencies toward improving man through programs of publicly sponsored social control. The future of society lay in the hands of the "intelligent, resourceful, original, forceful man" unencumbered by puerile and presumptuous restrictions.[7] Such controls blighted the potential contributions the individual could make to society and enthroned pious morality and mediocrity above real talent.[8] But Mencken was equally concerned by the controls of public officials and self-appointed puritan moralists in the 1920s. He seldom questioned the authority of a skillful and pretentious socioeconomic elite. For example, he commended James M. Beck's 1922 volume on the Constitution, a work which Thomas Reed Powell of the Harvard Law School referred to as a "prayer book."[9] The fact that it was written by a prominent citizen, had grown out of a series of lectures delivered at Gray's Inn in London, and had the sanction of the American bar, was enough to raise its meandering banalities above criticism.

Mencken was concerned by the heavy-handed attempts of ill-informed public officials, pandering to public pressures, to impose restrictions which hindered the really able individual from rising to a position of responsible leadership. A system which tricked Americans into placing high value on pointless, superficial, and transitory fads, fashions, and fancies obscured the more important objectives of American society. Mencken did not believe that all the "timorous, sniveling, poltroonish, ignominious mob of serfs and goosesteppers" had within them the potential to evolve into responsible leaders and citizens.[10] Yet intelligent leadership might well save the people from their own mediocrity and eventually restore proper values. Addressing himself directly to the question of free speech in a syndicated column in the *Chicago Tribune* in January 1926, he argued that

> the statute books are cluttered with oppressive legislation, most of it supported by penalties that clearly violate the guarantees of the bill of rights. Every one knows how the right of free speech, for example, has been invaded and made mock of. And the right to free assemblage. And the inviolability of domicile. . . . Under the pressure of ruthless fanatics, willing to go to any length to satisfy their lust to bludgeon and terrorize their fellow men, congress has violated every one of these rights, and some of them it has violated repeatedly.[11]

Mencken was confused. Certainly it was not Congress that had violated individual rights, but those wielding the weapons of informal control to enforce quiet conformity.

Mencken had come closer to the reality of the situation in a column the previous August. He argued that "one of the master delusions of the American people is to the effect that they are in favor of free speech. They are actually almost unanimously against it."[12] Free speech prevailed only where the majority faced minorities too strong to be put down. Otherwise, anyone dissenting from the ideas of the average community had no right to be heard, whether they be evolutionists in Tennessee, teachers whom the Lusk Laws proscribed in New York, or radicals in Los Angeles ("When a radical looses his balderdash there, the police first try to kill him and then railroad him to prison for the term of his natural life"). In his own experience in public controversy, he could "recall no combat that did not bring forth demands from the opposition that I be put down by force—that I be deprived forthwith of the bold right to state my case." Such demands seemed natural and inevitable in democratic societies.[13] Curiously, Mencken hailed Roger Baldwin of the American Civil Liberties Union as one of the few men in the country who actually believed in free speech. The statement betrayed a total lack of grasp that the actual purposes of the ACLU were sharp social reorganization. Mencken's admiration for Baldwin, who was then being assaulted by the "reds" for standing up for free speech for "reactionaries," was for devotion to freedom from any kind of arbitrary restraint by any kind of *homo boobien,* far right or far left.

Thus, the Mencken position on free speech was one of personal confusion mixed with cynicism.[14] Given his jaundiced view about the inability of the "booboisie" to make rational and responsible decisions, he hardly expected it to assist in shaping intelligent public policy. But at the same time, Mencken considered free speech a vital aspect of individuality, to be protected from the foolish restraints wielded by Watch-and-Ward Societies, Ku Klux Klans, American Legions, petty administrators and officials, DAR ladies, Babbitts from Maine to California, or "reds" and labor leaders, who were "mainly mountebanks . . . for themselves long before and after they are for labor."[15]

One of his few positive statements came in a March 1926 column which endorsed Chafee's pragmatic approach emphasizing as it did testing the dangerousness of ideas by their concrete effect (in essence Holmes's "clear and present danger" rule). "The real danger in free speech," he maintained, lay "in the fact that, not infrequently, it is not actually free—that is, that the attempt to exercise it is, in reality, an attempt to prevent its exercise by the other fellow."[16] Nonetheless, he called for open confrontation with no limitations except those imposed by the factors of common decency. Such a position, however, presupposed that the society of the 1920s was based upon Jeffersonian face-to-face relationships, although he knew that large groups were able to impose their puritanical, philistine will upon defenseless citizens. Governmental intervention would not help. From government came prohibition, which Mencken never lost a chance to assault, and the censorship and restriction representing the puritan values of the mediocre middle class. "The only way to make a government tolerant, and hence genuinely free is to keep it weak."[17]

While Mencken admired civil liberties, he had no positive program for enhancing them and no vision for infusing them with modern meaning. Mencken was the perennial nay-sayer who ridiculed American society, which both merited and enjoyed good-natured lampooning.[18]

It was a short but important step to the "lost generation" of predominantly literary intellectuals who lived high in an era of fragile and archaic values. This group felt totally alienated from its society and its world. It emerged from the war to find, in F. Scott Fitzgerald's words, "all Gods dead, all wars fought, all faith in man shaken." Their hideous caricatures of American society exaggerated the restraints upon the free spirit. Few realized that their very ability to strike such an iconoclastic pose demonstrated the openness of the society they rejected and many preferred to leave for the bohemias of the cities or the exotic hovels of an old world.

This group was not a product of the 1920s. Many of its members had developed patterns of rebellion long before the war; their revulsion with Victorian morality and puritan inhibitions was a reaction against the less desirable aspects of progressivism.[19] But the stultifying, hypocritical, and needless restraints of the 1920s were positively choking, and if Progressive concepts of Anglo-Saxon superiority were difficult to rationalize, comparable assumptions by people far less able to sustain them were infuriatingly presumptuous.[20]

Compounding this negative rejection, however, was an equally intense Menckenese revulsion with the stupidity of the American people. Their inability to rise above their own mediocrity was responsible for fostering the offensive restrictiveness. Free speech as a device for the exchange of ideas which would lead society to seek greater goals was as laughable to the intellectuals as to Mencken. A few years earlier certain philosophical anarchists and excitingly aggressive IWW leaders had been at least colorful. The iconoclasts of ten years earlier had staged a Madison Square Garden pageant, for example, in which the IWW-led Paterson textile strike was reenacted by the strikers with one of the workers' songs set to the tune of a Harvard college song.[21] By the 1920s, the unfortunate exploitation of the working class seemed due to its own stupidity, and few wished to waste creative energy to alleviate its distress. One might become seriously concerned over a flagrant miscarriage of justice, such as the Sacco-Vanzetti case, but to rally masses of irate little people behind a cause was pointless. Such an idea might make fine conversation, but its execution was difficult to contemplate seriously. Sinclair Lewis went through the decade vowing to write a proletarian novel. Yet, when confronted with a concrete labor conflict such as the violent textile strike in Marion, North Carolina, in 1929, with labor conditions in the closed towns of the Pittsburgh area, or with the Tom Mooney case, he was bored with a situation that was foreign to his comprehension and to his sympathies.[22]

The members of this group did not reject everything in their culture. Charles Hanson Towne, in a 1922 book, *Nonsensesorship*, resorted to American symbolism and the glories of the past in protesting against Prohibition, which he called a "symbol of the death of freedom."[23] Other authors in the volume—Dorothy Thompson, Heywood Broun, Ben Hecht, and Alexander Woollcott—accepted the rewards of commercial success which the system from time to time afforded. But generally it was more fashionable to agree with Harold Stearns, that "we have no heritage or traditions to which to cling except those that have already withered in our hands and turned to dust" and find in the whole of America and her complex history only "emotional and aesthetic starvation," only a "mania for petty regulation."[24] In such a context, freedom of speech became another piously mouthed symbol which previous generations had made meaningless by their own hypocrisy.

Thus, the lost generation, even though composed of the sons and daughters of secure upper middle-class families and infused with the "native cultural disposition of that class," had far less concern for freedom of speech as a positive value than even H. L. Mencken.[25] It was certainly an attribute of the free spirit and was to be kept as uninhibited by puritan restraint and philistine corruption as possible. But free speech was to be used in pursuing the sensitive individual's right to be erratic, erotic, esoteric, or liberated from the conventionality of a society whose frictions they were too tender to confront and too blasé to bother comprehending.

Obsessed as they were with the Freudian concept of repression as an inhibiting factor upon the human psyche, they ought instinctively to have favored free speech. But repression only seemed evil when it affected free spirits among their own group. The psychological damage to a radical agitator or a union organizer was hardly a cause for concern. Except for the occasional Marxist among them, few members of this group objected to subtle controls which actually kept society operating in rigid patterns and thereby insured the continuing political and economic power of the "establishment."[26] Restrictions on freedom of expression were only taken seriously when they were inhibitions upon an intelligentsia desirous of breaking down bourgeoisie mediocrity. Thus F. Scott Fitzgerald could only comprehend potential censorship when it stood to inhibit him. In 1922, he implored Edmund Wilson to take out a "soldier" incident in a piece Wilson was planning to publish about him.

> Ever since *Three Soldiers,* the New York Times has been itching for a chance to get at the critics of war. If they got hold of this, I would be assailed with the most violent vituperation in the press of the entire country (and you know what the press can do, how they can present an incident to make a man upholding an unpopular cause into the likeness of a monster—*vide* Upton Sinclair). And, by God, they would![27]

The reactions of the lost generation were not economic or political in nature, but cultural and moral. "The burghers offended in a thousand ways and made countless errors of taste."[28] Its members were sharp social critics and their criticism undoubtedly reached a larger segment of American population than did proletarian writers, but their narrow, pessimistic views were hardly geared to elicit relevant social reform. Primarily they vented their own self-pity and provided rationalizations for rejecting the social responsibilities with which their personal heritage had imbued them. Unlike the Menckens, then, the figures of the lost generation did possibly see freedom of speech as an instrument for attaining something new. But, like the sage of Baltimore, they hardly had any more concrete programs for realizing such attainment than their expression of devotion to the idea that liberating the free and creative spirit from unwarranted inhibitions would in turn open the way to salutary modernism.

Not all the critics were negative and unconstructive. Walter Lippmann stood for a group of thoughtful figures who felt that there were still ways in which civilization could be advanced. The fact that his solutions pointed in the direction of an authoritarian centralization which could destroy the type of society he espoused did not necessarily diminish his good intentions in the 1920s. He sought a better world for what he then was coming to feel were helpless Americans.

At a time when progressivism had tended to place almost complete emphasis upon the importance of social control and the sublimation of individual inclinations, Lippmann, through the pages of the *New Republic,* had frequently stood for the virtues of individual liberty. He expressed in *Drift and Mastery* in 1914 an amazingly prescient appreciation of the road to meaningful liberty through defying society. Urban in his orientation and sophisticated in his background, he appreciated the virtues of a culturally pluralistic society. He was sufficiently aroused over tendencies to eliminate diversity and coerce an ill-considered conformity to protest against both a variety of wartime restraints and the extension and intensification of suppression in the Palmer days. Writing a tribute in 1930 at the time of the death of Herbert Croly, he recalled with pleasure that "the most exhilarating experience we had, as I now look back, was the resistance of the *New Republic* in 1919 and 1920 to the Red hysteria."[29] But the red scare, and particularly the ability of callous and opportunistic leaders to manipulate public opinion through a variety of distored symbols and dishonest stereotypes contributed to the souring of Lippmann on the naive theory of democracy which assumed an intuitive grasp of the problems of government by every man and a spontaneous public opinion which welled up to move government on its currents. It also convinced him that "the traditional liberties of speech and opinion rest on no solid foundation." Speech could easily be suppressed or manipulated at will by men of bad faith. "Without protection against propaganda, without standards of evidence, without criteria of emphasis," he wrote in late 1919, "the living substance of all popular decisions is exposed to every prejudice and to infinite exploitation."[30]

In fact, the idea that the average man was competent to understand and judge public questions quickly came to be the "mystic fallacy of democracy." With society becoming ever more complex, the first-hand experiences essential to developing rational positions were possible only to a talented and favored few. The average man had to depend upon imperfect stereotypes and faulty premises in reaching public judgments. He could neither correct this condition by education nor argue forcefully against the judgment of his leaders. Greater participation in policy making by the average individual, then, was no solution at all. Public forums merely compounded public confusion and contributed at best to a governmental stalemate and at worst to a situation easily exploitable by power-driven demagogues. In this context, free speech had the unfortunate effect of creating the impression that better public opinion would result from the more frequent expression of ill-informed ideas. Thus, Lippmann had no more faith in policy making by public discussion than did the Menckens or the members of the lost generation.[31]

But the situation was not nearly as hopeless to him. Granted the "compounding of individual ignorances in masses of people" could solve nothing, expert opinion could move society in new and constructive directions by ascertaining the precise facts of economic, social, and political life and using them to clarify the desirable goals for the nation at large.[32] Properly controlled and managed, public opinion might well facilitate public policy making. By manipulating stereotypes responsibly and by carefully choosing examples with which to illustrate for an intellectually apathetic, incompetent, or deprived public the social needs of the state, one might be able to develop a managed democracy in which the people would feel they had a part, even though, in reality, it was one of approval, not creativity.

There was no validity for Lippmann, then, in restricting freedom of expression. On the contrary, censorship of books, the intimidation of educators, or the curtailment of freedom of the press might choke off public communication, and should (and did) call forth eloquent protest.[33]

Lippmann did not develop any blueprint for enhancing civil liberties. Individual violations might warrant some type of public action. Actually, many examples of the violation of a person's individual rights, while unfortunate, hardly needed to be blown into public causes. If one were to elicit the proper response, especially from great bodies of rational and decent people, it was essential that the episodes to be chosen and portrayed for public reaction involve clear-cut, uncompromised issues which would elicit a healthy reaction and thereby contribute to greater tolerance, reduction of tension, and broader justice in the future. Lippmann was either totally oblivious of or unconcerned with dozens of episodes involving the restriction of free speech in the 1920s. It was worse to play up an embarrassing episode than to resign unrewarding examples to quiet oblivion.

A clear-cut episode like the Sacco-Vanzetti affair was ideal. It involved neither Communists nor IWWs; it did not raise penetrating questions about a concrete labor situation or industrial exploitation; it was not an attempt to organize unions; it did not raise questions concerning the regimentation of labor through subtle private forms of coercion.[34] Sacco and Vanzetti could be cast as martyrs to raw individuality, restrained by the pompous hypocrisy of an excessively hysterical bourgeoisie society. It was possible to dwell honestly on the situation and keep it in the headlines in the hopes of reducing public prejudice and intolerance and creating a greater concern for meaningful liberty among large masses of the people. The same sort of headlines and stereotyping were, of course, possible with a safe situation such as the Scopes' "Monkey" trial or even the famed Leopold-Loeb thrill-killing case. In fact, the latter satisfied two basic emotions. One could convey to the public the amorality and ruthless aspects of the action, and, at the same time, take a certain, safe, crypto-delight in identifying with such free spirits who defied every aspect of the unwarranted restraints of their stodgy society in order to fulfill basic and liberating inner drives.

One example of Lippmann's reliance on expertise was revealing. As managing editor of the *New York World*, he evolved a working arrangement with Professor Thomas Reed Powell of the Harvard Law School, probably the leading constitutional law expert in the United States at the time, to write editorials on legal subjects, a number of them on celebrated Supreme Court civil liberties rulings of the 1920s. Powell in turn sought to elicit both the precise nature and overall implications of the decisions. The results were revealing. Although he did not share Zechariah Chafee's deep commitment to restriction being warranted only when speech created a "clear and present danger" of concrete damage, Powell explained with feeling the dangers in unwarranted restraint, approving, for example, of Holmes's and Brandeis's eloquent libertarian dissenting position in the case involving Benjamin Gitlow's unsuccessful appeal to the high bench.[35]

In the long run, Lippmann, while anxious to provide avenues for achieving a better society, was as alienated from government as a prime instrument for social engineering as were reconstituted Progressives and cynics from Mencken through the lost generation. Lippmann's impartial and independent intelligence bureaus might well be coordinated by a central agency, but they were to set the course for public policy. Only thus could men escape the oppressive and unenlightened forces of conformity and mediocrity.[36] Time was to show, however, that this position, shared by many Americans in the decade, was paradoxical.

> In the name of a waning diversity, they attacked the democratic order in which only it grows. Confronting the fact that most Americans submitted willingly to "normalcy," they leaped to the *non sequitur* that majority rule was the cause. Facing the universal centralizing tendencies of capitalism, the standardizing pressures of a consumer-oriented economy, the weakening of inherited moralities, they based their analysis on narrow political grounds or on invidious aesthetic objections. Having no faith in the progressive synthesis, their reply to solidarity by Rotarian bombast was diversity by social negation. The tragedy of their position was that they attacked democracy for being unified around banalities and indirectly gave aid to those forces which were unifying men still more thoroughly around the mysticism of race and war.[37]

The implications for free speech were clear. Even if the triumph of a talented elite was accomplished without racial theories and violence, the only practical avenue toward its goals called for discrediting and eventually curtailing the babbling of Mencken's "gaping primates."[38]

Although hardly systematic critics of the system, other influential free spirits in the 1920s had an effect upon their times. The 1920s was a great age of heroes: Henry Ford, Frank Lloyd Wright, and Gutzon Borglum defied convention in a variety of ways. But these men were hardly leaders in the civil liberties movement. The institutionalizing of liberty was as uncomfortable to such independent souls as public repression itself. The individual was responsible for protecting his own liberty which he himself defined. The results were at times bizarre.

Gutzon Borglum had assailed Nicholas Murray Butler's lack of social consciousness regarding labor's role in society immediately following the war. Yet Borglum, whose Mount Rushmore eventually became "the shrine of American democracy," also briefly found a berth in the Ku Klux Klan, assailing the enemies who would water down the purity of the American way of life.[39] Ford, who through cheap mass production methods certainly liberated many individuals from physical immobility, was celebrated as the finest product of the American atmosphere and condition of freedom.[40] He sponsored the *Dearborn Independent*'s vicious assault upon the Jews and, when upbraided, successfully prosecuted through a case in which the court upheld the sort of anti-Semitic expression which the paper was uttering as perfectly permissible free speech in light of the occasion.[41] Wright's private life, always hectic, was his own and was apparently the prerogative of the uninhibited genius.[42] Although such creative individuals raised questions concerning needless hindrances upon man's creativity, in the long run they had no positive commitment to advancing civil liberties through practical programs.

A third general group whose actions in the 1920s were relevant to free speech and free expression was comprised of those who either sought to change the system which the consensus was imposing or sought to alter their role within it by tampering with or otherwise curtailing certain of its operations.

Labor in the 1920s was not identical with the unions. Union membership at no time represented more than 12 percent of the civilian labor force and in 1930 dipped below 7 percent. Through the decade membership declined from over 5 million in 1920 to less than 3.5 million in 1930.[43] Yet labor's voice was frequently taken to be that of union leaders who had access to certain media of communication. The accuracy with which any leader spoke for workingmen varied in proportion to his ability to identify with their problems. While the voice of unorganized labor is difficult to record and measure, one can approach it through the motives and purposes of union leaders, the type of appeals they used, and their effectiveness in reaching workers.

The American Federation of Labor was certainly the principal national organizational body, but it was primarily a union for the elite. It served the interests of the skilled. Samuel Gompers maintained tight control until his death in 1924, brooking little opposition and using various sanctions to neutralize criticism.[44] William Green continued such policies with Matthew Woll, vice-president and carry-over from the Gompers's days, frequently presuming to posit the general position of labor on a variety of public issues. Woll was as much a spokesman for the employers as for labor and frequently pandered to the business community, assailing others who professed to have a more sincere interest in workingmen. Such a target was frequently the ACLU, whose goals and techniques he found especially suspect. Speaking to the New York Chamber of Commerce in December 1926, for example, he launched a bitter assault upon the organization and its free-speech position. He drew the position out of context from the Lusk Report of 1920, and he argued that it was "the most effective shield Communists could hope to find in our country in the promotion of their revolutionary propaganda and procedures."[45] Champions of industrial unions frequently fared as badly at his hands.

Gompers had been able to see very closely the threat of federal sedition legislation, and he had no trouble opposing the open-shop movement, or legislative and judicial actions against striking and picketing, to say nothing of interference by obedient local public officials or the constant wielding of the injunction. Further, he lost no opportunity to rally support by casting these questions as inherently involving the liberty of American citizens and their freedom of speech and expression. But Gompers was caught, as was his successor, between the twin dangers of enhanced business repression and the growth of militancy by nonorganized workers, chafing in their depressed position and urged toward positive action not only by Communists and Socialists, but by rival labor groups and reform-minded Americans. Hence Gompers made a hasty liaison with the National Civil Liberties Bureau in fighting the growing restraints upon labor which the red scare seemed to be bringing on. But when the successor Civil Liberties Union began making aggressive moves toward assisting unorganized labor in bettering its case, plugged for industrial unionism, or sought to sponsor labor schools and colleges, Gompers quickly turned on the ACLU and denounced it with great vehemence as working contrary to Americanism and the principles of sound, tried-and-true craft unionism.[46] Gompers wanted free speech for himself and took every occasion to utilize its symbolism. But here his free speech concern ended. Free speech for his enemies was a type of license, and it was un-American.

The more militant unions were not as cautious. The Amalgamated Clothing Workers, the Amalgamated Textile Workers, the International Ladies Garment Workers, and even certain of the Railroad Brotherhoods saw the issue in the broader context of wider participation by larger numbers of workingmen in policy-making through organized strength. Further, such strength could be more effectively gained with a wider degree of personal independence and individual liberty. *Advance,* the official organ of Sidney Hillman's Amalgamated Clothing Workers' organization, published a regular column on its editorial page entitled "The Week in the History of Freedom." This editorial column took strong positions on problems ranging from Justice Department and American Legion intimidation to malcarriage of justice through denial of individual rights and even to problems of censorship and academic freedom. *Labor* seldom missed an opportunity to raise the free-speech overtones of any question which tended to inhibit the average workingman in his normal relations with his employer or his society.

Such unions did not think of free speech only as an abstract concept. Anxious to grow and gain membership as well as power, such organizations were well aware of the antagonisms against them. Their problem, then, was to gain greater freedom of operation to enhance their own status and to provide greater freedom for those who might join the cause and generally enhance the lot of workingmen throughout the country.

Sidney Hillman found, however, as did other liberal labor leaders, that tolerance had to be tempered with practical self-interest. Unlike the AFL, his union did not hesitate to make liaisons with Communists or to endorse the workers' government of the Soviet Union. Further, Hillman was far more willing to tolerate a wide variety of critics and internal dissenters within his organization than the more conservative leaders, feeling that it had to practice democracy within its own ranks. Both positions altered with time. The destructive tactics and the general cynicism of the Communists wore down tolerance until Hillman along with other labor leaders came to distrust them almost as fully as Gompers had earlier.[47] Aggressive movements within the union tried to wrest leadership from the existing hands, eventually leading Hillman also to draw clear lines between private, nonconstitutional, back-biting criticism and public expression geared toward producing enlightened and equitable public policy.[48] The long-range goal then of Hillman, Dubinsky, and John L. Lewis was both personal and general. Unlike the AFL, which sought to protect its own membership and deal with other workingmen on its own terms only, these men felt a social obligation toward the working class and were willing, within the limits of their time and energy, to assume some of the responsibility for giving such people a greater opportunity to advance their self-interest and public status.

Communist cynicism eventually undercut any potential appeal to American workingmen. Communists were quick to appropriate the old free-speech fight techniques of the IWW and lost no opportunity to foster unrest and to pose as unselfish champions and martyrs to the working class. Yet workingmen quickly came to realize that communist assistance carried with it a high price. Martyrdom paid no grocery bills and the professed communist devotion to American ideals of freedom, liberty, and equality proved to be only means to ends. The classless society was quickly seen to lead to dictatorship of the proletariat in which much vaunted freedoms would be quickly sacrificed to higher goals. Free speech for anyone except sons and daughters of the revolution was to be quickly exterminated. The individual was expendable.[49]

The Socialists, while no less fervid in their desire to alter society, were nonetheless committed to revolution by peaceful and democratic means. But this meant placing a great importance upon communication as a device for pointing up the fallacies of the current economic system and the constructive utilization of free discussion to hasten the elimination of the archaic restrictions. These restrictions had previously lent far greater weight to the word of the elite than to any one of the depressed classes. In this respect, Socialists were less concerned with dramatic individual episodes of the violation of freedom of expression and more concerned with steady progress through educational programs geared to foster the need and desire for a new society.

The ACLU was thus a unique organization in this decade. As early as December 1919, the leaders of the body realized that, although it had certain moral obligations to fulfill earlier unfinished commitments, its future lay not in pacifism or antimilitarism but in constructive social democracy and economic equality geared clearly to create a more equitable balance of economic forces within society.

The history of the early organization was the history of the ideological and practical purposes and objectives of Roger N. Baldwin. Baldwin was a logical modern heir of the great New England reform tradition, channeling into the assault upon modern social problems much of the same emotional zeal, quasireligious fervor, and proclivity for sincere martyrdom of the abolitionists, intellectuals, and frequent revolutionists of that section's turbulent past. Undergoing wartime incarceration as an expression of his pacifist conscience, he sought identification with the laborer and his plight following the war. Through the device of becoming an itinerant workingman, moving from carrying bricks to laying rails to shoveling coal in a lead smelter, he pursued this goal. He got a firsthand taste of steel company autocracy when William Z. Foster made him a union spy in the Homestead plant during the steel strike.[50] By December, Baldwin was completely convinced and was able to convince the ACLU leaders that the future of the organization lay in the "cause of freedom of expression in the industrial struggle," but that although the "cause we should now serve is labor," such action would be advantageous for civil liberties.[51] The labor emphasis was a shorthand way of attacking the greater problem of creating meaningful civil liberties for all.

Ironically, however, labor membership, especially on the board of directors, was sparse and difficult to obtain. Labor was well aware of the wartime image of the old National Civil Liberties Bureau as a bunch of disloyal draft-dodgers still up to disruptive and "red" ends. Although labor leaders were frequently willing to praise its work and even join in its specific crusades, they preferred not to run the danger of being formally identified with the body. Much of the leadership, therefore, had to come from social reformers and liberals and even conscience-stricken conservatives. And such figures, ranging from Jane Addams and liberal theologian John Haynes Holmes to Felix Frankfurter, Arthur LeSueur of the Non-Partisan League, and Oswald Garrison Villard, editor of *The Nation,* would not have been in the movement had its purposes been solely to advance union organization. A great many members were even older Progressives, still seeking the brave new postwar world which had seemed so promising in late 1918 and early 1919 and which business had so mercilessly stopped. This world was still possible to attain, they felt, but only if the iron grip of the established consensus could be gradually and methodically loosened.

In a more general way, however, the vision of such people was far broader than simply freeing the individual from unwarranted restrictions. They were willing to face the fact that the country was no longer a nation of small farmers and shopkeepers with its personal contacts simple and face-to-face or with its economy organized in such a way that one could control and advance his own destiny through personal and individual self-determination. America was an industrial nation, and huge impersonal power blocks controlled the destiny of millions of its citizens. Such blocks manifested very little public responsibility in dealing with their employees or private citizens and cynically insisted that the old informal relationships were still available to solve the individual's problems. The ACLU members sought in essence a situation of countervailing power such as Madison projected in *The Federalist,* Number 10. The only way in which competing factions could actually have a fair opportunity for success was to remove the obstacles to effective organization and bargaining.

But those who willingly worked with the ACLU realized that they themselves would have to adopt well-coordinated organizational patterns to function effectively. It was no accident that the organization was referred to as a "union" or that it sought to function on a national scale and implement centrally determined programs through a national organization.

But this fact alarmed property-conscious citizens and apprehensive corporations, antagonistic toward the organization from the outset because of its war record. Its newly professed goals of making the Constitution work fairly for all smacked of a dangerous centralization and was quickly branded as un-American. The elimination of informal uses of power was needless meddling in local ways. It was easy to stereotype the organization as a meddlesome group of nosy outsiders and the enemy of sacrosanct local control, property rights, and individual freedom.

There was one further irony involved in the attempt to tar the

ACLU with the brush of impersonal centralization. The body was as laissez-faire in its attitudes toward government as almost any other group in the decade, and, until the late 1940s, the leadership of the organization continued to operate on the assumption that the way to attain meaningful, national patterns of equitable law and freedom was through assailing and assaulting governmentally imposed or sanctioned inhibitions. This could best be done by dedicated organizations of private individuals working to eliminate the inequities in society. Thus the ACLU's blueprint for bringing meaningful civil liberties to all Americans was unique in the 1920s in the organizational structure it evolved, in the assumptions on which it proceeded, in the tactics which it used, and in the long-range goals which it sought to attain. In fact, it was sufficiently unique and disruptive of ancient patterns that it inevitably brought the organization loud and frequently irresponsible public condemnation.

Finally, there were a great many individual citizens in the United States in the 1920s who turned to the symbol of free speech in hours of personal need and, consequently, had an effect upon its history. Many normally placid Americans, who were seldom crusaders and who even more seldom thought of civil liberties and free speech in the context of its meaning and utility in society at large, found that when their own toes were being stepped on, a free-speech context was effective in rallying support to their position. Teachers, although often meekly subservient to the school board or trustees, from time to time became irate over excessive meddling in course materials and content, particularly by self-appointed protectors of the community or defenders of 100 percent Americanism.[52] Similarly, individual examples of academic freedom involving friends or colleagues could bring forth solicitations for aid and support from liberals in general or even the ACLU in particular. Book publishers, normally associated with the business world and operating very much within it, could raise justifiable protests when one of their standard and widely adopted textbooks was condemned and removed from large numbers of classrooms. Freedom of information, in this instance, while inherently a dollars and cents business situation, stood a far better chance of triumphing if free-speech champions were rallied to the cause.

Radio broadcasters and movie producers, while also enjoying a businessman's role in many ways, found it equally useful to raise free-speech questions in the face of constant threats of censorship and insistent public pressure from modern-day Comstockery.[53] Birth control advocates, especially in their frequent run-ins with Catholic antagonists, relied heavily upon free-speech rationale,[54] while from

time to time disenchanted and silenced dissenters within functioning
organizations could and did attempt to continue the fight for their
minority position through raising the free-speech question.

The fact that such beleaguered individuals turned to free-speech
rhetoric in an attempt to preserve themselves once again demonstrated
the pertinacity of the concept in the American mind. But such examples also had the frequent effect of projecting individuals, otherwise
oblivious to the broader public problem of expression, into positive
action toward defending free speech.

The free-speech controversy of the 1920s, however, cannot be
defined solely in terms of defenders, cynics, and activists. With a
business culture dominant and with business leaders as power figures,
there were inevitably those sycophants who took it upon themselves
to offer unrequested protection against the opponents of the group
in power. A variety of such individuals and groups persisted into
the early 1930s. One of their principal targets was the ACLU. Few
organizations suffered from as much vituperative slander and assault
from ill-informed and frightened people as the ACLU in the 1920s.
"Free-speech faker" became a standard term in the vocabulary of
many organizations ranging from the American Legion to the DAR
and a wide range of professional patriots. Such bodies were both
pathetic and dangerous. Business, which had relied on them in 1919,
no longer needed their aid. Yet these gratuitous attackers, who failed
to comprehend the effectiveness of the "establishment's" informal
controls, felt they could serve the public cause by keeping the troublemakers in line. Business was at times embarrassed by such people.
But seeing their potential future value, businessmen occasionally
threw them crumbs of encouragement by quietly, informally, and even
financially endorsing their activities.[55]

Danger lay in the fact, however, that any sign of encouragement
from the business community seemed to activate such groups to
broader programs of 100 percent Americanism and repressive activities against dissenters—activities which frequently expanded to include harmless and innocent people and which proceeded on the
assumption that the status quo was unassailable. A standard contention of the spokesmen of such groups was "America is a free country,
and if you don't think so, you have the freedom to keep your mouth
shut or get out." Their desire to serve the cause of Americanism
frequently led them to advocate and foster forms of repression scarcely
complementary to the philosophy of the Declaration of Independence
or the Bill of Rights.

The significance of such groups did not lie in their connection
with the business community, but in the effect of their propaganda

upon America's concept of the role of free speech. To the extent that they continually forced redefinition of the issue, such groups kept the question in the public mind and aroused many more people to concern themselves with its meaning than might otherwise have been the case had it been primarily a bone of contention between militant labor and ACLU members on one hand and the socioeconomic elite who guided the nation on the other.

The meanings of freedom of speech in the 1920s were as divergent as those who sought to define it. Perhaps this suggests that free speech had little effective meaning; perhaps it implies that, since so many people were seeking to define it, it had a special attraction in the decade. In either event, looking at the period through the free-speech window raises doubts about the monolithic quality so often attributed to it. In the free-speech sense, at least, it was marked by more diversity than most eras before and since.

8

The Quest for
Equality Through
Free Speech

However important or significant may be the struggle for the political rights of fifteen million Negroes; however important or significant the defense of religious liberties; of academic freedom; of freedom from censorship of the press, radio, or motion pictures, these are on the whole trifling in national effect compared with the fight for the rights of labor to organize. From a larger view, these secondary issues dissolve into the primary.

Roger N. Baldwin, *Civil Liberties and Industrial Conflict*, 1928

When one considers the massive public apathy in the 1920s toward social progress, industrial democracy, and distribution of power through economic reorganization, the determination, energy, and constructive accomplishments of the small band of dedicated civil libertarians of the decade stand out. Even before the great depression in 1929, this group of Americans took limited but important steps in their struggle to nationalize certain minimum standards concerning the meaning and practice of constitutional principles. They had also touched the American conscience so that future progress toward their goals was easier. Central to this story was the free-speech issue.

The activists of the 1920s were a varied group. They had certain informal bonds in their common devotion to civil liberties through a more equitable dispersal of power within society. Such general goals attracted those dedicated reconstructionists of the immediate postwar period, and also other reform-minded critics seriously concerned with the preservation of American individuality through enhancing economic self-determination.[1]

The first National Committee of the ACLU, formed in early 1920, included the membership of the old pacifist-oriented executive committee of the National Civil Liberties Bureau and forty-five other individuals, among them prowar liberals, social workers, labor organizers, reform-minded churchmen, college professors, lawyers, authors, and publishers.

Yet a number of responsible and socially conscious people, often fully dedicated to liberal goals, declined to join the body, preferring to work for freedom through other channels. They were, ironically, often more outspoken than were ACLU members. Disagreement with ACLU policies was often instinctive in this group, which believed that revitalizing the symbolic American concepts would somehow be enough to put them into practice.[2]

A certain common sensitivity existed toward the problems to be confronted and toward the obstacles to them. The more aggressive activists were realists, and unlike many intellectual radicals, who, while alienated from their world, were content primarily to wallow in the mutual self-pity of such alienation,[3] were willing to work for limited objectives. Conscious that the nation's value orientation placed primary emphasis upon those ephemeral aspects of life symbolized in the jazz age, they realized the necessity of enlisting public support and popular endorsement. At times the activists were overly optimistic; yet they were shrewd students of the American psyche as well as of their times. They flushed out unexpected but sympathetic interest by touching deep-seated sentiments of previously unconcerned Americans. They deliberately sought to tap current public concern, ingrained devotion to American traditions, and a deep vein of individual self-interest hostile to governmental coercion. They seldom lost an opportunity to point to the needless extremes of the Palmer days, hoping to keep alive the concern for the rights of the individual and the dangers of official tyranny. Similarly, they emphasized the importance of preserving the American traditions of free speech and the Bill of Rights, while at the same time insisting that the road to the preservation of individual freedom lay in the curtailment of excessive governmental interference with individual freedom.

Yet they were highly realistic about the possibility of reaching all Americans with such appeals. They scarcely expected to draw large numbers from the business community. They seemed, to businessmen, to be underwriting "the unreasonable, unintelligent and ungrateful disposition of labor, its willingness in its own selfish interest to throw a monkey-wrench into the entire industrial machine."[4] Business had always provided the respectful hard-working citizen with opportunities and would continue to do so. It would also continue to resent any agent, government or private, telling it when and how this should be done or that its own prerogatives should be compromised to minister to the rights of citizens.[5]

Ironically, labor at times expressed a remarkably similar antipathy toward positive social control through legislation and governmental regulation. This scarcely was ground for any workable liaison, however. The civil libertarians' hostility to positive government came when it undermined individual liberties. They could, with equanimity, support national legislation to curtail child labor, or advocate maximum-hour and anti-injunction laws. Businessmen, on the other hand, saw the greatest threat of governmental intervention in unwarranted intrusion into their activities best symbolized by just such programs. But government certainly had an important positive function in curtailing "reds" and keeping labor in its place. The "danger of excessive governmental control" meant quite different things to different groups.[6]

Any appeal to the growing American middle class had to strike especially at the spirit of fair play and open opportunity. ACLU leaders hoped by identifying their objectives with the traditions of the Bill of Rights and the Declaration of Independence to set the movement within the basic American heritage, which these people publicly avowed to cherish. The fact that many average citizens had been able to identify personally with those traditions and protest when they were under serious assault meant that they were aware of the necessity for vigilant protection.

Thus ACLU leaders were highly conscious of the value of wrapping their general campaign for economic equality in the bunting of the fight for the preservation of the ancient tradition of American freedom. Pamphlets distributed widely by the ACLU were filled with quotations of famous Americans, from Jefferson and John Adams to Woodrow Wilson, on free speech.[7] The first six annual reports of the ACLU were all entitled "The Fight for Free Speech," or minor variations thereof, and ACLU leaders, convinced of the universality of devotion to that most basic attribute of man's individuality, sought to draw out the free-speech aspects of virtually every campaign they entered.

However, this conscious effort proved no assurance of any broad-gauge middle-class support. Americans instinctively considered that the path of meaningful individualism lay through freedom from authority, public or private.[8] The idea of group fulfillment—that the avenue to meaningful individual freedom lay through coordinated group action to create new means toward freedom for individuals to exercise—seemed frankly a confusing contradiction in terms. Arguments that liberty would only really emerge from enforced equality seemed to lead not to individualism, but to collectivism. The ACLU's position was too clearly prolabor and fostered disruptive social reorganization. The opportunities for upward social mobility in the decade still seemed sufficiently attainable that people who sought to give artificial advantages to any one element within society seemed to be interfering unjustly with natural developments.

Certainly middle-class citizens could scarcely have been expected to maintain a traditional tolerance for the virtues of dissent, particularly for reformers anxious to topple the existing order. There was nothing wrong with the order. Anyone could succeed within it who had the will and desire to do so. Anyone who did not, however, would have to bear full responsibility for his own condition. "Society could be expected to do no more than to interpose no obstacles in the path of success; it could not guarantee success. Failure remained a function of the individual for which society was not accountable."[9] In reality, therefore, although many civil libertarians never gave up hope of reaching such people, their relationship with them was far more often one of having to defend themselves against charges of irresponsible and unjustifiably disruptive actions.

There did, however, seem to be the possibility of winning some support from disgruntled groups which, for one reason or another, were not participating in the benefits of the big money decade. Liberal theologians of all three major faiths had issued optimistic statements concerning a reconstructed society based upon social justice in the period immediately following the Armistice. Such groups suffered much the same assault that other liberals did in late 1919 and early 1920, but that did not change their allegiance. It was still possible to chop away at peripheral wrongs and blemishes.

Thus the Federal Council of Churches continued to urge, after the war, the necessity to improve industrial and social relations and to apply Christian principles to industrial society. A number of elements in the social creed of the organization were clear-cut challenges to the business and industrial community. When, for example, the council spoke out against the aggressive open-shop drive of the early 1920s and defended labor's right to organize, various employers' groups called for a halt to contributions to churches that were associated with the Federal Council.

Religious bodies can hardly expect us to give them money for the purpose of manufacturing weapons with which to destroy industry.

The radical and Bolshevik elements in the churches seem to be in cooperation through the Federal Council of the Churches of Christ in America and many of our members are expressing themselves as determined to discontinue financial support of their respective churches unless they withdraw all moral and financial support from the Federal Council.[10]

As a result, the Federal Council tended to step up its concern with the alcohol-prohibition problem; the race problem, particularly lynching; foreign relations; and peace. At a time when the ACLU was intensifying its campaigns for economic equality, the council was soft-pedaling its concern with the same issues. A similar trend prevailed within American Catholicism.[11]

As to liberal Judaism, several prominent Jewish leaders played important roles within the ACLU, as the 1920s progressed. Individual Protestant leaders such as Harry Ward, John Haynes Holmes, and John Nevin Sayre, as well as the Catholic Father Ryan, did also. But like the Ryans, Wards, and Holmeses, figures such as Louis Marshall, Stephen Wise, and Judah Magnes did not attempt to commit the organs and organizations of their faith to any resolute civil liberties position. At the same time groups such as the American Jewish Committee, whose 1911 Act of Incorporation committed it to "prevent the infraction of the civil and religious rights of Jews . . . to render all lawful assistance and to take appropriate remedial action in the event of threatened or actual invasion or restriction of such rights,"[12] or the Anti-Defamation League of B'nai B'rith, whose objects were similar, interpreted their charges as committing them primarily to fight against legal and cultural discrimination against Jews, stereotyping, and various forms of overt anti-Semitism. There was no more willingness on the part of organized Judaism to give broad endorsement to campaigns of social equality than there was in the other faiths.[13]

Social workers and students of society in the 1920s generally were less aggressive in their desire to push the free-speech question than they had been prior to and, in some cases, during the war. In 1914, for example, four sessions of the annual convention of the American Sociological Society, plus the presidential address by Edward A. Ross, were devoted to the necessity for and the means of giving modern meaning and force to the traditional guarantees of free speech, press, and assembly.[14] Only one session of one convention of the body during the decade of the 1920s concerned itself with such problems, and in so doing drew its participants from the nonacademic world, hearing papers by Reverend Harry F. Ward, then chairman of the ACLU board, Father John A. Ryan, a member of the National Committee, and Lewis Gannett of *The Nation*.[15] Commitment to broad-scale social change through aggressive and disruptive campaigns for social justice made far less sense to a new profession than concern with analysis of the structure and problems of society and the most direct and effective way to ameliorate their symptoms. Freedom of expression did not seem an essential ingredient to those to whom social workers sought to minister or whom sociologists sought to analyze and categorize. The incentive was to take pride in the new role of being scientific ministers to society's massive needs, not aggressive advocates of its thorough reconstruction.

College professors and teachers generally, in a period of business domination in which salaries were poor, tenure was shaky, and public pressure for conformity was great, risked job and respectability in active participation in radical movements.[16] John Dewey did not participate actively in ACLU affairs until the depression years, and the few college professors on the National Committee—Harry Elmer Barnes, Scott Nearing, Edward A. Ross, and William E. Dodd—were financially independent men for whom tenure and local respectability were not serious considerations. Similarly, David Starr Jordan, as an academic administrator and nationally prominent and respected figure, could risk such activity with a comfortable insulation from personally damaging pressure.[17] The American Association of University Professors functioned during the decade as a defense society, not as an active challenger of the social and economic structure of the nation. Academicians were advised to be cautious in their own participation in civic campaigns for free speech: "the attempt to assimilate the doctrine of free speech into the doctrine of academic freedom aroused hostility . . . and seemed to demand a special protection for professors when they engaged in the rough give-and-take of politics," which large portions of the public were unwilling to afford them.[18]

Nor were farmers, in a period of intense agricultural depression and general economic beleaguerment, drawn toward voicing their complaints, bitterness, and frustration through the organized civil-liberties movement. Arthur LeSueur, attorney and onetime counsel for the Non-Partisan League, was an early and enthusiastic ACLU member, but he was more concerned with local officials who broke up meetings than in seeking solutions to general economic problems through civil liberties approaches.[19] The position of the American farmer in the 1920s tied him closely to the business community. Farm legislators had often been aggressive leaders in framing the criminal-syndicalism laws of the immediate postwar period. Farmers and farm organizations were among the most hostile and vicious opponents of IWW activities.

The American farmer, even in his most frenetic Granger and populist moods, had never thought of himself as a member of a rural proletariat or a peasant class. He was part of the mainstream of American citizenry, an essential part of the nation's social, economic, and political structure. Further, the business community was interested in cheap food and good markets for the industrial goods of the nation. In fact, the idea that the United States would soon outrun its food supply, an idea carried over from the Progressive era, led some to feel there was a pressing necessity to keep the farmers producing at all costs. This did not mean that the business community had any positive responsibilities to the farmer. When Calvin Coolidge responded to complaints of agrarian discontent with the statement that "the farmers never have made money anyhow," he was reflecting a widely held attitude that agriculture was not a business but a way of life. Farmers in the past had looked out for themselves and were expected to continue to do so.[20]

Such a "go-it-alone" policy created friction and hostility. But the discontented farmer renewed his efforts to gain a larger share of the pie, not to overturn the system. The farmer, the traditional producer, and now the manager and economist, stood to gain new status as the businessman of the rural community. An alliance with the liberal–radical–urban labor complex was unattractive, incorporating as it seemed to do an assault upon property and a way of life that had been vindicated and praised by politicians and national leaders from the days of Jefferson to the 1920s. The farmers were further frightened by the specter of un-American types: recent immigrants, the refuse of European cities, unfamiliar with American traditions, unappreciative of the value of the farmer's nobility, agitators and trouble-makers too lazy to work for themselves, resorting readily to violence, calling for revolution for their own benefit and often having records of disloyalty and draft evasion from the war period.[21] Those few farmers propelled into hasty alliances with labor quickly discovered the subordinate position that they would hold and the cynical attitude of those who used them for their own ends. The deliberate and callous infiltration by Communists of the effort to form a national Farmer-Labor party in 1923 further soured farmer opinion on the ultimate value of cooperation with an urban working class.[22]

The farmer, therefore, was little inclined to identify with the free-speech issue during the 1920s. He had little to fear from the current restrictions on radical expression, and he had no desire to change the system. His problem was not that he could not speak, but that few people paid any attention to him when he did. Further, the fact that the people who were manipulating the free-speech issue were doing so deliberately to upgrade the urban proletariat was hardly calculated to draw him into the movement. New and artificial benefits for such groups would only downgrade the farmer's status and increase the price he had to pay for manufactured goods. Farmer radicalism, therefore, exploded into demands for positive action in the 1920s as the McNary-Haugen movement, as a brief revival of Greenbackism, as movements for cooperative marketing, or as new pressure for railroad rate regulation. The farmer was willing to draw on the rhetoric of American free speech and constitutional rights. But when it came to implementation, he sought farmer relief, not broad-scale social reorganization and economic democratization.[23]

Like the farmer, the Negro in the 1920s saw no solution to his pressing economic, social, and political problems through organized free-speech campaigns. The ACLU's concern with such gross violations as lynching and peonage was so minor a part of its interests and focus that the Negro was hardly tempted to reciprocate through joining its crusades for union rights. James Weldon Johnson served briefly on the National Committee of the ACLU, but his actions there, while commendable, did little to support the action that Baldwin and the directors considered primary in the organization's general crusades.[24]

In the final analysis, then, the major thrust of the appeal of free-speech champions was toward the depressed classes, primarily industrial workers. The status of such groups most greatly concerned civil libertarians. Yet despite good intentions and pressing needs, it was no simple task to draw such individuals into the movement. Active challenges to the status quo opened workingmen to the risks of losing their meager subsistence and even endangered their lives. Furthermore, social and psychological inertia was a major stumbling block. Workers acted only when matters became hopeless, and employers were shrewd enough to throw sops to them in the form of company unions or new factory lunchrooms and to stress the possibilities of progress for all within a dynamic society. The hope, no matter how slight, that, by playing ball within the system the workingman might enhance his well-being, operated to reconcile him to the status quo. Since the expectation of bettering one's status was strongest among young people, the leadership of active campaigns against management fell to older persons. The appeal of the civil libertarians was most persuasive to those whose status was most desperate. To reach such individuals on the basis that their abstract civil liberties were being abrogated required careful strategy.

Civil libertarians were quick to pick up the deep-seated feeling on the part of such people that they had been wronged and that if they could only make their case known, people who cared would be willing to help.[25] Unlike the Communists, whose cynicism constantly created apprehensions, civil libertarians seriously attempted to reach the workers on their own terms. They sought to probe and publicize the actual facts about exploitative situations, and as their sincerity began to be respected and as they challenged local tyranny, the psychological barriers between self-proclaimed outside saviors and local citizens broke down. Few working-class people ever joined the ACLU, contributed to its campaigns financially, or understood the abstract principles of individual rights;[26] yet a spirit of trust, confidence, and warmth evolved, which encouraged working-class citizens and civil libertarians to feel that they were on the same side in the concern for a better world.

During the decade, forms of unsolicited support frequently emerged which had a clear effect upon the total outcome of the civil-liberties movement. Although the Communists tried to turn every tension-ridden situation into personal advantage for their own ends, the vigor with which they sought to provoke worker revolt encouraged the timid. Thus while it often fell to more sincere reformers to see such crusades through or some way mop up the damage, the fact that action had been forthcoming could not help but focus the spotlight upon deep-seated social and economic problems and thereby touch the consciences of sensitive Americans.

From time to time, overly zealous preservers of the status quo went too far and compromised the integrity of citizens who valued their individual freedom. Thus DAR assaults upon teachers or editors, campaigns by groups such as the National Security League, the American Defense Society, or the Better America Federation, for ridding a community of wrong thinkers, or vigilante action by the American Legion or the Ku Klux Klan backfired and called attention to the deep-seated American commitment to freedom.

The burden of the movement for equality through free speech in the 1920s, then, fell upon the ACLU. In many ways the key to its long-range objectives centered around the values, ambitions, and goals of Roger Baldwin. Baldwin, who had been instrumental in the reorganization of the body after the war, after returning from his incarceration and period of self-imposed exile as a manual laborer, hammered out the approach it would take to the new challenges confronting it.[27] Baldwin had been the prime mover in the transition period in which the ACLU was convinced of the necessity of directing its principal efforts toward labor. Similarly, it was he who in large part mapped the strategy that the body followed until 1930. His public relations work shaped its membership and support, and his sense of public needs very largely determined the challenges toward which it directed its energies.[28]

Beginning his professional career as a social worker in St. Louis, Baldwin had been influenced early by the eloquence of Emma Goldman and, while scarcely sharing the vehemence of her anarchism, felt many of the same apprehensions as she did about the feasibility of social change through government or law. With political power largely in the hands of those from whom concessions would have to be extracted, Baldwin thought it unrealistic to put much faith in reform through public instrumentalities. With the law solidly in the hands of a bench and bar pledged to maintain the status quo, it seemed unrealistic to hope for major concessions from that source.[29] The redistribution of power Baldwin sought would come by assailing the conservative and traditional legal structures which so regimented society as to prevent real social justice.[30] But the approach would have to be through a flank attack. Not until well into the 1930s was the ACLU sufficiently encouraged by outcroppings of legal sympathy to go directly to the courts for redress for civil liberty violations. In the 1920s, counseled by its own attorneys to expect little from courts whose concept of rights focused primarily upon property rights, the ACLU realistically focused its crusade for modernizing the law on the operational level. This meant attempting to arouse the public over instances of police brutality or the tyranny of arbitrary local restrictions. It meant fighting repressive legislation. It meant constant exposure of the inequality of the application of the law, especially to working-class people. It meant utilizing as fully as possible the symbolism of American democracy, emphasizing the necessity of public concern for its ancient liberties and casting every cause possible in a free-speech context.[31] In this regard, Baldwin frequently referred to himself as an "exponent of free speech for its own sake, who believes free speech should be used in fighting the fight of the exploited classes."[32]

This course frequently plunged civil libertarians into dramatic roles. To test restrictive local practices meant braving the fire of adverse publicity and public ridicule. Badgering congressmen and senators, appealing to presidents, petitioning governors, meant regular rebuff and frustration. If all else failed, there was always the option of drawing attention to the cause by undergoing incarceration in the name of principles more important than individual comfort or immediate personal freedom. In fact, in later years, in commenting upon the respectability that the organization had gained, Arthur Garfield Hays recalled the 1920s as a time when ACLU members "were all ex-jailbirds together."[33]

Those on the "firing line" in the 1920s were a courageous, argumentative, brash, and bold lot. While frequently their enthusiasm outran the sensitivity of their appraisal of hoped-for public support, nonetheless, by forcing out from under the rug much of the seaminess that the society of the day preferred to keep hidden, they needled the conscience of Americans.

Through the clipping of reported incidents from newspapers, the ACLU kept close track of every episode that seemed to raise civil liberties questions. Such incidents afforded the organization sufficient challenges to keep its small and underpaid staff busy deciding which deserved ACLU support and the best way to help.[34] The general strategy and long-range goal of the organization tended to dictate certain policy lines. Given the desire to focus attention upon the unfavorable position of working people, there was an instinctive tendency to respond to episodes growing out of labor problems.

But when an individual episode tended to dramatize a broad general legal problem, the ACLU was willing to work on it. The Scopes "Monkey Trial" in Tennessee did not involve any large number of working people, nor did it raise questions of economic exploitation or the lack of power of depressed individuals. It was, however, a useful opportunity to dramatize the dangers of local controls to freedom of expression and of conscience. Yet for every Scopes case, a dozen involved labor. In fact, Baldwin in 1929, in summarizing the work of the decade, wrote in the *Social Work Yearbook:* "Of the infringements of civil liberties against which organizations in this field protest, nine out of ten involve rights which labor asserts in its contest with employers or with civil authorities."[35]

The ACLU was unique in the sincerity of its concern for the individual. In contrast with the Lippmanns or even certain of the literary figures, who reacted sharply when civil-liberties violations threatened them personally or when the championship of rights was safe and popular, the ACLU concerned itself with every incident *and* the party involved in it whose rights were being abrogated. The contrast was equally marked with the Communists, whose interests lay only in episodes that tended to show the degradation of the capitalistic system and the necessity for its early overthrow. The Communists' concern for the individual was totally cynical and their ends totally irrelevant.[36] The ACLU members combined an honorable concern for the individual involved, no matter how obscure, with a long-range objective of bringing about sufficient change within society so that such episodes could not happen again to similar people in similar circumstances. Only by fighting for those composite ends did they feel civil liberties could be advanced along with the economic, political, and social equality to ensure their future protection.

9

The "Firing Line" in the 1920s

Free speech and the rights of labor to organize strike and picket will be assured just in proportion as the workers stand together when these rights are attacked. The aid of middle-class liberals and religious bodies helps secure them by decreasing "moral" prestige of employing interests and the government. Whether the industrial struggle will be waged without resort to violence and bloodshed depends entirely upon how far the right of agitation of new ideas can be won and held by the militant forces of labor and their allies.

Roger N. Baldwin,
"Who's Got Free Speech,"
Advance, May 18, 1923

The American Civil Liberties Union in almost every case is on the unpopular or disapproved side. We are seldom called upon for assistance otherwise. Therefore, in California, we are associated in the public mind with the I.W.W.; in the South with the Negroes or the atheists; in Pennsylvania, West Virginia and New Jersey with labor "agitators"; in Michigan and elsewhere with the Workers' party; in Albany with birth control; in Boston with the Ku Klux Klan and anarchists. Our enemies have little doubt that we are financed from Moscow.

Arthur Garfield Hays, *Let
Freedom Ring,* 1928

Problems left from the war and those created by labor were central in raising the issue of freedom of speech in the 1920s. Sometimes active civil libertarians inspired depressed people to raise the question. At other times action was taken to counteract aggressive restrictive movements. The public reaction showed that by 1929 a favorable climate for freedom of expression had been created, even though few civil libertarians then expressed optimism about their activities.

One of the first questions to confront the newly reorganized ACLU in 1920 was that of political prisoners. With the war well over a year past, men confined for the expression of unpopular beliefs were demanding and seemed to deserve freedom. A variety of organizations joined the battle. But it was of special interest to the ACLU, which grew out of wartime dissent and which hoped to use this opportunity to dramatize the free-speech question. The episode taught ACLU leaders that they would confront opposition from conservatives as well as from champions of civil liberty who questioned their techniques and purposes.

In 1919, while still members of the Justice Department, John Lord O'Brien and Alfred Bettman had reviewed numerous cases and had so drastically reduced sentences that two hundred prisoners went free in a short time.[1] Numerous amnesty committees worked for release of the others, and the Central Labor Bodies Conference for the Release of Political Prisoners (CLBC) attempted to rally the entire American labor movement behind the cause.[2] But conservative union leaders were unenthusiastic, and the CLBC had to appeal to individual locals throughout the country. It received encouraging support, both financial and moral.[3] Even Attorney General A. Mitchell Palmer met amnesty delegations with the reassurance that, as a Quaker, he understood the motives of the political heretic.[4] The red scare temporarily intimidated the supporters of freedom. By 1920, however, with national tensions abating, it was possible to reinvigorate the earlier movement. Many Americans were now clearly in a mood to forgive and forget. During the 1920 presidential campaign, Warren Harding approved a "generous amnesty for political prisoners,"[5] and the *Literary Digest* reported that even some conservative newspapers were supporting release.[6]

ACLU leaders hoped to gain the early release of federal prisoners, but not as an isolated and meaningless act of mercy. The distinction between amnesty and pardon was vital. Amnesty recognized that it was safe to let citizens express their right to criticize. Pardon carried with it no such implication but simply forgave "wrongs."[7] To the ACLU, then, it was important that the prisoners be released to show that dissent and even heresy were still alive. Oswald Garrison Villard, a member of the National Committee, wrote in *The Nation* in 1922:

Something very definite and important will have been lost by the American people if they persist in regarding amnesty as a matter of mercy or at best a grudging recognition that to release a few prisoners may silence an annoying clamor. Much of the hope for the future depends upon a clear recognition that since "heresy is the growing point of society" it is socially disastrous to punish it by legal penalties. All progress begins in a protest against generally accepted opinion, and the menace of the prophet or pioneer—even if in particular instances his theories do not stand the test of practice—is not comparable to the menace of the demagogue who caters to popular passion and ancient taboos.[8]

But to ask imprisoned men to sacrifice themselves to the abstract cause of free speech and refuse pardon on the basis of repentance was to ask a sacrifice that civil libertarians hardly seemed to be willing to make themselves. Similarly to ask those in a position to release such individuals to commit themselves to the stand that they had been wrong at the outset was to ask a form of political sacrifice that politicians were reluctant to make.

The widely revered Socialist leader Eugene V. Debs had not only gone to jail for his opinions during the war, but had run for the presidency while in Atlanta Penitentiary in 1920, polling nearly a million votes.[9] Now he was an old man in ill health. Many people felt the need for charity in his case. Although Wilson was relentless in his desire to keep Debs in prison, Harding was a far less vindictive man and began to respond to the mounting wave of public pressure for release, especially after July 2, 1921, when Congress officially terminated the state of war. Despite the objections of the American Legion and other right-wing groups, Harding consulted Attorney General Harry M. Daughtery in December 1921 as to the safest and most politic way to handle the Debs question.[10] Daugherty denied the charge that Debs was a "martyr to the cause of freedom of speech and the most conspicuous example of the illegal prosecution, and even persecution, of those who differed with the policy of this Government and the course pursued by it in the late war in Europe."[11] The forthcoming release, he argued, should be a "gracious act of mercy" to a sick man. It would stop the unsettling discussion and undercut the amnesty crusade "before the movement in that direction had succeeded or gone too far."[12] On Christmas Day, 1921, Eugene V. Debs was released through the grant of executive clemency in the form of a pardon.

ACLU leaders were disappointed. Although twenty-four other men were released at the same time,[13] such releases did not recognize the principle of free speech. Yet the ACLU could not object to the fact that Debs and the few others were free. It altered its position in early 1922 and decided to work for individual pardons, thus abandoning its overall goal of a general amnesty.[14]

Roger Baldwin, flushed with success, urged the seventy-six prisoners who remained in Leavenworth to apply for individual pardons. All refused. Dedicated to the amnesty position, they had suffered long and bitterly, solely for exercising their "constitutional right of free speech."[15] They assailed Baldwin and the ACLU for encouraging them to waive those civil liberties through the pardon process.[16] Even under such fire, however, the ACLU continued to submit frequent applications to the Justice Department asking for the release of the prisoners, and, in October, Harding eventually took steps to release any man who would promise "to be law-abiding . . . and not encourage, advocate, or be wilfully connected with lawlessness in any form."[17] A handful accepted.

In January 1923, dramatic action at the state level further forced the President's hand. Al Smith, upon taking office for a second term as governor of New York, called in his initial message to the legislature on January 1, 1923, for a repeal of the Lusk Laws and for a restoration of complete freedom of expression in the state.[18] On January 10, 1923, a group of over a hundred citizens met with Smith in his executive chambers and for an hour argued the case of such figures as "Big Jim" Larkin and Benjamin Gitlow. The first speaker, Jeremiah A. O'Leary, chairman of the Larkin Amnesty Committee, explained: "We feel that your message to the Legislature has given us light and shows us the way to the restoration of free speech, free assemblage and a free press."[19] He pointed out that eighteen Socialists convicted in Illinois under a similar law had been pardoned by Governor Small within six days after they started serving their sentences.[20] It was time for New York to follow suit. A prominent DAR member, Mrs. Malcolm Duncan, asserted that if the Constitution of the United States was strictly enforced there would be no political prisoners in this country. Smith lost little time acting. On January 18, he granted the application for executive clemency on behalf of James L. Larkin and made his position clear in a public statement. He utterly disagreed with the doctrines and principles of Larkin, but "political progress results from the clash of conflicting opinions. The public assertion of an erroneous doctrine is perhaps the surest way to disclose the error and make it evident to the electorate."[21]

Although the action drew vigorous criticism from Archibald Stevenson, Senator Lusk, the National Civic Federation, and the *The New York Times*, it also drew national commendation from many highly conservative and respectable agencies.[22] *Collier's Weekly* stated: "We are still listening for President Harding to say about the political prisoners in Leavenworth words as bold and ringing as those that Governor Al Smith of New York spoke in pardoning Big Jim Larkin."[23] Glenn Frank, soon to become president of the University of Wisconsin, argued persuasively that Smith's action should "set an example which should be followed by every Governor in the United States and by the President of the United States." Conservatives, he added, had "just as much at stake as radicals . . . in the preservation of the complete freedom of thought and speech." The temporary intolerance of wartime was waning; "a permanent organization of bigotry on a national scale" was a danger.[24] Harding was impressed by the growing pressure, particularly from Senators William E. Borah and George Wharton Pepper. Pepper assumed the responsibility "as an American lawyer . . . bound to take cognizance of their plight" of reexamining critically the record of each of the federal political prisoners and revealed to the Justice Department that in virtually every case the evidence upon which conviction had been made was insubstantial.[25] Harding, before his death on August 2, 1923, released sixteen more prisoners under the earlier conditions.

Harding's death aroused grave apprehensions on the part of amnesty leaders that a tough fight was ahead for the remaining thirty-six prisoners. Calvin Coolidge's role in the Boston Police Strike had hardly foreshadowed tolerance of dissent. Surprisingly, however, he appointed a committee of three prominent citizens to study the issue. And when, in December 1923, it recommended unconditional release of the remaining prisoners, the President ended the incarceration of the remaining opponents of the war. The action drew wide-scale commendation. Borah and other national leaders hailed it as a "vindication of the right of free speech and free press," and editorial comment widely praised the President for restoring the principles of American democracy.[26]

For the ACLU leaders, this was both a victory and a bitter disappointment. They hastened to proclaim publicly that the President's action recognized fully the principle of freedom of speech. Yet Coolidge failed to remove previous restrictions imposed by Harding upon earlier releases, and the number of state political prisoners still languishing in various penitentiaries indicated the further need for vigorous local campaigns. Coolidge's action made it possible for the ACLU to affirm that the principle of amnesty and hence free speech had been acknowledged, but it was not a victory in which it could take full satisfaction.[27]

Civil libertarians also threw themselves into concrete postwar labor issues. Action in the name of free speech came into hard, head-to-head confrontation with local repression. Three states especially cried for attention: West Virginia, Pennsylvania, and New Jersey. In each, employers used the law mercilessly to exploit working people; in each, the situation had become so desperate that discontent bubbled close to the surface. And a vital aspect of this discontent was the growing frustration due to the inability to assemble, plan group action, and publicly express their grievances.

The union movement in the coal mining region of West Virginia had been encouraged as a result of wartime gains, and the United Mine Workers hoped to expand organizational campaigns. Mine operators were just as adamantly opposed to any further unionization and in fact hoped to undo that which had already taken place. In West Virginia, the operators had a tremendous advantage, since 80 percent of the workers in the coal mining counties of Logan and Mingo lived in company-owned, company-financed, and company-dominated towns, and under the authority of local courts. Operators could therefore easily enforce rules such as one prohibiting miners from inviting union organizers into their homes and could legally evict an employee any time he quit work, regardless of cause.[28] In addition, in Local County, the operators "owned" the sheriff, a rough and tough rowdy named Don Chafin, who was paid $32,700 a year by the companies. Chafin ruled Logan County with tyranny, and he was hated and feared through the coal country.[29]

In February and March of 1920, after episodes in which operators refused to allow the few ACLU members in the coal region to assemble and speak freely, the United Mine Workers set out to bolster its few beleaguered members with an ambitious organizing campaign. The ACLU and Roger Baldwin promptly offered full cooperation, ostensibly because the rights of free speech and free assembly were clearly involved. Baldwin hired free-lance journalist John L. Spivak to represent the ACLU and to assist in organizing a "free-speech campaign" in Logan County. Spivak was shocked not only by what he saw of mine-owner tyranny in the region, but by the inability of ACLU officials in New York to comprehend the reality of the situation. Realizing that the unionization campaign would have to fight not only the mine officials and their hired gunmen, but the state Democratic governor, John J. Cromwell, who fully sympathized with them, he wrote to New York for strongly worded posters and pamphlets designed to arouse the workers by putting the issue in clear black and white terms. Albert De Silver, who handled the preliminary correspondence, felt that such sentiments as "the Thugs and Gunmen of Logan County Must Go!" were too violent and urged the circulation of material of a far more "quasi-judicial nature." Spivak was annoyed and amused. Writing to Roger Baldwin upon his return, he suggested that those in the New York office were apparently

> willing to do anything which would not hurt their tender feelings about civil liberties. They are still under the impression that there is some semblance of legal procedure here. There is not. You can't hold a meeting here, get pinched and then fight it out in the courts. If you try to hold a meeting in the southern counties, you'll never live to see the courts. . . . The state is on the verge of civil war, due to the suppression of the Constitutional rights of free speech and free assemblage. That's where you come in—or rather are supposed to come in, for the Union, besides sending me down, has *not* come in.[30]

By the time he reached Baldwin, local events had underlined the strength of his position.

Union efforts were succeeding surprisingly well in Mingo County. By mid-May of 1920, two locals of the UMW had been organized there. With organization, however, came systematic eviction of miners from company-owned property by Baldwin-Felts detectives in the employ of the operators. Tensions mounted precipitously until May 19, when trouble broke out in a sudden confrontation of detectives and union men. Shooting began, with Mayor Albert Felts of the town of Matawan, a detective official and six of his deputies, and three union men shot to death in a few minutes.[31]

The Matawan Massacre, quickly made national headlines and produced demands for federal intervention.[32] The ACLU promptly filed protests on behalf of the union with Governor Cromwell, President Wilson, and the Labor Department. There was no positive response. The UMW then appealed for protection to A. Mitchell Palmer, but the Attorney General, who had been ready to use federal troops in the 1919 coal strike on the side of the operators, quickly denied that any federal issue was involved here. "The laws of the State of West Virginia are involved," he told the UMW, "and you must look to the officers of that state to vindicate its laws."[33]

The operators placed the blame for the incident on Matawan Police Chief "Two Gun" Sidney (Sid) Hatfield and some twenty-three union men, all clearly associated in the public mind with the UMW. The issue was now clearly drawn. The UMW assumed responsibility for the defense, and Roger Baldwin and the ACLU agreed to manage the publicity for the trial, highly pessimistic at the outset, however, regarding the situation.[34] Baldwin's gesture was designed to show the ACLU's sincerity in its willingness to support the workers and the UMW. It was thus a calculated attempt at public image making. The risk was well worth the time and expense. Hatfield and his codefendants were freed by a jury of local miners, secretly delighted to strike a blow at their exploiters.[35]

The emboldened new union men in Mingo County decided to respond to the discharges and evictions by calling a strike. The operators refused to negotiate and instead used imported Negro and foreign-born strike breakers.[36] Soon civil war developed; a three-hour pitched battle on August 21, 1920, resulted in the death of seven men and the injury of dozens more. "Bloody Mingo" again made national headlines, and Woodrow Wilson responded to pleas from Governor Cromwell to send federal troops to the area. The ACLU protested, but to no avail. In the meantime, a local court issued a temporary injunction against further union recruiting, an action later upheld and made permanent by the state supreme court.[37] Intervention on the side of the operators drew national fire, however, and before the fall election, Wilson withdrew the troops. The newly elected Republican governor, Ephriam Morgan, declared martial law, using the state militia to break up union meetings and to suppress the UMW newspaper, *The West Virginia Federationist*.[38] The climax came on July 8, 1921, when state troops raided UMW headquarters and arrested union leaders, charging them with unlawful assemblage.[39]

The ACLU, anticipating little from the new Republican administration in Washington, publicly protested Morgan's actions and called for a congressional investigation. Other liberals and labor leaders endorsed the idea, and the Senate finally agreed to look into conditions in the mining area.

The subsequent hearings produced predictable testimony from each side.[40] Before hearings could be held in the mine region, however, Sid Hatfield and a UMW official were lured into a trap and shot in the back on the courthouse steps in Welch by a Baldwin-Felts detective, who later claimed, rather lamely, that he acted in self-defense.[41] Reaction among miners through the whole region was intense. Suspecting "King Don" Chafin's hand in the affair, mobs of union miners started to congregate in Boone County, just to the north of his Logan County fief, intent on taking law into their own hands and ending company tyranny. By late August, a force of four or five thousand men, many of them army veterans, began a carefully planned assault upon Logan County, and the nation's press spread the alarm. President Harding at once sent the army into the state, and the marchers disbanded. Governor Morgan then moved swiftly to prosecute the marchers. Grand juries in Mingo, Logan, and Boone counties returned hundreds of indictments, charging the local UMW president, Frank Keeney, and others with treason, conspiracy to incite riot, and many lesser offenses.[42]

The ACLU protested the indictments vigorously. Writing to President Harding, its leaders declared that the conflict was "due directly to the denial of civil rights to the miners by the employing interests and the officials whom they control." They urged the President to "bring together the parties to this conflict in order to arrive at a settlement which will insure peace and civil liberty."[43] Harding, whose sympathies were clearly with the operators, turned the communication over to the Justice Department, now under Harry M. Daughtery, but strongly influenced by former detective agency head and chief of the Bureau of Investigation, William J. Burns, and his assistant, J. Edgar Hoover. Their response was clear. "Communists" had been responsible for the trouble in West Virginia. The UMW and the ACLU had both long been suspect. Burns, in fact, regarded the ACLU as "one of the most dangerous organizations in the country" and kept it under as careful scrutiny as the Communist party.[44] Harding nevertheless shrank from a request by Governor Morgan to have the federal government assist in the prosecution of the marchers, fearing the national repercussions of such partisanship.

When the Senate committee visited West Virginia, it found no trouble, local conditions having sunk into a quiet, grudging truce. Don Chafin, whom Senator William S. Kenyon hoped to interview, had left for a long vacation. A few others were heard with indecisive results. The committee then held its final hearings in Washington and issued a noncommittal final report. Placing the blame equally on both sides, the committee hoped that early action would remedy the situation.[45] The ACLU was disappointed. The hearings did not give a clear picture of the miners' position. The outcome for the ACLU was gratifying only in the abstract as an occasion to fight against workers' exploitation.[46]

Federal troops remained in the Mingo and Logan areas into the fall of 1922, and the Mingo strike continued. There were no further overt violations of civil liberties in Mingo, however. Prosecution of the Logan marchers went on with the UMW supporting their legal defense. With calmer times, acquittals were systematically won, even in treason cases. The ACLU made fleeting attempts to push the free-speech issue in Logan in 1923, at one point sending Arthur Garfield Hays to speak in the town. But even a speech that assailed Don Chafin's autocratic reign, delivered with Chafin in the audience, produced no reaction, and Hays's hope of getting arrested to create a court test of local suppression failed.[47]

There was progress in the end, however. In 1924 a new Republican governor, Howard M. Gore, took office and, with a liberal attorney general joining him, shortly brought suit in the circuit court at Charleston attacking the Logan County system of armed guards paid by the companies and deputized as sheriffs. Action against Chafin ended in his conviction in the federal court at Huntington on a charge of bootlegging.[48] The result undercut the atmosphere of intimidation and bias which had prevailed in the state when state authority had been clearly lined up behind the operators. Ironically, with the UMW now totally free to go ahead with its campaigns, the bottom fell out of the coal market, and unionization fought a losing battle with unemployment and poverty until the days of the New Deal.

The situation in the Pennsylvania coal and iron regions was far more intricate and subtle, involving as it did many more powerful pressures. In 1919 and 1920 the postwar strikes, organizational campaigns, and free-speech fights were crushed. The elementary question of personal freedom was involved in all these incidents. As the Labor Defense and Free Speech Council of Western Pennsylvania stated in a 1923 pamphlet:

> In all their struggles, at Homestead, in the Great Steel strike of 1919, in the Mine Strike of 1922, to mention only a few, the workers were well aware that first of all they had to win free speech and free assemblage in order to even begin to organize. Hence the story of the heroic struggles of the workers in the District has to a large extent been the story of a bitter fight to secure the elementary civil rights supposedly accorded equally to all persons by the Constitution. The strong, burning desire of the workers for these rights could be matched in intensity only by the dogged determination of the bosses to deny these very rights, and stifle all freedom to meet and speak.[49]

The situation was naturally intriguing to civil libertarians. Hundreds of thousands of depressed citizens were not only being denied their basic civil liberties, but were often so intimidated that they were reluctant to protest.

Management had early been authorized to protect itself in its own fashion. An 1865 law allowed banks, railroads, and mining companies to organize their own armed police, which, commissioned by the governor, would act under state authority, even though paid by their employers and responsible only to them. Their chief function was to suppress labor unrest and they were recruited from those who could be counted upon to use strong-arm methods effectively. The brutal record of these Coal and Iron Police led to comparisons with the Russian Cossacks.

Such formal restraints, however, became inadequate when unionization gained strength in the region. In 1905, partially on the pretext of replacing the notorious Coal and Iron Police, the legislature set up the Pennsylvania State Constabulary, the first state police force in the country. The deeper motivation lay in employer complaints that the National Guard had been unsatisfactory during the great anthracite coal strike of 1902–1903. The meaning of the move quickly became clear, as no serious attempt was made to disband the Coal and Iron Police but rather an early working arrangement grew between them and the new constabulary so that workers were now terrorized by two organizations instead of one.

The State Federation of Labor protested early. Its Socialist president, James H. Maurer, had introduced an unsuccessful bill into the state legislature calling for abolishment of the constabulary in 1911, and the 1914 convention endorsed a book, *The American Cossack,* which gave explicit data regarding its activities.[50] The protest was of little avail. In the postwar period Pennsylvania added to its repressionist machinery a rigid state sedition law in 1919 and a growing use of private deputy sheriffs to maintain proper law and order. The unsuccessful strikes of 1919 and 1920 led to a further tightening of local restrictions.

During the steel strike the Reverend William M. Fincke, director of the Presbyterian New York Labor Temple, a citadel of free speech, was arrested along with a number of strikers for trying to hold a street meeting.[51] The ACLU protested that local antiassembly ordinances violated the fundamental guarantees in the federal Bill of Rights and the state constitution. This charge was summarily dismissed by the state supreme court, which argued that such provisions did not give "the right to assemble with others and speak wherever he and they choose to go." A person who wished to address an assemblage had to "gather his audience together in places where he and they have the right to be for this purpose."[52] The ruling gave local officials complete control over all meetings in public places. They could act through vagrancy laws, prosecutions for rioting and inciting to riot, sedition, or unlawful assembly. In a public disturbance, the sheriff, on his own discretion, had the power to take any action necessary to preserve law and order. Such proclamations were issued freely in the counties around Pittsburgh during the coal and steel strikes, and the conviction of violators was consistently upheld in the courts where local judges and prosecutors were often part-time company employees.[53]

But even further weapons were available to Pennsylvania employers. Large portions of the state, especially in the coal regions, were made up of closed company towns similar to those in West Virginia. Here traditional forms of compulsion and the danger of expulsion contained dissension. The injunction, revived with vigor in the 1920s, also became a useful weapon against actions threatening the status quo.[54]

Various business interests of the state worked together to check unionization and union activities. With the exception of the governorship of former Progressive Gifford Pinchot in 1923–1927, the state throughout the decade was in the hands of politicians obedient to the Mellon interests in Pittsburgh and the Vare interests in Philadelphia. The Pennsylvania Railroad refused to buy coal from operators who submitted to unionization. Companies that kept their contracts with the union were warned by their bankers not to do so. One firm, which tried to operate on a union basis despite such threats, had its mortgages foreclosed and was forced into bankruptcy.[55] The press of the state was almost entirely employer oriented; even ACLU leaders found it virtually impossible to get local happenings correctly reported.

The challenge of Pennsylvania, then, was ominous; yet conditions in the mines and the steel industry were sufficiently intolerable and civil libertarians were sufficiently aghast at the unchallenged despotism that it had to be met. The ACLU lent all the financial and moral support it could to working men willing to challenge the system. It sent its own officials into the state to assist in free-speech fights. It publicized local conditions as vigorously as possible and, despite sharp rebuff by the Wilson administration, continued to demand federal investigation of civil liberties.[56]

The 1920s opened with a strong drive by John L. Lewis and the UMW for increased wages in both the bituminous and anthracite coal fields. The operators resisted with equal vigor. Initially, in 1920, the UMW agreed to accept arbitration of wage demands from a government-appointed commission, but quickly found the commission loaded against them, and struck for two weeks before grudgingly accepting its low wage raise. In 1922, disillusioned with arbitration, the miners struck for five months rather than accept a 20 percent wage cut, but were finally forced after a long period of harassment to accept a greatly reduced one-year contract, all the while seething as company profit margins rose.[57]

The United States Coal Commission, which came into existence in September, 1922, was directed by Congress to study the industry and recommended constructive legislation. The members, while unconnected with mining interests, were largely of the cut of its conservative chairman, John Hays Hammond, who in later conversations with Pinchot indicated that the best immediate solution to the union problem was to use substitute miners to get the coal out.[58] Anticipating that the commission might very well overlook the civil-rights aspect, the ACLU and the League for Industrial Democracy sponsored a joint Committee of Inquiry on Coal and Civil Liberties to supply facts to the federal commission concerning the violation of civil liberties. The Committee of Inquiry, consisting of Zechariah Chafee, Father John A. Ryan, Reverend Arthur Holt, and Miss Kate H. Claghorn, made its findings public in a widely distributed pamphlet by Winthrop D. Lane entitled *The Denial of Civil Liberties in the Coal Fields.*[59] The action undoubtedly prodded the federal commission to include as part of its concern the civil-liberties question. Yet, the commission qualified the free-speech question by stating in its final report:

> Men have, of course, the inalienable American right to go into strange communities and diagnose the evils under which the community suffers and offer remedies for a cure. But many times it is not expedient to exercise this right. Men not connected with the industry have no right to make inflammatory speeches leading to the use of violence.[60]

Further, the commission went out of its way to insist that it had no responsibility to take any action that might affect the civil-liberties situation.

Prior to the expiration of the 1922 contract on September 1, 1923, other federal authorities did seek effective action. On April 27, 1923, a squad of federal Department of Justice agents working closely with city police and county detectives staged a "red raid" on Workers' party headquarters in Pittsburgh, ransacking the files and seizing nine party leaders and a dozen other workingmen found on the premises. All were held without bail, and many subsequently lost their jobs. The assistant district attorney justified the arrests by the charge that party officials "were trying to get the mine and steel workers into the Workers' Party," a legally recognized political organization. The Pittsburgh press fell into line, announcing that a May Day plot had been nipped in the bud.

The ACLU wired a strongly worded protest to newly elected Governor Giffort Pinchot protesting the action as a flagrant violation of the right of freedom of speech. The newspapers reported the ACLU wire in conjunction with a story indicating that the arrested workers had planned to dynamite public buildings and worded the account so that it seemed that the ACLU objected to the arrest of persons intent upon violence. City police shortly raided the home of the chairman of the Pittsburgh branch of the Labor Defense Council, arresting him and two New York attorneys residing with him while they prepared briefs for the victims and held all three in an act of calculated intimidation. Among others subsequently held was a UMW official in the Pittsburgh area.[61]

Protests to Pinchot and the state attorney general brought assurances of an early investigation.[62] The governor, however, concentrated on efforts to arbitrate the wage situation before the expiration of the one-year contract on September 1. The ACLU, growing impatient, sent Arthur Garfield Hays to the state in late May to establish a beachhead for freedom of speech through public meetings in one of the most tightly controlled company towns in the coal region, Vintondale. Hays quickly got a taste of company power.[63] His experience, however, encouraged a group of Workers' party members, including Robert W. Dunn, a member of the ACLU's National Committee, to attempt to hold a public meeting in McKeesport in September without a permit from the mayor. The subsequent furor that its arbitrary denial produced further pressured Pinchot to concern himself seriously with statewide conditions.[64] After successfully arbitrating between mine operators and workers (gaining for all miners a new contract including an eight-hour day and a 10 percent wage increase), he appointed a state commission to investigate the state constabulary, the Coal and Iron Police, the use of privately paid deputy sheriffs, and the general status of civil liberties and free speech in the mining areas.[65] The subsequent report of the commission, presented by one of its members, John P. Guyer, and entitled *Pennsylvania's Cossacks and the State Police*, was a devastating exposé of company tyranny, revealing over a hundred detailed cases in the single strike year of 1922 of lawless violence—the riding down of men, women, and children at meetings or on the sidewalk, ingenious tortures in jail, the shooting up of tent colonies of evicted union miners, and even murder.[66] Governor Pinchot cut the Coal and Iron forces in half, and, during his enlightened administration from 1923 to 1927, the mining districts enjoyed calm for the first time since the war.[67]

Unfortunately for the workers, however, Pinchot could not succeed himself as governor, and, although UMW head John L. Lewis campaigned for him, he was unsuccessful in his bid for the United States Senate. His successor, John S. Fisher, conservative Republican and later Mellon associate, had little concern for working people, and, at a time when governmental statesmanship could have been highly salutary, he made no attempt to arbitrate the labor situation. From 1927 to 1931, pre-Pinchot conditions returned to Pennsylvania with a vengeance.

Coal was a "sick industry" in the 1920s, and the UMW was caught between pressures from its members and from management.[68] Public opinion, while sympathetic, was nonetheless apprehensive, for the Herrin massacre in which irate miners in Illinois killed nineteen strike-breakers turned the public against the union.[69] John L. Lewis was forced to make concessions in 1924 to management in the three year, wage-holding "Jacksonville Agreement"; however, the operators began to evade it almost immediately. The Mellon-controlled Pittsburgh Coal Company and one hundred other Pennsylvania operators repudiated it openly and established the open shop, a movement against which the UMW was powerless. A "Save the Union" campaign developed among the miners under left-wing auspices, and management, delighted with internal dissension among its opponents, determined to gain further wage reductions and concessions in the 1927 contract negotiations. In that year, the UMW was forced to authorize negotiation by districts. Certain local unions did agree to lower wages, but the net outcome was a wide-scale strike, particularly in Pennsylvania and parts of Ohio. Promptly the Coal and Iron Police were expanded even beyond the previous size, and, with the "Cossacks" and deputy sheriffs cooperating fully, an assault was launched so systematic and ruthless in its effectiveness that eventually Lewis was forced to cancel the strike to spare workers further brutality.[70]

The ACLU sent representatives and funds to raise the civil-liberties aspect sufficiently to reach the national conscience. The American Federation of Labor summoned a special convention in Pittsburgh to spur efforts to provide strike relief. Congressman Fiorello H. La-Guardia of New York, visiting the area, was so aghast at the brutality of Coal and Iron Police that he called for a congressional investigation of conditions in the mining region. A Senate committee subsequently looked into charges that John D. Rockefeller of Consolidated Coal in West Virginia, General W. W. Atterbury of the Pennsylvania Railroad, and the Mellons of Pittsburgh Coal were responsible for hunger and radicalism of the "reddest kind" in the mine fields. It eventually produced a documented account filling 3,414 pages.[71]

Response to the committee varied. Governor Fisher refused to answer questions about state licenses for the Coal and Iron Police. He was chief of a sovereign state, he maintained, and did not have to heed senatorial requests. J. D. A. Morrow, president of the Pittsburgh Coal Company, painted a picture of contented workers happily living in well-kept villages, until stirred up by the un-American agita-

tion of outsiders. Senator Frank Gooding of Idaho, a member of
the committee, was skeptical. Having visited several of the company's
camps, he felt that

> conditions which exist in the strike-torn regions of the Pittsburgh district
> are a blotch upon American civilization. It is inconceivable that such
> squalor, suffering, misery, and distress should be tolerated in the heart
> of one of the richest industrial centers in the world. The committee
> found men, women, and children living in hovels which are more unsani-
> tary than a modern swinepen. They are breeding places of sickness
> and crime.[72]

John L. Lewis declared that Pittsburgh Coal miners had been "evicted
from their homes and a reign of terror and intimidation inaugurated
that excelled for brutality and lawlessness any union-busting endeavor
this nation has witnessed in recent years."[73] Scores of miners and
their families gave the details of beatings and of police tyranny.
    The hearings touched the consciences of a good many more citizens.
As novelist Fannie Hurst, who had done some investigating on her
own (finding conditions "more appalling and more degrading and
more humiliating . . . than anything I saw in Russia two years ago
under the stress of revolution"), told the committee, even the suggested ameliorative measures would merely be "putting iodine to
a cancer."[74] And an event immediately following the departure of
the committee indicated that ameliorative steps were far in the future.
    The Coal and Iron Police, kept in the background by strict orders
from the companies, beat John Barkoski, a miner and prounion man,
to death in a company barracks with blackjacks, knucklers, and a
poker which was bent double on his body. The hard-boiled district
attorney who investigated the case said, "It was the most brutal
murder I have ever investigated."[75] Although the Mellon Company
defended the attackers so successfully that they were given light
sentences, reaction was nationwide and even rumbled through the
middle-class elements of Pittsburgh.
    Pittsburgh had now been invaded by the Hearst and Scripps-
Howard newspaper chains, which reported the episode with horror.
The Constitutional Rights Committee composed of liberal clergymen,
college professors, and lawyers moved against the Coal and Iron
Police. Frederick Woltman and William L. Nunn, in *The American
Mercury* of December 1928, commented somewhat cynically upon
the committee's timidity and ended their article by insisting that
"the one agency which had proved to be the courageous friend of

working people and of civil liberties and of human rights in the entire crisis was the A.C.L.U."[76]

The ACLU, while undoubtedly flattered by the compliment, was only partly encouraged by its efforts in Pennsylvania. During the strike, attempts to challenge anti–free-speech ordinances led only to arrests and expulsions from the cities involved. Frederick Woltman, the new secretary of the ACLU's Pittsburgh local, arrested while speaking at a defense meeting in early 1929, elicited a ruling of the city law department that no police permit was required to hold meetings in the future. And Miss Sophia Dulles, executive secretary of the ACLU's Philadelphia branch, reported in March 1929 that "widespread interest in legislative action designed to curb the abuses of the Coal and Iron Police has led to the plan for establishing branches in Reading, Scranton, and Wilkes-Barre."[77] But these acts were more significant in conception than in operation. The ACLU did join the AFL in demanding that the 1929 legislature enact anti–injunction and anti–yellow-dog contract legislation, laws providing for state regulation of private detective agencies engaged in "industrial sabotage," and abolition of the Coal and Iron Police. Instead, Senator W. D. Mansfield introduced a "substitute" measure legalizing the powers that the mine guards already frequently exercised of making arrests without warrant from a magistrate and of placing prisoners in their own private jails. Governor Fisher hailed the measure as a great step forward in eliminating previously "illegal" activity.[78]

In actuality, then, the Pennsylvania situation did not improve appreciably during the decade. As late as 1929, the ACLU still stated that Pennsylvania was the worst state in the country in the denial of basic civil liberties. This condition continued until the depression years, and the return to office of Governor Pinchot in 1931 brought some measure of relief.

The Colorado coal fields also saw violence in the late 1920s. But the outcome of the confrontation there was different. Highly responsible IWW leaders and a dramatic local Joan of Arc rallied the workers, and a general strike of the miners succeeded.

A State Industrial Commission to mediate labor controversies had been set up after the Ludlow Massacre. The 1915 law authorizing it made a crime of striking any industry affected by a public interest before the commission made an inquiry and reported its findings. The commission had the power to determine whether a legitimate labor dispute existed and whether workers were being represented by a bona fide spokesman.[79] Such provisions, combined with a state antipicketing law and a wartime-created state police force of "Rangers," effectively curbed further worker discontent.

In the mid-1920s, in action paralleling that of Governor Al Smith in New York and Pinchot in Pennsylvania, the Rangers were abolished by gubernatorial edict, so that the companies, particularly the Rockefeller-owned Colorado Fuel and Iron Company, depended on their own guards to curtail worker unrest. Discontent nevertheless grew. In 1922, wages were lowered, and the UMW was forced out of the region altogether. IWW leaders filled the vacuum; in 1925, the Wobblies began organizational work among the miners from a headquarters in Walsenburg.[80] In August of 1927, an IWW protest strike in sympathy for Sacco and Vanzetti got an unexpectedly enthusiastic response from workers. In September, delegates representing forty-three mines and properties met at Aguilar to formulate an extended list of demands, including improvement of wages and working conditions and an insistence that labor organizers be allowed to come and go in company-owned camps.[81] Leaders, scrupulously abiding by the law, notified the State Industrial Commission of their intention to strike in one month if their conditions were not met.

The Industrial Commission promptly declared the proposed strike illegal, claiming that the IWW did not represent the miners. Company police were mobilized, and an active campaign of direct repression against IWW leaders and sympathizers began. Organizers were arrested, meetings were broken up, and in various communities IWW halls were ransacked or burned. Yet intimidation did not frustrate the strike plans. In October, half the state's miners walked out. The Industrial Commission promptly declared the action illegal and prohibited picketing.

At this point, Governor Adams reconstituted the state police under the leadership of a former army captain, Louis N. Scherf, who had led the Rangers in active strike-breaking activities in 1922.[82] That, however, merely steeled the strikers' determination. "Flaming Milka" Sablich, a colorful nineteen-year-old girl, moved from location to location in a bright red dress insisting with vigor, "They can't dig coal with bayonets" and "We must stop every miner from working. We can win if every miner stays away from the mines."[83] Ridden down by a mounted policeman, who dragged her half a block by the wrist, she was jailed as a dangerous agitator. But the young girl's encouragement propelled miners into daring acts of defiance, even though a new Douglas bomber equipped with machine guns and antipersonnel bombs was furnished to the reactivated constabulary.[84]

Public opinion, theretofore callous to Cossack tyranny in Pennsylvania, became incensed. When state police on November 21 opened fire at close range on several hundred unarmed picketers at the Columbine Mine of the Rocky Mountain Fuel Company, killing six and wounding twenty, even the local press protested the tyrannical methods.[85] Two religious bodies spoke out vigorously. *The Register,* a Denver Catholic weekly, supported the right of men to unionize. The Social Service Commission of the Colorado Conference of the Methodist Episcopal Church protested in "the name of Americanism against the abridgement of fundamental civil liberties. Interference with free speech and peaceful assembly and the arrest of strike leaders as such were not only gross violations of constitutional rights, but also provoked violence on the part of those not given an equal opportunity before the law."[86]

The ACLU, which had been active in defending Denver Judge Ben Lindsey against bitter attacks by the Ku Klux Klan, issued a pamphlet, *The War on Colorado Miners,* indicating to its national membership that it had been fighting to get the civil-liberties feature of the strike into the foreground and setting forth clearly and factually the general issues in the controversy.[87]

The Industrial Commission now agreed to investigate and thus provided a forum from which newspaper reporters gathered much material, all of which weighed heavily against the operators.[88] By January, conditions had calmed, and the strike was gradually terminated. Employers agreed to substantial wage increases and met so many demands of the workers that the IWW leadership felt a sense of victory.

One of the most effective rallying cries of the IWW was the tyranny of the antipicketing law. In calling for its violation, the IWW contended that that statute was an unconstitutional infringement of personal liberty contrary to the First Amendment. No clear resolution of this ever emerged from Colorado courts, but thereafter there was little attempt to enforce this provision.

The free-speech issue was an integral part of other labor controversies of the 1920s. The Paterson, New Jersey, silk strike of 1924 afforded the ACLU a situation in which to act enthusiastically. Paterson had a long history of arbitrary police control of workers. In strikes in 1913 and 1919, men had been sentenced to jail for exercising their freedom of expression. Paterson was almost "unique among industrial communities in this form of police dictatorship backed up by local officials and the courts."[89]

The clear pretext the ACLU needed came in August 1924, when 6,000 members of an independent local union, the Associated Silk Workers, walked out on strike. In September, Chief of Police John M. Tracey suddenly decided to close Turn Hall, the organizational headquarters, to further meetings. The union turned to the ACLU for help in getting their hall open again. The ACLU moved to rent the hall for a meeting of its own. But the 500 to 600 people who turned out for the meeting found a cordon of police around the building. Frustrated, the crowd moved to the steps of the City Hall, where John C. Butterworth, a Socialist candidate for public office, managed only to say, "Fellow workers" before police demanded his permit. Holding up the Bill of Rights of New Jersey he stated, "This is my permit," and his supporters angrily demanded he be allowed to continue. At this point 50 police charged with nightsticks, injuring a number of people and effectively breaking up the gathering. Eleven persons were arrested for disorderly conduct, blocking traffic, resisting an officer, and holding a meeting without a permit.[90] Roger Baldwin, upon his insistence that he was responsible for the meeting, was held by the police pending investigation. All the charges were dismissed the next day in the police court except that of disorderly conduct, for which small fines were levied.

Baldwin and Butterworth had no intention of letting the issues drop there, but insisted upon pushing a test case in connection with their own arrest under a 1796 New Jersey unlawful assembly law, never tested in court, but available as a potential club over any form of public meeting unsavory to local officials.[91] Baldwin was indicted by a Grand Jury under the blanket charge of instigating hundreds to disturb the public peace and thus violate the unlawful-assembly statute. The Ku Klux Klan of Passaic County passed a resolution endorsing a proposal of the mayor of Paterson to deport troublesome strikers.[92] Klan endorsement, however, hardly proved a benefit to local officials, already smarting from a strong "I am the law" statement by Police Chief Tracey.[93] The light in which his comment threw Tracey was so poor that he promptly agreed to reopen Turn Hall to striker meetings, thereby restoring the right of peaceful assembly.[94]

Yet Baldwin was also determined to make his legal point. After a local judge upheld his conviction in December 1924, he appealed to higher New Jersey courts and eventually was vindicated. After an eloquent plea by attorney Arthur Vanderbilt of Newark, the highest court of the state ruled that the common-law test for unlawful assembly on which the unlawful-assembly statute was based illustrated "the futility of attempting for future guidance to adopt an inflexible definition of all circumstances and conditions which might arise." Judge Samuel Kalisch then reversed the convictions. Making clear that each case should depend "upon the object and character of the meeting and whether or not the overt acts done by the participants therein . . . are of such a nature as to inspire well-grounded fear in persons of reasonable firmness and courage of a riot, rout, affray, or other breach of the peace," he held that "from the record before us, we find nothing in the statement of the facts to have warranted the finding by the trial judge that the accused were guilty of the offense of unlawful assembly."[95]

The ACLU hailed the action as "the only liberal state Supreme Court decision in a civil liberties case in recent years."[96] Further, editorial comment, with the exception of the employer-oriented Paterson papers and the ultraconservative press, was surprisingly warm. The *Newark Evening News* editorialized that the action should "put an end to this disgraceful interference with the right of the people of this state." The *St. Louis Post-Dispatch* hailed the decision as a great victory for freedom of speech. *The New York Times*, although maintaining clearly that the action did not "vindicate incendiary speech," still had to admit that Baldwin had established an important point of law in undercutting the arbitrariness of local police rule.[97]

The situation in the famous Passaic textile strike in 1926 was less clear-cut and involved the ACLU not only with the local suppression of strike activities but with Communists and red baiting.

The woolen textile industry in the 1920s was among the most depressed in the country. Wool was hit not only by growing competition from newer fabrics, but by changes in style and by the growth of central heating. A 1925 report of the National Industrial Conference Board reported that the average weekly wage for American workers in the twenty-two largest national industries was $27.13, while the average for American textile workers was $21.84; few Passaic workers reached this level.[98] In addition, they suffered from long hours, unsanitary working conditions, speedups, sudden layoffs for indefinite periods, spies infesting the factories, blacklisting, and fingerprinting of employees; and since many of the workers had large families, women and children often worked the night shifts to eke out a bare existence for those at home.[99]

In October 1925, nine woolen mills in Passaic and neighboring Garfield announced a 10 percent wage cut for their workers. Through the rest of the year already distressed workers seethed with renewed discontent, and an explosion was near; it merely needed a good catalyst. The AFL United Textile Workers had little interest. Depressed, inarticulate, often immigrant mill hands would hardly complement the thin layer of skilled workers then in the UTW.[100] But for the Communists, now anxious to make a strong frontal move into organization, the situation was inviting, and the party then mapped a careful strategy for the situation, sending into Passaic an explosive young intellectual and recent graduate of Harvard Law School, Albert Weisbord. The result was the formation of a United Front Textile Committee under Communist guidance. Employers countered by discharging workers identified with the union movement.

On January 25, a committee of forty-five workers, composed of representatives of each department of the Botany Mills who presented written demands to the company management, were discharged. The other workers in the mill poured out with them, and within four weeks all major companies in Passaic and Garfield had been struck, with a total of sixteen thousand workers out.[101]

The demands presented included abolition of the wage cut, plus a 10 percent increase over the old scale, a forty-four-hour week, with time-and-a-half for overtime, a cleanup of working conditions, no discrimination against union workers, and recognition of the union.[102] The last point finally became the central issue of the strike.

The strikers were quickly mobilized into picket lines, and mass meetings were held periodically to bolster strike morale.[103] Initially employers attempted to divide workers by appeals to religious and national differences and by hinting at the cynicism of Communist leadership, but solidarity was great and the police were quickly turned to for assistance. Strikers were beaten, fire hoses threw icy streams of water at them, and Police Chief Richard O. Zober used tear gas bombs to break up meetings and picket lines. Police also rode down strikers with horses and motorcycles. Union halls were closed, and nearly a thousand arrests were made. Male strikers headed picket lines clad in World War I steel helmets and gas masks, and women strikers pushed their infants in carriages.[104]

Policy tyranny did not go unnoticed. The press filled columns with pictures and stories of life on the picket lines. Since many stories were written by left-wing and liberal journalists favorable to the strikers, police hostility developed. The *New York Herald Tribune* pointed out in March that over $3,000 worth of photographic equipment had been smashed. The *New York World* called for thorough investigation of "the outrageous 'Cossack' methods" of the police, and eventually newsmen began surveying the strike from inside armored cars or from low-flying airplanes rather than face further personal danger.[105]

After some twelve weeks, the police decided to ban all strike meetings. Mayor William A. Burke of Garfield, an employee of one of the mills, called in Sheriff George P. Nimmo of Bergen County, who decided on the basis of a state law of 1864 to use the "Riot Act." He plastered the city of Garfield with notices forbidding public assemblages.[106] Since the authorizing law provided for the reading of the Riot Act only when trouble was clearly brewing, his action was totally unwarranted and gave the police an excuse for dispersing crowds even before meetings could start.

The ACLU had engaged in local relief work and had cooperated in feeding starving strikers and raising money on their behalf. In late March it instituted civil suits against Zober and twelve of his officers on the grounds of "atrocious assault" and battery. "We insist upon observance of the law by those who enforce the law," read a statement from national headquarters which also revealed that the ACLU investigation had uncovered not less than one hundred cases of unlawful police violence.[107] It gained the free-speech issue for which it had been waiting when Norman Thomas, one of its members and leader of the League for Industrial Democracy, attempted to speak in a vacant lot in Garfield. Thomas found himself talking, however, almost exclusively to fifty police armed with sawed-off shotguns and managed to say only a few sentences before a sheriff shouted to his deputies: "Clean 'em out; lock that bird up." Thomas was hustled off to Hackensack to face indictment by a local insurance agent who acted as Justice of the Peace, Louis N. Hargreaves. The action drew sharp public criticism from conservative as well as liberal sources.[108]

On April 22, a conference of representatives of the various organizations including the Communists, the ACLU, the International Labor Defense, the League for Industrial Democracy, and various local makeshift emergency relief organizations set up the Joint Committee for Passaic Defense and Free Speech. It unanimously decided that the International Labor Defense would conduct the defense of Albert Weisbord and all the others arrested as a direct result of their activity. Cases involving free speech would be handled by the ACLU, and both organizations would be supported in their work by the joint committee and all other participating organizations.[109]

Thomas was quickly released, but the $10,000 bail that had been imposed upon him plus the $30,000 on Weisbord had proved too much for a good many conscious-stricken Americans. New York Attorney Bainbridge Colby, former Bull Moose Progressive and cabinet contemporary of A. Mitchell Palmer under Woodrow Wilson, came to New Jersey to argue personally against such tactics, strongly condemning "the unfavorable light in which free speech and free assemblage are thrown by these actions."[110] The ACLU in the meantime started proceedings before Vice Chancellor John Bentley of Jersey City to enjoin Sheriff Nimmo and his men from any similar action. Senators Borah and La Follette urged congressional investigation. The Senate Committee on Manufactures took testimony, and New York attorney Samuel Untermyer's argument against the denial of the civil rights of strikers clearly impressed it and received considerable public attention as well. In fact, fear of action by Congress

eventually helped to check much of the lawlessness by the employers
and public officials.[111]

The ACLU, eager for dramatic action, decided upon another test
of "Riot Law" restraint and in late April scheduled a meeting in
Belmont Park, near Passaic, with the Reverend John Haynes Holmes
and Arthur Garfield Hays as speakers. Sheriff Nimmo's response was
fast and clear: "They think they are going to hold their meeting
but they are positively not going to hold it if they discuss the strike."
Recently released Albert Weisbord retorted: "We are going to force
these peanut politicians to restore the constitutional rights of the
people."[112] On April 30, as dozens of police stood with shotguns
on their shoulders, injunction papers signed by Vice Chancellor Bentley
were served upon Sheriff Nimmo and his deputies, restraining them
and local police from interfering with the meeting or with peaceful
picketing. Nimmo withdrew his forces and acceded to the order.
From then on the strikers were unmolested. Although the strike
dragged on and was eventually terminated with only minor concessions to the workers, the effectiveness of the free-speech argument
was again demonstrated.[113]

On the West Coast in 1923, similar techniques challenged uninhibited local power and pushed the issue into a test case. California
was unique, especially Los Angeles. That city's antiunion press, stimu-
lated by the local American Legion and by the Commercial Federation
of California, later and more popularly known as the Better America
Federation, continued its demands for extended red hunting even
after national hysteria had calmed. Although there was an active movement in behalf of leniency for Anita Whitney and consistent pressure
for repeal of the state's criminal-syndicalism law, such opinion was
clearly in the minority. Prosecutions under the law declined in 1920
and 1921, but not because of liberalism. A combination of the growing
success of a vigorous open-shop movement and a sharp economic
depression kept employers busy and undermined the strength and
will of the militant IWW elements.[114]

The years 1922 and 1923, however, saw both a revival of economic
prosperity and a resurgence of IWW organizational and strike activity
in California, particularly among construction workers in Sacramento
and Fresno counties, in scattered agricultural districts throughout
the state, and among the marine transport workers at San Pedro,
the port area for Los Angeles. By the spring of 1923, the IWW
felt strong enough to attempt a general strike, the objectives of which
were to bring pressure for the release of remaining state political
prisoners, to protect "Fink Halls"—antiunion employment offices in
various areas—and to demand the repeal of the criminal-syndicalism

law, as well as higher wages. On the San Pedro waterfront, some 3,000 longshoremen answered the strike call, completely tying up the port while many ships loaded with high-demand goods for the Los Angeles area were in the harbor.[115]

The local police, fully sympathetic with employers, had been arresting known Wobbly troublemakers for six months before the strike. On April 26, they turned back outstate Wobblies attempting to join the demonstration and arrested and ordered out of town as many strikers as could easily be singled out. A special "Wobbly squad" raided IWW halls, making many arrests and seizing and confiscating much literature. Two days after the strike began, four asserted leaders were arrested on charges of criminal syndicalism. After a May Day mass meeting in the harbor district, police Captain C. R. Plummer announced that in the interests of "public security," no more street meetings would be permitted. Thereafter those attempting to start public gatherings were arrested and charged with violating the criminal-syndicalism law. Street meetings, however, continued and took on the character of "free speech" meetings, particularly on "Liberty Hill," a vacant lot on a rise in the harbor district owned by a woman who sympathized with the strikers. Being private property, the hill presumably could be utilized as its owner saw fit. But the police broke up meetings there as well, again arresting large numbers of defiant strikers.[116]

On the fifteenth day of the strike, Chief of Police Louis D. Oaks of Los Angeles took charge, with the aid of 500 policemen, and arrested under various charges of vagrancy, traffic violations, and criminal syndicalism over 400 men, packing two Los Angeles jails and placing the rest in a specially constructed stockade, ordering other "bull pens" built to accommodate further prisoners.[117] At this point the ACLU decided that the time was overdue for a head-on test of such arbitrary police rule.

Upton Sinclair had been a member of the ACLU since its reorganization in 1920. He and a group of libertarians from Los Angeles and Pasadena secured permission from the mayor to hold a free-speech meeting at San Pedro. They informed the chief of police that they intended to read the Bill of Rights of the Constitution of the United States from Liberty Hill and had the mayor's permission. Chief Oaks, who Sinclair later testified was intoxicated, warned him that "this Constitution stuff does not go at the Harbor" and that if he tried to read the Constitution even on private property, he would be thrown in jail and held without bail. Such a confrontation increased Sinclair's determination that to challenge such "lawbreakers in office . . . was the highest duty that a citizen of this community can perform."[118]

Arriving at Liberty Hill on the evening of May 12, Sinclair mounted the lantern-lit platform and proceeded to read to a large mass of strikers and several hundred policemen the First Amendment: "Congress shall pass no law abridging freedom. . . ." He got no further but was seized and dragged from the platform. His brother-in-law, Hunter Kimbrough, then mounted the platform and started to read the Declaration of Independence; he was promptly arrested. Prince Hopkins then stepped on the platform and stated "We have not come here to incite to violence," and was immediately arrested. Hugh Hardyman then followed Hopkins and cheerfully announced: "This is a most delightful climate" and was hauled down. The four men were hurried off to jail and held incommunicado for eighteen hours. Their lawyer, John Beardsley, later a judge of the superior court of Los Angeles County, tried frantically to discover where they were being held. He finally succeeded in serving a writ of habeas corpus, and the next day they were all released. Sinclair promptly launched a public attack upon the legal authorities, and the ACLU filed suits for damages for unlawful arrest against the police, but later dropped the charges when private assurances were given of no further persecution of prisoners and all but twenty-eight of the six hundred IWWs then being held were ordered released also. The challenge to local tyranny had had significant and immediate results. And such firm retaliatory action had the further effect of restoring and reviving a measure of respect for civil liberties in the area. The unfavorable publicity given the episode raised the hackles of many decent citizens against the brutality and arbitrariness of the police.[119]

Sinclair and the ACLU were unwilling to stop there. He and his local supporters immediately rented a large auditorium in Los Angeles and scheduled a series of open meetings to express public grievances. The meetings underlined the need for a permanent watchdog over California civil liberties, and from those in attendance came promises of support for a southern California branch of the ACLU. The branch was quickly organized, incorporating generally the sense of the meetings:

> There are many groups of people formed for the purpose of bringing about industrial changes; and these people apparently cannot get together upon a program. But there is one platform upon which it should be possible to get every true American to stand, and that is the platform of free discussion of our problems. This ideal was carefully embodied by our forefathers in the fundamental law of our nation and of every one of our separate States. There are constitutional provisions, granting

to the people the rights of freedom of speech and of the press, also the right to assembly and petition the government for redress of grievances. This is the true 100 percent Americanism, and we have taken this for our sole program.[120]

The Reverend Clinton J. Taft, a local Congregational minister, resigned from his pulpit to serve as regional director, a post he held for over twenty years.[121]

The episode led to the firing of Police Chief Oaks. But the Los Angeles area continued to be one of the dark spots for civil liberties throughout the decade. Although peace was restored temporarily, the IWW continued to suffer from police raids. The Better America Federation continued its red baiting and antiunion crusades, eventually inducing the city of Los Angeles to establish a "Red Squad" under the leadership of Captain William ("Red") Haynes to keep the city free from "subversives" of all sorts.[122] Ernest J. Hopkins, in summarizing the report of the Wickersham Commission, which investigated the abuse of law enforcement machinery late in the decade, found the Los Angeles police, stirred on by "hysterical propaganda," unable to "distinguish between the economic dissenter and the criminal."[123] Yet the membership of the new ACLU chapter grew as police repression continued and with efficient organization and considerable support, and through the pages of its paper, *The Open Forum*, it often served as the conscience of the community.[124]

The ACLU's action in behalf of depressed workers in the mines, in the mills, and on the waterfront contrasted with its inactivity in the greatest strike of the decade, that of nearly 400,000 railway shopmen in the summer of 1922. The government broke the strike through a massive injunction and infringed free speech more than at any other time in the decade. Perhaps the public protest was so immediate and massive that ACLU leaders felt that their limited resources and energies were not needed. The ACLU concentrated on mopping up peripheral issues.[125]

The strike grew out of a 12 percent wage cut ordered by the management-oriented Railway Labor Board. Immediate response to the strike was hostile, with most of the nation's newspapers opposing the unions, especially since the chairman of the Railway Labor Board declared their action illegal. The strikers refused to retreat and management refused to talk.[126] As the strike wore on toward autumn, public apprehension and administration panic grew. On September 1, Attorney General Harry M. Daugherty obtained an order from a Chicago federal court, headed by ultraconservative Judge James H. Wilkerson, forcing the six striking shop unions and their officials to refrain from combining to interfere with railroad transportation or with any persons employed by the roads or desirous of such employment. Wilkerson also forbade union officials to aid anyone "by letters, telegrams, telephones, word of mouth, or otherwise" to commit any of the forbidden acts. They must keep off railroad property; they must not try "to induce by the use of threats, violent or abusive language, opprobrious epithets, physical violence, or threats thereof, intimidation, display of numbers of force, jeers, entreaties, arguments, persuasion, rewards or otherwise," anybody to stop work in railroad shops. Picketing was prohibited. Union officials were restrained from issuing any strike directions or saying anything that might keep any strike-breaker from work, nor were they to use any union funds to do any of the things forbidden in the injunction writ.[127]

Public reaction was immediate, and largely hostile. Liberal publications were unanimous in denouncing the action as a flagrant violation of fundamental rights. The *Survey* suggested that the injunction was directed chiefly against peaceful picketing, and the demand of the *New York World* for the impeachment of both Daugherty and Wilkerson received the support of various labor groups, including the 800,000 member New York Central Trades and Labor Council.[128] The *New York Globe* insisted that the action was bound to produce strong public hostility since "liberty is not dead, and the right to free speech, a free press, and unhampered assemblage will not be lightly surrendered by the American people."[129] Zechariah Chafee, in a piece written for distribution by the New York League of Women Voters, warned:

> No matter how great the national danger was, it could not warrant a judge in acting contrary to law. Justice according to law is the foundation of our liberties; when the sovereign himself, whether Stuart king or American people, comes into his courts, he shall be shown no more favor by the judge than the poorest citizen; he shall receive nothing but what the law allows him. If the emergency required new law, Congress was in session. While the law remained unaltered, it was the duty of judges to decide controversies in accordance therewith, and not to depart from it, even to save the nation from disaster.[130]

Newspapermen were quick to spot the implications of the action for themselves. "If the spokesmen for the strikers can be enjoined from writing about the strike, or from talking about it for publication," wrote the *Brooklyn Eagle*, "newspapers can also be enjoined from publishing interviews and statements which have any color favorable to the strikers or adverse to the railroads."[131] The influential trade journal, *Editor and Publisher*, stated categorically, "The constitutional guarantees of a free press and free citizenship . . . were taken away last Saturday when the First Amendment to the Constitution was abridged by Federal Injunction."[132]

Daugherty and President Harding were taken aback by the suggestion that they were trampling upon individual freedom. Harding stated publicly that the injunction "would not be used to abridge personal liberty" and that "the only purpose and the only use that will be made of it will be to restrain violence and compel obedience to law and order." Daugherty hastened to agree. But he also felt compelled, in an unfortunate attempt at self-justification, to state that "the decent press of the United States, which includes ninety percent of the newspapers published in America, supports my action." The statement was vigorously deplored by Democratic Senator Joseph T. Robinson of Arkansas, who maintained that when the government sought to coerce opinion media through subtle pressure it was departing from its legitimate role.[133]

Republican Congressman Oscar E. Keller of Minnesota called for Daugherty's impeachment on the floor of the House of Representatives on the grounds that he had used his high office to violate the Constitution by abridging freedom of speech, press, and the right of the people to assemble peaceably. The startled Republican Old Guard, fearing a record vote, quickly referred Keller's charges to a committee of the judiciary. Two days later, however, a preliminary strike settlement was reached, and when the committee finally met in December, the immediate issue was no longer pertinent.[134]

The conservative press generally defended Daugherty. *The Railway Review* explained that the courts could forbid "The kind of free speech that incites to crime and violence. . . . When the privilege of free speech becomes the weapon of the cowardly conspirator inciting aliens to acts of violence against life and property, no law-abiding citizen will suffer by its abridgment in such cases."[135] But when the crisis was safely over, Daugherty addressed himself to the issue in some depth. Speaking to an audience at Canton, Ohio, on October 21, he likened the United States in 1922 to the Roman Empire and insisted that the government had a right to forestall its destruction by curtailing the activities of the barbarian hordes seeking its downfall. He insisted that he was no enemy of free speech, but "the freedom of speech guaranteed under the Constitution" was "not that freedom of speech which incites mob violence, destruction of life and property and attacks on government." Daugherty insisted also that the injunction had been salutary to free speech. It guarded the honest American workingman from criminal action, and thereby preserved his own freedom and individuality. The only question was one of maintaining public security under the Constitution. With the forces of evil frustrated, "God reigns and the government at Washington still lives."[136]

Samuel Gompers responded by calling the Attorney General an "irresponsible agitator," insisting that his remarks were "absolute falsehoods, filled with hatred, exaggeration, and calumny." He also renewed the call for Daugherty's impeachment for "violating Constitutional guarantees to which the people are entitled."[137]

Two concrete and related episodes involved newspaper editors. William Allen White of the *Emporia Gazette* was no flaming liberal. He defended the Kansas industrial court, a move to compulsory arbitration, as an enlightened step toward eliminating strikes. Many national figures had felt that some such arrangement might well be the answer to labor disputes at the time, although they were aware that the courts might "fall into the hands of capital, just as many of our civil courts have done, and thus predominantly serve the interests of capital instead of labour."[138] White's suspicions that the Kansas court might move in that direction were confirmed during the shopmen's strike. Governor Henry J. Allen issued an order based on the Industrial Court Act prohibiting strikers in Kansas from picketing.[139]

White, although an old friend of Allen's, protested through the unusual device of printing posters supporting the strikers and asking friendly merchants to display them in their store windows. One promptly went up at the *Gazette* office. The attorney general of Kansas ruled that this was another form of picketing, and Allen ordered all posters removed. On July 19, White denounced Allen's order as an "infamous infraction of the right of free press and free speech." He also refused to back down on the poster. Allen, maintaining that neither free speech nor liberty of the press was involved, swore out a warrant for White's arrest for violating the antipicketing law and conspiring with the strikers.[140]

White's arrest, combined with his continuing insistence that the issue was free speech and that he was fighting for its preservation, attracted widespread newspaper and magazine comment, overwhelmingly sympathetic to him. The local Kansas press, however, was critical, with certain editors wondering out loud whether White was not putting abstract principles above immediate local needs. His response was an editorial in the *Gazette* on July 27, entitled, "To an Anxious Friend." Subsequently winning the Pulitzer Prize, it stands as one of the most eloquent statements on freedom of speech issuing from the decade. White wrote:

> You say that freedom of utterance is not for time of stress, and I reply with the sad truth that only in time of stress is freedom of

utterance in danger. No one questions it in calm days, because it is not needed. And the reverse is true also; only when free utterance is suppressed is it needed, and when it is needed, it is most vital to justice.[141]

Within a few days after his arrest, White had offers of legal aid from the ACLU and from other devoted civil libertarians, including Felix Frankfurter, William E. Borah, and Albert J. Beveridge. White was prepared to carry the case to the United States Supreme Court and protested vigorously and bitterly when the Kansas attorney general dropped it before an actual showdown.[142]

Other newspaper editors, however, did not fare as well. Shortly after Wilkerson issued his famous injunction, United States Judge J. W. Ross issued an implementing injunction, requested by the Frisco, Illinois Central, and Yazoo and Mississippi Railroad companies, enjoining the criticism and molestation of strike-breakers. Jacob Cohen, editor of the 7,500-circulation *Memphis Labor Review*, defied the order in a Labor Day editorial entitled "Dirty Scabs," in which he denounced strike-breakers as "snakes," "traitors," and "industrial scavengers"; he was promptly arrested and sentenced to six months in jail and fined $1,000 for contempt of court.[143] G. V. Sanders, editor of the large daily *Memphis Press*, while not accepting Cohen's opinions, came out strongly for his right to express those opinions. A resounding anti-Daugherty editorial, "The King Forbids," stated:

Mr. Cohen possibly was not thoroughly up to date on questions of fundamental rights in this country of the free. No doubt he is one of those old-fashioned souls who believe there is something real in those words the Constitution contains about free speech and free press. He probably thought that antiquated doctrine would protect him in giving his opinion to the world. Ha! Ha! We shall see about that. Fetch him before the throne.[144]

The editorial was published while contempt proceedings were pending. Sanders was promptly charged with contempt on the grounds that his editorial had a direct tendency to interfere with the courts and the determination of the Cohen case. The matter then fell for defense to the ACLU, which provided legal aid. Roger Baldwin got funds from the American Fund for Public Service and eventually obtained a reversal of the Cohen case in the court of appeals.[145]

The ACLU played a significant role in other issues of the decade. It was the instigator of the Scopes "Monkey Trial" in Dayton, Ten-

nessee, which challenged that state's antievolution law. Although
Baldwin felt that attorney Clarence Darrow, in "hamming up" the
defense, missed an opportunity to dramatize the free expression issue
clearly, the ACLU nonetheless was widely supported by otherwise blasé
critics such as H. L. Mencken and by liberals of the Lippmann
variety.[146]

The ACLU fared far less well in championing birth-control advocates. It assisted Margaret Sanger in her legislative campaigns to
introduce birth-control bills in New York, Connecticut, and New
Jersey and participated in an attempt to modify Section 1142 of
the New York penal code which punished the dissemination of such
information. Massachusetts was equally restrictive, especially Boston
under its colorful Catholic mayor, James M. Curley.[147]

Curley also successfully challenged the ACLU in a situation in
which it felt moral commitment. Curley was adamant against allowing
the Ku Klux Klan to parade in Boston. The ACLU maintained the
rights of Americans to express themselves, even if in a distasteful
way.

> Baldwin himself wrote Mayor Curley in the usual manner: we are
> opposed to the Klan but every American citizen is entitled to the
> right of assemblage. As Jefferson said . . . as Lincoln said . . . as
> Theodore Roosevelt said . . . as Woodrow Wilson said.
>
> The Boston mayor replied briefly: My dear sir, I know perfectly
> well what these great statesmen said, but I also know what they *did*.[148]

Baldwin was so amused that he gave in; his heart was not in the
cause in any case.

He was, however, deeply involved in the Sacco-Vanzetti case. Many
radicals and liberals were convinced that the men had been convicted
not for their role in a payroll robbery, but because they were anarchists who spoke their doctrines openly and vigorously. The ACLU
supported their defense. It also frequently confronted situations in
which protest meetings for Sacco and Vanzetti were banned, canceled,
or broken up by local police, who had in this situation set "an all-time
all-American record for the ruthless violation of the constitutional
rights of free speech and assemblage."[149] In Boston at the time of
the execution in August, 1927, such prominent figures as John Dos
Passos, union organizer and social reformer Powers Hapgood, Professor
Ellen Hayes of Wellesley College, journalist and editor Katherine
Huntington, Dorothy Parker, and Edna St. Vincent Millay learned
painfully the limits to freedom of expression set by overly sensitive

public officials. There was backlash from the episode, however, as misgivings and second thoughts filled many American minds, and again the ACLU gained sympathy if not support.[150]

Heywood Broun, widely quoted and popular columnist, had sought a position on Pulitzer's liberal *New York World* at the beginning of the decade because he was convinced that the *World* was the most independent of all the New York dailies and that as a member of its staff he would be given the greatest freedom of expression. Broun was no crusader, generally producing in his column "It Seems to Me" pithy but detached and good-natured commentary on the passing American scene. He, like many other Americans, had an instinctive commitment to fair play. He rose in wrath when the city withdrew Margaret Sanger's permission to speak. "Free speech might as well be a card in the hands of a conjurer. Now you see it, now you don't."[151] Broun was an acid foe of the Klan and of censorship in any form, insisting that censorship actions, almost without exception, covered private interest in the cloak of public welfare. But Broun certainly had no desire to alter the power structure.[152]

The exception proved to be the Sacco-Vanzetti episode. With his wife Ruth Hale actively organizing pickets in the last stages of the protest, Broun turned his pen on Massachusetts justice, vitriolically accusing the governor of having "no intention in all his investigation but to put a new and higher polish upon the proceedings." "The justice of the business was not his concern," Broun went on. "He called old men from high places to stand behind his chair so that he might seem to speak with all the authority of a high priest or a Pilate." Broun concluded the first of two rousing pieces on the case, "We have a right to beat against tight minds with our fists and shout a word into the ears of the old men. We want to know, we will know—'Why?' " The second essay hinted that the mind of Massachusetts had been closed on the situation because the men were radicals and foreigners and because criticism had been so sharp from outside the state. Broun concluded with a blast at Harvard, which he dubbed "Hangman's House."[153]

The normally liberal Ralph Pulitzer was not pleased by the results. While the mail bags from readers brought much favorable comment, the business office of the *World* was besieged by irate advertisers, demanding the suppression of Broun's wild outbursts and threatening to cancel contracts if the paper insisted on continuing to print his material. Influential alumni voiced loud protest against the assault upon Harvard. As a result Pulitzer omitted Broun's column and refused to print anything further on the situation. A statement on the editorial page explained that although the *World* believed in allowing the fullest possible expression of individual opinion, it had gone as far as it intended to with Broun on this subject.[154]

Broun was furious and refused to write anything further. A brief statement of his position acknowledged that a columnist did not have the liberty to say whatever came into his mind, given the laws of libel, obscenity, and blasphemy, but suggested that such had not been the nature of the material that the *World* was censoring. The controversy simmered for some months, with Broun writing pieces for *The Nation* and *New Republic* and eventually returning to the *World,* only to be dismissed permanently for a *Nation* piece in which he bemoaned the absence of a liberal press in the United States and criticized the *World's* lack of courage and tenacity in giving way to business pressures in his own case and in many similar instances.

"The *World* has decided to dispense with the services of Haywood Broun. His disloyalty to this paper makes any further association impossible,"[155] read an announcement in the *World* on May 5, 1928, and a none-too-surprised Broun found himself looking for a new employer.

The episode raised important abstract questions about the freedom of the press. It was not the sort of public question, however, in which the ACLU could play a role. *The Nation* sent questionnaires to writers, publishers, and editors asking how free a writer should be to criticize the paper that paid his salary. Nine replies were selected for publication. Three writers and two editors found the action of the *World* unjustified. Four who defended the *World* were publishers and editors. William Allen White wrote that the Broun case raised no important point that he could see.

> The editor still is boss, the employee still has his royal right to resign or be fired. It is just another newspaper row, and the friends of each participant have a right to uphold their favorite. No cause is involved, no principle at stake.[156]

The episode was revealing as a demonstration of what constituted a permissible freedom of speech issue at the time. White was right in calling it "another newspaper row," for certainly it was a hothouse situation with no major issue of the right of inarticulate and deprived working people involved.[157]

The record of civil libertarians from the red scare days of January 1920 until panic and depression changed the entire atmosphere of the nation, was one, then, of constant frustration and frequent setback, but in the long run, of subtle and at times remarkable success. The evidences of that success, although seldom dramatically obvious, were substantial.

The growth of the ACLU was in itself an index. Its membership and budget increased, its affiliates grew in number, and the range of its activities expanded. Far more important, however, was the growing number of people who came to accept the fact that its aims were not only legitimate, but were indeed geared to preserving and implementing the abstract ideals of the Declaration of Independence and the Bill of Rights.[158]

Other manifestations of growing tolerance included the quiet suspension of the use of the state criminal-syndicalism and sedition legislation in all but a few remote areas and the diminished application of local controls. Perhaps the rather rigid consensus of the decade had triumphed so thoroughly that local dissenters had given up trying to alter it. But the fact remains that the same critics were criticizing in 1928 and 1929 who had been throughout the decade and were doing so with far less fear of assault and suppression than was the case in the years of the Shopmen's Strike, San Pedro, Paterson, and Passaic.

There was a far more receptive climate for national standards of free speech and for other constitutional guarantees of equal rights than in the earlier days when nervous citizens clung to local restrictions and sought reinforcement through positive federal intervention either in the form of punitive national legislation or stepped-up federal interference and restraint. The constant reiteration by civil libertarians of the symbols of American democracy undoubtedly reached many. Granted, the average citizen had little technical knowledge of the concept of free speech in its complex legal sense or of freedom of the press or due process of law, but as historical first principles, as essential parts of the rhetoric of American democracy, he saw their preservation as essential to his own freedom and to perpetuation of the American way of life. Here, the sincerity of the civil libertarians' desires to make such concepts function stood out in contrast with others, from far right to far left, who mouthed them loudly, only to abrogate them when they became an obstacle to their particular ends. Thus while Herbert Hoover, Republican leaders, and the business community generally spoke in 1928 as if a completed nation were in view and the full culmination of the American dream was realizable with only minor improvements in the economic system, civil libertarians insisted that it would not be until economic equality and justice could be attained by millions of depressed citizens that anything resembling the American dream could be expected, and that it was not until such depressed citizens gained the right of free expression, in its fullest modern sense, that such economic justice could be realized.

Similarly, when business spokesmen used the term "liberty," a problem of definition arose. To them this meant the open shop, "freedom of contract," a kind of classical "civil liberty" that assumed the inability of the individual to save himself from his own weakness or the relentless external societal forces beyond his control, and emphasized the importance of subjection to enlightened authority as the true path toward meaningful freedom. Such assumptions hardly displayed any deep-seated faith in the ability of the average individual either to govern himself or to utilize in his own way the attributes of the democratic system. Civil libertarians, on the other hand, by trying to liberate the individual from artificial economic and social restrictions and increase his personal power, emerged as true believers in the democratic process, with faith in the common sense and good judgment of the individual.

One explicit manifestation of the degree to which the civil libertarian position reached the consciences of Americans was the amount of financial support it elicited. Charles Garland, eccentric scion of a millionaire security broker, for example, in 1921 turned his inheritance over to a group headed by Roger Baldwin to be spent as rapidly as possible in the support of liberal and radical causes. Baldwin and the Board of the American Fund for Public Service, which was created to administer the $2 million bequest, dispensed a good deal of the amount to legal defense, strike relief, and publicity (over $25,000 was devoted to the Passaic strike, plus $40,000 bail). They also used a smaller sum to put new ACLU representatives in the field, create local affiliates, and support free-speech fights in a variety of areas where effective labor union organization was being blocked.[159]

The ACLU and other civil libertarian groups also received large sums from respectable citizens. The MacMurtrie sisters left all their property, real estate worth roughly $200,000, equally to the ACLU and the NAACP. They were "rather elegant Philadelphia ladies of an old and wealthy family . . . not Quakers, but doubtless influenced by their Quaker friends—free thinkers, rather."[160] Mrs. Willard Straight's annual contributions through the early years of the 1920s to social welfare and liberal causes ran well over $300,000. Mrs. Agnes Brown Leach, Mrs. Kate Crane Gartz, Mrs. Robert C. Lillie, Mrs. Elizabeth Glendower Evans, and Miss Fanny T. Cochran, who also contributed, were educated, sensitive, insulated upper-class citizens, convinced of the validity of the free-speech position.[161] They were also people of older wealth, not employers, and sufficiently divorced from the pell-mell money-making world to be appalled by its callousness. The money and prestige the "parlor pinks" lent to the civil-liberties movement was significant in its growing successes. They "made possible pioneering and experimental work where a general public appeal would not yield results."[162]

Such support had a profound effect upon millions of working-class citizens, to say nothing of liberal editors and journalists whose publications drew extensive support from such sources. Such ventures as the ambitious research program of the Rand School in New York and its annual publications, especially the valuable *American Labor Year Book*, could not have continued without help.[163] The same was true of the Brookwood and the Denver labor colleges as well as of the League for Industrial Democracy, the American Birth Control League, and the Cooperative League of America. Although the attempt to foster a news service which would have sympathetic labor tone was less successful, the Federated Press did serve a variety of liberal union publications.[164]

One interesting example of mutual assistance was the establishment of a labor-oriented radio station dedicated to the memory of Eugene V. Debs and bearing the call letters WEVD. The station, which had great difficulty maintaining its license because of bitter criticism of its liberal programming, was defended by the ACLU and in turn gave ACLU spokesmen the opportunity to publicize their work.[165]

In addition to the direct appeal civil libertarians made to the altruism as well as the self-interest of definable individuals and groups, the strategy of civil libertarians emphasized the value system of the period. Advocating full protection of private individual rights through private instrumentalities and chary of any form of governmental intervention in individual freedom, they were nearer to the overall laissez-faire assumptions of the decade than were the frenetic patriots who constantly called for massive state interference in the affairs of private citizens. Thus, just as many Americans had resented the governmental tyranny of the red scare, and came, as the decade progressed, to develop an increasing hostility toward prohibition and antievolution laws, many could then look with a certain sympathy upon an organization whose avowed purpose was to protect the individual against arbitrary use of public authority. The position was particularly appealing to those disillusioned with governmental leadership in the decade that revealed the dangers inherent in a tyranny of little minds.

In the same decade in which new theories concerning the raising of children led to vigorous assaults upon all artificial restraints, Americans developed a new hostility toward many previously accepted restrictions and a new desire for liberation and fulfillment of individuality.[166]

Growing disillusionment with World War I was indirectly beneficial to civil libertarians. The ACLU, which had been one of the most outspoken opponents of the wartime restrictions, seemed to have represented true democratic principles better than leaders of the government. Time showed not only the courageousness but also the value of its position. That conclusion underlay much of the popular sympathy for the release of arrested radicals, from Jim Larkin, Benjamin Gitlow, and Anita Whitney to Sacco and Vanzetti.

Somewhat ironically, the materialism and technological progress of the decade afforded new avenues for the dispersal of civil-libertarian sentiments. The automobile, radio, syndicated columns, newspaper chains, and the movies reduced the insulation of variants so as to bring formerly independent value systems into direct conflict with each other. Inevitably the result was the erosion of excessively deviant patterns in the name of the desirability of national standards.

Lynching in the South was an early target. Lynchings became national news, widely reported, and offended national sensitivities. The workers' conditions in the Pennsylvania and West Virginia mining regions, the repressive actions at Paterson and Passaic, or the massacre at Columbine in Colorado might well have remained "local business" or remote incidents a quarter of a century earlier. Now they became subjects nagging the national conscience, with a broad general cry that something must be done about those who do not live by the standards to which American citizens accede. To the extent, then, that civil libertarians in general and the ACLU in particular became acknowledged as legitimate instrumentalities through which to better accomplish such an extension of standards, they came to stand for constructive outlets through which positive steps toward proper national standardization might be taken.

One last measure of the success of the activist-libertarians in winning both concessions and supporters in the decade was the constant and progressively growing apprehensiveness of their conservative and right-wing enemies, whose attacks grew in passion and intensity as the civil-liberties movement gained strength and power. Conservatives were not content merely to assail and criticize; they organized counterattacks on virtually every front, attempting to reverse patterns dangerous to their interests and those of the nation. Thus the microcosmic struggle of the reconstruction months, following November 11, 1919, was reenacted in a broader drama during the sweep of the 1920s, and this time with decidedly differing results.

10

The Quest for
Security Through
Proper Free Speech

Free Speech

Yielding allegiance to an alien flag
    Red with the blood of millions foully slain:
Holding our banner but a worthless rag,
    Seeking to rend it, though as yet in vain.
Aiming envenomed daggers at the heart
    Of Freedom: singing their hymns of hate
Against the land we love: striving to start
    Our nation down the dark road to Russia's fate.

Plotting our early downfall, sowing the hateful seed
    Of treason in the people's minds: grasping to reach
By violence the posts of power for tyranny and greed:
    In their behalf misguided fools demand "free speech"!
Freedom to murder Freedom: freedom to steal and kill!
    Freedom to extirpate the home, the church and state!
Freedom to rear a despot o'er the public will!
    Wake, sleeping land of Freedom, ere it be too late!
                   The National Republic,
                   February 1926

The crusades and campaigns that were mounted in the 1920s against
the civil libertarians' campaigns for meaningful free speech both paralleled and diverged from those of the immediate postwar reconstruction
years of 1919–1920. The same groups were generally assailed, fre-

quently with the same techniques and using the same rationalizations, and with the same sort of repressive ends in mind. But a different group of Americans with differing motivations, goals, and ambitions was involved. The business community and propertied conservatives generally were content with normalcy and the restored set of informal controls. The center of power in the nation had shifted away from Washington with the notable exception of the Supreme Court and certain regulatory bodies, now safely in the control of property conscious figures, often stalwart members of the business community themselves. The labor movement was clearly in retreat. Open-shop and Americanization campaigns attained considerable success, a new child labor law fell before the judiciary, and the labor injunction was revitalized and extended. The assumption that the business of America was business had become widely acknowledged. The idea that those who might criticize or assault the system posed a serious danger casually slipped into the background. In fact, it was now possible for business leaders to suggest that progress was in order and that important changes did have to be made. Business leaders were even willing to make certain concessions to working people in the form of shorter hours and better pay.[1] There was nothing to be feared from such concessions and at times much to be gained, especially in placating worker discontent and building worker loyalty and productivity. Sharp criticism of the new consensus certainly continued, as did the activity of those who sought to change it. But business itself seldom bothered with such critics after 1921.[2]

Large numbers of Americans did feel the necessity for assailing the critics, dissenters, and disbelievers, particularly the civil libertarians. The motives for such frequently gratuitous assault were extremely varied, even though there were common patterns in their behavior and in their campaigns. Many editors, writers, and publicists chose to work independently, some even turning the process of assailing the critics of normalcy into virtually a business proposition. Others worked through identifiable groups such as the American Legion, the DAR, the National Civic Federation, and the Ku Klux Klan. Still others operated from within the framework of established bodies, such as the American Federation of Labor or, in the early years of the decade, the Bureau of Investigation. All conceived of themselves as true patriots. Most proclaimed deep devotion to the fundamental principles of the Constitution, the Bill of Rights, and the Declaration of Independence, feeling themselves to be the true interpreters, if not the most qualified guardians, of such documents.[3]

Such citizens sometimes entered these campaigns to secure financial contributions. Others, particularly various national organizations, obligated to deliver a wide variety of favors to their membership, sought broader concessions. For still others, the mere acknowledgment that they were preservers of the ancient ways was adequate to propel them into more feverish activity. This was particularly true of ambitious members of superpatriotic bodies, seeking status within the body as well as within the nation.

Few politicians in the 1920s still saw the feasibility of projecting themselves into the role of master-defender of the endangered order in order to obtain nomination to high office. But scattered congressmen, such as Thomas L. Blanton of Texas, John B. Sosnowski of Michigan, and Arthur M. Free of California, continued to seek political power through striking the pose of defender against left-wing activities, particularly those of civil libertarians.[4] Certain bureaucrats also persisted in such actions. William J. Burns, the head of the Bureau of Investigation through the early years of the decade, used his office to guide public fears in order to enhance his own public status and to stimulate a brisk private business for the Burns International Detective Agency. But generally speaking, renewed red baiting and hysteria manufacturing was not a useful path to political power.

The American Legion epitomized the many service-oriented organizations, publicly committed and devoted to assailing the "reds" and their "fellow travelers." Legion leaders hoped that demonstrations of loyalty would convince congressional leaders of the deservedness of their persistent annual appeals for pensions, bonuses, and a variety of other concessions for veterans.[5] As the decade progressed, the same leaders apparently got the cue that their raucousness was offensive to many members of the "establishment," and in 1927 called conspicuously for a toning down of overt suppression since it "defeats its own ends in the vast amount of advertising it bestows on the person suppressed and on the case it represents."[6] Such newly professed faith in the right of dissent apparently had little effect upon the activities of many individual members, since the ACLU in its annual report for the same year maintained that the Legion had "replaced the Klan as the most active agency of intolerance and repression in the country."[7] The activities of other veterans' groups frequently paralleled those of the Legion.[8]

The Daughters of the American Revolution had far less materialistic motives, seeking generally to "take a firm and active stand against all forms of attack, whether open or insidious, against the Constitution of the United States, American institutions and against our national society and its leaders."[9] The position was open to some question, since the DAR ladies seemed to ignore the fact that freedom of speech was a professed American institution. Equally embarrassing was the fact that the body's general respectability, combined with its naiveté, made it an attractive pawn for more selfishly motivated groups.

The "professional patriots" had simpler and often highly dubious motives. They formed primarily propaganda organizations and were the mouthpieces of single leaders or small cabals; their central purpose was to ingratiate themselves with large private or corporate donors and thereby insure their own continuation. This meant showing results, not only in broad distribution of literature but in providing speakers to help in mobilizing large elements of the general public against all manner of enemies of "the American way." Few were as frank as Harry A. Jung of the powerful National Clay Products Industries Association and later the American Vigilant Intelligence Federation, who wrote to a potential subscriber in 1926:

> We cooperate with over 30 distinctly civic and patriotic organizations. . . . It would take me too long to relate how I "put over" this part of our activities, namely, "trailing the Reds." Should you ever be in Chicago, drop in and see me and I will explain. That it has been a paying proposition for our organization goes without saying,[10]

or Fred R. Marvin, head of the Keymen of America, who stated to a reporter of the *New York World* in 1928: "We are just getting somewhere now. . . . We are coming to the position where we can lay a reasonable charge for surveys and researches of radical activities."[11] Well over thirty such organizations appeared and disappeared during the decade.[12]

The Ku Klux Klan played a unique role. Although it was geared to financial gain, it was content to draw large portions of its money and support from private citizens in small towns and rural communities, a fact that set it apart from most other intolerance purveyors in the 1920s. This meant that it operated upon poorly underpinned grounds, a fact graphically illustrated by its rapid collapse well before the onset of the economic crisis of the depression years. It further meant that its appeal, while frequently patriotic, was generally designed not to woo large corporations or wealthy business leaders, but to appeal to the rural or small-town establishment with its own peculiar forms of status and power to protect.[13]

Individuals and groups engaged in counterattack activities seldom lost an opportunity to proclaim their devotion to American democracy, including freedom of speech and expression. Their free-speech line differed very little from that of the activist-repressionists of 1919 and 1920. In fact, one basic source of charges against activist-libertarians continued to be the famous and long since discredited, although seemingly governmentally sanctioned, Lusk Report of 1920. It became the standard documentation for how "red" the ACLU was, for how dangerous various labor bodies and pacifist groups were, and for measures to instill "the proper interpretation of America's ideals of freedom and service" in all citizens.[14] The report was still being used by congressional committees, particularly the 1930 Fish Committee,[15] in the depths of the depression, even though the conditions it spoke of were no longer pertinent or its recommendations applicable.

Certain new themes were added in the 1920s. As the civil libertarians' campaigns for equality through free speech gained in favor and success, it became essential to prove that such a use of free speech was wrong. The term "free-speech faker" was coined early in the decade by Ralph M. Easley of the National Civil Federation to characterize the ACLU in particular and civil libertarians in general. Those who wanted to utilize free speech as a device for creating social justice and economic equality were, it was argued, prostituting the concept. There was no freedom in America to destroy freedom as it had traditionally existed. And those who insisted that there was should at the very least be silenced.

The argument that equality was not the basic birthright of every American was also used. Coerced equality led to the destruction of liberty and human individuality. Such a view had been widely expressed in the nineteenth century.[16] The 1920s, with its focus upon material accumulation and new opportunities for the ambitious and talented citizen to rise under reinstituted conditions of economic individualism, gave renewed emphasis to the old theme. Mounting contempt for the common man and focus upon the need for elite leadership to preserve American institutions from being drowned in the mediocrity of his basic instincts and behavior strengthened its appeal. Americans from H. L. Mencken and Walter Lippmann through Everett Dean Martin, Will Durant, James Harvey Robinson, Harry Elmer Barnes, and Frank R. Kent explored the theme. Such a distinguished man of letters as Irving Babbitt, an early admirer of Mussolini and the new fascist regime in Italy, summarized the position when he maintained vehemently in 1924 that "equality as it is currently pursued is incompatible with true liberty."[17] He further warned:

> if we do not develop a sounder type of vision than that of our "uplifters" and "forward-lookers," the history of free institutions in this country is likely to be short, and, on the whole, discreditable. . . . The time may come, with the growth of false liberalism, when a predominant

element in our population, having grown more and more impatient of the ballot box and representative government, of constitutional limitations, and judicial control, will display a growing eagerness of "direct action." . . . The democratic contention that everybody should have a chance is excellent provided it means that everybody is to have a chance to measure up to high standards. If the democratic extension of opportunity is, on the other hand, made a pretext for lowering standards, democracy is, so far, incompatible with civilization.[18]

Such a view drew upon the commonly held assumption, particularly of middle-class Americans, that the "booboisie" was ineligible for full participation in the democratic process. Translated into terms understandable to Legionnaires and Klansmen, this meant undesirable people getting favors they did not deserve and would not appreciate. Giving freedom and liberty to citizens who had not earned them was actually destroying their real meaning.

Patroits were also highly apprehensive of the techniques of their chosen enemies, feeling an exaggerated and at times almost neurotic fear of propaganda and its devious use by the activist-libertarian element. Many Americans after World War I were distressed to discover that not only had the Germans used propaganda effectively during the war, but that the British and even their own government had done so as well.[19] The government had never fully masked its activities in this regard, but had candidly undertaken to mobilize American opinion behind the war effort. Nonetheless the realization by many Americans that they had been victimized by this type of device was shocking and unsettling. The postwar period saw a tremendous outpouring of literature on the subject.[20] All propaganda was not categorically decried. In fact in the 1920s it quickly became the staple instrument for public opinion makers, public relations men, and advertisers. But in its political context, its use was still highly disturbing. This was particularly so when one combined it with the alleged scientific wartime findings of army psychologists who had tested the general intellectual level of American servicemen and had produced such findings as the fact that 24.9 percent of all inductees were illiterate,[21] that the average mental age of the country's military manpower was around thirteen,[22] and that only 30 percent of Americans appeared capable of finishing high school.[23] Projecting such figures to all Americans seemed to prove clearly, as William Allen White wrote, highly disturbed, in an article after the war, that the "majority of Americans are morons."[24] Little wonder that feverish concern developed among the nation's superpatriots to protect such citizenry against the guileful machinations of sinister propagandists.

The materialism of the decade also figured in the propaganda fear. Irresponsible social reconstructionists, advocates of industrial democracy, liberal churchmen, and civil libertarians were now attempting to convince the average man that foreign "-isms" would bring him more of his share of the pie than the current system. Their propaganda bypassed man's rational and responsible inclinations and played deviously upon his greed and venality. It was essential, therefore, to expose these insidious propagandists.

The problem was that so many of the advocates of responsible reform and social justice were highly respectable citizens whose arguments hardly suggested the need for immediate violent revolutionary action. To prevent the average well-meaning but none-too-bright American from being duped, it was essential to show that these people were not innocent reformers and that their ideas were actually masks for revolutionary social destruction. It was equally vital to demonstrate the evil sources of these ideas.[25] If this was not enough to discourage people from listening to them, it was essential to show the interlinking ties of such seemingly innocent citizens with corrupting foreign ideologies and conspiracies.

Such a position had within it elements of sincere and traditional social responsibility and stewardship; it also had ingredients of clear elitism. Everett Dean Martin, one of the leading advocates of this position, whose book, *Liberty,* was a choice of the Book-of-the-Month Club late in the decade,[26] stated frankly that the liberties of the people could be protected only by a responsible and elite group of Americans. The concept that experts, whether they be army generals, industrial leaders, managerial specialists, or self-appointed propaganda analysts, were not to be questioned was equally implicit in their thinking. Policy by such specialists was in the interests of all citizens, and the chronic malcontent, to say nothing of the average citizen, should not challenge it.

But even this attitude could be exploited by the professional patriots themselves. Many of those who were delighted to furnish exposé material to any American body wishing to assail critics of the system lost little time in proclaiming themselves "experts" in this field. Conversely, those who challenged their expertise were charged with seeking to undermine the true protectors of the nation.

However, there were difficulties involved in such a pose. While the superpatriots decried the callous manipulation of propaganda as highly un-American and maintained that its dispensers must be silenced or discredited, propaganda techniques became their own approach. Their defense was that their type of propaganda was salutary, and emanated from red, white, and blue citizens who were also experts. But such contentions failed to convince many Americans.

The effectiveness of the combined series of repressionist appeals, lumped together as basic ammunition against the "free-speech fakers," was measurable in a variety of different ways. Business, the group whose approval was most earnestly sought, was moved very mildly. Although the counterattackers were convinced that they were aiding the establishment, the establishment needed such aid very little and found much of it gratuitous, patronizing, and frequently annoying. Certain business leaders were willing to tolerate such unrequested assistance and throw occasional crumbs of financial encouragement to such bodies. As Sidney Howard caustically wrote in the *New Republic* in 1924, business might well again wish to turn to the "services of radicalism in almost any one of their patriotic clashes with social liberalism, or rambunctuous unions, or, even, child labor reformers."[27] Such willing allies might be useful if such an exigency actually arose.

The record of the National Civic Federation is revealing in this regard. Its ebullient and frequently irrepressible secretary, Ralph M. Easley, drawing upon the goodwill that the organization had established with prominent American figures in the Progressive era,[28] followed a regular pattern of issuing strongly emotional denunciations of liberals, reformers, and civil libertarians. He then attempted to gain endorsement from distinguished figures on the organization's membership lists for such unexpected and frequently irresponsible positions. The net result was hardly favorable. Such former stalwarts as William Howard Taft, Woodrow Wilson's Secretary of Commerce William C. Redfield, and labor leaders Warren S. Stone and Timothy Healy of the Railroad Brotherhoods, first denounced Easley for his presumptuousness in assuming that they would endorse statements without having seen them previously, and when he persisted they quickly and abruptly resigned their membership. Taft, for example, wrote Easley a curt letter stating: "I can not be drawn into discussion such as you have evoked by your articles . . . and I can not afford to have my name figure in any controversial matter of this sort."[29] Thus Easley, an abrasive man who craved conviviality and enjoyed staging luncheon meetings with prominent members of the body in New York City, found as the decade progressed that luncheon attendance dwindled and that the support that continued to come came primarily in the form of impersonal donations from large corporations.[30]

Another measure of the qualified success of such bodies lay in the personal jealousy they felt for one another. Business was willing to put up only a limited amount of funds to endorse such activities, and, since many self-styled patriots were anxious to get as large a chunk of money as possible, frequent jockeying went on between such groups. Each maintained that its efficiency was greater than that of its rivals. Each kept close track of the activities of other comparable bodies, to be sure that its own prerogatives in the area of "free-speech faker" baiting were observed and respected. National Civic Federation correspondence shows Easley's determination to keep his body high in the hierarchy of effective organizations, and an uneasiness and resentfulness toward newer rivals. When he learned of their existence, he never failed to inform them that they were latecomers to the field and should respect the prerogatives of the older and more established organizations.[31]

If repressionist appeals were lost on large portions of the business community, they reached the membership of many of the service and social organizations. American Legionnaires, Sons and Daughters of the American Revolution, and members of other veteran and service bodies endorsed such programs and derived personal satisfaction out of belonging to organizations that launched and pursued them. The same was true of many members of the AFL. Such patriotism afforded concrete opportunities for members to demonstrate and articulate their faith and allegiance to basic ideals and institutions, and thereby to gain acceptance and status with those who felt a similar need. In a period of changing values this was both gratifying and stabilizing. Further, there is strong evidence that such appeals reached large masses of Americans who in no way maintained formal connections with the activist counterattackers. The reasons are best explained in the light of the problems and tensions of the decade and its general value orientation.

The period from the inauguration of Warren G. Harding to the great crash of 1929 differed greatly from that of 1919 and 1920. Normalcy meant stability and easygoing but firm public policy, geared to minimize discontent and to foster the ideal of America as the land of boundless opportunity, every day, in every way, getting better and better. The return of prosperity, although a development that was felt in the pocketbooks of only selective Americans, affected the psyches of almost all. America's business society was succeeding, and surely those who had not as yet partaken of the rewards of such success would do so in good time.

Unemployment no longer disturbed many people. The danger of returning veterans taking away jobs gradually melted away as new opportunities opened. Immigration was halted by the restrictive national quotas act of 1924, with its safeguards against "nonassimilable" South and East Europeans—those in the public mind most commonly

associated with radical and left-wing activities.[32] Domestic communism, which had seemed so horrendous a threat in 1920, faded
as a spectre of public disruption. With the death of Eugene V. Debs,
socialism's most dangerous and effective crusader vanished, and with
him went much of the fear formerly felt for his party. The rapid
decline of the IWW, the breakup of the Non-Partisan League, and
the abject failure of the Communists to work out a successful farmer-
labor alliance were reassuring.

Even unions ceased to create strong apprehensions among the new
emerging middle class. Membership declined rapidly during the decade. The government had clearly shown its hand in breaking the
Shopmen's Strike and in the renewed use of the labor injunction.
The effective use of local law enforcement officials in San Pedro,
Lawrence, New Bedford, Passaic, Paterson, and Colorado convinced
many that even the most aggressive strike action would be handled
appropriately, firmly, and successfully.[33] The postwar fear of strangers
in formerly isolated communities or in self-contained neighborhoods
diminished as time went on. The enhanced mobility made possible
by the automobile was producing many surprising but understandable
developments, and with society confortably controlled at all times
by the right people, such individuals could be ignored with equanimity rather than viewed with alarm.[34]

But if postwar tensions of this sort declined, new and more pressing
ones emerged. The 1920s was a period of immense disruption of
prior norms, and its dynamism and the rapidity of the changes taking
place were enough to cause sleepless nights for millions of ostensibly
contented citizens. The accepted moral and social codes fell in the
face of a new technological society geared toward bringing mass
communication, mass transportation, mass automation, and mass entertainment to all with a few dollars down and few dollars a month
for life. Whereas the blessings of this new civilization seemed glam-
orous to many, their impact was distressing to others. The enhanced
mobility of the automobile produced a moral revolution and a breakdown in traditional sanctions of family and community structure such
as the country had never seen.[35] The radio, in reaching the ears
of rural America, raised renewed discontent in the minds of rural
youth. The movies proved to be far more than entertainment, so
shattering moral standards as to evoke calls for national censorship.[36]

The new national standards that such new technological developments were fostering seemed at every turn to be callous, brittle,
and meaningless, producing, particularly in youth, a lower moral
tone. Why else were major scandals in government, such as those
of the Harding administration, casually brushed off and carelessly

ignored? Why was a meaningful national standard such as the "noble experiment," prohibition, so vigorously defied?[37]

Many conservative and respectable Americans had trouble appreciating the fact that subtle informal controls were working in the economic area when they clearly were not working, in fact were being flouted and defied at every turn, in the moral and social areas. They sought scapegoats on which to blame the troubles of the new generation and the rapidly dissolving world over which they had had such firm and comfortable authority. Such people wanted simple scapegoats. One scarcely blamed the fathers of the new technology and the business revolution for the evils they created, particularly since their arguments were so convincing that potentially the new technology could create a virtually utopian society. The troublemakers were obviously those who were trying to break down the whole system, to pervert it to improper ends, or to alter it to their benefits. The nature of such detractors' and dissenters' wishes and actions was so unclear, the reasons for their behavior so incomprehensible, and the vigor of their activities so great that the public mind was not sure of much beyond the fact that they were dangerous and probably to blame for society's evils. Many were easily convinced of this, however, especially since the superpatriot counterattackers never lost a chance to cast them as a conspiratorial alliance, working deviously and feverishly to undermine fundamental American values and destroy the good life of the 1920s.[38]

The inconsistency of one set of critics of society suspecting another is easily reconcilable. The former did not basically reject either dominant American values or the values of the new order. Babbitt loved his car and his movies, and few rural or small-town housewives objected to being emancipated from age-old chores through new appliances and labor-saving devices now readily available in every local store. Such citizens wanted to maintain the blessings of this society while returning to former strictures and sanctions which would insure that such blessings would not be abused and become the instruments for social and moral decay.

The advanced critics, by contrast, called for a complete breakdown of these very informal standards, assailing prohibition, castigating censorship in any form, championing radicals from Sacco and Vanzetti down. Some even condemned both men of wealth and American values that turned money-making into a religion and a morality. Even worse, some hypocrites sought to gain wealth unjustifiably and then turn its use to improper ends.

Two types of Americans thus underwent critical assault—those who aspired to succeed within the system, but whose success large numbers resented, and those who openly rejected the values of the system. The former group, particularly ambitious, non-Anglo-Saxon, non-Protestant, immigrants with tendencies to overachieve drew, most overtly, Klan antipathy. And the quiet consensus of the 1920s backed up the Klan's overt censuring with a type of coercion that was often far more effective, especially if a Jew wanted admission to the local country club or a Catholic wanted the presidency of the nation. The deviators, on the other hand, although small in number, were even more of a threat. Radicals, militant labor leaders, civil libertarians—all were critics of the system and the programs that might hopefully return some measure of morality to it. They and the honest but misguided average citizens whom their propaganda seemed to be perverting had to be clamped into place quickly and thoroughly and by virtually any means possible.[39]

Inherent in such a set of attitudes were vital and, at times, contradictory assumptions regarding freedom of speech. On one hand, there was little willingness on the part of conservative Americans to come to terms with the arguments, the rationale, and the positions that the champions of social justice and economic equality maintained. Such people were categorically wrong by the very nature of the posture they were assuming. Certainly their supposed utilization of free speech to destroy society and the conditions in which free speech was meaningful were clear evidence of their cynicism and their danger. Their ability to express their foreign, radical, un-American views clearly had to be limited. Advocacy of ideas and programs designed to chop away at the basic underpinnings of society, especially when it led naive dupes to take violent action in their name, could hardly be tolerated.

Yet, on the other hand, much of the fear of such "radical" groups stemmed from the conviction that such groups were conspiratorial and were working in some sinister fashion to undermine the basic patriotism and loyalty of many Americans. Many were convinced that such critics were deviously concealing their ideas from the cleansing currents of public opinion and not fully utilizing their freedom of speech by refusing to engage in open discussion. They refused to accept the healthy Protestant tradition, it was frequently charged, of placing their ideas where they could be examined, weighed, and, in their critics' minds, obviously rejected when the balance was struck.

But whether one assaulted such critics by curtailing their ability to advocate their ideas or by forcing them to speak more openly and freely about their plots and schemes, there was no question that action had to be taken. Such "free-speech fakers" had to be some way dealt with by the true free-speech advocates before their ideas spawned any further damage. This was particularly true if their subversive actions led to some new national standard in the area of free speech which could not be modified selectively by local pressures when local "establishments" felt the need.

The irony of such a position lay in the fact that the majority of the free-speech instrumentalists were seeking to strengthen the new American system by eliminating its many defects. Their critics, by blindly assailing as potentially Bolshevik such organizations as the ACLU, the Federal Council of Churches, various social justice elements within specific religious groups,[40] and explicit social reform organizations like the American Birth Control League, the Consumer's League, and the National Child Labor Committee, sharply undercut the potential sources of constructive reform in the period.

The battle over the proper meaning of freedom of speech in the United States in the 1920s once again centered on definitions designed to serve best the self-interest of ambitious and energetic Americans. The self-appointed eradicators of the perverters of the concept clearly sought to assuage insecurity and set the nation right for themselves and those like themselves.

11

The Counterassault
Against the
"Free Speech Fakers"

Beneath the Constitution's shade,
    A boon and shield of peerless worth,
We stand erect and unafraid,
    Unmatched in all the teeming earth.

The Constitution: still it stands
    August, majestic, lofty, alone;
No fabric wrought by human hands
    Such strength and symmetry has shown.

To us belongs the pious task
    To ward from it its gathering foes,
Both those who lurk 'neath friendship's mask
    And those who deal it hostile blows.
                Archibald Hopkins for the
                National Security League, 1924

The leaders of the Harding administration, with a few notable exceptions such as Charles Evans Hughes and possibly Herbert Hoover,
interpreted their mandate as one of underwriting business control
and eliminating undue boat rocking. Unfortunately, some underlings
in the executive branch were not content with such an easy approach
to public administration. One was William J. Burns, head of the
Bureau of Investigation.

Burns came into the Bureau in mid-August of 1921, the appointment

coming both on the basis of his public image as a "famous international sleuth" and as a boyhood chum and crony of Attorney General
Harry M. Daugherty.[1] As head of the Burns International Detective
Agency, he had gained the confidence of business over the years by
affording personnel for strike-breaking work for large corporations. The
agency had flourished during the red scare, since the fear of radicals
had impelled many employers to seek private protection for which they
paid well. Burns was certainly not oblivious to the fact that many
apprehensive Americans still needed dramatic public gestures which
would indicate that their government was prepared to keep radicals
in check through the most advanced forms of law enforcement.

Yet Burns could never disengage his sense of obligation to effective
crime control from his own venality and vanity. Even worse, he
failed to read the general public mood, which was clearly calling
for a quiet end to red-hunting excesses and a focus upon the positive
attributes of the new business civilization. Burns liked nothing better
then to don his checked and colored frock coat and play the public
role of the supersleuth, ferreting out enemies of the republic. But
he began early to become an embarrassing anachronism. As his
heavy-handedness, personal opportunism, and ineptitude grew, his
presence became a liability, even to those who had earlier welcomed
his appointment. Although his aggressive role in intimidating strikers
during the Shopmen's Strike of 1922 was revealing of his attitudes,[2]
and his active work in clandestinely searching out incriminating information on critics of the Harding administration was revealing of
his techniques,[3] his part in the famous Bridgman communist raids
of 1922 best encapsulated the many aspects of the man's approach.

Communism in the United States in the early 1920s was a weak
protest against capitalist economic exploitation, an ineffective, faction-
ridden dialogue among a few thousand alien radicals and native
American malcontents. The movement began as an illegal, underground operation, seeking the gradual conversion of dissident Americans to its policies.[4] Its leadership rejected early the approach of
infiltrating existing labor unions to gain power through direct economic pressure. Rather, the principal internal issue was whether the
organization should seek open legal status as a formal organized
political party, and, if so, whether actual control should come from
those affiliated with it in its legal capacity or from its underground
inner core. The party, in the hopes of undermining its crippling
factionalism, scheduled a secret convention for the summer of 1922.
Agents from the Communist Internationale were scheduled to meet
with American leaders to agree upon future policy.[5] Among those
requesting the opportunity to participate were several Marxists, promi-

nent among them William Z. Foster, organizer of the 1919 steel strike, who, while persona non grata to the leaders because of their desires to work through economic coercion, was nonetheless allowed to take part.

Burns had been defending the bureau's mounting appropriation by stressing the growing need for protection against the radical menace. Secret red plots, he maintained, were growing in number, as evidenced especially by subtle red penetration into new corners—education, religion, the news media, even the movies and vaudeville.[6] He now saw an opportunity for validating his claims and set out to trap the Communists at Bridgman. His problems here were more serious than he realized. There was no federal statute under which the government could move. But Burns, in this matter as in others, was not deterred by legal fine points. He quickly and quietly sought the cooperation of private red hunters, particularly Ralph Easley and the National Civic Federation, who in turn set out to raise private funds to assist the government.[7] Burns assigned a secret government operative, K-97, to infiltrate the party and be present at the convention. He then encouraged Michigan authorities to move on the group in a cooperative effort with Bureau of Investigation agents.

The results of the Bridgman raid were far from satisfactory. The American Civil Liberties Union promptly described the seizing of delegates and of party records as a serious threat to the rights of free speech and assembly. A statement from national headquarters read:

> No overt criminal act of any sort is charged. No evidence is offered except the doctrines advocated by the Communists. The Michigan criminal syndicalism law punishes the mere expression of prohibited opinions. The essence of the charge against the men is that, holding communist views, they dared meet together for discussion. While we thoroughly disagree with the Communist attitude toward free speech, with their melodramatic secret tactics and with their talk about revolutionary violence, we shall defend their right to meet and to speak as they choose.[8]

The Communists promptly retained as counsel ACLU national committeeman Frank P. Walsh, former cochairman of Woodrow Wilson's War Labor Board and cosigner of the National Popular Government League's indictment of the Palmer raids. Walsh, in preparing their defense, dramatized the free-speech aspects of the situation,[9] winning acquittal of Foster by drawing a sharp line between predicting that violence would have to be used before social and industrial revolution could be achieved and the actual advocacy of violent acts themselves.[10] He also, however, took the occasion to introduce a witness who not only challenged the legality of the federal government's intervention, but accused Burns of utilizing the episode to shake down business firms for protection money through the creation of false hysteria and unwarranted apprehensions. He further charged that the Justice Department, in Bridgman as in the Palmer raids earlier, had actually written many of the seized documents upon which the Communists were now being tried.[11]

Embarrassed but undaunted, Burns's voice became shriller and his appeals for private support more insistent. In early February of 1923, he addressed the Allied Patriotic Societies in New York City, indicating not only that red propagandists had to be silenced, but also that the government could not carry on this fight alone and needed the help of 100 percent Americans.[12] In his appearance before the House Appropriations Committee in March, he insisted that the Bridgman raids had proved that "radicalism is becoming stronger every day in this country." Now, however, he linked its growth with the increasing influences of the "parlor Bolsheviks" who had "sprung up everywhere, as evidenced by this American Civil Liberties Union of New York." "Wherever we seek to suppress these radicals," Burns complained, "a civil liberties union promptly gets busy."[13]

Burns argued that only if the radicals advocated force and violence were they guilty of violating the law. He then took the occasion to point out that this was the main purport of their literature and that the Third Internationale had systematically been sending in incendiary instructions to strikers in all of the large national strikes of the previous three or four years. His bureau had seized most of them and had copies of others.[14]

From then on, however, Burns's public career and prestige ran a downhill course. The *New York World* summarized his position in an incisive editorial entitled "The Tragic Figure of W. J. Burns," stating:

> He is the only man in the United States who can still see that famous Red revolution coming. He has called attention to it repeatedly; he has shown that liberals are capturing some of the colleges, that radicals are occasionally allowed to speak on street corners, that the Civil Liberties Union has defended free speech for communists as well as for other people. But he has failed miserably to arouse the citizens to a sense of their own danger. They are not aware of the cataclysm

impending. It is the tragic fate of Mr. Burns that nobody is aware of it but himself.[15]

But Burns, apparently still counting heavily upon support from his ultraconservative, superpatriotic constituency, courageously blazed away, telling the Shore Kiwanis Club in Atlantic City in May 1923 that his goal was to "drive every radical out of the country and bring the parlor Bolsheviks to their senses." He warned that American schools and colleges were turning out "parlor Bolsheviki" in increasing numbers and insisted that the "loop holes of American jurisprudence" prevented American courts from functioning properly.[16]

However, Burns's days were numbered. The growing scandals of the Harding administration focused attention on the nationwide spy system in the Justice Department and on the quasi–police-state activities of Burns and many of his agents. Many Americans welcomed "Silent Cal" Coolidge and his image of detached honesty and efficiency. Among Coolidge's first appointees was a new Attorney General, Harlan Fiske Stone, former dean of Columbia University Law School, who willingly and aggressively assumed the job of cleaning house in the Justice Department. Among the first to fly before Stone's new broom was William J. Burns, protesting like Harry M. Daugherty that his ouster was the fault of the reds.[17] In appointing Burns's successor, Stone made very clear that the Bureau of Investigation was to be taken out of politics, a move that its new temporary head, J. Edgar Hoover, endorsed fully. Far more significantly from the standpoint of free speech, however, Stone ordered an end to the Bureau's radical-chasing activities. In a public statement on May 14, Stone stated:

> There is always the possibility that a secret police may become a menace to free government and free institutions because it carries with it the possibility of abuses of power which are not always quickly apprehended or understood. . . . it is important that [the Bureau of Investigation's] activities be strictly limited to those functions for which it was created and that its agents themselves be not above the law or beyond its reach.
>
> The Bureau . . . is not concerned with political or other opinions of individuals. It is concerned only with their conduct and then only with such conduct as is forbidden by the laws of the United States.[18]

Further, the *Annual Report of the Attorney General* for 1924 stated: "Investigations conducted by the bureau are confined exclusively to possible violations of the Federal statutes and such administrative matters as clearly are incidental to the administration of the Department of Justice."[19]

The demise of the "Burns Idea"[20] and the end of governmental radical hunting was warmly welcomed by a majority of Americans.[21] It removed the executive branch of the government from the task of monitoring opinion and public expression, a situation that characterized the remainder of the decade. It was testimony to the fact that informal controls, when improperly used or used by the wrong people, were anathema to many. The action, however, in no way rejected the proper use of such controls by responsible citizens. It also reflected a new desire, characteristic of the decade, for professionalism and efficiency. Such a move had tactical advantages. Handling Burns and Daugherty by institutionalizing them out of the system with the pose that security problems could now be handled more efficiently by a professionalized service was a sop to the red-hunters, who could hardly argue with the need for greater efficiency. It was also a sop to the critics, who could interpret the move as a whole new tack on law enforcement which would eliminate the type of gross behavior that had formally been not only offensive but inefficient.

The move was also in harmony with renewed laissez-faire attitudes. Curtailing the activities of a government agency complemented Coolidge's frequently quoted statement that the business of America was business and removed government agents from meddling with radicals, on one hand, and with congressional or senatorial files and businessmen's private papers and records on the other.

The only sizable element of opinion not mollified by such action was the ultra-right-wing superpatriots, for whom professional detachment was little solace. For such people, scientific, aloof public servants in Washington handling the massive red threat statistically and impersonally did not inspire the same kind of confidence that Burns's headline-hunting exposure and supersleuthing did. A passive approach to problems of this nature seemed the height of incaution. Positive, aggressive action was essential. Consequently, a variety of superpatriotic organizations now found themselves with the ponderous task of saving the nation and rallying others in the face of its impending collapse.[22]

The new crusade of what Norman Hapgood came to call, rather cynically, the professional patriots was new in the targets it sought and the charges it made rather than in leadership, techniques, or eventual objectives.[23] Its first objective was to silence public expression of pacifist sentiment as an abuse of free speech.

Pacifism in the 1920s had growing popular support, complementing international disarmament conferences and aggressive pleas for the outlawry of war by a number of leading American statesmen and policy makers. Such an interest was also tied to growing disillusionment with the failure of World War I to make the world safe for democracy, particularly in light of the domestic sacrifices of civil liberties and personal freedom which had been demanded ostensibly to achieve that purpose.[24] A wide range of peace organizations were the beneficiaries of this sentiment, ranging from conservative bodies like the generously financed Carnegie Endowment for International Peace, the World Peace Foundation, the Church Peace Union, and the World Alliance for International Friendship through the Churches to highly aggressive pacificist groups. Some of these, like the Fellowship of Reconciliation, had their origins prior to World War I; some, like the Women's International Conference (later, League) for Peace and Freedom, were wartime products; and some, like the Fellowship of Youth for Peace, emerged in the 1920s. So strong was pacifist sentiment among liberals that the National Council for the Prevention of War, a clearinghouse for over thirty organizations, maintained by the mid-1920s that membership in its various suborganizations could be counted in the millions.[25]

Similarly, there was a great upsurge of pacifism in the churches. Many religious leaders had been stampeded into supporting wartime hysteria. Now, with the objectivity of peacetime, they could compensate for their prior desertion of the principles of the "Prince of Peace."[26] In fact, by the mid-1920s, A. J. Muste claimed, in an article in *Fellowship,* the organ of the Fellowship of Reconciliation, that "in the larger denominations (with the exception of the Lutheran and, in much less degree, the Episcopalian), the pacifist position was the prevalent one among the leaders of theological thought, in the Student Christian movement, the seminaries and the upper grades in the Sunday School."[27]

In addition, many Socialists, labor leaders, educators, and a sizable portion of the membership of the ACLU were ready to remove the vestiges of militarism from American life early in the decade. These often included the postwar reconstructionists and the activist-libertarians of 1918 and 1919, now seeking to strike a blow for a better world though international programs of peaceful cooperation. Typical was Kirby Page, editor of *The World Tomorrow,* whose book, *War: Its Causes, Consequences and Cure,* was sent out by the thousands of copies by Sidney L. Gulick, executive secretary of the Commission on International Justice and Good Will of the Federal Council of Churches.[28]

Such pacifism was frightening to many Americans, who saw it

weakening national security and crippling the nation's strength to fight off destructive enemies. With the Justice Department no longer having responsibility for curtailing radical expression and propaganda, crippling the military, which seemed to be the pacifists' goal, wiped out one further symbol of stability and security in a rapidly changing and confusing world.

The self-appointed saviors of America quickly rallied against the mounting pacifist crusade. In the process, they not only furthered their own self-interest but also served the forces for whom pacifism posed a serious financial or professional threat, particularly military and business leaders.

The most obvious interrelationship among business leadership, the army, and the pacifist-baiters of the far right involved the connection among leading chemical producers in the United States, the Chemical Warfare Service of the War Department, and a number of specific superpatriotic organizations, especially the American Defense Society, the Reserve Officer's Association, the American Legion, and the DAR. Following postwar disarmament and the disarmament conferences of 1921–1922, a good many Americans were intrigued with making war more scientific, in the same way that technology was bringing new blessings to peacetime society. Chemical warfare seemed to eliminate the need for large numbers of troops and for massive costly armament programs. The chemical industry exploited such sentiments to its advantage. Elon H. Hooker, a multimillionaire who fought with Henry Ford during the early years of the 1920s for control of Muscle Shoals, was head of Hooker Electro-Chemical Company, the nation's largest producer of gases used in warfare, and a director of a number of closely connected corporations, as well as a member of the executive committee of Ralph Easley's National Civic Federation. Major General Amos H. Fries, head of the Chemical Warfare Service of the War Department, was also one of the most ambitious military men in Washington. Fries, whose wife was publicity chairman of the DAR during the period, was closely tied with leading chemical manufacturers and was highly enthusiastic that this type of warfare would not only be effective, but would popularize his department and increase his power and status.[29] Yet Fries anticipated early trouble from both growing pacifism and pacifist leadership. As early as December 1922, he fired the opening salvo in the war against the pacifists in a speech in Kansas City, in which he maintained that he had incontrovertible proof that the National Council for the Prevention of Was was "financed, inspired and directed from Moscow" and proposed "to establish communism in America."[30]

Almost simultaneously, Fries gave his blessing and encouragement to the compilation by Mrs. Lucia R. Maxwell, librarian of the Chemical Warfare Service, of an elaborate Spider Web Chart, which purposed to show the interlocking directorate of pacifist organizations and leaders. It was headed by a quotation from the Lusk Report: "The Socialist-Pacifist Movement in America Is an Absolutely Fundamental and Integral Part of International Socialism." The chart, aimed primarily at women's organizations, assumed that women especially were naive, blundering, often well-meaning, but innocent dupes of the "red menace." As such, they were agents for the spreading of propaganda whose only purpose could be the destruction of the nation.

In taking on a widely based movement, Fries and Mrs. Maxwell apparently did not count on a sharp negative reaction. Leaders of the National Farmers' Union, the League of Women Voters, the National Women's Trade Union League, and the American Association of University Women formed a delegation to call on Secretary of War John W. Weeks to point out the impropriety and unfairness of the attacks apparently emanating from the War Department.[31] The Spider Web Chart had branded as "red" such organizations as the General Federation of Women's Clubs, the Women's Christian Temperance Union, the National Congress of Mothers and Parent-Teachers Associations, the American Home Economics Association, the National Federation of Business and Professional Women, and the YWCA, as well as the League of Women Voters and the AAUW. It had been reprinted and widely distributed by Henry Ford's *Dearborn Independent* with an accompanying article entitled "Why Don't Women Investigate Propaganda: Vigorous House-cleaning to Prevent Further Duping of Organizations."[32] It was now so vigorously assaulted that Secretary Weeks promised that he would warn his officers against future unjustified remarks and would demand the destruction and the end of further dissemination of the chart.[33]

Weeks's restrictive posture was not heeded by his officers nearly as fully as his further statement that he would still "encourage them to discuss public questions and would not rebuke them for saying anything so long as it was the truth."[34] Brigadier General Albert J. Bowley, commander of Fort Bragg, North Carolina, had been speaking widely to patriotic groups, but always cautiously stipulating that there should be no publication of anything he said. On March 7, 1924, he addressed a highly receptive chamber of commerce in Columbus, Ohio. Five of his listeners, including Franck C. Caldwell, a professor of electrical engineering at Ohio State University, Mrs. Caldwell, and Mrs. W. E. Henderson, chairman of the Ohio League of Women Voters' Committee of International Cooperation to Prevent

War, swore out affidavits indicating that Bowley had charged that Frederick J. Libby of the National Council for Prevention of War was a Moscow-trained Communist and that the National Council had as its "impelling motive" the overthrow by violence of the American government.[35] Mrs. Henderson and Mrs. Caldwell then began a vigorous letter-writing campaign, joined by members of the League of Women Voters, nationally directed at Bowley and at Secretary Weeks, irately demanding proof of the charges.

Bowley first fell back on the Spider Web Chart and the *Dearborn Independent* articles supporting it.[36] When it was pointed out that the chart had been rejected as erroneous by the Secretary of War and ordered destroyed, he then indicated that documentary evidence would be furnished by three antired experts, Fred R. Marvin, editor of the red-exposing "Searchlight" column of the vigorously open-shop *New York Commercial*, R. M. Whitney of the American Defense Society, and J. S. Eichelberger, editor of *The Woman Patriot*. All proved frail reeds. Their sources were highly dubious. Marvin was keyman of the Keymen—and women—of America. He was openly on record as having documentary proof that

> "Brotherly Love," "Internationalism," "No More War," "Peace and Freedom," "Industrial Democracy," are all beautiful expressions in the abstract, but not one of those slogans originated in the mind of an American. All of them were manufactured in other lands and sent across the water to this country to destroy the morale of the American people that we, in the end, might, as a nation be destroyed.[37]

However, in this instance, he hedged. He wrote Mrs. Caldwell that he was preparing a brief of probably ten to fifteen typewritten pages supporting Bowley's charges, but no brief was ever forthcoming, and in the long run, Marvin admitted that "it is possible that in his address . . . he used expressions which, if literally construed, he could not prove. But, as to his real purpose, no honest citizen can question him."[38]

Whitney dodged completely. "It is absurd to say that all his information was obtained from me," he wrote Mrs. Henderson; "I cannot comply with your request to supply you with documents which I possess. I would be a greater fool than my worst enemies accuse me of being, were I to let such documents out of my possession."[39]

Eichelberger proved even more of a disappointment. He spoke primarily for the remnants of a disgruntled element of those who opposed woman suffrage, still devoted to "the defense of the family and the state against feminism and socialism."[40] In seeking to achieve such ends, *The Woman Patriot* apparently sought to scare women out of further active participation in public life and back into the kitchen and nursery by "reddening" their causes. It thus attacked with abandon pacifism, women's peace movements, social welfare, Judge Ben Lindsey, the Federal Children's Bureau, and especially the advocates of the child labor amendment.[41] Indicating that he had no information as to whether Libby had ever been in Russia, he continued: "We have not charged him with being a Communist, as we do not charge anybody with anything unless we can prove it."[42] Thus, as even Bowley's friends admitted, he was in a tight place.

But the general discrediting of red baiting and pacifist baiting by military officials, much like the undercutting of the Burns approach in the Justice Department, aroused private superpatriots to new heights of activity. And while Secretary Weeks and Attorney General Stone may have been well-intentioned in seeking to terminate further official indiscriminate use of "red files," Lusk Reports, Spider Web Charts, "Searchlight" columns, and military broadsides, the patriots did not interpret such action as applying to them.

The American Defense Society rose to the challenge and attempted to authenticate the evidence. Like the National Security League, the Defense Society had sprung into existence during the preparedness agitation preceding World War I.[43] During the war it had assailed pacifists, conscientious objectors, and alleged pro-Germans, and through its famed "Flying Squadron of Speakers" had been prepared to propagandize any reluctant American behind the war effort. Its honorary president, Theodore Roosevelt, had aroused it to new postwar responsibilities. In his last public message in January 1919, he had insisted that "there must be no sagging back in the fight for Americanism merely because the war is over. . . . We have room for but one flag, the American flag, and this excludes the red flag, which symbolizes all wars against liberty and civilization."[44] The membership was quick to respond. Elon Hooker, chairman of the board, and Franklin Remington, a director of the Great Western Chemical Corporation and chairman of its finance committee, were worried about the pacifist menace. When radical baiting seemed no longer to arouse feverous response, they were delighted to be off in pursuit of the reds on a different but equally pernicious charge.[45]

Hooker was particularly delighted by a series of articles in the *Boston Transcript* in late 1922, by newspaperman R. M. Whitney, which explored in detail the communist menace in America. Whitney claimed to base great portions of his exposé on "privileged" information, which he had secured from William J. Burns's "red file" in the Justice Department, drawing particularly upon the records seized in the Bridgman raid.[46] Hooker promptly offered to circulate the articles as a pamphlet through the auspices of the Defense Society under the title *The Reds in America*. He was particularly pleased with Whitney's clear demonstration of the sinister connection between Russian bolshevism and American pacifism. Americans agitating for universal peace, Whitney declared again and again, were only playing into the hands of Moscow—breaking down national resistance against red conquest. Those who continued to work to guarantee the dissemination of such treasonous propaganda, particularly an organization like the ACLU (to which he devoted a full chapter), were as red as the pacifists themselves.[47]

Whitney went on the payroll of the Defense Society as head of its Washington office and quickly became its official spokesman. He set out to add further "documentation" to his antipacifist charges by publishing a pamphlet in 1923 at the time of the annual conference of the American segment of Jane Addams's Women's International League for Peace and Freedom. He described the meeting as "probably the most subversive, certainly the most insidiously and cleverly camouflaged, thoroughly anti-American and un-American public meeting that has ever been held in the country since the United States entered the European war."[48] He subsequently added a work entitled *The Youth Movement in America* in which he assailed the National Student Forum, a clearinghouse of information on public issues (which, while liberal-left, sought consciously to maintain an impartial stand) for seeking "to undermine and sink, or overthrow, the Government of the United States, and to set up in this country a soviet form of government, such as Russia now boasts."[49] Whitney's material was still being used in the late 1930s by superpatriotic groups to attack Roosevelt and his "Communist" New Deal.[50]

Efforts thus to silence Americans with controversial viewpoints were frequent.[51] The Women's International League for Peace and Friendship (WIL) had sprung from a body organized at The Hague in 1915 with Jane Addams as its international president.[52] In the postwar period it established permanent headquarters at Geneva to be near the headquarters of the League of Nations. It met regularly in international congresses and channeled most of its work into disarmament and pacifist programs. After R. M. Whitney alerted Americans to the "communistic" purposes of the WIL in 1923, it became more and more a target of those seeking to save the nation from the reds. Despite its small membership of 12,000 and its limited resources, its critics labeled Jane Addams, whose ties with the ACLU were also widely known, as "the most dangerous woman in America."[53]

By 1924, the WIL had become increasingly disturbed about the dangers and evils of chemical warfare. One of its leaders, Emily Greene Balch, later to win the Nobel Peace Prize, was prepared to introduce a resolution condemning such warfare in the Fourth International Congress in Washington, D.C. Further plans called for a number of the international delegates to tour America in a special railroad car, the "Pax Special," and speak in a number of cities where invitations were forthcoming.[54]

The forces of Americanism jumped into action. The WIL had been prominently mentioned in the Spider Web Chart and had been singled out for attack by organizations ranging from the American Legion to the Reserve Officers' Association. The American Legion joined with the DAR in trying to block the convention. When this was unsuccessful, its membership was alerted to repress the irresponsible propaganda soon to be forthcoming. Again, however, women also manned the barricades. A number of patriotic women's organizations met in Washington on the eve of the WIL congress and adopted a resolution urging Congress to investigate "pacifist and unpatriotic propaganda."[55] When the congress actually opened on May 1, following an initial reception at the White House by President Coolidge, numerous officers in mufti were seen attending its sessions, visibly disturbed, especially by its assault on gas warfare. At the close of the congress, Republican Congressman Clarence McLeod of Michigan asked Attorney General Stone to investigate allegations that the WIL was "allied with the Soviet Government of Russia . . . maintained by funds from Russia . . . with a view of eventually overthrowing the American government, and displacing it with a Soviet form." McLeod was especially disturbed because "the members spent one whole day of the Congress attacking the United States government." He proposed that the organization be broken up and its leaders jailed.[56]

Such appeals for governmental action fell on deaf ears. Superpatriots were forced to resort to their own devices. The "Pax Special" became a prime target. At Cincinnati, the train was met by members of the Ku Klux Klan, armed with clubs, and had to be diverted to another station. Eventually certain delegates spoke, but to a virtually secret conference of local women in a private home. At Dayton, Ohio, a meeting scheduled at the YMCA was cancelled since many local businessmen, large contributors to that body, threatened to withdraw their financial support if it sponsored the group.[57] In Chicago, the *Chicago Tribune* conducted an effective preventative campaign. In St. Louis, the DAR and the Colonial Dames put strong pressure on a local church, which had promised facilities for a meeting. In

Detroit, a local physician, closely connected with the ROTC, stated that the members of the "Pax Special" should be placed in an insane asylum. Subsequently, the city council was presented with a suggestion from the floor that the "Pax Special" should be derailed and the women tarred and feathered. In Cleveland, the Chamber of Commerce, the ROTC, and the American Legion passed censorious resolutions based upon evidence provided by General Bowley. Cleveland women, however, were not to be denied and arranged a successful meeting at the Women's City Club, with public endorsement by the Gold Star Mothers, the YWCA, and the local Federation of Churches. Thus, even against the strongest local opposition, the WIL's position was heard, though often clandestinely, since, as the official report of the congress stated, "a few courageous radicals in each city which upheld the Constitutional right of free speech" held firm in the face of such heavy pressure.[58]

Such a limited victory disturbed many superpatriots. The DAR, which had maintained a relatively apolitical pose in the early years of the decade, was particularly upset. But immediately after the WIL Washington congress, the executive committee voted unanimously that "our society would not be true to its lofty ideals of patriotic service if it did not take more active measures than it has yet taken in opposing the disloyal individuals and organizations that are striving to pervert our national ideals." A year later, the president-general, Mrs. Anthony W. Cook, became more explicit and publicly deplored "the spirit of pacifism and the undermining of our ideals of national service by foreign agencies and by our native-born emotional theorists who have been swept from stable moorings by skillful propaganda."[59]

The most determined and successful leaders in turning the DAR into an active red-hunting instrument were Mrs. Alfred J. Brosseau, wife of the president of Mack Truck, Inc., who served as president-general from 1926 to 1929, and Mrs. William Sherman Walker of Seattle, who became first chairman of a newly created National Defense Committee. The two moved the organization into active participation in an organization called the Women's Patriotic Conference on National Defense. The alignment enabled Mrs. Brosseau to channel the organization's activities during her incumbency into national defense work and an equally vigorous war against the "Communist menace." It led also to peculiar liaisons which eventually produced national reaction.

Mrs. Walker claimed to have gathered independently the country's outstanding display of information about subversive forces in it. A quick analysis of her sources indicated that they were a general pastiche of data compiled from the Lusk Report, the Spider Web Chart, the works of R. M. Whitney, and particularly the writings of Fred R. Marvin and J. S. Eichelberger.[60] Marvin established an early liaison with both Mrs. Brosseau and Mrs. Walker, placing the former on the advisory council of the Keymen. Then the National Defense Committee issued a pamphlet Marvin had prepared entitled *The Common Enemy,* with Mrs. Walker listed as its author, since she read it practically verbatim to the Ohio State Conference in Columbus on March 16, 1927. The heading acknowledged, however, that the information was "supplied by the Key Men of America, a national bureau of information on radical and subversive movements, forces, organizations and individuals. Every statement of fact contained in this booklet can be substantiated by documentary evidence."[61] The pamphlet began:

> Communism, Bolshevism, Socialism, Liberalism, and Ultra-Pacifism tend to the same ends:
> 1. The abolition of government,
> 2. the abolition of patriotism,
> 3. the abolition of property rights,
> 4. the abolition of inheritance,
> 5. the abolition of religion, and
> 6. the abolition of family relations.

It was mailed out by the thousands to members and interested friends of the organization and with it went a long excerpt from the *Congressional Record,* constituting a typical Eichelberger assault from *The Woman Patriot* on advocates of the child labor amendment, linking them with Russia and domestic reds, especially the WIL. It "proved" that Mrs. Grace Abbott, chief of the Children's Bureau, was a "notorious pacifist" and that the recently enacted Sheppard-Towner Maternity Act was a special red weapon for getting into the American home and brainwashing American housewives with sinister propaganda.[62] DAR endorsement through distribution put the organization on record as one of the few women's groups in the country opposed to the then widely supported amendment.

Carrie Chapman Catt, the famed suffragette, roasted the DAR for this action in her widely circulated "Open Letter to the DAR" in mid-1927.[63] And criticism mounted when the DAR blacklist of speakers was revealed. The DAR had been assailing pacifist speakers for some time in the hopes of preventing their propaganda from being heard. One such typical target was Frederick J. Libby of the National Council for the Prevention of War.[64] But the blacklist included over 60

organizations and, by implication, all their officers. It also listed the
names of over 200 men and women of liberal tendency, branding
them as "undesirable speakers," with brief comments after their names
to indicate why they were undesirable and whether they were "communist," "socialist," "radical," "pacifist," or a combination. Prominent
were such names as Jane Addams; Judge George W. Anderson of
the United States Circuit Court of Appeals, Boston; Methodist Episcopal Bishop William F. Anderson of Boston; Senator William E.
Borah of Idaho; recently "excommunicated" Carrie Chapman Catt,
now branded as an "internationalist, feminist"; Clarence Darrow;
Irving Fisher, professor of political economy at Yale; and Felix Frankfurter. Also included were the Reverend John Haynes Holmes; David
Starr Jordan, president emeritus of Stanford University; Methodist
Bishop Francis J. McConnell, prominent official in the Federal Council
of Churches and chairman of the Commission of the Church and
Social Service; Reverend Charles S. Macfarland, general secretary
of the Federal Council and prominent member of the World Alliance
for International Friendship through the Churches; President William
A. Neilson of Smith College, who had permitted various "unde-
sirables" to speak on the Smith campus and had sanctioned the famous
Smith "sex questionnaire"; Roscoe Pound; Reverend E. Talmadge Root,
executive secretary of the Massachusetts Federation of Churches;
Kansas editor and prominent Republican leader William Allen White,
who had been instrumental in driving the Ku Klux Klan out of the
state; Rabbi Stephen Wise of New York's Free Synagogue, a leader
in exposing the falsity of the anti-Semitic, Henry Ford-distributed
and DAR-endorsed *Protocols of the Elders of Zion*, and prominent
in defending free speech for the Passaic strikers; and President Mary
E. Woolley of "red infiltrated" Mount Holyoke College.

The list was compiled from all the familiar and by now widely
discredited sources plus some new ones that the DAR found particularly appealing. It included a long list of over 270 individuals and
organizations compiled by E. H. Hunter of the Industrial Defense
Association, a body organized in 1926 in Boston to keep communism
out of industry in Massachusetts and initially supported by a number
of wealthy local industrialists. It included the AAUW, which Hunter
interpolated for his readers as the American Associated University
of Women; the hundred-year-old American Peace Society; the Church
Peace Union, of which a prominent director was William Howard
Taft; the Foreign Policy Association; the Association for International
Conciliation, headed by Columbia University president and prominent
Republican Nicolas Murray Butler; and the World Alliance for International Friendship through the Churches.[65]

The Massachusetts Public Interest League, headed by Mrs. Margaret Robinson, was a Boston local-action organization to support the principles enunciated by Eichelberger's *The Woman Patriot.* Mrs. Robinson printed her own blacklist in 1928 and exposed a new group of enemies by following up Calvin Coolidge's suggestion that the reds were endangering women's colleges.[66] In addition, both organizations proscribed Boston's famous Ford Hall Forum, a twenty-five-year-old institution that provided facilities for the public discussion of all vital questions and maintained a speakers' bureau to serve smaller forums throughout the country in towns where public interest encouraged current issues explored from all angles.

Many local chapters of the DAR used the blacklist. By early 1928 at least eight lists, including a long one by Scabbard & Blade, an instrument of ROTC, were circulating.[67] But the frequent cancellations of scheduled addresses roused increasing hostility to the use of such lists. In February, the *New York World* published a series of detailed articles based upon extensive research, exposing the shabby methods of the "heresy hunters" and detailing numerous examples of the effectiveness of their muzzling of any controversial discussion of public questions.[68] In March, a Unitarian minister in Milton, Massachusetts, the Reverend Vivian T. Pomeroy, roused a Boston audience with a stirring denunciation of the "Blue Menace." "There is in this city," said Reverend Pomeroy, "too much stupid interference with matters which properly belong to the realm of free individual conscience and choice, and to the realm of responsible common council and conference." And he went on, "This petty intolerance has succeeded in magnifying its otherwise insignificant self by claiming a monopoly of the American flag and the historic fame of this people." Pomeroy further pointed out that it was mostly women who "operate this machine of intolerance. . . . They are quite respectable educated women [who] appoint themselves the guardians of our national virtue . . . and attempt to prohibit all intelligent discussion by vilifying any speaker who shows a gleam of freedom in thought and who disregards the bounds set by their own suffocating narrowness."[69]

Shortly thereafter, the Reverend E. Talmadge Root learned of his presence on the blacklist and extended Reverend Pomeroy's condemnation in speeches to meetings of Congregational and Baptist clergymen, denouncing a "countrywide system of espionage, semi-military in character, invoked in the name of Americanism and patriotism, apparently aimed at censorship and suppression of free speech." Root warned that "if once we admit that our army and navy and those formerly connected therewith are, by the fact, constituted censors of public opinion, their power will insensibly grow, and the liberties of America will be lost."[70]

Again, indignant women played the most effective role. Mrs. Helen T. Bailie, a Cambridge, Massachusetts, DAR member, herself a pacifist and descendant of a Revolutionary War hero, had long chafed under the growing tendency of high DAR leadership to commit the entire body to a supermilitaristic position. She was particularly aroused over Mrs. Walker's casual endorsement in early 1928 in the name of the entire national body of the "Big Navy Bill" then before Congress. Mrs. Bailie thus began vigorous research on her own, utilizing especially the ACLU's extensive private files on the patrioteering organizations. In early April she had ready for distribution a pamphlet entitled *Our Threatened Heritage.* It not only exposed the leadership's subservience to military jingoists and professional patriots but deplored "the un-American blacklist," the abuse of which meant that "D.A.R. chapters listen to only one side of certain questions of national and international importance." Mrs. Bailie insisted that "our officers are not really our pilots. Those who determine our course are people like Marvin and Hunter." "Fellow members," she concluded, "I appeal to you to throw off this foreign domination, so at variance with our ideals—a domination that has already brought our society into disrepute, and if continued, will destroy its usefulness."[71]

Other irate Daughters were equally incensed. Mrs. Mary P. Macfarland, wife of blacklisted church leader Charles S. Macfarland, wrote Mrs. Brosseau that it was high time she realized she was being duped by self-seeking "professional propagandists."[72] Mrs. Brosseau's reply was crisp and cutting. "I do not know to whom you allude when you say 'professional propagandists,'" she wrote, "but I must remark in passing, that a man who has served his country on the field of battle is I think well fitted to offer advice on matters of national defense."[73] Mrs. Macfarland, however, would not be so easily turned off. She charged Mrs. Brosseau with putting forward the inexcusable blacklist and thereby "violating the principle of the first amendment to the Constitution of the United States by insistent, repeated, and continuous efforts to suppress freedom of speech when such speech was clearly within legal rights." "By 'professional propagandists,'" she stated, "I mean persons whose sole or main occupation is the production and distribution of this sort of literature." She concluded that the entire matter should be a major agenda item at the DAR's forthcoming Continental Congress.[74]

Such dissenters, however, paid for their disloyalty and were steamrollered at the convention. Mrs. Bailie was censured, suspended, and finally expelled.[75] The body voted down overwhelmingly even a mild resolution by a Kansas delegate, asking that local chapters be able to choose their own speakers and hear all sides of public issues.[76] But while the leadership controlled its minions, it was helpless in the face of public condemnation and repudiation. Newspaper comment was almost universally hostile, so much so, in fact, that Mrs. Brosseau at one point denied that the blacklist existed and at another charged Mrs. Bailie with attempting to deny free speech to the DAR by trying to prevent its use.[77]

In the long run the most effective response was ridicule. William Allen White devastated the leaders with good-natured scorn. "Mrs. Brosseau is a lovely lady with many beautiful qualities of heart and mind," he wrote in a widely reprinted editorial, "but in her enthusiasm she has allowed several lengths of Ku Klux Klan nightie to show under her red, white and blue. . . . The DAR had yanked the Klan out of the cow pasture and set it down in the breakfast room of respectability, removing its famous hood and putting on a transformation." He rebuked the Daughters for having been "lured into the Red-baiting mania by the tea gladiators of Washington . . . apoplectic old gentlemen in red flannels who escape the boredom of their rich wives by sitting in club windows and bemoaning the decadence of the growing world."[78]

The Nation quickly picked up the cue and scheduled a "Blacklist Party" in early May, sending invitations beginning "Dear Fellow Conspirator" to all whose names had appeared on the blacklist and to members of organizations that had been so honored. The response was overwhelming. Over a thousand people jammed the Level Club in New York City on May 10 to take part in the high jinks. Typical was Rosika Schwimmer, who had played a leading role in the ill-fated 1918 Henry Ford Peace Ship mission, who sent along with her acceptance a copy of a document allegedly in possession of the Military Intelligence Association of Chicago proclaiming her an agent of bolshevism in Europe and Asia, writing that she hoped this would make her eligible for the title of "Ambassador of Ill-Will." Heywood Broun, by contrast, was incensed that he should have been omitted by the DAR from the blacklist and wrote to the party sponsors that he was planning to bring a libel suit against the Daughters for criminal omission. The suit was tried during the evening with blacklisted Clarence Darrow and Arthur Garfield Hays acting as counsel and Groucho Marx as the leading character witness. Mrs. Brosseau was invited, but ironically she was at the time in England being presented at court to the king and queen, thus attaining the "height of her social ambition."[79]

A year later the Ford Hall Forum held a notable "Free-Speech Rally," attended by 700 people and presided over, as "Chief Roastmaster and Master of Revelries," by Harvard history professor Arthur M. Schlesinger, whose books at the time were being flayed as anti-

American and pro-British by Mayor "Big Bill" Thompson of Chicago. Margaret Sanger, forbidden to speak in Boston, appeared at the head table with a gag over her mouth. While the evening was focused most directly upon the ludicrousness of book censorship in Boston, the theme of uninhibited public expression was dominant throughout.[80]

Such actions by no means terminated the activities of direct-action groups. The Ku Klux Klan still had sufficient momentum to pressure unpopular types and unpopular statements. The American Legion, with well over a half million members, was also vigorous. Legion leaders, while certainly not ignoring blacklists, generally eschewed the type of controversy that their use aroused and preferred to use various forms of direct coercion in keeping the air pure from corruptive and controversial ideas. Officially, this excluded the type of heavy-handed vigilantism that had marked the activities of many posts and individual Legionnaires during the red scare.[81] Such policies had frequently brought vigorous public criticism and given the organization a bad name. Yet the Legion was well aware of the demand and need of local members to take part in patriotic radical smashing. Thus, at the Second National Convention, the vigorous Americanism Committee was formed to give radical hunting a formal sanction and official direction. In the following year it became official that all Legion posts were to "keep a watchful eye on radical propagandists and use all lawful means to prevent the fulfillment of their plans." This meant

> that owners of halls and auditoriums in which radical meetings might be held be urged not to lease their property to such persons for such purposes . . . that officials of Legion posts be urged to notify peace officers of all such contemplated meetings coming under their observation, that such meetings may be prevented or dispersed if they transgress on our laws.[82]

The nature of the enemy was also fairly clear. In addition to the usual advocates of bolshevism, communism, sovietism, IWWism, anarchy, and revolutionary radicalism, the Americanism Commission prepared a pamphlet entitled *Preparedness versus Pacifism*, in which members were assured that "no brief can be held for the Pacifist; his views are dangerous—no matter how sincere he may be, or how rational he may be otherwise. Pacifism leads inevitably to forcible and organized resistances to government authority, both civil and military." "The American Legion," ran the argument, "can never watch unconcerned the abuse of freedom of speech. We, of the Legion, take our citizenship seriously [and are] ever working to keep America a place where there is political and economic justice for all." But "the right of the entire nation to free speech may be endangered by the flagrant abuse of the right by a few." Thus the Legion had a special duty to silence those who did not "realize the priceless value of the Constitution . . . and the danger of carelessly departing from its spirit and purpose."[83]

The Legion also declared the ACLU suspect. In March of 1924, Garland W. Powell issued a bulletin to all state organizations calling on members to combat all efforts of that body, and, incidentally, to oppose repeal of "anti-sedition [sic] laws in various states." "These people," wrote Powell, "are advocating 'free speech,' speech of the kind that would allow the advocacy of the overthrow of our government by forces of arms, which means the overthrow of a government which guarantees 'free speech.' Free speech up to a certain point is an excellent thing, but free speech that would destroy our nation and the servicemen who defended it cannot be tolerated."[84]

Most members needed a few more cues than these. All pacifists became fair game from Frederick Libby and Lucia Ames Mead (who was also a feminist), to Jane Addams and Sherwood Eddy. Eddy, a close friend of Kirby Page and prominent official in the national YMCA, was particularly anathema to Legionnaires, since he was not only a highly popular speaker, but one who coupled his dangerous pacifism with open advocacy of the recognition of Soviet Russia. Eddy found his meetings blocked so frequently that he eventually journeyed to Legion headquarters in Indianapolis and obtained an audience with Commander Edward Spafford, later a great admirer of Adolph Hitler.[85] Spafford assured Eddy that the Legion certainly believed in free speech. He stated, however, that "he would do all in his power to prevent people from coming to hear me," and would seek to have his engagements cancelled "because proper pressure was brought to bear." Eddy also succeeded in obtaining copies of two letters mailed out from National Headquarters which he quoted in *The Christian Century,* instructing local posts in how to handle him.[86]

Again, courageous souls protested. Reverend J. A. Ellis, a Legionnaire and formerly a post chaplain, wrote from Raleigh, North Carolina, to Commander Spafford:

> How can the Legion pledge itself to support the Constitution of the United States, and then deny one of the fundamental things in that Constitution? How can the Legionnaires who are going up and down the land, as spokesmen for the Legion, boast that it stands for one hundred percent Americanism? Does not a one hundred percent Ameri-

canism demand a one hundred percent support of one hundred percent of the Constitution of the United States?

Similar protest was forthcoming when the organization sought to prevent Albert Einstein from visiting America, even though one Los Angeles Legionnaire convincingly revealed him to the local post as nothing more than a "pacifist travelling in the guise of a mathematician."[87]

The effect of such criticism was normally to steel Legion leaders in their determination to pursue their patriotic course. Legion suppression tailed off appreciably by the late 1920s because leaders felt it defeated the intended purpose and gave needlessly excessive publicity to those it was seeking to suppress.

One of the more intense and ticklish campaigns to silence the "free-speech fakers" was the war on the churches. Here the challenge was great. Not only were some highly prominent religious leaders in the forefront of movements for social justice and industrial democracy, to say nothing of being intimately involved with the pacifist crusade; they were at least partially insulated from superpatriotic pressure because of the particular nature of their professional operations. Only the Ku Klux Klan on rare occasions would think of attempting to interfere directly with a church service. Such actions would provoke obvious backfire.[88] But public assault and exposure was possible by showing the interlocking connections, especially of those clergymen and those church bodies, that demonstrated any liberal tendencies. The Interchurch World Movement was effectively destroyed by conservative criticism of its *Report on the Steel Strike* in 1920, and the authors of this report, particularly Bishop Francis J. McConnell, never shook off the stigma attached to them. The Federal Council of Churches was early labeled "a large, radical pacifist organization, disseminating sugar-coated radicalism to church and labor organizations."[89] The fact that many churchmen were active in the ACLU was raised as a damning factor in itself. Rabbis Harry Levy of Temple Israel, Boston, Abba Hillel Silver of Cleveland, and Stephen Wise were listed on most blacklists, as was Father John A. Ryan of the National Catholic Welfare Council, who not only was on the national board of the ACLU but had crusaded vigorously for an end to Palmerism and Burnsism in the Justice Department. The Union Theological Seminary, whose staff was joined in the period by the "notorious radical pacifist" Reinhold Niebuhr, was normally classified as "revolutionary Socialist" and a "training school for radical theological students."[90]

Ralph Easley, Fred Marvin, R. M. Whitney, J. S. Eichelberger

II, and E. H. Hunter never lost an opportunity to damn "our crimson clergy." A widely reprinted editorial in the *New York Commercial* on April 11, 1926, read:

> Too many ministers have forsaken the spiritual feature of their work. They have been led astray to wander into the fields of economics, politics, social welfare and business. They have engaged their time and attention with those who are seeking to destroy, rather than to build. Ministers must become the humble servants of a spiritual God rather than seek to be the roaring leaders of a material god.[91]

The widely circulated magazine, *The National Republic,* initially an organ of the Republican National Committee, kept its readers alert to the dangerous ties of their clergymen and church organizations with a regular monthly column, "The Enemy Within Our Gates," presided over by Marvin. Frequent articles condemned the red activities of church leaders and their supposed ties with Moscow.

The Better America Federation of Los Angeles enjoyed a peculiar role among superpatriot groups in the decade, since it was one of the few that maintained an open relationship with the business community. Its activities ran the full spectrum from assailing labor unions, crusading for the open shop, encouraging strike-breaking activities, and seeking to put all IWWs in jail to crusading for a peacetime sedition law. It fought against all legislation that constituted an opening wedge for bolshevism, such as child labor laws, compulsory education up to the sixteenth year, the eight-hour day, the forty-hour week, minimum wage laws, the initiative and the referendum, and public utility regulation. It interfered in school curricula, banning books by such dangerous authors as H. G. Wells, Sinclair Lewis, and James Harvey Robinson and plays by George Bernard Shaw and Eugene O'Neill. It carried on such activities while waving the flag frenetically and looking condescendingly at the inefficiency of other bodies in the same field.[92]

The organization had, as early as 1920, launched a vigorous campaign against the YWCA in Los Angeles for taking as its platform the postwar statement of industrial principles adopted by the Federal Council of Churches and endorsed by the National Catholic Welfare Council. It distributed, with approval, R. M. Whitney's *Reds in America* pamphlet. Its *Behind the Veil* went through more than ten editions and demonstrated that the "inner circle at Moscow" was behind everything from strikes and the child labor amendment to demands for the release of political prisoners and "LaFollettism." Among its other publications were Woodworth Clum's *Making Social-*

ists Out of College Students, and the "Drifting Series," which included
Let the Pee-pul Rule, Over the Tea Cups, Professors Astray, and
Ministers Astray.[93]

In 1927 the editor of its biweekly *Bulletin,* Colonel LeRoy F.
Smith, and a Washington journalist, E. B. Johns, published a series
of articles in a short-lived magazine called *Patches* under the general
title "Does the Federal Council of Churches Speak for 20,000,000
Church Members on Political Questions?" The articles were a bitter
exposé of the Council on Churches and its membership, as well
as that of other church groups working for world peace and were
subsequently reprinted in a book entitled *Pastors, Politicians, Pacifists.*
The volume was eagerly picked up and distributed not only by the
Better Americans but by bodies from E. H. Hunter's Industrial Defense Association and the Massachusetts Public Interest League to
Harry A. Jung's American Vigilant Intelligence Federation of Chicago.
While going through the same gestures of demonstrating the interlocking directorate of the bolshevist-radical-pacifist conspiracy, the work
also leveled broad charges against numerous church organizations
as well as their financial sponsors. The Federal Council particularly,
it charged, was "attempting to control affairs of the civil government."
It was "opposed to every measure of adequate defense for the nation,"
was using its supposed respectability to push for such thoroughly
undesirable ends as unlimited immigration, United States participation
in the World Court and the League of Nations, tariff tinkering, and
fostering subversive youth movements, while maintaining a covert
relationship with the ACLU, which had a clear contact with Moscow.[94]
The book also found great favor among many Legionnaires, irate
that many churches were providing a "religious cloak" behind which
many enemies of the country could hide as conscientious objectors,
or opponents of compulsory military training in the school ROTC
programs.[95] Another target of this study as well as of the general
hierarchy of superpatriots was the Methodist Federation for Social
Service, of which Harry F. Ward, a high official of the "red" ACLU,
was a prominent member.

The churches were disturbed by the charges and hastened to repudiate them. The Department of Research and Education of the
Federal Council authorized a thorough study of patriotic propaganda,
which analyzed the sources from which its attackers derived their
dubious information.[96] The response to the report among clergymen
particularly was one of both outrage and reassurance. The flimsiness
of the charges, the dubiousness of their origins, and the extravagantly
gratuitous way in which they were thrown about seemed to reopen
the way for logical and devastating counterassault. By 1930, Colonel

LeRoy Smith and the Better Americans were devoting far more energy to assailing the ACLU then to raising new charges regarding "crimson clergymen" and the red activities of church leaders.[97]

One final, but by no means insignificant, activity of the superpatriots of the 1920s was the consuming concern with education and educators. Since the youth of America was tender and gullible, every effort had to be made to eliminate the slightest tinge of radicalism, liberalism, and, as the decade progressed, pacifism from the schools. Simultaneously, there was urgent need to indoctrinate the young, new immigrants and even workers in industrial plants with the proper concepts of Americanism.

The red scare had placed pressure on school boards to dismiss teachers who held any but the most conservative and orthodox views. Loyalty oaths had been prevalent, and, by the end of the decade, more than thirty states were insisting upon affirmations of 100 percent Americanism from every public school instructor.[98] The American Defense Society, in a mailing of February 28, 1920, set forth an objective, shared either overtly or tacitly by most of the organizations:

> Purge the public schools of all teachers who are in sympathy with Bolshevism, Socialism, I. W. W.ism, Sovietism, or any other fundamentally un-American theories or doctrines, and make it impossible for disloyal persons to teach in any educational institution or to conduct public lectures or services or to carry on any propaganda of violence against the institutions or government of the United States.

Simultaneously, however, the body urged school authorities to

> Make public buildings available after school hours, and particularly in the evening, for patriotic meetings, to the end that these public buildings and plants be fully used for Americanization work and may serve as community meeting houses for citizens who are opposing radicalism, anarchy and crime.[99]

The DAR, in speaking for itself, also again enunciated commonly held ideas, in stating: "We want no teachers who say there are two sides to every question including even our system of government; who care more for their academic freedom of speech and opinion (so-called) than for their country." In fact, as the president general stated in a speech to the Thirty-second Continental Congress of the DAR in 1923:

> Academic freedom of speech has no place in school, where the youth of our country are taught and their unformed minds are developed.

There are not two sides to loyalty to this country and its flag. . . .
Freedom of speech does not give the right to teach disloyalty to our
children and college youth.[100]

The same concern was reflected regarding the introduction into
the schools of subversive materials. The Better American Federation
of Los Angeles and many similar groups poured energy and money
into attempts to eliminate radical literature from schools and public
libraries. By "radical" the federation meant not only such magazines
as *The Nation* and the *New Republic,* but history textbooks by such
authors as David S. Muzzey, Willis M. West, and Albert Bushnell
Hart, and the writings of such authors as Upton Sinclair, E. A.
Ross, Henry George, and Jane Addams.[101] During the early years
of the decade especially, the body carried on a running battle with
California's state superintendent of public instruction, Will C. Wood,
seeking on one hand to eliminate radical materials but on the other
to flood the classrooms with its own kinds of patriotic propaganda.[102]
The National Civic Federation urged continuing examination by true
patriots of all schoolbooks used with an eye to the immediate elimination of those "seeking to de-Americanize our institutions and sap
the foundations of the Constitution." "Otherwise," wrote Talcott Williams, "liberty and human rights and the rule of the majority will
be wounded to death in the house of their friends the public schools
of America."[103]

For college students, the ideal was one of nonquestioning conformity. Military training was given particularly high priority since
"the enobling spirit engendered by military training and the potent
influence of exact discipline become important auxiliaries to religion
in fostering and completing the moral education of boys. . . . Educators are generally agreed," continued a typical piece in the *National
Republic,* "that respect for authority is our greatest national need."[104]
Similarly, fraternities and sororities were considered salutary. In 1924,
in a public pronouncement, Mrs. Mary Love Collins, president of
the National Pan-Hellenic Congress, assured William J. Burns that,
in his crusade for private assistance to combat radicalism, he could
certainly "look to the Greek world." "Fraternities and sororities are
but a part of the middle class," stated Mrs. Collins." The middle
class is a stable one. You find no radicals therein. Hence, in my
opinion, these school groups are bands of clear thinking young people
already organized to uphold the United States Government in any
crisis."[105]

Individual instances of the effectiveness of the campaign to purge
the schools of un-American teachers, texts, materials, and ideas were
abundant. Howard K. Beale's *Are American Teachers Free?* (1936)

and Bessie L. Pierce's *Citizens' Organizations and the Civic Training
of Youth* (1933) devoted the major part of their coverage to the
1920s.[106]

The positive side of Americanization was equally frenetic and revealing. "Students," stated the Americanism Committee of the American Bar Association, "must not be taught but indoctrinated with
gratitude and pride and love of country. . . . No student should
be graduated from an American school who lacks faith in our government."[107] But the faith had to be one in the omniscience of military
leaders and businessmen, to say nothing of the unassailable correctness
of the Supreme Court and its proper function, the glorification of
property rights.[108] At the same time there was a necessity for allegiance
to abstract symbols. The Constitution, for instance, was regarded
as static, standing as a bastion of protection for the status quo.

Explicitly, the implementation of these positions took many forms.
The National Security League launched a campaign of patriotism
through education, circulating leaflets and pamphlets by the hundreds
of thousands encouraging Constitution worship, promoting an annual
Constitution Day, and working for state laws to require Constitution
instruction in the public schools. Eventually, with assistance from
other sympathetic groups, the League secured passage of such laws
in over thirty states.[109] The organization's position on the proper meaning of free speech was predictable and was stated in a 1919 pamphlet
Our Charter of Liberty: What It Means to Every American: "Free
Speech is for the law-abiding." Controversial views on a variety of
public issues could be expressed, but the prior condition for such
expression was that it be set in an American context. "We must
make everyone think in terms of our own nation," ran the pamphlet,
"and say so everywhere, at every time we have an opportunity to
speak."[110]

Oratorical contests were held in the schools along with contests
for the best story interpretive of the Constitution ("We are looking
for a 'Robinson Crusoe,' 'Alice in Wonderland,' or 'Treasure Island,'
to help perpetuate the Constitution in its integrity").[111] And when
a number of leading newspapers suggested an annual national oratorical contest on the Constitution, the group was enthusiastic. The pros-
pect of a million and a half young people "studying the Constitution
and thereby learning a respect for it," as Thomas J. Norton of the
Cooperating American Citizenship Foundation told the Indiana Bar
Association in 1926, shows "these young people are on the way."[112]

The American Legion was particularly active in Americanization
work. Many Legionnaires agreed with the report of the National
Americanism Commission at the 1923 convention that "to make good

citizens of our children, the most effective study in our schools is HISTORY, our own history." "Our past," ran the report, "despite its occasional mistakes, has been so glorious that its proper study must inspire any child to patriotism and to 'constructive' desire for the future." This led Legionnaires not only to root out of the schools' textbooks teaching "disloyalty" and to sponsor an annual national essay contest (the first subject was "How the American Legion Can Best Serve the Nation," the second, "Why America Should Prohibit all Immigration for Five Years"), but to commission the writing of a proper textbook for school use. The work was to "inspire the children with patriotism, preach on every page a vivid love of America and preserve the old patriotic legends." It was to carry no propaganda and be "non-partisan, giving each state full space and value for the achievements of each, not centralize upon any one section, and give each political party praise for what the party has accomplished." In brief, read the blueprint, "the book is intended to encourage patriotism, strengthen character, stimulate thought and impress the worth of Truth."[113]

The resultant two-volume treatise, *The Story of Our American People,* by Charles F. Horne, with careful acknowledgments to the National Civic Federation, the National Security League, the DAR, Archibald E. Stevenson, R. M. Whitney, and a wide variety of other patriots, was a panegyric of unqualified praise for American achievements, guaranteed to stir the heart of any superpatriot. It was, as C. H. Van Tyne wrote after its publication, "so maudlin and sentimental about 'our' virtues and 'our' superiority to the rest of the world that if universally used 'our' next generation would behave like an insufferable cad toward the rest of the world."[114]

But the authors knew their job, and did not miss an occasion to superimpose the values of their sponsors on the history they were preparing. The text's position on the proper meaning of free speech was that of the various superpatriotic groups. The Alien and Sedition Acts were viewed with admiration since "France and Britain had been sending propagandists here to rouse our people against the national government. These strangers took advantage of our 'free speech' to hurl against our officials every sort of false charge and evil slander." The author explained the proper meaning of free speech and its limits: "The moment anyone threatens to do injury so as to compel others to adopt his views, the moment he uses or urges others to use any form of violence or bribery or compulsion in opposition to our laws, he becomes a criminal. . . . Such limit, is obviously necessary to save us from the constant internal warfare which has ruined other lands."[115]

Others who joined in the call for greater Constitution worship and the uncritical study of history had far more explicit personal ambitions to assuage than the Legion, the DAR, or the Security League. J. S. Eichelberger, the American Constitutional League, and the Sentinels of the Republic were intent that a proper appreciation of the Constitution include the understanding that the child labor amendment would be a socialistic sore on that great document, that the Children's Bureau was equally against its spirit in seeking to "impose international and European standards on every section of the country," and that any type of social welfare program was foreign in origin and a total contradiction both to American institutions and traditions.[116] Any attempt at public regulation was un-American, the Better American Federation maintained in its campaign to flood the California schools with its pamphlet *America Is Calling*, including particularly any form of public ownership of any type of public utility.

The Better Americans failed in their immediate purpose in California, but the public utility campaign succeeded admirably on a national level. This campaign, which eventually resulted in a massive investigation by the Federal Trade Commission in 1928, was launched in 1920 largely at the inspiration of Samuel Insull, who in that year established the Illinois Public Welfare and Public Utility Educational Service. The National Electric Light Association quickly responded and in 1923 began to storm the schools with propaganda against public ownership or regulation.[117] Committees of utility men reviewed textbooks, assailed authors and publishers, sought to force adoption of texts of their own choosing, flooded the schools with pamphlets and paid lecturers, and eventually so overplayed their hands that they brought down the ire of even conservative citizens upon them. This was especially true when the trade commission hearings became a matter of wide public knowledge.[118] By 1928, even the superpatriotic *National Republic* endorsed the National Education Association's resolutions condemning "the policy and efforts of agencies to put propaganda into the schools."[119]

Several organizations devoted considerable energy to Americanization of immigrants. Part of the inspiration for such work stemmed from a distressing vacuum created by the government's withdrawal from this area. The Bureau of Education had been forced as early as 1919 to discontinue the programs it had launched. The overworked and understaffed Bureau of Naturalization remained the government's sole instrument in this field. The National Security League and the Inter-Racial Council, a lineal descendant of the Committee for Immigrants in America and the National Americanization Committee, which had been disbanded at the end of the war, were the two bodies most active in leading the new crusade to "forestall the indoctrination of this important part of the populace with Bolshevistic principles."[120] Both vigorously pursued programs to disseminate to the newcomers the "right ideas about American business, American life, and American opportunity."[121] Both sought to flood the foreign language press with superpatriotic propaganda, pointing out the benefits that would accrue from loyalty and service in the new homeland and the evils that would ensue from improper affiliations and activities. Many sensible and high-minded citizens joined willingly in advancing the more reasonable and constructive aspects of such work. Others, less sensitive, were far more concerned about the wrong ideas that immigrants might absorb. They urged the elimination by any means possible of foreign ideas alien to American traditions and were not reluctant to use red baiting as a device.

In addition, a number of states appropriated funds for Americanization programs. In most cases, such funds were earmarked less for propaganda and more for the purpose of training teachers to instruct the foreign born—in evening, factory, home, and community classes—to extend educational facilities for the training of illiterates and to prepare immigrants for naturalization. Such state programs were far more effective in achieving the desired ends than those of groups such as the American Citizenship Foundation, which aimed its efforts particularly at the Americanization of workers in industrial plants through special study courses and through the use of its own textbooks. Its frank intent was to show industrial managers that "loyal and contented workers mean cheaper costs, that cheaper costs mean larger output, that larger output means greater markets, and that greater markets mean bigger profits." By the mid-1920s, the Citizenship Foundation was attempting to tap businessmen in the Chicago area for $2 million to continue its efforts. Its leadership, however, admitted that it seemed to be getting greater response from its campaigns for exposing and blacklisting labor, liberal, and pacifist leaders than its Americanization work.[122]

The balance sheet on the efforts of the superpatriots to discredit the "free-speech fakers" was, by the eve of the great depression, unimpressive. Given the amount of money spent, the amount of propaganda distributed, and the number of people actively involved, the total credits were pitifully low. Certainly such a campaign had had pronounced influence and impact. But it did as much to produce strong public hostility, even arousing many people from lethargy or other preoccupations, as it did to mobilize substantial and influential portions of the American public against the "free-speech fakers."

The campaigns, even when sincere, were out of harmony with the times.

The patriots were too raucous, especially in a decade when Americans looked to silent Cal Coolidge as the most desirable type of public figure. They were also undiscriminating, never willing to accept any gradations when assailing the enemies of the republic, lumping together all who opposed their versions of proper patriotism as part of a sinister, treasonable conspiracy with no other motives than to destroy the nation. This produced positions which were not only implausible but, even to the average uninformed citizen, foolish and exaggerated. To label the Carnegie Endowment for International Peace or the World Peace Foundation, headed by such prominent, respectable, and conservative Americans as Nicholas Murray Butler and Boston publisher Edwin Ginn, as "pinko" and linked with Moscow was beyond common sense. So was the lumping together with clearly socialistic and crypto-communistic groups bodies such as the PTA, the YMCA, the BPW, and the AAUW. Such charges were clearly irresponsible and far-fetched even though "documented" from impressive looking sources. Further, the patriots found to their frequent shock and embarrassment that the leaders of such bodies would not hold still while the tarbrush was applied. Often among the most respectable and articulate people, both in their own communities and the national community, such citizens launched vigorous counter-assaults and were regularly joined by other sympathetic Americans. Such reaction was often more effective than the charges, couched, as with White's attack on Mrs. Brosseau, in common-sense terms with an added dash of ridicule, or devastatingly destructive, such as Taft's indignant resignation from the National Civic Federation as a gesture of disaffiliation from Ralph Easley's vitriolic assault upon Frederick J. Libby and pacifists generally.[123]

In addition, the dangers of the secret conspiracy that the patriots conjured up never materialized into any concrete damage that the average citizen could observe. Even the Communists in the 1920s were notoriously unsuccessful in advancing their plans and programs, and the worst sins that could be pointed to in assailing the ACLU were that a few political prisoners were freed from jail, the handful of men arrested at Bridgman got a fair trial, and strikers in West Virginia, Pennsylvania, and Passaic were able to keep facilities closed longer than management found comfortable.[124] Probably the most concrete damage that the members of this imagined conspiracy achieved was the success of the pacifists in curtailing armaments, giant naval programs, and compulsory military training in the decade. But with the great majority of the American public pacifist-minded itself, such developments were not out of harmony with national goals and ideals.[125]

The heinous secret conspiracy that the patriots sought to expose was also highly implausible to men of goodwill and common sense. Such a conspiracy theory assumed the ignorance of the common citizen and a general lack of rational direction in public affairs. Only the Communist party, of the many red groups assailed, actually behaved in a remotely conspiratorial fashion (and in the 1920s the Communists themselves were at times brashly open and vocal as to their short- and long-range objectives). The groups that were conspiratorial in keeping their liaisons hidden, their benefactors anonymous, and their actual objectives ambiguous and obtuse were the superpatriot groups themselves.

The gradually revealed insincerity of many of the patriots, to say nothing of their frequent crudeness, grossness, and total lack of fair play, militated against them. Marvin's unscrupulousness, which became evident as time went on, the near illiteracy of Hunter, the autocratic insensitivity of Jung, the charlatan quality of Easley, the arbitrary vindictiveness of Brosseau or Spafford were unattractive. Conversely, the gentle altruism of Jane Addams, the aggressive but good-willed pacifism of Frederick Libby, the dignity and grace of Sherwood Eddy, or the intellectual respectability of Neilson or Wooley or Butler all too often cast the drama as a motley group of frustrated, self-seeking individuals assaulting, with no taste or restraint, decent and responsible citizens. When the prodding and advocacy of violence against the "free-speech fakers" burst out into Ku Klux Klan or American Legion vigilantism, even some extreme patriots were somewhat chagrined.

The arbitrariness of the patriots' means and the dubiousness of their ends were often so transparent as to be self-defeating. Although self-styled advocates of freedom and human individuality, they expected of their minions blind and unquestioned acquiescence. On the other hand, they felt they had unqualified license to assail as misguided dupes anyone who adhered to different views, especially devotees of pacifism, social justice, economic reorganization, and an instrumentalist view of free speech. But they were even more vulnerable in their insistence that they sought to restore good old-fashioned American morality, to revitalize good old-fashioned American principles and sanctions—in other words, to recreate an older, purer America. Most had no desire or intention of living in such a world themselves. They sought a comfortable and influential position in the new materialistic society of the 1920s, with its urban trappings, tinsel glamor, and artificiality. This hypocrisy did not escape criticism. One has only to recall William J. Burns's high-handed tactics as national "snoop" and his later jailing for jury tampering; Fred Marvin's loud public contention that Albert J. Fall was "clean as a hound's tooth . . . and the victim of a gigantic international conspiracy;" the indictment of Harry M. Haldeman, president of the Better America Federation, for usury; or the removal of Jacob S. Cash of the United States Patriotic Society from his office of city marshall for malfeasance in office to see why many Americans agreed with the editor of the Methodist *Social Service Bulletin* when he groaned "such patriots!"[126]

There were more profound miscalculations by the patriots. All too often they gratuitously presumed to speak for a majority of the American people. Such a position was blindly obtuse and was often belied by totally contradictory attitudes. The patriots never sought to consult with the majority and actually operated on the assumption that the average American was so stupid he had to be protected against forces he was innocently ignoring. To a sizable American middle class, pricked at times by the charges of Babbittry or anxious to refute the stereotype of Mencken's "booboisie," such presumptuousness was infuriating, particularly when such individuals then blithely equated Americanism with censorship of books and plays, antievolution laws, the rapid conclusion of the Sacco-Vanzetti case, an extension of the methods of Burns and Palmer, the vigilantism of the Ku Klux Klan, the 100 percentism of the American Legion and the DAR, or the firing of teachers who dared to teach two sides of controversial issues.

The attacks on the clergy and the Federal Council of Churches were felt unwarranted by far more than those who supported such attacks. A sprinkling of liberal clerics existed in the decade at a few theological seminaries and in certain urban congregations, but the average clergyman was a conservative conformist, trained almost exclusively in Biblical, ecclesiastical traditions, with inadequate background for the interpretation of the political, economic, and sociological conditions among which he and his parishioners lived. His selection for the position had normally been carried out by the more affluent and influential businessmen of the congregation, who had a stake in his success and his conservatism. Thus when agitated local laymen set out to carry on an antired campaign, there was often no one plausible or advisable to assault, and only when an occasional Sherwood Eddy came to town or a Frederick Libby visited under the auspices of a religious body was a logical religious target even present. The patriots' overenthusiasm for charging churchmen with excessive leanings toward Godless communism left them in the untenable position of having to prove that the religious leaders of the nation were atheists at heart.

The patriots' approach to education and educators hardly showed greater sensitivity. Placing themselves in the officious position of knowing that what was taught in the schools was subversive on one hand and claiming to be the proper agents to administer the antidote on the other could hardly have been better calculated to produce violent and hostile reaction among the members of a harried and underpaid but generally proud profession. The average educator of the 1920s tended to be highly respectable and highly conservative. But educators, while cautious, were not unwilling to express their reaction through their own channels. Although the National Education Association was carefully detached and the American Association of University Professors was primarily a defense organization, the latter grew in membership and in the courage of its defense of academic freedom as the decade progressed. The American Historical Association, the American Sociological Society, and the more scientific groups denounced the bogus Americanism and misinterpretation of American institutions that the patriots were advocating.[127] Liberal speakers found ready audiences on many campuses, often in defiance of local DAR or American Legion pressure. Significantly, a sizable number of the national debate topics set forth as official during the decade encouraged students to explore all sides of such issues as freedom of expression, censorship, individual rights, and individual self-determination.[128]

The American Legion's flag-waving text found few adoptions and was assailed vigorously in professional journals and mass periodicals. The filiopietistic study of the Constitution that Legionnaires and others encouraged found poor reception in the classroom, either from deliberate disregard of the flag-waving techniques that its purveyors wished followed or from the pure sterility of its approach.[129] The patriots' version of freedom of speech went so strongly against the basic concepts of liberal education that few dedicated academics could resist quoting famous men to refute them. In this regard, the educators found a surprising ally in one segment of the business community: the textbook industry, despite its commercial nature, lined up behind freedom of information and against damaging censorship which stood to hurt both author and company stockholder.[130]

The patriots' pitch could hardly have been better calculated to offend and antagonize the average student of the decade. To the serious student, the attempt at deprivation of intellectual options was infuriating. To the less serious, the rote memorization of sterile ancestor-worship material was boring, impractical, and pedantic.

Flag-waving campaigns of patriotism could not still the natural inclination of intelligent youth to be iconoclastic about hoary truths,
which had little relevance to everyday reality. And while the "youth
movement" in the 1920s, despite the worst apprehensions of Ralph
Easley and R. M. Whitney, gained few adherents among students,
the movement against compulsory military training did. Occasionally
a few enterprising students were even moved to action; for example,
nineteen Yale men in 1927, having prepared a careful analysis of
the poor working conditions in a local neckwear plant, picketed a
New Haven newspaper for refusal to publicize the workers' side
of a local labor dispute protesting such conditions. They were jailed
briefly and censored for their indiscretion, but they had the satisfaction of creating a dramatic case for free speech and stimulating new
controversy about the proper meaning of that concept.[131]

The Americanization work among the immigrants felt the blight
of the insensitivity of the 100 percenters. The superpatriots conducted
themselves in a manner of superiority and self-importance which
deeply hurt the feelings of the immigrants, causing resentment and
antagonism. The constant insistence that Americanism was essential
to pry the immigrant loose from his radical and foreign ideas was
insulting to his integrity and patriotism and abrasively condescending
toward his culture and background. The passage of state laws prohibiting the teaching of the common branches of study in foreign
languages and the efforts to enact legislation prohibiting the use
of the mails to foreign-language publications deeply offended the
more sensitive and led to the growth of hostility to the Americanization
groups.[132]

On a more abstract level, the patriots betrayed themselves and
undermined their cause by their ignorance of American symbolism,
traditions, and values. Few Americans accepted the monolithic,
dithyrambic, my-country-right-or-wrong interpretation of Americanism
which the patriots insisted was the only one possible. For example,
in a 1926 contest, the editors of *The Forum* magazine found at
least seven major categories of definition of Americanism among hundreds of entries, one contestant even suggesting that "Americanism
is the national inferiority complex of the citizens of the United
States."[133]

Remarkably few Americans accepted the American Legion–DAR–
Better American–Daily Data Sheet interpretation of the proper meaning of free speech. The patriots' actual implementation was all too
revealing of what that meaning implied—blacklisting, censorship,
Comstockery, anti-intellectualism, the freedom to libel pacifists, liberals, reformers, and left-wingers, with little opportunity for those

so libeled to respond. Even those who passively accepted the definition and waved off blacklisting with a nonchalant amusement could see little if any validity in active campaigns of suppression in the years of the late 1920s. Life was too good; prosperity was too sweet; success was too easy; utopia was too near. Let the dissidents and the grouches and the pinks and even the reds babble. A country with as great and as optimistic a future as the United States could tolerate such a minor annoyance.

12

The Depression and Repression of Free Speech

Things got worse quickly. The incidents of real violation of free speech grew by leaps and bounds and our office was swamped with a greater number and variety of cases than in all previous years.

Interview with Roger Baldwin,
June 1962

I would say that if anything, restrictions on free speech loosened up in the depression years. The public authorities were certainly watchful and apprehensive, but they also seemed to realize that discontent was growing and spreading and that to clamp the lid on too fast and too hard might well lead to a real explosion. I certainly had no trouble speaking anywhere in those years, which had certainly not been the case earlier.

Interview with Norman Thomas,
June 1962

Even before the stark reality of the depression, subtle but important changes began to alter the free-speech climate. The election of Herbert Hoover brought to the White House a dedicated public servant and a man of eminent common sense and goodwill. Hoover, a Quaker, was not moved by the pacifist-baiting exhortations of the superpatriots nor was he overly sympathetic with their chauvinistic militarism. Early in his administration, he called for a loosening of the restrictive quota system in the National Origins Act of 1924. When he met denunciation for such actions by Fred Marvin, through the columns of the *National Republic,* he responded by making clear that that party organ no longer spoke for Republicanism.[1] DAR criticism resulted in his curtly declining an invitation to address the body's continental congress in 1929.[2] In addition, early in his administration he called for the appointment of a national commission to make extensive studies into the problems of law enforcement in the United States with an eye to greater efficiency.[3] When the commission began its operations in November 1929, one of its prominent consultants was Zechariah Chafee of Harvard Law School, whose book *Freedom of Speech* had been the bête noire of the professional patriots through the decade. Another was attorney Walter Pollak, well known as a regularly retained counsel to the American Civil Liberties Union, whose legal skill and eloquence had had pronounced effect upon the Supreme Court in the Gitlow and Whitney cases of the previous years.[4] Further, it fell early to Hoover to chose a successor to William Howard Taft as chief justice. He named Charles Evans Hughes, one of the leading critics of the blatant refusal to seat the Socialists in the New York legislature in 1920 and to be a voice for sanity during the decade.[5]

Hoover, in his early years as President, was also refreshingly level-headed when it came to confronting a concrete challenge. When communist pickets stormed the White House in December 1929 and were subsequently arrested by Washington police, Hoover promptly ordered their immediate release, stating publicly that the confinement of such malcontents for their unpopular views merely made needless martyrs.[6]

The President's posture had a salutary impact upon the climate of the times. In late 1928 a clergyman in Boonton, New Jersey, frankly challenged Fred Marvin's sources as malicious, contrived, and bogus. A resolute DAR promptly brought suit against him for libeling such a stalwart patriot, and Arthur Garfield Hays of the ACLU entered the case on the clergyman's side. The court subsequently ruled that the charges against Marvin were not libelous because Marvin was highly unreliable.[7] Hays was almost simultaneously instituting a suit for "libel by innuendo" against an American Defense Society pamphlet which contained the usual charge of communism by interlocking directorate of liberal–pacifist–left-wing bodies. Although he lost the case on final appeal, the lower court verdict had awarded him a sizable sum. The net effect was not lost on the super-patriots, as evidenced by the subdued nature of their later activities.[8]

On the other hand, 1929 also saw a major setback for the liberal-pacifist cause when the Supreme Court refused to grant citizenship to Mrs. Rosika Schwimmer on the grounds that she, as an alien pacifist, would not swear to bear arms for her country. Although the majority merely ruled that two sections of the oath clauses of the Naturalization Act of 1906 did require such a display of willingness, thus validating the earlier legislation, the ruling was susceptible to an interpretation by the superpatriots that pacifists generally were not qualified to enjoy the rights of full American citizenship.

But even such a loss had certain redeeming aspects. Oliver Wendell Holmes, Jr., in protesting the ruling, made an eloquent plea for freedom of thought, especially for "the thought we hate."[9] His dissent led those sympathetic with the pacifist cause to start pushing for congressional modification of the legislation under which Mrs. Schwimmer was barred. Further, Mrs. Schwimmer went down fighting. In the months before the ruling she had been persuaded by many friends, especially in the ACLU, to file a massive libel suit against Fred Marvin, who for years had been calling her a German spy and Bolshevik agent. In June 1929, she was awarded damages of $17,000, even though Marvin's American Defense Society attorney, Joseph Cashman, waved the flag and dragged the red herring through the courtroom. The suit cost Marvin his job with the *New York Commercial* and brought an end to the further publication of the Daily Data Sheets. The court's ruling that the Lusk Report was not privileged and could not be regarded as authoritative also undercut the usefulness of one of the professional patriot's chief "official" sources for their allegations and had a further sobering effect upon their raucous and irresponsible propaganda.[10]

Meanwhile the ACLU and aggressive civil libertarians were beginning to have sobering experiences of their own. ACLU leaders had been far too placid and unprotesting in allowing irresponsible extremists to speak in their name or to make pronouncements and commit them without consent. Now responsible ACLU leaders of the center-left, who had waved aside communist activities as irrelevant, began to see the folly in failing to disassociate themselves from such extremists. One strong, head-clearing experience came during the series of southern textile strikes in 1929. The ACLU's role was a logical sequel to West Virginia, Pennsylvania, Passaic, and Colorado. But the earlier "united front" atmosphere was never successfully attained. Communist deceit and cynicism was far more open and early became obvious. The Communists' callous manipulation of ACLU assistance and money produced short-term and long-range reorientation of the ACLU's future course of action.

The outburst of trouble in the southern textile regions was late in coming and shocking to management upon its arrival. The migration of substantial parts of the industry to the South had seemed to management successful in maintaining a high level of productivity with an extremely penurious wage scale and in the effective paternalism that management was able to establish and underwrite through a variety of forms of local control.[11] There was wide general confidence that, unlike the more vociferous and aggressive immigrants of the North, the southern workman was more docile, more American, and, when aroused, more inclined to solve grievances through individual action on an every-man-for-himself basis rather than by turning to any form of effective collective behavior. But in 1927, management callously began to utilize the stretch-out system in which workers were given additional machines to tend without commensurate increases in pay. This proved too much for even cowed southern operatives, and in the early half of 1929 unconnected strikes and vocal worker dissent broke out in Tennessee, North Carolina, and South Carolina.

In the first of these actions, in Elizabethton in east Tennessee, strikers issued a call to the weak and timid AFL United Textile Workers for assistance. The union sent organizers south to recruit members, quickly signing up a substantial number of the workers in both plants of the struck American Glanzstoff Corporation, a German rayon firm. Even such innocuous steps seemed symbolic of grave danger to southern operators. AFL recruiters were kidnapped, taken across the state line, and threatened with death. The governor of Tennessee apparently supported such action by dispatching two companies of the National Guard to the scene upon call from the corporation's president. As George Fort Milton, editor of the *Chattanooga News*, wrote at the time: "Tennessee manufacturers were apprehensive of a labor success at Elizabethton; they looked upon it as an entering wedge for the unionization of the South. . . . There is every reason to believe that the troops went to Elizabethton to quiet this apprehension."[12] Elizabethton was quickly quieted through the intervention of federal mediators and the pleas of AFL officials to accept company terms in order to preserve what few successful gestures at unionization had been achieved.

No such simple result was attained at Gastonia, North Carolina, a town of over a hundred cotton mills, where similar trouble had begun in early April. There the Communists had sent Fred Beal, a recent convert and an effective organizer fresh from the battlefield of New Bedford, Massachusetts, to fill the vacuum left by conservative union indifference. Beal was no intellectual; he was a textile worker and had rallied large numbers behind the Communist-led National Textile Workers Union to fight a potential wage cut by New Bedford employers in 1928.[13] He then had begun secretly recruiting workers into the NTWU at Gastonia's huge Loray Mill, the largest in the world under one roof. When the management of the Rhode Island-based Manville-Jenckes Company learned of that fact, it discharged many such workers. This action triggered a massive walkout and the organization of a strike committee, which promptly set forth terms for return. Management dug in its heels and a stalemate resulted. In the ensuing uproar, "the South and the Communists brought out the worst in each other: both thought of the strike as a symbolic test in which fundamental issues would forever be settled. And meanwhile the strikers faced a reign of terror, and the demand for better wages was almost forgotten."[14]

The Communists promptly set up a strike headquarters in Gastonia as an agency to distribute aid and propaganda to the strikers. They needlessly flaunted the race issue when it was a negligible factor in the situation. They then prepared for a long propaganda campaign. The employers responded in kind, waving the red flag, encouraging in every subtle way possible the early retribution by the "patriotic" elements in the community and obtaining from Governor Max Gardner, himself a mill owner in another part of the state, the commitment of a large detachment of National Guard, ostensibly to maintain law and order in the supercharged atmosphere, but tacitly to protect mill property and bring pressure on the dissident elements.

The Guard's bias became evident on the night of April 18, when a mob of armed and masked men demolished union headquarters, destroyed the workers' commissary, and burned their food. The troops, only 500 feet away, managed to sleep through the action, but arrived just after the vandals had left and seized a group of strikers whom they turned over to the police for destroying their own property. Even local courts would not support such a charge and the workers were released. The action, however, did bring the ACLU into the fray, although primarily in a defense capacity. The body offered rewards for information leading to the arrest and conviction of the raiders.[15] But a grand jury of Gaston County was unable to find enough evidence to indict anyone and the issue was closed. Feeling that the strike was broken, the National Guard was removed. In the face of recalcitrant worker defiance, management of the plant organized the committee of 100, a body of strong-armed, nonstriking workers and strikebreakers, many deputized as sheriffs or policemen, to protect the factory and intimidate the opposition. The management-oriented city council enacted an ordinance prohibiting parades.

In the meantime the local press, clergy, and business and professional organizations had a field day. Gastonia and other southern newspapers were filled with stories and editorials denouncing not only the Communists, but unionization and strikes in general. All of the typical charges against the ACLU were aired with monotonous regularity.[16] On May 13, after ACLU proposals for a "free-speech fight" became known, the Gastonia *Daily Gazette* printed a long piece, citing with approval a statement by Senator William King in the *Congressional Record* that the Bill of Rights guaranteed no federal protection of free speech and that this area was meant to be left strictly to the needs, the responsibility, and the definition of local authorities.[17] On June 7, local authorities, tired of "seditious talk," decided to exercise their prerogatives. Moving on the strikers' tent village at the edge of town, police officials were challenged by private striker guards. A scuffle ensued, shots were fired, and one striker and four officers, including Police Chief O. F. Aderholt, fell wounded, Aderholt fatally. A hoarse cry of retribution promptly reverberated through the community. Eventually seventy-one strikers were arrested and sixteen indicted for murder, including all the principal organizers of the NTWU.

Promptly the communist legal organ, the International Labor Defense, injected itself into the case. The ACLU was reluctant to intervene openly in a legal test, since according to ACLU leaders the issue was solely self-defense, with no clear issue of freedom of conscience or denial of civil liberties.[18] It did agree to finance the ILD, through ACLU funds, an urgent appeal for public support, and a substantial grant from the Roger Baldwin administered Garland Fund. The ACLU rather unwisely agreed to do so on the Communists' terms, allowing the ILD "to represent itself to the United States as conducting the defense and financing the defense."[19] Much of the money raised for the ILD did not go for striker defense but was used in advertising and propaganda for the communist organization locally and throughout the country. This did not prevent the ACLU at the time from affording legal counsel, but that counsel which came was to follow strategy set forth by the ILD.[20]

Even under such handicaps legal proceedings initially went well. A change of venue was granted. The judge assigned to the case in Charlotte, where the trial was moved, attempted from the first to conduct a respectable and responsible proceeding. He rejected the prosecution's attempt to introduce the political, religious, and economic commitments of the plaintiffs as evidence of their guilt. Fireworks were inevitable and a mistrial ensued, to the secret pleasure of both the Communists and their antagonists. The latter, upon learning that five of the jurors would have voted for acquittal, covertly encouraged a reign of terror and vigilantism in Gaston County which did not end until numerous strikers had been threatened, assaulted, and beaten, and Mrs. Ella May Wiggins, the strikers' "minstrel" who wrote a number of ballads about this strike, was shot and killed. This brought wide condemnation from the North and from large segments of the responsible South.[21]

Encouraged, the ACLU came more into the open. It called upon Governor Gardner for action against the terrorists and offered a reward for information leading to the conviction of the murderers of Mrs. Wiggins.[22] The ACLU even employed an investigator to run down clues and witnesses. But despite the fact that the killing had taken place in broad daylight in the presence of more than fifty people, the five Loray employees eventually charged with the crime were acquitted.

Not so the alleged killers of Chief Aderholt. In the first trial the flamboyant prosecutor, John G. Carpenter, had a black-shrouded, life-sized, bloodstained dummy of Aderholt suddenly wheeled into the courtroom. One juror became hysterical, thus necessitating a new trial. Then Carpenter succeeded in introducing evidence of the defendants' beliefs. This prodded the ACLU to support the defendants openly, though vainly. In October a jury out only forty-five minutes convicted all of them. Carpenter's courtroom histrionics (praying, lying on the floor, clasping the widow's hand, and promising that faith would be kept with the dead) were successful with the jury, but were roundly condemned by southern newspapers, which deplored such tactics as a parody on responsible southern justice. The ACLU thus met little hostility when it promptly provided bail and retained former Senator Thomas W. Hardwick of Georgia as counsel in a futile appeal to the North Carolina supreme court. In the meantime the convicted Communists visited Russia, the "workers' paradise," where the Soviets paraded them about as proletarian martyrs of capitalist injustice. When word came that their appeal had failed, all remained in Russia, forfeiting a sizable chunk of the bail raised by the Garland Fund and ACLU.[23]

The outcome of the episode was painfully unrewarding. The Communists failed miserably in another attempt to bring organization to helpless and beleaguered workers and failed also in the propaganda campaign to win the working class to their cause. The ruthlessness of their tactics stood out far too clearly, as did the complete lack of concern for the individual. So also did the fact that the ability to pin "red" charges on a legitimate campaign against legitimate grievances was the kiss of death.

The ACLU in turn got a bitter lesson in the futility of further cooperation with the Communists. It was particularly irate about the perfidy involved in the bail jumping. Such action strengthened the position of the courts, already inclined to set bail for radicals at excessively high figures, decreased the amount available for future emergencies, and caused radical sympathizers to hesitate before coming to the rescue in similar cases. When it became clear that the Communists would assume no responsibility for repaying such a loss, the body announced that it would issue no further bail bonds to members of the Communist party.[24] The workers, large numbers of whom were now discharged, learned the futility of action that was not underwritten in advance with firm prior guarantees of personal protection in case honest demands could not be fully met.

The victory of the employers was not as sweet as they might have desired, especially as criticism of their ruthless tactics grew. This ruthlessness was especially obvious when one looked compositely at the entire set of strikes and added the concluding one at Marion, South Carolina, for full perspective.

Following Gastonia, southern employers frequently protested that they had no argument with unionization, but merely opposed communism. When, however, the AFL launched a vigorous organizational campaign shortly thereafter, employer response in Marion hardly complemented such allegations. A labor injunction was used immediately to curtail an AFL-organized walkout in local textile mills there, and strikebreakers were imported. When strikers continued to picket plants, police and company guards monitored them constantly, with tension mounting so high that eventually violence broke out. On the morning of October 2, 1929, sheriffs and deputies stationed in a plant of the Marion Manufacturing Company fired into a group of pickets, killing six and wounding twenty-four; the pickets were promptly arrested and charged with riot and insurrection because of their refusal to obey the sheriffs' order to disperse.[25] Eight deputy sheriffs were eventually tried. The ACLU, possibly hoping to recoup some of its tarnished reputation from Gastonia, took the initiative in financing a private prosecution. Defended by Clyde Hoey, brother-in-law of Governor Gardner, the men pleaded self-defense; all were acquitted. In separate actions a number of the strikers indicted for insurrection were convicted and sentenced to long terms. The ACLU, in an attempt to keep faith with the workers, promptly announced that it would aid the families of the men killed and wounded to file civil suits for damages against the mills and officials. All such action seemed of little lasting importance, since by that time the strike had been broken. However, the Marion developments certainly gave lie to the operators' pious talk of supporting conservative and reasonable unionism and being only hostile to the Communists.[26]

The net results of the southern textile uprisings seemed discouraging to workers and reformers, but there were signs of future hope. Roger Baldwin was fond of saying that civil liberties might not win in an immediate fight, but in the long run it never lost when an issue was dramatized. The revolt of the "lint-heads" brought the attention of sensitive members of an affluent and self-satisfied nation to a disgraceful human situation. Large elements of the liberal clergy were moved as much by Gastonia as by any other labor outbreak in the 1920s. The liberal press was full of extensive analysis of the situation. Considerable maturity was also evidenced in the public reaction to the Communists. In sharp contrast to Passaic, where all action had been roundly condemned as evil because of the Communists' role, talk now grew of the necessity for concrete and constructive action to relieve the hopelessness that gave communism such an alarming foothold. And as time passed, well over a dozen monographs appeared on various aspects of the strikes, to say nothing of a half dozen novels and at least fifteen graduate dissertations, the majority at southern universities. The employers, never properly tried in southern courts, were thus tried literarily and academically with few favorable verdicts rendered.[27]

Employers learned to their surprise and distress that their supposedly individualistic workers were not docile, subservient, and manipulatable dregs of humanity who would submit to any form of exploitation. The labor movement was beaten back, but its slight foothold in southern industry was not broken. Rather, the crushed strikes now stood out "as a sort of Boston Massacre—the point at which something which had been essentially unthinkable before suddenly began to be more thinkable. . . . Hereafter, the notion of labor unionism would distinctly be more present to the mind of Southern workers."[28] Such maturing represented a moderate move which asked reasonable reform and progress from responsible conservatives. The way was left open for gradual, grudging, but by no means insignificant accommodations, expedited when the National Industrial Recovery Act of 1933 provided authority with its Code of Fair Competition for the cotton textile industry. Significantly, the resulting employer-drawn code provided for a maximum forty-hour week for workers in both South and North, with a minimum weekly wage of twelve dollars. Child labor was banned, and a section headed "Collective Bargaining Rights" prohibited interference, restraint, or coercion to prevent unionization or discrimination against union members. When a liberal reporter visited the South in 1933, he found that the Loray Mill in Gastonia had been one of the first to eliminate child labor and establish model conditions.[29]

But if the discrediting of the raucous and irresponsible superpatriots on the far right and the Communists on the far left had the effect of changing the attitudes and tactics of the moderate activist elements, so also did the deepening depression, with mounting unemployment and human suffering, and the loss of fortunes, businesses, bank accounts, and general financial stability. The major assumptions of those who had attacked the "free-speech fakers" were that the American economy was basically sound, that business leadership was wise, stable, and responsible, and that critics were not only unjustified but misguided and malicious in their constant assaults upon the system. The depression undercut many of the factors upon which such assumptions rested. The glories of the great business civilization had proven fragile. Business leadership was now seen to have been short-sighted and faulty and was even regarded by many as misguided and callously self-seeking. The financial collapse of great tycoons, such as Samuel Insull, who had been one of the chief and open supporters of the superpatriots, merely footnoted such an argument. The equalizing factors produced by common poverty, adversity, and suffering cleared away many barriers which had formerly insulated groups in positions of extreme wealth or extreme poverty. It made open dialogue more common.

Such contact was also salutary in removing many previous stereotypes stemming from lack of such contact. It was far easier for the means to come together when the stakes were lower—when it was not so much a battle of haves versus have-nots as of one type of have-nots versus another. There was a natural tendency in the depression years to "rub it in" to the businessmen for creating the hard times. But the concrete motivation of the deprived classes for hating such people, that is, their wealth and their abuse of it, was frequently no longer present. Scapegoating hardly offered constructive cures for the nation's ills.

The same reaction was certainly a factor in the growing rejection of the claims of the Marvins and Jungs on one hand and the Communists on the other. All muddied the waters at a time when national cooperation was essential. The depression would not be solved if the responsible elements encouraged irresponsible charges by the extremists. The results were salutary. The center gradually disassociated itself from the ideological tar smearing of churchmen, pacifists, liberals, honest Socialists, and even college professors on one hand and became far more realistic about the Communists on the other.[30]

The depression afforded other bases for eliminating much prior misunderstanding and hostility between responsible right and left. With the world of normalcy in a shambles, former liberal critics ceased to seem irresponsible disruptionists and took on the color

of concerned and foresightful prophets. Conversely, such critics, now
with a larger responsible and concerned audience, were far less shrill.
With the economy collapsing, a new need for the discussion of alterna-
tives was clearly present. To silence even the purveyor of the wildest
scheme made little sense, since the rulers of the country seemed
to have few plausible and constructive panaceas. Theorists on the
campuses gained a new status, not so much because of the answers
they afforded, but because the crisis upgraded the importance of
their skills in analyzing the evils so clearly plaguing the nation.

Such a growing tolerance was not necessarily reflected at the everyday procedural level. With social turmoil and upheaval, unemployment parades, and demonstrations and hunger marches taking place
with disturbing regularity, restriction grew sharply. Employers who
no longer saw any need for expending large amounts from tight
budgets on the Marvins and upon propaganda generally felt very
pressingly the need for supporting direct repression of strikers in
a plant, pickets around it, or public marchers capable of arousing
hostility which might result in destruction of property. Money was
turned to company guards, arms, and private police. More significantly, extra effort was made to encourage local police and law enforcement officials to use every form of local regulation from vagrancy
laws to laws against disturbing the peace to insurrection statutes
and criminal-syndicalism and sedition laws, to cut off dangerous protest before it had an opportunity to gain momentum and erupt into
direct action.[21] Such activity, in most cases premature and seldom
really warranted, was often understandable, particularly given the
Communists' great penchant for painting the smallest manifestation
of local protest as the first snowballing step in the coming revolution
and exploiting every grievance in the hopes of discrediting the capitalist system.

The response of civil libertarians was equally significant. With
tolerance growing, they diverted their energies away from pushing
the free-speech issue as a basis for major social reorganization. They
concentrated their efforts in direct defense work, protecting individuals whose civil rights had clearly been violated by overzealous local
police or local courts, or by strong-arm methods utilized by nervous
employers. The result for the ACLU was remarkable. As it ceased
to project the image of a disruptionist, trouble-making, Communist-
dominated body and became an agency for human relief at a time
in which such relief was a crying need, its membership grew sharply,
its income rose, further local affiliates began to be planned, and
its business multiplied astronomically. The press it received became
increasingly favorable, with not only liberal magazines but moderate

newspapers taking a long second look and deciding that the body served a real function, especially in a period of public tension.[32]

This hardly suggests that warm cooperation developed between businessmen and civil libertarian activists. All too often the cases the ACLU defended had been brought on directly by business repression. It does suggest that the responsible elements within each spectrum of opinion were working to minimize the extreme disruption of depression years and were seeking to avoid the hysterical misunderstanding that had prevented even formal dialogue a few years earlier.

Several major events of the depression years and their resultant outcome provide useful case studies of the new attitudes. The loss of conservative support did not lead the superpatriots to alter their modes of behavior. The American Legion and the DAR intensified their war on pacifists, "free-speech fakers," and liberals. One concrete manifestation was the Fish Committee hearings of 1930. Equally revealing was the new public response to their efforts.

Since the mid-1920s, superpatriots had exploited every opportunity to draw the federal government back into the red-hunting business. The depression now afforded a new excuse. If the collapse of the national economy could be blamed upon the Communists and those who had attacked normalcy, the government actions that such patriots favored might be achieved. These included deporting all alien radicals, tightening the immigration laws, recreating a radical bureau of the Justice Department, closing the mails to all communist publications, a federal peacetime sedition law, and an end to all relations with the Soviet Union. Basic to the success of such a move would be the recreation of the atmosphere of public apprehension and antired hysteria of the immediate postwar period. In the free-speech area this meant reviving most of the repressionist arguments and discrediting the libertarian position.

The campaign began early. At its annual convention in 1929, the American Legion demanded a federal investigation of pacifists, Communists and "parlor pinks."[33] At the same time, Ralph Easley induced Elihu Root to call publicly for a special federal police force to combat the reds.[34] Congressman Hamilton Fish of New York, one of the founders and heroes of the Legion, called for a massive investigation of Communist activities in the House of Representatives in 1930 and urged creation of a special committee to take testimony. Fish, in assuming the chairmanship of the committee, implied openly that economic troubles would disappear when the Communists were all driven from the United States. This simple and direct approach appealed instantly to many frightened and depression-ridden people who hastened to appear before the committee with reports ranging from responsible to fantastic allegations of communist deceit and treachery.

The committee heard many such people and even reluctantly took testimony from such hostile critics as Roger Baldwin, who claimed to its face that its inquiry was not genuine "in that you have prejudged the evidence by announcing your remedies before you heard the testimony."[35] It seemed to have the greatest empathy for the professional and superpatriot organizations and their representatives. Its hearings were dominated by such individuals as Harry Jung; E. H. Hunter; Matthew Woll; Walter S. Steele, editor of Marvin's outlet, the *National Republic;* Francis Ralston Welch, a Philadelphia businessman and standard source of blacklist and Spider Web Chart information; and Captain Will F. Hynes of the Los Angeles police force, head of that city's "red squad," which regularly railroaded radicals from the city and maintained proper open-shop conditions for Los Angeles employers. Representatives of the DAR, the American Legion, the National Security League, the American Vigilant Intelligence Federation, and the Better America Federation were given every opportunity to fill the committee's public hearings with irresponsible charges against organizations from the ACLU to the Federal Council of Churches. When published, the committee's records rivaled the Lusk Report of ten years earlier in size and irresponsibility.

Gaily anticipating the publication of the committee's report and eagerly hoping to speed its adoption, representatives of many of the superpatriot bodies held a "Deport the Reds" rally in Carnegie Hall in early January 1931. They were a bit taken back to hear a cautious Fish warn that communist propaganda fed on human suffering and discontent, which also had to be attacked and removed from the nation. But the bejewelled audience cheered Martin Littleton, pamphleteer for the American Defense Society, when he called not only for deportation of alien radicals but for strong federal action to restore sense and loyalty to those natives who had strayed from the true patriotic way.[36]

The depression was not a propitious time for drawing the federal government into a campaign against dissenters. Popular hostility to the committee burst forth with vehemence when its findings and recommendations were announced in late January. The committee's general assumption that elimination of communist propaganda was one of the most serious challenges facing the nation was sharply repudiated not only by liberals but by large segments of conservative opinion as well. As an editorial in the *Milwaukee Leader* stated: "If the exploring expedition wants to do our country a real service it will stop running down the 'agitators' and run down our national problems instead."[37] The *New York Evening Post* regretted that the investigation of such serious subjects as domestic radicalism and its influence had been put into the hands of "our most muddle-headed statesman, Mr. Hamilton Fish, Jr., of New York" and called the committee's fourteen recommendations "mostly un-American, and mostly rather cowardly."[38] The *New York World* opined that "the whole maneuver had benefitted the communists" and pointed out that they were delighted to have Fish rate their "piddling strength, influence, and general capacity for mischief so highly."[39] This sentiment was repeated by Professor Jerome Davis of Yale, who charged in a nationwide radio address, sponsored and later reprinted and distributed by the ACLU, that Fish had "unwittingly become the master communist press agent in this country" and that the recommendations of the committee would be a "severe blow at free speech."[40]

The ACLU and free speech both fared well as a result of the committee's abrasive tactics and claims. One of the committee members, conservative Republican Congressman John E. Nelson of Maine, had provided an initial rallying point in refusing to sign the committee's report. "There was no cause for hysteria on the question of communism," Nelson stated. "It could best be met with economic and social justice for American workers."[41] He also told a reporter: "I did not feel that American democracy should attempt to defend itself by abandoning the institutions of a democracy, or that the situation was serious enough to warrant a major operation on our Bill of Rights."[42] Eight prominent liberals, acting in behalf of the ACLU, and including such figures as John Dewey, Zechariah Chafee, Jr., Reverend John A. Ryan, Rabbi Stephen A. Wise, and Professor Alexander Meiklejohn, sent a letter to a list of citizens urging them to express their opposition to the committee's proposals on the grounds that they struck "so clearly at the right of freedom of speech, press, and assemblage that they cannot, in our judgment, be too strongly condemned."[43] The free-speech factor, so dramatized, was picked up and elaborated upon in newspaper editorials across the country, with many also repudiating the committee's categorical charge that the ACLU was nothing but a Communist front whose belief in free speech was insincere and clearly hypocritical.[44] "It is difficult to see how anyone could be farther from the truth than the author of this statement," ran an editorial in the *Brooklyn Standard Union*. "When a Committee brings in a report tainted as is the Fish Committee Report, its findings are suspect and its recommendations have little weight."[45] In addition, the point was frequently made that protecting American liberty by setting up a federal spy system and encouraging constant federal intervention in the lives of private citizens was a contradiction in terms. As the *Portland* (Maine) *News* warned: "if the Red Baiters have their way, the state will be everything and the individual nothing."[46]

But the coup de grace for American Legionnaire Fish came in May 1931. That body's Americanism committee, through which he had tried to railroad prior commitment to the committee's proposals, recommended to national leadership that it withhold any endorsement and recommended to Congress that the report and its proposals be quickly tabled. Taking the position that there was adequate legislation on the books for handling the communist menace, the body merely encouraged its more rigorous enforcement.[47] Such action hardly created the type of momentum necessary for formal congressional approval. Congressman Martin Dies from Texas was able to push the deportation provisions of the measure through the House. But the rest of the proposals met flat rejection and the Senate negated Dies's efforts.

The aloofness of business leaders throughout the entire struggle was significant. They could see little utility in its support. As hardheaded realists, they saw clearly the real irrelevancy of its proposed remedies to the nation's economic necessities.[48]

Depression activities at the operational level presented a totally different picture. New York City was not only the center of explosive public demonstrations, it was also the headquarters of communist efforts. Further, the city in the early depression years was under the loose and good-natured control of "Gentleman" Jimmy Walker. In late 1928, Mayor Walker named as police commissioner the general manager of John Wanamaker's department store, Grover Whalen. Whalen promptly set up a special intelligence squad of plainclothesmen, whose responsibility was to infiltrate communist organizations and immediately report potential law infractions.[49] The result was that the police were on hand with billy clubs ready at the slightest public disturbance, and as early as July 1929, civil libertarians were publicly condemning Whalen as a bully with no sensitivity for civil liberties or freedom of expression.[50]

The Communists quickly saw the situation as an ideal one in which to foment unpopular action and thus gain martyrdom as victims of capitalist tyranny. They took every occasion to provoke violent police response, quickly seeking support of civil libertarians in their efforts to dramatize their martyrdom. Mayor Walker kept his head admirably and tried to establish working ground rules, proclaiming the virtue of frank freedom of expression and public protest but drawing a line between it and malicious disturbing of the peace and the spreading of irresponsible propaganda in a deliberate attempt to trigger violence. The distinction was endorsed by the local press as one that respected responsible ordered liberty.[51] Whalen promptly agreed to uphold it, with tear gas if necessary. Learning of a massive unemployment demonstration planned for City Hall Plaza in early March 1931, he informed Communist leaders William Z. Foster, Robert Minor, and Israel Amter that a permit was required for such a public meeting. The Communists' reaction was one of complete defiance, and although the rally was moved to Union Square, where it denounced police brutality and capitalist tyranny, there was no overt action to break it up until the Communist leaders proposed a march on City Hall in cynical defiance of Whalen and Walker. Whalen at this point ordered the police to move in with no holds barred. Foster, Minor, and Amter were arrested, jailed, and held on high bail for breaking the city's antiparade ordinance, normally a violation that carried a small fine.[52]

Whalen, sensing his power, offered publicly to make available to local employers a police department blacklist of known local Communists who deserved to be discharged. The ACLU promptly sought an injunction to prevent Whalen's proposed action and denounced his encouragement of police brutality. Its leaders approached the New York Bar Association, pointing to his poor record as one in defiance of the elementary principles of common justice and urging its parallel condemnation. Eighteen members of the Columbia University Law School faculty signed a protest against Whalen's blacklisting proposal. Charles A. Beard and a number of other local liberal leaders, including Norman Thomas, Rexford G. Tugwell, John Dewey, and Max Lerner, signed a strongly worded ninety-six-man petition calling for Whalen's immediate ouster. Whalen's principal public defense came from a handful of superpatriotic army officers and from Fred Marvin, currently seeking to regain his public status through a newly created superpatriotic body to be known as the New York City Chamber of Commerce.[53]

Whalen casually shrugged off all negative criticism, and the Communists continued to bait and taunt him with hunger marches, May Day demonstrations, and Union Square rallies, inevitably calling upon the ACLU for legal support when the invited crackdown came and then refusing to go into capitalist courts to testify when one of their alleged victims was being tried. On May 19, one hundred nationally prominent literary figures, including H. L. Mencken, Sherwood Anderson, Edmund Wilson, John Dos Passos, and Carl Van Doren, issued a strong public statement calling for an end to arrests for the expression of opinions. Whether this or the mounting pressure from all sides was responsible, a disgruntled Whalen submitted his resignation the following day and returned to his department store post, unfortunately seeking public vindication by attempting to broadcast through the Fish Committee widespread proof of the aggravated and dangerous activities of the Communists in this country as contained in revealing secret documents he had obtained from highly questionable former Czarist agents. Even the Fish Committee would not accept such questionable information, and Whalen's public image was only resuscitated when he later emerged as New York's official morning-coated, white-boutonniered greeter and arranger of ticker-tape parades and public ceremonies.[54]

The episode focused further attention upon the national problem of police brutality and the police as arbitrary judges of the extent of permissible public expression and protest. The subject was one which the ACLU had attempted to analyze on two different occasions in the 1920s and which the Wickersham Commission was currently exploring. Its report, issued in 1931, coincided with the less ambitious ones of the ACLU.[55] It confirmed a wide range of variation, with only a few pockets of law enforcement forces in the country that were conscious of civil liberties. These were found in cities with a great internal heterogeneity of cultural makeup and wide internal division of social and political forces whose proper balance was essential to domestic peace and cooperation. As R. L. Duffus wrote in a general summary article at the time: "The more a city is divided, the more tolerant are its diverse elements. United, they fall into intolerance; divided they stand anything. The most excitable towns are those with a dominant, well-fixed middle class, like Los Angeles, or a solid intolerant majority, like Boston."[56] The publication of such findings confirmed the growing concern of responsible middle elements about needless repression and their willingness to speak out against those who induced it, whether cynical Communists or heavy-handed law enforcement officials.

A dramatic example of this concern was the passage of the Norris-LaGuardia Act in February 1932, outlawing the labor injunction and seeking to make management-labor accommodation reasonable. The ACLU had long been an open and vigorous critic of the labor injunction, which represented to its leaders a flat denial of freedom of expression.[57] The injunction reflected the values of the 1920s. Its operation demonstrated the effectiveness of business's desires for informal controls and, at the same time, lack of responsibility for the conditions that led to those controls. The application of the injunction proceeded on the assumption that property should be protected at all costs from any type of infringement, while defense against its abuse was strictly the responsibility of the injured individual. The result was that business was able to operate freely without fear of restrictive public regulation. Those who suffered were free to organize and protest only to the extent to which local law enforcement officials were willing to tolerate such protest. The result "made violence inevitable. Even the techniques of strike conduct—mass picketing, strikebreaking, and strike guards—were a hazard to the preservation of peace. No other advanced nation in the world conducted its industrial relations with such defiance of the criminal law. In 1926, for example, the lowest strike year of record in the United States and the highest for Britain, culminating in the general strike, the American display of violence far exceeded the British."[58]

Responsible voices throughout the decade had publicly deplored the situation and urged a more equitable application of the law to ease tension between management and labor. It was not until depression undercut business's arrogance that there were substantial steps toward the goal. Senator George Wharton Pepper of Pennsylvania, who in his apprehension over the growing bitterness of organized labor had conducted a personal survey of injunctions, reported with concern in 1924:

> The injunction orders have become more and more comprehensive in their provisions until they culminate in the Shopmen's Injunction Order . . . during the shopmen's strike in 1922 nearly every one of the two hundred and sixty-one "Class I" railroads and a number of shortline railroads applied for injunctions in the various federal courts. No applications were denied. In all nearly three hundred were issued. Naturally enough . . . there have been bitter protests from the ranks of labor. To the striker it seems like tyranny to find such vast power exercised—not by a jury of one's neighbors—but by a single official who is not elected but appointed, and that for life, and whose commission comes from a distant and little understood source.[59]

Similarly, Newton D. Baker warned that judges invited disrespect if justice became too obviously one-sided. Republican Senators William E. Borah and George Norris spoke frequently upon the necessity for equal justice for both the workingman and the business community. In November 1928, Congressman Fiorello LaGuardia told a session of the American Academy of Political and Social Science that the time was near when the power of granting injunctions in all labor cases would be taken from the courts. "If the future of our republic depends upon the suppression of free speech," LaGuardia maintained, "there is no future."[60]

The mounting pressure reached the halls of Congress. In late 1927, Senator Henrik Shipstead of Minnesota introduced an anti-injunction bill. A subcommittee of the Senate Judiciary Committee, with Norris as its chairman, began a public assault upon government by injunction. Prominent among those who testified at length were William Green, president of the AFL, Andrew Furuseth, president of the International Seamen's Union, and Morris Ernst, counsel for the ACLU.[61] But although both party platforms in 1928 expressed concern that injunctions in labor disputes had been abused, the Shipstead bill languished and failed.

By 1930, a substitute measure written by Norris began gathering support from widely divergent sources. That year the ACLU, seeking to publicize the issue and involve more public figures in it, created a National Committee on Labor Injunctions at the suggestion of Donald Richberg and Alexander Fleischer, a Philadelphia civil libertarian. The committee, composed of 400 people from all parts of the country, was headed by a former federal judge, Charles F. Amidon, whose eloquent opinion in the Brosseau case had been one of the few rallying points for anti-injunction sentiment during the decade. The committee set out to educate the public on the necessity for Norris's amended bill and to draw congressional support behind it. It also framed a model anti-injunction bill for the states and solicited support for such a measure in various legislatures.[62]

The AFL had shrunk from pushing an aggressive program for outlawing the injunction during the 1920s and had flatly rejected cooperation on any issue with the ACLU. It now joined that body in supporting such legislation at both the federal and state level. The Federal Council of Churches publicly urged curtailment of the injunction, especially in cases of peaceful picketing. James W. Gerard, chairman of the Commission on Industrial Inquiry of Ralph Easley's National Civic Federation, while certainly not linking hands with ACLU leaders, independently but publicly espoused similar goals in the name of that body. Other superpatriots, however, denounced the entire movement as communist-inspired and a vicious assault upon capital. The Communists were equally uncooperative, rejecting legislative relief as a devious capitalist plot and asking mass violation of injunctions as the only method of preventing their being issued.[63]

Enactment by Congress of the Norris-LaGuardia Act in March 1932 and the approval by President Hoover represented a concrete achievement of responsible center-oriented cooperation. Those results were especially gratifying to ACLU leaders, since the terms of the measure wrote into federal law many of the concrete objectives for which the body had been working and agitating for the previous dozen years. The key section, Section Four, read:

> No court of the United States shall have jurisdiction to issue any restraining order or temporary or permanent injunction in any case involving or growing out of any labor dispute to prohibit any person or persons participating or interested in such dispute from doing, . . . any of the following acts: . . . Giving publicity to the existence of, or the facts involved in, any labor dispute, whether by advertising, speaking, patrolling, or any other method not accompanied by force or violence; assembling peaceably to promote an interest in a labor dispute; advising or notifying any person of an intention to do any of the acts heretofore specified; agreeing with other persons to do or not to do any of the acts heretofore specified; and advising, urging, or otherwise causing or inducing without fraud or violence the acts heretofore specified.[64]

Coupled with the enactment of a number of state statutes, the measure was a major step forward in undercutting the legal basis for the implementation, at least by courts, of local controls to silence various forms of freedom of expression of working class people and their champions.[65] It injected the federal government between the citizen and a number of forms of overt legal coercion in such a way as to give him access to concrete relief when he felt his personal rights were clearly being abridged. It was a harbinger of future assault upon other forms of local control.

The measure was not self-implementing. Attorney General William D. Mitchell immediately announced that such a "controversial" law would have to await judicial clarification before executive enforcement could proceed categorically.[66] Civil libertarians were prepared to continue direct challenge to local restrictions in the interim. So were the Communists. Union leaders were more anxious than ever to evoke social and economic reorganization as a means for making Bill of Rights guarantees more meaningful. The Communists were growing more cynical and opportunistic as they became convinced that internal revolution was imminent. An increasingly sharper dichotomy developed over the proper meaning of free speech between the two groups.

The national headline-producing struggle in Harlan County, Kentucky, in 1931 and 1932 drove the wedge deeper and proved to be one of the last "united front" free-speech fights in which civil libertarians challenged entrenched local controls through direct intervention and confrontation.[67] Harlan County and its neighboring counties of Bell, Knox, Hazard, and Breathitt were in the heart of the southern soft coal region. With coal a sick industry and declining more rapidly as depression conditions intensified, they were the centers of acute depression and human exploitation. Management of the absentee-owned mines retrenched by reduction of wages and employment. The miners had been bypassed by union organizers, because of sheer timidity. The United Mine Workers and the IWW began to take a few fleeting and generally futile steps in late 1930 and early 1931. They were encouraged by clear outbursts of local sentiment, with miners maintaining openly that they might as well "strike while we starve as work while we starve."[68] The results were unsatisfactory. Harrassed by local officials, UMW representatives led a number of miners out on strike and made some attempts at mass recruitment, only to lose their nerve and depart after violence erupted, leaving the workers high and dry with neither jobs nor union support.

With discontent seething, Communist organizers from the National Miners Union promptly moved in. The Communists were surprisingly successful at the outset because they were militant, and they were the one group taking any aggressive action ostensibly to relieve human suffering. In the months following the first protest walkout in February, miners, urged on by Communist organizers, went from mine to mine in Harlan County holding "speak-ins" at which other miners were urged to join the movement. The fact that communism was present in any form in Kentucky was enough to place the red stigma upon every miner and every action he took and to rouse the ire of local leaders from law enforcement officials through businessmen, religious leaders, newspaper editors, and willing vigilantes, who quickly called for direct action. The early result was a complete breakdown in communication between ownership and management on one side and striking workers with legitimate complaints on the other. The Communists took every opportunity to intensify such tension and misunderstanding. Harlan County quickly became a powder keg.[69]

In early May at Evarts, Kentucky, a gun battle ensued with 3 deputies and 1 miner killed and a number injured. Wholesale indictments for murder and conspiracy to murder were quickly brought against the miners. Governor Flem D. Sampson promptly ordered 325 National Guardsmen in, complete with an armored tank, to begin making arrests. Eventually 29 men were indicted for the killing of the 3 deputies and for the interesting and novel additional charge of "banding and confederating," an action punishable under Kentucky's 1920 criminal-syndicalism law.[70] Even though a number of key strike leaders were among those indicted, owner-inspired violence against the miners continued. On June 14, the ACLU protested in a futile telegram to Governor Sampson against the continued wanton and unpunished killing of union miners by company guards.[71] Three days later the body sent a young Union Theological Seminary student, Arnold Johnson, to the region as an observer.

The reaction of local authorities was typified very clearly by Judge David Crockett Jones, in whose court the murder indictments were to be tried. Jones made clear prior to trial that no "red" had any right "to look to this court or to any other court in the country for justice."[72] He further stated that Harlan County did not need "anyone from Russia or any warped twisted individuals from New York to tell us how to run our government."[73] Local officials implemented the sentiment by arresting Arnold Johnson in early August for criminal syndicalism for possessing an ACLU pamphlet entitled *What Do You Mean—Free Speech?* Simultaneously, Mrs. Jesse Wakefield, an agent for the International Labor Defense, was also jailed on the same charge. Both were summarily convicted and given long sentences. But both were quickly offered complete freedom if they would leave the region promptly and permanently.[74]

Further extensive arrests for criminal syndicalism enabled the ACLU to raise the freedom of expression question and condemn widely what its leaders now legitimately claimed to be the flagrant violation of both the rights of workers and American citizens seeking to aid them.[75] The Communists moved quickly to seize this weapon for themselves and exploit it fully for their own purposes. In the autumn of 1931, at the prodding of the International Labor Defense, author Theodore Dreiser, not yet a Communist but moving rapidly in that direction, sent out a solicitation to a number of leading American liberals to join him in a private investigation of conditions in Kentucky. His telegram read "Free Speech Free Assembly United States Constitution Suspended."[76] His response was nil. He then set out with a handful of members of the recently formed National Committee for the Defense of Political Prisoners to hold on-the-spot investigations of local conditions. Dreiser quickly found himself arrested for violating a local morals statute. He managed to beat this charge, but after leaving the area to return to New York to compile a formal record of his findings, he and nine others of the investigating writers and Communists were indicted for criminal syndicalism. Governor Franklin D. Roosevelt announced that no extradition would be granted on the charge, but the action was a direct threat and intimidation to future investigators.[77]

The issue created national headlines and broad indignation, with Kentucky officials pictured as having interest in nothing but repression. A second independent group of New York writers promptly set out to raise large quantities of food to take to starving miners and their families. The trucks were met outside the beleaguered counties and run off the road, and their drivers were arrested. Waldo Frank, who along with Allen Taub of the ILD had been prominent in the maneuver, was taken by local vigilantes to the state line, severely beaten, and told not to return. Such martyrdom only intensified national concern. One hundred and seventy-five New York City educators, including Franz Boas, John H. Randall, Jr., Rexford G. Tugwell, Harry Carman, Lionel Trilling, Sidney Hook, and Henry Sloane Coffin signed an open letter assailing Harlan and Bell County officials for the "suspension of liberties under a supposedly constituted regime, the institution of a reign of lawlessness and violence connived at and abetted by those who are looked upon as the guardians of the law."[78] The National Student League recruited students from thirty universities throughout the country to go to Kentucky to investigate conditions and protest against the pending trial of Dreiser. The students, physically ejected from the area, headed for Washington to urge a Senate investigation, a maneuver that members of the Columbia University faculty publicly endorsed in late March 1932.[79]

Up to this point the ACLU had been cautious, taking every public occasion to disassociate itself from the Communists, but not wanting to seem callous about obvious free speech violations. The treatment of the students brought forth a strong position paper from the body in early April 1932.[80] This elicited a contemptuous response from an ambitious local Kentucky figure, Walter B. Smith, public prosecutor in Pineville, county seat of Bell County, into which miner revolt had spread in late January 1932. Smith, a local product but a Harvard graduate, had been among the earliest to wave the red flag and proclaim the 100 percent Americanism of the mine operators, while denouncing the Moscow-led assault upon them. He now wrote a letter to Arthur Garfield Hays which he promptly released to the press, daring the ACLU to come to Bell County.[81] Citing the Lusk and Fish Committee reports as concrete evidence that the organization was communist, he wrote:

> It seems a funny thing to hear one who is the head of an organization, the purpose of which is the overthrow of the government and the constitution, setting up such an awful clamor about constitutional rights such as freedom of speech and of the press. . . . If a mad dog has a constitutional right to run rampant in Bell County, biting people and scattering hydrophobia, then the American Civil Liberties Union has the same right. But—just as we would suppress the mad dog, we will suppress this un-American Union. [We] are little impressed . . . with the cackling of your Union over "freedom of speech"

and "freedom of the press" and "freedom of movement." We also
believe in those fundamentals of liberty, but we believe that "freedom
of speech" should be limited by a man's knowledge of what he talks
about.

To Smith's surprise and distress, local opposition to his posture
erupted immediately. His own minister started in the pulpit the following Sunday: "The deadliest, dirtiest, darkest, meanest menace
that confronts our land today is the disposition of every man to be
a law unto himself."[82]

Smith prevailed in his subsequent struggle with the ACLU. Its integrity publicly questioned, the body had no choice but to respond,
and, on April 10, its leaders announced that it would send a team
to investigate Bell County. However, in an effort to protect those
representatives and draw national attention to the partisanship of
local law enforcement, ACLU leaders sought an injunction from courts
in the state to prevent local officials and vigilantes from interfering
with its legitimate right to move freely in the area. A countersuit
denied that there had been any violations of civil liberties, maintaining
that any action taken had been perfectly legitimate efforts to maintain
law and order. At the very same time, the Reverend Reinhold Neibuhr
and a team of ministers, who had personally investigated conditions,
were issuing a public statement calling for a Senate investigation
in the area because of the extensive violation of the civil liberties
of people therein by local officials.[83]

The local judge refused to issue the injunction, maintaining that
no such legal writ could prevent public hostility against unwanted
investigations by nosy outsiders. He insisted that Bell and Harlan
counties had to be "protected from free speech."[84] But Arthur Garfield
Hays and Dudley Field Malone, heading the ACLU's actions, decided
to start without it. With a team of eleven investigators, including
Broadus Mitchell, Ernest Sutherland Bates, Carol Weiss, and two
clergymen "who came along to lend respectability to the enterprise,"
they publicly declared their intention to force the free-speech issue
in Bell County. They set out by car, only to be turned back at
the county line by a hostile band of armed men led by Walter
B. Smith himself. The committee promptly filed suit for $100,000
against Bell County officials and those in the city of Pineville for
denial of their rights as American citizens. The action induced certain
students who had been physically beaten earlier to launch suits also
and prompted spontaneous demonstrations of sympathy for ACLU
goals in Chicago, New York, Boston, and Philadelphia.[85]

The episode dramatized the tyranny of local authority and drew national sympathy and public response from intellectuals, writers, religious leaders, students, and legislators. Nonetheless, it proved futile in its immediate results. The local strike was broken completely, and the National Miners Union was driven out of the area. The sincerity of its professed desire to eliminate the human suffering of the workers was seriously questioned. John Dos Passos, who had been a prominent member of the Dreiser Committee, wrote some years later:

> I had the feeling that there was something a little too offhand about the way these human engineers were handling the Kentucky miners. There was something about the boss communist's sneering tone that made it a little too obvious that he enjoyed making monkeys of the warm-hearted liberals. The miners were even more pawns than we were. A whole series of small incidents in Kentucky made me feel that the communists were treating the misery and revolt of the Harlan County miners with the same professional's sneer . . . the way they handled the cases of the miners in jail, denying help to men who wouldn't play their game.[86]

As with Gastonia, the ACLU learned a bitter lesson. Honest utilization of the free-speech issue could be undermined both by the red smear and by the reds themselves. The latter had as their actual objective the destruction of the structure in which free speech could be vitalized as a meaningful concept for all Americans.

Relief gradually and grudgingly reached Harlan miners. The La Follette Committee of the mid-1930s probed carefully and insistently into the abuse of local power in the area. The New Deal codes afforded relief to the textile workers as well as the miners. Its more general efforts to create conditions of broader prosperity and elevation of standards of human decency alleviated a situation which Communists had hoped would be the "powder box where a well-placed fuse could blow a hole in the Capitalist System."[87]

Broad legal assault upon the abuse of local authority and arbitrary enforcement of a variety of forms of local control came much sooner in other areas. The events in the Kentucky mine region offended the sensibilities of many Americans. Two decisions of the Supreme Court, at the same time, indicated that the members of that body were not oblivious to such abuse of local power.

The cases of *Near* v. *Minnesota* and *Stromberg* v. *California* had reached the Court during the 1930–1931 term and had been argued on January 30 and April 15, 1931, respectively.[88] In each the abuse of local controls had been flagrant and the ACLU had taken an early concern. The Near case involved a local scandal sheet in Minneapolis which had been piquing a number of local officials through sharp criticism of their public conduct and general lack of ethics.[89] Angered officials sought to close down the clearly anti-Semitic organ through the enforcement of an obscure state law declaring certain types of publications a nuisance and providing for injunctions to prevent their circulation. Civil libertarians sensed a direct challenge to freedom of the press, and newspaper editors throughout the country quickly saw the implications. The ACLU offered assistance to the beleaguered editor. But the body willingly and incredulously stepped aside when attorneys for Colonel Robert McCormick's *Chicago Tribune* indicated that they were prepared to throw the full weight of that ultraconservative organ's resources behind a challenge.[90]

The Stromberg case raised issues fully as vital. The Better America Federation, in its zeal for eliminating all dangerous dissent in southern California, had conspired with willing American Legionnaires to attack a remote youth camp in the San Bernardino hills at which it suspected communist doctrine was being taught to youths six to sixteen years old. Five young women and an elderly camp caretaker, a gas victim as a soldier in World War I, were physically manhandled and dragged off to jail. There the district attorney of San Bernardino County, himself a Legionnaire, sat down with local officials to figure out the charges on which they could be held. It was proposed at first to charge them with criminal syndicalism, but prosecutions under that law in California had not been popular since the early years of the decade. Then the 1919 anti–red-flag law, which had never been used, was discovered. The raiders had found a small red flag at the camp and had discovered by questioning the children that it was part of the daily ceremony to give a morning pledge of allegiance to such a flag. The camp leaders were indicted for violation of the law and subsequently given prison terms of from six months to five years. Yetta Stromberg, a young former political science student at the University of California at Los Angeles and camp discussion leader, received ten years. The confused and despondent caretaker promptly committed suicide, but the women began serving their terms until the International Labor Defense, with the ACLU at its side, filed an appeal. The ACLU largely footed the bill, and the case went from the district court of appeal in California directly to the United States Supreme Court, after petition for hearing by the supreme court of California was denied.[91]

The Supreme Court, in late May and early June of 1931, sustained the defendant against the state in each case. By a five to four majority, it ruled the Minnesota Gag Law effected an unconstitutional infringement of freedom of the press as safeguarded by the due process clause of the Fourteenth Amendment. Basing its ruling on a qualified endorsement of the broad Blackstonian principle of "no prior restraint," the majority nonetheless came down hardest on the fact that under the statute a single violation invoked the threat of permanent suppression of a periodical, whatever its contents thereafter. Four of the justices disagreed, however, protesting against the use of the Constitution to give partial immunity to any person guilty of offenses such as those described. Less objection arose to holding the key section of the California red-flag law unconstitutional. Here seven justices agreed that the law was so vague and indefinite as to permit punishment of the fair use of opportunity for free political discussion, and therefore, as enforced, effected a denial of liberty without due process. Only McReynolds and Butler felt that this was an area where federal relief was not in order.

While the actions at the time seemed largely victories over disparate examples of unwarranted state restrictiveness, they were also significant legal moves by the Court.[92] In both the Court rejected continuation of such controls over freedom of speech and of the press. It thus made clear that the federal government was prepared to be a national monitor over both areas. The action afforded new avenues of legal redress to injured parties when local authorities trampled their rights by formal and informal restrictions.[93]

The decisions marked, in an almost anticlimactic way, a further legal triumph for the position which the activist-libertarians had been seeking to establish for the last dozen years. The depression years finally brought home to a majority of the American people the fact that it was no longer possible, within a highly complex, industrial society, for every man to take care of himself on an individual basis. Society had a responsibility for the individual and could create conditions in which liberty could meaningfully flourish. In the depression years it became absolutely essential that society aid certain individuals through bread lines, soup kitchens, relief centers, and even, under a highly reluctant Herbert Hoover, through governmental underwriting of various forms of private relief. Such action validated the free-speech position of the civil libertarians that steps had to be taken by society to enhance the status of people so that their individuality would be assured and hence their civil rights made meaningful.

The position was an important but realistic modification of the historic tradition of American liberalism running from Roger Williams, John Wise, and Thomas Jefferson through the later American devotees of John Stuart Mill. It adhered to the premise that rational man that he did not need to be protected against his own human frailties should be free to follow the dictates of his own conscience and by a paternalistic state. It added the legitimate qualification that when private forces within society were sufficiently powerful and repressive to make it impossible for the individual to enjoy his freedom, another type of paternalistic action could be used to create the new freedom central to the exercise of individuality. Such a position moved civil libertarians far from the laissez-faire assumptions of nineteenth-century liberalism and at times opened them to charges of a lack of confidence in rational man's ability to manage his own destiny. But civil libertarians, who had been realists about those forces that actually undermined individuality, regarded such diversionary criticism as merely a desperate last alarm.

The question remains as to the motivation of the Supreme Court justices. This chapter of the history of free speech in the 1920s is vital. Although the concept's legal meaning was little understood by the layman, that meaning could not help but reflect the moral imperatives of the layman. The justices' translation of them into legal principles represented their concept of broadly held national needs and desires.

13

The Legal Community
and the Meaning of
Free Expression

> Historians [like judges] . . . attach significance to those things which
> are significant to them. . . . Contributing causes cannot be subject,
> like a chemical combination in a test tube, to qualitative and quantitative
> analysis so as to weigh and value the various elements.
>
> Louis D. Brandeis, dissenting,
> *Pierce* v. *United States,* 1920

A variety of forces shaped the legal meaning of freedom of speech
in the 1920s. Before World War I, there had been only scattered
legal adjudication of this subject. With the exception of the 1798
Sedition Act, there was no federal legislation. Provisions in most
state constitutions were similar to that in the First Amendment so
that few statutes limited the practice directly.

The operational rule of thumb of the permissible limits of free
speech turned on an imprecise delineation between the proper use
of utterance and its abuse. A line existed between "liberty" and
"license." The former was permissible, the latter punishable. That
conception broke down quickly when any body of litigation began
confronting the bench and bar. Clearly, obscenity, profanity, and
defamation of individuals fell toward the "license" side of the ledger.
Where sedition and libel against the government fell was unclear.
Here the courts were of little help. "There were practically no satisfactory judicial discussions before 1917 about the meaning of the
free speech clauses. The prewar courts in construing such clauses
did little more than place obvious cases on this or that side of the

line. . . . But when we asked where the line actually ran and how they knew on which side of it a given utterance belonged, we found little answer in their opinions."[1]

If an attorney was seeking precise meaning of the concept, he went to works on the common law, or to various commentaries and treatises commonly used at the time. These included Ernst Freund's *The Police Power: Public Policy and Constitutional Rights* (1904) and the current edition of Thomas M. Cooley's classic, *Treatise on the Constitutional Limitations Which Rest Upon the Legislative Powers of the States of the American Union*.[2] These, however, presented the same problem. No precise legal opinions drew the line in the areas in which the free-speech issue was relevant.

World War I changed this situation radically. The federal government legislated in such a way as to curtail expression contrary to the national interest. The states acted similarly. The result was massive arrests of American citizens for the violation of such laws and many legal appeals from initial convictions. Attorneys for such appellants, however, found themselves in legal difficulty. With no judicial interpretation of the meaning of free speech under the new statutes as yet, there was little material ground for briefs against them. Most judges felt the few existing precedents irrelevant. Further, it was a thankless task to challenge statutes enacted to advance the war effort while the fighting continued. Members of the legal profession, so beleaguered, looked anxiously to the first interpretations of the statutes which would not come until calm had once again descended upon the nation.

Others were concerned about the legal implications of the wartime statutes, especially since they seemed to be violations of First Amendment rights and similar guarantees in most state constitutions. In the first major case to reach the Supreme Court, Justice Oliver Wendell Holmes, Jr., with the acquiescence of the eight other justices, attempted to inject into interpretation of freedom of speech a new precision which would enable those confronted with cases under it to make a clearer distinction between "liberty" and "license."[3] Holmes's "clear and present danger test" seemed to exclude nonpolitical speech at the outset ("The most stringent protection of free speech would not protect a man in falsely shouting fire in a theatre and causing a panic"). In the political area, he placed emphasis upon the difference between the advocacy of abstract theory or even hypothetical action (which was liberty) and situations in which the words used by a speaker were used "in such circumstances and were of such a nature as to create a clear and present danger that they would bring about the substantive evils that Congress has a right to prevent." "It is a question of proximity and degree," Holmes wrote. "When a nation is at war many things that might be said in time of peace are such a hindrance to its effort that their utterance will not be endured as long as men fight and that no Court could regard them as protected by any constitutional right."[4]

In retrospect, the success of Holmes's ruling resided more in the practical fact that it sustained conviction of a persistent vocal critic of the war than in the subtlety of the delineation Holmes sought to inject into First Amendment interpretation. Subsequent cases waved the distinction aside. Conviction after conviction was sustained at both the federal and state level by the courts' turning to a "bad tendency test," taking the position that there was no necessity of showing a clear relationship between advocacy and any overt act.[5] Advocacy of wrong action or even theory which might "bring the form of our present government into contempt or disrepute" was clearly "license" and therefore punishable under the sedition law.[6] The line between "liberty" and "license" placed any but the most docile expression close to the latter category. Such was the case in the initial convictions of Benjamin Gitlow, William Bross Lloyd, and Anita Whitney. The same was true in cases involving Eugene Debs at the federal level and in the most significant test of comparable state legislation, *Gilbert* v. *Minnesota,* which reached the Supreme Court in 1920.[7]

Many members of the legal community inveighed against this tendency at the time. Holmes, seeing his attempt at careful distinctions ignored, protested vigorously, reiterating his conviction, this time in dissent, that only emergency circumstances and advocacy that clearly led to direct, dangerous action fell in the area of "license." It was only the "present danger of immediate evil, or intent to bring it about" he argued, which warranted Congress's setting a limit on the expression of opinion.[8] Congress certainly could not forbid all effort to change the mind of the country. Turning to history, he expressed his firm conviction, as did Cooley's *Treatise,* that the First Amendment had been adopted to repudiate the English law of seditious libel and to give the people broad freedom of speech.

By his side was Louis Brandeis. His dissenting opinion in the Gilbert case reiterated similar sentiments and introduced the radical suggestion that such a basic right of national citizenship as freedom of speech might well deserve the benefit of federal protection if state authorities abused it too arbitrarily. Brandeis pointed out, somewhat sarcastically, that the liberty guaranteed by the Fourteenth Amendment had been held to assure the right of an employer to discriminate against a workman who was a member of a trade union and the right of a businessman to conduct a private employment agency, even though strongly supported state legislation had deemed both inimical to the public interest. He now wondered why such liberty did not include the right of peaceful dissent, stating: "I cannot believe that the liberty guaranteed by the Fourteenth Amendment includes only liberty to acquire and to enjoy property."[9]

Courageous defiance of the repressive momentum also came from a handful of besieged lower court justices. In North Dakota, Charles F. Amidon, under heavy wartime fire by conservative opponents in his district, stood fast for fair treatment of member of the Non-Partisan League.[10] George W. Anderson denounced the red scare so effectively in *Colyer* v. *Skeffington* in 1920 as to turn public opinion against the Bureau of Investigation and the Justice Department.[11] In Montana, George M. Bourquin had publicly opposed enactment of that state's criminal syndicalism law during the war. He continued his opposition to its excesses in his rulings.[12] Orrin N. Carter's dissent in the Lloyd case in the Illinois Supreme Court was a tour de force almost as eloquent as Holmes's Abrams dissent and was far more thoroughly documented. It was the basis for Governor Small's pardon of Lloyd.[13] Similar courageous behavior marked the activities of Learned Hand and Cuthbert Pound in New York and Kimbrough Stone in Missouri.[14] Most of these judges, raised on Cooley and familiar with Freund, found the movement toward construing virtually all critical speech as "license," both legally indefensible and legally impractical. Carter wrote in the Lloyd case, for example, that under such a construction "many public utterances of the great leaders in our past history would have been punishable."[15] In a dissenting opinion in the Gitlow case in the New York Supreme Court, Pound, joined by Justice Benjamin N. Cardozo, stated that "the rights of the best men are secure only as the rights of the vilest and most abhorrent are protected."[16]

Many other nonjudicial members of the legal community joined the fray. Appalled by the excesses and fearing that such a trend might become permanent, they fought vigorously against the proposed federal peacetime sedition legislation. In a position to take a partisan public posture, they jumped into the fray against the Lusk Laws and the refusal to seat the Socialists in the New York Assembly. They deplored the sedition and criminal-syndicalism laws proposed elsewhere as deceitful and superfluous and as precautionary legislation, giving unwarranted power to local authorities to check free expression virtually at their discretion.[17] In general, they openly stated their apprehension that if every public protest became a form of license, the concept of free speech would have little positive legal meaning. Such citizens included a number of liberal attorneys from

Clarence Darrow and Frank P. Walsh to John Lord O'Brian, Louis
Marshall, Walter Nelles, Francis Fisher Kane, and Swinburne Hale
and a small, but influential, element within legal education, many
of whom were impressed strongly by Zechariah Chafee's persuasive
treatise and brief for the liberal view, *Freedom of Speech,* published
in 1920.[18] Similarly, respected lawyers in Congress, William E. Borah,
Joseph I. France, Robert M. La Follette, and George Huddleston
spoke up. Former Senator Albert J. Beveridge, hailed for his masterful
work on John Marshall, carried the message of a proper rule of
law to the American Bar Association at its 1920 meeting.[19]

The outcome of such protest left two potential legal definitions
of free speech available to bench and bar. The prevalent one grew
out of the application of the "bad tendency test" both at the federal
level in the various Espionage and Sedition Act rulings of 1919 and
1920 and in the multifarious lower court rulings sustaining convictions
under those laws and under the state criminal-syndicalism and sedition
measures.[20] Further, Justice Sanford, in the Gitlow case, had bolstered
the restrictive side through an additional consideration. Sanford
acknowledged that the "clear and present danger test" had been
useful and valid as a device for deciding how far the Espionage
Act, which dealt primarily with acts, should extend to words. But
he emphasized that the rule was intended to apply only to cases
where the statute "merely prohibits certain acts involving the danger
of substantive evil without any reference to language itself."[21] He
rejected it altogether as a test of the constitutionality of a statute
expressly directed against words of incitement. Words could be punished for their bad nature, he insisted, regardless of the Court's opinion that there was no danger of bad acts, if legislative findings had
resulted in statutes aimed clearly at curtailing the dissemination of
sentiments destructive to the ends of society. Judicial restraint, so
lacking when society sought to legislate economic controls, was a
virtue when society set out to correct its evils through suppression
inimical to the public welfare.

But the liberal tradition and definition had not been destroyed.
Enough cases in the federal district and circuit courts had applied
the "clear and present danger test" precisely and clearly to state
statutes to make a defense of the libertarian interpretation available
for the attorney who sought an argument emphasizing strongly the
"liberty" side of the ledger. The fact that this position was held
by such eminent and respected members of the bench and bar
as Holmes, Brandeis, Pound, Hughes, Borah, and even, in a modified
way, by such a conservative as Henry W. Taft, brother of the Chief
Justice, made it impossible to ignore the liberal tradition.[22]

The Normalcy years tended to push the issue of a precise definition of freedom of speech into the background. The repeal of the Sedition Amendment to the wartime Espionage Act in March 1921 and the termination of further attempts to enact peacetime substitutes removed the possibility of any further federal indictments for dangerous talk. The issue continued only in connection with the states whose criminal-syndicalism, sedition, and occasional red-flag legislation was not revoked. Here calm was not so quickly restored, even though normalcy weakened the determination to protest and dissent. From 1919 until early 1924, prosecutions under the laws were fairly active, especially in California, and the Gitlow and Whitney indictments were still pending before the Supreme Court as late as 1925 and 1927, respectively.

The situation in California was unique. With IWW activity vigorous, and a small, but vocal, Communist Labor party intent upon making its weight felt, more people were indicted there than in any other state. Public demand for the punishment of seditionists, encouraged by the Better America Federation and the American Legion, seldom diminished. But as time went on, charge after charge was disproved. California then turned to the callous use of paid witnesses.[23] Even so, conviction in California became more and more difficult. Public criticism of the unfairness of trials grew. Longtime Republican leader and editor Chester Rowell, attorneys Eustace Cullinan, John Francis Neylan, and Warren Olney, all highly respected counsels for large organizations, the Right Reverend Edward L. Parsons of the San Francisco diocese of the Episcopal church, David Starr Jordan, and Max Radin not only vigorously condemned such proceedings but fought for repeal of the California criminal-syndicalism law. Juries became more cautious in handing out blanket convictions, and the state sought legal action to avoid further embarrassment.

In 1923, a California judge, Charles O. Busick, issued an injunction, subsequently upheld by the state supreme court, that enjoined the various acts classed as crimes under the criminal-syndicalism law.[24] Members of the IWW and the Workers party were thus prohibited from circulating pamphlets and books, advocating their doctrines orally, or organizing any group to do so. The Busick injunction thus removed offenders from the control of juries and gave the judge the direct power to sentence them for contempt of court for their actions. The result was that equity proceedings tended to replace direct prosecutions under the act. This eliminated the growing embarrassment of using dubious witnesses or having to rely upon juries. There was prompt protest against the use of such a legal device

to prohibit free speech and deny due process of law. George Kirchway, former Kent Professor of Law at Columbia University and respected criminologist, summarized the position of a growing number
of Californians condemning "the law, coverted in ˙many instances
by maladministration into an instrumentality of injustice and oppression." Not only the courts of first instance, Kirchway charged, but
the appellate courts have "failed to make good in action the doctrines
to which they have given allegiance in principle."[25]

By 1924, criminal syndicalism had become a virtual dead letter,
even in California. In subsequent years, many states attempted to
repeal such legislation. These attempts were led particularly by labor
leaders, who feared that the club would be revived against them
at any time. In all but one instance such attempts failed.[26] On the
other hand, labor apprehensions generally proved groundless, and
suppression of freedom of expression by the application of formal
statute had virtually ended. Such calm, however, was highly illusion-
ary. Although the use of obvious legal weapons to silence dissent
was largely discontinued, the quiet consensus of the decade, which
was fully as efficient in its operation as the older more overt methods,
subtley sanctioned the quasilegal silencing of too vocal critics. With
the ascendancy of William Howard Taft to the nation's supreme
legal position, the national atmosphere for freedom of speech clouded.
The concept was quickly downgraded in the face of other more
pressing and, to Taft, more essential legal needs.

The values that Taft brought to the Supreme Court in 1921 and
the iron hand with which he ran the high bench and the federal
judiciary are well known.[27] At best a reluctant Progressive even during
his presidency, Taft was obsessed in the postwar years with the
necessity to restore proper control of the country to the men of
property who could best manage its resources and divide and distribute its largesse. He retained that element of progressivism which
felt that the moral tone and better general functioning of society
could best be achieved by a responsible upper class of talent and
wealth. Conscious of the felt need of Americans in his class for
the imposition of stable forces to hold together a turbulent and distressingly dynamic and changing society, he was happy to answer
the call of opinion makers from business tycoons to disillusioned
Progressives like Walter Lippmann for counteracting such tendencies
through a potent and stable legal structure. Yet, while welcoming
power himself, he hardly conceived of it as being wielded solely
by juridical kings. Sharing broad popular disillusionment with democracy, he was still a Republican, cognizant of the need for a leadership,
which the people would feel represented their wishes. He sought

to throw the weight of the law on the side of creative and imaginative leadership by freeing private individuals from the sort of inhibiting restrictions which undermined their ingenuity and creativity. As he wrote to Elihu Root in 1922, "the cornerstone of our civilization is the proper maintenance of the guarantees of the 14th Amendment and the 5th Amendment."[28] In application, this meant curtailment of federal child labor laws, maximum hour legislation, anti-injunction statutes, and similar forms of social control designed to interfere with the "liberty" of property without due process of law.

The positive function of the state was to protect those same individuals against radical agitators and unwarranted demands of labor leaders and social reformers out to undermine the nation's confidence in their ability, sincerity, and inherent paternalism. This was warranted by either formal legislation or informal sanctions. Financiers, manufacturers, industrialists, and private entrepreneurs were already holding society together in the economic area; the state could certainly assist them in this respect. Thus, to Taft or Van Devanter, Sutherland, Butler, or McReynolds, there was positive validity in the application of repressive legislation, when its enforcement acted to keep the natural leaders of society and the economic order free to concentrate on the central issues of the times. Although Brandeis, or even Holmes, might question a legal structure that left the states free to deprive United States citizens of their liberties in the free-speech area, to Taft, and those of his orientation, such a situation was not only natural but valid. So was the application of subtle forms of informal local control if these seemed necessary to the protection of private property and its uninhibited use.

Throughout his tenure as Chief Justice, Taft was able to wrap this set of legal assumptions around the concept of free speech. He threw his weight behind rulings that would endorse it, both on the high bench and in the lower courts, and lobbied subtley and informally for appointment of judges who would maintain it. He also fought, at times ruthlessly, against critics of such judicial supremacy— congressmen and senators seeking to limit the awesome power of the judiciary; public figures, including Presidents, who manifested too great a concern for social welfare and the right of dissent; or dissenters on his own Court, to whom he made clear his resentment and whose positions he attempted to undermine.[29] Taft gave his legal position protective camouflage. As chairman of the ultraconservative American Bar Association's committee to draw up the Canons of Judicial Ethics, he took pains to make clear that the role of a judge was a passive one, an arbiter of disputes between individual litigants. Such a role was certainly not one of assuming responsibility for active policy making. "The judges constituting a court of last resort should use effort and self-restraint to promote solidarity of conclusion and the consequent influence of judicial decision. A judge should not yield to pride of opinion or value more highly his individual reputation than that of the court to which he should be loyal. Except in case of conscientious difference of opinion on fundamental principle, dissenting opinions should be discouraged in courts of last resort."[30] Such a denial of power sought to cover its patent exercise.

The result for the attorney who argued First Amendment cases was vital to freedom of speech in the decade. During the red scare, he was disturbed by the frivolous and imprecise application of the law molded by public officials to fit their immediate need to expose and hunt down radicals. Now no such legal uncertainty existed. Clearly aware that a narrowly restrictive interpretation of freedom of speech was the one consistently followed by the courts, he was equally aware of the limited success he might attain in any challenge to that concept. His reaction was to advise clients in advance of the near futility of taking a legal position based upon a highly libertarian view. The result was to discourage clients interested in pursuing the point. If the average court was unwilling to listen to such a line of argument, there seemed little reason for spending valuable time and money pushing it. Taft and those intimate with him and his views were able, through the peculiar forms of communication available to the legal community, to convey to members of the bar the sort of decisions they could expect in the free-speech area. The result was that the number of such cases reaching courts diminished sharply as the decade progressed. It is little wonder that ACLU leaders were totally callous in their attitudes toward the courts as agencies of redress for clients whose civil liberties had been violated. The way to get free speech, militant civil libertarians charged, was not by claiming it was a legal right but by taking it by force and driving off the police when they tried to make arrests.[31]

In many ways, Taft's tenure was a form of nervous holding action despite the efficacy with which he maintained his major legal premises. Despite Taft's pose of judicial impartiality, there was a gnawing feeling among many sensitive Americans that such a calm was only in the minds of insulated, remote judges, unwilling to confront the realities of the time.

There were too many obvious contradictions to reconcile. At the ideational level, the legal meaning that the courts were giving to freedom of speech was highly restrictive, in many ways a denial of traditional interpretations of that concept. The fact that those who supported the Court's interpretation were identified in the public mind with repressive attitudes—the American Legion, the DAR, the professional patriots and their spokesmen—raised serious questions.

At the legal-ideational level, there were grounds for questioning the professed omniscience of the Court in its claim of rendering impartial justice. The Court willingly sustained various pieces of state police power legislation which curtailed radicals, undermined critics of the system, and silenced dissent. At the same time, it threw out an exaggerated number of state police power laws applying various forms of social control to employers and propertied interests. These, it contended, were unwarranted violations and limitations upon the liberties and privileges of property.[32] Such inconsistency seemed even more glaring in face of the Court's constant posture of self-restraint and frequent denial of any policy-making function. Such a position clearly relegated liberties which many Americans felt traditional and basic, prominently freedom of speech, press, and assembly, to a second-class status. It elevated the rights of property even beyond the state's ability to control such liberties when they became "license" in the form of antisocial conduct. Such a double standard defied the realities of the power structure in the decade. Its effect was to throw the weight of the law on the side of the scale where massive private economic power was already adequate to allow men of property to protect their interests, with no effort at any commensurate weighting of the law in behalf of powerless, propertyless, lobbyless citizens with few resources to protect their personal rights.[33]

The posture of the judiciary and its supporters was even more vulnerable when one compared their professions of free-speech devotion with the violations which they condoned. The Court upheld virtually every conviction made under the various criminal-syndicalism and sedition laws even though in many cases the action so curtailed often constituted little more than raucous public dissent.[34] The confidently assumed paternalism of employers and the general assurance that they would be sensitive and responsible in the use of private power was hardly vindicated by actions in West Virginia, Pennsylvania, Colorado, San Pedro, Paterson, Passaic, New Bedford, Gastonia, and Marion. Leaving free speech to the mercy of informal local controls virtually underwrote any form of repression that a local "establishment" felt essential to apply to protect its self-interest.

Critics and opponents of the Court, unable to alter its position as long as its leadership and membership remained the same, engaged in a variety of slanting assaults upon it. Such attacks were geared to discredit its professed omniscience and lay the groundwork for a more sensitive legal position. Such critics and opponents came from the nonlegal and the legal community. The former relied more heavily upon a barrage of criticism geared to popular consumption and arousing general hostility and distrust of courts, hoping thereby to undermine legal irresponsibility. The latter sought through more subtle and specialized means to maintain the validity and strength of the activist-libertarian view of freedom of speech, as well as to structure other portions of the law, to bring them into harmony with the social needs and realities of the period.

The former took on a variety of interesting forms. The bias of courts had been one of the earliest forms of public criticism in the sober "morning after" following the red scare. Judicial behavior, it was seen in retrospect, had given in to the frenetic repressionists. Not only had most lower court judges fallen in line to sustain convictions for highly dubious forms of radicalism, they had tacitly underwritten the vigilantism which had been overt in the episode. The high bench, at the same time, had acquiesced fully in turning Holmes's moderate and responsible "clear and present danger test" into a "bad tendency rule," making reversal of lower court convictions virtually impossible. Senator Thomas J. Walsh of Montana and a subcommittee of the Senate Judiciary Committee sought to alert Americans to very real dangers in this area. "It is only in such times," the report maintained, "that the guarantees of the Constitution as to personal rights are of any practical value. . . . If in such times the Constitution is not a shield, the ecomiums which statesmen and jurists have paid it are fustian."[35] The Senate refused to adopt the Walsh report, but its supporters injected it into the *Congressional Record,* and its frankness was cheered by many elements of the liberal community.

From the outset of the 1920s, the labor press made the courts a prime target. An editorial in the *American Federationist* in 1921 sounded the cry: "The time has come when freedom cannot afford to suffer longer under the encroaching tyranny of judicial usurpation. It must be stopped."[36] And Taft's appointment and his iron-handed use of judicial power intensified the criticism. So did the massive use of the injunction in the shopmen's strike and thereafter. The organ of the Railroad Brotherhoods, *Labor,* maintained: "Freedom of speech and action is a joke in any number of states. Judges and the courts are in large part to blame. Occasionally they intervene to protect the citizens, but immediately they are overruled by a higher court."[37] An aging Samuel Gompers, only shortly before his death, charged: "The courts have abolished the Constitution as far as the rights and interests of the working people are concerned."[38]

Labor leaders and other liberals urged positive action as well. In 1923, Donald Richberg, writing in the Amalgamated Clothing

Workers' organ *Advance*, called for an easier way to remove judges who rendered unpopular and unjustified opinions. Gompers frankly advocated giving power to Congress to enact any measure by a two-thirds majority after it had been declared unconstitutional by the Supreme Court. He coupled such a proposal with another for the direct election of federal judges.[39] Various liberal congressmen and senators proposed, and in some cases introduced, legislation seeking to curtail the power of the federal judiciary. One such maneuver by Senator George Norris of Nebraska aroused Taft, who set out to rally the conservative bench and bar, especially the American Bar Association, in opposition. The Senate—"a most Bolshevik body," with a highly untrustworthy judiciary committee—would, he warned, "have to be kept under constant barrage and constant surveillance in this regard."[40]

The greatest national fervor over the question developed when it became a major campaign issue in the election of 1924. Senator Robert La Follette, seeking to appeal to a broad strata of working-class and liberal citizens, opened his platform with a categorical assertion that the fundamental rights of Americans were endangered by the tyranny of the monopoly system. The principal instrument for maintaining such a system on the backs of the people, he insisted, was its sanction by a judiciary usurping their power and their rights. Such an assertion was not accompanied by any revolutionary proposals, the remedies proposed being implementation of Gompers' demands. But they found themselves in a cross fire of criticism from the candidates for both major parties. The Republicans suggested that such demands clearly showed La Follette's identification with the Russian Bolshevists. Democrat John W. Davis argued that keeping the court system intact was the most important issue in the campaign.[41]

La Follette's disappointing showing dimmed the hopes of those seeking responsibility from the courts through legislative reforms. It did little to diminish the continuing undertone of criticism, however. Hostility to rulings such as those in the Gitlow case, the Whitney and Burns cases in 1927, and especially the handful of state criminal-syndicalism actions in the depths of the depression, made clear that defeating the opponents of the courts had in no way insured public confidence in their objectivity. As the decade moved toward conclusion, critics from H. L. Mencken to the Communists continued to decry judicial unconcern for individual rights, particularly freedom of speech and press.[42]

Those within the legal community, discontented and upset with the conservative judicial monolith, relied on different techniques. Such individuals also had forms of specialized legal communication which even conservative legalists could not ignore. Brandeis and Holmes, and, as the decade progressed, Stone had a loyal constituency within the legal community, a fact which distressed Taft, but about which he could do little. The heart of Brandeis's jurisprudence lay in a sociological law which would realistically and honestly confront the social needs of all members of the community. Such a view conceived of the law as a sensitive instrument to be applied with endless variation to changing and differing circumstances as human needs in those circumstances dictated. Guaranteeing the enlightened self-interest of the business community would not take care of all those dependent upon it. The former Wilson confidant, in a widely quoted dissent in a case in which Taft assailed a state anti-injunction law as an assault on property, wrote: "Few laws are of universal application. . . . And the law of property is not appropriate for dealing with the forces beneath social unrest."[43] Brandeis was an early and vocal critic of the attitude that property was more important than human rights. He rejected the conservative contention that "Hard cases make bad law": "It was a short way of saying that in a case where ideas of common sense and justice collided head on with established legal principle or precedent it was better to reach an unjust result than to disturb or modify the precedent." He also decried the notion "that judges could not correct their own mistakes: *stare decisis*—right or wrong the decision must stand."[44]

Brandeis saw the Court's position on free speech as particularly inappropriate and inconsistent. To gauge the limits of free speech in such a way that what determined permissibility was the potential danger to property interests was to use a negative, biased, and unwarranted scale. Like Holmes, he felt that the criteria should be the extent to which the speech was or was not serving the general welfare of the whole community. Hence, the test should evolve vis-à-vis broad social needs, and, unless free speech posed a clear and present danger to society at large, there was more to be lost in its suppression than in its expression. Members of society, in other words, might better find, as Holmes wrote in a masterful piece of legal Darwinism in his Abrams dissent, "that the ultimate good desired is better reached by free trade in ideas—that the best test of truth is the power of the thought to get itself accepted in the competition of the market, and that truth is the only ground upon which their wishes safely can be carried out."[45] Or, as Holmes reiterated in his Gitlow dissent, the fact that speech might be incitement was no grounds for repression. "Every idea is an incitement. It offers itself for belief and if believed it is acted on unless some other belief outweighs it." And he added: "If in the long run the beliefs expressed in proletarian dictatorship are destined to be accepted by the dominant forces of the community, the only meaning of free speech is that they should be given their chance and have their way."[46] Brandeis went one step further in his eloquent concurring opinion in the Whitney case, proposing an even more explicit way of determining the cutoff point. No danger flowing from speech can be deemed clear and present, he wrote, "unless the incidence of the evil apprehended is so imminent that it may befall before there is opportunity for full discussion. If there be time to expose through discussion the falsehood and fallacies, to avert the evil by the process of education, the remedy to be applied is more speech, not enforced silence."[47] Thus, Brandeis, even in affording more precise ways to limit, was at pains to make clear that limitation was warranted only when general social needs were threatened by a type of expression that might lead directly to serious damage to society.

His concern was not merely that of finding a salutary method of control. Like Holmes, he deplored the unfortunate impact which the persistence of a double standard in the area of freedom had on the law. In legislation regulating labor contracts, freedom was the rule and regulation the exception. Why should not the same principles apply to limitations on speech and press? The state was assuming responsibility for curtailing the freedom of individuals to express themselves either orally or in print, or to assemble to discuss their grievances, in the name of checking actions potentially dangerous to property and hence to society. Why should the state be curtailed in its power to regulate a variety of antisocial activities in the economic area which in the long run robbed men of their individualism and created the conditions which fostered dissent and protest in the first place? Such persuasive convictions, wrapped as they were with a strong element of social responsibility and a serious concern for the needs of society, went far toward keeping alive the libertarian position on free speech.[48]

Those who subscribed to such views scored certain minor legal breakthroughs in spite of the Taft Court's intransigence and conservatism. Walter H. Pollak, a brilliant attorney and frequent counsel for the ACLU, building upon Brandeis's dissent in *Gilbert* v. *Minnesota*, convinced a reluctant Court through an eloquent brief in *Gitlow* v. *New York* that there should at least be legal avenues for undermining local controls over individual liberties when they became obsessively arbitrary. As Pollak wrote: "Liberty of expression is a right which the due process clause protects against state action. This is established (a) by the authoritative determinations of the meaning of 'liberty' as used in the Fourteenth Amendment; (b) by the as-

sumptions of this Court in dealing with the precise question; and
(c) by its explicit declaration with respect to the related right of
free assemblage."[49] The Court refused to use such a device in the
immediate case, either to reverse Gitlow's conviction or to strike
down the New York criminal anarchy law (which Pollak had vigorously argued rested on the theory of the older common law of seditious libel which had become obsolete even in England).[50] The justices
accepted it, however, as a viable interpretation of the First and
Fourteenth amendments and as an acceptable legal device, thus making it available for attorneys and judges should local actions become
so arbitrary as to warrant curtailment.

Pollak was unwilling to rest on such minor laurels. In a 1927
case, *Burns* v. *U.S.*, involving indictment of an IWW organizer under
the California criminal syndicalism law, he took further occasion to
clarify what he contended was the "Invidious Charter of Classification
on Which the Act is Based."[51] The measure's only concern, he charged,
was to protect property. It betrayed no parallel concern with the
individual rights of those who might feel compelled to protest the
way that property was being used. Its general definitions of what
constituted improper expression were so vague and imprecise that
it was easily turned into a blanket weapon against any dissenter
which any local law enforcement official might wish to silence or
otherwise proscribe.[52]

Legal education in the 1920s, if not undergoing marked reorganization, was feeling the impact of this new emphasis upon the social
role of law. Roscoe Pound's researches and writings earlier in the
century had gone far toward reorienting the Harvard curriculum.
Pound had vigorously spoken out against red scare excesses. He was
a major force at Harvard along with such distinguished liberals as
Zechariah Chafee, Felix Frankfurter, whose work on the labor injunction was a classic indictment of that form of judicial power, James
M. Landis, and Thomas Reed Powell.[53] The activities of such men in
behalf of a modernized law extended well beyond the classroom.
Powell had come to Harvard from Columbia University, where, as a
teacher of constitutional law, he had earned a reputation for radical
unconventionality through his realistic suggestion that in deciding
cases judges were moved not merely by legal arguments but also by
social, economic, and psychological biases of which they were usually
quite unconscious. His views had ruffled the conservative members of
the Columbia law faculty, many of whom felt such a position im-
pugned the honor of the judiciary. He had been defended vigorously
by Dean Harlan Fiske Stone, however, who demonstrated his own
awareness of judicial venality by condemning the adverse effect the

red scare had had upon the courts in 1920. Underhill Moore, another Columbia advocate of the new legal realism, kept alive his iconoclasm.[54]

Elsewhere, a similar pattern developed. Alongside legal traditionalists and conservatives there came to sit on the faculties of most leading law schools vigorous and often aggressive advocates of judicial realism. Ernst Freund adhered to such a position at the University of Chicago. Herbert J. Goodrich, who early in the decade had called for a new day in the area of freedom of speech in a widely quoted article in the *Michigan Law Review*, moved from Ann Arbor to become dean of the University of Pennsylvania Law School in the later years of the 1920s.[55] Max Radin had been an early opponent of the California criminal-syndicalism laws and had headed several committees advocating their repeal. He worked in other ways to attain a practical approach to legal questions at the University of California. Probably the most advanced movement in this direction among academic legalists took place at Taft's old alma mater, Yale, where young Dean Robert M. Hutchins was not only surrounding himself with such legal iconoclasts as William O. Douglas, Thurman Arnold, Walton H. Hamilton, Morris Cohen, and Walter Nelles, prominent ACLU attorney who had assisted Pollak, but was insisting that law be viewed as part of a larger science of human relations, with the older emphasis on precedent sublimated to its functional impact.[56]

Such teachers and scholars were in an advantageous position to bring about significant effects upon the law in the period. Divorced from the necessity of rendering justice from a bench under the strong influence of legal conservatism and the pressure of the conservative "establishment" and not reliant upon steady fees for their income, they could see the legal picture in the country with an objective clarity seldom available to bench and bar. Scholarship demanded analysis of the interrelationships of the whole broad legal structure. Few such legal scholars failed to see the detrimental nature of the highly restrictive concepts of freedom of expression currently being followed. Many condemned the double standard in the area of economic due process and individual and personal freedom which current interpretations of the Fourteenth Amendment incorporated.

This frequently extended beyond the classroom to the larger legal community. Many scholars addressed bar associations. In a widely reported speech in February 1927, Dean Frank H. Sommer of the New York University Law School, called for the creation of a new body of liberties through legal implementation of the abstract rule set forth in the Gitlow ruling. Not only First Amendment freedoms, but those of the other eight amendments as well, should be protected against state interference, he contended. "Experience has shown that the danger to 'liberty' comes rather from the States than from the Federal Government. . . . If the ideas of the founders are to continue to dominate, the fundamental individual rights must be restored to their former high estate in popular regard."[57] The Busick injunction drew contemporary condemnation in the *California Law Review.* Another journal included a call for a new emancipation for freedom of expression by "obtaining a Supreme Court whose personnel will guarantee a good application of the rule of reasonableness."[58]

A number of legal scholars attempted to set the record straight for the scholarly world through incisive pieces in the *Encyclopedia of the Social Sciences* on liberty, free speech, criminal syndicalism, the injunction, and other related topics.[59] Powell's regular editorials for Walter Lippmann's *New York World* gave a popular interpretation of the meaning of leading decisions of the day. He also assailed the simplemindedness of the conservative legal community, especially the American Bar Association, dissecting popular interpretations of the Constitution for the lay public. He categorized the widely circulated volume by James M. Beck as a "prayer book." ("Most volumes on the Constitution make you tired because you have to try so hard to think; the book Mr. Beck has written is different. You can read it without thinking.")[60] Felix Frankfurter wrote frequent articles in the *New Republic* and the *Atlantic Monthly* condemning such overt violations of liberty as Judge Wilkerson's injunction in the shopmen's strike, the State Department's treatment of Count Karolyi, and the miscarriage of justice in the Sacco-Vanzetti case.[61]

By the late 1920s, such pithy and sharp legal comment was beginning to have an impact upon the bench. Liberal justices, especially, dissatisfied with the few standard precedents in the First Amendment area, looked for other less rigidly legalistic types of data to document their views. The main body of writing, they discovered, was in the activist-libertarian vein. The trend was present in other areas of the law as well. In 1928 Max Radin pointed out that while precedent law was still primary authority in influencing the behavior of judges and while older commentaries still held sway, these were now being joined by recent treatises and by articles in legal periodicals. Radin was frank to urge that the courts be more sanguine toward utilizing the writings of men of "authoritative calibre" whose works appear "frequently enough in our law reviews, often in treatises, rarely elsewhere."[62]

Certain acceptance was evident. As an attorney, Brandeis had pioneered in using socioeconomic data to accompany a formal brief based upon precedent. He boldly documented his concurring opinion in the Whitney case with allusions not only to a liberal line of free-speech decisions but to Chafee's book, *Freedom of Speech*, a quotation from Thomas Jefferson drawn from Charles A. Beard's article, "The Great American Tradition," in *The Nation*, Harold Laski's *Grammar of Politics*, and a law review article by Charles Warren exploring the new concept of bringing individual liberties under the protection of the Fourteenth Amendment.[63] Use of such material suggested that factors other than precedent were relevant considerations and indicated that the courts had an obligation to explore the history of a statute for light upon its meaning. Judicial acceptance, while originally slight, grew with time. "Where there had been absolutely phrased rules of competency that barred use of hearings, debates, committee reports, there appeared by the 1930s more or less explicit recognition that almost any official source contemporary with the passage of a statute might be used in its interpretation. The effect of such background evidence was to be gauged by its credibility, and not be its compliance with formal rules of competence."[64] Thus the activist-libertarian concept of the proper legal meaning of free speech was nurtured from many legal sources.

Early actions of the Hoover administration indicated that its leaders were not unrealistic about the flawless way the law was functioning. In fact, various of Hoover's actions seemed to challenge the confident assumption that since all was well with the business community, all was well with America at large. The setting up of the Wickersham Commission was a significant step. It was acknowledgment that control at the local level in the hands of virtually uninhibited local authorities was not producing a high pattern of law observance. Rather, Hoover indicated a growing distress with both the excesses of local authorities and the growing disrespect for the law which such heavy-handedness seemed to produce.[65] The same spirit was manifested in the President's attitude toward the communist pickets in December 1929, an attitude which, if legally implemented, would have necessitated turning to more liberal precedents in the free-speech area.

Growing public awareness of the necessity for more sensitive figures in positions of judicial authority also became obvious as the depression progressed. When Taft reluctantly stepped down in early 1930 due to ill health and President Hoover named Charles Evans Hughes to take his place, large segments of the liberal public protested. Waving aside the courage of Hughes's earlier red scare opposition, they applauded Senator Wiliam E. Borah when he indicated that the crying need was for judges who would stop treating the Fourteenth Amendment as a sole protection for property and elevate it as a guarantee of individual liberty. "When during the last sixteen years has corporate wealth had a contest with the public that Mr.

Hughes has not appeared for organized wealth and against the public?" Borah asked.[66] Senator George Norris raised other liberal doubts
about Hughes, maintaining: "He has not seen the man who suffers,
the man who knows what it is to be hungry and not have the
necessary money with which to buy food. His vision has extended
only to that limited area which is circumscribed by yellow gold."
Robert M. La Follette, Jr., took the occasion to relaunch his father's
campaign of 1924, declaring the Hughes's appointment once again
reopened the issue of usurpation of power by the Courts.[67] Hughes,
a sensitive public servant, reassumed his chair on the high bench
with a strong awareness of the public's demand that his new power
be wielded with a high sense of social responsibility.

Such public pressure did not subside. Later in the same year Hoover
nominated John J. Parker, a prominent North Carolina Republican,
to fill the post vacated by Justice Sanford. Public wrath was sufficient
to defeat the nomination. The reasons were significant. Parker not
only had a strongly antilabor record, he was prominently endorsed
by Governor Max Gardner, whose name was associated with management intransigence and brutality in Gastonia and Marion. He had
condoned local discrimination against Negroes, was a champion of
the labor injunction, and was on record as believing that the role
of a judge within society was "the protection of private property,
not alone from the fury of the mob, but from ill-advised majorities
activated by envy or hatred or malice."[68] Even a usually conservative
Senate balked, and Hoover had no choice but to withdraw the nomination. The much less well-known Philadelphia attorney, Owen J. Roberts, was quietly inserted in Sanford's slot.

Even the opposition to Parker was mild when in the latter years
of his presidency, a besieged Hoover named to the Seventh Circuit
Court of Appeals Judge James H. Wilkerson of Chicago, whose name
was synonymous with the hated injunction of the shopmen's strike.
Wilkerson's record was probably more outrageous than that of any
other judge in the country. In the face of such fire, Hoover withdrew
the nomination. Its impact, coming when it did, was salutary. The
amount of protest it aroused against abuse of the labor injunction
in general came when the Norris-LaGuardia act was before Congress.
It was not an irrelevant factor in its final enactment.[69]

The judicial behavior of Hughes and Roberts in the area of state
police power quickly aroused criticism from conservatives as each
moved cautiously but steadily toward liberal legal positions. A great
variety of disparate factors were involved in such a change of attitude.
Hughes and Roberts, as sophisticated, eastern, urban, and urbane
legalists, instinctively tended to associate with similar types. On the

high bench as it was then constituted, this did not mean McReynolds from Tennessee, Sutherland from Utah, Van Devanter from Wyoming, or Butler, who had grown up in rural Minnesota. Rather, they empathized more readily with Holmes, Brandeis, and, to a lesser degree, Stone. These men viewed life and society from a perspective which encompassed the many problems of a pluralistic social structure. The importance of such a delineation was intensified as the depression progressed.[70]

Earlier, a person such as Hughes or Roberts might have found little difficulty in defending the Taft court's positions. They could now see that changing times no longer made such positions viable. Responsible men of property no longer exerted salutary social control in such a way as to benefit large segments of society. The dramatically changed social situation necessitated a change in legal assumptions. Other responsible leaders would have to reassert responsible authority through such instruments of public control as courts, assemblies, or executive agencies. But, to function effectively, it would be necessary to undermine wide-scale public distrust in the courts and deeply felt convictions regarding the social irresponsibility of the law. This could be done only by a sharp and sincere move toward making it applicable to the broad range of problems confronting the nation and affording through it new avenues of relief and redress for depressed people. To persist in a callous attitude of legal unreality would push the discontented toward extralegal or even revolutionary actions, which might well destroy the entire structure.

There was also calculated risk in continuing a blind adherence to a set of legal assumptions and precedents, through which socially responsible public action was blighted and criticism silenced. The continued use of such a questionable legal abstraction as freedom of contract to throw out child labor laws, maximum hour and minimum wage laws, anti-injunction statues, and various other forms of social welfare legislation was increasingly hard to defend.

Holmes for some time had maintained that if the people wanted to do something and there was nothing in the Constitution which prevented them from doing so, they should be encouraged to go ahead and the courts should keep hands off. He had spoken favorably, albeit in dissent, of the desirability of social experiments in the insulated chambers afforded by the several states, in which peculiar solutions to peculiar local problems might be hammered out.[71] With the depression not only creating more problems but intensifying older ones, a degree of leniency in permitting experimentation, even when it meant curtailment of the rights of private property, was now widely urged. And consistency seemed to dictate an equal leniency toward those who would experiment, orally or in print, with a wide range of proposals for solving the nation's problems. If property and its use could be regulated, it could be criticized. The latter, in the long run, was certainly far less immediately damaging and challenging than the former.

To give the green light to expanded use of state regulatory authority in the economic area required a shift from the prevailing assumption that freedom of contract was the general rule, restraint the exception. Judges would have to concede that statutes were not to be annulled unless invalidity was clearly proved. In a case decided in early January 1931, a new five-man majority, over the bitter protest of McReynolds, Sutherland, Van Devanter and Butler, took this very position.[72] Legal commentators did not miss the implication of this obscure ruling. Shortly thereafter, the *Yale Law Journal* stated: "Recent developments have indicated that our economic organization has not the skill of conveniently curing its ills. Governmental aid appears inevitable. Man is not born into our society free of economic constraints. Legislation relaxing them may more likely be an enhancement of than a restriction upon the 'liberty of contract.' The Court is not to stand in the way of experimentation. The addition of two vigorous thinkers to the Bench has carried the day for pragmatism and liberal tolerance of legislative experiment with control for the purpose of advancing a large capacity for individual freedom."[73]

Removing legal restrictions on free discussion, however, could not be achieved by such an easy shift of emphasis. Here, legal realists realized that formal governmental enforcement of restrictive laws was only rarely the avenue used for limiting free expression. Rather, the functionally effective approach for censuring too militant or dissident protest was through subtle forms of local control applied by individuals and groups, public and private, in positions to exert power at the local level. What was needed was a legal device for undermining such control, whether exercised through the implementation of a vagrancy, ordinance or trespass law or through inducing higher officials to apply to local dissenters criminal-syndicalism, sedition, or red-flag statutes. This involved new legal avenues for affording those victimized to obtain legal relief when their fundamental civil liberties were denied. Here even a literal and accurate translation and application of Holmes's "clear and present danger test" was not a highly viable or relevant mechanism. Challenging the application of formal statutes because they placed more emphasis upon proscribing license than authorizing liberty was not the answer. The need was for a national standard which would make clear that the First Amendment not only protected freedom of speech and press from formal federal governmental restraint, but more subtle forms of local restraint. State action could not be counted upon. Although most state constitutions guaranteed such rights in one form or another, simultaneous protective action in the form of forty-eight legislative enactments providing a common way to ensure that such national standards be guaranteed was clearly out of the question.

The Court had an easy tool at hand, one not far divorced from that involving state police power at the economic level. This was Pollak's device, making the First Amendment freedoms part of the "liberty" guaranteed against state encroachment by the due process clause of the Fourteenth Amendment. The legal path followed by Hughes in the Stromberg and Near cases in 1931 was significant in this regard. In reversing the conviction of Yetta Stromberg, Hughes condemned the dragnet action which the looseness of the first section of the California red-flag law seemed clearly to condone and encourage and which had been dramatized by Miss Stromberg's attorney.[74] He emphasized that such a statute would have to measure up to the basic guarantees of the federal constitution. Focusing particularly upon the First Amendment guarantee of freedom of speech, he stated: "The maintenance of the opportunity for free political discussion to the end that government may be responsive to the will of the people and that changes may be obtained by lawful means, an opportunity essential to the security of the Republic, is a fundamental principle of our constitutional system. A statute which upon its face, and as authoritatively construed, is so vague and indefinite as to permit the punishment of the fair use of this opportunity is repugnant to the guaranty of liberty contained in the Fourteenth Amendment."[75]

Stromberg proscribed one kind of local action unwarranted by its clear abrogation of national standards. Hughes's equally direct and incisive opinion in the Near case undercut another. Here the Chief Justice, in "the most important decision rendered since the adoption of the First Amendment," stated categorically that "it is no longer open to doubt that the liberty of the press, and of speech is within the liberty safeguarded by the due process clause of the Fourteenth Amendment from invasion by state action." Hughes also clearly related this development to the Court's new attitude toward freedom of contract, insisting that liberty generally needed new definition and that "liberty of contract is not an absolute right . . . the wide field of activity in the making of contracts is subject to legislative supervision."[76]

Hughes's technique in the Near case was also significant. Turning sharply from reliance upon straight legal precedent, he made clear that a concept such as freedom of the press had a long history which was highly relevant to its modern application. To gain proper historical prospective, he turned to historical materials—Thomas E. May's *Constitutional History of England*, Clyde A. Duniway's *Development of Freedom of the Press in Massachusetts*, the *Journals of the Continental Congress*, the writings of the founding fathers, particularly James Madison, and, not insignificantly, Zechariah Chafee's *Freedom of Speech* and an article in the *Harvard Law Review* by Roscoe Pound entitled "Equitable Relief Against Defamation and Injuries to Personality."[77]

There was a certain legal irony in elevating speech and press to a new legal height by wrapping them both with the protection of the due process clause of the Fourteenth Amendment and a new surveillance of the federal judiciary. Coming almost simultaneously with a downgrading of the blanket protection of property and liberty of contract through the same due process clause, Hughes seemed not to be merely challenging the former double standard in this area but creating a new one with emphasis reversed and the law now weighted in behalf of individual and personal rights. Further with the wide public reporting of such rulings, the new tack of the court became commonly known. The *Literary Digest* opened an article shortly after the Near decision with the comment that the shift of a majority of the Court to the "liberal" side was "just about the biggest Washington news of the decade. . . . The cleavage between liberal and conservative and the dominance of the former appear particularly in two areas of decisions. One, speaking broadly, emphasizes human rights and constitutional guarantees to the individual, such as freedom of speech. These human rights the liberals of the Court tend to protect or enlarge. The other group of decisions . . . tends to restrain private property rights and to enlarge the powers of State governments in dealing with private property."[78]

The general acceptance of such a sharp legal move and the singular lack of broad-scale criticism seem surprising. The reasons, however, are not difficult to understand. The creation of a national floor of uniform elemental decency in general human relations had been a liberal theme for years. The depression with its human suffering had merely reemphasized the need. Police brutality in the cities, assaults upon unemployment demonstrations and other gatherings of malcontents, shocking disregard for the rights of workers in the Carolina and New England textile strikes and in the mining regions of Illinois and Kentucky became questions of national concern. Americans could see the need for new avenues of legal redress through which such beleaguered citizens could gain equitable consideration in struggling for their rights. The massive condemnation of the Fish

Committee's call for a new wave of national repression further showed that the public wanted tolerance not coercion and restriction.

The new responsibility of moderate elements and their willingness to cooperate for constructive social change made acceptance of this legal shift easier. it encouraged the left to take further actions within the context of the law. It encouraged the right to engage in constructive dialogue and problem solving with those of more radical view, rather than running to the courts and demanding suppression. For a Court chronically accused of substituting its own narrow will for the democratic process, it served to remove that stigma by indicating a renewed faith in that process.[79]

The move was natural and logical for judges in the power sense as well. Their status and prestige was clearly threatened by continued adherence to Taftian principles in a period of intense social disruption. Rather than guaranteeing the sanctity of property, the depression legitimized new public goals—equal opportunity, equal justice, social responsibility, the dignity and the rights of the individual. The courts were not only qualified to develop legitimate avenues of attainment, but traditionally were responsible for insuring them at all times. Maximization of judicial power, both individually and collectively, could best proceed by opening new and easier legal avenues toward such goals.[80]

Many men of property viewed such general legal reorientation with alarm. Millions of other Americans responded with pleased surprise. Civil libertarians were pleased, especially in Hughes's Near opinion, to see the Supreme Court taking action to complement their own desires. A great many middle-class citizens could hardly object when a public servant of the caliber, reputation, and respectability of Charles Evans Hughes took legal action to undercut unseemly local behavior and disrespect for the law.

As to the professional patriots and other ultraconservative 100 percent Americans, the Court's heresy had been carried out in such a way as to leave such citizens small room to protest. They had been proclaiming for a dozen years, in the most overtly chest-thumping fashion, their devotion to such American institutions as the Constitution, the Bill of Rights, and freedom of speech and press and had insisted that these historic rights be guaranteed. The Court's move to afford practical legal protection of them, couched as it was in its own new emphasis upon the importance of the history of such concepts and their proper modern application, left little ground for open protest.

For the average practicing attorney, the move was a real legal boon. The Court had now suggested new avenues by which counsel might challenge a variety of forms of local restriction and hence defend those victimized by it. It had made fairly clear the rules to follow in pursuing such cases. Further the path was now clearly open into federal courts, so that the possibility of the loss of a lawsuit at the local level was now ameliorated by the suggestion that if national standards were involved and were not being enforced, federal authorities would like to hear about it and were prepared to take appropriate action.[81]

Thus, the quiet, legal, free-speech revolution of 1931 was a comparatively simple and logical one. In many respects it was also a highly beneficial one. The Court for the first time in well over a decade had looked at freedom of expression and considered it practically and sensibly. It had admitted that the legal meaning that prior justices had attached to freedom of speech would not bring realistic solutions to problems which arose in that area. It inferred, however, that solutions for problems in that area could not be hammered out by any single legal tool. Courts could at best afford workable legal devices by which men of goodwill, who did believe in the vitality and viability of such concepts, could themselves take positive steps to defend and extend them. The justices, cognizant that legal precepts cannot change human nature, thus did not reject their potential power as symbols of man's decency and desire to conduct his affairs in an equitable way. But they acknowledged realistically that if such symbols were to elicit such salutary behavior, modern ways would have to be afforded whereby their practical day-to-day practice would be in some reasonable harmony and logical relationship to their avowed and espoused principles.[82]

In establishing the tenuous beachhead of 1931, the courts, the most logical agency to give a practical working meaning to freedom of speech, looked both backward and forward. History was turned to in a search from a proper and traditional ideological meaning. Present reality was confronted for a functional meaning which would lead to the successful and proper operation of that concept within modern society. The question remained whether such a beachhead could be held and what steps should be taken to secure and extend it. Here, too, the courts would play a major role. In assuming a new responsibility for translating immediate human and national needs into workable law in the free-speech area, they would be under constant pressure to keep such law relevant to the fast changing challenges of burgeoning national government, war, cold war, and the inevitable complexities created by such developments.

14

Epilogue

The ultimate responsibility for the protection of freedom of speech and press rests upon people like ourselves, the ordinary citizens whose ideas and feelings taken together constitute what we call American public opinion. . . . Within the legal barriers set up by the Constitution and the courts to protect free speech and a free press, there remains ample room for the play of legislative and executive intolerance and repression when supported or instigated by an excited and brutal opinion. Freedom of speech and freedom of press will be effectively preserved in this country only if people themselves value these vital civil liberties and demand that they be protected.

Robert E. Cushman in
Boston University Law Review,
1943

About three fourths of the people interviewed [in a C.B.S. poll] said extremist groups should not be permitted to organize demonstrations against the Government, even if there appeared to be no clear danger of violence. Over half of those questioned would not give everyone the right to criticize the Government if the criticism were thought to be damaging to the national interest, and 55 percent added that newspapers, radio and television should not be permitted to report some stories considered by the Government to be harmful to the national interest.

The New York Times,
April 19, 1970

The implications of the beachhead of 1931 and 1932 differed for the members of the high bench as their assumptions about the proper role of government and individual liberties varied. To the conservative, property-rights-first wing, it was a move fraught with dangerous implications; to the liberal, it was a reaffirmation of historical principles of individual freedom and a needed incentive for responsible people to take action in its name. This meant, on one hand, standing up against local tyranny and, on the other, moving to the logical implications of Brandeis's eloquent concurrence in the 1927 Whitney case and working through local democratic bodies to revoke restrictive laws and substitute for them a healthy new policy of tolerance and pluralism. Legislative creativity and a healthy, reinvigorated federalism would once again reassure individual rights.

Civil libertarians responded accordingly. There could be no relaxation in the struggle against informal restrictions. The Court had opened an encouraging door. There was no guarantee that this represented a permanent change until a set of consistent cases created a firm bastion of legal precedent in the liberal idiom. Nor was there any greater assurance that legislative bodies would pick up such a cue. Since neither of the 1931 rulings involved the rights of labor in its struggle for economic power, civil libertarians were convinced they would have to remain on the firing line, endowed with new hope but sobered by the reality of twelve years of frustration.

This is indicated by the initial jaundiced apprehensions of the American Civil Liberties Union toward Franklin D. Roosevelt's new government. The new President's call for "broad Executive power to wage a war against the emergency, as great as the power that would be given to me if we were in fact invaded by a foreign foe," created apprehensions in the minds of those who recalled the World War I government as one ruthlessly unconcerned with freedom of speech and press.[1] The new administration at first did little to prevent employers from encouraging company unions and engaging in repressive tactics against working people. This led ACLU leaders, in their first annual report under the New Deal, to insist that New Deal policies carried with them "inevitable fears of inroads on the rights of agitation. . . . Alarms are widely expressed over alleged dictatorship by the President, the abrogation of States' rights and the vast economic powers of the federal government," the report continued. Suppression had not yet come because there was as yet "no significant opposition to suppress."[2] There were dangers of federal censorship of everything from the mails and radio to the movies; the only bright development was the Labor Department's abolition of the secret service section, permitting radical aliens to visit the country for the first time in ten years and speak while here.

The 1935 report voiced the same views. Convinced that the New Deal was moving ever further toward the right, it listed as the leading civil liberties issue the increased attack on workers' rights and noted the revival of many of the professional patriot groups with wide use of the Fish Committee Report to maintain an atmosphere of continued suppression. The only favorable reaction toward government was the grudging acknowledgment that the administration had been cordial toward an ACLU-sponsored conference held in Washington to discuss general plans for ending violations of the rights of dissenters.[3] By 1936, the body had shifted positions sharply. The administration was no longer the seat of repression. "The greatest single attack upon American liberties is the resort to force and violence by employers, vigilantes, mobs, troops, private gunmen and compliant sheriffs and police. These bulk far larger and more serious than restrictions by law." If the ACLU was more sanguine toward the proper use of federal authority, it was positively ebullient over the forthcoming La Follette hearings to investigate violations of free speech and assembly and interference with the rights of labor. Its leaders hopefully predicted these would "for the first time put the reactionaries on the defensive."[4]

In the long run the ACLU was to be disappointed in the lack of concrete results from that committee's investigations of company espionage, strikebreaking, and use of private arms.[5] It was thoroughly gratified, however, by the dramatic movement toward attainment of functional freedom of speech for workingmen. This came with the enactment of the Wagner Act, the setting up of the National Labor Relations Board, the subsequent board action in arranging and enforcing collective bargaining and the Supreme Court's consistent upholding of the legality of this whole new development. Although such rulings turned on the commerce clause and not on the First Amendment, ACLU leaders considered them the most important single step toward the attainment of meaningful freedom of speech in modern times.[6] When a later court moved further to surround peaceful picketing with the guarantees of First Amendment freedom of speech, the old complaints of the conservative judicial property bias virtually dropped from their vocabulary. In fact, the annual reports of the late 1930s and early 1940s were paeans of praise for the Supreme Court, the Roosevelt administration, the La Follette Committee, and the salutary actions of Congress in enacting legislation to better advance individual rights and security.[7]

The changed reaction reflected an awareness of important shifts in the relationships of government to the individual. The Roosevelt administration seemed to have rejected the old Progressive assumption that individual rights were to be sublimated to the good of the whole defined by a socially responsible elite. Rather, it emphasized the government's responsibility for insuring economic stability and protecting the individual in order that he might attain the fullest life which his capacity permitted. That emphasis lessened civil libertarians' responsibility for working to protect laborers' rights from abrogation by government. If the federal government would insure full respect for individual liberties, private groups could work for meaningful freedom by fighting repression by local authorities.[8]

Such confidence was reflected in the ACLU's increased concern with segregation, the denial of voting and other rights to the Negro, persecution of the Jehovah's Witnesses, academic freedom, teacher loyalty laws, and the rights of American Indians and citizens in American colonies. Significantly, this still included protecting from hostile opponents the freedom of speech of highly dissident groups from the Nazi-American Bund and the various shirt organizations to the Communists and plain citizens with offbeat panaceas for the cure of the as yet unsolved depression.[9]

The new climate was also the product of a variety of other divergent forces. The dictatorial regimes in Germany and Italy with their emphasis upon total loyalty to the state, the Moscow purge trials, and the threatening militarism, which reached around half the globe to the Far East, renewed the devotion of Americans to the vigilant protection of personal freedom in their own country. Few political leaders, from Communists to ultraconservatives, failed to see the value of boasting that a major American concern had to be the finding of new ways to secure and guarantee such liberties to all Americans.[10] Franklin D. Roosevelt had a compelling need to demonstrate that big government in America did not have to mean suppression of individual rights and coerced loyalty to the state. Anticipating America's role as vital in any challenge to European tyranny, the President was convinced that there were basic international reasons for making democracy work at home. Hopefully, this would renew confidence in it as a viable and workable system for a modern industrial nation. Even various anti-Semitic, pro-Nazi, hate-Roosevelt groups saw the value of using such symbols to gain an audience and callously demanded free speech to propagandize for a system which, if instituted, would make liberty its first casualty.[11]

Even the conservative American Bar Association was caught up in the spirit and, in a desire to demonstrate its enthusiasm for the

First Amendment, established a special Committee on the Bill of Rights in 1938, whose membership included Zechariah Chafee, Jr., Lloyd K. Garrison, John Francis Neylan, and Charles P. Taft. The committee took its first action by filing an amicus curiae brief against the tyrannical local government of Mayor Frank Hague of Jersey City, thereby siding with the ACLU, to say nothing of the Socialists, the Communists, and the Congress of Industrial Organizations, in what proved to be the last major direct action challenge to local restrictions on First Amendment freedoms.[12]

Some evidence suggests that the unwillingness of Congress to provide strong machinery to carry out fully the recommendations of the La Follette committee induced the executive branch to assume a partial role in that regard. "I am anxious that the weight and influence of the Department of Justice should be a force for the protection of the people's liberties," Attorney General Frank Murphy wrote Roger Baldwin on February 3, 1939.[13] The same day Murphy issued Order No. 3204 announcing the establishment of the Civil Liberties Unit in the Department of Justice which would "direct, supervise and conduct prosecutions of violations of the Constitution or Acts of Congress guaranteeing civil rights to individuals." The government, in other words, not only pledged itself to respect the Bill of Rights as a shield against the activity of its own agents which might endanger civil liberties, but to wield a powerful sword to cut away at such encroachments when carried on by state and local governments.[14] Few civil libertarians would have predicted that the vital struggle against local informal controls would be taken over by so unlikely an agency as the federal government, particularly a Justice Department now apparently dedicated to carrying the struggle into the newly opened doors of the courts. All enjoyed what seemed official vindication of their crusades.

With war fears and the challenge of foreign tyranny growing daily, other agencies did their share. In 1940, the United States Office of Education prepared a series of booklets, *Our Freedoms*, "in answer to the increasing appeal of teachers and civic leaders for material on democracy." Beginning with the pamphlet, *The Right of Free Speech*, pitched to secondary school level, the series took a virtually unqualified activist-libertarian position on the fundamental freedoms, insisting that in the case of free speech "we are interested in the principle of free trade in ideas, believing that dangerous proposals are best defeated by sound argument."[15] For those at a more sophisticated level, Zechariah Chafee updated and gave modern relevance to his 1920 classic study, *Freedom of Speech*, hoping to remind Americans of the folly of their abuse of personal liberties in the prior war and anxious to forestall a sharp movement toward defining permissible expression as "license" in any future struggle.[16]

The climate had a pronounced influence upon the Supreme Court. The Court had continued the sharp downgrading of the old concept of freedom of contract, hardly an unpopular move in an era when social regulation seemed essential to most Americans. It had attempted to build a more substantial legal rationale for positive legal protection of Bill of Rights' freedoms, always in the initial stages, however, continuing to leave to administrative and legislative discretion the proper techniques of implementation. Curiously, such decisions, when emanating from the pre-Roosevelt bench were written almost exclusively by Hughes and Roberts, with more categorically recognized libertarians, such as Brandeis, Stone, and Cardozo, silently acquiescing.[17]

Whether the eloquence of Hughes was motivated by a desire to strike an indirect blow at the New Deal and excessive governmental power is conjectural. On the eve of Roosevelt's announced intent to curtail unwarranted judicial policy making, he rose to new heights in proclaiming the right and necessity for the people to stand against legislative encroachment upon their fundamental liberties, in order "to preserve inviolate the constitutional rights of free speech, free press and free assembly in order to maintain the opportunity for free political discussion, to the end that government may be responsive to the will of the people and that changes, if desired, may be obtained by peaceful means. . . . Therein lies the security of the Republic, the very foundation of constitutional government."[18] Early the following year, after the court-packing tempest had died down, Justice Stone wrote to Judge Irving Lehman: "I have been deeply concerned about the increasing racial and religious intolerance which seems to bedevil the world, and which I greatly fear may be augmented in this country. For that reason I was greatly disturbed by the attacks on the Court and the Constitution last year, for one consequence of the program of judicial reform might well result in breaking down the guarantees of individual liberties."[19]

The court-packing crisis encouraged justices to reaffirm their commitment to civil liberties at the same time that they sustained federal social and economic legislation. In such reaffirmation, freedom of speech gained new judicial emphasis. Cardozo, writing in a case in late 1937, emphasized the "social and moral values" of freedom of thought and speech, insisting that they existed on a different plane from the other rights set out in the first eight amendments and maintaining that freedom of speech especially "is the matrix, the indispensable condition, of nearly every other form of freedom."[20]

The justices were still stinging from charges of failing to adhere to judicial self-restraint. Consequently they did not immediately assume the role of determining whether the seriousness of a supposed evil from speech was sufficiently great to produce the social necessity for suppression of that speech. Caution was still the greater part of wisdom. Yet the desire to join the national civil liberties' crusade was not absent, and, in an inconspicuous footnote in an inconspicuous 1938 ruling, Justice Stone suggested a possible legal rationale. Proposing what would later evolve into a "preferred freedoms" concept, Stone suggested that legislation regulating economic matters should have a higher presumption of constitutionality than that restricting individual freedom. Yet even here he was quick to add: "it is unnecessary to consider now whether legislation which restricts those political processes which can ordinarily be expected to bring about repeal of undesirable legislation, is to be subjected to more exacting judicial scrutiny under the general prohibitions of the Fourteenth Amendment than are most other types of legislation."[21]

By 1940, with membership of the bench shifting sharply, the Court was prepared to undertake the "more exacting judicial scrutiny" to which Stone had referred. It now struck down statutes restricting peaceful picketing and peaceful distribution of leaflets.[22] Both cases, significantly, required wrapping the protection of the First Amendment around situations not previously considered in that context. In the picketing case of 1940, the Court took one more positive legal step, revealing both its current temper and its future intentions. Application of the preferred freedoms concept pushed the legal line between liberty and license far in the direction of underwriting virtually every type of utterance except that clearly dangerous to society. In seeking a legal tool to do this, the logical and most accessible one was Holmes's "clear and present danger rule," applied in its literal sense as Holmes had originally conceived it. The rule became one of the key grounds for throwing out the Florida antipicketing statute and a number of comparable restrictions as violations of free speech. It thus gained, for almost the first time since its enunciation, a meaning close to Holmes's original intent.[23]

The administration lost no opportunity to capitalize on the intensified public concern for personal freedom. Roosevelt, sensing the climate of the period proclaimed six months before Pearl Harbor, "Free speech and a free press are still in the possession of the people of the United States and it is important that it should remain there. For suppression of opinion and censorship of news are among the mortal weapons that dictatorships direct against their own peoples and direct against the world. . . . It would be a shameful use of patriotism to suggest that opinion should be stifled in its service."[24]

The President shortly expanded the theme. With the nation only a few weeks at war, he virtually cast the struggle with Hitler and his allies as an international crusade for the principles of the American Bill of Rights. In enunciating with Winston Churchill the "four freedoms" as primary war aims, he designated these, in order, as freedom of speech and expression, freedom of worship, freedom from want, and freedom from fear.[25]

At the more practical level, administration leaders set precedents, both formal and informal, to protect domestic dissent. On December 17, 1941, Attorney General Francis Biddle informed United States attorneys throughout the country that "prosecution of persons arrested for alleged seditious utterances must not be undertaken unless consent is first obtained from the Department of Justice."[26] Four days later, Biddle, a prominent friend and member of the ACLU, dismissed complaints lodged against three men for alleged seditious utterances, stating categorically: "Free speech as such ought not to be restricted."[27] *The New York Times*, which had been highly sanguine about restrictions on sedition in World War I, editorially endorsed such action, commending the Congress, the people, and the courts for their absence of hysteria in regard to this war, urging "a deeper toleration of the thought we hate" as a "course not only sound philosophically, but practically beneficial."[28]

The nation emerged from the war unscathed in its commitment to freedom of speech. Given the totalitarian nature of the enemy and the general unity of Americans behind the war's purposes, dissent, except from a handful of intransigent Nazi supporters, was minimal. The few wartime prosecutions which resulted in curtailment of liberty were virtually nonprecedent making. Even so, such a widely approved action as the curtailment of Father Coughlin's pro-Nazi, anti-Semitic organ, *Social Justice*, drew protest as an abrogation of traditional liberties, as did the indictment of eighteen leaders of the Trotskyite Socialist Workers party under the Smith Act, with, in this instance, Attorney General Biddle's approval.[29] But by the time the United Nations charter was adopted, with its eloquent endorsement of personal freedom, and military action victoriously ended, Americans faced a brave new world, hopeful of extending the four freedoms into peacetime society.

The cold war and new concerns with national security as early as 1947 played upon the apprehensions of Americans and began a sharp movement back toward restriction. Before that tendency in turn led to a new national revulsion, it came close to returning freedom of speech to the precarious position of the dark days of January 1920. The depression had undermined the professional patriots, and many such groups dissolved. The philosophy of repression remained, however, fed by a growing fear of man's inability to preserve his own independence and integrity against such relentless impersonal forces as tyranny and dictatorship against which it was the duty of government to shield him. Distressed by Roosevelt's lack of restrictive action and by his tendency to move toward economic statism, demoralized professional patriots found new opportunities for exploiting public apprehensions.

Hatred of Roosevelt and fear by business leaders of the growing power of the federal government emerged in such organizations as the Liberty League. The situation seemed made to order for super-patriots once again to make available their services. Fred R. Marvin, after a futile attempt to gain power through a new American Coalition of Patriotic Societies, turned to grinding out pamphlets for the League for Constitutional Government, levying against Roosevelt and the New Deal many of the same charges he had dispensed in the 1920s.[30] Despite the threat of libel suits, Harry A. Jung stepped up the activities of his American Vigilent Intelligence Federation, adding to his pitch against the reds and pinks a new anti-Semitic twist combined with charges of national dictatorship.[31] The American Legion remained, in the eyes of the ACLU at least, the principle instrument for the suppression of dissent in the country on a direct basis, even though Legionnaires at the higher echelons found it useful to strike an ideological pose for free speech as an abstract national value. Futher Coughlin and a variety of openly or clandestinely pro-Nazi groups, from the Silvershirts to the Black Legion, found Hitler's assault upon Jews and Communists a pattern to be emulated by those who would rid America of her internal corruptionists and seditionists.[32]

Roosevelt's smashing victory in the election of 1936 illustrated the futility of this kind of opposition to New Deal programs and policies. It spurred those hostile to the President and his administration into seeking the creation of public instruments with which to combat New Deal liberalism. Such an antiadministration spirit undoubtedly underlay the successful effort to get Congress actively into the anticommunist business. On August 12, 1938, a special House Committee on Un-American activities, chaired by Representative Martin Dies, one of the most aggressive champions of the earlier Fish Committee hearings and recommendations, held its first public hearing. The committee began with great bravado, suggesting that it hoped to rid America of all subversive influences from communism to nazism. Its early actions made it evident that its primary intent was to strike out at the wide range of activist-libertarian groups in the country which had been the target for repression for nearly twenty years, hoping, if possible, to tar the Roosevelt administration with the "red" label which it hoped to attach to them.[33]

The committee, however, although enjoying wide support from dissident right-wing groups and well supported by congressional appropriations, was decried and rejected by the administration from the outset. When, for example, it sought to drag red herring charges across the La Follette Committee's activities, Roosevelt's response was to call for higher appropriations for the latter.[34] Lacking official support, the committee was hamstrung by the usual limitations on the authority of a congressional committee. With the federal courts actively and openly concerned for the protection of the liberties of the individual, the committee was also limited in its ability to pursue its victims. It was thus pushed into stimulating new forms of informal and local controls as devices for implementing its desires to punish and restrict too liberal citizens. Ironically, the very success of the activist-libertarians in getting legal protection in one sphere encouraged activist-repressionists to create new techniques of extra-legal violation in others.

Significantly, given its orientation and the assumptions of many of its members, the Dies Committee was particularly prone to proscribe group-connected activities and individuals. It was particularly motivated by ancient and traditional fears of conspiratorial action by private associations able, supposedly through rigid discipline and insulated indoctrination, to coerce their membership into acts antagonistic to the republic. It focused sharply on such groups, taking in the extreme the position that once one joined such a group his individualism disappeared and with it, by his own act of voluntary rejection of accepted principles, he surrendered his basic right to utilize such principles as free speech, press, and assembly. He also abrogated his ability to enjoy all the procedural guarantees of the American legal system.[35] The idea that an individual could belong to such a group and still retain his Americanism uncorrupted was generally rejected. The idea that there were any individual differences between members of a group on matters of opinion inevitably seemed to be ignored. Such groups, which were clearly up to no good, should have their real purposes revealed and their members should be held up to public exposure so that they might be subjected to proper sanctions, either public or private.[36]

The Federal Council of Churches, various pacifist and social action bodies, militant trade unions, a great variety of left-wing political organizations, and the ACLU quickly came in for condemnation from the committee. With the exception of the Nazis, with which the committee bothered little, and the Communists, who by the late

1930s were anathema to almost all Americans, there were few bodies to which the committee was successfully able to make subversive charges stick. Such difficulty was clearly illustrated by Dies's capitulation in 1939, when, after many veiled innuendoes, he finally was forced to admit publicly that "there was no evidence that the American Civil Liberties Union is a communist organization."[37]

The Communists themselves were fair game. Although the action came totally apart from committee activity, Congress, in mid-1940, enacted the first peacetime sedition act since 1798, adhering to the same type of assumptions regarding group role. It carefully proscribed those who adhered to communism's tenets, belonged to its organizations, or sought to advance its policies by any but the most abstract methods.[38] With the Soviet Union as an essential and much needed wartime ally and a new burst of united-frontism demonstrated by domestic Communists during the war period, the Smith Act, despite grave apprehensions by such free-speech devotees as Zechariah Chafee and others, did not become a major instrument for suppression of freedom of expression during the war period. Yet, like Franklin Roosevelt's quiet 1938 revival of the once discredited General Intelligence Division in the Justice Department and renewed information collecting and classifying by the FBI,[39] it was available when cold war stresses came. It was quickly turned into a ready instrument for suppression, especially in the hands of a new administration which shared little of the previous one's concern and devotion for the primacy of free speech and civil liberties.

As cold war tensions grew, the Truman administration quickly came to rival its right-wing critics in new calls for strengthening national security. The result was the inevitable sublimation of individual liberty to social need. Congress, in the Taft-Hartley Act, joined the growing tendency to insure loyalty and curtailment of dissent through test oaths being demanded by many states.[40] Republicans, especially, strongly supported a Mundt-Nixon bill that would expand the proscriptions of the Smith Act even further and demand multifarious new forms of internal security legislation. The executive branch, not to be outdone, instituted broad-scale federal loyalty clearance programs and, particularly anxious to extricate itself from growing charges of softness on communism and dangerous affiliation with red and pink groups, called for active prosecution under the Smith Act of the top leaders of the Communist party in the country on charges of open advocacy of overthrow of the government by force and violence.[41]

From a legal standpoint, such a repressive climate once again focused attention upon the courts as the agency charged with setting

forth a proper legal definition of the permissible limits of freedom
of expression. The adaptability of the law to current tensions was
demonstrated as the Court quickly improvised legal ways to reverse
what had until that time been an ongoing trend of permissibility
extending from the wartime period. The Court, dominated by Roosevelt appointees, especially since the addition of Justice Wiley Rutledge
in 1943, had adhered rigidly to the "clear and present danger test"
in free-speech cases. In the years between 1943 and 1949, it had
broadened the concept by extending it into a variety of new areas.[42]
As late as 1949, in a case in which a defrocked priest had provoked
violence by his intemperate anti-Semitic remarks, it ruled that even
speech which "invites dispute . . . induces a condition of unrest,
creates dissatisfaction with conditions as they are, or even stirs people
to anger" is permissible. "There is no room under our Constitution,"
wrote Justice Douglas for the Court, "for a more restrictive view."[43]

Such was not true for Communists. The ability to single out the
Communists as part of an identifiable group, and one which Congress
was maintaining through its legislation was the instrument of a foreign
enemy, somewhat eased the pain of capitulation which the membership of the bench clearly saw was the only safe course, given the
tensions of McCarthyism, McCarranism, and loyalty-security hysteria.[44]

Chief Justice Vinson's opinion upholding the Smith Act convictions
of the communist leaders was a clear turn to restrictive free-speech
precedents. Vinson began by insisting that Congress had full power
to enact legislation to prohibit acts intended to overthrow the government by force and violence. The question, he contended, following
Sanford's reasoning in the Gitlow case, was thus not the validity
of the statute but whether, when the statute was used to restrict
speech, a First Amendment violation resulted. In answering, Vinson
stressed the relative quality of free speech, insisting that it was not
an unlimited and unqualified right, but one which must, on occasion,
be subordinated to other values and considerations. As to the point
of proper limitation, he was willing to concede that the "clear and
present danger test" might be viable if the interest that the state
was attempting to protect was insubstantial; however, he questioned
whether the test was practical when that interest was great and
national survival was involved. Here, he argued, a more workable
statement of the rule would be that proposed by Judge Learned
Hand at the lower court level; that "in each case [courts] must
ask whether the gravity of the 'evil,' discounted by its improbability,
justifies such invasion of free speech as is necessary to avoid the
danger." Using such a test, he was easily able to show that the
speech of the Communists did not warrant First Amendment protec-

tion, the implication being clear that legislation applying to such a group could restrict speech if it conformed to such a test. This view he justified, in the hope of garnering some liberal support, as being within the proper spirit of Holmes's and Brandeis's free-speech philosophy.[45]

Many civil libertarians protested vigorously as did members of Vinson's own bench. Justice Black was particularly adamant about what he considered an ignominious maneuver. With Justice Douglas agreeing, he charged that the Chief Justice's somewhat lame rationalizing established a doctrine that "waters down the First Amendment so that it amounts to little more than an admonition to Congress" and contended that "the Amendment as so construed is not likely to protect any but those 'safe' or orthodox views which rarely need its protection." But Black was forced to acknowledge realistically that, public opinion being what it then was, few would protest such a departure from fundamental principles of free speech, and could only hope, with obvious discouragement, that "in calmer times, when present pressures, passions and fears subside, this or some later Court will restore the First Amendment liberties to the high preferred place where they belong in a free society."[46] The "clear and present danger rule" was seen to be a frail reed for underwriting a policy of broad permissiveness in the free-speech area. It was incapable, like courts themselves, of guaranteeing the right of free self-expression in the face of strong public pressure to curtail it.[47] The actions of the government here, as well as in its often highly arbitrary loyalty-security programs, rekindled many of the deep-seated apprehensions of traditional civil libertarians that while the government might be an agency for protecting civil liberties, it could still, with little effort, be turned into an efficient weapon for suspending them.

Black's calmer times came sooner than many thoroughly depressed civil libertarians expected. The downfall of McCarthy, the election of a Republican President clearly seeking national calm and a new normalcy, and especially the appointment of a new Chief Justice, committed in philosophy to a policy of social progress, restored some of the balance. The Court had not retreated from keeping legal channels open for challenging misapplication of a variety of restrictions and inhibitions on individual freedom. In cases in 1957 and 1958 it moved to restrict the overzealous application of such weapons opting for free speech and the importance of its protection in a number of divergent areas.[48] It then went on to question sharply certain of the overaggressive and repressive tactics of congressional committees, particularly the House Un-American Activities Committee.[49] In the face of a new wave of right-wing criticism, however, it was again forced to retreat to safer ground in the latter years of the decade, thus seeming to swing the pendulum quickly from permissiveness to restrictiveness as public pressures dictated.[50]

The fact that the meaning of freedom of speech had become primarily a concern of judges, attempting to define it through the technique of splitting fine legal hairs over the precise and proper limits of its operation, was in itself highly revealing.[51] The free-speech issue might have been one of the major instruments for the redefinition of fundamental social relationships in the 1920s and a major rallying cry for democracy in the late 1930s and war years. In the 1950s, it was no longer a public issue which excited or even aroused the great concern of a new generation. Free-speech symbolism, especially as a catalyst for producing a variety of active and constructive forms of social action, had scarcely survived the war. It had hung on among certain civil libertarians for whom it had a special meaning and had become a temporary device for opposing McCarthyism. Even this action was defensive and often uncreative and partook far more of the old orientation of freedom from unwarranted restraint than freedom for the full realization of meaningful social values. The reasons were obvious and important.

The burgeoning and broad based prosperity of the 1940s, 1950s, and 1960s was grounded upon the emancipation and growth in status and power of the class for which earlier civil libertarians had fought free-speech fights in the 1920s and 1930s. The courts were open and prepared to adjudicate challenges to overly restrictive informal local controls. ACLU attorneys were ready to provide legal counsel when a client could not afford it. The increasing development of a massive, pluralistic, urban society made informal local controls both irrelevant and unnecessary. The average person did not feel sufficiently deprived of First Amendment freedoms to become involved in any crusade that had their preservation and extension as its major rallying cry. Strictures to economic success were not that great, and free-speech campaigns would hardly topple the remaining ones.

Such an attitude certainly constituted an indirect victory for the activist-libertarian philosophy. It represented acceptance of the position that only positive programs of intervention could eliminate age-old forces and strictures that inhibited an individual's economic opportunities. Only by freeing the individual from forces against which he was personally unequipped to fight successfully could conditions be created wherein he could enjoy meaningful individuality and the opportunity to take advantage of boasted rights and freedoms which a democratic system held up as his birthright.

By the 1950s, those in a position to use this new individuality found little incentive to continue extending old programs into more and more peripheral areas. More obvious frustration of human potential and the opportunity to fully utilize democracy's instruments was being carried out through the denial of political, educational, and social opportunities. In this regard, an obvious situation cried for relief; namely, the plight of the southern Negro and, all too often, his northern counterpart.

A new generation of Americans, finding the concerns and crusades of their fathers irrelevant, felt called upon to redefine the symbols of democracy in terms applicable to the challenges of their day. For them, giving coherent meaning to the traditional symbols of liberty, freedom, and equality meant attacking the age-old skeleton in the democratic closet, the professed equality and dignity of all men, tarnished by the refusal to extend such theories in practice to over 10 percent of the population.

The fight to obtain full rights for the Negro was happily devoid of the embarrassing complications of national security. The possibilities of inducing broad charges of disloyalty which fighting for free speech for the Communists inevitably produced was also avoided. On the contrary, America, as leader of the free world, was involved in a life and death struggle with a new totalitarianism abroad, and in a rivalry for the minds of millions of peoples in newly emerging areas of Africa and Asia. Such activity was considered by many to be a primary weapon in the cold war. By the 1950s, as some cynics remarked, times were never so bad for civil liberties or so good for civil rights. But despite massive governmental support from the administration, from Frank Murphy's old Civil Liberties Unit, now reconstituted as the Civil Rights Section, and with a greatly expanded staff actively moving to secure civil rights, and eventually from Congress, the battle was still a long and frequently bloody one, given the strength of entrenched local interests and their skill and willingness in using every type of diversionary measure to frustrate its success.

Whether conscious of the fact or not, this civil rights movement owed much to the free-speech crusade of the 1920s and early 1930s. Like that movement, it maintained philosophically that only through insuring conditions of equality could man enjoy and utilize his liberties. Like that movement, it recognized that in daily operation one of the major factors preventing Americans from enjoying the full use of their heritage of liberty, freedom, and equality was the application of local, informal controls. Like that movement, its leaders utilized as their weapons direct challenges to those applying such strictures, boldly inviting violence, incarceration, and retaliation by hostile law enforcement officials, local courts, and vigilante groups. Unlike that movement, the new generation had the encouragement of broad assistance unavailable to its predecessors. Federal courts, Justice Department officials, burgeoning legal tools authorized by congressional civil-rights measures, the encouragement of Presidents, and massive public sympathy for its immediate and long-range objectives, strongly missing before, were now clearly available. For many of these, debts were owed to the earlier free-speech movement.

The challenge of making traditional American symbolism meaningful in the context of immediate social problems thus temporarily moved away from free speech as a priority as equality eclipsed the activist attention. Yet the eclipse was brief. As a new generation of restless youth set out to challenge national and local policies, which they felt were instruments for the undermining of human freedom, dignity, and individuality, they quickly came to realize the centrality of free speech as a concept, a practice, and a vital instrument for accomplishing social goals. Thus, while often viewing their problems as unique and their situation as peculiarly frustrating, in actuality, many were reliving the experience of an earlier day and reenacting a significant segment of the recent American past.

Notes

Chapter 1

1. "Text of President Kennedy's Commencement Address to Yale's Graduating Class," *The New York Times*, June 12, 1962, p. 20.

2. Alfred N. Whitehead, *Symbolism: Its Meaning and Effect* (New York, 1927), p. 88.

3. This statement was carried on the masthead of the newspaper *Communist Labor* during the early years of the decade.

4. Robert E. Cushman, "Ten Years of the Supreme Court: Civil Liberties," *American Political Science Review* 42 (February 1948): 42–43.

5. Jerold S. Auerbach, "The Patrician as Libertarian: Zechariah Chafee, Jr. and Freedom of Speech," *New England Quarterly* 42 (December 1969): 511–531.

Chapter 2

1. Archibald MacLeish, "Loyalty and Freedom," *American Scholar* 22 (Autumn 1953): 397–398.

2. Seymour M. Lipset, *Political Man: The Social Bases of Politics* (Garden City, 1963), p. xxiii.

3. John P. Roche, "American Liberty: An Examination of the 'Tradition' of Freedom," in Milton Konvitz, ed., *Aspects of Liberty* (Ithaca, 1958), p. 138.

4. Max Farrand, ed., *The Records of the Federal Convention of 1787* (New Haven, 1911–1937), I, p. 49.

5. Jacob E. Cooke, ed., *The Federalist* (Middletown, Conn., 1961), pp. 351–352.

6. Leonard W. Lévy, *Legacy of Suppression: Freedom of Speech and Press in Early American History* (Cambridge, 1960).

7. Levy particularly objects to Zechariah Chafee's contention that it was the intention of the founding fathers who ratified the First Amendment to "wipe out the common law of sedition, and make further prosecutions for criticism of the government, without any incitement to law-breaking, forever impossible in the United States of America." Zechariah Chafee, Jr., *Free Speech in the United States* (Cambridge, 1948), p. 21.

8. Donald Meiklejohn, "Review of *Legacy of Suppression,*" *Southern California Law Review* 35 (Fall 1961): 111–120; William O. Douglas, "The Bill of Rights Is Not Enough," *New York University Law Review* 38 (April 1963): 218. Justice Black, in response to government's argument to the contrary, reiterated the Chafee position from the bench in 1961. Communist Party of the U.S. v. Subversive Activities Control Board, 81 S. Ct. 1357, at 1143, n. 46.

9. James Morton Smith, "Review of *Legacy of Suppression,*" *William and Mary Quarterly*, 3d ser., 20 (January 1963): 158–159.

10. Leonard W. Levy, "Liberty and the First Amendment: 1790–1800," *American Historical Review* 68 (October 1962): 22–37.

11. Francis N. Thorpe, *The Federal and State Constitutions* (Washington, 1909), V, p. 3083.

12. David B. Davis, "Some Ideological Functions of Prejudice in Ante-Bellum America," *American Quarterly* 15 (Summer 1963): 118.

13. Rudolf Rocker, *Pioneers of American Freedom* (Los Angeles, 1949), p. 57.

14. Quoted in Paul A. Freund, *On Understanding the Supreme Court* (Boston, 1950), pp. 15–16.

15. Quoted in Roger N. Baldwin, "The Myth of Law and Order," in Samuel D. Schmalhausen, *Behold America* (New York, 1931), p. 659.

16. Russel B. Nye, *Fettered Freedom: Civil Liberties and the Slavery Controversy: 1830–1860* (East Lansing, 1949), p. 139. For an intimate view of the role freedom of speech played in the life of a northern abolitionist family, see Hermann R. Muelder, *Fighters for Freedom: The History of Anti-Slavery Activities of Men and Women Associated with Knox College* (New York, 1959), pp. 172–188.

17. Commonwealth v. Barrett, 9 Leigh 665 (1839).

18. Arnold E. K. Nash, "The Judicial Defense of Liberalism in the South Atlantic States: 1831–1861" (Senior Honors thesis, Harvard University, 1958), was able to document rather fully Clement Eaton's contention that "the surprising fact about Southern laws curtailing freedom of discussion is that they were so rarely invoked. The courts . . . tended to moderate the harshness of the written code, and to throw the mantle of protection around minorities." Clement Eaton, *Freedom of Thought in the Old South* (Durham, 1940), p. 143. Nash feels that the ruling of a Virginia Judge Lomax in 1850 (Jarvis v. Bacon, 7 Grattan 602), upholding a Methodist minister who had criticized slavery on the grounds that to convict for the expression of a moral opinion was to contravene the Bill of Rights of Virginia, "was sufficiently successful to forestall further cases before the war."

19. Nye, *Fettered Freedom*, p. 61.

20. D. H. Lawrence, *Studies in Classic American Literature* (London, 1924). A curiously similar sentiment was expressed a decade earlier by Walter Lippmann, *Drift and Mastery* (New York, 1914).

21. James Bryce, *The American Commonwealth* (New York, 1909), II, p. 349.

22. The relationship between freedom of speech and freedom of assembly, while not inevitable, is close since frequently meaningful expression gains its greatest impact while addressed to an audience. A suggestive study of restrictions on the right to assembly is found in James M. Jarrett and Vernon A. Mund, "The Right of Assembly," *New York University Law Quarterly Review* 9 (September 1931): 1–31.

23. Baldwin in Schmalhausen, *Behold America*, p. 659.

24. Lillian Symes and Travers Clement, *Rebel America: The Story of Social Revolt in the United States* (New York, 1934), p. 159. Most's pamphlet, *Science of Revolutionary Warfare: A Manual of Instructions in the Use and Preparation of Nitroglycerine, Dynamite, Gun-cotton, Fulminating Mercury, Bombs, Fuses, Poisons, etc., etc.,* setting forth detailed information on how and where to plant bombs in churches, palaces, ballrooms, and similar gathering places in order to obtain the "happiest" results, reveals some of his values. See James B. Christoph, "Alexander Berkman and American Anarchism" (Master's thesis, University of Minnesota, 1952), pp. 25–27.

25. William Preston, *Aliens and Dissenters: Federal Suppression of Radicals: 1903–1913* (Cambridge, 1963), p. 21. For a later codification and summation of what had often been a previously unarticulated sentiment regarding free speech and the immigrant, see Henry P. Fairchild, *The Melting-Pot Mistake* (Boston, 1926), pp. 255–256.

26. Merrill D. Peterson, *The Jeffersonian Image in the American Mind* (New York, 1962), pp. 330ff.

27. Although too much can easily be made of it, the appointment by President Wilson of Anthony Comstock, the ancient Victorian vice exposer and symbol of Puritan inhibition and snooping pruriency, as United States delegate to the International Purity Congress at the San Francisco Exposition in 1915 is worthy of comment. See Heywood Broun and Margaret Leech, *Anthony Comstock: Roundsman of the Lord* (New York, 1927), pp. 258ff. On the other hand, Charles Forcey is quite correct in pointing out the danger of taking a monolithic view of Progressive authoritarianism. In such men as Croly, Weyl, and Lippmann, such authoritarianism was belied by their strong concern for civil liberties. In fact, they "were considerably more strenuous in their defense of individual rights than the prophet of the New Freedom in the White House." Charles Forcey, *The Crossroads of Liberalism* (New York, 1961), p. 214. See also Henry May, *The End of American Innocence* (New York, 1959), pp. 351–352.

28. The stated purpose of the organization was to "Promote such judicial construction of the Constitution of the United States, and of the several states, and of the statutes passed in conformity therewith, as will secure to every person the greatest liberty consistent with the equal liberty of all others, and especially to preclude the punishment of any mere psycho-

logical offense; and, to that end, by all lawful means to oppose every form of governmental censorship over any method for the expression, communication or transmission of ideas, whether by use of previous inhibition or subsequent punishment; and to promote such legislative enactments and constitutional amendments, state and national, as will secure these ends." See Theodore Schroeder, *Free Speech for Radicals* (New York, 1916). On the League, see also Hutchins Hapgood, *A Victorian in the Modern World* (New York, 1939), p. 279; Lincoln Steffens, "An Answer and An Answer," *Everybody's Magazine* 25 (November 1911): 717–720.

29. U.S., Congress, Senate, *Industrial Relations, Final Report and Testimony Submitted to Congress by the Commission on Industrial Relations,* S. Doc. 415, 64th Cong., 1st sess., 1916, XI, p. 10841. For a popular expression of the same sentiment, see Courtenay Lemon, "Free Speech in the United States," *Pearson's Magazine* 36 (December 1916): 531.

30. Senate, *Industrial Relations,* p. 10842.

31. Although Black's views are best assessed from a reading of his judicial opinions, a brief summary on his free-speech position can be found in "Justice Black and First Amendment 'Absolutes': A Public Interview," *New York University Law Review* 37 (June 1962): 549–563.

32. Significantly, the Free Speech League was primarily a letterhead organization with little if any organizational structure and no concrete program other than "educating" through a vigorous pamphleteering service. The standard statement of the League's purposes (*n.*28 above) ended, "If you are interested send a contribution to THE FREE SPEECH LEAGUE, 56 East 59th St., New York City."

33. Paul F. Brissenden, *The I.W.W.: A Study of American Syndicalism* (New York, 1920), pp. 351–352.

34. The technique antedated the IWW, however. Richard Drinnon, *Rebel in Paradise* (Chicago, 1961), pp. 121–123, gives numerous examples of Emma Goldman's use of the device in her campaign to propagate her views, and cites a variety of press reactions to the approach.

35. Brissenden, *The I.W.W.,* p. 265. See also Donald M. Barnes, "The Ideology of the Industrial Workers of the World: 1905–1921" (Ph.D. diss., Washington State University, 1962), pp. 147ff.

36. Brissenden, *The I.W.W.,* p. 264. For the futility of police violence in an effort to suppress these affairs at Los Angeles and San Diego, see U.S. National Commission on Law Observance and Enforcement, *Report on Police, No. 14* (Washington, 1931), p. 24.

37. Brissenden, *The I.W.W.,* p. 367, cites a "partial list" of twenty-six such fights in the years between 1909 and 1916, indicating that "the most important of these disturbances was that at San Diego, which broke out about February 1, 1912, and continued until late the following summer" (p. 265). The San Diego fight was reported at length in the *New York Call.* A republishing of those reports is contained in Schroeder, *Free Speech for Radicals,* pp. 116–190. See also Symes and Clement, *Rebel America,* pp. 260ff.; Joyce L. Kornbluh, *Rebel Voices: An I.W.W. Anthology* (Ann Arbor, 1964), chap. 4.

38. By 1916 and 1917, the IWW was making significant strides in

its organizational campaigns and its income was steadily increasing. Philip Taft, "The IWW in the Grain Belt," *Labor History* 1 (February 1960).

39. "After the Battle," *Survey* 28 (April 6, 1912): 1–2. The general problem of the refusal to accept unquestioningly the rationale of the system and work dutifully within it is explored in detail in Reinhard Bendix, *Work and Authority in Industry: Ideologies of Management in the Course of Industrialization* (New York, 1956), pp. 254–340.

40. Ray Stannard Baker, *Woodrow Wilson, Life and Letters, Facing War, 1915–1917* (New York, 1937) IV, pp. 506–507. The authenticity of this statement has been challenged, however. See Jerold S. Auerbach, "Woodrow Wilson's 'Prediction' to Frank Cobb: Words Historians Should Doubt Ever Got Spoken," *Journal of American History* 54 (December 1967): 608–617.

41. Chafee, *Free Speech in the United States*, pp. 39–41.

42. Philip Taft, "The Federal Trials of the IWW," *Labor History* 3 (Winter 1963): 57–91. Carol E. Jenson, "Agrarian Pioneer in Civil Liberties: The Non-Partisan League in Minnesota During World War I" (Ph.D. diss., University of Minnesota, 1968). For a numerical summary of Espionage Act prosecutions, see Harry N. Scheiber, *The Wilson Administration and Civil Liberties* (Ithaca, 1960), pp. 61–63. For examples of the effectiveness of informal controls in this regard, see O. A. Hilton, "The Minnesota Commission of Public Safety in World War I, 1917–1919," *Bulletin of the Oklahoma Agricultural and Mechanical College* 68 (May 15, 1951): 27, 29, 36.

43. In June 1917, Wilson warned those who opposed the war: "For us there is but one choice. We have made it. Woe be to the man or group of men that seeks to stand in our way in this day of high resolution." Flag Day Address, June 14, 1917, quoted in Scheiber, *The Wilson Administration*, p. 27. For Theodore Roosevelt's reaction to Wilson's crackdown on criticism, see Elting E. Morison, ed., *The Letters of Theodore Roosevelt* (Cambridge, 1954), VIII, pp. 1320–1321.

Chapter 3

1. *Congressional Record*, 65th Cong., 3d sess. (1919), p. 5066.

2. Charles N. Fay, *Business in Politics: Suggestions for Leaders in American Business* (Cambridge, 1926), pp. 166ff. For a general assessment of business attitudes in the 1920s, see James W. Prothro, *Dollar Decade: Business Ideas in the 1920's* (Baton Rouge, 1954).

3. Nicholas Murray Butler, *The Real Labor Problem: An Address Delivered before the Institute of Arts and Sciences, Columbia University, October 13, 1919* (New York, 1920), p. 12. Butler attacked labor for its lack of patience and reasonableness in demanding too much too soon. Gutzon Borglum, in responding to Butler for a "Committee of Twelve" wrote: "It is a keen disappointment that although a known disciple of reactionary politics and the laissez faire principle, he should not himself have offered some of the 'far reaching and instrumental reforms (he admits) easily possible' or indicated some direction toward which equitable coopera-

tion should be established in the producing world. Instead, he pleads especially for the attitude of 'reasonableness' with no reference to equity, and once rebukes Labor for having made to date no single constructive suggestion. This together with his sweeping intolerance of free speech, organization by those not of his belief, has left an unfortunate impression." *The Labor Problem,* no. 1, December 10, 1919, p. 1, copy in Widener Library, Harvard University.

4. Quoted in Savel Zimand, *The Open Shop Drive: Who Is Behind It and Where Is It Going?* (New York, 1921), p. 1.

5. Butler candidly admitted in his Columbia University address that "the experience of the war taught us that propaganda can do almost anything with public opinion, at least for a time," but while apparently condoning that experience, expressed alarm that "at this moment propaganda of all kinds is well under way all about us except as regards the one essential subject of the State's own preservation," Butler, *Real Labor Problem,* p. 12.

6. *Proceedings of the National Association of Manufacturers,* "Our Industrial Platform" (New York, 1920), p. 272. See also Albion G. Taylor, *Labor Policies of the National Association of Manufacturers,* University of Illinois Studies in the Social Sciences, XV (Urbana, 1928).

7. Committee on Free Speech, Free Press and Peaceable Public Assembly, miscellaneous papers, National Civic Federation Papers, New York Public Library.

8. "Freedom of Speech and Press vs. License," *National Civic Federation Review* 5 (April 1, 1920): 2–3.

9. P. Tecumseh Sherman, quoted in "The Answer—Root Out Revolutionary Radicalism," *National Civic Federation Review* 5 (September 25, 1920): 3–4.

10. The attitude was not without merit. The biographer of William E. Borah speaks of "the Senator's opposition to the repressive war measures," but adds: "He knew that if the Government itself did not enact stringent legislation the local 'patriots,' acting under no authority would take vigorous measures to stamp out every conceivable form of disloyalty. His files contained many letters from persons who were being persecuted by local guardians of the Republic. . . . Although the Senator could not bring himself to support the severe restrictions Congress placed upon freedom of expression, his opposition to them was tempered with the realization that such legislation might give local vigilantes less excuse for roughness." Claudius O. Johnson, *Borah of Idaho* (New York, 1936), p. 215.

11. *Anarchism on Trial, Trial and Speeches of Alexander Berkman and Emma Goldman in the U.S. District Court in the City of New York, 1917* (New York, n.d.), p. 73. See also Richard Drinnon, *Rebel in Paradise* (Chicago, 1962), pp. 193–194.

12. Theodore Draper, *The Roots of American Communism* (New York, 1957), traces the early history of the rise of the Communist party in the United States. As a typical example of liberal enthusiasm for the Russian experiment, see Evans Clark, "Americanism and the Soviet," *The Nation* 108 (March 22, 1919): 424, in which the author compared the

United States and Soviet governments to show that the Soviet state was more in keeping with American ideals of democracy and popular control than the American government with its institutions "frankly designed to check and balance the popular will" rather than give expression to it. See also Christopher Lasch, *The American Liberals and the Russian Revolution* (New York, 1962).

13. By 1919 at least 50 domestic communist publications in 26 different languages were in existence. In New York City alone, 25 circulated weekly, and the Justice Department indicated that in late 1919 there were 471 radical newspapers or periodicals in the United States advocating the violent overthrow of capitalism. See Robert K. Murray, *Red Scare: A Study in National Hysteria, 1919–1920* (Minneapolis, 1955), p. 53.

14. Stanley Coben, *A. Mitchell Palmer: Politician* (New York, 1963), p. 155, drawing upon cross-cultural analysis, especially Anthony F. C. Wallace, "Revitalization Movements," *American Anthropologist* 58 (April 1956): 264–281, contends, of the immediate postwar period, "never had the American people as a whole responded more unrealistically to the problems they faced."

15. U.S., Immigration Commission, *Abstracts of Reports of the Immigration Commission* (Washington, 1911), I, p. 48.

16. George E. Robert, vice-president of The National City Bank of New York, addressing the Iowa Bankers' Convention, June 24, 1919 stated: "These are troubled times. The whole system of industry and fabric of society are threatened with disorganization. Nobody has made society what it is by any plan. It has come to be what it is by development, a process of growth, constantly changing with the needs of society and the development of the people. It tends always to become more complex and highly organized, more interdependent. . . . I sometimes wonder if the development has not gone beyond the comprehension of the people, if we have not developed a machine that the great body of the workers do not understand." And not understanding the new complex structure, the worker "gets suspicious and antagonistic toward [his employer] with the result that a large part of the efficiency of the system is lost in friction." *Causes Underlying the Social Unrest* (New York, n.d.).

17. Not irrelevant is the fact that one byproduct of the war was to drive radicalism into the somewhat more tolerant atmosphere of the cities, since the wartime expression of unorthodox views was virtually suicidal in smaller towns and rural communities. Since it tended to remain there after the war and often concentrated on the depressed conditions of immigrant groups, to associate it with *gesellschaft* values was instinctive, if not always accurate. See Lillian Symes and Travers Clement, *Rebel America* (New York, 1934), pp. 301–302.

18. Scott Nearing, writing in the official journal of the Amalgamated Clothing Workers in early 1920, bitterly queried: "What is the purpose of this frenzied attack on the 'reds'? It has but one purpose—to 'save civilization'; to preserve law and order; to safeguard the inalienable rights of the parasite and the profiteer. When will this salvation be assured? After all the members of the IWW have been lodged in jail. After all

the Communists have been raided and beaten and deported. After all of the Socialists have been given 10 year sentences, or sent to the projected 'penal colony' in the Philippines. After every man or woman who has ideas that differ from the by-laws of the Union League Club or the Charter of the National City Bank or the articles of incorporation of the United States Steel Corporation, and who dares to make those ideas known, has been muzzled or banished or throttled." *Advance* (January 30, 1920): 6.

19. A revitalization movement, according to Professor Wallace, is a "deliberate, organized, conscious effort by members of a society to construct a more satisfying culture," its object, as well as a new cultural system, being new relationships and traits. Wallace, "Revitalization Movements," p. 265.

20. Theodore Schroeder to Roger N. Baldwin, November 27, 1917, American Civil Liberties Union Papers, microfilm reel 1, New York Public Library.

21. Roger N. Baldwin to Theodore Schroeder, December 7, 1917, ACLU Papers, microfilm reel 1, New York Public Library.

22. Quoted in Kirby Page, *Christianity and Economic Problems* (New York, 1922), p. 108. For the statements of the various religious groups in detail, see W. Jett Lauck, *Political and Industrial Democracy* (New York, 1926), pp. 27ff.

23. Kirby Page, *Industrial Facts: Concrete Data Concerning Industrial Problems and Proposed Solutions* (New York, 1921), p. 27.

24. Aaron I. Abell, *American Catholicism and Social Action: A Search for Social Justice, 1865–1950* (New York, 1960), p. 203.

25. In commenting on the Bishops' Program, Frank P. Walsh, cochairman of the National War Labor Board, acknowledged with approval that the Bishops "take for granted . . . that the man who is physically brutalized by long hours of toil and a scant leisure spent amid squalid surroundings . . . is in no condition to respond to the spiritual appeals to which every healthy and normal man readily responds." Frank P. Walsh, "The Significance of the Bishops' Labor Program," *National Catholic Welfare Council Bulletin* 1 (August 1919): 18–19, quoted in Abell, *American Catholicism and Social Action*, p. 203.

26. Zechariah Chafee, *Freedom of Speech* (Cambridge, 1920), p. 165.

27. Charles T. Sprading, *Freedom and Its Fundamentals* (Los Angeles, 1923), p. 38.

28. Swinburne Hale, "The Force and Violence Joker," *New Republic* 21 (January 21, 1920): 232.

29. "Gerard Flays Traitors," *The New York Times*, November 14, 1917, p. 3.

30. American Civil Liberties Union, *Who May Safely Advocate Force and Violence?* (New York, 1922), p. 5. See also Forrest R. Black, "Debs v. The United States—A Judicial Milepost on the Road to Absolutism," *University of Pennsylvania Law Review* 81 (December 1932): 171–172.

31. John M. Blum, *Joe Tumulty and the Wilson Era* (Boston, 1951), p. 197.

32. Although Wilson, then in Europe, promised to study Tumulty's program on his way home (Blum, *Joe Tumulty*, p. 198), little, if any, positive action was taken in this direction under his leadership.

33. "There Is But One Agitator—Injustice," *World Tomorrow* 3 (February 1920): 43.

34. Hannis Taylor, former American minister to Spain, constitutional law expert, and author of various widely used legal texts, published a pamphlet in early 1920 entitled *Shall We Perpetuate the Wilson Dictatorship as a System of Government* (privately printed). In it he charged that the "real motive for the absurd prolongation of a technical state of war, for years after it has ceased to exist in fact, is to enable the Executive Power to perform many abnormal acts, under the cover of war statutes, manifestly illegal in time of peace." The American people "resent the grave and scandalous assaults upon the sacred writ of habeas corpus made by the Executive power; the harsh enforcement of un-American sedition laws generally regarded by all calm and non-Partisan jurists as unconstitutional; the many violent and indefensible encroachments that have been made upon our system of representative government, and upon the right of freedom of speech. By such unbearable conditions, which are rapidly undermining our entire fabric of 'constitutional morality,' we are admonished that the time has arrived for us to advance by falling back. Let us return to the faith of our fathers; let us reestablish the Constitution as they made it; let us employ once more American methods of legitimate statesmanship."

35. A debater's point, suggested to college debaters later in the period, ran: "European countries have attempted to suppress [radical] propaganda in the past. As a result anarchism, syndicalism and communism have spread faster in Europe than the United States." Lamar T. Beman, ed., *Selected Articles on Censorship of Speech and the Press* (New York, 1930), p. 55. The attempt to demonstrate by empirical proof the suggested cause and effect relationship must have given various collegians some difficulty when challenged.

36. "An Infamous Measure," *New York World*, January 22, 1920, p. 12.

37. John L. Heaton, ed., *Cobb of "The World"* (New York, 1924), p. 355.

38. Ibid., pp. 356–357.

Chapter 4

1. There had been various vigorous, although unsuccessful, moves during the war to augment the federal espionage and sedition laws. Representative Burton L. French of Idaho had initially introduced a proposed federal criminal-syndicalism law (*Congressional Record*, 65th Cong., 1st sess. [1919], p. 6551), while Senator William L. King of Utah introduced legislation to amend the Espionage Act and, by expanded use of the postal power, to extend the penalties of the measure to cover material which, by implication at least, advocated IWW policies. *Congressional Record*, 65th Cong., 2d sess. (1919), p. 5933. See also ibid., p. 5117.

2. Walter Nelles, *A Liberal in Wartime: The Education of Albert DeSilver* (New York, 1940), p. 173.

3. The measure had four main provisions. It would prohibit: first, the advocacy of the overthrow of the United States government by force or violence; second, the advocacy of such overthrow by means of a shutdown in industrial production (i.e., by means of syndicalist techniques); third, the display of a red flag, which symbolized these sentiments; and fourth, the distribution of seditious and revolution-preaching material through the United States mails. Donald Johnson, *The Challenge to American Freedoms: World War I and the Rise of the American Civil Liberties Union* (Lexington, Ky., 1963), pp. 126–127.

4. U.S., Congress, Senate, Committee of the Judiciary, *Brewing and Liquor Interests and German and Bolshevik Propaganda, Hearings,* before a subcommittee of the Committee of the Judiciary, 65th Cong., 2d sess. (1919), II, p. 2778.

5. Ibid., III, pp. 839–840.

6. Ibid., p. 644. The following revealing exchange took place between John Reed and Senator Josiah O. Wolcott of Delaware:

Mr. Reed: We do not have to change our Constitution in the phrase which says that the right of free speech shall not be abridged and annulled; yet it is both abridged and annulled.
Senator Wolcott: I do not know where it is. If you mean by the right of free speech that you can preach violence and incendiarism, it ought to be annulled.
Mr. Reed: Why is not the Constitution changed?
Senator Wolcott: That is not free speech.
Ibid., p. 588.

7. Savel Zimand found the open-shop movement operating locally through 240 Open Shop Associations active in 44 states and in every principal city in the country. Savel Zimand, *The Open Shop Drive: Who Is Behind It and Where Is It Going?* (New York, 1921), p. 55.

8. Idaho, *Laws* (1917), chap. 145.

9. Iowa, *Laws* (1917), chap. 372. The New Jersey and Louisiana laws were copies of the Iowa law.

10. New York, *Laws* (1917), II, chap. 416; (1918), II, chap. 246.

11. *Idaho Statesman* (Boise), February 27, 1917, p. 7, March 2, 1917, p. 15, March 8, 1917, p. 7.

12. Eldridge F. Dowell, *A History of Criminal Syndicalism Legislation in the United States* (Baltimore, 1939), p. 86. Three senators opposed the bill with George H. Curtis, Democrat of Boise, speaking against it on the ground that it dealt severely with anyone who might advocate a cause, questioning this as an unwarranted restraint on free speech. *Idaho Statesman*, March 2, 1917, p. 5.

13. *Minneapolis Tribune,* January 31, 1917, p. 10. See also *Chicago Solidarity,* March 10, 1917, p. 3; Willis H. Raff, "Civil Liberties in Minnesota: World War One Period" (Ph.D. diss., University of Minnesota, 1950), chap. 2.

14. *Minneapolis Tribune*, March 20, 1917, p. 7; Minnesota, House, *Journal* (1919), pp. 955–956, 972–973.

15. Minnesota, House, *Journal* (1917), p. 1616; *Minneapolis Journal*, April 3, 1917, p. 13.

16. City of Duluth, *Council Proceedings* (1917), p. 237 (Ordinance No. 917).

17. See Ex parte Jackson, 263 U.S. 110; Ex parte Starr, 263 U.S. 145; Ex parte Radivoeff, 278 U.S. 277.

18. Montana, House, *Journal* (1918), pp. 1–2; *Anaconda Standard*, February 2, 1918, p. 1.

19. *Anaconda Standard*, February 9, 1918, p. 1; February 15, 1918, p. 1; *Helena Independent*, February 4, 1918, p. 1, February 17, 1918, p. 4; *Montana Record Herald*, February 7, 1918, p. 1, February 9, 1918, p. 4.

20. *Anaconda Standard*, February 16, 1918, p. 1; *Helena Independent*, February 18, 1918, p. 1; *Montana Record Herald*, February 7, 1918, p. 1.

21. Oswald Garrison Villard, *The Press Today* (New York, 1930), p. 80.

22. Herbert S. Schell, *History of South Dakota* (Lincoln, Neb., 1961), pp. 271–273.

23. Walter C. Smith, *The Everett Massacre* (Chicago, 1916); Edwin E. Witte, *The Government in Labor Disputes* (New York, 1932), pp. 166–167. For the IWW version of the affair, see Ed Delaney and M. T. Rice, *The Bloodstained Trial* (Seattle, 1927), pp. 82–85.

24. Accounts of the trial by Anna Louise Strong were carried in "Everett's Bloody Sunday—A Free Speech Fight That Led to a Murder Trial," *The Survey* 37 (January 27, 1917): 475–476; and "The Verdict at Everett," *The Survey* 38 (May 19, 1917): 160–162.

25. *Tacoma Ledger*, February 27, 1917, p. 1.

26. *Kitsap County Herald* (Poulsbo, Wash.), August 8, 1924, p. 4. The account was by Marion Garland of Bremerton, Washington, who was minute clerk in the Senate at that time and recorded the proceedings as they took place.

27. Washington, Senate, *Journal* (1917), pp. 389–390.

28. Washington, House, *Journal* (1917), p. 489.

29. Washington, Senate, *Journal* (1919), pp. 14–17.

30. *Seattle Post-Intelligencer*, March 22, 1917, p. 6.

31. Pennsylvania, *Laws* (1919), no. 275.

32. Connecticut, *Laws* (1919), chap. 312.

33. Dowell, *History of Criminal Syndicalism*, pp. 48, 143.

34. Washington, House, *Journal* (1919), p. 16.

35. *Seattle Times*, January 14, 1919, p. 1; *Spokane Spokesman-Review*, January 15, 1919, p. 3.

36. *Kitsap County* (Poulsbo, Wa.) *Herald*, August 8, 1924, p. 4. The watering-down of the criminal-syndicalism law was at most an empty gesture. To the phrase, "Whoever shall advocate, advise, teach or justify

crime, sedition, violence, intimidation or injury as a means or way of effecting any economic, social or industrial change," the words "or resisting" were inserted, following "effecting." Its supporters claimed that this made the act as applicable to reactionaries as to revolutionists, and was thereby a victory for labor. Labor remained dubious. *Proceedings of the Washington State Federation of Labor* (1919) (report of legislative agent, W. M. Short).

37. Alexander Trachtenberg and Benjamin Glassberg, eds., *The American Labor Year Book, 1921–1922* (New York, 1922), p. 10.

38. Nevada, Senate, *Journal* (1919), p. 15.

39. U.S., President's Mediation Commission, *Report on the Bisbee Deportations* (Washington, 1918); Delaney and Rice, *The Bloodstained Trail*, pp. 102ff.

40. Vernon H. Jensen, *Heritage of Conflict: Labor Relations in the Nonferrous Metals Industry Up to 1930* (Ithaca, N.Y., 1950), p. 426.

41. Arizona, Senate, *Journal* (1919), pp. 49–50 (Joint Resolution No. 5).

42. *Republican* (Phoenix, Ariz.), June 11, 1918, p. 5.

43. On the Mooney-Billings situation, see Richard H. Frost, *The Mooney Case* (Stanford, 1968).

44. California, Senate, *Journal* (1917), p. 2457; *Los Angeles Times* (April 24, 1917), sec. 1, p. 4; *Chicago Solidarity*, May 5, 1917, p. 2.

45. Philip Taft, "The Federal Trials of the I.W.W.," *Labor History* 3 (Winter 1962): 76–79. See also Woodrow C. Whitten, "Criminal Syndicalism and the Law in California, 1919–1927" (Ph.D. diss., University of California, 1946).

46. Franklin Hichborn, *The Case of Charlotte Anita Whitney* (privately published, 1920), p. 1.

47. Ibid.

48. "In 1638 my ancestors came to America in order that they might have the right to believe as they chose, to teach as they chose, and to speak as they chose. After three centuries there still lives in me the same belief in freedom of speech and thought. I do not believe in destruction or violence of any kind. But neither do I believe that we can rid ourselves of the menace of sabotage by a return to the methods that drove our ancestors from their homes into the wilderness of an unknown land. I believe the only cure for I.W.W.ism is a removal of the cause of I.W.W.ism. When we have done away with oppression, there will be no need of suppression. When we have industrial democracy as well as political democracy, I.W.W.ism will vanish as the dew before the morning sun. Such suppression as is contemplated in this bill will, in my opinion, not do away with I.W.W.ism, but rather spread it." California, Assembly, *Journal* (1919), p. 2019.

49. George P. West, "After Liberalism Had Failed," *The Nation* 116 (May 30, 1923): 629.

50. The literature on Ludlow is voluminous. See Robert Perkin, *The First Hundred Years* (New York, 1959), pp. 440ff; Barron B. Beshoar, *Out of the Depths: The Story of John R. Larson* (Denver, 1942), pp. 166ff; Eugene O. Porter, "The Colorado Coal Strike of 1913—An Interpreta-

tion," *Historian* 12 (Autumn 1949): 3–27. Ludlow led to the passage of a novel industrial disputes investigation act in 1915, which prohibited strikes and lockouts in industries affected with a public interest pending investigation and report by the Colorado Industrial Commission. For the operation of the measure, see Colston E. Warne and Merrill E. Gaddis, "Eleven Years of Compulsory Investigation of Industrial Disputes in Colorado," *Journal of Political Economy* 35 (October 1927): 657–683. The measure also induced the Rockefellers to turn to a professional publicist, Ivy Lee, in an attempt to erase the poor public image created by the episode. See Ivy Lee Papers, Princeton University.

51. *United Mine Workers Journal* 28 (December 6, 1917): 4. See also Benjamin M. Selekman and Mary Van Kleeck, *Employees' Representation in Coal Mines* (New York, 1924).

52. Warne and Gaddis, "Compulsory Investigation," p. 672.

53. A bill for an ordinance to suppress seditious utterances and street meetings of the IWW and membership therein was introduced into the Denver City Council on November 18, and a delegation from Pueblo called on the governor and urged legislation November 21. The American Legion was also active in the campaign, a Denver post going on record as opposing illegal raids on radicals, but favoring a "lawful movement" against them. *Rocky Mountain News* (Denver, Colo.), November 23, 1919, p. 1.

54. Colorado, *Laws* (1919), chap. 1; *Proceedings of the Colorado Federation of Labor* (1920), p. 26.

55. *Social Service Review* 1 (January–March 1920): 3.

56. *Rocky Mountain News*, December 17, 1919, p. 1; *The New York Times*, December 19, 1919, p. 7.

57. Shank indicated that he took pleasure in assuring the governor that the legislation "accords with the principles of the I.W.W.," and sent him literature to prove the point. *Chicago Solidarity* (January 24, 1920): 3.

58. The second section of the preamble read: "Recent occurrences in Russia and elsewhere warn us that toleration of such unbridled licenses of speech and of such practice involves a great danger to civilization and to organized society and threatens a possible lapse into barbarism." Indiana, *Laws* (1919), chap. 125.

59. Iowa, Senate, *Journal* (1919), pp. 665, 777–778, 817–818; *Des Moines Register*, April 18, 1919, p. 2.

60. *Detroit Free Press*, March 2, 1919, p. 9; *Proceedings of the Michigan Federation of Labor* (1923), p. 9.

61. *Omaha World-Herald*, January 15, 1919, p. 6.

62. Ibid., April 4, 1919, p. 8.

63. *Columbus Evening Dispatch*, April 29, 1919, p. 14.

64. *Portland Oregonian*, January 30, 1919, p. 7; *Oregon Journal* (Portland), January 29, 1919, p. 5. After passage of the measure, one paper decried it as an unfortunate way to root out IWWism, suggesting that the really practical way "would seem to be with speakers and other educative processes rather than with standards which may silence not only

the IWW's free speech, but the free speech of all citizens." *Oregon Journal,* January 31, 1919, p. 10.

65. Charles C. Bush, "The Green Corn Rebellion" (Ph.D. diss., University of Oklahoma, 1932). See also James Morton Smith, "Criminal Syndicalism in Oklahoma: A History of the Law and Its Application" (Ph.D. diss., University of Oklahoma, 1946), p. 9.

66. *Oklahoma Leader,* March 15, 1919, quoted in Smith, "Criminal Syndicalism," pp. 60–61.

67. *Salt Lake Tribune,* February 9, 1919, p. 8.

68. Utah, House, *Journal* (1919), p. 175.

69. West Virginia, Senate, *Journal* (1919), pp. 14–15. In supporting the constabulary law, the Democratic governor, John J. Cornwall, justified it on the ground that if enacted it would "eliminate the private guards and the company-paid sheriffs and substitute real public officials in their stead." Charles H. Ambler and Festus P. Summers, *West Virginia: The Mountain State,* 2d ed. (New York, 1958), p. 386.

70. *Wheeling Register,* March 12, 1919, p. 1.

71. "Vicious Propaganda is Repudiated by District 17," *United Mine Workers Journal* 30 (April 1, 1919): 13.

72. U.S., Congress, House, Committee of the Judiciary, *Amnesty for Political Prisoners, Hearings,* before a subcommittee of the Committee of the Judiciary, on H.R. 60, 67th Cong., 2d sess. (1919), pp. 32, 37. This contains the testimony of Caroline A. Lowe.

73. The three "ex-IWW" witnesses, Jack Dymond, Elbert Coutts, and Frank Wermke, who also testified against the IWW in the Chicago and Sacramento trials, were used prominently in a variety of cases against the IWW particularly in indictments under the California criminal-syndicalism law. See Whitten, "Criminal Syndicalism," pp. 37, 40, 59–60. In one California case, the following exchange took place between Coutts and an attorney cross-examining him:

Q. Where do you get your money to live on now mostly?
A. Well, I guess through these trials.
Q. That has been the case now for how long?
A. I guess practically ever since they started prosecutions under the criminal syndicalism law.

People v. Thompson, Reporter's Transcript, pp. 525–526, quoted in George W. Kirchwey, *A Survey of the Workings of the California Criminal Syndicalism Law* (Los Angeles, 1926), p. 40. For the judicial rationalization for the use of such evidence, see the opinion of Justice Plummer in People v. Cox., 66 California App. 293.

74. The Legion was especially active in Kansas, affording the press especially great quantities of privately secured information on statewide subversion. See *Witchita Daily Capitol,* June 5, 1919, p. 5, June 20, 1919, p. 12, June 21, 1919, p. 4, July 27, 1919, p. 6B, August 24, 1919, p. 6B, September 8, 1919, p. 1, September 9, 1919, p. 3.

75. Kansas, *Laws* (1919), chap. 184; the 1917 legislature had enacted

a vagrancy law, chap. 167, which applied to persons loitering without visible support, to those engaged in an unlawful calling, and to those threatening violence or personal injury to fellow workmen or employers of labor.

76. Kansas, House, *Journal* (1920 ext. sess.), pp. 11–12.

77. Kansas, Senate, *Journal* (1920 ext. sess.), pp. 14–15.

78. *Proceedings of the Kansas Federation of Labor* (1920), p. 17.

79. *Topeka Daily Capitol*, January 15, 1920, p. 4. The editorial also cited with approval Justice Holmes' eloquent dissent in the Abrams case.

80. *Topeka Daily State*, January 22, 1920, p. 4.

81. Kentucky, Senate, *Journal* (1920), pp. 12–13.

82. Kentucky, House, *Journal* (1920), pp. 41, 1067–1068; *Louisville Courier Journal*, February 26, 1920, p. 1.

83. To counter Palmer's influence, Campbell quoted earlier statements of the attorney general in which he had maintained that too radical legislation would defeat its own purpose and had insisted that the only legislation necessary were laws to better safeguard free speech. Kentucky, House, *Journal* (1920), pp. 1563, 1695, 1799, 2139, 2496.

84. *Louisville Courier-Journal*, March 23, 1920, p. 4.

85. Ibid., March 26, 1920, p. 1; *Proceedings of the Kentucky Federation of Labor* (1920), p. 65. The controversial Section 10 of the measure read in part: "it shall be unlawful for any person or persons by speech, writing or otherwise to arouse, incite or fix or attempt to arouse, incite or fix enmity, discord, or strife or ill feeling between classes of persons for the purpose of inducing public tumult or disorder in order to cause the forcible or violent change or overthrow of the Government of the United States, or of the Government of the Commonwealth of Kentucky, or for the purpose of inciting resistance to the Courts, laws, officers, or constituted authorities of the Commonwealth of Kentucky." Kentucky, *Laws* (1920), chap. 100.

86. Alexander Trachtenberg, *The American Labor Year Book, 1919–1920* (New York, 1920), p. 286.

87. *Proceedings of the North Dakota Federation of Labor* (1921), p. 36.

88. Wisconsin, Assembly, *Journal* (1919), pp. 1696, 1738; *Milwaukee Journal* (July 1, 1919), p. 1, (July 2, 1919), p. 8.

89. Dowell, *History of Criminal Syndicalism*, p. 145.

90. Quoted in Francis Downing, "Graham Greene and the Case of 'Disloyalty,'" *Commonweal* 45 (March 14, 1952): 565.

Chapter 5

1. "A City Set on a Hill: An Account of the First American Conference on Reconstruction Problems, Rochester, November 20–22," *The Survey* 41 (November 30, 1918): 242. The platform of the conference is printed on p. 266.

2. Lewis L. Lorwin, *The American Federation of Labor* (Washington, 1933), p. 174.

3. "The Forum, Bulwark of Free Speech," *The Survey* 41 (December 7, 1918): 327–338.

4. "The Churches and Reconstruction," *The Survey* 41 (December 21, 1918): 375–376.

5. "The Conference on Demobilization," *The Survey* 41 (December 7, 1918): 287–288.

6. John A. Fitch, "Labor Reconstruction: The Conference of the Academy of Political Science," *The Survey* 41 (December 14, 1918): 335.

7. Ibid.

8. Ibid., p. 336.

9. Ibid., p. 338.

10. William H. Johnston, "How Labor Defines Democracy," Address Delivered at the Reconstruction Conference of the National Popular Government League, Washington, 1919, sec. 4, pp. 9–10. For another broad and general contemporary exploration of such goals, see Frederick A. Cleveland and Joseph Shafer, eds., *Democracy in Reconstruction* (Boston, 1919).

11. Louis F. Post, "Democracy in Industry," Address Delivered at the Reconstruction Conference of the National Popular Government League, Washington, 1919, sec. 4, pp. 7–8.

12. Philip Taft, *The A. F. of L. in the Time of Gompers* (New York, 1957), pp. 369–372.

13. "Reconstruction from Above and Below," *The Survey* 41 (November 23, 1918): 224–226.

14. The eleventh of the fourteen demands of the federation was for the restoration of free speech, free press, and free assemblage, the removal of all wartime restraints, and the "liberation of all persons held in prison or indicted under charges due to their championship of the rights of labor or their patriotic insistence upon the rights guaranteed to them by the constitution." "Labor's Fourteen Points," *The Survey* 41 (November 30, 1918): 265.

15. Ida M. Tarbell, *The Life of Elbert H. Gary: A Story of Steel* (New York, 1925), p. 299.

16. There were few exceptions to this employer monolith. See W. Jett Lauck, *Political and Industrial Democracy* (New York, 1926), pp. 59–62.

17. Eric F. Goldman, *Two-Way Street: The Emergence of the Public Relations Counsel* (Boston, 1938), pp. 12–13. Advertising men themselves, proud of their success in "selling" the war, were reluctant to surrender their newly won prestige and tended to stress that advertising had few bounds. George French, editor of the trade journal *Advertising and Selling*, maintained in 1920: "As a motive power in social, economic, religious and commercial life, advertising is more effective than any other in disseminating the truth," while others stressed the possibility of "merchandising on a national scale not only medicine and pianos but 'ideas' such as hygiene, Santa Claus, patriotism, and a distrust of subversives." Otis Pease, *The Responsibilities of American Advertising: Private Control and Public Influence, 1920–1940* (New Haven, 1958), pp. 17–18.

18. Basil M. Manly, "Some Underlying Facts of the Labor Situation,"

Address Delivered at the Reconstruction Conference of the National Popular Government League, Washington, 1919, sec. 4, p. 41.

19. Ibid.

20. Quoted in William Preston, *Aliens and Dissenters* (Cambridge, 1962), p. 198.

21. Ole Hanson, *Americanism versus Bolshevism* (New York, 1920), p. 87.

22. "Bolsheviki in the United States," *Literary Digest* 60 (February 22, 1919): 11–13. The most thorough treatment is Robert L. Friedheim, *The Seattle General Strike* (Seattle, 1964).

23. All quotations cited in Robert M. Miller, *American Protestantism and Social Issues, 1919–1939* (Chapel Hill, 1958), pp. 258–259.

24. Senator Knute Nelson of Minnesota implored his colleagues: "It is our duty as legislators to protect the American people against this poisonous spirit of anarchy and sedition. The Constitution never was intended for the protection of people of that kind. To my mind it is idle to invoke the liberty of speech and press for those classes of people." *Congressional Record*, 65th Cong., 3d sess. (1919), p. 2943. See also ibid., p. 2915.

25. Robert K. Murray, *Red Scare: A Study in National Hysteria, 1919–1920* (Minneapolis, 1955), pp. 111–112.

26. *The Nation* 108 (January 25, 1919): 108.

27. This seems to have been one of the few controversies with a fair press. Miller states: "It was in this strike . . . that the State Conference of Congregational Churches of Massachusetts selected Dean Charles R. Brown of the Yale Divinity School to investigate conditions." His report, adopted by the conference after heated debate, vindicated the workers and severely criticized the mill owners. It was printed at the conference's expense and given wide circulation, and this perhaps explains why a number of church journals carried accounts of the strike very favorable to the workers. Miller, *American Protestantism*, pp. 260–261.

28. Hanson also wrote a series of articles for the *American Legion Weekly* in which he grossly exaggerated the extent of radical activity in the United States. Murray, *Red Scare,* p. 90.

29. Among those on the bomb honor roll were Attorney General Palmer, Postmaster General Burleson, Justice Holmes, and Judge Landis, Secretary of Labor Wilson, Senator King, J. P. Morgan, and John D. Rockefeller.

30. May Day was an annual rallying point for militant labor. As to its background, see Sidney Fine, "Is May Day American in Origin?" *Historian* 16 (Spring 1954): 121–134.

31. Murray, *Red Scare*, p. 77. Liberals and radicals moved quickly to deny any responsibility for the violence and bombings, with the idea frequently put forward that such action was deliberately planned by reactionaries to arouse public hostility toward their critics. Max Eastman wrote at the time: "The capitalist papers may shout 'Bolshevism' whenever an explosion occurs, but their shouting only strengthens the always plausible hypothesis that it was for the purpose of the shouting that the explosion occurred." "More Bombs," *The Liberator* 2 (July 1919): 7.

32. Zechariah Chafee, "Legislation Against Anarchy," *New Republic*

19 (July 23, 1919): 379–385, summarizes a wide variety of proposed federal laws, state statutes, and city ordinances being pushed at the time.

33. People's Freedom Union, *The Truth About the Lusk Committee* (New York, 1920), pp. 7–8. Evans Clark, *Facts and Fabrications About Soviet Russia* (New York, 1920), makes a serious attempt to prove at the time that the wealthy and more conservative the individual or group the greater the inclination to deception and deceit.

34. Lawrence H. Chamberlain, *Loyalty and Legislative Action: A Survey of Activity by the New York State Legislature, 1919–1949* (Ithaca, 1951), p. 52.

35. Chamberlain, *Legislative Action*, p. 21, includes a copy of such a warrant.

36. Algernon Lee, educational director of the school, although opening it to full search demanded a specific warrant to open its safe. This necessitated a two-day delay and produced an interesting episode in which Lee pointed out to later safe raiders that the material they had seized had nothing to do with advocacy of violence, to which reply was made, "Oh, that ain't what we're after. We want to get the source of the financial support of the Rand School." *New York Sun*, June 24, 1919, quoted in People's Freedom Union, *Truth about Lusk*, p. 21.

37. In the eventual four-volume report of the Committee, a section entitled "Revolutionary Industrial Unionism" condemned the IWW, Brotherhood of Metal Workers' Industrial Union, the Amalgamated Clothing Workers', and the International Ladies Garment Workers' Union among others and while generally suggesting that trade or craft unions had some validity condemned all industrial unions as subversive. *Report of the Joint Legislative Committee of the State of New York Investigating Seditious Activities* (New York, 1920), I, pp. 872ff. This Lusk Committee Report, popularly titled "Revolutionary Radicalism," although demonstrated time after time to be fraught with error and misrepresentation, became a standard source of "exposé" material of labor, pacifist and otherwise liberal or radical groups throughout the 1920s and well into the 1930s. Opponents of the ACLU, for example, constantly waved the Lusk Committee's findings as conclusive proof of its red leanings.

38. Quoted in People's Freedom Union, *Truth about Lusk*, p. 27.

39. Chamberlain, *Legislative Action*, p. 40.

40. The instrument was a measure which provided that no individual, group, or organization could establish or conduct a school or offer instruction without first receiving a license from the University of the State of New York, and no license was to be granted unless the Board of Regents was "satisfied that the instruction proposed to be given will not be detrimental to public interest." Also such a license could be revoked if the institution was acting in such a detrimental way. Ibid., pp. 40–41.

41. *Progressive Democracy: Addresses and State Papers of Alfred E. Smith* (New York, 1928), p. 277.

42. In his early months in office, Palmer had been far less disposed to suppression than his predecessor Thomas W. Gregory, who had strongly advocated that the wartime statutes regarding sedition be kept on the

books and violators prosecuted in order to prevent harm to the public morale during the discussion of peace terms. Gregory had even encouraged private organizations such as the American Protective League and the American Defense Society, to contiinue their work of amateur spying on "subversives," after the war. Harold M. Hyman, *To Try Men's Souls: Loyalty Tests in American History* (Berkeley, 1959), pp. 290–291.

43. Stanley Coben, *A. Mitchell Palmer: Politician* (New York, 1963), pp. 155–156, is undoubtedly correct when he argues that the New Freedom had conditioned Americans to depend upon the federal government to solve national problems and look to Washington when positive action was needed, a heritage of progressivism which certainly helps explain the cry for national suppression at this time.

44. Quoted in Donald Johnson, *The Challenge to American Freedoms: World War I and the Rise of the American Civil Liberties Union* (Lexington, 1963), p. 132.

45. Ibid., p. 133. Although few senators were clearly hostile to such legislation, two, Joseph France of Maryland and Robert M. La Follette of Wisconsin, were members of the Judiciary Committee which considered them.

46. Quoted in Max Lowenthal, *The Federal Bureau of Investigation* (New York, 1950), p. 72.

47. Ibid., p. 84.

48. Coben, *A. Mitchell Palmer*, p. 207.

49. Lowenthal, *The F.B.I.*, chaps. 8–23 passim. On Lowenthal, see Harry and Bonaro Overstreet, *The FBI In Our Open Society* (New York, 1969).

50. U.S., Congress, Senate, *Report on Conditions of Employment in the Iron and Steel Industry in the United States*, S. Doc. 110, 62d Cong., 1st sess. (1911), III, pp. 118–119.

51. *The New York Times*, October 3, 1919, p. 2.

52. William Z. Foster, *The Great Steel Strike and Its Lessons* (New York, 1920), chaps. 3–5.

53. Quoted in David Brody, *Steelworkers in America: The Non-Union Era* (Cambridge, 1950), p. 222. Brody also points out that most of the new amalgamated lodges took names like "Democracy," "Liberty," and "Old Glory." Ibid., pp. 222–223.

54. *Gary Tribune*, September 18, 1918, II, p. 9. A facsimile of a portion of the story was printed in *The Survey* (November 2, 1918): sec. II, VI.

55. *The Survey* (November 2, 1918): sec. II, VI.

56. S. Adele Shaw, "Closed Towns," *The Survey* 41 (November 8, 1919): 63. John A. Fitch had as early as 1910 reported for *The Pittsburgh Survey* that "measures . . . intended to preserve industrial efficiency . . . have resulted in a thorough-going and far reaching censorship that curtails free speech and the free activity of citizens. The effect of these measures is seen in every department of community life wherever, in Allegheny County, steel is made." John A. Fitch, *The Steel Worker: The Pittsburgh Survey* (New York, 1910), p. 6.

57. John A. Fitch, "Democracy in Steel: A Contrast Between the Rhine and the Monongahela," *The Survey* 41 (January 4, 1919): 453. See also Foster, *Great Steel Strike,* pp. 54–57.

58. Quoted in Fitch, *The Steel Worker,* p. 453.

59. Ibid., p. 454.

60. Brody, *Steelworkers,* p. 232.

61. Also included were abolition of twenty-four-hour shifts, reinstatement of all men discharged for union activities, with pay for time lost, check-off for collecting union dues and assessments; the principle of seniority in maintaining, reducing, and increasing the working force; abolition of company unions; and abolition of the physical examination of applicants for employment, the latter because of experience in having it used by company physicians as an instrument for blacklisting men active in the unions. Taft, *The AF of L,* p. 388.

62. The Interchurch report underlined the solidarity among employers and the dominance of the U.S. Steel Corporation as policy maker in the crisis. "The 'independent' steel companies gave the Corporation solid speechless support; not a spokesman was heard but Mr. Gary." Commission of Inquiry, The Interchurch World Movement, *Report of the Steel Strike of 1919* (New York, 1920), p. 177.

63. The Interchurch report cited instructions of the Sherman Service, Inc., a company-retained labor-detective agency, to its operatives: "We want you to stir up as much bad feeling as you possibly can between the Serbians and Italians. Spread data among the Serbians that the Italians are going back to work. Call up every question you can in reference to racial hatred between these two nationalities; make them realize to the fullest extent that far better results would be accomplished if they will go back to work. Urge them to go back to work or the Italians will get their jobs." Ibid., p. 230.

64. Brody points out, however, that in areas where steel was not so vital a product and element in the economy, such suppression could not be as vigorously imposed on all labor. *Steelworkers,* pp. 252–253.

65. Mary Heaton Vorce, "Civil Liberty in the Steel Strike," *The Nation* 109 (November 15, 1919): 635. The second volume of the Interchurch report, *Public Opinion and the Steel Strike* (New York, 1921), included an extensive, town-by-town study by George Soule, "Civil Rights on Western Pennsylvania," of the violation of individual rights during the strike. Steel's subsequent "reply" to the report, Marshall Olds, *Analysis of the Interchurch World Movement Report on the Steel Strike* (New York, 1923), in rebutting the charges, stressed that "liberty is not license," pointed out towns (normally outside the Pittsburgh area) where meetings were not closed and argued that the Interchurch report was attempting to "make its sensational appeal to the national government and national public opinion against the judicially approved exercise of the rights of local self-government in Pennsylvania." p. 308. See also Ernest W. Young, *Comments on the Interchurch Report on the Steel Strike of 1919* (Boston, 1921). Young, who supported fully the steel company position, did point out a significant shortcoming in the Interchurch report in its tendency

to treat the steel strike as an isolated event, wholly spontaneous in origin (p. 80).

66. The famed Boston police strike, which aroused the nation, had just been broken a week earlier. Frederick M. Koss, "The Boston Police Strike of 1919" (Ph.D. diss., Boston University, 1966).

67. Charles G. Miller, "Pittsburgh's Prostituted Press," *The Nation* 112 (January 5, 1921): 9. A revealing case of press values occurred in *The New York Times* in early October. In a front-page story on October 1, "Foster's Arrest Held No Violation of Free Speech," the *Times* quoted with apparent approval the ruling of a Pennsylvania judge that Foster's arrest for defying a local ordinance in speaking in Duquesne represented no violation of free speech; but two days later in an editorial "They Disgraced Their State," the *Times* condemned as a violation of the "sacred principle" of freedom of speech the action of an Ardmore Oklahoma audience in hissing and booing and causing the early end of an anti-League of Nations address by Senator James A. Reed. *The New York Times*, October 3, 1919, p. 14.

68. Samuel Harden Church, *The Criminal Leadership of Labor* (Pittsburgh, 1919), p. 3.

69. U.S., Congress, Senate, *Report Investigating Strike in Steel Industries*, S. Rept. 289, 66th Cong., 1st. sess. (1919), p. 14.

70. U.S., Congress, Senate, Committee on Education and Labor, *Investigation of Strike in Steel Industries*, 66th Cong., 1st sess. (1919), I, pp. 10–13, 41, 65, 85.

71. Only later did they admit that they had found hardly any connection between radicalism and the strikers. Robert K. Murray, "Communism and the Great Steel Strike," *Mississippi Valley Historical Review* 38 (December 1951): 459.

72. An account of much of the inner workings of the federation at the time is included in the autobiography of its then president James H. Maurer, *It Can Be Done* (New York, 1938), pp. 238ff.

73. The National Committee estimated that altogether the industry received between 30,000 and 40,000 such black workers before the strike was over, with steel officials later gloating in the face of victory that "Niggers did it." Brody, *Steelworkers*, p. 255.

74. "Back to the 12-Hour Day," *The Survey* 43 (January 17, 1920): 421.

75. "Red Forces Disrupting American Labor," *Literary Digest* 63 (October 25, 1919): 11–14. When T. T. Brewster, a spokesman for the coal industry, charged that Lenin engineered and Moscow financed the affair, John L Lewis pressed him for proof, but to no avail. Saul Alinsky, *John L. Lewis: An Unauthorized Biography* (New York, 1949), pp. 32–33.

76. *Los Angeles Times*, November 8, 1919, II, p. 3.

77. *Congressional Record*, 66th Cong., 1st sess. (1919), p. 7063.

78. McAlister Coleman, *Men and Coal* (New York, 1943), p. 97. The Lever Act's use was dubious in itself. A wartime measure, which during the war period had not been applied to labor activities, it was generally assumed that its vitality had ended with the armistice.

79. A straw in the wind at the time was the Supreme Court's action in a massive antitrust suit filed by the government against U.S. Steel. The case, originally argued March 9, 1919, was sent back for reargument which took place while the strike was on, October 7–10, 1919, and was decided favorably to the company on March 1, 1920. 251 U.S. 417 (1920). The decision left little doubt that the courts were unconcerned about both steel's size and its power. See Melvin I. Urofsky, *Big Steel and the Wilson Administration* (Columbus, 1969).

80. *Advance* (June 11, 1920): 4. Selig Perlman wrote in this regard "The vehemence with which the leaders of the American Federation of Labor have denounced Sovietism and Bolshevism, and which has of late been brought to a high pitch by fear lest a shift to radicalism should break up the organization is doubtless sincere. But one cannot help feeling that in part at least it aimed to reassure the great American middle class on the score of labor's intentions. The great majority of organized labor realize that, though at times they may risk engaging in unpopular strikes, it will never do to permit their enemies to tar them with the pitch of subversionism in the eyes of the great American majority. Selig Perlman, *A History of Trade Unionism in the United States* (New York, 1937), pp. 203ff.

81. The Interchurch report, in assessing the impact upon workingmen's attitudes concluded: "To the steel workers the import of the violation of civil and personal rights resulted as follows: Great numbers of workers came to believe—that local mayors, magistrates and police officials try to break strikes; that state and Federal officials, particularly the Federal Department of Justice, help to break strikes, and that armed forces are used for this purpose; that most newspapers actively and promptly exert a strike-breaking influence; most churches passively." Commission of Inquiry, The Interchurch World Movement, *Report of the Steel Strike*, p. 238. See also Leon N. Flint, *The Conscience of The Newspaper* (New York, 1930), in which the author states categorically: "Perhaps in no field is the charge of news distortion so often made as in that of industrial controversy. The advocates of the interests of labor express entire lack of confidence in the verity of the news in which they denominate the "capitalistic press" (p. 61). Although not to achieve significant national results, labor's move after the strike to set up its own news service, the Federated Press, the first national news service owned by labor unions, was an indication of its attitude toward standard news sources. Commission of Inquiry, The Interchurch World Movement, *Public Opinion and the Steel Strike*, p. 89.

Chapter 6

1. From a statement by A. Mitchell Palmer, quoted in William Preston, *Aliens and Dissenters* (Cambridge, 1963), p. 193.

2. *Advance* (January 30, 1920): 1.

3. *Congressional Record*, 66th Cong., 1st sess. (1919), p. 193.

4. In August, William J. Flynn, director of the Bureau of Investigation,

had sent confidential instructions to all special agents and employees of the Justice Department to begin an investigation "particularly directed to persons not citizens of the United States, with a view of obtaining deportation cases." Agents were urged in making reports to include "all information of every nature, whether hearsay or otherwise," although Flynn warned: "Inasmuch as gossip or said hearsay evidence is of no value in making technical proof, agents are hereby instructed to trace every piece of information to its source." Special agents were also warned to "constantly keep in mind the necessity of preserving the cover of our confidential informants," for "in no case shall they rely upon the testimony of such cover informants during deportation proceedings." National Popular Government League, *To The American People: Report Upon the Illegal Practices of the United States Department of Justice* (Washington, 1920), p. 37.

5. 40 Stat. 1012 (1918).

6. Preston, *Aliens*, p. 219.

7. Ibid., p. 220.

8. Donald Johnson, *The Challenge to American Freedoms* (Lexington, 1963), p. 138.

9. Alexander Trachtenberg and Benjamin Glassberg, eds., *The American Labor Year Book: 1921–1922* (New York, 1922), p. 26, claimed that "over 1400 members of the IWW alone" were indicted. See also Selig Perlman and Philip Taft, "Labor Movements," in John R. Commons, *History of Labor in the United States, 1896–1932* (New York, 1935), pp. 429–430, and John S. Gambs, *The Decline of the I.W.W.* (New York, 1932), pp. 29–30. One careful local study in California showed that by August 1924, 531 persons had been charged on information or indictment. Woodrow C. Whitten, "Criminal Syndicalism and the Law in California, 1919–1927" (Ph.D. diss., University of California, 1946), p. 1. See also Daniel F. Callahan, "Criminal Syndicalism and Sabotage," *Monthly Labor Review* 14 (April 1922): 803–812.

10. Fortunately for the state, the latter charge was dropped before the men came to trial. Irving Howe and Lewis Coser, *The American Communist Party: A Critical History, 1919–1957* (Boston, 1957), p. 55.

11. Judge Weeks, in commending the jury on its verdict, seemed to indicate that a person's worth was to be measured by the property he had accumulated. "A young man, twenty-eight years of age, of intelligence, a striking example of the educational system of this country, able-bodied, of full intellect, confesses he owns no property. Employed at forty-one dollars a week the last time he was employed and never accumulated any property!" Benjamin Gitlow, *I Confess: The Truth About American Communism* (New York, 1939), p. 73.

12. Howe and Coser, *Communist Party*, p. 56.

13. Trachtenberg and Glassberg, *American Labor Year Book: 1921–1922*, p. 19.

14. Ibid., p. 20.

15. "The Law and the Alien Radical," *The Social Service Bulletin* 10 (February 1920): 2.

16. The facts of the case are well covered in People of Illinois v. Lloyd, 304 Ill. 23 (1922). See also Chicago Civil Liberties Committee, *Pursuit of Freedom: A History of Civil Liberty in Illinois, 1787–1942* (Chicago, 1942), pp. 87–89.

17. Arthur Weinberg, ed., *Attorney for the Damned* (New York, 1957), p. 172.

18. Upon the introduction of this evidence, state's attorney Barnhart tearfully cried out to the jury, "My God, can it be?" Howe and Coser, *Communist Party*, p. 58.

19. People v. Lloyd, at 69.

20. Weinberg, *Attorney*, pp. 155ff. In the process Darrow referred to Hanson as a "cheap, advertising, money-mad man," and a "cheap poser." Ibid., pp. 159–160.

21. There is voluminous literature on the Centralia affair. For the American Legion view, see Ben Hur Lampman, *Centralia: Tragedy and Trial* (Tacoma, 1920); for the IWW version, see Ralph Chaplain, *The Centralia Conspiracy* (Chicago, 1924). More impartial assessments include Federal Council of Churches, Committee on Social Relations, *The Centralia Case* (n.p., 1930), and Robert L. Tyler, "Rebels of the Woods," *Oregon Historical Quarterly* 55 (March, 1954): 29ff. See also State of Washington v. Smith, 115 Wash. 405 (1921).

22. Whitten, "Syndicalism in California," p. 140.

23. *Oakland Tribune,* February 22, 1920. The following day the *Tribune* editorialized: "The conviction of Charlotte Anita Whitney should serve as a warning to 'Parlor Bolshevists' not only in this [state] but throughout the nation. It is a striking demonstration that the normal American community simply will not endure conduct upon the part of any individual or social group based on assumption of exaltation above the law, either by reason of wealth, social station, or intellectual attainment." Ibid., February 23, 1920, quoted in Whitten, "Syndicalism in California," p. 182.

24. "Free Speech in the United States," *The Social Service Bulletin* 10 (December 1920): 1, 3.

25. State v. Workers' Socialist Publishing Co., 185 N.W. 931 (1921).

26. Trachtenberg and Glassberg, *American Labor Year Book: 1921–1922*, pp. 21–22.

27. State v. Gabriel, 95 N.J. 338 (1921).

28. New Mexico, *Laws* (1919), chap. 140.

29. State v. Diamond, 27 N.M. 477 (1921).

30. Preston, *Aliens,* p. 231.

31. "Free Speech in the United States," p. 3; Callahan, "Syndicalism and Sabotage," p. 203.

32. "Free Speech in the United States," p. 4.

33. Johnson, *Challenge to Freedoms,* pp. 134–135. Wilson's statement on this and repressive legislation generally, although emphasizing that the best road to the elimination of radicalism was through liberal programs of economic reform to eliminate the sources of discontent, was: "With the free expression of opinion and with the advocacy of orderly political change, however fundamental, there must be no interference, but towards

passion and malevolence tending to incite crime and insurrection under guise of political evolution there should be no lenience. Legislation to this end has been recommended by the Attorney General and should be enacted." *Congressional Record,* 66th Cong., 2d sess. (1919), p. 30.

34. "A New Alien and Sedition Law," *New Republic* 20 (November 26, 1919): 366.

35. Kate Holladay Claghorn, "Aliens and Sedition in the New Year," *The Survey* 43 (January 17, 1920): 423.

36. "Plot to Turn Steel and Coal Strikes Into a Real Revolt Revealed in 'Reds' Arrest," *St. Louis Post-Dispatch,* January 4, 1920, p. 1.

37. Johnson, *Challenge to Freedoms,* p. 136.

38. "Penalty of Death in Sedition Cases Urged Upon House," *New York World,* January 13, 1920, p. 2.

39. "Wholesale Raids on Alleged Reds Anger Senators," *New York World,* January 14, 1920, p. 2. The story also indicated a growing move among senators to assail the Graham bill.

40. Anderson was hardly the type who could be assailed as an unpropertied Bolshevik. Respected Boston attorney, he had been a member of the faculty of the Boston University Law School, a member of the Massachusetts Public Service Commission and the Interstate Commerce Commission, and former United States District Attorney for Massachusetts, when he was appointed to the United States bench in November 1918. He was also a member of the Cosmos Club, the New York City Club, and four Boston country clubs. *National Cyclopaedia of American Biography* (1926), A, p. 412.

41. "Prating Patriots Worse Than Reds," *New York World,* January 13, 1920, p. 2. The *World* used the statements as the basis of an editorial the following day, stating: "It is time to get back to the first principles of free government and stay there, in equal defiance of radicalism and reaction." *New York World,* "Government by Hysteria," January 14, 1920, p. 10.

42. "Keepers of the Faith: Men and Women Who Recently Broke Silence and Revealed a Great Body of Public Opinion Ready to Uphold the Liberties of the Founders," *The Survey* 43 (February 7, 1920): 537.

43. Ibid., p. 536.

44. Paul U. Kellogg to Chester Rowell, January 23, 1920, Chester Rowell Papers, Bancroft Library, University of California, Berkeley. In resigning, Kane wrote Woodrow Wilson: "I am obliged to take this step because I feel out of sympathy with the anti-radical policies of Mr. Palmer and his methods of carrying them out. I am strongly opposed to the wholesale raiding of aliens. I am also utterly opposed to the enactment of a new Espionage Act 'with teeth in it,' now that we are, to all intents and purposes at peace. I believe that the enforcement of such a new act as Mr. Palmer has proposed would lead to an entirely unnecessary repression of free speech and interference with freedom of the press." American Civil Liberties Union Papers, vol. 117, New York Public Library.

45. The principal force behind this move seemed to be the Associated Industries of New York State, which acted through a number of professional

lobbyists and through the New York League for Americanism. Particularly prominent were many of those who had fought hardest for passage of the Lusk laws, including especially Archibald Stevenson, attorney and influential member of the National Civic Federation. See Louis Waldman, *Labor Lawyer* (New York, 1944), p. 97.

46. "Education from Albany," *The Nation* 110 (May 8, 1920): 613.

47. "Albany's Ousted Socialists," *Literary Digest*, 64 (January 24, 1920): 20. See also "Assembly's Actions Rebuked by Press," *New York World*, January 13, 1920, p. 3; Thomas E. Vadney, "The Politics of Repression: A Case Study of the Red Scare in New York," *New York History* 49 (January 1968): 56–75.

48. "Barred Socialists Again Attack Lusk," *The New York Times*, January 11, 1921, p. 21.

49. "Dr. Grant's Policy Under Scrutiny of Vestrymen," *The New York Times*, January 12, 1920, p. 1. For the Grant situation generally, see "The Way to Unconstitute Authority," *New Republic* 21 (February 11, 1920): 306–308; "Dr. Grant Faces a Possible Trial; Can't Use Pulpit for Radical Opinions," *New York World*, January 13, 1920, p. 1.

50. "Savages Still, Shaw Says of Americans," *New York World*, January 13, 1920, p. 1.

51. "Albany's Ousted Socialists," p. 19.

52. Other members included Morgan J. O'Brien, a former judge of the New York Court of Appeals; Joseph M. Proskauer, later a judge of the Appellate Division of the New York State Supreme Court; and attorney Louis Marshall. Marshall's various actions at the time are valuably revealed in Charles Reznikoff, ed., *Louis Marshall: Champion of Liberty* (Philadelphia, 1957), II, pp. 977–985.

53. Attempts had been made to introduce a resolution supporting the refusal to seat, but the resolution was castigated for its restrictiveness, especially with regard to free speech, and defeated. *Report of the New York State Bar Association* 43 (1920): 531.

54. "This Little Story is Entitled 'God Bless the Lusk Committee,'" National Civil Liberties Bureau (January, 1920). A portion of this flier is quoted in "The Sedition Bills," *The Survey* 43 (February 7, 1920): 549.

55. William Hard, "Perhaps the Turn of the Tide," *New Republic* 21 (February 11, 1920): 313.

56. "Sterling-Graham Sedition Measure is Widely Opposed; Flood of Protesting Letters and Telegrams Pour in Upon House Rules Committee," *New York World*, January 22, 1920, p. 2. See also *Congressional Record*, 66th Cong., 2d sess. (1920), p. 9624.

57. *Congressional Record*, 66th Cong., 2d sess. (1920), pp. 1782–1783. Blanton went on after the hearing to read into the record a denunciation of Samuel Gompers, which, if there had been doubt of the repressionists' having labor for a target before, left no further doubt. Ibid., p. 2209.

58. Ibid., p. 1680.

59. Senator Robert L. Owens of Oklahoma, president of the National Popular Government League stated at a League meeting January 21:

"It is high time to discount hysteria and return to normal thinking. We have serious tasks ahead of us to perform. . . . We cannot have social intercourse without free discussion. But free discussion has, as a result of the war, been partially suppressed for two years. But now when peace has come, for us to attempt to endanger free discussion, as the Graham Bill does is folly and worse than folly." "Sterling-Graham Measure Is Widely Opposed." Ibid.

60. *Congressional Record*, 66th Cong., 2d sess., 1920, 59, p. 1968.

61. U.S., Congress, House, Committee on Rules, *Rule Making in Order the Consideration of S. 3317, Hearings*, 66th Cong., 2d sess. (1920), p. 112. See also Hard, "Turn of the Tide," p. 314.

62. Albert De Silver, "Mr. Palmer Shudders," *World Tomorrow* 3 (March, 1920): 74.

63. *New York World*, January 23, 1920, p. 3. On January 24, 1920, p. 14, the *St. Louis Post-Dispatch* printed a Fitzpatrick cartoon entitled: "Mr. Palmer Drops Something," the "something" in his instance being a hot potato labeled "Sedition Bill." This culminated a steady campaign against the Graham bill which had begun with a Fitzpatrick cartoon on January 12, showing an old world tyrant in the American Congress advocating "Laws to Suppress Free Speech."

64. *Congressional Record*, 66th Cong., 2d sess. (1920), p. 1970. Husted came from Westchester and Rockland Counties, where, according to Albert De Silver, "they like to believe all sorts of things about the wicked city of New York." De Silver, "Mr. Palmer Shudders," p. 75.

65. The position was one which Palmer took regularly. In a January 27, 1920, letter to the magazines of the nation, Palmer had made a similar statement adding: "but nothing so endangers the exercise of a right as the abuse thereof." National Popular Government League, *To The American People*, p. 66.

66. U.S., Congress, House, Committee on the Judiciary, *Hearings*, on Sedition, 66th Cong., 2d sess. (1920), pp. 10–11, 25.

67. Ibid., pp. 164ff.

68. "Labor's Attitude Toward the 'Red' Agitators," *Literary Digest* 64 (March 20, 1920): 21.

69. Samuel Gompers, "The Graham-Rice 'Sedition Bill' Would Manufacture Law-Breakers," *American Federationist* 27 (February 1920): 138. The labor press waxed eloquent over the dangers of the measure. See "Sedition Bill Is a Blow to Liberty," *International Molders' Journal* (February 1920): 97; "Glenn R. Plumb on the Sedition Bill," *Locomotive Engineers Journal* (June 1920): 480; *The Garment Worker* (January 23, 1920): 4ff; *Brotherhood of Locomotive Firemen and Engineers Journal* 79 (1920): 7ff. Widely reprinted in various labor journals was an article by Sidney Howard, "Baiting the Bolshevist," *Collier's Weekly* 65 (January 10, 1920): 15ff., in which Howard indicated a large degree of employer-sponsored red literature, issued and deviously distributed in such a way as to stigmatize the workers, and also claimed that the "violence" attributed to the strikers in the autumn 1919 strikes was largely the creation of the antilabor press. One of the most stinging pieces at the time, John T.

Quinn, "Trusts to Blame for the Red Agitators," *The Carpenter* (January–February 1920): 17ff, argued persuasively that management had imported cheap foreign labor. "It did not make any difference to them if these men were never made good Americans. It did not make any difference if they had any sympathy with our American institutions or not, nor did it make any difference if they brought their bombs with them or not." And now that the harm was done, they had to find some way to "blame all this on the labor unions, to blame it on the only people who have ever raised their voice against this crime."

70. Hard, "Turn of the Tide," p. 314.

71. John Higham, *Strangers in the Land* (New Brunswick, 1955), p. 232.

72. The Lusk Committee especially sought to regiment newspaper opinion behind its actions. See Jean Gould, ed., *Homegrown Liberal: The Autobiography of Charles W. Ervin* (New York, 1954), pp. 75–77.

73. Palmer, in his enthusiasm for his Davey Bill, had stated early in January that "the patriotic press of virtually every state has endorsed the Bill" to which the *St. Louis Post-Dispatch* retorted editorially: "We do not believe the patriotic press of any state has expressed any such opinion. The American newspaper which holds that the supremacy of our free government depends upon drastic sedition laws or any kind of laws by which loyalty is enforced by political activity or arrest or imprisonment is a journalistic anachronism, out of place in this country and in this age." "Palmer's Palaver," January 7, 1920, p. 24.

74. "The Road to Revolution," *St. Louis Post-Dispatch*, January 23, 1920, p. 26. See also Representative Huddleston's remarks in *Congressional Record*, 66th Cong., 2d sess. (1920), 1969.

75. "A Severe Bill," *The New York Times*, January 7, 1920, p. 18.

76. Robert M. Miller, *American Protestantism and Social Issues* (Chapel Hill, 1958), p. 190.

77. As Miller points out: "Virtually all the major churches put on drives at the end of the war to fatten their membership lists and coffers, and one of the most effective—or at any rate, widespread—techniques was to present organized religion as the chief bulwark against bolshevism." Ibid., p. 186.

78. Ray H. Abrams, *Preachers Present Arms* (New York, 1933), pp. 126–142.

79. "Freedom of Opinion and the Clergy," *New Republic* 21 (February 11, 1920): 304. See also Paul A. Carter, *The Decline and Revival of the Social Gospel* (Ithaca, 1954), pp. 26–27.

80. William G. McLoughlin, *Billy Sunday Was His Real Name* (Chicago, 1955), p. 276.

81. William F. McKee, "The Social Gospel and the New Social Order, 1919–1929" (Ph.D. diss., University of Wisconsin, 1961), pp. 150ff.

82. National Popular Government League, *To The American People*, p. 8.

83. "Professor Chafee Says Sterling Bill Gag on Free Speech," *Boston American*, January 14, 1920, p. 3.

84. House, Committee on Rules, *Rule Making of S. 3317, Hearings,* p. 29.

85. Zechariah Chafee, *Freedom of Speech* (New York, 1920).

86. *St. Louis Globe-Democrat,* February 2, 1920, quoted in Forrest R. Black, "Debs v. the United States—A Judicial Milepost on the Road to Absolutism," *University of Pennsylvania Law Review* 81 (December, 1932): 171.

87. House, Committee on the Judiciary, *Hearings,* on Sedition, pp. 231ff.

88. Ibid., pp. 262ff.

89. Ibid., pp. 189ff.

90. Grimke, a Negro, placed heavy emphasis upon the danger involved currently in advocating such things as equal suffrage, the reduction of southern representation for denial of voting rights, and antilynching legislation, arguing that the legislation "would suppress more than exists now of the right of free speech, free press, and the right of assembly." Ibid., pp. 263ff.

91. In the *Survey* piece, "Keepers of the Faith," various leaders were quoted on the current problem, each with a statement of his own faith in freedom of expression. The list was one of eminent respectability.

92. The American Bar Association then represented less than 10 percent of the lawyers in the United States. "Open Forum," *Reports of the American Bar Association* 45 (1920): 26–27.

93. Albert J. Beveridge, "The Assault Upon American Fundamentals," *Reports of the American Bar Association* 45 (1920): 191.

94. Edward M. Burns, *David Starr Jordan: Prophet of Freedom* (Stanford, 1953), p. 62.

95. See, for example John Lord O'Brian, "Civil Liberty in War Time," in *Proceedings of the New York State Bar Association, Forty-second Annual Meeting* (Albany, 1919), pp. 279ff.

96. A typical and revealing statement was that of Frank I. Cobb, close friend and supporter of Woodrow Wilson, in April 1920: "While we were engaged in destroying our political and moral influence throughout the world, we were likewise engaged in destroying our personal liberty at home, in wrecking the police powers of the States, in nullifying local self-government and in establishing the Federal authority as the supreme arbiter over what men shall eat and what they shall drink and what the family doctor may prescribe for the influenza. From that to the complete extinguishment of freedom of opinion is only a step; it is a step which all the demagogues of reaction are urging the country to take." John L. Heaton, *Cobb of "The World"* (New York, 1924), p. 359.

97. One fairly revealing index was afforded by Hornell Hart, "Changing Social Attitudes and Interest," in *Recent Social Trends in the United States, Report of the President's Research Committee on Social Trends* (New York, 1933), pp. 429–430. Hart reported that "every thousand articles indexed in the *Reader's Guide* from 1915 to 1918 included 1.36 dealing with communism and bolshevism. This number rose to 5.51 for the years 1919–1921, dropping to 1.53 the following three years."

98. Charles H. Ambler and Festus P. Summer, *West Virginia: The Mountain State*, 2d ed. (Englewood Cliffs, 1958), pp. 454ff.

99. Lewis S. Gannett, "The Constitution by Candlelight," *The Nation* 110 (April 3, 1920): 425.

100. Kirk H. Porter and Donald B. Johnson, *National Party Platforms, 1840–1956* (Urbana, 1956), p. 224; see also pp. 220, 236, 240.

101. John D. Hicks, *Rehearsal for Disaster: The Boom and Collapse of 1919–1920* (Gainesville, 1961), p. 32. Business had "covered its bet" thoroughly in the 1920 Republican convention with such men as Elbert M. Gary, Harry F. Sinclair, Cornelius Vanderbilt, T. Coleman Dupont, and various J. P. Morgan partners playing a major role in shaping Republican policy. William Allen White, loyal Republican editor of the *Emporia Gazette*, was disturbed, writing: "Never had I seen a convention so completely dominated by sinister predatory economic forces as was this." Wesley M. Bagby, *The Road to Normalcy: The Presidential Campaign and Election of 1920* (Baltimore, 1962), p. 86.

102. Samuel D. Schmalhausen, ed., *Behold America!* (New York, 1931), p. 660.

103. Walter Nelles, *A Liberal In Wartime: The Education of De Silver* (New York: 1940), p. 204.

Chapter 7

1. The question of who actually governs a society as contrasted to who holds the formal positions of leadership has concerned political scientists and sociologists more and more in recent years. The Lynds's famous studies of Muncie, Indiana, in the 1920s and 1930s were a pioneer American attempt at getting to the roots of informal and actual power, and generally revealed that, beneath the facade of democratic politics, a social and economic elite actually ran the community. Robert S. Lynd and Helen M. Lynd, *Middletown* (New York, 1929), and their, *Middletown in Transition* (New York, 1937). Floyd Hunter, especially in his work on Atlanta, reached similar conclusions. Floyd Hunter, *Community Power Structure* (Chapel Hill, 1953), and his, *Top Leadership, U.S.A.* (Chapel Hill, 1959). The best-researched and, in many ways, most revealing study is Robert A. Dahl, *Who Governs? Democracy and Power in an American City* (New Haven, 1961), which, drawing on other investigations of New Haven, Connecticut, attempts both to reach some general conclusions based on one case study and to explore the general problem as well. See especially Dahl's brief survey of the subject as an area for research and concern, pp. 1–8. A revealing and related investigation of the wielding of power is Reinhard Bendix, *Higher Civil Servants in American Society: A Study of the Social Origins, the Careers, and the Power-Position of Higher Federal Administrators* (Boulder, 1949).

2. In some ways the position of the radical dissenter was more tenuous after business's objectives became more closely identified with national goals. In sharply challenging those objectives, he now ran the risk of engaging in an even more insidious disloyalty and lack of patriotism than

at an earlier time when such a massive consensus and identification had not been reached. The term "consensus" here, and in this chapter, is being used in the more formal sociological sense of the acceptance of a system of values which establishes the discipline and shared understanding which permit human activity to be carried on with a minimum of friction. See Sigmund Diamond, *The Reputation of the American Businessman* (Cambridge, 1955), pp. 177, 202.

3. "Association Holds Memorable Meeting at Detroit," *American Bar Association Journal* 11 (September, 1925): 569.

4. Charles Evans Hughes, "Liberty and Law," *American Bar Association Journal* 11 (September, 1925): 567.

5. Ibid., p. 569.

6. See Mencken's bitter piece on postwar hysteria, "Star-Spangled Man," *New Republic* 14 (September 29, 1920): 119–120.

7. H. L. Mencken, "Nietzsche," *Chicago Sunday Tribune*, August 23, 1925, sec. 4, p. 1.

8. For Mencken, it was only people of talent who could appreciate and utilize the attributes of a free society. As to the inferior democratic man, "He simply cannot formulate the concept of a good that is not his own good. The fact explains his immemorial heat against heretics, sacred and secular. His first thought and his last thought, contemplating them, is to stand them up against a wall, and have at them with musketry. Go back into history as far as you please, and you will find no record that he has even opened his mouth for fairness, for justice, for decency between man and man. Such concepts, like the concepts of honor and of liberty, are eternally beyond him and belong only to his superiors." H. L. Mencken, *Note On Democracy* (New York, 1926), p. 31.

9. Morton Keller, *In Defense of Yesterday: James M. Beck and the Politics of Conservatism, 1861–1936* (New York, 1958), pp. 158–159.

10. H. L. Mencken, "On Being an American," in *Prejudices: Third Series* (New York, 1926), pp. 11–12.

11. H. L. Mencken, "The Bill of Rights," *Chicago Sunday Tribune*, January 17, 1926, sec. 4, p. 1.

12. H. L. Mencken, "On Free Speech," *Chicago Sunday Tribune*, August 9, 1925, sec. 4, p. 1.

13. Ibid.

14. The editor of the *Chicago Tribune* apparently wanted this fact spelled out clearly. Under the picture of Mencken in the column, a caption stated: "Writing for toleration and personal liberty." Ibid.

15. H. L. Mencken, in *A Carnival of Buncombe*, ed. Malcolm Moos (Baltimore, 1956), p. 87.

16. H. L. Mencken, "On Liberty," *Chicago Sunday Tribune*, March 21, 1926, sec. 4, p. 1.

17. H. L. Mencken, "Reflections on Government," *Chicago Sunday Tribune*, September 18, 1927, sec. 4, p. 1.

18. Alfred Kazin, *On Native Grounds* (New York, 1942), pp. 201ff. Mencken certainly professed to value the various principles in the Bill of Rights highly. Yet when it came to facing the question of who was

to protect these rights he had no answer except the judges. But in the next breath, he would contend that judges were corrupt, especially elective judges, and that the politics of democracy churned mediocrity and hypocrites to the top. "The demogogue," he wrote in *Notes on Democracy* (p. 103), "is one who preaches doctrines he knows to be untrue to men he knows to be idiots. The demaslave is one who listens to what these idiots have to say and then pretends to believe it himself. Every man who seeks elective office under democracy has to be either the one thing or the other, and most men have to be both."

19. Henry F. May, *The End of American Innocence: A Study of the First Years of Our Own Times, 1912–1917* (New York, 1959). Allen Tate's comments on the "nonsense" of the term "lost generation," are revealing. Allen Tate, "Random Thoughts on the 1920s," *Minnesota Review* 1 (Fall 1960): 56.

20. May emphasizes that "the Young Intellectuals, rejecting many parts of traditional ideology, turned against the doctrine of Anglo-Saxon superiority with special delight and enthusiasm. For them the only hope for American culture lay in the influx of cheerful Italians and soulful Slavs. For opposite reasons, many of them agreed with the extreme racists in disliking the idea of the melting-pot. Immigrant cultures must be preserved to leaven the solid Anglo-Saxon lump. Disregarding sociologists like Ross, the Young Intellectuals turned instead to the Boas school of anthropology. From it they learned, with pleasure, that there was no sound reason for assuming that any one culture was superior to another." May, *End of American Innocence*, p. 350.

21. Ibid., p. 313.

22. Mark Schorer, *Sinclair Lewis: An American Life* (New York, 1961), pp. 522ff. Lewis's attitude toward the Sacco-Vanzetti episode is not atypical of others of his group. He felt that the affair could profitably remind Americans that they were not "so just, so free, so honest, nor even so efficient as we like to think." But aside from being willing to assist in picquing American consciences, he had little other interest in positive action regarding people of this ilk.

23. Heywood Broun, et al., *Nonsenseorship: Sundry Observations Concerning Prohibitions, Inhibitions and Illegalities* (New York, 1922), p. 37.

24. Harold E. Stearns, ed., *Civilization in the United States: An Inquiry by Thirty Americans* (New York, 1922), p. vii.

25. Frederick J. Hoffman, "Philistine and Puritan in the 1920's," *American Quarterly* 1 (Fall 1949): 253. See also Henry F. May, "Shifting Perspectives on the 1920's," *Mississippi Valley Historical Review* 43 (December 1956): 414, 424.

26. Bernard DeVoto, in writing later of the period, castigated the writers not only for their inability to observe what was taking place in front of them but for their added irresponsibility in distorting the picture. "The truth is that literature's repudiation of American life during the Twenties shut it away from the realities of that life, the evils as well as the good. The verdict of those future historians is likely to be that

the evils of American society are not portrayed or even reflected in the literature which, some historians may say, should have accepted the obligation to explore them." Bernard DeVoto, *The Literary Fallacy* (Boston, 1944), pp. 18, 67–68.

27. "Love To All of You, of All Generations," *Esquire* 60 (July 1963): 87. See also Malcolm Cowley's amusing discussion of the threat of postal censorship in *Exile's Return: A Literary Odyssey of the 1920's* (New York, 1951), pp. 186ff.

28. Hoffman, "Philistine and Puritan," p. 254.

29. Walter Lippmann, "Notes for a Biography," *New Republic* 63 (July 16, 1930): 252.

30. Walter Lippmann, "The Basic Problem of Democracy: I. What Modern Liberty Means," *Atlantic Monthly* 124 (November 1919): 616–617.

31. Lippman had no illusions about the people's continued devotion to democracy themselves. Their own lack of willingness even to try to make democratic processes function undoubtedly compounded his disillusionment about them. Writing an essay in 1927 on the popularity of Sinclair Lewis, he stated: "The election of 1920 marked the close of that period of democratic idealism and of optimism about the perfectability of American society, which began in its modern phase with Bryan, was expressed for a while by Roosevelt, and culminated in the exaltation and the spiritual disaster under Wilson. By 1920 the American people were thoroughly weary of their old faith that happiness could be found by public work, and very dubious about the wisdom of the people. They had found out that the problem of living is deeper and more complex than they had been accustomed to think it was." Walter Lippmann, *Men of Destiny* (New York, 1927), pp. 71–72.

32. Walter Lippmann, *The Phantom Public* (New York, 1925), p. 39.

33. Advocates of censorship were, to Lippmann, "muddle-headed and therefore not clear as to why they were doing what they were doing. . . . When you look at censorship as a whole it is plain that it is actually applied in proportion to the vividness, the directness, and the intelligibility of the medium which circulates the subversive idea." "The battles of liberty are organic conflicts between the adjusted and the unadjusted." Lippmann, *Men of Destiny*, pp. 100, 106.

34. Lippmann's attitude toward labor was one of detachment and a certain aloofness. He at no time in his early career identified himself with labor as a class. He did argue that labor should secure "recognized industrial power in the management of industry," in the years before the war (*The Stakes of Diplomacy* [New York, 1915], p. 214), and spoke of the need of organized labor and militant liberalism for representation in the existing news organization (*Liberty and the News* [New York, 1920]), but the desirability of plunging into active programs to protect labor against discrimination and exploitation was minimized by his qualified views toward the role of the state and the individual. See Howard Edward Dean, "Walter Lippmann and the Good Society: A Study in Political Ideas" (Ph.D diss., Columbia University, 1950), pp. 85ff.

licly, did not teach constitutional law at the Harvard Law School. Powell
35. Chafee, although vitally concerned with civil-liberties problems pub-
continued to hold this position until his retirement. Among his editorials
for the *World* were "Clear and Present Danger," *New York World*, February 7, 1925, p. 10; "Karolyi Again," *New York World*, October 23, 1925,
p. 11; "Go North, Young Man, for Freedom," *New York World*, April 15,
1923, p. 10; "Free Speech," *New York World*, May 24, 1926, p. 10. Drafts
for these and other *World* pieces are contained in the Thomas Reed
Powell Papers, Treasure Room, Harvard Law School Library.
36. Lippmann's 1929 statement on liberty and government could as
well have been made by Mencken: "The advancement of human liberty
has as a matter of practical politics consisted in building up centers of
resistance against the absolutism of the reigning sovereign. For experience
has shown that liberty is most ample if power is distributed, checked,
and limited up to the point where it is paralyzed and unable to maintain
order." Walter Lippmann, *American Inquisitors* (New York, 1928), p.
111. On Lippmann's attitude toward this problem over the years, see
Oscar Handlin, "Does the People's Rule Doom Democracy?" *Commentary*
20 (July 1955): 1–8.
37. Walter Metzger, "American Social Thought in the Twentieth Century," in May Brodbeck, James Gray, and Walter Metzger, *American Non-
Fiction: 1900–1950* (Chicago, 1952), p. 178.
38. Lippmann here found room to take Mencken to task: "If Mr.
Mencken really wishes an aristocracy he will have to give up liberty
as he understands it; and if he wishes liberty he will have to resign himself
to hearing *homo boobiens* speak his mind." Lippmann, *Men of Destiny*,
p. 67. For a broad and useful survey of disillusion with democracy in
the United States in the 1920s, see Joseph Edward Clark, "The American
Critique of the Democratic Idea, 1919–1929" (Ph.D. diss., Stanford University, 1958).
39. Borglum was one of the members of the Klan's cabinet, or Imperial
Koncilium, and a member of the executive committee which finally completed the transfer of power from William J. Simmons to Hiram W. Evans
(*Minutes of the Imperial Koncilium of the Knights of the Ku Klux Klan,*
May 1–2, 1923, Atlanta, Georgia). He was a defendant in the Rittenhouse
case (*The New York Times*, June 1, 1923) and a close friend and advisor
to D. C. Stephenson (Gutzon Borglum to D. C. Stephenson, July 3, 1924,
Borglum Papers, Library of Congress). I am indebted for these references
to Professor David Chalmers of the University of Florida.
40. Diamond, *Reputation of the American Businessman*, pp. 147–149.
41. The Dearborn case, Dearborn Publishing Co. v. Fitzgerald, 271
Fed. 484 (1921), was one of the few in the early 1920s which produced
a ringing defense of free speech. Emphasizing that "Jews are too law
abiding that this kind of anti-semitic attack would arouse them to violence,"
District Court Judge Westenhaver stated: "If defendants' action were sustained (i.e. the attempt to interfere with distribution of the newspaper),
the constitutional liberty of every citizen, freely to speak, write, and publish
his sentiments on all subjects, being responsible only for the abuse of

that right, would be placed at the mercy of every public official who for the moment was clothed with authority to preserve the public peace and the right to a free press would likewise be destroyed." Such an exaggerated concern for the application of *gemeinschaft* sanctions was as unusual as the free speech position. On Ford and the Jews generally, see Keith Sward, *The Legend of Henry Ford* (New York, 1948), pp. 146ff.

42. On personal freedom, Wright was adamant. He later wrote in his autobiography: "A free country and democratic in the sense that our forefathers intended ours to be free, means *individual* freedom for each man on his own ground." Frank Lloyd Wright, *An Autobiography* (New York, 1943), p. 325.

43. Irving Bernstein, "The Growth of American Unions," *American Economic Review* (June 1954): 303.

44. The most conspicuous example of Gompers's treatment of opposition came in the 1923 AFL Convention in Portland, Oregon, in regard to William F. Dunne, avowed Communist, editor of the *Butte Bulletin,* and aggressive champion of amalgamation and industrial unionism. When move was made by Philip Murray to revoke Dunne's credentials as a delegate, Gompers insisted that Dunne be heard. His resultant speech, which was a bitter assault on union leadership and policy was then heard before vote was taken revoking his credentials. *Report of Proceedings of the Forty-Third Annual Convention of the American Federation of Labor* (Washington, 1923), pp. 256–259. For a discussion of the implications of the action by a contemporary defender of Gompers, see Edward P. Mittelman, "Basis for American Federation of Labor Opposition to Amalgamation and Politics at Portland," *Journal of Political Economy* 32 (February 1924): 89–91. Dunne's speech was later published by the Trade Union Educational League with an introduction, which said of the action: "This arbitrary unseating of a regularly elected delegate from an affiliated body by the officialdom of the A.F. of L. was in violation of every principle of free speech and expression of opinion to which the A.F. of L. professed allegiance." *Wm. F. Dunne's Speech at the A.F. of L. Convention* (Chicago, 1923), p. 3.

45. Matthew Woll, "Subversive Forces in Our Country," *Bulletin of the Chamber of Commerce of the State of New York* (January 1927): 7.

46. Samuel Gompers, "Sittin' in a Corner," *American Federationist* 31 (September 1924): 750.

47. There is no single adequate treatment of the attempt of noncommunist unions to throw off communist influence and extricate themselves from obligation to Communists who had at times assisted in organizational drives and strikes. See, however, David J. Saposs, *Communism in American Unions* (New York, 1959). See also Matthew Josephson, *Sidney Hillman: Statesman of American Labor* (Garden City, 1952), pp. 274ff.

48. The question arose at the 1926 Montreal Convention of the ACW as to freedom of speech for those who wanted to overthrow the then current leadership of the organization, and refusal of the official organ

of the organization, the newspaper, *Advance,* to give extended space to opinion by critics of official policy. Hillman called upon J. B. S. Hardman, editor of the Amalgamated's organs to outline policy. Hardman indicated to the delegates that "Freedom of the press . . . does not mean freedom to every one to use the Union's press for the purpose of weakening our own organization. In the life of the organization . . . there are times when free discussion is possible, but there are also occasions when it is necessary to refrain from coming out into the open with discussion which could not bring the Union any good, but which might conceivably bring the organization much harm." "The Editorial Policy of Our Papers Discussed," *Advance* (May 28, 1926): 6. On the general question of the rights of the dissenter within union structure, see the suggestive discussion in Seymour Martin Lipset, Martin A. Trow, and James S. Coleman, *Union Democracy* (Glencoe, Illinois, 1956), pp. 238–261, 259–260.

49. A revealing statement was that of William Z. Foster in 1926: "Militant tactics can be used with good effect when the companies, through their city government agencies, attempt to prohibit free speech and the holding of public meetings during strikes or organizing campaigns. The thing to do is to hold meetings anyhow and go to jail if necessary. A well-waged free-speech fight is never lost. . . . Free-speech fights are an excellent means to unite and inspire the workers in such situations, provided the campaigns are conducted so that the workers realize their direct connection with the wage struggle. Care must be taken not to precipitate such free-speech fights prematurely, before the workers realize what is at stake, else they will not support them." William Z. Foster, *Strike Strategy* (New York, 1926), pp. 63–64.

50. Donald Johnson, *The Challenge to American Freedoms* (Lexington, 1963), p. 145.

51. Baldwin Memorandum (December 8, 1919), quoted in Barton Bean, "Pressure for Freedom: The A.C.L.U." (Ph.D. diss., Cornell University, 1955), p. 82.

52. Richard Hofstadter and Walter P. Metzger, *The Development of Academic Freedom in the United States* (New York, 1955), p. 403.

53. There is a large body of literature on the peculiar problems regarding freedom of expression and free speech as they related to radio and its use, especially as abuse of the airlines brought growing demands for public regulation. See especially Walter B. Emery, *Broadcasting and Government* (East Lansing, 1961), p. 244. See also Elmer E. Smead, *Freedom of Speech by Radio and Television* (Washington, 1959); Llewellyn White, *The American Radio* (Chicago, 1947). Movie censorship raises different problems. See, for example, Ruth A. Inglis, *Freedom of the Movies* (Chicago, 1947), and Bosley Crowther, *Movies and Censorship* (New York, 1962).

54. Margaret Sanger was a favorite target of those who would silence the planned parenthood movement. When her announced Town Hall appearance in New York in November 1921 was blocked by city policemen acting on orders from the Catholic Archbishop of New York and a resultant demonstration resulted, the anti–free-speech position of the church drew

national attention and as Miss Sanger wrote later, aided the movement. "The clumsy and illegal tactics of our religious opponents broadcast to the whole country what we were doing. Even the most conservative American newspapers were placed in the trying position of defending birth control advocates or endorsing a violation of the principle of freedom of speech." Margaret Sanger, *My Fight for Birth Control* (New York, 1931), p. 220.

55. Few of the professional patriot groups were more aggressive in assailing the ACLU specifically and "free-speech fakers" generally than the influential National Civic Federation which in its earlier days had numbered among its members such figures as William Howard Taft, Alton B. Parker, Elihu Root, Samuel Gompers, and William Green. During the 1920s the organization set up the special Committee for the Study of Subversive Movements and focused much of its energies on exposing "reds" in all areas of American life. The body drew regular annual donations from such business organizations as American Telephone and Telegraph Corp., Travelers Insurance Co., Metropolitan Life, New York Edison Co., Edison Electric Illuminating Co. of Boston, Kuhn Loeb Co., Stone & Webster, Carnegie Corporation of New York, National Cash Register, Otis Elevator, DuPont, Shell Union Oil, and such private donors as V. Everet Macy, Cyrus McCormick, Bernard Baruch, John Hays Hammond, Helen C. Shepard, and Samuel Insull. National Civic Federation, Receipt Book, National Civic Federation Papers, New York Public Library.

Chapter 8

1. In this regard, John Dewey wrote in mid-1920: "Freedom of speech and of the franchise is now significant because it is part of the struggle for freedom of mind in industry, freedom to participate in its planning and conduct." And Dewey went on to urge erecting monuments to such men as Palmer and Sweet for dramatizing the fact with their repressive actions. "Freedom of Thought and Work," *New Republic* 22 (May 5, 1920): 317.

2. Learned Hand, "Sources of Tolerance," in Irving Dilliard, ed., *The Spirit of Liberty* (New York, 1960), p. 80; John Haynes Holmes, "What Is Worth Fighting for in American Life?" *The Survey* 57 (February 1, 1927): 605ff.

3. See Christopher Lasch, *The New Radicalism in America, 1889–1963* (New York, 1965).

4. Dewey, "Freedom of Thought," p. 316.

5. The businessmen on the National Committee of the ACLU were either independent entrepreneurs or well insulated from reprisals. For an analysis of committee members in the 1920s and after, see Barton Bean, "Pressure for Freedom: The American Civil Liberties Union" (Ph.D. diss., Cornell University, 1955), pp. 158ff.

6. John Haynes Holmes, rather ironically, extended the realm of permissible social control to rigid enforcement of prohibition. Freedom of thought, speech, assembly, and freedom to vote were, to him, "the principles

of freedom which are the foundations of our temple of liberty, but when
you have named those principles of freedom you have come to the end.
Outside of those fundamental principles, all the people acting as a democratic body can pass their laws as expressions of their will, and the minority
in such case which disagrees is a good sport and representing the true
principles of democracy, join hands with the majority in trying out the
experiment and working it through." Ransom H. Gillett, *Repeal of the
Prohibition Amendment* (New York, 1923), p. 44.

7. Typical of such widely distributed pamphlets was one edited by
John Haynes Holmes entitled *Freedom of Speech and of the Press: Striking
Passages from Distinguished Champions of Freedom of Expression* (New
York, 1922), which included not only American authorities but world
figures from John Milton and John Locke through Herbert Spencer and
Lord Bryce.

8. David M. Potter, "American Individualism in the Twentieth Century," *Texas Quarterly* 6 (Summer 1963): 148.

9. Sigmund Diamond, *The Reputation of the American Businessman*
(Cambridge, 1955), p. 170.

10. Quoted in Charles S. Macfarland, *Christian Unity in the Making:
The First Twenty-five Years of the Federal Council of Churches of Christ
in America* (New York, 1941), p. 207.

11. The 1919 Catholic "Bishop's Program," a general blueprint for
postwar economic justice and social cooperation, met with similar assault.
Ralph M. Easley, secretary and self-professed spokesman for the National
Civic Federation alleged that its authors were "near Bolsheviki" and spoke
only for themselves, not their fellow bishops, while the Lusk Committee
in New York made similar charges, focusing its wrath particularly on
Father John A. Ryan, one of its architects and subsequently a prominent
member of the ACLU. "Civic Federation 'Witch Hunting,'" *Labor* (February 26, 1921): 4. Thus, as Aaron Abell has pointed out, "not a single
remedial or transforming proposal in the Bishop's Program was adopted
during the 1920s. Whereas in the idealistic afterglow of the war, Catholic
and other progressives confidently expected economic democracy to be
the basis of the forthcoming peace and reconstruction, they were soon
to find their country in the grip of a frenzied reaction which wiped out
the recent gains of union labor and imperiled the whole structure of
prewar social legislation." Aaron Abell, *American Catholicism and Social
Action: A Search for Social Justice, 1865–1950* (New York, 1960), p.
204. Ryan's role is further elaborated in Francis L. Broderick, *Right Reverend New Dealer: John A. Ryan* (New York, 1963), pp. 104–109.

12. Nathan Schachner, *The Price of Liberty: A History of the American
Jewish Committee* (New York, 1948), p. 217.

13. See Morton Rosenstock, *Louis Marshall, Defender of Jewish Rights*
(Detroit, 1965), pp. 7ff. There was growing dissatisfaction with such
cautiousness, however, by the rising East European immigrant Jew who
was far more ready to support economically "radical" positions. For example, the United Hebrew Trades was among the most active groups supporting economic equality for the working class and in its heavy donations

to civil liberties causes, especially the campaign for the release of political prisoners. See the tables of donors in the appendix of Lucy Robins, *War Shadows: A Documental Story of the Struggle for Amnesty* (New York, 1922).

14. *The Survey* 33 (January 9, 1915): 406.

15. Harry F. Ward, "Repression of Civil Liberties in the United States (1918–1923)," *Papers and Proceedings of the American Sociological Society* 18 (1923): 127–146. Professor E. A. Ross had sought to get Ralph Easley of the National Civic Federation to debate Ward, but Easley refused to appear on any platform with a representative of the ACLU, which, he believed, stood for "license in labor disputes—not liberty." Ralph M. Easley to E. A. Ross, December 14, 1923, ACLU Papers, microfilm reel 333, New York Public Library.

16. George E. Mowry, *The Twenties: Fords, Flappers and Fanatics* (Englewood Cliffs, 1963); Arlington J. Stone, "The Dawn of a New Science," *The American Mercury* 8 (August 1928).

17. See Edward M. Burns, *David Starr Jordan: Prophet of Freedom* (Stanford, 1953), pp. 44ff. Jordan was a leader in the movement to secure repeal of the California criminal-syndicalism law. On May 17, 1924, for example, he sent a letter to a large number of leading Californians urging common action in this regard. Jordan Papers, Hoover Library, Stanford University.

18. Richard Hofstadter and Walter P. Metzger, *The Development of Academic Freedom in the United States* (New York, 1955), p. 405.

19. Meridel LeSueur, *Crusaders* (New York, 1955), pp. 55–56; Theodore Saloutos and John D. Hicks, *Agricultural Discontent in the Middle West, 1900–1939* (Madison, 1951), pp. 191–195.

20. James H. Shideler, *Farm Crisis, 1919–1923* (Berkeley, 1957), pp. 35ff; See also Ronald E. Michel, "Patterns of Agrarian Self-Consciousness in the 1920's" (Ph.D. diss., Wayne State University, 1961), chap. 7.

21. During the height of the red scare in 1919, Secretary of Agriculture Houston, apparently seeking to join Palmer and Burleson on the bandwagon, called on farmers to join or form farm bureaus in order to fight "bolshevism." Later, Houston overgenerously gave the Farm Bureau the credit for "stopping 'bolshevism' in 1919." Such flattery was not lost on Farm Bureau President J. R. Howard, who worked during his tenure to insure that the bureau behave "responsibly" in rejecting radicalism. Such action was effective in keeping the Bureau conservative through the decade, and as Grant McConnell has pointed out, "complemented business solicitude for the farmer sufficiently to divert farm organizations away from 'radical' channels." Grant McConnell, *The Decline of Agrarian Democracy* (Berkeley, 1959), pp. 48, 56.

22. Irving Howe and Lewis Coser, *The American Communist Party: A Critical History* (New York, 1962), pp. 121ff. See also Kenneth C. MacKay, *The Progressive Movement of 1924* (New York, 1947), pp. 80ff.

23. Saloutos and Hicks, *Agricultural Discontent*, pp. 192–193.

24. Johnson did participate in the struggle to break the speaker ban in New York schools in the famous episode involving Stuyvesant High

School, a case which the Annual Report of the ACLU for 1927, *Free Speech, 1926* (New York, 1927), referred to as "the most important 'free speech fight' of the year." James Weldon Johnson, *Along This Way* (New York, 1933), pp. 385–386.

25. See the brief and impressionistic, but revealing sketch of civil libertarians and Passaic workingmen in John Dos Passos, *The Theme is Freedom* (New York, 1956), pp. 5–7.

26. See Bean, *Pressure for Freedom*, p. 168, 395ff.

27. Dwight McDonald, "The Defense of Everybody, I," *New Yorker* 29 (July 11, 1953): 31.

28. The periodical literature on Baldwin's career is voluminous and generally adulatory. See R. L. Duffus, "The Legend of Roger Baldwin," *American Mercury* (August 1925): 408–414; "Galahad of Freedom," *World Tomorrow* 13 (January 1930): 33–36; Travis Hoke, "Red Rainbow," *North American Review* 234 (November 1932): 431–439; Oliver Jensen, "The Persuasive Roger Baldwin, *Harper's* 203 (September 1951): 47–55; Willie Morris, "Barely Winded at Eighty: Roger Baldwin," *New Republic* 150 (January 25, 1964): 8–10.

29. American Civil Liberties Union, *State Political Prisoners* (New York, 1924), p. 4; Henry Pringle, *The Life and Times of William Howard Taft* (New York, 1939), I, p. 536; Dwight McDonald, "The Defense of Everybody, II," *New Yorker* 29 (July 18, 1953): 57.

30. American Civil Liberties Union, *The Fight for Free Speech* (New York, 1924), p. 3.

31. In 1928, ACLU leaders published a tactics manual with strategy suggestions, Clement Wood and McAlister Coleman, *Don't Tread On Me: A Study of Aggressive Legal Tactics for Labor* (New York, 1928), leading portions of which were issued as an ACLU pamphlet, American Civil Liberties Union, *Legal Tactics for Labor's Rights* (New York, 1930).

32. "Baldwin In Plea For Free Speech," *Madison* (Wisc.) *Journal*, March 18, 1929, p. 3. Baldwin was little concerned with the theoretical aspects of the civil liberties movement, being eminently a practical, hard-headed man of action.

33. McDonald, "Defense, II," p. 57.

34. See Lucille Milner, *Education of an American Liberal* (New York, 1954), pp. 144–145. The ACLU scrapbooks are housed in the Princeton University Library, Princeton, New Jersey. A complete microfilm copy of them is available in the New York Public Library.

35. Fred S. Hall, ed., *Social Work Year Book, 1929* (New York, 1930), p. 86.

36. Joseph Freeman, *An American Testament: A Narrative of Rebels and Romantics* (New York, 1936), pp. 326–327.

Chapter 9

1. Albert De Silver, "The Great Battle for Amnesty," *The Nation* 117 (January 2, 1924): 10.

2. Examples were the League for Amnesty of Political Prisoners; the

Washington, D.C., Citizens' Amnesty Committee; the Amnesty League, a branch of the IWW General Defense Committee; and many smaller local organizations. See H. C. Peterson and Gilbert C. Fite, *Opponents of War, 1917–1918* (Madison, 1957), pp. 267–268; "Borah Speaks for Politicals," *Advance* (October 6, 1922): 1.

3. Lucy Robins, *War Shadows, A Documentary Story of the Struggle for Amnesty* (New York, 1922), pp. 53–54, quotes numerous examples.

4. De Silver, "Amnesty," p. 10.

5. "Harding Declines to Plead for Debs," *The New York Times*, July 25, 1920, p. 3.

6. "Free Speech and Jailed Speakers," *Literary Digest* 77 (June 16, 1923): 11–13. The article also reported a strongly worded amnesty petition, which had been sent to Harding, signed by forty-eight prominent men and women, among them five state governors, eleven college presidents, several editors, and many well-known Protestant, Catholic, and Jewish clergymen, and recorded a vigorous and effective speech by Senator William E. Borah, in which he stated that "at the bottom of the controversy there lies the question of what constitutes free speech and free press under the American flag."

7. A bitter editorial in the *Washington Times* spoke to this point. Pointing out that all of the wartime profiteers, wealthy draft evaders, and capitalists who had defrauded the government on wartime contracts had not so much as tasted penalty, while the radicals whose "crime" had been primarily speech were still in jail, the paper suggested that this hardly was a flattering image of a nonpartisan government. "Today the 'radicals' are able to say to the striking coal miners and to the striking railroad shopmen: 'Look! The government imprisons war-time offenders who represent capital. Are you going to submit your grievances in this strike to any arbitration by any such government?' " Release, the paper argued, would be the best way to undermine social unrest and recreate an atmosphere of respect for both government and basic American traditions. Quoted in General Defense Committee, *Public Opinion: Where Does It Stand on the Question of Amnesty for Political Prisoners?* (Chicago, 1924), pp. 5–6.

8. Oswald Garrison Villard, "Why Amnesty Matters," *The Nation* 114 (January 25, 1922): 87–88.

9. Debs's jailing had raised basic questions of free speech, which had particularly disturbed Oliver Wendell Holmes, Jr., who had written the decision upholding his conviction. See Otto Kirchheimer, *Political Justice: The Use of Legal Procedure for Political Ends* (Princeton, 1961), pp. 390–391. See also Ray Ginger, *The Bending Cross: A Biography of Eugene Victor Debs* (New Brunswick, 1949), p. 400. David Starr Jordan wrote Harding at the time: "Debs immediate pardon would serve to mark the end of the period of un-American intolerance which has made an indelible stain on the record of the Wilson administration and which contributed so largely to its final downfall." Jordan Papers, Hoover Library, Stanford University.

10. The leader of one veteran's group took the Legion to task for

its position and activities. Marvin Gates Sperry, national president of the Private Soldiers and Sailors Legion of the United States, wrote letters to both Harding and Daugherty in 1921 condemning "the lawless swash-buckling American Legion Officers and their immediate circle of addle-pated followers" for stating that Debs's pardon would constitute "license to dis-regard all law and order," and charging the Legion with "resorting to mob violence against both men and women in hundreds of cases in all parts of the United States . . . until their depraved and deliberate lawless-ness has become a national scandal and disgrace to our country; where freedom of press and speech and peaceable assemblage, which these Ameri-can Legion officers and their dupes would destroy, are the very treasures of the ark of the covenant of American Liberty." Quoted in Robins, *War Shadows*, p. 342.

11. Peterson and Fite, *Opponents of War*, p. 278.

12. Daugherty to Newcomb Carlton, quoted in William Preston, *Aliens and Dissenters* (Cambridge, 1963), p. 259. Daugherty's movement suc-ceeded since numerous bodies supporting amnesty, especially the AFL, now thinking the victory was won, promptly curtailed further efforts in this regard.

13. Philip Taft, "The Federal Trials of the IWW," *Labor History* 3 (Winter 1962): 84–85.

14. Donald Johnson, *The Challenge to American Freedoms* (Lexington, 1963), pp. 185–189.

15. Pierce C. Wetter, "The Men I Left at Leavenworth," *The Survey* 49 (October 1, 1922): 31.

16. "Amnesty and the Civil Liberties Union," *The Nation* 118 (March 26, 1924): 346; "Against Compromise," *The Nation* 118 (May 7, 1924): 534.

17. Johnson, *Challenge*, p. 190.

18. "Text of Gov. Smith's Message to the Legislature on Pressing State Issues," *The New York Times*, January 1, 1923, p. 10.

19. "Smith May Pardon Larkin and Others," *The New York Times*, January 10, 1923, p. 25.

20. See "Governor Small's Pardon," *Advance* (December 8, 1922): 4.

21. "Larkin Pardoned, Leaves Sing Sing; Others May Follow," *The New York Times*, January 18, 1923, p. 1. The initiative in the action to free Larkin had been taken by the ACLU, whose counsel, the law firm of Hale, Nelles & Shorr had been the attorneys in the case.

22. "Condemn Pardon of Jim Larkin," *The New York Times*, January 19, 1923, p. 19; "The Pardon of Larkin," *The New York Times*, January 19, 1923, p. 16. See also *Advance* (January 26, 1923): 5.

23. "Fresh Air Blows Away Hot Air," *Collier's Weekly* 71 (February 10, 1923): 16.

24. Glenn Frank, "Al Smith Pardons Jim Larkin," *Century Magazine* 105 (March 1923): 798–799.

25. George Wharton Pepper, *Philadelphia Lawyer: An Autobiography* (Philadelphia, 1944), p. 184; Preston, *Aliens*, pp. 262–263.

26. "Coolidge Releases All War Offenders," *The New York Times,*
December 16, 1923, p. 2. *The New York Times* was a prominent exception.
In an editorial entitled "Free Speech Was Not Involved," December 17,
1923, p. 16, the *Times* insisted that Coolidge's action in no way inferred
pardon of the men's misdeeds and that the men were not, and never
had been, "martyrs to free speech," since the type of speech they had
uttered was certainly not protected by the First Amendment.

27. "Political Convicts May Be Freed Soon," *The New York Times,*
November 29, 1923, p. 1; Robins, *War Shadows,* pp. 366–373.

28. See Winthrop D. Lane, *The Denial of Civil Liberties in the Coal
Fields* (New York, 1924), pp. 5–9; Homer L. Morris, *The Flight of the
Bituminous Coal Miner* (Philadelphia, 1934), pp. 85–97; Zechariah Chafee,
The Inquiring Mind (Boston, 1928), pp. 172–182; Arthur Gleason, "Company Owned Americans," *The Nation* 110 (June 12, 1920): 794–795.

29. Winthrop D. Lane, *Civil War in West Virginia* (New York, 1921),
p. 17.

30. Spivak to Baldwin, June 11, 1920, ACLU Papers, quoted in Donald
Johnson, "The American Civil Liberties Union: Origins, 1914–1917" (Ph.D.
diss., Columbia University, 1960), pp. 307–308. Baldwin recalls Spivak
as "one of the most colorful and adventurous newspapermen I ever
knew . . . who incited news by being provocative . . . and revelled in
drama and danger." Roger N. Baldwin to Paul L. Murphy, September
14, 1964. See also John L. Spivak, *A Man in His Times* (New York,
1967), chaps. 3–5.

31. Although exact details of the conflict are impossible to obtain,
Virgil C. Jones makes a serious attempt to recreate the situation in *The
Hatfields and the McCoys* (Chapel Hill, 1948), pp. 233–237. See also
John L. Spivak, *The Devil's Brigade* (New York, 1930), pp. 303ff.

32. "Twelve Men Killed in Pistol Battle in West Virginia," *The New
York Times,* May 20, 1920, p. 1; "Demand Action by Governor: Miners'
President and Civil Liberties Union Criticize His Policy," *The New York
Times,* May 21, 1920, p. 2; "10 Killed in Fight Between Miners and
Company Detectives," *St. Louis Post Dispatch,* May 20, 1920, p. 1. See
also Robert Miner, "The Wars of West Virginia," *Liberator* 3 (August
1920): 7–13, and his, *John L. Lewis and the International Union, United
Mine Workers of America* (New York, 1952), pp. 29–30.

33. Palmer to Frank Keeney, June 1, 1920, Justice Department Archives,
quoted in Johnson, "American Civil Liberties Union," p. 308.

34. Baldwin to Harold Houston, September 13, 1920, ACLU Papers
quoted in ibid., p. 311.

35. "United Miners Raise $1,000,000 for Strikers," *The New York
Times,* January 10, 1921, p. 2; "Jury Acquits 16 of Coal Strike Murder,"
The New York Times, May 22, 1921, p. 6; Charles H. Ambler and Festus
P. Summers, *West Virginia, The Mountain State,* 2d ed. (Englewood
Cliffs, 1958), pp. 454–455.

36. Local reaction to such scabs was strong, however, with even women
and children harrassing them. See McAlister Coleman, *Men and Coal*
(New York, 1943), p. 103.

37. The ruling restrained organizers from interfering with individual contracts that miners had made with their employers and since these were in large part "yellow dog" contracts, upheld by the Hitchman Coal Case (245 U.S. 229 [1917]), little could be done to counter it short of starting a test case in already antilabor courts. See Ambler and Summers, *West Virginia*, pp. 449–450.

38. Winthrop D. Lane, "Conflict on the Tug," *The Survey* 46 (June 18, 1921): 398–399.

39. "Twelve Union Leaders Arrested in Mingo," *The New York Times*, July 9, 1921, p. 20.

40. U.S., Congress, Senate, Committee on Education and Labor, *Hearings to Investigate Recent Acts of Violence in the Coal Fields of West Virginia*, 67th Cong., 1st sess. (1921–1922), I, pp. 5–8, 8–14. The ACLU petitioned the committee to restore in West Virginia "the rights guaranteed all citizens by the Federal Constitution." Ibid., p. 558.

41. Jones, *Hatfields*, p. 244; Ambler and Summers, *West Virginia*, p. 456.

42. Coleman, *Coal*, pp. 103–104; Winthrop D. Lane, "The Labor Spy in West Virginia," *The Survey* 47 (October 29, 1921): 110–112; "The Blame for West Virginia's War," *Literary Digest* 70 (September 10, 1921): 16–17; Arthur Warner, "Fighting Unionism with Martial Law," *The Nation* 113 (October 12, 1921): 395–396; Heber Blankenhorn, "Marching Through West Virginia," *The Nation* 113 (September 14, 1921): 288–289; J. W. Hess, ed., *Struggle in the Coal Fields* (Morgantown, W. Va., 1967).

43. Harry F. Ward et al. to Harding, October 19, 1921, Justice Department Archives, quoted in Johnson, "American Civil Liberties Union," p. 322.

44. Burns to Daugherty, October 19, 1921, and Burns to Crim, October 25, 1921, Justice Department Archives, quoted in ibid., pp. 322–323.

45. U.S., Congress, Senate, Committee on Education and Labor, *Personal Views of Senator Kenyon et al*, 67th Cong., 1st sess. (1922), pp. 6–7.

46. The UMW was not impressed with ACLU support. Houston to Baldwin, September 27, 1923, ACLU Papers; Johnson, "American Civil Liberties Union," p. 329.

47. Arthur Garfield Hayes, *Let Freedom Ring* (New York, 1928), pp. 128–129.

48. American Civil Liberties Union, *Free Speech in 1924* (New York, 1925), pp. 20–21. For mid-1920 conditions, see also Labor Research Department, Rand School of Social Science, *The American Labor Year Book, 1926* (New York, 1926), pp. 214–215.

49. Labor Defense and Free Speech Council of Western Pennsylvania, *Free Speech in Western Pennsylvania* (Pittsburgh, 1923), p. 3.

50. James Hudson Maurer, *It Can Be Done: The Autobiography of James Hudson Maurer* (New York, 1938), pp. 150–155; Pennsylvania State Federation of Labor, *The American Cossack* (Philadelphia, 1914).

51. Fincke was the moving force behind the establishment of the Brookwood Labor College, a not insignificant factor in union organization and

education in the 1920s, having donated the buildings and grounds of his family estate at Katonah, New York, for this purpose. See Coleman, *Coal,* pp. 108–109.

52. Duquesne v. Fincke, 112 Atl. 130 (1920).

53. American Civil Liberties Union, *The Shame of Pennsylvania* (New York, 1928), p. 10; Frederick Woltman and William L. Nunn, "Cossacks," *The American Mercury* 15 (December 1928): 403.

54. Winthrop D. Lane, *The Denial of Civil Liberties in the Coal Fields* (New York, 1924); Powers Hapgood, *In Non-Union Mines: The Diary of a Coal Digger* (New York, 1922).

55. ACLU, *The Shame of Pennsylvania,* pp. 20–21.

56. David Brody, *Steelworkers in America: The Nonunion Era* (Cambridge, 1960), p. 271.

57. Labor Research Department, Rand School of Social Science, *American Labor Year Book, 1926,* pp. 208–209; United Mine Workers of America, *John L. Lewis and the U.M.W.,* p. 24.

58. Nelson McGeary, *Gifford Pinchot* (Princeton, 1960), p. 308.

59. Lane, *Denial.*

60. U.S., Congress, Senate, *Report of the United States Coal Commission,* Sen. Doc. 195, 68th Cong., 2d sess. (1925), I, pp. 176, 179.

61. *Free Speech Council of Western Pennsylvania,* pp. 6–10.

62. Ibid., p. 13.

63. Hayes, *Freedom,* pp. 102–110; Labor Research Department, Rand School of Social Science, *American Labor Year Book, 1923–1924* (New York, 1924), p. 211. Hapgood, *Mines,* pp. 27–30, gives a graphic, firsthand description of a worker's role in Vintondale. See also "Right to Talk Is Still Denied in Pennsylvania," *Labor* (December 9, 1922): 1.

64. "Pennsylvania Justice," *The Nation* 117 (October 10, 1923): 381–382.

65. See "Coal Dealers Score Pinchot For Deal," *The New York Times,* September 13, 1923, p. 23; "Assail Coal Settlement," *The New York Times,* September 23, 1923, p. 6.

66. John P. Guyer, *Pennsylvania's Cossacks and the State Police* (Reading, 1924), p. 4.

67. Labor Research Department, Rand School of Social Science, *American Labor Year Book, 1926,* p. 210.

68. The broad outlines of the situation are drawn in Joseph G. Rayback, *A History of American Labor* (New York, 1964), pp. 307ff.

69. On Herrin, see Cecil Carnes, *John L. Lewis, Leader of Labor* (New York, 1936), pp. 94–95, 113ff; Coleman, *Coal,* pp. 115–125.

70. *Biennial Report of the Pennsylvania State Police for 1927–1928* (Harrisburg, 1928), p. 5; Woltman and Nunn, "Cossacks," give a graphic eyewitness account of much of the brutality. See also Mary Donovan-Hapgood, "Fascism in Pennsylvania," *The Lantern* 2 (March–April 1928): 14–16; Harbor Allen, "Coal, Steel, and 'Sedition,'" *The Nation* 124 (February 23, 1927): 205–206.

71. U.S., Congress, Senate, Committee on Interstate Commerce, *Condi-*

tions in the Coal Fields of Pennsylvania, West Virginia, and Ohio, Hearings,
70th Cong., 1st sess., 1928.

72. Ibid., pp. 562, 1363, 2529, 2539.

73. Ibid., pp. 2549, 2550.

74. Ibid., pp. 982, 989.

75. Harvey O'Connor, *Mellon's Millions: The Biography of a Fortune*
(New York, 1933), p. 224; Coleman, *Coal*, p. 135; *Advance* (March
1, 1929): 1.

76. Woltman and Nunn, "Cossacks," p. 406. Woltman and Nunn, then
instructors at the University of Pittsburgh, were forced to resign as a
result of the article. John O. P. Hall, *A Miner's Life: John Brophy* (Madison,
1964), p. 223.

77. American Civil Liberties Union, *The Fight for Civil Liberty,
1928–1929* (New York, 1929), p. 17; *Reading* (Pa.) *Eagle*, March 13,
1929. See also *Fresno Bee*, March 2, 1929, and *Tatentum* (Pa.) *News*,
February 19, 1929, all ACLU Papers, microfilm reel 362, New York Public
Library.

78. Commonwealth of Pennsylvania, *Administrative Code of 1929* (Harrisburg, 1945), art. VII, sec. 712, p. 67.

79. Samuel Yellen, *American Labor Struggles* (New York, 1936), pp.
248–249; Mary Van Kleeck, *Miners and Management* (New York, 1934),
pp. 63ff.

80. Donald J. McClurg, "The Colorado Coal Strike of 1927—Tactical
Leadership of the IWW," *Labor History* 4 (Winter 1963): 70.

81. Ibid., pp. 73–74.

82. American Civil Liberties Union, *The War on Colorado Miners*
(New York, 1928), pp. 8–10.

83. "Picturesque Girl Strike Leader of Colorado Untamed by Jail,"
Advance (December 16, 1927): 8; "The Blood-Spilling in Colorado," *Literary Digest* 95 (December 3, 1927): 5–7.

84. McClurg, "Coal Strike," p. 81.

85. News coverage of the Pennsylvania situation, which involved many
times more people and much more tyrannical repression, was virtually
negligible, with even the liberal journals carrying little. The remote Colorado situation, by contrast, drew anguished protests, especially from the
eastern press. See, "Bloody Colorado," *The Nation* 125 (November 16,
1927): 534; "Colorado Coal Battle," *Outlook* 147 (December 7, 1927):
422; Frank L. Palmer, "War in Colorado," *The Nation* 125 (December
7, 1927): 623–624; M. M. Rice, "Bloody Monday Again in Colorado,"
Independent 119 (December 31, 1927): 655–656; "Rebellion in Colorado,"
The Nation 126 (January 11, 1928): 33; Frank L. Palmer, "Solidarity
in Colorado," *The Nation* 126 (February 1, 1928): 118–121; Erwin F.
Meyer, "Six Killed, Twenty Wounded: A Case Study of Industrial Conflict,"
The Survey 54 (February 15, 1928): 644–646.

86. "Two Church Views of the Colorado Strike," *Literary Digest* 95
(December 17, 1927): 31–32.

87. ACLU, *War on Miners*, p. 12. On Lindsey and the Klan, see Ben
B. Lindsey and Rube Borough, *The Dangerous Life* (New York, 1931),
pp. 388ff; Ben B. Lindsey to Roger Baldwin, September 12, 1925, American

Fund for Public Service, Miscellaneous Correspondence, 1923–1933, New York Public Library.

88. Industrial Commission of Colorado, *Tenth Report* (Denver, 1928), especially pp. 48–49; Van Kleeck, *Miners and Management,* pp. 60, 64.

89. Grace Hutchins, *Labor and Silk* (New York, 1929), pp. 137–144; American Civil Liberties Union, *Unlawful Assembly in Paterson* (New York, 1925), p. 11.

90. State v. Butterworth, 139 Atl. 161, 162 (1927); American Civil Liberties Union, *The New Jersey Case Against Roger N. Baldwin* (New York, 1928).

91. ACLU, *Unlawful Assembly,* pp. 10–11.

92. The resolution stated: "Another of the great principles of our noble order . . . is the protection and preservation of the constitutional rights [sic] of free speech to the end that it shall remain a matter of liberty, and not of license to spread propaganda for the overthrow of orderly constitutional government and the establishment of Bolshevism and a state of chaos and anarchy." "Klan Votes on Strike," *The New York Times,* October 22, 1924, p. 9.

93. ACLU, *Unlawful Assembly,* p. 8.

94. American Civil Liberties Union, *Free Speech in 1924* (New York, 1925), p. 26.

95. State v. Butterworth, 142 Atl. 57, 59, 61 (1928).

96. ACLU, *Free Speech in 1924,* p. 26.

97. Quoted in ibid., pp. 15, 17. For an appreciation of the ACLU's role, see Charles Reznikoff, *Louis Marshall: Champion of Liberty* (Philadelphia, 1957), II, p. 987. See also Clement Wood and McAlister Coleman, *Don't Tread on Me: A Study of Aggressive Legal Tactics for Labor* (New York, 1928), pp. 64–65.

98. Beulah Amidon, "An Old Fashioned Strike," *The Survey* 56 (April 1, 1926): 11.

99. See "Passaic Textile Workers Fight for Their Right of Free Speech," *The Advance* (April 30, 1920): 13. Albert Weisbord, in his contemporary analysis of the strike, made much of the fact that the mills, almost without exception, were owned by Germans who had come to the United States at the turn of the century to "escape the labor and social insurance laws that the German trade unionists and socialists had compelled the government of the empire to enact." Albert Weisbord, *Passaic* (Chicago, 1926), p. 12.

100. Irving Howe and Lewis Coser, *The American Communist Party: A Critical History* (Boston, 1957), pp. 239–240.

101. Benjamin Gitlow, *I Confess: The Truth About American Communism* (New York, 1940), pp. 363–377, and his, *The Whole of Their Lives: Communism in America* (New York, 1948), pp. 130–133.

102. Labor Research Department, Rand School of Social Science, *American Labor Year Book, 1927* (New York, 1927), p. 105.

103. Joseph Freeman captures much of the spirit of the situation in his memoir, *An American Testament: A Narrative of Rebels and Romantics* (New York, 1936), pp. 395–400.

104. Detailed accounts of Passaic are many. Albert Weisbord wrote

his own version, *Passaic. The Christian Century* devoted an entire issue to exploring every facet of the strike including the proper role of the church regarding it, "The Passaic Strike: A Study in Contemporary America," *The Christian Century* 43 (August 5, 1926): 964–990. See also Mary Heaton Vorse, *Passaic* (Chicago, 1926), pp. 11–12.

105. "Battle of Passaic," *Literary Digest* 88 (March 20, 1926): 11–12.

106. The posted notices read: "By Virtue of an Act of this State entitled 'An Act to prevent routs, riots, and tumultous assemblies,' I am directed to charge and command all persons, being here assembled, immediately to disperse themselves and peaceable to depart to their habitations or to their lawful business, upon the pains and penalties contained in the said Act. GOD SAVE THE STATE." Vorse, *Passaic,* p. 7.

107. "Seek Arrest of Passaic Chief," *The New York Times,* March 28, 1926, p. 9.

108. Harry Fleischman, *Norman Thomas: A Biography* (New York, 1964), p. 106.

109. Vorse, *Passaic,* p. 23.

110. "Thomas Gives Bail in 'Riot Act' Arrest," *The New York Times,* April 16, 1926, p. 1; "Weisbord Freed, Then Jailed Again," *The New York Times,* April 18, 1926, p. 1.

111. "Moore and Aids Plan to Mediate Strike," *The New York Times,* April 21, 1926, p. 27.

112. "To Bar Dr. Holmes from Riot Act Test," *The New York Times,* April 30, 1926, p. 7.

113. "Writ Defeats Guns: Mill Strikers Meet," *The New York Times,* May 1, 1926, p. 19; Howe and Coser, *Communist Party,* pp. 242–243.

114. Edwin Layton, "The Better America Federation: A Case Study of Superpatriotism," *Pacific Historical Review* 30 (May 1961): 137–147; General Defense Committee, *The Shame of California* (San Francisco, 1923).

115. Hyman Weintraub, "The I.W.W. in California: 1905–1931" (Ph.D. diss., University of California, Los Angeles, 1947), pp. 226ff.

116. Woodrow C. Whitten, "Criminal Syndicalism and the Law in California, 1919–1927" (Ph.D. diss., University of California, Berkeley, 1946), p. 219. See also Louis B. Perry and Richard S. Perry, *A History of the Los Angeles Labor Movement, 1911–1941* (Berkeley, 1962), pp. 183–186; Weintraub, "The I.W.W.," p. 291; "A Visit to Liberty Hill," *Industrial Pioneer* 1 (August 1923): 35–36.

117. George P. West, "After Liberalism Had Failed," *The Nation* 116 (May 30, 1923): 629.

118. Upton Sinclair, *The Autobiography of Upton Sinclair* (New York, 1962), pp. 229–230; U.S., Congress, House, *Investigation of Communist Propaganda, Hearings,* before a Special Committee to Investigate Communist Activities in the United States, 71st Cong., 2d sess. (1930), III, pt. 5, pp. 325–326.

119. Wood and Coleman, *Don't Tread on Me,* p. 64; American Civil Liberties Union, *The Record of the Fight for Free Speech in 1923* (New York, 1924), p. 14; "Upton Sinclair Held for Breach of Peace," *The*

New York Times, May 17, 1923, p. 20; John S. Gambs, *The Decline of the I.W.W.* (New York, 1932), pp. 44–45.

120. Upton Sinclair, "Protecting Our Liberties," *The Nation* 117 (July 4, 1923): 10.

121. Clinton J. Taft, *Fifteen Years on Freedom's Front* (Los Angeles, 1939), p. 5.

122. Sinclair, *Autobiography*, pp. 231–232; Upton Sinclair, "Civil Liberties in Los Angeles," *Industrial Pioneer* 1 (August 1923): 27–29; American Civil Liberties Union, *Mob Violence on the Rampage in San Pedro* (Los Angeles, 1924); Ed Delaney and M. T. Rice, *The Bloodstained Trail* (Seattle, 1927), pp. 152–161; John W. Caughey, *Their Majesties the Mob* (Chicago, 1960), pp. 127–129; Perry and Perry, *L. A. Labor*, pp. 190–191; Carey McWilliams, *Southern California Country* (New York, 1946), pp. 291–292.

123. Ernest J. Hopkins, *Our Lawless Police: A Study of the Unlawful Enforcement of the Law* (New York, 1931), p. 154. See also United States National Commission on Law Observance and Enforcement, *Report on Lawlessness in Law Enforcement* (Washington, 1931), XI, pp. 143ff.

124. ACLU, *Free Speech in 1924*, pp. 17–20.

125. Irving Bernstein, *The Lean Years: A History of the American Worker, 1920–1933* (Boston, 1960), p. 211; ACLU, *Free Speech in 1923*, p. 10.

126. Management had on frequent occasion refused to abide by the rulings of the Board, but with no penalty. See Zechariah Chafee, *The Inquiring Mind* (New York, 1928), pp. 208–209.

127. A full statement of the injunction order is carried in Felix Frankfurter and James M. Landis, "Power of Congress Over Procedure in Criminal Contempts in 'Inferior' Federal Courts—A Study in Separation of Power," *Harvard Law Review* 37 (June 1924): 1101–1113.

128. Philip Adler, "The Daugherty Injunction," *The Survey* 48 (September 15, 1922): 702; "Impeachable Offenses," *New York World*, September 7, 1922, p. 10. The AFL and Gompers initially talked of a nationwide general strike ("General Strike to Be Considered by A.F. of L. Chiefs," *New York World*, September 1, 1922, p. 1) to support the shopmen, but when the general council met it quashed such talk, contenting itself with offering "full sympathy" to the strikers. "A. F. of L. to Dodge General Strike Call," *New York World*, September 4, 1922, p. 1.

129. "Smothering a Strike by Injunction," *Literary Digest* 74 (September 16, 1922): 7.

130. Chafee, *Inquiring Mind*, p. 214.

131. "Smothering a Strike," p. 8.

132. "Trifling With Freedom," *Editor and Publisher* 55 (September 9, 1922): 26.

133. "Harding Hedges on Injunction," *New York World*, September 6, 1922, p. 1; "The World and Mr. Daugherty," *New York World*, September 7, 1922, p. 1.

134. U.S., Congress, House, Committee on the Judiciary, *Charges of*

Hon. Oscar E. Keller Against the Attorney General of the United States, Hearings, 67th Cong., 3d sess. (1922), p. 2.

135. "Smothering a Strike," p. 8.

136. *Address by the Attorney General of the United States, Harry M. Daugherty at Canton, Ohio, October 21, 1922* (n.d.), pp. 11, 14, 15.

137. "Gompers Condemns Daugherty Defense," *The New York Times,* October 23, 1922, p. 17.

138. John Haynes Holmes, *Is Violence the Way Out of Our Industrial Disputes?* (New York, 1920), p. 104. On the court's history, see Domenico Gagliardo, *The Kansas Industrial Court: An Experiment In Compulsory Arbitration* (Lawrence, 1941).

130. Walter Johnson, *William Allen White's America* (New York, 1947), p. 362.

140. Helen O. Mahin, *The Editor and His People: Editorials by William Allen White* (New York, 1924), p. 346.

141. Ibid., pp. 348–349; "Justice Will Bring Peace: Force Is Decried by White," *Labor* (September 9, 1922): 4.

142. Johnson, *White's America,* p. 368; *Labor* (December 16, 1923): 4; "This Week," *New Republic* 32 (December 27, 1922): 106.

143. "Labor Editor Gets Six Months for Scoring Scabs," *Labor* (September 23, 1922): 1; "Memphis Editor Held," *The New York Times,* September 5, 1922, p. 2.

144. "Contempt of Court," *Law and Labor* 5 (June 1923): 153.

145. American Civil Liberties Union, *A Year's Fight for Free Speech* (New York, 1923), pp. 34–35, and its, *Free Speech in 1924,* p. 14.

146. The ACLU entered the New Bedford, Massachusetts, textile strike in 1928, where peaceful picketing was constantly being disrupted by local authorities. American Civil Liberties Union, *The Fight for Civil Liberty, 1928–29* (New York, 1929), pp. 12–13. See also Howe and Coser, *Communist Party,* pp. 243–245; Robert W. Dunn and Jack Hardy, *Labor and Textiles* (New York, 1931), pp. 225–227; Dwight McDonald, "The Defense of Everybody, II," *New Yorker* 29 (July 18, 1953): 38.

147. Lawrence Lader, *The Margaret Sanger Story* (New York, 1955), pp. 226–227; Hayes, *Freedom,* p. 130.

148. Freeman, *American Testament,* p. 329; ACLU, *Free Speech in 1923,* p. 17.

149. "Assails the Police in Sacco Disorders," *The New York Times,* September 3, 1927, p. 17.

150. G. Louis Joughin and Edmund. M. Morgan, *The Legacy of Sacco and Vanzetti* (New York, 1948), pp. 312–313; Miriam Gurko, *Restless Spirit: The Life of Edna St. Vincent Millay* (New York, 1962), pp. 179–189. Hayes, *Freedom,* pp. 130–146; Daniel Aaron, *Writers on the Left* (New York, 1961), pp. 170–173; "A Boston Jury Surprises," *The Lantern* 2 (January 1928): 7; Labor Research Department, Rand School of Social Science, *American Labor Year Book, 1929* (New York, 1929), p. 203. See also McClurg, "Coal Strike," pp. 71–72; "Some Left Over Morals," *The New York Times,* August 24, 1927, p. 22.

151. Lader, *Margaret Sanger Story,* p. 227.

152. Harvey Goldberg, ed., *American Radicals: Some Problems and Personalities* (New York, 1957), p. 58.

153. Heywood H. Broun, *Collected Edition of Heywood Broun* (New York, 1941), pp. 198, 201, 204.

154. James W. Barrett, *Joseph Pulitzer and His World* (New York, 1941), p. 392; Broun, *Collected Edition*, pp. 204–205.

155. Heywood Broun, "It Seems to Heywood Broun," *The Nation* 126 (May 4, 1928): 532; Broun, *Collected Edition*, pp. 206–209; "The Rights of a Columnist," *The Nation* 126 (May 30, 1928): 607–609.

156. "The Rights of a Columnist," p. 607.

157. There was much internal criticism of the lack of independence of the press during the decade. See, for example, Silas Bent, *Ballyhoo* (New York, 1927); "Sell the Papers! The Malady of American Journalism," *Harper's* 151 (June 1925); "The Myth of a Free Press," *The Nation* 128 (May 15, 1929); John T. Flynn, "News by Courtesy: Our Commercially Owned Press," *Forum* 82 (March 1930).

158. See Edward M. Snider, "The American Civil Liberties Union, A Sociological Interpretation" (Master's thesis, University of Missouri, 1937), pp. 81ff. American Civil Liberties Union, *The Fight for Civil Liberty, 1927–1928* (New York, 1928), p. 3.

159. American Fund for Public Service, Inc., *Report for the First Year of Operation Ending July 31, 1923* (New York, 1923), p. 18; Merle Curti, "Subsidizing Radicalism: The American Fund for Public Service, 1921–1941," *The Social Service Review* 33 (September 1959): 277, 278, 286.

160. Roger N. Baldwin to Paul L. Murphy, July 16, 1962.

161. The predominance of female donors is striking. Roger Baldwin and Stuart Chase in their 1923 survey reported that "individual givers who contribute largely and generally to enterprises within our field are exclusively women of large means. There is not a single man in the country whose gifts to such enterprises total $5000 a year. There are four or five women who give as much or more." "Survey of the Enterprises in the Liberal, Labor and Radical Movements in the United States," in American Fund for Public Service, Inc., *Miscellaneous Reports, 1922–41*, VI, p. 320, New York Public Library.

162. Ibid.

163. Curti, "American Fund," p. 282.

164. The split between Samuel Gompers, AFL leadership, and the ACLU came as the direct result of Garland Fund money. The ACLU and the AFL had been cooperative colleagues in the battle against red scare repression, but when Gompers applied for a sizable Garland Fund grant for his Workers Education Bureau and was turned down on the grounds that the fund only supported "those organizations and institutions which instilled into the workers the knowledge and the qualities which fit them for carrying on the struggle for the emancipation of their class in every sphere," he assailed the fund as a red revolutionary conspiracy against public order, and expanded his assault to the ACLU charging that it was behind the fund's operations and that both were "clearly

connected with perhaps 50 or more leading pacific, pro-Bolshevist and parlor pink organizations." "Gompers Charges Garland's $800,000 Helps Revolution," *The New York Times,* April 13, 1923, p. 1. See also Baldwin's response, "Denounce Gompers for Attack on Fund," *The New York Times,* April 14, 1923, p. 15, and Curti, "American Fund, p. 292.

165. The Radio Act of 1927 had given to the Federal Radio Commission wide discretionary authority to refuse renewal of broadcast licenses as "public interest, convenience, or necessity" may require, although the measure was careful to add "no regulation or condition shall be promulgated or fixed by the licensing authority which shall interfere with the right of free speech by means of radio communications." 44 Stat. 1172 (1927). See also "Previous Restraints Upon Freedom of Speech," *Columbia Law Review* 31 (November 1931): 1153. On the controversy, see "Meeting to Protest Move to Bar WEVD," *The New York Times,* June 25, 1928, p. 26; "Socialist Station Continued on Air," *The New York Times,* August 23, 1928, p. 26; "Labor Groups Plead for Station WEVD," *The New York Times,* March 2, 1931, p. 28; "Edging Toward Radio Censorship," *Labor* (September 1, 1928): 4. For other examples of radio arbitrariness, see Labor Research Department, Rand School of Social Science, *American Labor Year Book, 1928* (New York, 1928), pp. 189–190.

166. Oscar Sternback, "Sexual Liberation and the Child," *Current,* no. 25 (May 1962): 28.

Chapter 10

1. Big steel was an important exception. Under the leadership of Elbert H. Gary, steel not only slashed wages in the postwar period, but clung tenaciously to the twelve-hour day until public pressure eventually forced capitulation in late 1923. See David Brody, *Steelworkers in America: The Nonunion Era* (Cambridge, 1960), pp. 268–275.

2. One observer noted "proponents of the status quo let prosperity speak for itself, and it spoke loudly enough to drown out talk about . . . unpleasant aspects of the twenties." Granville Hicks, *Where We Came Out* (New York, 1954), p. 24.

3. Earle L. Hunter, *A Sociological Analysis of Certain Types of Patriotism* (New York, 1932), pp. 44ff, 83ff, 113ff.

4. Blanton, characterized later in the decade as "the premier blatherskite of American public life" ("Exit Garrett, Blanton and Black," *Labor* [August 11, 1928]: 4), was responsible for one of the most vicious and widely quoted assaults on the ACLU in the decade, reading into the *Congressional Record* a long letter from Francis Ralston Welsh, a Philadelphia "red hunter," which among other things referred to the organization as the "Un-American Criminal License Union." *Congressional Record,* 69th Cong., 1st sess. (1925), pt. 2, pp. 1217ff. The story of the assault was widely reprinted. Harry A. Jung of the National Clay Products Industries wrote to 600 trade secretaries urging support for Blanton in his fight against the ACLU. ACLU Papers, microfilm reel 333, New York Public Library. Sosnowski also assailed the ACLU and a wide variety of liberal, labor, and pacifist organizations in early 1927, maintaining that the ACLU

"proclaims in loud terms its purpose to protect the citizen in his right of free speech and assemblage. A careful survey of its work indicates that it has never sought to give protection save to agitators who are seeking to subvert the government," and urging a congressional investigation of communistic activities in the United States. *Congressional Record*, 69th Cong., 1st sess. (1925), pp. 4599, 5463. Free, in what turned out to be a widely quoted and vigorously attacked Flag Day address before the Palo Alto, California, Elks Club, repeated a similar charge: "The American Civil Liberties Union is, in my opinion, the most dangerous organization in America because of its radical character. It pretends to favor free speech, but it really means to stand up for radicals everywhere." He also challenged the integrity and patriotism of David Starr Jordan of Stanford University, one of the leaders in the movement to repeal the California criminal-syndicalism law. "Congressman Flays Liberals," *Palo Alto Times*, June 15, 1927, p. 1.

5. An early assault on the Legion's callousness and calculating use of superpatriotism was Marcus Duffield, *King Legion* (New York, 1931). See also Rodney G. Minott, *Peerless Patriots: Organized Veterans and the Spirit of Americanism* (Washington, 1963). Morris Janowitz touches peripherally on the issue as it applies to the conservatism of military men in his, *The Professional Soldier: A Social and Political Portrait* (Glencoe, 1960), pp. 233–255.

6. "The Emporia Way," *American Legion Monthly* 3 (July 1927): 28. This editorial set the stage for a feature article in the same issue by Rupert Hughes entitled "There's Only One Kind of Americanism," *American Legion Monthly* 3 (July 1927): 12ff, which made a fervent plea for the importance not only of dissent but freedom of expression even for ideas of which we disapprove.

7. American Civil Liberties Union, *Free Speech, 1926* (New York, 1927), p. 2. Such a statement was widely criticized. Even an editorial in Joseph Pulitzer's liberal *New York World* wondered: "With scores of different organizations seeking to curtail liberty in scores of different ways, it is a wise man who can say that one is more active than any of the others." "The American Civil Liberties Union," *New York World*, May 17, 1927, p. 12. Forrest Bailey, director of the ACLU responded by merely pointing out that this was the consensus of all the state units reporting to national headquarters for the year. Letters column, *New York World*, May 18, 1927, p. 12.

8. Minott, *Patriots*, passim.

9. Resolution of the New Jersey delegation to the national DAR convention, April, 1928, quoted in Hunter, *Patriotism*, p. 50.

10. Jung to Henry E. Niles, March 23, 1926, ACLU Papers, microfilm reel 333, NYPL.

11. "Inquiry Points to Spy System Muzzling U.S.," *New York World*, February 12, 1928, p. 25.

12. Norman Hapgood, ed., *Professional Patriots* (New York, 1927), concentrates on twenty-five or so of the major ones, although Fred R. Marvin, *Our Government and Its Enemies* (New York, 1932), by adding

a variety of local auxiliaries, lists fifty-four organizations as making up the American Coalition of Patriotic Societies at the height of the movement.

13. In a recent study of the Klan, Arnold S. Rice, *The Ku Klux Klan in American Politics* (Washington, 1962), p. 14, emphasizes that "the secret fraternity drew its millions primarily from the villages and small towns which had been left rather undisturbed by the immigration, industrialization, and liberal thought of modern America." Such was undoubtedly true in the South, to which this study is largely confined, but Klan activity in the North in the same period is well known, especially in relation to planned intimidation of striking workers. See David M. Chalmers, *Hooded Americanism: The First Century of the Ku Klux Klan* (Garden City, 1965); William P. Randel, *The Ku Klux Klan: A Century of Infamy* (Philadelphia, 1965); Kenneth T. Jackson, *The Ku Klux Klan in the City, 1915–1930* (New York, 1967).

14. *Revolutionary Radicalism: Its History, Purpose and Tactics,* Report of the Joint Legislative Committee Investigating Seditious Activities, Filed April 24, 1920 in the Senate of the State of New York (Albany, 1920), especially III, pp. 2570ff.

15. U.S., Congress, House, *Investigation of Communist Propaganda, Hearings,* before a Special Committee to Investigate Communist Activities in the United States, 71st Cong., 2d sess. (1930), pts. 1–6 passim.

16. The view was a carefully analysed theme by both de Tocqueville (see Yehoshua Arieli, *Individualism and Nationalism in American Ideology* [Cambridge, 1964], pp. 188–190) and Bryce (see Henry A. Myers, *Are Men Equal?* [New York, 1945], pp. 146–148). It was an essential theme of the late nineteenth-century defenders of economic laissez-faire. See Abbott Lawrence Lowell, *Essays on Government* (Boston, 1889), pp. 15–17.

17. Irving Babbitt, *Democracy and Leadership* (Boston, 1924), pp. 298, 308. See Henry L. Mencken, *Notes on Democracy* (New York, 1926); Walter Lippmann, *The Phantom Public* (New York, 1925); Everett Dean Martin, *The Behavior of Crowds: A Psychological Study* (New York, 1920), a portion of which was published as an ACLU pamphlet in 1921 entitled *The Mob Mind vs. Civil Liberty;* Everett Dean Martin, *Liberty* (New York, 1930); Will Durant, "Is Democracy a Failure?" *Harpers* 153 (October 1926): 553–565; James Harvey Robinson, "Freedom Reconsidered," *Harpers* 147 (November 1923): 769–777; Harry Elmer Barnes, *History and Social Intelligence* (New York, 1926); Frank R. Kent, *The Great Game of Politics* (New York, 1923), and his, *Political Behavior* (New York, 1928). See also Lucille Birnbaum, "Behaviorism in the 1920's," *American Quarterly* 7 (Spring 1955): 15–30.

18. Babbitt, *Leadership,* p. 321.

19. Rush Welter, *Popular Education and Democratic Thought in America* (New York, 1962), pp. 303–310, and especially Barry A. Marks, "The Idea of Propaganda in America" (Ph.D. diss., University of Minnesota, 1957).

20. See Harold D. Lasswell, Ralph D. Casey, and Bruce L. Smith, *Propaganda and Promotional Activities: An Annotated Bibliography* (Minneapolis, 1935), and, for an analysis of such material, see Welter, *Education*

and Thought, Marks, "Propaganda," and Joseph E. Clark, "The American Critique of the Democratic Idea, 1919–1929" (Ph.D. diss., Stanford University, 1958), pp. 249–305.

21. Robert M. Yerkes, ed., *Pyschological Examining in the United States Army*, (Washington, 1921), pp. 743–744. See also Daniel J. Kevles, "Testing the Army's Intelligence: Psychologists and the Military in World War I," *Journal of American History* 55 (December 1968): 565–581; Clark, "American Critique," pp. 255–256.

22. Yerkes, ed., *Psychological Examining*, pp. 785, 789–790. There was much contemporary controversy regarding the concept of mental age, even Walter Lippmann, at the time thoroughly disillusioned with popular democracy, questioning the concept as an abstract creation of the psychologist's imagination, applied according to an arbitrary scale. Walter Lippmann, "The Mental Age of Americans," *The New Republic* 32 (October 25, 1922): 213–215. Clark, "American Critique," pp. 257–259, summarizes the controversy.

23. Clarence S. Yoakum and Robert M. Yerkes, *Army Mental Tests* (New York, 1920), pp. 17, 22–23.

24. William Allen White, "What's the Matter with America," *Colliers* 70 (July 1, 1922): 4. White made much of the debasing role of the recent immigrants and their tendency to fall prey to the wiles of political bosses in assailing the political irresponsibility of this "moronic majority."

25. The DAR summarized the view of many patriots on the propaganda menace in its handbook, *National Defense Through Patriotic Education* (Washington, 1927).

26. Everett Dean Martin, *Liberty* (New York, 1930). See the analysis of Martin's work in Welter, *Education and Thought*, pp. 305–306; Marks, "Propaganda," pp. 76ff.; Clark, "American Critique," pp. 303–305.

27. Sidney Howard, "Our Professional Patriots: V. The New Crusade," *New Republic* 40 (September 24, 1924): 93.

28. On the early years of the organization, see Marguerite Green, *The National Civic Federation and the American Labor Movement, 1900–1925* (Washington, 1956).

29. William Howard Taft to Ralph M. Easley, July 26, 1922. See also William C. Redfield to Alton B. Parker, April 25, 1923; Warren S. Stone to Easley, June 5, 1922, May 6, 1924; Timothy Healy to Easley, February 27, 1924: all National Civic Federation Correspondence, New York Public Library.

30. Among the large annual donors in the years before the depression were such organizations as American Telephone and Telegraph Corp., Carnegie Corporation of New York, DuPont Corporation, Edison Electric Illuminating Company of Boston, General Electric Corp., Kuhn Loeb Co., Metropolitan Life Insurance Co., National Cash Register, New York Edison Co., Otis Elevator, Shell Union Oil Co., Stone & Webster, Traveler's Insurance Co., and such private donors as Bernard Baruch, Nicholas F. Brady, John Hays Hammond, Samuel Insull, Cyrus McCormick, V. Everet Macy, and Helen C. Shepard. National Civic Federation, Receipt Book, National Civic Federation Collection, New York Public Library.

31. See, for example, Easley to Woodworth Clum of the Better America Federation, July 26, 1921; Easley to Jerome A. Myers of the Constitutional League of America, January 27, 1923; Easley to Lewis Harthill of the American Constitution Association, June 22, 1927; Easley to John R. Quinn, Commander of the American Legion, May 21, 1924: all National Civic Federation Correspondence, New York Public Library.

32. Robert A. Divine, *American Immigration Policy, 1924–1952* (New Haven, 1957), pp. 17ff.

33. For a fictional, but not untypical local response to a strike situation in the 1920s, see Sinclair Lewis, *Babbitt* (New York, 1922), pp. 311–314.

34. Margaret M. Wood, *The Stranger: A Study in Social Relationships* (New York, 1934).

35. Frederick Lewis Allen, *Only Yesterday: An Informal History of the Nineteen-Twenties* (New York, 1931), pp. 99–100, places the automobile, with the confession and sex magazines and the movies, as a force which accelerated the revolution in manners and morals of the decade. A more explicit assessment of its impact was that of the Lynds in a typical small American town, Robert S. Lynd and Helen M. Lynd, *Middletown: A Study in American Culture* (New York, 1929), pp. 114, 253ff.

36. Raymond Moley, *The Hays Office* (Indianapolis, 1945), pp. 25ff.

37. The public concern for the breakdown of law enforcement, particularly prohibition, was a broadly held one in the decade. See Louise Duus, "There Ought To Be A Law: Public Attitudes Toward Law Enforcement in the 1920's" (Ph.D. diss., University of Minnesota, 1967).

38. Lewis, *Babbitt,* pp. 345–346.

39. Babbitt's liberal phase led him to a fairly advanced position on free speech (ibid., pp. 303–304) but the effective application of informal local controls brought him rapidly into line (pp. 371–390).

40. The Methodist Federation for Social Service, Unitarian Fellowship for Social Justice, Church League for Industrial Democracy (Episcopal), National Catholic Welfare Council, and Central Conference of American Rabbis are leading examples.

Chapter 11

1. Don Whitehead, *The FBI Story: A Report to the People* (New York, 1956), p. 56. On Burns' appointment, see Max Lowenthal, *The Federal Bureau of Investigation* (New York, 1950), pp. 269ff.; Fred J. Cook, *The FBI Nobody Knows* (New York, 1964), p. 118; and Frederick L. Collins, *The FBI in Peace and War* (New York, 1943), pp. 4ff.

2. U.S., Department of Justice, *Lawless Disorders and Their Suppression, Appendix to the Annual Report of the Attorney General of the United States for the Fiscal Year 1922* (Washington, 1924), p. 8. See also Lowenthal, *The FBI,* pp. 272–273.

3. "William J. Burns Quits Federal Service, Long Under Fire," *The New York Times,* May 10, 1924, p. 1. See also Whitehead, *FBI Story,* pp. 64, 332, and Lowenthal, *The FBI,* pp. 290–292. Gaston B. Means, a department underling, particularly roused the senators when, in testifying

before a Senate committee, he explained the techniques department officials used in rifling their offices and their mail. See American Civil Liberties Union, *The Nation-Wide Spy System Centering in the Department of Justice* (New York, 1924).

4. Theodore Draper, *The Roots of American Communism* (New York, 1957), pp. 345ff.; Daniel Bell, "The Background and Development of Marxian Socialism in the United States," in Donald D. Egbert and Stow Persons, *Socialism and American Life* (Princeton, 1952), I, pp. 334ff.

5. Irving Howe and Lewis Coser, *Communist Party: A Critical History* (New York, 1962), p. 99.

6. U.S., Congress, House, Subcommittee on Appropriations, *Department of Justice Appropriations, 1923*, 67th Cong., 4th sess. (1923), pp. 127, 129–131, 145.

7. Burns especially approached Howard E. Coffin of the Hudson Motor Car Co. in an appeal for funds writing him: "We have been asked to look into the matter of raising a fund to meet this exigency. An official from Washington is going to meet with some of our people . . . to see what, if anything, can be done." Easley to Coffin, October 9, 1922. Later Easley wired Coffin that he had arranged for him to see Burns in Washington "to explore avenues of private support, even though the State of Michigan has still agreed to pay expenses of the trial." Easley to Coffin, October 29, 1922, National Civic Federation Correspondence, New York Public Library.

8. Roger Baldwin, in agreeing to lend ACLU support, extracted a grudging prior promise from Foster that the occasion would not be used for pushing party propaganda, and that the free-speech issue, on the ACLU's terms, not the Communists', would be the only issue dramatized. Donald Johnson, *The Challenge to American Freedoms* (Lexington, 1963), p. 167.

9. One key juror who voted for acquittal did so admittedly because Walsh convinced her that "this trial was far bigger . . . than merely determining whether Mr. Foster was guilty or not . . . it was really a big battle for human rights." "Tells Why Her Vote Was to Free Foster," *The New York Times,* April 7, 1923, p. 16.

10. "Foster's Fate in Jury's Hands By This Evening," *Chicago Tribune,* April 3, 1923, p. 14.

11. "Charges Inciting of Red Outrages," *The New York Times,* February 13, 1923, p. 1; "Death Threats Here Laid to Burns Man in Spy Testimony," *The New York Times,* February 14, 1923, p. 1. See also "Memorandum on Albert Balanow," and "Deposition of Albert Ballin Alias Albert Balanow," February 12–17, 1923, Frank Walsh Papers, New York Public Library.

12. "Burns Calls for Aid in Fighting Radicals," *The New York Times,* February 8, 1923, p. 20.

13. U.S., Congress, House, Subcommittee on Appropriations, *Department of Justice Appropriations, 1925*, 68th Cong., 1st sess. (1924), p. 93.

14. Ibid., pp. 93–94.

15. *New York World,* February 9, 1923, p. 8.

16. "Burns Would Drive Out Every Radical," *The New York Times,* May 25, 1923, p. 44.

17. *The New York Times,* May 10, 1924, p. 1; Lowenthal, *The FBI,* p. 274.

18. ACLU, *Nation-Wide Spy System;* Lowenthal, *The FBI,* p. 298.

19. U.S., Department of Justice, *Annual Report of the Attorney General of the United States for the Fiscal Year 1924* (Washington, 1924), p. 60.

20. "The Burns Idea Passes," *American Federationist* 32 (January 1925): 33.

21. "Why Daugherty is Out," *Literary Digest* 81 (April 12, 1924): 5–8; "Vanderlip Favors a 'Housecleaning,' " *The New York Times,* May 11, 1924, p. 14. See also Alpheus T. Mason, *Harlan Fiske Stone: Pilar of the Law* (New York, 1956), pp. 149ff.

22. Ralph M. Easley was especially distressed over the curtailment of governmental authority to expose radicals. He barraged Burns's successor, J. Edgar Hoover, with letters in late 1924 and early 1925 urging him to follow up a number of leads he had on the activities of the "reds," particularly the "Civil Liberties Bureau [sic] crowd which gets its funds from Moscow." Easley to Hoover, September 16, 1925, National Civic Federation Correspondence, New York Public Library. Hoover responded to all correspondence thanking him politely, but promising him nothing. Apparently none too optimistic, Easley, at the same time, was also urging the American Legion to "quit worrying about Americanism and concentrate on exposing the red menace." Easley to National Commander, James A. Drain, November 5, 1924, National Civic Federation Correspondence, New York Public Library.

23. Norman Hapgood, *Professional Patriots* (New York, 1928).

24. Robert H. Ferrell, *Peace in Their Time: The Origins of the Kellogg-Briand Pact* (New Haven, 1952), p. 14. For a general assessment, see John K. Nelson, *The Peace Prophets: American Pacifist Thought, 1919–1941* (Chapel Hill, 1967).

25. No accurate figures exist for such membership. See Merle Curti, *Peace or War: The American Struggle* (New York, 1936), pp. 272–273, for estimates. Ferrell, *Peace,* pp. 26–28, includes a list of many of the most familiar bodies with a rough estimate as to their individual membership.

26. Donald B. Meyer, *The Protestant Search for Political Realism, 1919–1941* (Berkeley, 1961), pp. 350–351.

27. Quoted in Nat Hentoff, *Peace Agitator: The Story of A. J. Muste* (New York, 1963), p. 138.

28. "A Study of Patriotic Propaganda," *Information Service* (Federal Council of Churches of Christ in America) 7 (May 5, 1928): 2. The pacifists did not hesitate to wrap their cause in patriotism. See John Haynes Holmes, *Patriotism is Not Enough* (New York, 1925), pp. 135ff.

29. The service was highly publicity conscious, flooding the news media with stories of its accomplishments. See "War's Deadly Gas Is Used by

Science to Help Humanity," *New York World,* June 8, 1924, Sec. 2, p. 1. See also Brooks E. Kleber and Dale Birdsell, *The Chemical Warfare Service* (Washington, 1966), pp. 24ff.

30. Leonard L. Cline, "Others Carry on War Department's Attack on Women," *New York World,* June 8, 1924, Sec. 2, p. 1. See also Will Irwin, "Patriotism That Pays," *The Nation* 119 (November 12, 1924): 514.

31. Leonard L. Cline, "The War on the Peace Seekers, II," *New Republic* 39 (July 9, 1924): 185.

32. *Dearborn Independent,* March 22, 1924, p. 10. The article was part of a two-part series by "An American Citizen" (actually Mrs. Haviland H. Lund, of the Institute of Government) the first of which was entitled: "Are Women's Clubs 'Used' by Bolshevists?" *Dearborn Independent,* March 15, 1924, p. 9. The chart was printed in the second article, omitting only Mrs. Maxwell's famous accompanying poem, "Miss Bolsheviki." Hapgood, *Professional Patriots,* p. 104.

33. Hapgood, *Professional Patriots,* pp. 105–106.

34. Leonard L. Cline, "Army Fights Women's Societies Because They're in War on War," *New York World,* June 10, 1924, Sec. 2, p. 1.

35. Leonard L. Cline, "Spider-Web Orator's Charges Aren't Supported by Informants," *New York World,* June 9, 1924, Sec. 2, p. 1. Libby was quick to validate for his defenders that he had never visited Russia.

36. Ibid.

37. Sidney Howard, "Our Professional Patriots: II. Patriotic Perils," *New Republic* 40 (September 3, 1924): 14.

38. Cline, "Spider Web Orator," p. 1.

39. Quoted in Frederick E. Lumley, *The Propaganda Menace* (New York, 1933), pp. 267–268.

40. Hapgood, *Professional Patriots,* p. 90. See also Leonard L. Cline, "The War on the Peace Seekers, I," *New Republic* 39 (July 9, 1924): 149.

41. The *Woman Patriot* group was by no means alone in such effort. See the piece by Joseph T. Cashman, spokesman for the National Security League, "The Child Labor Amendment and Socialism," *Iron Age Review* 127 (August 13, 1925): 377–379. This article was part of a series entitled, "The Reds: Are They a Real Menace to American Industry?" designed to provide industrial managers with "sound and authentic information on the radicals" and prepared by "the best informed students and writers on the subject." These turned out to be Fred Marvin and Ralph Duncan of the *New York Commercial,* Hermine Schwed, propagandist for the Better American Foundation and the National Association for Constitutional Government, Margaret C. Robinson of the Massachusetts Public Interest League, and Captain Corydon B. Hopkins, a prominent member of the Reserve Officers Association. Scabbard and Blade, a division of the latter group, reprinted the series as a "Special Situation Bulletin" in 1927 mailing it out with a covering letter to show "that the Anti-Military Training agitation has as its origin purely communistic ideas." "To Each and Every Member of Scabbard and Blade from Ralph Royal Bush, Colonel, Com-

manding the Division," February 15, 1927, ACLU Papers, New York Public Library.

42. Cline, "Spider Web Orator," p. 1.

43. On the origins of the National Security League, see Sidney Howard, "Our Professional Patriots: III. Sweeping up the Crumbs," *New Republic* 40 (September 10, 1924):39. See also Hapgood, *Professional Patriots*, pp. 39–44, 49–51 passim; Fred G. Morgner, "The National Security League" (Master's thesis, University of New Mexico, 1965); U.S., Congress, House, Special Committee to Investigate the National Security League, *Investigation of National Security League*, 65th Cong., 3d sess. (1920), Report 1173, pp. 4–7. The ACLU files contain large quantities of information on the various superpatriotic bodies, including analyses of their structure, their pamphlets, bulletins, and various releases. See especially microfilm reels 327, 331, 332, 333, 334, 341 in the ACLU Papers, New York Public Library.

44. Elting E. Morison, *The Letters of Theodore Roosevelt* (Cambridge, 1954), VIII, p. 1422.

45. This is not to say the organization gave up other activities. Its assault on the ACLU's role in the Passaic strike, charging it with being the "coordinating medium for Communism," was particularly sharp and widely distributed. American Defense Society, *What Is the American Civil Liberties Union?* (New York, 1926).

46. Irwin, "Patriotism That Pays." Most of the patriotic organizations had access to such files. See Marguerite Green, *The National Civil Federation and the American Labor Movement, 1900–1925* (Washington, 1956), p. 421.

47. Richard M. Whitney, *The Reds in America* (New York, 1924), p. 124. Whitney's pamphlet, in book form, contained added material including a chapter by Fred Marvin on the Bridgman trials.

48. Richard M. Whitney, *Peace at Any Old Price* (New York, 1923), p. 3. The pamphlet also contained a list of the delegates with their subversive ties. Ibid., pp. 26–32.

49. Richard M. Whitney, *The Youth Movement in America* (New York, 1923), p. 3. For the general assault on the youth movement, see Sidney Howard, "Our Professional Patriots: VI. Bigger and Better Americans," *New Republic* 40 (October 1, 1924): 119–123. Ralph M. Easley was particularly upset by a widely distributed fund raising letter by the National Student Forum, seeking speakers of divergent views to visit college campuses since "fair and open minded discussion of the great problems of contemporary life . . . will afford inestimable encouragement to the students in their movement for intellectual liberty . . . ," and sent copies to his mailees as horrible examples of the "red takeover" of many campuses. National Civic Federation Correspondence, New York Public Library.

50. See Elizabeth Dilling, *The Roosevelt Red Record and Its Background* (Chicago, 1935), pp. 85, 90 and passim. American Vigilant Intelligence Federation, *The Man Behind the President* (New York, 1936), pp. 15–16.

51. For the Civic Federation's activities in this regard, see "A Fake

'Friend of Labor' Exposed," *Locomotive Engineers' Journal* 60 (June 1926): 408–409.
52. The American wing of the movement was the principle source of financial support. See Ferrell, *Peace*, p. 19n. For Miss Addams' role, see John C. Farrell, *Beloved Lady: A History of Jane Addams' Ideas on Reform and Peace* (Baltimore, 1967), pp. 198–200.
53. Sidney Howard, "Our Professional Patriots: I. Ralph Easley: Dean of the Prodigy," *New Republic* 39 (August 20, 1924): 348; "Inquiry Points to Spy System Muzzling U.S.," *New York World*, February 12, 1928, p. 1; Margaret Tims, *Jane Addams of Hull House* (London, 1961), p. 137.
54. Mercedes M. Randall, *Improper Bostonian: Emily Green Balch* (New York, 1964), p. 300. The fear of foreign speakers led to a number of successful actions to stifle such expression. When a communist British Member of Parliament was invited to attend an international conference of the Interparliamentary Union in Washington in 1925, Secretary of State Frank Kellogg revoked his invitation on the grounds that "his admission is inconsistent with the immigration laws because of his inflammatory and revolutionary speeches." Many Americans cheered such a decision but it also drew strong condemnation both in Congress and in a large segment of the press. American Civil Liberties Union, *The State Department's Ban on Saklatvala* (New York, 1925). Liberal Count Michael Karolyi, deposed First President of the Hungarian Republic, was granted admission to the country only upon pledging the State Department that he would not speak publicly while here. The ACLU fought the ban unsuccessfully, but with strong public support. Charles A. Beard, "Count Karolyi and America," *The Nation* 120 (April 1, 1925). Carlo Tresca, left-wing Italian editor and outspoken critic of Mussolini's new fascist regime in Italy, which was popular with many American business leaders (Judge Elbert H. Gary was an honorary member of the Fascisti) was railroaded to jail and his newspaper closed in 1925 by government action. John P. Diggins, "Mussolini's Italy: The View From America" (Ph.D. diss., University of Southern California, 1964), pp. 156–164. See also American Civil Liberties Union, *Foreign Dictators of American Rights* (New York, 1925).
55. William Gellermann, *The American Legion as Educator* (New York, 1938), pp. 88–89; "Women in Uproar Over Peace Gathering," *The New York Times*, April 28, 1924, p. 5.
56. "Would Investigate Women's Peace Plan," *The New York Times*, May 12, 1924, p. 31; Elizabeth McCausland, *The Blue Menace* (Springfield, Mass., 1928), p. 4. This pamphlet constituted a collection of articles printed in the *Springfield Republican*, March 19–22, 1928. See also Martha Strayer, *The D.A.R.: An Informal History* (Washington, 1958), p. 123.
57. *Report of the Fourth Congress of the Women's International League for Peace and Freedom* (Washington, 1924), p. 134. In Dayton the delegation was taken to visit a federal experiment station for aircraft where "we were shown how the poison gases of the Chemical Warfare Department can be distributed by airplanes through their exhaust."

58. Cline, "The War on the Peace Seekers, I," p. 150; *Report of the Fourth Congress of the W.I.L.,* p. 134.

59. Strayer, *The D.A.R.,* p. 124. As Carrie Chapman Catt pointed out during the heated debate over the blacklist, this actually represented a new departure since the body in the past had been pacifist oriented. "Denies He Supplied D.A.R. 'Blacklist,'" *The New York Times,* April 10, 1928, p. 9.

60. Marvin had a broad variety of outlets for his material. See the "Enemy Within Our Gates" column in the *National Republic,* 1924–1929 passim; R. N. Larson, "Shall Communism Rule America?" *The Federation News* [Official Publication of the Insurance Federation of America, Inc.] 10 (April 1927): 3–4. The Military Intelligence Association (see Hapgood, *Professional Patriots,* pp. 176–177) pointed out in its public statement of purposes: "Allied with this organization in its work of keeping track of the subversive activities in America, there exists the Searchlight Department of the 'New York Commercial,' . . . conducted by Mr. Fred R. Marvin, who has more information relative to the plans, purposes and activities of the destructive forces that undermine American institutions, than any other person in America." ACLU Papers, microfilm reel 333, New York Public Library. See also *Congressional Record,* 70th Cong., 1st sess. (1928), pp. 3603–3609.

61. Mrs. William Sherman Walker, *The Common Enemy* (Columbus, 1927), p. 1. Marvin had in turn taken this material from the work of an Englishwoman, Mrs. Nesta Webster, *World Revolution* (Boston, 1921), p. 22. See Lumley, *Propaganda Menace,* pp. 270–271. Another pamphlet widely distributed by the DAR reprinted an address which Melvin M. Johnson, a Boston attorney, delivered to the New Jersey State Bar Association in 1927, which contended, categorically, that "one of the most active and successful of the movements initiated by the Communists in America is the pacifist movement." DAR, *Red, White and Blue or Red Pink and White* (Boston, 1927), p. 12.

62. *Congressional Record,* 68th Cong., 1st sess. (1924), pp. 9962–9977. The DAR tried persistently to draw the National Congress behind their antired activities. See E. Pendleton Herring, *Group Representation Before Congress* (Baltimore, 1929), pp. 230–232.

63. Carrie Chapman Catt, "Open Letter to the D.A.R.," *Woman Citizen* 12 (July 1927): 10–12. Mrs. Catt had also roasted Ralph Easley earlier in the decade for his "over-frightened" anti-pacifism. Catt to Ralph M. Easley, July 20, 1922, National Civic Federation Correspondence, New York Public Library. See also Ferrell, *Peace,* p. 29.

64. Libby collected two filing cabinet drawers filled with clippings and other materials dealing with efforts to prevent his speaking. Strayer, *The D.A.R.,* p. 128. Ralph M. Easley set out to silence Libby by "reasoning" with him through the mails, insisting to Libby that if he were a "good, square, loyal, patriotic American," he would give up this treasonous pacifism. Easley to Frederick J. Libby, September 5, 1922, National Civic Federation Correspondence. Libby had stated: "it seems to me that your activities of the past few years have had a bad effect upon your judgment"

Libby to Easley, August 25, 1922. National Civic Federation Correspondence.

65. McCausland, *The Blue Menace*, p. 2; Frederick Lynch, "Frenzied Militarism" *Christian Century* 44 (February 10, 1927): 172–174.

66. McCausland, *The Blue Menace;* "Heresy Hunters' Blacklist Seen to Cover Wide Range," *New York World*, February 13, 1928, p. 13.

67. "Heresy Hunters," p. 13; "Blacklists Spur Patriot Bodies to Bar Speakers," *New York World*, February 16, 1926, p. 13.

68. *New York World*, February 12–15, 1928. Congressman Victor Berger, Wisconsin Socialist, was so aroused by the series that he introduced a bill in the U.S. House of Representatives, aimed at the blacklisters, making violation of the First Amendment punishable by law. "That First Amendment," *Advance* (February 17, 1928): 4.

69. McCausland, *The Blue Menace*, p. 5.

70. "Boston Minister Decries 'Espionage'," *The New York Times*, April 1, 1928, Sec. 3, p. 1.

71. Helen T. Bailie, *Our Threatened Heritage* (Cambridge, Mass., 1928), pp. 12, 15, 17. For her cooperation with the ACLU, see ACLU Papers, microfilm reel 341, New York Public Library.

72. Mary P. Macfarland, *To Members of the Daughters of the American Revolution* (Mountain Lakes, N.J., 1928), p. 4.

73. Mrs. Alfred J. Brosseau to Mrs. Mary P. Macfarland, March 12, 1928, Arthur M. Schlesinger Papers, through the courtesy of Professor Schlesinger.

74. Mrs. Mary P. Macfarland to Mrs. Alfred J. Brosseau, March 20, 1928, Schlesinger Papers.

75. "D.A.R. Votes Down 'Blacklist' Protest," *The New York Times*, April 21, 1928, p. 19. Mrs. Bailie's pithy response was "Mrs. King George Brosseau and Lord North Walker have won only a momentary victory."

76. "D.A.R. is Defended on Big Navy Policy," *The New York Times*, April 20, 1928, p. 25. Following the defeat and the expulsion of various of the dissident Daughters, eleven members of the New Haven, Connecticut, chapter, including Mrs. Irving Fisher, Mrs. William Lyon Phelps and Mrs. Edward B. Whitney, resigned, issuing a widely reprinted public statement that they felt "the organization had adopted a policy which strikes at the root of American freedom and is contrary to the spirit of the First Amendment to the Constitution which it has sworn to uphold. "Women Leave D.A.R. as Protest on Blacklist," *New York World*, May 3, 1928, p. 1; "Eleven Women Quit New Haven D.A.R.," *The New York Times*, May 3, 1928, p. 1.

77. "D.A.R. Disciplines Insurgent Member," *New York Times*, April 22, 1928, p. 8; "What is Behind the D.A.R. Blacklist?" *Literary Digest* 97 (April 14, 1928): 5–6; "More Light on the D.A.R. Blacklists," *Literary Digest* 97 (April 21, 1928): 9. See also Strayer, *The D.A.R.*, pp. 137–139; Earle L. Hunter, *A Sociological Analysis of Certain Types of Patriotism* (New York, 1932), pp. 137–138; "D.A.R. Head Defends Orders' Blacklist," *The New York Times*, April 3, 1928, p. 31. Mrs. Brosseau had apparently anticipated trouble on the issues early and had written to Ralph Easley

almost a year earlier attempting to prepare her defenses. Mrs. Alfred
J. Brosseau to Easley, July 7, July 24, 1927, National Civic Federation
Correspondence.
   78. "More Light on the D.A.R. Blacklist," p. 9; Everett Rich, *William
Allen White: The Man from Emporia* (New York, 1941), pp. 258–261.
   79. "Speakers 'Blacklisted' to Defy D.A.R.," *The New York Times*,
May 1, 1928, p. 32; "Blacklist Party," *The Nation* 126 (May 23, 1928):
580; Strayer, *The D.A.R.*, p. 174.
   80. "Boston Hit By Liberals' Wit," *Boston Herald*, April 17, 1929,
p. 30. See also Paul S. Boyer, "Boston Book Censorship in the Twenties,"
American Quarterly 15 (Spring 1962): 22.
   81. Gellerman, *American Legion*. See also Harry K. Schwartz, "The
American Legion, 1919–1939: A Case Study in the Nature of Americanism"
(Honor's thesis, Harvard University, 1955), p. 58.
   82. Marcus Duffield, *King Legion* (New York, 1931), p. 206.
   83. National Americanism Commission [American Legion], *The Threat
of Communism and the Answer: With Questions and Answers on Preparedness v. Pacifism* (Indianapolis, 1927), pp. 9–11.
   84. *New Castle* (Indiana) *Times*, March 11, 1924; ACLU Papers,
microfilm reel 331, New York Public Library.
   85. Minott, *Patriots*, p. 93.
   86. Sherwood Eddy, "The Legion and Free Speech," *Christian Century*
45 (March 1, 1928): 277–278. See also Duffield, *King Legion*, p. 219,
for general instructions on all such controversial speakers.
   87. Duffield, *King Legion*, pp. 217, 218.
   88. On the KKK's activities in this regard, see Everett R. Clinchy,
All in the Name of God (New York, 1934), chap. 10.
   89 The charge was leveled in a chart widely distributed by Harry
A. Jung, a Chicago businessman, initially connected with the National
Clay Products Industries Association and later the American Vigilant Intelligence Federation, which had been founded in 1919 and was the "oldest
continuous anti-subversive research organization in the U.S.A." On Jung,
see Hapgood, *Professional Patriots*, pp. 162–165.
   90. John A. Ryan, *Social Doctrine in Action: A Personal History* (New
York, 1941), pp. 168–171.
   91. "Our Crimson Clergy," *New York Commercial*, April 11, 1926, p. 4.
   92. Howard, "Our Professional Patriots: VI. Bigger and Better Americans," *New Republic* 40 (October 1, 1924): 120.
   93. Edwin Layton, "The Better America Federation: A Case Study
of Super-patriotism," *Pacific Historical Review* 30 (May 1961): 142–143.
The Better America Federation Papers, at the Haynes Foundation in
Los Angeles, contain copies of all such pamphlets and considerable correspondence and clippings of the body.
   94. LeRoy F. Smith and E. B. Johns, *Pastors, Politicians, Pacifists*
(Chicago, 1927), p. 169.
   95. Duffield, *King Legion*, p. 224.
   96. "A Study of Patriotic Propaganda," p. 1.
   97. LeRoy F. Smith, *The American Civil Liberties Union: Its Mental
Processes, Its Chums, Its Program and Purpose* (Los Angeles, 1930). The

Legion, however, which certainly understood its own self-interest, did not relax its assault on the pacifists. See Duffield, *King Legion*, pp. 244ff.

98. Howard K. Beale, *Are American Teachers Free?* (New York, 1936), pp. 65–66.

99. Henry Marsh to ACLU members, ACLU Papers, microfilm reel 331, New York Public Library. One of the most famous and widely publicized "free-speech fights" of the decade took place in May 1926, when the ACLU sought to test the speaker ban in the New York public schools by requesting the right to use Stuyvesant High School for a public meeting. After a year of fighting the Board of Education for permission, the meeting was held with Congressman Fiorello LaGuardia as one of the speakers, along with Harry F. Ward and Charles N. Lathrop. The speakers were assailed bitterly by the Military Order of the World War and quoted out of context in the press (Howard Zinn, *LaGuardia in Congress* [Ithaca, 1958], pp. 100–101), but the principle was established that the schools could be used for public meetings of other than superpatriot or nonpolitical, noncontroversial groups. See American Civil Liberties Union, *School Buildings As Public Forums* (New York, 1934).

100. Quoted in Bessie L. Pierce, *Citizens' Organizations and the Civic Training of Youth* (New York, 1933), p. 21.

101. Bessie L. Pierce, *Public Opinion and the Teaching of History in the United States* (New York, 1926), p. 297.

102. Wood remained firm despite a barrage of abuse from both the Better Americans and other superpatriots, writing characteristically to one attacker: "Your proposition to introduce partisanship in the schools strikes directly at the foundation of the public school system of America. No public school system could stand under such a strain. In taking the stand you have . . . you have not advocated 'free and open discussion,' you have insisted upon the misuse of the schools for partisan purposes. I have no objection to the impartial presentation of the single tax question or socialism or the protective tariff or any other public question, but there is unanswerable objection to the partisan presentation of partisan questions in the public schools of America." Will C. Wood to Samuel Leask, February 4, 1921, ACLU Papers, microfilm reel 331, New York Public Library.

103. Talcott Williams, "Loyalty to Constitution, Test in Education," *National Civic Federation Review* 5 (April 1, 1920): 23.

104. Joseph A. McNulty, "War on Military Training," *National Republic* 18 (March 1931): 27. See also Arthur A. Ekirch, *The Civilian and the Military: A History of the American Antimilitarist Tradition* (New York, 1956), pp. 220–225.

105. "Greek Letter Patriots," *The Nation* 118 (January 2, 1924): 12. See also Upton Sinclair, *The Goose Step: A Study of American Education* (Pasadena, 1923), and Upton Sinclair, *The Goslings: A Study of the American Schools* (Pasadena, 1924).

106. Howard K. Beale, *A History of Freedom of Teaching in American Schools*, (New York, 1941), pp. 235–236.

107. "Program for Promoting American Ideals," *American Bar Association Journal* 8 (September 1922): 587.

108. A typical example of this sentiment was expressed by Thomas James Norton, who, in addressing the Indiana State Bar Association, revealed that he had received letters from high school students "whose letterheads had this un-American theory: 'Resolved, that the Supreme Court of the United States should not have power to declare an act of Congress unconstitutional.'" As Norton observed: "That is making them anti-American at a very early age." "Our Bounty of Constitutional Government," *American Law Review* 61 (January–February 1927): 133.

109. Howard K. Beale, *Are American Teachers Free?* (New York, 1936), pp. 321ff.; Pierce, *Public Opinion*, pp. 188–189; C. Lewis Fowler, editor of a leading Ku Klux Klan publication in the period, endorsed Constitution worship as a vital devise for showing how the document's "provisions of freedom of conscience, freedom of speech and of the press . . . are the antithesis of Romanism." "Constitution Day," *The American Standard* 2 (September 15, 1925): 420.

110. National Security League, *Our Charter of Liberty: What It Means to Every American* (New York, 1919), pp. 71–72.

111. Sidney Howard, "Our Professional Patriots: VIII. The Constitution Worshipers," *New Republic* 39 (October 15, 1924): 173.

112. Norton, *Bounty*, p. 133. See also "This Week," *Advance* (March 23, 1923): 7; "Saving the Constitution," *Labor* (August 12, 1922): 4.

113. "Report of the National Americanism Commission of the American Legion," *Reports to the Fifth Annual Convention of the American Legion* (Indianapolis, 1924), pp. 23, 16–17, 25–26.

114. Beale, *Are American Teachers Free?* p. 527n. See also Pierce, *Citizens' Organizations*, pp. 37ff.

115. Charles F. Horne, *The Story of Our American People* (New York, 1926), pp. 48, 55.

116. Howard, "Constitution Worshippers," p. 172; Hapgood, *Professional Patriots*, pp. 175–176.

117. Ernest Gruening, *The Public Pays: A Study of Power Propaganda* (New York, 1931), pp. 18ff. See also Jack Levin, *Power Ethics: An Analysis of the Activities of the Public Utilities in the United States* (New York, 1931), and Judson King, *The Challenge of the Power Investigation to American Educators* (Washington, 1929).

118. Carl D. Thompson, *Confessions of the Power Trust* (New York, 1932). As a defense, the utilities turned to constitutional rights, demanding the privilege of putting their views forward in their own manner. See Harper Leech, "Is American Business Entitled to the Rights of Free Speech?" *Seattle Utility Users Magazine* (January 1929): 8–10.

119. "The Enemy Within Our Gates," *National Republic* 16 (December 1928): 42. William Allen White's comment was widely reprinted at the time: "If Americanism means anything, it means freedom of speech, freedom of thought, freedom of press. Every wicked, greedy force in America today is trying to strangle discussion under the guise of promoting Americanism." David Hinshaw, *A Man from Kansas* (New York, 1945), p. 237.

120. Edward G. Hartmann, *The Movement to Americanize the Immigrant* (New York, 1948), p. 218.

121. National Security League, *Americanization: What Is It?—What to Do?* (New York, 1923), p. 3.

122. Hartmann, *Americanize*, pp. 235–252; Hapgood, *Professional Patriots*, pp. 160–162.

123. Libby had written Taft directly protesting Ralph Easley's violent assault on the pacifists in his, *The War Against Patriotism* (New York, 1922). Frederick J. Libby to William Howard Taft, July 20, 1922, National Civic Federation Correspondence. Taft's response was to demand that Easley immediately "take my name down from your letter head." W. H. Taft to R. Easley, July 26, 1922, National Civic Federation Correspondence.

124. Matthew Woll, vice president of the AFL, insisted that the ACLU had been instrumental in "the padlocking of the Bureau of Investigation of the U.S. Department of Justice." Matthew Woll, *Subversive Forces in Our Country* (New York, 1927), p. 7.

125. Armin Rappaport, *The Navy League of the United States* (Detroit, 1962), pp. 107–108.

126. "Speaking of Patriots," *The Social Service Bulletin* 19 (March 15, 1929): 3; Smith and Johns, *Pastors, Politicians, Pacifists*, pp. 1–2.

127. Beale, *Are American Teachers Free?* p. 313; Pierce, *Public Opinion*, pp. 294ff.

128. These included such subjects as: suppression of propaganda for the overthrow of the United States government; repeal of the California criminal-syndicalism law; governmental restriction of individual liberty; legislative control of curricula in educational institutions; freedom of speech on political and economic questions; and the abolition of legal censorship. Edith M. Phelps, ed., *University Debaters' Annual* (New York, 1921–1931), VI, pp. 293ff.; X, pp. 59ff.; XII, pp. 143ff.; XIII, pp. 265ff.; XV, pp. 231ff.; XVI, pp. 287ff. Some of the college debaters who participated prominently in debating such subjects were Henry R. Luce, Walter Millis, William S. Holbrook, Lawrence Dennis, Arthur Flemming, and Thomas A. Bailey.

129. Norton, *Bounty*, p. 133.

130. Ginn and Company's November 1921 circular, "What the Colleges Are Doing," contained a vigorous broadside on those seeking to silence liberalism and radicalism on the campus, quoting, with approval, Dr. S. P. Duggan in the *Vassar Quarterly* (August 1921), that "not radicalism but suppression of free speech is the greatest danger facing the colleges today."

131. "19 Yale Men Arrested by New Haven Police," *Yale News*, January 11, 1928, p. 1; "Freedom of Speech and Press," *Yale News*, January 14, 1928, p. 2.

132. Hartmann, *Americanize*, pp. 252ff.

133. "What is Americanism?" *The Forum* 75 (June 1926): 802, 804.

Chapter 12

1. "Hoover Frowns on GOP Attack on Radicalism," *New York Telegram*, June 26, 1929, p. 1; "Squelching a Drive," *The New York Times*,

June 27, 1929, p. 24. The magazine had endorsed a call for a national anti-Bolshevik campaign to be spearheaded by the Republican party.

2. "D.A.R. Leader Calls Atheists Menace," *New York Telegram*, April 15, 1929, p. 1. Hoover made it clear that the militarists had every right to criticize his policies but denounced such criticism when it was purely a cover for special interest. William S. Myers, ed., *The State Papers and Other Public Writings of Herbert Hoover* (New York, 1934), I, pp. 98–99.

3. The body known as the National Commission on Law Observance and Enforcement was headed by George W. Wickersham, former Attorney General under William Howard Taft. Hoover was particularly concerned about the defiance of prohibition. "Crime Board Names Two Aides to Probe Lawless Officers," *New York World*, October 6, 1928, p. 1.

4. On Pollak, see Zechariah Chafee, Jr., "Walter Heilprin Pollak," *Dictionary of American Biography* (New York, 1958), XXII, pp. 534–535.

5. On Hughes's appointment, see Irving Bernstein, *The Lean Years: A History of the American Worker, 1920–1933* (Boston, 1960), pp. 403–405; Gregory Hankin, *Progress of the Law in the U.S. Supreme Court, 1930–1931* (New York, 1931), pp. 1–25.

6. "Hoover Frees Reds Seized at Capital," *The New York Times*, December 15, 1929, p. 1; "Cheap Martyrdom," *The New York Times*, December 16, 1929, p. 28; "Mr. Hoover and the Communists," *New York World*, December 16, 1929, p. 12. For the contrast with his later behavior, see W. W. Waters and William C. White, *B.E.F.* (New York, 1933); John H. Bartlett, *The Bonus March and the New Deal* (Chicago, 1937); Harris G. Warren, *Herbert Hoover and the Great Depression* (New York, 1959), pp. 224–236.

7. Hays describes the situation in his, *Trial By Prejudice* (New York, 1933), pp. 328–333. See also "Radicals Testify in D.A.R. Libel Suit," *The New York Times*, October 7, 1928, p. 33; "Mrs. Baldwin of the D.A.R.," *The Outlook* 150 (October 24, 1928): 1019.

8. Arthur Garfield Hays, *City Lawyer* (New York, 1942), pp. 277–278. Hays' brief in the case is contained in American Civil Liberties Union, Papers, microfilm reel 341, New York Public Library. See also Arthur G. Hays v. American Defense Society, 252 N.Y. 266 (1928); "The Hays Libel Suit," *Information Service* (Federal Council of Churches) 8 (February 16, 1929): 4.

9. U.S. v. Schwimmer, 279 U.S. 644 (1929), pp. 654–655. For detail on the case and the ruling, see Rocco J. Tresolini, *Justice and the Supreme Court* (Philadelphia, 1963), pp. 60–76, 169–170.

10. Schwimmer v. Commercial Newspaper Co., 228 N.Y.S 220 (1928). See also "The 'Blacklist' Again," *Information Service* 7 (November 6, 1928): 1–2; "Wanted: A New Scandal Expert," *World Tomorrow* 11 (August 1928): 324; "The Trial of Fred R. Marvin," *World Tomorrow* 11 (September 1928): 377–378; Ray Tucker, "Marvin, Red Baiter, Loses Backing for His Daily Alarum," *Washington* (D.C.) *News*, July 1, 1927, p. 1; "Marvin, Key Man Fink, Must Pay Out 17 'Grand,'" *Industrial Solidarity* (July 3, 1927): 1. Sensing an opportunity to strike at other malicious critics, the ACLU filed two suits in 1930 and 1931 against

Harry A. Jung. American Civil Liberties Union, *The Fight for Civil Liberties* (New York, 1931), p. 29. Jung was also denounced publicly by the Greater Chicago Area Ministerial Association in early 1932 for his phony patriotism and anti–free speech attitudes. See ACLU Papers, microfilm reel 541, New York Public Library.

11. Jennings J. Rhyne, *Some Southern Cotton Mill Workers and Their Villages* (Chapel Hill, 1930), pp. 194–199; Liston Pope, *Millhands and Preachers: A Study of Gastonia* (New Haven, 1942), pp. 143ff.

12. George Fort Milton, "The South Fights the Unions," *New Republic* 59 (July 10, 1929): 202. See also Sherwood Anderson, "Elizabethton, Tennessee," *The Nation* 128 (May 1, 1929): 527; Tom Tippett, *When Southern Labor Stirs* (New York, 1931), pp. 54–75; Bernstein, *Lean Years*, pp. 13–20.

13. Irving Howe and Lewis Coser, *The American Communist Party: A Critical History* (New York, 1962), pp. 243–245. See also "A Case of Reputation," *The Lantern* 2 (March 1929): 1.

14. Howe and Coser, *Communist Party*, p. 259. One communist spokesman was quoted as having declared: "North Carolina is the key to the South, Gaston County is the key to North Carolina, and the Loray Mill is the key to Gaston County." Robin Hood, "The Loray Mill Strike" (Master's thesis, University of North Carolina, 1932), pp. 33–34.

15. American Civil Liberties Union, *Justice—North Carolina Style* (New York, 1930), p. 3.

16. Paul Blanshard, "Communism in the Southern Cotton Mills," *The Nation* 128 (April 24, 1929): 500; Tippett, *Southern Labor*, p. 92; Margaret Larkin, "Tragedy in North Carolina," *North American Review* 108 (December 1928): 689. A typical outburst was an article in the *Gastonia Daily Gazette*, "Civil Liberties Union is Un-American," April 22, 1929, p. 4, in which Marvin, Jung, and the Lusk Report were quoted extensively to show the communistic nature of the body. See also "American Civil Liberties Union Unmasked," *Gastonia Daily Gazette*, May 6, 1929, p. 4.

17. "What Guarantee Have We of the Right of Free Speech," *Gastonia Daily Gazette*, May 13, 1929, p. 4. For King's speech, see *Congressional Record*, 71st Cong., 1st sess. (1929), p. 356. Howard Odum in his revealing impressionistic work, *An American Epoch: Southern Portraiture in the National Picture* (New York, 1930), p. 260, captures the attitude.

18. ACLU, *Justice—North Carolina Style*, p. 8.

19. U.S., Congress, House, *Investigation of Communist Propaganda, Hearings*, before a Special Committee to Investigate Communist Activities in the United States, 71st Cong., 2d sess. (1930), I, pt. 6, p. 75.

20. Forrest Bailey, "Gastonia Goes to Trial," *New Republic* 59 (August 14, 1929): 332; Bernstein, *Lean Years*, p. 25; House, *Investigation of Communist Propaganda*, I, pt. 6, p. 73.

21. "Fighting Communism with Anarchy," *Literary Digest* 102 (September 28, 1929); Odum, *American Epoch*, pp. 259–260.

22. ACLU, *Justice—North Carolina Style*, p. 8.

23. Tippett, *Southern Labor*, pp. 103–104. The best description of the legal proceedings is "Gastonia Striker's Case," *Harvard Law Review*

44 (May 1931): 1118–1124. See also "The Gastonia Strike Murder Verdict," *Literary Digest* 103 (November 2, 1929): 14; State v. Beal, 199 N.C. 278 (1930).

24. American Civil Liberties Union, *The Fight for Civil Liberty, 1930–1931* (New York, 1931), pp. 38–39; "Ends Bonding Reds Due to Bail Jumping," *The New York Times,* October 11, 1931; p. 20. A considerably sobered Albert Weisbord wrote a few years later that the Communists' role in depression strikes lost them any advantage they had with working people. Albert Weisbord, *The Conquest of Power* (New York, 1937), II, pp. 1115–1116.

25. Duane McCracken, *Strike Injunctions in the New South* (Chapel Hill, 1931), pp. 79–82; Sinclair Lewis, *Cheap and Contented Labor* (Philadelphia, 1929); Tippett, *Southern Labor,* pp. 109–155.

26. American Civil Liberties Union, *The Story of Civil Liberty, 1929–1930* (New York, 1930), p. 21.

27. See the extensive annotated bibliography in Pope, *Millhands and Preachers,* pp. 337–357.

28. Wilbur J. Cash, *The Mind of the South* (New York, 1941), pp. 346–347.

29. George Libaire, "Gastonia: Outpost of Recovery?" *New Republic* 76 (October 11, 1933): 233–235.

30. Curiously the attraction of Italian fascism also declined in depression years. Although civil libertarian antagonism toward Mussolini's suppression of free speech was but one factor, it was one raised with vigor and frequency. See, for example, "Fascism Foes Riot at Protest Rally," *The New York Times,* November 16, 1931, p. 3; ACLU, *Story of Civil Liberty—1929–1930,* pp. 29–30; ACLU, *Fight For Civil Liberty, 1930–1931,* pp. 28–29.

31. Mauritz A. Hallgren, *Seeds of Revolt* (New York, 1933), pp. 164–170. See also Eldridge F. Dowell, "A History of the Enactment of Criminal Syndicalism Legislation in the United States" (Ph.D. diss., Johns Hopkins University, 1936), pp. 866ff.

32. ACLU Papers, microfilm reels 362, 464, 465, 541, 542, New York Public Library, contain a growing number of clippings from newspaper and magazines sympathetic with the body and its work.

33. *Proceedings of the Eleventh National Convention of the American Legion* (Washington, 1930), H.D. 217, 71st Cong., 2d sess. (1930), p. 115. See also "Legion Demands Pacifist Inquiry," *The New York Times,* October 3, 1929, p. 33; "The American Legion's Foolish Demand," *New York World,* October 4, 1929, p. 12.

34. "Elihu Root Wants Special Police Force to Combat Reds," *The New York Times,* July 14, 1930, p. 1; "Is Such a Force Needed?" *The New York Times,* July 15, 1930, p. 22.

35. House, *Investigation of Communist Propaganda,* IV, pt. 1, p. 407.

36. "Anti-Red Rally Asks Deporting of Communists," *New York Tribune,* January 10, 1931, p. 1; "70 Groups Fight to Outlaw Reds," *New York World,* January 10, 1931, p. 1. Press reaction was hostile. Typical was an editorial in the *Providence* (R.I.) *New Tribune,* January

10, 1931, p. 8, entitled "Communist Species," which maintained: "such meetings as last night's with its demands for further spy systems and further restrictions of free speech are of far more value as propaganda for the Communists than is anything the Communists themselves say or do."

37. "Hunt Down Our Problems Instead," *Milwaukee Leader*, January 22, 1931, p. 8; American Civil Liberties Union, *Call to Action! Help Beat The Fish Committee's Program* (New York, 1931). For congressional opposition, see *Congressional Record*, 71st Cong., 2d sess. (1930), pp. 9390–9393.

38. "Fish Report Should Be Disregarded," *New York Evening Post*, January 20, 1931, p. 7.

39. "Curbing Radicalism," *New York World*, January 19, 1931, p. 12.

40. Jerome Davis, *Liberty, Censorship and the Fish Committee* (New York, 1931), p. 5. See also "Fish is Attacked as Red Press Agent," *The New York Times*, March 14, 1931, p. 11.

41. "Fish Report Asks Outlawing of Reds As National Menace," *The New York Times*, January 18, 1931, p. 1.

42. Quoted in Davis, *Liberty*, p. 3.

43. *American Civil Liberties Union Bulletin* (January 22, 1931): 1.

44. See, for example, "Something to Forget," *Knoxville* (Tenn.) *News Sentinel*, January 10, 1931, p. 6; "Ham Fish's Nonsense," *New Leader* (January 24, 1931): 39; "The Fish Report and Free Speech," *Daily News and Knickerbocker* (Albany, N.Y.), February 24, 1931, p. 6; "Fish Investigations Over," *Advance* (January 23, 1931): 1.

45. "Mr. Fish Reports," *Brooklyn Standard Union*, January 29, 1931, p. 7.

46. "A Typical Case of Red-phobia," *Portland News*, January 23, 1931, p. 6.

47. *Reports to the Thirteenth Annual Convention of the American Legion* (Indianapolis, 1931), pp. 318–319. Fish had later problems with the Legion. As an early admirer and supporter of Adolph Hitler, he drew fire and was censured by the 1943 Omaha convention for abuse of his congressional franking privilege by spreading Nazi propaganda. Rodney G. Minott, *Peerless Patriots* (Washington, 1962), p. 93.

48. S. Stanwood Menken, chairman of the board of directors of the National Security League, in early September had startled the committee by urging recognition of Soviet Russia and minimizing any communist danger here. When Ralph Easley publicly denounced him, he replied: "I feel that your effort to alarm the business men of this country into contributions for a campaign against Communism is entirely on a false basis. The undue exaggeration may fill the coffers of the National Civic Federation but that does not in any sense relieve your position from absurdities or warrant your attacks on representative citizens." "Menken Defends His Shift on Soviet," *The New York Times*, September 7, 1930, Sec. 2, p. 2.

49. Whalen was clearly impressed with the quasi-Gestapo-like tactics which Captain William Hynes had pursued so successfully in Los Angeles.

For his version of his activities, see *Mr. New York: The Autobiography of Grover Whalen* (New York, 1955), pp. 151ff.

50. Reverend John Haynes Holmes preached a widely reported sermon in early July 1929 in which he accused Whalen of encouraging police brutality, especially against union workers. "Dr. Holmes Scores Whalen as 'Bully,' " *The New York Times*, July 1, 1929, p. 32.

51. "Walker Warns Reds Stern Curb Awaits Lawless Outbreaks," *The New York Times*, March 4, 1930, p. 1; "Free But Responsible," *The New York Times*, March 5, 1930, p. 22.

52. American Civil Liberties Union, *Police Lawlessness vs. Communists in New York* (New York, 1930), details the episode. See also Whalen, *Autobiography*, pp. 154–158; House, *Investigation of Communist Propaganda*, III, pt. 3, pp. 1–17. On Whalen's delight at headcracking, see "Reds Boring into Business, Schools, City Bureaus," *The New York Times*, March 9, 1930, p. 2.

53. "Whalen Tells Employers of 300 Reds They Hired," *The New York Times*, March 11, 1930, p. 1; ACLU, *Police Lawlessness*, pp. 6, 9; "Whalen is Assailed for Drive on Reds," *The New York Times*, March 12, 1930, p. 3; "Whalen's Removal Urged in Petition," *The New York Times*, March 17, 1930, p. 3; "Opens Fight Here to Curb Radicals," *The New York Times*, April 3, 1930, p. 50.

54. " 'Red Scare' Protest Issued by Liberals," *The New York Times*, May 19, 1930, p. 19; U.S., Congress, House, *Investigation of Communist Propaganda*, H. Rept. 2290, 71st Cong., 3d sess. (1930), p. 50. Criticism of the documents had been vigorous since their introduction; see "Whalen Data Under Fire," *The New York Times*, July 18, 1930, p. 11; "Says Reds 'Planted' Papers on Whalen," *The New York Times*, August 17, 1930, p. 19.

55. National Commission on Law Observance and Enforcement, *Publications* (Washington, 1931), 14 vols. The ACLU reports were *The Police and Radicals: What 88 Police Chiefs Think and Do About Radical Meetings* (New York, 1921), and *Blue Coats and Reds* (New York, 1929). The latter began with the statement: "Nine Tenths of the attacks on freedom of speech and assembly are made by the local police. The police are the steady, year-in-and-year-out censors and dictators . . . ready at a moments' notice to decide who may meet and speak, and when and where . . . The difficulty in opposing this police censorship of speeches and meetings is that it is commonly outside the law—or, rather, that the law is so indefinite that the police can act as they please. They are the judges of what is 'disorderly conduct,' 'disturbing the peace,' 'inciting to riot,' etc., and the courts ordinarily will sustain them—almost certainly against reds and strikers."

56. R. L. Duffus, "Civilization in American Cities," *Scribner's Magazine* 90 (October 1931): 357. Duffus was also impressed by the fact that liberal mayors had a pronounced effect on civil liberties climate, pointing particularly to Frank Murphy in Detroit as an outstanding example. Murphy in late 1930 had called for a public forum in the city where divergent views could and should be readily expressed, an action which led the

Indianapolis Times to praise Murphy for an honest belief in free speech and wonder sardonically, why he was not "in constant telephonic connection with Ham Fish, Ralph Easley, Harry Jung and Father Coughlin." "A Fairy Tale From Detroit," *Indianapolis Times*, January 26, 1931, p. 6.

57. American Civil Liberties Union, *The Fight for Civil Liberty* (New York, 1929), pp. 18–19. See also Albert DeSilver's earlier piece "The Injunction—A Weapon of Industrial Power," *The Nation* 114 (January 25, 1922): 89–90.

58. Bernstein, *Lean Years*, p. 204.

59. George Wharton Pepper, *Men and Issues: A Selection of Speeches and Articles* (New York, 1924), p. 159.

60. "LaGuardia Urges Liberty of Speech," *The New York Times*, November 17, 1928, p. 12.

61. U.S., Congress, Senate, Committee of the Judiciary, *Limiting Scope of Injunctions in Labor Disputes, Hearings*, before a subcommittee of the Committee of the Judiciary, 70th Cong., 1st sess. (1928), I, p. 157. Ernst made it clear at the outset that his main concern with the issue was "from the point of view of maintaining the liberties set forth in the Bill of Rights," and filled his testimony with multifarious examples of the way injunctions had been used to infringe upon a great variety of forms of freedom of expression. On Norris's general role, see George W. Norris, *Fighting Liberal, The Autobiography of George W. Norris* (New York, 1945), pp. 308ff.; Bernstein, *Lean Years*, pp. 391ff.

62. ACLU, *Fight For Civil Liberty, 1930–1931*, p. 21; Labor Research Department, Rand School of Social Science, *American Labor Year Book* (New York, 1928), IX, pp. 168–170; Thomas J. Norton, "Further Light on Pending Anti-Injunction Measure," *American Bar Association Journal* 17 (January 1931): 60.

63. For a typical AFL statement, see Green's address to the National Civic Federation, May 25, 1927. William Green, *Labor and Injunctions* (Washington, 1927). See also "Church Body Urges Curb on Labor Writs," *The New York Times*, March 10, 1930, p. 23; National Civic Federation Correspondence, New York Public Library; "Gerard For Check on Labor Writs," *The New York Times*, January 12, 1931, p. 13; "Ask Mass Violations of Labor Injunction," *The New York Times*, April 19, 1930, p. 9.

64. U.S., *Statutes at Large*, XLVII, p. 70. The measure passed the Senate, 75 to 5, and the House, 362 to 14.

65. See Edwin E. Witte, *The Government in Labor Disputes* (New York, 1932), pp. 77–81.

66. Myers, ed., *State Papers of Hoover*, II, pp. 145–146.

67. There still remained the bitter fight for freedom of assembly which called ACLU forces to the firing line against Mayor Hague in Jersey City in the late 1930s. See Zechariah Chafee, Jr., *Free Speech in the United States* (Cambridge, 1948), pp. 409–431.

68. Bernstein, *Lean Years*, p. 378. On the miner's plight, see U.S., Congress, Senate, Committee on Manufactures, *Conditions in Coal Fields in Harlan and Bell Counties, Kentucky, Hearings*, before a subcommittee of the Committee on Manufactures, 72d Cong., 1st sess. (1932); National

Committee for the Defense of Political Prisoners, *Harlan Miners Speak* (New York, 1932).

69. NCDPP, *Harlan Miners Speak*, pp. 277–297. The miners were rather sardonically amused at being constantly called "red." See John Dos Passos, *The Theme is Freedom* (New York, 1956), p. 82.

70. Malcolm Ross, *Machine Age in the Hills* (New York, 1933), pp. 171ff.

71. "Protests Killing in Mines," *The New York Times*, June 14, 1931, p. 6.

72. American Civil Liberties Union, *The Kentucky Miners' Struggle* (New York, 1932); "Mine Reds Warned by Kentucky Judge," *The New York Times*, August 18, 1931, p. 16.

73. Bernstein, *Lean Years*, p. 379.

74. Senate, Committee on Manufactures, *Conditions in Coal Fields*, pp. 217, 221–224; NCDPP, *Harlan Miners Speak*, pp. 69–74.

75. "Kentucky Blames Reds for Outbreaks," *The New York Times*, August 23, 1931, Sec. 3, p. 5; "Agree to Leave Mine Area," *The New York Times*, September 13, 1931, Sec. 2, p. 5; "Harlan War Traced to Pay Cut Revolt," *The New York Times*, September 29, 1931, p. 3.

76. NCDPP, *Harlan Miners Speak*, pp. 5–6, contains the entire telegram. On the extent of Dreiser's communist commitment at the time, see Daniel Aaron, *Writers on the Left: Episodes in American Literary Communism* (New York, 1961), pp. 178, 183, 419–420; Robert H. Elias, ed., *Letters of Theodore Dreiser* (Philadelphia, 1959), pp. 587–588, 625–626.

77. "Dreiser Indicted for Syndicalism," *The New York Times*, November 17, 1931, p. 14; "Free and Easy Indictments," *The New York Times*, November 18, 1931, p. 22; "Governor to Hear Dreiser," *The New York Times*, November 18, 1931, p. 27; W. A. Swanberg, *Dreiser* (New York, 1965), pp. 383–389.

78. "175 Educators Sign Kentucky Protest," *The New York Times*, March 3, 1932, p. 24; ACLU, *Kentucky Miners' Struggle*, pp. 19–20. Senate, Committee on Manufactures, *Conditions in the Coal Fields*, pp. 37ff.

79. "30 Colleges to Study 'Terror' in Kentucky," *The New York Times*, March 13, 1932, Sec. 2, p. 3; "Ejected Students Leave Kentucky," *The New York Times*, March 30, 1932, p. 3.

80. American Civil Liberties Union, *The History of the Miners' Struggle in Harlan and Bell Counties* (New York, 1932).

81. "Judge to Escort Tour in Kentucky," *The New York Times*, May 13, 1932, p. 22.

82. Quoted in Ross, *Machine Age*, pp. 186–188.

83. "Federal Aid Sought for Kentucky Visit," *The New York Times*, April 27, 1932, p. 15; "Hays Party Defers Visit to Kentucky," *The New York Times*, April 28, 1932, p. 42; "A Kentucky Mine Town Speaks Its Mind," *The New York Times*, May 1, 1932, Sec. 9, p. 2; "Ask Harlan Inquiry Order," *The New York Times*, May 4, 1932, p. 9; "Harlan Charges Denied," *The New York Times*, May 10, 1932, p. 10; "Pastors Ask Action by Senate on Miners," *The New York Times*, May 8, 1932, Sec. 2, p.

1; "Asserts Religion Dulls Conscience," *The New York Times*, May 9, 1932, p. 13.

84. ACLU, *Kentucky Miners' Struggle*, p. 29; "Kentucky Inquiry Rebuffed by Court," *The New York Times*, May 14, 1932, p. 10.

85. Hays, *Trial By Prejudice*, pp. 334–335; "Leave to Test Curb on Harlan Mine Aid," *The New York Times*, May 12, 1932, p. 21; Senate, Committee on Manufactures, *Conditions in Coal Fields*, pp. 237ff.; ACLU, *Kentucky Miners' Struggle*, p. 23; "Kentucky County Bars Civil Liberties Group," *The New York Times*, May 15, 1932, p. 1.

86. Dos Passos, *Freedom*, pp. 86–87. See also "The Kentucky Miners Statement," *The Road to Freedom* 8 (November 1931): 8; Bernstein, *Lean Years*, p. 380; Aaron, *Writers on the Left*, pp. 178–179.

87. Ross, *Machine Age*, p. 173.

88. 283 U.S. 697 (1931); 283 U.S. 359 (1931).

89. For the background of the Near case, see Transcript of Record, J. M. Near, Appellant, v. State of Minnesota ex rel Floyd B. Olson, Filed April 25, 1930, pp. 8ff.; John E. Hartmann, "The Minnesota Gag Law and the Fourteenth Amendment," *Minnesota History* 27 (December 1960): 161–173.

90. American Civil Liberties Union, *The Fight For Civil Liberty, 1928–1929* (New York, 1929).

91. Transcript of Record, Yetta Stromberg, Appellant, v. People of the State of California, Filed December 9, 1930, pp. 24ff.; American Civil Liberties Union, *The California Red Flag Case* (New York, 1930).

92. Newspaper reaction was mixed. Some editors (see, for example, "Our Imperiled 'Liberties,'" *Indianapolis Star*, August 8, 1931, p. 7) were quick to point out that in Stromberg, at least "the ruling was largely technical and did not upset the basic right of the state to proceed against disloyal and subversive groups." Others (see, for example, "Free Speech: Safe in the Courts, Yet Imperiled by Official Stupidity," *Philadelphia Record*, May 20, 1931, p. 7) were impressed with such "vindication of the right of free speech" and were convinced the decisions indicated that "constitutional rights and liberties are secure in the custody of the highest Courts," although were disturbed that they were still "endangered by hysteria, stupidity, or malice on the part of 'village constable' authorities, whether they are in office in cities, towns, boroughs or legislatures."

93. The case had marked effect on the newspaper profession. The case in its early stages had spawned a freedom of press committee within the American Newspaper Publishers Association (see Edwin Emery, *History of the American Newspaper Publishers Association* [Minneapolis, 1950], pp. 222–223), and the ruling encouraged the committee to extend its efforts and become a constant participant in cases involving the constitutional rights of newspapers. See J. Edward Gerald, *The Press and the Constitution, 1931–1941* (Minneapolis, 1948). Disturbed by the narrowness of the 5 to 4 ruling and feeling it was "an indication that there was real danger of subversion of the principle of freedom of the press unless those particularly interested in its maintenance . . . were ready at all times to come to its defense," Claude G. Bowers led in the organization

of a Freedom of Press Committee under the auspices of the Jefferson
Memorial Foundation, which complemented the work of the ANPA. "New
Group to Fight for Free Press," *The New York Times,* July 31, 1931,
p. 10. Both seemed to indicate a faith among newspapermen that the
courts were a new avenue of relief against forms of local pressure and
censorship.

Chapter 13

1. Zechariah Chafee, Jr., *Free Speech in the United States* (Cambridge, 1941), pp. 14–15. See also Harry Kalven, Jr., *The Negro and
the First Amendment* (Columbus, 1965), pp. 18–19.

2. Ernst Freund, *The Police Power: Public Policy and Constitutional
Rights* (Chicago, 1904), pp. 502–514; Zechariah Chafee, *Freedom of
Speech* (Boston, 1920), cited the seventh edition. For a later assessment,
in the Cooley tradition, of the wartime sedition cases, see Walter Carrington,
ed., *Thomas M. Cooley, A Treatise on the Constitutional Limitations Which
Rest upon the Legislative Power of the States of the American Union,*
8th ed. (Boston, 1927), esp. pp. 876–959. The various legal cyclopedias
of the period, *Corpus Juris,* the *Cyclopedia of Law and Procedure,* and
Ruling Case Law were of little more help than Cooley or Freund.

3. Holmes's earlier rulings in the free-speech area had indicated no
such concern. Typical was Commonwealth v. Davis, 162 Mass. 510 (1895).
See also Patterson v. Colorado, 205 U.S. 454 (1907), and Fox v. Washington, 236 U.S. 273 (1914). Max Lerner speculates that Holmes earlier
took the narrow view in upholding state restriction since "he was writing
in a relatively less turbulent social context, when no concrete issues of
freedom of speech had arisen, and he was loath to launch on the broad
sea of social philosophy." Max Lerner, *The Mind and Faith of Justice
Holmes* (New York, 1943), p. 106.

4. Schenck v. U.S., 249 U.S. 47, 52 (1919).

5. With Schenck, the leading Supreme Court rulings were: Frohwerk
v. U.S., 249 U.S. 204 (1919); Debs v. U.S., 249 U.S. 211 (1919); Abrams
v. U.S., 250 U.S. 616 (1919); Schaefer v. U.S., 251 U.S. 468 (1920);
and Pierce v. U.S., 252 U.S. 239 (1920). For lower federal and state
court rulings, see Chafee, *Free Speech in the United States,* pp. 50–60, 100–
102, especially his analysis of the role the ruling in Masses v. Patten, 246
Fed. 24 (1917), had in establishing the bad tendency doctrine at the
district court level.

6. Abrams v. U.S., 250 U.S. 616, 617, (1919).

7. Gilbert v. Minnesota, 254 U.S. 325 (1920).

8. Abrams v. U.S., 250 U.S. 616, 628 (1919).

9. Gilbert v. Minnesota, 254 U.S. 325, 343 (1920). On the background
of the case see Dwight W. Jessup, "Joseph Gilbert and the Minnesota
Sedition Law" (Master's thesis, University of Minnesota, 1965).

10. See especially his opinion in U.S. v. Schutte, 252 Fed. 212 (1918),
Rietz v. U.S., 257 Fed. 731 (1919), and U.S. v. Fontana, Bull. Dept.
of Justice No. 148, 1. The impact of Chafee's writings upon Amidon
is clear from their correspondence. As Amidon wrote shortly after the

1920 election, "I do not see any brilliant outlook for freedom of speech. The federal government and the dull and massive administration of Mr. Harding seems to be sliding down on the American people like a glacier and wiping out whatever ths little sanhedrin of senators who are to be in control may be pleased to call 'radicalism.' . . . I am glad you are young and will be here to stand for human liberty and the downtrodden. I have no doubt whatever as to what the result will be. Democracy will go on its triumphant course. It will be a redeemed democracy and not the accursed economic oligarchy that we have had in the United States and England and France and Germany." Charles F. Amidon to Zechariah Chafee, Jr., November 22, 1920, Charles F. Amidon Papers, University of North Dakota Library, Grand Forks, North Dakota. See I. Kenneth Smemo, "Progressive Judge: The Public Career of Charles Fremont Amidon" (Ph.D. diss., University of Minnesota, 1967).

11. Colyer v. Skeffington, 265 Fed. 17 (1920). As U.S. District Attorney in Massachusetts, Anderson had refused to institute a single prosecution under the espionage and sedition legislation. Chafee, *Free Speech*, p. 60.

12. Among Bourquin's more eloquent protests against wartime hysteria were his opinions in U.S. v. Hall, 248 Fed. 150 (1918) (see Arnon Gutfeld, "The Ves Hall Case, Judge Bourquin, and the Sedition Act of 1918," *Pacific Historical Review* 37 [May 1968]: 163–178); Ex parte Jackson, 263 Fed. 110 (1920); and Ex parte Starr, 263 Fed. 145 (192). In his Starr ruling, he contended the continual cry for conviction in vague cases gave "color if not justification to the bitter comment of George Bernard Shaw . . . that during the war the courts in France, bleeding under German guns, were very severe; the courts in England, hearing but the echoes of those guns, were grossly unjust; but the courts of the United States, knowing naught save censored news of those guns, were stark, staring, raving mad."

13. People v. Lloyd, 304 Ill. 23 (1922).

14. Masses Publishing Co. v. Patten, 244 Fed. 535 (1917); U.S. v. Nearing, 252 Fed. 223 (1918); U.S. v. Eastman, 252 Fed. 232 (1918); People v. Gitlow, 234 N.Y. 132 (1922); Wolf v. U.S., 259 Fed. 389 (1919); Enfield v. U.S., 261 Fed. 141 (1919); Granzow v. U.S., 261 Fed. 172 (1919). Stone did not waver in his commitment to human rights and gave an eloquent address to the annual meeting of the American Bar Association in 1932 encouraging its members to support the Supreme Court's new move to undercut encroachment on individual liberties by the states. Kimbrough Stone, "The Greatest Function of the Courts," *American Bar Association Journal* 18 (November 1932): 715–720.

15. People v. Lloyd, 304 Ill. 23, 110 (1922).

16. People v. Gitlow, 234 N.Y. 132, 158 (1922).

17. Percy L. Edwards, "Criminal Syndicalism," *Central Law Journal* 89 (November 7, 1919): 337. See also "Criminal Syndicalism," *Columbia University Law Review* 20 (February 1920): 232.

18. See *n.* 3 above. Chafee's personal activities in seeking public implementation of his position also impressed liberal legalists. This was especially true of his testimony against proposed federal sedition legislation, his

participation on the Committee of Inquiry on Coal and Civil Liberties in the West Virginia and Pennsylvania area, and his courageous and insistant condemnation of the violation of civil liberties involved in the abuse of the labor injunction. For the latter see especially Zechariah Chafee, Jr., *The Inquiring Mind* (New York, 1928), pp. 198ff. Legal conservatives were apprehensive of Chafee from the beginning, however, at one point seeking to force him out of his Harvard Law School position. See Jerold S. Auerbach, "The Patrician as Libertarian: Zechariah Chafee, Jr., and Freedom of Speech," *The New England Quarterly* 42 (December 1969): 524ff.

19. Albert J. Beveridge, "The Assault Upon American Fundamentals," *Reports of the American Bar Association* 45 (1920): 188–216.

20. The conservative line of precedents normally included People v. Most, 171 N.Y. 423 (1902); State v. Boyd, 86 N.J. Law 75 (1914); State v. Gibson, 189 Iowa 1212 (1919); State v. Kahn, 56 Mont. 108 (1919); State v. Tachin, 92 N.J. Law 269 (1919); State v. Hennessy, 114 Wash. 351 (1921); State v. Sinchuk, 96 Conn. 605 (1921); People v. Steelik, 187 Cal. 361 (1921); State v. Laundy, 103 Ore. 443 (1922); People v. Lloyd, 304 Ill. 23 (1922); State v. Dingman, 37 Idaho 253 (1923); People v. Ruthenberg, 229 Mich. 315 (1924); and Berg v. State (Okla.), 223 Pac. 497 (1925). The Most case, which was probably relied on as much as any other to justify the punishment of mere advocacy, was in some ways a dangerous one since Most had been indicted under an existing New York penal law, not under anything resembling the later criminal-anarchy or criminal-syndicalism laws. This was itself an admission of their superfluousness and could well have been used to demand an explanation for their real purpose.

21. Gitlow v. New York, 268 U.S. 652, 669 (1925).

22. For the liberal precedents see *n.* 10–16 above. See also State v. Diamond, 27 N. Mex. 477 (1921); State v. Gabriel, 95 N.J. Law 337 (1921). On Henry W. Taft, see "Freedom of Speech and the Espionage Act," *American Law Review* 55 (September–October 1921): 720.

23. See chap. 3, *n.* 73 above. Chafee in a later work maintained that "the California Syndicalism Law made the American people familiar for the first time with what had long been an odious feature of political trials in Europe—the renegade as a chief witness for the government. . . . At last even jurymen ceased to believe these renegades and convictions stopped." Zechariah Chafee, Jr., *The Blessings of Liberty* (New York, 1954), pp. 75–76.

24. For the text of the injunction, see In re Wood, 194 Cal. 49 (1924).

25. George W. Kirchwey, *A Survey of the Workings of the Criminal Syndicalism Law of California* (San Francisco, 1926), pp. 25, 37.

26. Such attempts are chronicled thoroughly in Elbridge F. Dowell, "A History of the Enactment of Criminal Syndicalism Legislation in the United States" (Ph.D. diss., Johns Hopkins University, 1936), II, p. 1165 and passim. By the late 1920s the Scripps-Howard newspapers had centered on the laws as a standard and regular subject of hostility, although a number of independent papers in Oregon, Ohio, California, and Nevada also openly supported repeal campaigns.

27. Alpheus T. Mason, *William Howard Taft: Chief Justice* (New York, 1964); Walter F. Murphy, "In His Own Image; Mr. Chief Justice Taft and Supreme Court Appointments," *Supreme Court Review* (1961): 159–193; Walter F. Murphy, *Elements of Judicial Strategy* (Chicago, 1964).

28. William Howard Taft to Elihu Root, December 21, 1922, Taft Papers, Library of Congress.

29. Murphy, *Elements,* p. 61. The business community was highly cognizant of what Taft was doing and seldom lost an opportunity to display its approval and gratitude. President John E. Edgerton of the National Association of Manufacturers in his annual address in 1924 expressed gratification that the one place where there was not the faintest echo from the "babel voices of the mob" was the Supreme Court of the United States. There, Edgerton maintained, "one may expect to find the safest repository of power and, at the same time, the most important check upon the power of agencies more responsible to the demands of the crowd." John E. Edgerton, "Annual Address of the President," *Proceedings of the National Association of Manufacturers* (New York, 1924), 114–115.

30. Quoted in Murphy, *Elements,* pp. 177–178.

31. Roger N. Baldwin, "Who's Got Free Speech," *Advance* (May 18, 1923): 10. The ACLU attitude was further reflected in its filing few, if any, amicus curiae briefs in this period, a common procedure by the late 1930s. See Samuel Krislov, "The Amicus Curiae Brief: From Friendship to Advocacy," in Gottfried Dietze, *Essays on the American Constitution* (Englewood, N.J., 1964), p. 97.

32. The Court between 1919 and 1931 ruled 161 pieces of state legislation unconstitutional, the great majority of which were economic regulatory statutes. See Norman J. Small, ed., *The Constitution of the United States of America: Analysis and Interpretation* (Washington, 1964), pp. 1449–1477. See also Thomas Reed Powell, *The Supreme Court and State Police Power—1922–1930* (Charlottesville, Va., 1932).

33. See Zechariah Chafee, Jr., "The Law," in Harold E. Stearns, *Civilization in the United States* (New York, 1922), pp. 75–76.

34. The one prominent exception would be Fiske v. Kansas, 274 U.S. 380 (1927), but even here the Court proscribed the improper application of the Kansas criminal-syndicalism law in reversing a conviction under it and did not challenge it directly. Thomas Reed Powell told his Harvard Law School class in constitutional law: "Fiske is the one man in the decade whom the free speech clause saved. All that saved him was that his pamphlet was dull and didn't incite." Herbert S. Marks, class notes, Thomas Reed Powell Papers, Treasure Room, Harvard Law School Library.

35. *Congressional Record,* 67th Cong., 4th sess. (1923), p. 3027. See also Louis Post *The Deportations Delirium of Nineteen-Twenty* (Chicago, 1923), pp. 302–304.

36. "American Freedom Must Be Maintained," *American Federationist* 28 (July 1921): 568.

37. "Saving the Constitution," *Labor* (August 19, 1922): 4. See also "The New Chief Justice," *Labor Clarion* 20 (July 8, 1921): 3–4.

38. Samuel Gompers, "The Courts vs. Natural Rights and Freedom," *American Federationist* 31 (November 1924): 865.

39. Donald G. Richberg, "The Labor Injunction," *Advance* (May 18, 1923): 11; Gompers, "Natural Rights."

40. Quoted in Murphy, *Elements,* p. 167. The sponsor of an earlier such measure Taft had castigated as "one of these small barrelled criminal lawyers and ambulance chasers who have gotten into the Senate." Ibid., p. 163.

41. Kirk H. Porter and Donald Bruce Johnson, *National Party Platforms* (Urbana, 1956), p. 252; John D. Hicks, *Republican Ascendancy, 1921–1933* (New York, 1960), p. 100.

42. See Dowell, "Criminal Syndicalism," pp. 982–1003; "This Is Tyranny," *New York Telegram,* April 7, 1930, p. 6; "Making Needless Martyrs," *Cleveland Press,* November 21, 1929, p. 8; "Repeal It," *Akron Times Press,* December 5, 1930, p. 4; "A Common Sense Decision," *Cleveland Plain Dealer,* May 25, 1930, p. 12; "A Defeat for Free Speech," *Cleveland Press,* March 17, 1931, p. 1; "A Vicious Law," *Ohio State Journal* (Columbus), April 29, 1931, p. 4. See also State v. Kassay, 126 Ohio St. 177 (1932); H. L. Mencken, "The Bill of Rights," *Chicago Sunday Tribune,* January 17, 1926, Sec. C, p. 1; Labor Research Association, *Labor Fact Book* (New York, 1931), pp. 155–156.

43. Truax v. Corrigan, 257 U.S. 312, 367, 376 (1921). See also Samuel J. Konefsky, *The Legacy of Holmes and Brandeis* (New York, 1956), pp. 129–136; Murphy, *Elements,* pp. 53–54; Mason, *Taft,* pp. 294–296.

44. Thurman Arnold, *Fair Fights and Foul: A Dissenting Lawyer's Life* (New York, 1965), p. 58.

45. Abrams v. U.S., 250 U.S. 616, 630 (1919).

46. Gitlow v. New York, 286 U.S. 652, 673 (1925).

47. Whitney v. California, 274 U.S. 357, 377 (1927). On Brandeis's concept of a dissenting (in this case concurring) opinion's educational value, see Alpheus T. Mason, *Brandeis: A Free Man's Life* (New York, 1946), p. 518.

48. Brandeis did not advocate massive federal intervention, however, as the solution to the civil liberties problem. Rather, he remained convinced even into New Deal days that the great bulwark of liberty was federalism and if states were carrying out their proper duties, they would be the greatest bastion for the protection of individual rights. Mason, *Taft,* p. 558.

49. Brief for Plaintiff-in-Error, Gitlow v. New York, 11. See Chafee's comments on Pollak in *The Blessings of Liberty,* p. 73.

50. Brief for Plaintiff-in-Error, Gitlow v. New York, p. 37.

51. Burns v. U.S., 274 U.S. 328 (1927).

52. Brief for Plaintiff-in-Error, Burns v. U.S., p. 28.

53. Felix Frankfurter and Nathan Greene, *The Labor Injunction* (New York, 1930); Felix Frankfurter and James M. Landis, *The Business of the Supreme Court: A Study in the Federal Judicial System* (New York, 1928).

54. Columbia University, Foundation for Research in Legal History, *A History of the School of Law, Columbia University* (New York, 1955),

pp. 241–242, 262. See also John W. Hopkirk, "The Influence of Legal Realism on William O. Douglas," in G. Dietze, *Essays,* pp. 60–61.

55. See Thomas Reed Powell, "The Recruiting of Law Teachers," *American Bar Association Journal* 13 (January 1927): 69–72. Freund's highly influential colleague, James Parker Hall, took a more cautious, but also more self-assured, position. In a convocation address at the University of Chicago in 1921, he maintained, much like Sidney Hook three decades later, that common sense should dictate when freedom of speech should be permitted and that no one should worry about its periodic suspension, since when there was public need for it, it could be revived. James Parker Hall, "Free Speech in War Time," *Columbia University Law Review* 21 (June 1921): 526–537; Herbert F. Goodrich, "Does the Constitution Protect Free Speech?" *Michigan Law Review* 19 (March 1921): 487–501.

56. Arnold, *Fair Fights and Foul,* p. 59, cites an alleged conversation between Hutchins and Justice James C. McReynolds: "I understand that at Yale you are teaching your students that the decisions of the Supreme Court are all nonsense." To which Hutchins replied: "Not at all, Mr. Justice. We simply give them the decisions to read and let them judge for themselves." For the personnel of law school faculties, see the annual volumes of the Association of American Law Schools, *Directory of Teachers in Member Schools* (St. Paul, 1921–1932).

57. Frank H. Sommer, "The Fading Bill of Rights," *New York University Law Review* 4 (February 1927): 10–34. The address was reported fully in all the New York newspapers.

58. Hugh E. Willis, "Freedom of Speech and of the Press," *Indiana Law Journal* 4 (April 1929): 455; Henry W. Ballantine, "Injunctions: Extension of Criminal Equity: Criminal Syndicalism Punishable as Contempt of Court," *California Law Review* 12 (November 1924): 63–68.

59. Adhering especially to the activist-libertarian positions were the following articles: A. A. Berle, Jr., "American Legion," II, pp. 31–32; Zechariah Chafee, Jr., "Injunction," VIII, pp. 53–57, "Right of Assembly," II, pp. 275–276, "Sedition," XIII, pp. 636–639; Francis W. Coker, "Patriotism," VII, pp. 26–29; Robert Cushman, "Civil Liberties," III, pp. 509–513; Ernst Freund, "Constitutional Law," IV, pp. 247–255; Walton H. Hamilton, "Freedom of Contract," VI, pp. 451–455, "Judicial Process," VIII, pp. 450–457; James M. Landis, "Freedom of Speech and of the Press," VI, pp. 455–459; Harold Laski, "Freedom of Association," VI, pp. 447–450, "Liberty," IX, pp. 442–447; Harold D. Lasswell, "Propaganda," XII, pp. 521–528; Lewis L. Lorwin, "Criminal Syndicalism," IV, pp. 582–584; Walter Nelles, "Blacklist," II, pp. 576–578. *Encyclopedia of the Social Sciences* (New York, 1930).

60. Thomas Reed Powell, "Constitutional Interpretation and Misinterpretation," *New Republic* 33 (February 7, 1923): 297–298.

61. A number of such pieces were later collected in Archibald MacLeish, ed., *Law and Politics: Occasional Papers of Felix Frankfurter* (New York, 1939). See also Chafee, *Inquiring Mind,* pp. 183ff.

62. Max Radin, "Sources of Law—New and Old," *Southern California Law Review* 1 (July 1928): 416, 421. A possible measure of the effective-

ness of liberal legal views was the report that in Alabama "a good many legal textbooks, and such Red reviews as the *Columbia* and *Harvard Law Reviews* cannot circulate in the state." William Seagle, "The Technique of Supression," *American Mercury* 7 (January 1926): 40.

There was also a substantial body of legal periodical writing which supported the conservative position on free speech, especially in *The American Bar Association Journal* and the *American Law Review*, and a substantial number of pieces in the latter which maintained that the only protection for free speech was laissez-faire, with the state a potential instrument of tyranny in the area of individual liberty as well as in the economic area. See, for example, Albert C. Ritchie, "Which Shall It Be: A Government of Laws or a Government of Men?" *American Law Review* (November–December 1927): 932–943. There is no indication that such material came to be relied on by the bench. See Chester A. Newland, "Legal Periodicals and the United States Supreme Court" (Ph.D. diss., University of Kansas, 1958), pp. 275–280.

63. Whitney v. California, 274 U.S. 357 (1927), pp. 375–377. Brandeis had a direct connection with law review material. The 1890 article, Samuel D. Warren and Louis D. Brandeis, "The Right to Privacy," *Harvard Law Review* 4 (December 15, 1890): 193–220, had virtually created the law of privacy in the United States.

64. James Willard Hurst, *The Growth of American Law: The Law Makers* (Boston, 1950), p. 187.

65. William S. Myers and Walter H. Newton, *The Hoover Administration: A Documented Narrative* (New York, 1936), p. 390.

66. *Congressional Record*, 71st Cong., 2d sess. (1930), pp. 3440–3450.

67. Ibid. pp. 3566, 3563. For a general discussion of the controversy, see Richard L. Watson, "The Defeat of Judge Parker: A Study in Pressure Groups and Politics," *Mississippi Valley Historical Review* 50 (1963): 213–234.

68. John J. Parker, "The Lawyer in a Democracy," *West Virginia Bar Association Reports* (1928): 131. See also Joseph P. Harris, *The Advice and Consent of the Senate* (Berkeley, 1953), pp. 124–127.

69. Irving Bernstein, *The Lean Years: A History of the American Worker* (Boston, 1960), pp. 411, 550–551.

70. Holmes and Brandeis had their own self-chosen constituencies with which they interacted. These were by and large made up of scholars, writers, men of affairs of a liberal cut; for example, one of Brandeis's old friends was Norman Hapgood, editor of the incisive exposé of the superpatriots, *Professional Patriots* (New York, 1928). See Mason, *Brandeis*, pp. 599–601 and passim. Holmes was clearly impressed with such scholars as Chafee and Frankfurter, Konefsky, *Legacy of Holmes and Brandeis*, and in his private correspondence was bluntly frank in his support of free discussion. See Mark D. Howe, ed., *Holmes-Pollock Letters* (Cambridge, 1941), II, pp. 7, 28–29, 61, 65, 90, 163. Lacking the self-assurance of a Holmes or Brandeis, Stone was constantly looking to influential friends and journals for endorsement of his positions. See Alpheus T. Mason, "The Core of Free Government: Mr. Justice Stone and 'Preferred Free-

doms,'" *Yale Law Journal* 65 (April 1956): 597–628. See also Mason, *Taft*, p. 228.

71. Truax v. Corrigan, 257 U.S. 312, 344 (1921).

72. O'Gorman v. Hartford Insurance Co., 282 U.S. 130 (1931).

73. Harry Shulman, "The Supreme Court's Attitude Toward Liberty of Contract and Freedom of Speech," *Yale Law Journal* 41 (December 1931): 276. For other legal comment, see George Foster, Jr., "The 1931 Personal Liberty Cases," *New York University Law Quarterly Review* 9 (September 1931): 64–81; Maurice S. Culp, "Constitutional Law—Freedom of the Press—Restraints on Publication," *Michigan Law Review* 30 (December 1931): 279–281; "Previous Restraints Upon Freedom of Speech," *Columbia Law Review* 31 (November 1931): 1148–1155; Malcolm P. Sharp, "Movement in Supreme Court Adjudication: A Study of Modified and Overruled Decisions," *Harvard Law Review* 46 (January 1933): 360–403; Pendleton Howard, "The Supreme Court and State Action Challenged Under the Fourteenth Amendment, 1930–1931," *University of Pennsylvania Law Review* 80 (February 1932): 483–521; Eberhard P. Deutsch, "Freedom of the Press and of the Mails," *Michigan Law Review* 36 (March 1938): 703–751; Walton H. Hamilton, "The Jurist's Art," in Felix Frankfurter, ed., *Mr. Justice Brandeis* (New Haven, 1932), pp. 171–192.

74. Brief for Appellant, Stromberg v. California, pp. 24–25. Her attorney, John Beardsley, also quoted extensively from Chafee's *Freedom of Speech*, pp. 24ff.

75. Stromberg v. California, 283 U.S. 359, 369 (1931).

76. See Eberhard P. Deutsch, "Freedom of the Press and of the Mails," *Michigan Law Review* 36 (March 1938): 748.

77. Near v. Minnesota, 283 U.S. 697, 707, 713 722 (1931).

78. "The Supreme Court's Shift to Liberalism," *Literary Digest* 109 (June 13, 1931): 8. Similar sentiments were expressed in D. E. Wolf, "Supreme Court in a New Phase," *Current History* 34 (July 1931): 592–593. See also Alpheus T. Mason, *Harlan Fiske Stone: Pillar of the Law* (New York, 1956), p. 314.

79. It should be noted that in both the Near and Stromberg cases, Hughes put heavy emphasis upon the abuse of local controls. His Stromberg ruling carefully struck at only that portion of the California red flag law that had dragnet implications and left the state free to try Miss Stromberg again under the other sections if it chose, which it did not. The rulings thus implied that when, but only when, local controls became arbitrary, the court would move against them. Contemporary newspaper opinion at the time, generally favorable, was quick to stress this point. "The Red Flag Decision," *Literary Digest* 109 (June 6, 1931): 9.

80. For an example of the application of game theory to judicial decision making, see Glendon A. Schubert, Jr., "The Study of Judicial Decision-Making as an Aspect of Political Behavior," *American Political Science Review* 52 (December 1958): 1007–1025. For an assessment of its limited utility for the historian, see Edward N. Saveth, *American History and the Social Sciences* (New York, 1964), p. 21.

81. The next extension of the principle of "nationalizing" of the Bill of Rights was equally encouraging. With the Scottsboro cases focusing attention upon the perversion of justice in the South, the Court brought under federal surveillance the Sixth Amendment guarantees of the right to counsel, Powell v. Alabama, 287 U.S. 45 (1932), and to an impartial jury, Norris v. Alabama, 294 U.S. 587 (1935).

82. The Court clearly felt implementation would have to come from outside. However, if it was cautious and none too optimistic that such action would result, others were not. See Robert A. Horn, *Groups and the Constitution* (Stanford, Calif., 1956), pp. 16–17.

Chapter 14

1. Samuel Rosenman, ed., *The Public Papers and Addresses of Franklin D. Roosevelt* (New York, 1938–1950), II, pp. 11–12.

2. American Civil Liberties Union, *Liberty Under the New Deal: The Record for 1933–34* (New York, 1934), pp. 3, 9–10.

3. American Civil Liberties Union, *Land of the Free* (New York, 1935), pp. 3–4, 8–9.

4. American Civil Liberties Union, *How Goes the Bill of Rights?* (New York, 1936), pp. 5–6, 7.

5. Jerold S. Auerbach, *Labor and Liberty: The La Follette Committee and the New Deal* (Indianapolis, 1966), pp. 197ff.

6. American Civil Liberties Union, *Let Freedom Ring* (New York, 1937), pp. 4–5; American Civil Liberties Union, *Eternal Vigilance* (New York, 1938), pp. 3–4, 7. The process was extended at the state level with strong civil libertarian approval as well. See "State Labor Relations Boards," *International Juridical Association Monthly Bulletin* 7 (August 1938): 13; "Little Wagner Acts—Amended Style," *International Juridical Association Monthly Bulletin* 7 (June 1939): 137.

7. Thornhill v. Alabama, 319 U.S. 88 (1940); Grenville Clark, "Civil Liberties: Court Help or Self Help," *Annals of the American Academy* 195 (January 1938): Supp. 1.

8. The ACLU was particularly jubilant over developments regarding injunctions, commenting especially upon the Court's unprecedented move in the Jersey City situation to use an injunction to protect free speech. American Civil Liberties Union, *The Bill of Rights 150 Years After* (New York, 1939), pp. 13–14.

9. Florence C. Hanson, "Loyalists' Oaths," *The Social Frontier* 2 (November 1935): 47, noted the flourishing of such oaths in the early 1930s and their intimidating influence. See also Harold M. Hyman, *To Try Men's Souls: Loyalty Tests in American History* (Berkeley, 1959), p. 325.

10. Alfred M. Landon, for example, warned Roosevelt against abrogating free speech in any war, insisting, in an allusion to the President's overt annoyance with the American Firsters, particularly Charles Lindbergh: "I am going to insist on the freedom of others to speak their minds, whether in all points or no points I agree with them." "Landon Hits Attempt

'to Smother Debate,'" *The New York Times,* August 31, 1941, p. 20.

11. See, for example, "Have You Been Hoaxed on Silvershirts," *Liberation: Facts Behind the Crisis* 9 (September 28, 1938): 1–3; Roy Tozier, "Christian-Front, Bund-Klan Americanism," *Twice A Year* 1 (Spring-Summer 1941): 533–534; and especially Alfred McClung Lee and Elizabeth B. Lee, eds. *The Fine Art of Propaganda: A Study of Father Coughlin's Speeches* (New York, 1939), pp. 51–52.

12. The resolution defining the duties of this committee included authorization, "To investigate, or cause to be investigated instances of seeming substantial violations or Bills of Rights, whether by legislative or administrative action or otherwise." *Reports of the American Bar Association* 64 (1939): 285–286. For the later retreat of the ABA, see Zechariah Chafee, Jr., *The Blessings of Liberty* (New York, 1956), p. 86. See also Norbert Brockman, "The Politics of the American Bar Association" (Ph.D. diss., Catholic University, 1963), chap. 6. The brief is reprinted in 307 U.S. 678–682 (1938).

13. The subject is well handled in Jerold S. Auerbach, "The La Follette Committee: Labor and Civil Liberties in the New Deal," *Journal of American History* 51 (December 1964): 455–456.

14. *Annual Report of the Attorney General of the U.S.* (Washington, 1939), p. 2. Auerbach, *Labor and Liberty,* p. 455. The development of this conscious shield–sword concept is well traced in Robert K. Carr, *Federal Protection of Civil Rights: Quest for a Sword* (Ithaca, 1947).

15. Chester S. Williams, *Right of Free Speech* (Evanston, 1940), p. 2. United States exhibits at the various fairs of the 1930s, especially the San Francisco, Dallas, and New York exhibitions, systematically stressed American rights and liberties. See Edgar Bernhard et al., eds., *Pursuit of Freedom* (Chicago, 1942), pp. 154–155.

16. Zechariah Chafee, Jr., *Free Speech in the United States* (Cambridge, 1941). Roosevelt also sought to forestall a repeat of World War I local suppression, urging the 1940 Governor's Conference and a Conference of Law Enforcement Officials to leave matters of national internal security to national officials. Rosenman, ed., *Papers and Addresses of Franklin D. Roosevelt,* IX, pp. 317–318.

17. See, for example, Grosjean v. American Press Co., 297 U.S. 233 (1936); DeJonge v. Oregon, 299 U.S. 353 (1937); Herndon v. Lowry, 301 U.S. 242 (1937); and Lovell v. Griffin, 303 U.S. 444 (1938). On freedom of contract, see Nebbia v. New York, 291 U.S. 502 (1934).

18. DeJonge v. Oregon, 299 U.S. 353, 364–365 (1937).

19. Harlan Fiske Stone to Irving Lehman, April 26, 1938, Harlan Fiske Stone Papers, Library of Congress.

20. Palko v. Connecticut, 320 U.S. 319, 326–327 (1937).

21. U.S. v. Carolene, 304 U.S. 144, 152–153 (1938). See also Alpheus T. Mason, "The Core of Free Government, 1938–1940: Mr. Justice Stone and 'Preferred Freedoms,'" *Yale Law Journal* 65 (April 1956): 597–628; Herbert Wechsler, "Stone and the Constitution," *Columbia Law Review* 46 (September 1946): 764–796.

22. Thornhill v. Alabama, 310 U.S. 88 (1940); Cantwell v. Connecticut,

310 U.S. 296 (1940). See also Sidney Fine, "Frank Murphy, the Thornhill Decision and Picketing as Free Speech," *Labor History* 6 (Spring 1965): 99–120.

23. The rule had been cited only twice in the 1930s, once in dissent, and in both instances in a highly peripheral way. See Wallace Mendelson, "Clear and Present Danger: From Schenck to Dennis," *Columbia Law Review* 52 (March 1952): 313–333. See also Phillip L. Sirotkin, "The Evolution of the Clear and Present Danger Doctrine" (Master's thesis, University of Chicago, 1947).

24. "President Pledges Liberty of Speech," *The New York Times,* April 18, 1941, p. 8.

25. "President's Bill of Rights Speech," *The New York Times,* December 16, 1941, p. 30.

26. "Consent of Dept. of Justice Needed for Prosecution of Seditious Speech," *The New York Times,* December 17, 1941, p. 24.

27. "Sedition Cases Dropped," *The New York Times,* December 21, 1941, p. 21. For Biddle's version of this and other wartime free-speech problems, see Francis Biddle, *In Brief Authority* (New York, 1962), pp. 233–251.

28. "Civil Liberties," *The New York Times,* December 21, 1941, Sec. 4, p. 6. For other revealing statements of wartime commitment, see "Free Speech in War Time," *Commonweal* 35 (March 27, 1942): 547–548; "Legal Techniques for Protecting Free Discussion in Wartime," *Yale Law Journal* 51 (March 1942): 798–804.

29. Dunne v. U.S., 138 F. 2d 137 (8th Cir., 1943) cert. denied, 320 U.S. 790 (1943). Biddle, in commenting on the case some years later, stated: "I was opposed to the sedition and other provisions of the Smith Act, and doubted their constitutionality. From this point of view it seemed to me wise to test them promptly. I therefore authorized the indictment. The case was tried fairly, and the sentences were moderate." Francis Biddle to Thomas L. Pahl, December 28, 1964, letter in Mr. Pahl's possession. For critical contemporary response, see "Justice Denied," *The Nation* 158 (January 15, 1944): 60–61. On the postwar climate of optimism for free speech, see Zechariah Chafee, Jr., *Government and Mass Communications* (Chicago, 1947), pp. 318–320.

30. Typical of Marvin's efforts were *Fools Gold: An Exposé of Un-American Activities and Political Action in the United States Since 1860* (New York, 1936), and his, *United We Stand or Divided We Fall* (New York, 1939).

31. Jung's earlier monthly newsletter, *The Vigilante,* whose masthead carried the statement "Everything printed in this paper is supported by reliable documentary evidence," was replaced in the mid-1930s by *Items of Interest on the Patriotic Front,* which carried on its editorial page the more cautious claim: "The statements herein, while not guaranteed, are based upon information from sources regarded by us as entirely reliable."

32. See Rodney G. Minott, *Peerless Patriots: Organized Veterans and the Spirit of Americanism* (Washington, 1962), pp. 64–65. See also "Federal Sedition Bills: Speech Restriction in Theory and Practice," *Columbia Law*

Review 25 (June 1935): 922; William E. Leuchtenburg, *Franklin D. Roosevelt and the New Deal*, (New York, 1963), pp. 275–277.

33. On the committee's organization and activity, see August R. Ogden, *The Dies Committee* (Washington, 1945); William Gellermann, *Martin Dies* (New York, 1944); Robert K. Carr, *The House Committee on Un-American Activities* (Ithaca, 1952).

34. Auerbach, *Labor and Liberty*, pp. 451–452; Gellermann, *Martin Dies*, pp. 179–180.

35. Such a view had been a central assumption of the fomenters of the red scare in 1920 and was well expressed in Archibald Stevenson's scathing review of Zechariah Chafee's volume *Freedom of Speech*—"The World War and Freedom of Speech," *The New York Times Book Review*, February 13, 1921, p. 16.

36. The problem of the legal complexities of dealing with groups, especially regarding civil liberties, is explored in Robert A. Horn, *Groups and the Constitution* (Stanford, 1956), especially pp. 122–151. See also Robert S. Hartman, "Group Membership and Class Membership," *Philosophy and Phenomenological Research* 13 (March 1953): 353–369, and Chafee, *Free Speech in the U.S.*, pp. 481–483.

37. American Civil Liberties Union, *In The Shadow of War* (New York, 1940), p. 19.

38. U.S., *Statutes at Large*, LIV, p. 19.

39. Donald F. Whitehead, *The FBI Story* (New York, 1956), pp. 157–161; Fred J. Cook, *The FBI Nobody Knows* (New York, 1964), pp. 241–245.

40. Walter Gellhorn, ed., *The States and Subversion* (Ithaca, 1952).

41. The impact of such repressive pressures was especially great when it came to squaring their implications with what had become a fairly literal translation of such concepts as freedom of speech and press. See John H. Schaar, *Loyalty in America* (Berkeley, 1957), pp. 112ff. See also Charles R. Nixon, "Free Speech for Anti-Democratic Groups?" (Ph.D. diss., Cornell University, 1947); Horn, *Groups*, p. 123.

42. See Burton C. Bernard, "Avoidance of Constitutional Issues in the United States Supreme Court: Liberties of the First Amendment," *Michigan Law Review* 50 (December 1951): 261–296. Bernard is particularly concerned with the application of the "preferred freedom" concept in this period. On the use of the "clear and present danger rule," see Mendelson, "Danger," pp. 320–325.

43. Terminiello v. Chicago, 337 U.S. 1, 4–5 (1949).

44. President Truman was highly distressed over the anti–free-speech implications of much of the legislation, especially the Internal Security, or McCarran Act, which he characterized in his veto as "the greatest danger to freedom of press, speech, and assembly since the Sedition Act of 1798." *Congressional Record*, 81st Cong., 2d sess. (1950), p. 15630. Congressman Rankin promptly characterized the veto message as "Communist propaganda." Ibid., p. 15632.

45. Dennis v. U.S., 341 U.S. 494, 503–511 (1951).

46. Ibid., 580–581.

47. The development led to various post-mortems on the clear and present danger rule, most concurring with Earl Latham's contention of the prior year that "judicial protection of free speech is as vulnerable as judicial protection of the economic version of civil liberty enforced by the judges in the 1920's." Earl Latham, "The Theory of the Judicial Concept of Freedom of Speech," *Journal of Politics* 12 (November 1950): 649–650. See especially Chafee, *Blessings of Liberty*, pp. 84–89, and Chafee's review of Alexander Meiklejohn, *Free Speech: And Its Relation to Self-Government* (New York, 1948), in *Harvard Law Review* 42 (March 1949): 895–896; Edward S. Corwin, "Bowing Out 'Clear and Present Danger,'" *Notre Dame Lawyer* 27 (Spring 1952): 325–359; Robert S. McKay, "The Preference for Freedom," *New York University Law Review*, 34 (1959): 1203–1227.

48. Yates v. U.S., 355 U.S. 66 (1957); Staub v. City of Baxley, 355 U.S. 313 (1958); NAACP v. Alabama, 357 U.S. 449 (1958); Speiser v. Randall, 357 U.S. 513 (1958).

49. U.S. v. Rumely, 345 U.S. 41 (1953); Watkins v. U.S., 354 U.S. 178 (1957). See also Sweezy v. New Hampshire, 354 U.S. 234 (1957), in which the Court moved sharply to undercut the too zealous operations of a comparable state un-American investigatory body which had prevented an invited campus speaker from being heard.

50. These developments are well treated in Walter F. Murphy, *Congress and the Court: A Case Study in the American Political Process* (Chicago, 1962); C. Herman Pritchett, *Congress Versus the Supreme Court, 1957–1960* (Minneapolis, 1961); Alexander M. Bickel, *Politics and the Warren Court* (New York, 1965).

51. Such a process led to little resolution. Thomas I. Emerson writing as late as 1963 said that we have "no really adequate or comprehensive theory of the First Amendment." Thomas I. Emerson, "Toward a General Theory of the First Amendment, *Yale Law Journal* 72 (April 1963): 877. See also Emerson's more ambitious treatise, *The System of Freedom of Expression* (New York, 1970).

Note on Sources

In his novel, *Walden Two* (New York, 1948), B. F. Skinner's character, Frazier, castigates history, citing among its shortcomings the fact that the historian "has no scientific vocabulary or technique for dealing with the real facts of history—the opinions, emotions, attitudes; the wishes, plans, schemes; the habits of men." The behavioral sciences have, in recent years, taken important steps to correct this fact, particularly through attitudinal surveys, opinion polls, and, more subtly, scaling techniques. But the difficulty in reconstructing the human sentiments of an earlier generation, especially when such data are unrecorded and when the parties involved may not have been wholly conscious of their own internal values and assumptions, while central to proper historical understanding, is not that easily solved. It is dubious, for example, whether, even were the results of opinion polls available, one would be able to gain an accurate evaluation of earlier personal values. Conscious answers to abstract questions have been demonstrated to be poor indices to people's deeper values, and, as expressions from which no action is intended to follow, even poorer data with which to predict the type of action people might actually take faced with a real challenge. (Sir Lewis Namier, *Crossroads of Power* [New York, 1963], has gone far to demonstrate that the motives of many historic figures were seldom the ones they professed.) But absence of this kind of data has seldom discouraged the historian from generalizing on the basis of recorded actions, and the historical literature on the 1920s is particularly replete with attempts to speak of "the values of the decade," "the assumptions upon which people acted," "the standards which governed the lives of Americans," to say nothing of studies of popular attitudes toward everything from prohibition to the breakdown of public morals. Historians, in other words, as Arthur M. Schlesinger, Jr., has written, have not been dazzled by the mystique of empirical social research "which

377

leads its acolytes to accept as significant only the questions to which quantitative magic can provide answers." Rather, they have operated on the stubborn and possibly naive assumption "that almost all important questions are important precisely because they are *not* susceptible to quantitative answers," and have prowled about in their own eclectic way seeking to reconstruct something resembling accurate past reality using any technique that looked as if it might produce fruitful results. (Arthur M. Schlesinger, Jr., "The Humanist Looks at Empirical Social Research," *American Sociological Review* 27 [December 1962]: 768–771.)

In attempting to reconstruct public attitudes toward freedom of expression, particularly the permissible limits of dissent in the 1920s and the impact of these attitudes upon policy makers, with special emphasis on judicial ones, it was necessary to evolve a research pattern that attempted to sift as wide a range of extant materials as seemed in any way pertinent. Such a process also included a fairly subjective sliding factor, wherein expression, or evidences of expression, previously recorded as having been influential, were instinctively given more weight until, at least, other evidence was obtained to upgrade material about which there was not this initial surety. Further, it was necessary, since the average American of that day normally did not deliver himself of pronouncements on free speech except in personal reaction to a specific circumstance or event, to assess public statements carefully in an attempt to determine whether the response reflected transitory annoyance or approval, or constituted the surfacing of deep-seated and deeply held convictions. Here, an element of subjectivity had to come in, yet elementary career-line analysis frequently proved useful in this regard.

Fortunately, for the 1920s the range of material available is enormous, even if not processed in very sophisticated fashion for the student of attitudinal research and the impact of public opinion. (See Harold D. Lasswell, Ralph D. Casey, and Bruce L. Smith, *Propaganda and Promotional Activities: An Annotated Bibliography* [Minneapolis, 1935] for an early acknowledgment of the role opinion influencing played in the decade.) The following sources were turned to for this study. A serious attempt was made to explore and extrapolate pertinent material from a wide range of national newspapers of all political persuasions, both large city dailies and small town weeklies. This included not only the general press, but specialized organs of labor, business, and religion. Particular attention was paid to editorials, syndicated columnists, and letters to the editor, with cartoons and even, at times, advertising proving revealing. The magazines of the decade proved a useful source since the period afforded a rich range, with a high reader interest, until, at least, radio and the depression began chopping away at circulation. Radio broadcasts themselves seem to have been bland and geared to the mindlessness of a mass audience, yet, although little is extant, important addresses on nationwide hookups inevitably got newspaper play or were frequently reprinted by the special interest to whom they most greatly appealed. The pamphlet literature from the decade, while highly ephemeral and the plague of most conscientious librarians, is nonetheless enormous and much was examined as it related to dissent and protest. Here the Widener Library, the library of the Harvard Law School, the New York Public Library, the Hoover Library at Stanford, and the University of Minnesota libraries were of immense help. Further, the files of the American Civil Liberties Union at Princeton University and at the New York Public Library (including the Garland Fund material at the latter) proved rich sources of preserved pamphlet material, both official reports of that body and also material from organizations, particularly of the far right, hostile to the body and to libertarian free speech and civil liberties generally. Specialized articles in learned journals, particularly law reviews, were also helpful, even though numerous contemporary scholars seemed at times to manifest a distressing myopia regarding the broader implications of the free-speech issue.

Other forms of overt expression, which provided reactions and fruitful insights, included the addresses of leading figures, particularly executive messages, at the national and state level; statements of congressional and legislative members, on the floor, in committee, and on the stump (unfortunately even the legislative libraries of larger states contain only scattered information on speeches and interim actions); testimony before congressional committees and observations by committee members on that testimony. Private bodies' and their members' attitudes were also probed through statements in official organs, published minutes, and convention resolutions on public issues, with consideration given a great range of organizations as diverse as the Communist party, the American Federation of Labor, the National Council of Churches, the American Legion, and the American Historical Association. Statements of organizational policy fell into somewhat the same category, as did party platforms, local and national.

Values, however, often emerge in less overt ways. The college, high school, and even grade school textbooks of the decade frequently reveal a value structure which is a comment both on their authors and those authors' perceptions of the proper values regarding dissent to be taught the young. Similar revelations occur in high school and college debate, as debate points on the free-speech issue (a frequent official and unofficial topic) clearly reflected a range of attitudes both innate and implanted. Similar results were obtained by evaluating sermons, Sunday school lessons, addresses to bodies such as Chautauqua, and comparable public affairs caucuses, as well as luncheon addresses to service clubs or speeches to youth organizations. While the lecture notes of most professors who taught either law in the law schools or politics and government in the colleges have been mercifully destroyed, some, surprisingly, remain. These are also revealing. Much more so is the literature of the decade—not only works of high literary merit but best sellers with a wide popular audience—its drama, its general artistic expression, its humor and satire, the movies it produced, to say nothing of its popular movements, from the Ku Klux Klan and immigration restriction to pacifism and freedom through technological emancipation.

All of these were examined with a conscious eye to impact, as well as to content and assumptions. At the impact level more attention was paid, particularly since the central question of this study involved the

380 Note on Sources

ways in which judicial behavior reflected popular attitudes, to legal briefs, case transcripts, addresses to juries, and ultimately opinions rendered, at the state, lower federal, and Supreme Court levels. And finally, in a decade in which disillusionment with democracy was rampant and in which · elite leadership, whether in the business community, the intellectual community, the legal community, or the governmental community was widely accepted, the activities of men and women prominently wrapped up in the free-speech issue were especially relevant. Here, research was made more pleasant due to the fact that a number of leading figures were still alive and augmented the written record by granting gracious interviews. I am particularly indebted to Roger N. Baldwin, Joseph Freeman, Alfred A. Knopf, Broadus Mitchell, Norman Thomas, and Pierce Wetter, as well as to valuable correspondence with Thomas A. Bailey, Malcolm Cowley, Mary Farquharson, William S. Holbrook, Matthew Josephson, Robert Littler, Walter Lippmann, Henry Luce, William J. McNally, and Walter Millis. In addition, the private papers of a number of deceased figures proved revealing, as well as the contemporary public writings of a wide range of free-speech activists, right and left.

Here the published literature is unusually rich. Useful autobiographical memoirs and/or published papers exist for the following figures: Jane Addams, Thurman Arnold, John Dos Passos, Max Eastman, Charles W. Ervin, William Z. Foster, Felix Frankfurter, Joseph Freeman, Benjamin Gitlow, Emma Goldman, Arthur Garfield Hays, John Haynes Holmes, Oliver Wendell Holmes, Jr., James Weldon Johnson, Louis Marshall, James H. Maurer, Lucile Milner, George Norris, John Lord O'Brian, George Wharton Pepper, James A. Ryan, Louis Waldman, William Allen White and Stephen Wise.

Valuable biographical studies are available of Jane Addams, Charles F. Amidon, Emily Greene Balch, James H. Beck, William E. Borah, Louis D. Brandeis, Frank I. Cobb, Clarence Darrow, Eugene V. Debs, Albert De Silver, Felix Frankfurter, Henry Ford, Emma Goldman, John Haynes Holmes, Oliver Wendell Holmes, Jr., Charles Evans Hughes, David Starr Jordan, Ben B. Lindsey, Tom Mooney, A. J. Muste, George Norris, A. Mitchell Palmer, Gifford Pinchot, John A. Ryan, Sacco and Vanzetti, Harlan Fiske Stone, William Howard Taft, Norman Thomas, Grover Whalen, Charlotte Anita Whitney, William Allen White, Stephen Wise, Leonard Wood, and Art Young.

Since so much of free-speech response was to major developments of the decade, a number of prior studies of those developments were particularly valuable, providing the initial points from which this study took off. On the war period and immediate postwar years, I found invaluable such works as the following:

Chamberlain, Lawrence H. *Loyalty and Legislative Action: A Survey of Activity by the New York State Legislature, 1919–1949.* Ithaca, 1951.
Dowell, Eldridge F. *A History of Criminal Syndicalist Legislation.* Baltimore, 1937.

Higham, John. *Strangers in the Land.* New Brunswick, 1955.
Johnson, Donald. *The Challenge to American Freedoms: World War I and the Rise of the American Civil Liberties Union.* Lexington, 1963.
Murray, Robert K. *Red Scare: A Study in National Hysteria, 1919–1920.* Minneapolis, 1955.
Peterson, Horace C., and Fite, Gilbert C. *Opponents of War 1917–1918.* Madison, 1957.
Preston, William. *Aliens and Dissenters: Federal Suppression of Radicals, 1903–1933.* Cambridge, 1963.
Roche, John P. *The Quest for the Dream: The Development of Civil Rights and Human Relations in Modern America.* New York, 1963.
Scheiber, Harry N. *The Wilson Administration and Civil Liberties, 1917–1921.* Ithaca, 1960.

The labor scene, not only in terms of specific organizing activities, and formal disputes, but attempts by a range of bodies from the Communists to the National Civic Federation to influence working men, has been explored with useful results in the following:

Auerbach, Jerold S. *Labor and Liberty: The La Follette Committee & the New Deal.* Indianapolis, 1966.
Bernstein, Irving. *The Lean Years: A History of the American Worker, 1920–1933.* Boston, 1960.
Brody, David. *Steelworkers in America: The Nonunion Era.* Cambridge, 1960.
Coleman, McAlister. *Men and Coal.* New York, 1943.
Draper, Theodore. *The Roots of American Communism.* New York, 1957.
Dubofsky, Melvyn. *We Shall Be All: A History of the Industrial Workers of the World.* Chicago, 1969.
Gambs, John S. *The Decline of the I.W.W.* New York, 1932.
Green, Marguerite. *The National Civic Federation and the American Labor Movement, 1900–1925.* Washington, 1956.
Howe, Irving, and Coser, Lewis. *The American Communist Party: A Critical History.* New York, 1962.
O'Connor, Harvey. *Mellon's Millions: The Biography of a Fortune; The Life and Times of Andrew W. Mellon.* New York, 1933.
Yellen, Samuel. *American Labor Struggles.* New York, 1936.

In addition, specific studies focusing on depression time labor activities, particularly in the South, were examined. Especially valuable in this regard were:

McCracken, Duane. *Strike Injunctions in the New South.* Chapel Hill, 1931.
Odum, Howard. *An American Epoch: Southern Portraiture in the National Picture.* New York, 1930.

Pope, Liston. *Millhands and Preachers.* New Haven, 1942.
Rhyne, Jennings J. *Some Southern Cotton Mill Workers and Their Villages.* Chapel Hill, 1930.
Ross, Malcolm. *Machine Age in the Hills.* New York, 1933.
Tippett, Tom. *When Southern Labor Stirs.* New York, 1931.

The activity of formal and informal agencies and groups, at a number of levels, from official federal bodies, to private voluntary organizations, to movements, especially among cultural and literary types has been the subject of valuable monographs. Here I found particularly useful:

Abell, Aaron. *American Catholicism and Social Action: A Search for Social Justice, 1865–1950.* New York, 1960.
Beale, Howard K. *A History of Freedom of Teaching in American Schools.* New York, 1941.
Bean, Barton. "Pressure for Freedom—The American Civil Liberties Union." Ph.D. dissertation, Cornell University, 1954.
Boyer, Paul S. *Purity in Print: Book Censorship in America.* New York, 1968.
Brockman, Norbert. "The Politics of the American Bar Association." Ph.D. dissertation, Catholic University, 1963.
Brodbeck, May et al. *American Non-Fiction: 1900–1950.* Chicago, 1952.
Carter, Paul A. *The Decline and Revival of the Social Gospel.* Ithaca, 1954.
Duffield, Marcus. *King Legion.* New York, 1931.
Duus, Louise. "There Ought To Be A Law: Public Attitudes Toward Law Enforcement in the 1920's." Ph.D. dissertation, University of Minnesota, 1967.
Gibbs, Margaret. *The D.A.R.* New York, 1969.
Gellerman, William. *The American Legion as Educator.* New York, 1938.
Hapgood, Norman. *Professional Patriots.* New York, 1927.
Hartmann, Edward G. *The Movement to Americanize the Immigrant.* New York, 1948.
Herring, E. Pendleton. *Group Representation Before Congress.* Baltimore, 1929.
Hopkins, Ernest J. *Our Lawless Police: A Study of the Unlawful Enforcement of the Law.* New York, 1931.
Hunter, Earle L. *A Sociological Analysis of Certain Types of Patriotism.* New York, 1932.
Lowenthal, Max. *The Federal Bureau of Investigation.* New York, 1950.
Lumley, Frederick E. *The Propaganda Menace.* New York, 1933.
Macfarland, Charles S. *Christian Unity in the Making: The First Twenty-five Years of the Federal Council of the Churches of Christ in America.* New York, 1948.
Markmann, Charles L. *The Noblest Cry: A History of the American Civil Liberties Union.* New York, 1965.
Marks, Barry A. "The Idea of Propaganda in America." Ph.D. dissertation, University of Minnesota, 1957.

May, Henry F. *The End of American Innocence: The First Years of Our Own Time, 1912–1917.* New York, 1959.
Meyer, Donald B. *The Protestant Search for Political Realism, 1919–1941.* Berkeley, 1961.
Miller, Robert M. *American Protestantism and Social Issues.* Chapel Hill, 1958.
Minott, Rodney G. *Peerless Patriots: Organized Veterans and the Spirit of Americanism.* Washington, 1962.
Nelson, John K. *The Peace Prophets: American Pacifist Thought, 1919–1941.* Chapel Hill, 1967.
Pierce, Bessie L. *Citizens' Organizations and the Civic Training of Youth.* New York, 1933.
————. *Public Opinion and the Teaching of History in the United States.* New York, 1926.
Strayer, Martha. *The D.A.R.: An Informal History.* Washington, 1958.
Welter, Rush. *Popular Education and Democratic Thought in America.* New York, 1962.
Whitehead, Don. *The FBI Story: A Report to the People.* New York, 1956.

The utilization of all these works once again involved a process of exegesis of the record both explicit and implicit by the writer. If there are bad errors of "translation" in this regard, however, this is not a commentary on the works "translated" but more likely an inadvertent verification of the validity of Frazier's condemnation of history. Nonetheless, the author hopes that the results here, and future and better ones, will one day prove him wrong.

Index

Abbott, Mrs. Grace, 198
Abolitionists, 15
Adams, Governor (Colorado), 150
Addams, Jane, 118, 195, 199, 204, 209, 215
Aderholt, O. F., 225, 226
Advance, 115
Alien and Sedition Act, 13, 22
Allen, Henry J., 55, 162
Amalgamated Clothing Workers, 31, 115, 116
Amalgamated Textile Workers, 115
America Is Calling (pamphlet), 212
American Academy of Political Science, 60
American Association of University Professors, 127, 217
American Association of University Women, 192, 199, 214
American Bar Association, 210, 252, 259, 264, 276
American Birth Control League, 169, 183

American Citizenship Foundation, 213
American Civil Liberties Union, 31, 83, 98, 99, 106, 114, 115, 117, 118-119, 120, 121, 124- 127, 129-132, 133, 134-141, 143-147, 173, 175, 183, 186, 187, 190, 195, 201, 204, 205, 207, 208, 214, 221, 222, 224- 227, 230-233, 235-236, 238, 240-245, 256, 274-277, 280- 283, 286
growth of the, 167
National Committee of the, 123-127, 129
southern California branch, 158-159
American Coalition of Patriotic Societies, 281
American Constitutional League, 212
American Cossack, The, 143
American Defense Society, 130, 191, 194-195, 208, 221
American Federationist, 258

385

American Federation of Labor, 41, 45, 49, 61-62, 64, 70-71, 75, 114, 149, 153, 172, 179, 223, 227, 238
American Fund for Public Service, 163, 168
American Historical Association, 217
American Home Economics Association, 192
Americanization, 30, 67, 212-213, 218
American Jewish Committee, 126
American Labor Year Book, 169
American Legion, 7, 29, 41, 55, 56, 82, 107, 115, 120, 130, 135, 156, 172, 173, 179, 191, 196, 197, 203-205, 207, 210-211, 212, 215, 216, 217, 218, 231, 232, 234, 245, 253, 257, 281
American Peace Society, 199
American Protective Association, 17
American Revolution, freedom and the, 12, 21
American Security League, 63
American Sociological Society, 217
American Vigilant Intelligence Federation, 207, 232, 281
Amidon, Charles F., 238, 251
Amter, Israel, 235
Anarchism, 18
Anderson, A. B., 51
Anderson, George W., 86, 199, 251
Anderson, Sherwood, 235
Anderson, William F., 199
Anti-Defamation League of B'nai B'rith, 126
Anti-Semitism, 113, 126, 199, 245, 281, 284
Are American Teachers Free? (Beale), 209

Arizona, 48-49
Arizona Federation of Miners, 48
Associated Employers of Indianapolis, 52
Associated Silk Workers, 151
Association for International Conciliation, 199
Association of the Bar of the City of New York, 88
Atterbury, W. W., 147
Attrition of right of free speech (1919), 59-76

Babbitt, Irving, 25, 175-176
Bailie, Mrs. Helen T., 201-202
Baker, Newton D., 237
Bakunin, Mikhail, 18
Balch, Emily Greene, 196
Baldwin, Roger N., 31-32, 47, 99, 106, 117, 122, 129, 130-131, 133, 136, 138, 139, 140, 152, 163, 164, 168, 220, 225, 228, 232
Barkoski, John, 148
Barnes, Harry Elmer, 127, 175
Barrett, Lysander, 15
Bates, Ernest Sutherland, 243
Beaghen, B. L., 72
Beal, Fred, 223
Beale, Howard K., 209
Beard, Charles A., 59, 235, 265
Beardsley, John, 158
Beck, James M., 105, 264
Beecher, Henry Ward, 16
Behind the Veil, 206
Benjamin, Raymond, 50
Bentley, John, 155, 156
Berger, Victor, 56, 87
Berkman, Alexander, 19, 28, 85
Better America Federation, 130, 156, 159, 206, 207, 208, 209, 212, 216, 218, 232, 245, 253
Bettman, Alfred, 134
Beveridge, Albert J., 97, 163, 252
Biddle, Francis, 280

Billings, Warren K., 65
Bill of Rights, 13, 21, 123, 124, 143, 157, 167, 172, 225, 277, 280
Bisbee, Arizona, 48
Black, Hugo, 20, 285
Black Legion, 281
Blanton, Thomas L., 89, 173
Boas, Franz, 242
Bolshevism, 66, 81, 92, 93
"Booboisie," 105, 106, 176, 216
Borah, William E., 85, 137, 155, 163, 199, 237, 252, 265-266
Borglum, Gutzon, 113
Borquin, George, 43, 251
Boston Police Strike, 137
Boston Transcript, 194
Botany Mills, 154
Bowley, Albert J., 192-194, 197
Boyle, Emmet D., 47
Brandeis, Louis D., 112, 248, 250, 252, 255, 260-261, 264, 267, 274, 278, 285
Brooklyn Eagle, 160
Brooklyn Standard Union, 233
Brosseau, Mrs. Alfred, 197, 198, 201, 202, 214, 215
Broun, Heywood, 108, 165-166, 202
Buford (ship), 85, 87
Bureau of Investigation, 172, 173, 184-188, 251
Burke, William A., 154
Burleson, Albert, 84
Burns, William J., 141, 173, 184-189, 194, 209, 216
Burns International Detective Agency, 173, 185
Burns v. U.S., 262
Busick, Charles O., 253, 264
Butler, Nicholas Murray, 25, 26, 113, 199, 214, 215
Butler, Pierce, 246, 255, 267, 268
Butte Daily Bulletin, 44
Butterworth, John C., 152

Caldwell, Franck, 192
Caldwell, Mrs. Franck, 192, 193
Calhoun, John C., 14
California, 82, 156-159, 245, 253-254
criminal-syndicalism law, 49-51
California Federation of Labor, 49, 61
California Law Review, 264
Campbell, Peter, 56
Campbell, Thomas E., 48, 49
Cardozo, Benjamin N., 251, 278
Carman, Harry, 242
Carnegie Endowment for International Peace, 190, 214
Carnegie Hall, rally in (1931), 232
Carnot, President (France), assassination of, 18
Carpenter, John G., 226
Carter, Orrin N., 251
Cash, Jacob S., 216
Cashman, Joseph, 222
Catholicism, 126
Catholic War Council's Reconstruction and After-War Activities Committee, 32
Catt, Carrie Chapman, 198, 199
Censorship, 15, 19, 84, 86, 103, 109, 111, 119, 165, 166, 181, 203, 216
opposition to, 20
Central Conference of American Rabbis, 32
Central Labor Bodies Conference for the Release of Political Prisoners, 134
Central Labor Union of Silver Bow County (Montana), 44
Chafee, Zechariah, 9, 34, 107, 112, 145, 160, 221, 233, 252, 262, 265, 270, 277, 283
Chafin, Don, 138, 140, 141, 142
Chaplin, Ralph, quoted, 38
Chemical warfare, 191, 196

Chicago Daily News, 93
Chicago Federation of Labor, 62, 70
Chicago Tribune, 196, 245
Children's Bureau, Federal, 194, 198, 212
Christian Century, The, 204
Church, Samuel H., 73
Church Peace Union, 190, 199
Citizens' Organizations and the Civic Training of Youth (Pierce), 210
Citizens' Protective Leagues, 74
Civil liberties, U. S. Supreme Court and, 8
Civil rights, property and, 14-15, 31
Civil rights movement, 287
Claghorn, Kate H., 145
"Clear and present danger rule," 9, 107, 249, 252, 279, 285
Clum, Woodworth, 206
Coal and Iron Police, 142-143, 146, 147, 148, 149
Coal strike (1919), 69, 75
Cobb, Frank, 36, 86, 93
Cochran, Fanny T., 168
Coffin, Henry Sloane, 242
Cohen, Jacob, 163
Cohen, Morris, 263
Colby, Bainbridge, 155
Collective bargaining, 61, 62, 69, 70
Collier's Weekly, 137
Collins, Mrs. Mary Love, 209
Colonial Dames, 196
Colorado, 51, 149-151
Colorado Conference of the Methodist Episcopal Church, 151
Colorado Federation of Labor, 51
Colorado Fuel and Iron Company, 150
Colorado Industrial Commission, 149, 150, 151
Colyer v. *Skeffington,* 251

Commercial Federation of California, 156
Committee for Immigrants in America, 212
Committee of Inquiry on Coal and Civil Liberties, 145
Committee on Public Information, 71
Common Enemy, The, 198
Communist Labor Party, 80-81, 82, 83, 253
Communist party, American, 29, 185-186, 215
Communists, 80, 82, 114, 115, 116, 128, 129-130, 141, 153, 155, 185-186, 214-215, 221, 222-241, 259, 276, 282-284, 287
Conference of American Industries, 60
Conference of Demobilization and the Responsibilities of Organized Social Agencies, 60
Congress of Industrial Organizations, 277
Connecticut, 46, 83
Conscientious objectors, 22, 31
Conspiracy, 41, 78
Constitutional Convention, 12, 13
Constitutional Rights Committee, 148
Consumer's League, 183
Cook, Mrs. Anthony W., 197
Cooley, Thomas M., 249, 250, 251
Coolidge, Calvin, 99, 128, 137, 188, 189, 196, 200, 214
Cooperative League of America, 169
Coughlin, Father, 280, 281
Counteraction of restrictions on freedom of expression, 4-5
Counter-propaganda, 63
Croly, Herbert, 110
Cromwell, John J., 138, 139, 140
Cullinan, Eustace, 253

Curley, James M., 164
Cushman, Robert E., 7, 273

Daniels, Josephus, 60
Darrow, Clarence, 80, 81, 164, 199, 202, 252
Daughters of the American Revolution, 52, 107, 120, 130, 172, 173-174, 179, 191, 196, 198-202, 208, 211, 212, 216, 217, 218, 221, 231, 232, 257
Daughtery, Harry M., 100, 135, 141, 159, 161-162, 185, 188, 189
Davey, Martin, 84
Davey bill, 91, 96
Davis, Jerome, 233
Davis, John W., 259
Dearborn Independent, 113, 192, 193
Debs, Eugene V., 135-136, 169, 180, 250
Declaration of Independence, 124, 158, 167, 172
Dell, Floyd, 19
Democracy, 25, 59
  direct, fear of, 12
  disillusionment with, 7
  economic, 69
  industrial, 61-62, 70, 205
  World War I and, 22
Denial of Civil Liberties in the Coal Fields, The (Lane), 145
Depression, and repression of free speech, 220-247
DeSilver, Albert, 68, 89, 99, 138
Detroit Free Press, 93
Dewey, John, 127, 233, 235
Diamond, Jack, 83
Dies, Martin, 234, 281
"Disturbing the peace," 17
Dodd, William E., 127
Dorris, Grace S., 50
Dos Passos, John, 164, 235, 244

Douglas, William O., 263, 284, 285
Dreiser, Theodore, 241, 242
Drift and Mastery (Lippmann), 110
Dubinsky, David, 116
Duffus, R. L., 236
Dulles, Sophia, 149
Duncan, James A., 63
Duncan, Mrs. Malcolm, 136
Duniway, Clyde A., 270
Dunn, Robert W., 146
Dunne, William F., 44
Durant, Will, 175

Easley, Ralph M., 27, 175, 178, 179, 186, 205, 214, 215, 218, 231
Eddy, Sherwood, 32, 204, 215, 216
Editor and Publisher, 160
Education, 208-212
Education, Bureau of, 212
Education, U.S. Office of, 277
Eichelberger, J. S., 193, 198, 200, 205, 212
Einstein, Albert, 205
Ellis, J. A., 204
Emerson, Ralph Waldo, 16
Emery, James A., 25, 27
Employers Association of Pittsburgh, 73
Emporia Gazette, 162
Encyclopedia of the Social Sciences, The, 8
Equality, 175
  quest for, free speech and, 122-132
Ernst, Morris, 238
Espionage Act (1917), 22, 43, 86, 87
Evans, Mrs. Elizabeth Glendower, 168

Fall, Albert J., 216

Farmer-Labor party, 99, 128
Farmers, 127-130
Farm organizations, 127
Federal Bureau of Investigation, 68, 69, 283
Federal Council of Churches, 32, 59, 125-126, 183, 205, 206-207, 216, 232, 238, 282
Federalist, 13, 118
Federated Press, 169
Federation of Churches (Cleveland), 197
Fellowship, 190
Fellowship of Reconciliation, 190
Fellowship of Youth for Peace, 190
Felts, Albert, 139, 140
Ferguson, Isaac A., 79, 80
Fifth Amendment, 255
Fincke, William M., 143
"Fink Halls," 156
First Amendment, 13, 14, 21, 39, 96, 151, 158, 161, 248, 249-250, 256, 262, 263, 264, 268, 269, 275, 277, 284, 285, 286
abridgement of, 4
Supreme Court and the, 5, 7
Fish, Hamilton, 231-234
Fish Committee, 175, 231, 233, 236, 270-271, 275, 281
Fisher, Irving, 199
Fisher, John S., 146, 147, 149
Fitch, John A., 60
Fitzgerald, F. Scott, 107, 109
Fitzpatrick, John, 70, 74
Fleischer, Alexander, 238
Flynn, William J., 68, 69
Ford, Henry, 113, 191, 192
Ford Hall Forum (Boston), 200, 202
Foreign Policy Association, 199
Forum, The (magazine), 218
Fosdick, Raymond B., 101
Foster, William Z., 70, 71, 73, 75, 117, 186, 235

Founding Fathers, freedom and the, 12-13, 21
"Four freedoms," 280
Fourteenth Amendment, 246, 250-251, 255, 261, 262, 263, 265, 269, 270
France, Joseph I., 86, 252
Frank, Glenn, 137
Frank, Waldo, 242
Frankfurter, Felix, 95, 118, 163, 199, 262, 264
Free, Arthur M., 173
Freedom of Speech (Chafee), 96, 221, 252, 265, 270, 277
Free Speech (poem), 171
"Free Speech, a Nuisance" (pamphlet), 27
"Free Speech Fakers," 175-183
counterassault against, 184-219
Free Speech League, 19, 20, 31
Freund, Ernst, 95, 249, 251, 263
Fries, Amos H., 191-192
Fries, Mrs. Amos H., 191
Furuseth, Andrew, 238

Gabriel, Walter, 83
Gannett, Lewis, 126
Gardner, Gilson, quoted, 23
Gardner, Max, 224, 226, 266
Garland, Charles, 168
Garland Fund, 225, 226
Garrison, Lloyd K., 277
Gartz, Mrs. Kate Crane, 168
Gary, Elbert H., 62, 72, 74
Gary Tribune, 71
Gastonia, North Carolina, 223-227, 228
Gastonia Daily Gazette, 225
General Federation of Women's Clubs, 192
George, Henry, 209
Gerard, James W., 34, 238
German-Americans, 22, 34
Gilbert v. Minnesota, 250, 261

Gilson, Gardner, 93
Giltow, Benjamin, 79, 80, 112, 136, 170, 250, 251, 252, 253, 259, 261, 262, 263
Ginn, Edwin, 214
Goldman, Emma, 19, 28, 85, 131
Gold Star Mothers, 197
Gompers, Samuel, 60, 70, 72, 75, 85, 90, 92, 96, 114-115, 116, 162, 258, 259
Gooding, Frank, 148
Goodrich, Herbert J., 263
Gore, Howard M., 142
Graham, George S., 86
Graham bill, 86, 89-94, 96
Grammar of Politics (Laski), 265
Grant, Percy Stickney, 87
Green, William, 114, 238
Greenbackism, 129
Green Corn Rebellion, 53
Grimke, Archwood H., 97
Gulick, Sidney L., 100
Guyer, John P., 146

Haddock, Sheriff, 73
Hague, Frank, 277
Haldeman, Harry M., 216
Hale, Ruth, 165
Hale, Swinburne, 90, 95, 252
Hamilton, Walton H., 263
Hammond, John Hays, 145
Hand, Learned, 251, 284
Hanson, Ole, 64, 65, 81
Hapgood, Powers, 164, 189
Hard, William, 93
Harding, Warren, 24
Harding, Warren G., 99, 101, 134, 135, 136, 137, 140, 141, 161
Hardwick, Thomas W., 65, 226
Hardyman, Hugh, 158
Hargreaves, Louis N., 155
Harlan County, Kentucky, 239-244
Hart, Albert Bushnell, 209

Hatfield, Sidney, 139, 140
Hayes, Ellen, 164
Haymarket Affair, 18
Haynes, William ("Red"), 159
Hays, Arthur Garfield, 131, 133, 141, 146, 156, 202, 221, 242, 243
Hays office, 103
Haywood, "Big Bill," 80
Healy, Timothy, 178
Hecht, Ben, 108
Henderson, Mrs. W. E., 192, 193
Herrin massacre, 147
Hill, Joe, 53
Hillman, Sidney, 115, 116
History, American, theory and practice of free speech in, 11-22
Hitler, Adolf, 280, 281
Hodgdon, George N., 46-47
Hoey, Clyde, 227
Holmes, John Haynes, 118, 126, 156, 199
Holmes, Oliver Wendell, 9, 10, 80, 86, 97, 103, 107, 112, 222, 249 250, 252, 255, 260, 267, 279, 285
Holt, Arthur, 145
Homiletic Review, 64
Hook, Sidney, 242
Hooker, Elon H., 191, 194-195
Hooker Electro-Chemical Company, 191
Hoover, Herbert, 167, 184, 220-221, 238, 246, 265, 266
Hoover, J. Edgar, 68, 69, 79, 141, 188
Hopkins, Archibald, 184
Hopkins, Ernest J., 159
Hopkins, Prince, 158
Horne, Charles F., 211
House Committee on Un-American Activities, 281-283, 285
Howard, Sidney, 178
Huddleston, George, 89, 90, 252

Hughes, Charles Evans, 88, 89, 97, 98, 103, 104, 184, 221, 252, 265-266, 267, 269, 270, 271, 278
Hunt, George W. P., 48
Hunter, E. H., 199, 201, 206, 215, 232
Huntington, Katherine, 164
Hurst, Fannie, 148
Husted, James W., 90-91
Hutchins, Robert M., 263
Hynes, Will F., 232

Idaho, 82
criminal syndicalism law (1917), 41-42
"Illegal Practices of the United States Department of Justice," 95-96
Illinois, 80-82, 251
Illinois Public Welfare and Public Utility Educational Service, 212
Illinois Sedition Act (1919), 80, 81
Immigration, 29-30, 211
Immigration Bureau, 83
Independent, 85
Indiana, 52
Industrial Defense Association, 199
Industrial Workers of the World (IWW), 20, 21, 22, 24, 27, 29, 31, 34, 41, 42, 44, 45, 48, 49, 50, 51, 53, 54, 55, 63, 64, 66, 71, 73, 78, 79, 81, 82, 91, 95, 97, 108, 116, 149-151, 156-159, 206, 240, 253
decline of the, 180
opposition of farm organizations to activities of the, 127
Ingersoll, Robert, 16
Injunctions, 237-238
Insull, Samuel, 212, 229

Interchurch World Movement, 74, 205
International Labor Defense, 155, 225, 241, 242, 245
International Ladies Garment Workers, 115
Inter-Racial Council, 212
Iowa, 52
sedition law (1917), 41
Iverson, Peter, 45, 47

Jackson, Andrew, 15
"Jacksonville Agreement," 147
Jefferson, Thomas, 246, 265
Jehovah's Witnesses, 276
Jerome, Arizona, 48
Jesus Christ, 32
Jews, 113, 126, 182, 281
Johns, E. B., 207
Johnson, Arnold, 241
Johnson, Hiram, 50
Johnson, James Weldon, 129
Johnson, William H., 60
Joint Committee for Passaic Defense and Free Speech, 155
Jones, David Crockett, 241
Jones, Mother, 54, 59
Jones, Richard, 42
Jordan, David Starr, 97, 127, 199, 253
Judaism, 126
Jung, Harry A., 174, 207, 215, 232, 281
Justice Department, U.S., 68, 77, 78, 79, 83, 84, 85, 87, 90, 93, 95, 99, 115, 136, 137, 141, 145, 187, 188, 189, 191, 195, 205, 251, 277, 280, 283

Kalisch, Samuel, 152
Kane, Francis Fisher, 87, 90, 92, 95, 97, 252
Kansas, 54-55, 82, 162-163
Kansas Anti-Bolshevik Campaign, 55

Kansas Federation of Labor, 55
Karolyi, Count, 264
Keeney, Frank, 141
Kehoe, William H., 50
Keller, Oscar E., 161
Kellog, Paul U., 87
Kennedy, John F., commencement
  address (Yale, 1962), 3
Kent, Frank R., 175
Kentucky, 56, 239-244
Kenyon, William S., 141
Key Men of America, 198
Kimbrough, Hunter, 158
King, William, 54, 67, 225
King Bill, 67, 68, 94
Kirchway, George, 254
Kropotkin, Peter, 18
Ku Klux Klan, 17, 29, 107, 113,
  130, 151, 152, 164, 165, 172,
  173, 174, 182, 196, 199, 202,
  203, 205, 215, 216

Labor, 59-66, 69-73, 92, 114-118,
  124, 138, 172, 180, 223
Labor (periodical), 258
Labor Defense and Free Speech
  Council of Western Pennsyl-
  vania, 142
Labor Defense Council, 146
Labor Department, U.S., 83, 139,
  274
La Follette, Robert M., 155, 252,
  259
La Follette, Robert M., Jr., 266
La Follette Committee, 244, 275,
  277, 282
"LaFollettism," 206
LaGuardia, Fiorella H., 147, 237
Laissez-faire policy, 7, 17, 25, 26,
  119, 189
Landis, James M., 262
Landis, Kenesaw Mountain, 96
Lane, Franklin D., 60
Lane, Winthrop D., 145
Langtry, Albert P., 34

Larkin, "Big Jim," 79, 136, 137,
  170
Larkin Amnesty Committee, 136
Laski, Harold, 8, 265
Lawrence, D. H., on freedom, 16
Lawrence, Massachusetts, textile
  strike in, 65
Leach, Mrs. Agnes Brown, 168
League for Constitutional Gov-
  ernment, 281
League for Industrial Democracy,
  145, 155, 169
League of Nations, 25
League of Women Voters, 192,
  193
Left-Wing Manifesto, 80
Legal meaning of freedom of
  speech, 248-272
Lenroot, Senator, 60
Leopold-Loeb thrill-killing case,
  112
Lerner, Max, 235
Le Seuer, Arthur, 60, 118, 127
Let the Pee-pul Rule, 207
Level Club (New York City), 202
Lever Act, 75
Levy, Harry, 205
Lewis, John L., 75, 116, 144, 146,
  147, 148
Lewis, Sinclair, 108, 206
Libby, Frederick J., 193, 194, 198,
  204, 214, 215, 216
Libel, seditious, 13
Liberty, Laski, Harold, quoted
  on, 8
Liberty (Martin), 177
Liberty League, 281
Lillie, Mrs. Robert C., 168
Lindsey, Ben, 151, 194
Lippmann, Walter, 110-112, 175,
  254, 264
Lister, Ernest P., 45, 46
Literacy tests, 29
Literary Digest, 92, 134, 370
Littleton, Martin, 232

Lloyd, William Bross, 81, 250, 251
Loeb-Leopold case, 112
Loray Mill (Gastonia, N. C.), 224-226, 228
Los Angeles Times, 49, 75
"Lost generation," 107-110
Louisville Courier-Journal, 56
Lowenthal, Max, 69
Loyalty League, 48
Loyalty oaths, 208
Ludlow massacres (Colorado), 51
Lusk, Senator, 136
Lusk Committee, 79, 89, 91
Lusk Laws, 39
Lusk Report, 175, 198, 222
Lynching, 129, 170
Lysle, Mayor (McKeesport, Pa.), 72

Macfarland, Charles S., 199, 201
Macfarland, Mrs. Mary P., 201
MacMurtrie sisters, 168
Madison, James, 13, 118, 270
Magnes, Judah, 126
Making Socialists Out of College Students (Clum), 206-207
Malone, Dudley Field, 243
Manly, Basil M., 60, 63
Mansfield, W. D., 149
Manville-Jenckes Company, 224
Marion Manufacturing Company, 227
Marsh, Benjamin C., 96
Marshall, Louis, 88, 126, 252
Martin, Everett Dean, 175, 177
Marvin, Fred R., 174, 193, 198, 201, 205, 206, 215, 216, 220, 221, 222, 235, 281
Marx, Groucho, 20
Mason, George, 12
Massachusetts, 165
Massachusetts Public Interest League, 200, 207
Matawan Massacre, 139

Maurer, James H., 143
Maxwell, Mrs. Lucia R., 192
May, Thomas E., 270
McAvoy, John V., 66
McCarthy, Joseph, 285
McConnell, Francis J., 199, 205
McCormick, Robert, 245
McKinley, William, assassination of, 18
McLeod, Clarence, 196
McNary-Haugen movement, 129
McReynolds, James, 246, 255, 267, 268
Mead, Lucia Ames, 204
Meiklejohn, Alexander, 233
Mellon interests, 144, 147, 148
Mencken, H. L., 105-109, 113, 164, 175, 216, 235, 259
Methodist Federation for Social Service, 207
Methodist Social Service Bulletin, 84
Michigan, 52, 186
Michigan Manufacturers Association, 52
Military Intelligence Association of Chicago, 202
Mill, John Stuart, 246
Millay, Edna St. Vincent, 164
Miller, Nathan L., 99
Mills, Ogden L., 88, 103
Milton, George Fort, 223
Milwaukee Leader, 232
Ministers Astray, 207
Minnesota, 82, 244, 245-246
    criminal-syndicalism legislation, 42
Minor, Robert, 235
Missouri, 251
Mitchell, Broadus, 243
Mitchell, William D., 239
Montana, 83, 251
    criminal syndicalism legislation, 42, 43-44
Montana State Federation, 44

Mooney, Tom, 65, 108
Mooney-Billings case, 49
Moore, John D., 91
Moore, Underhill, 263
Morgan, Ephriam, 140, 141
Mormons, 15, 16
Morrow, Edwin P., 56
Morrow, J. D. A., 147
Most, Johann, 18
Mount Rushmore, 113
Movie industry, censorship of, 103
Muckrakers, 19
Murphy, Frank, 277, 287
Muste, A. F., 65, 190
Muzzey, David S., 209
"My country, right or wrong," 22

Nation, 85, 166, 202, 209
National Americanization Committee, 212
National Association for the Advancement of Colored People (NAACP), 92, 168
National Catholic Welfare Council, 206
National Child Labor Committee, 183
National Civic Federation, 27, 28, 63, 136, 172, 178-179, 186, 191, 209, 211, 214, 238
National Civil Liberties Bureau, 40, 53, 67, 68, 85, 89, 115, 117, 123
National Committee for the Defense of Political Prisoners, 241
National Congress of Mothers and Parent-Teachers Associations, 192
National Council for the Prevention of War, 190, 191, 193
National Defense Committee, 197, 198
National Defense Society, 63

National Education Association, 212, 217
National Electric Light Association, 212
National Farmers' Union, 192
National Federation of Business and Professional Women, 192
National Guard, 143, 223, 224, 240
National Industrial Conference (1919), 62
National Industrial Conference Board, 153
National Industrial Recovery Act, 228
National Labor Relations Board, 275
National Miners Union, 240, 244
National Municipal League (Rochester, N.Y.), 59
National Origins Act (1924), 220
National Pan-Hellenic Congress, 209
National Popular Government League, 60, 63, 90, 92, 95
National Republic, The, 171, 206, 209, 212, 221
National Security League, 29, 130, 210, 211, 212, 232
National Student Forum, 195
National Student League, 242
National Textile Workers Union, 223-224
National War Labor Board, 63, 70, 71
National Women's Trade Union League, 192
Naturalization, Bureau of, 212
Naturalization Act (1906), 222
Nearing, Scott, 127
Near v. Minnesota, 244, 245-246, 269, 271
Nebraska, 53
Negroes, 129, 287
Neilson, William A., 199, 215

Nelles, Walter, 39, 252, 263
Nelson, John E., 233
Nelson, Knute, 84
Nevada, 47-48, 83
Newark Evening News, 153
New Deal, 244, 274, 275, 278, 281
New Era Magazine, 64
New Jersey, 83, 138, 151-156
New Mexico, 83
New Republic, 85, 95, 110, 166, 209
Newton, Charles D., 91
New York American, 93
New York Bar Association, 235
New York Central Trades and Labor Council, 160
New York City Chamber of Commerce, 235
New York Commercial, 193, 206
New York Evening Post, 233
New York Globe, 93, 160
New York Herald Tribune, 154
New York League of Women Voters, 160
New York State, 41
New York State Bar Association, 88, 89
New York Supreme Court, 80, 251
New York Times, 67, 77, 93, 136, 153, 273, 280
New York World, 36, 66, 85, 86, 90, 154, 160, 165-166, 187, 200, 233, 264
Neylan, John Francis, 253, 279
Niebuhr, Reinhold, 205, 243
Nimmo, George P., 154, 155, 156
Non-Partisan League, 22, 29, 31, 43, 55, 57, 180, 251
Nonsensesorship (Towne), 108
Norris, George, 60, 237, 238, 259, 266
Norris-LaGuardia Act (1932), 236-239
North Carolina, 223-224

North Dakota, 57, 251
Norton, Thomas J., 210
Nunn, William L., 148

Oaks, Louis D., 157, 159
O'Brian, John Lord, 88, 97-98, 134, 252
Ohio, 53
Ohio State Federation of Labor, 61
Oklahoma, 53
Oklahoma Leader, 53
O'Leary, Jeremiah A., 136
Olney, Warren, 253
Omaha World-Herald, 53
O'Neill, Eugene, 206
Open Forum, The, 159
Open-Forum National Council, 60
Open shop, 41, 49, 115, 147, 156, 172, 206
Oppenheim, Benjamin W., 42
Oregon, 54
Otis, Harrison Grey, 49
Our Charter of Liberty: What It Means to Every American (pamphlet), 210
Our Freedoms, 277
Our Threatened Heritage (pamphlet), 201
Over the Tea Cups, 207
Overman, Lee S., 39, 40
Overman bill, 40, 66, 84
Owen, Robert Dale, 14
Owens, Arvid, 81
Owens, Edgar, 81

Pacifism, 34, 189-215, 222
Page, Kirby, 32, 190
Palmer, A. Mitchell, 7, 51, 56, 67, 68, 69, 75, 78, 84, 85, 87, 90, 91, 92, 93, 100, 102, 134, 139
Parker, Alton B., 27
Parker, Dorothy, 164
Parker, John I., 266
Parsons, Edward L., 253

Pastors, Politicians, Pacifists, 207
Patches (magazine), 207
Patriotism, 23, 34, 35, 69, 179, 182, 210, 211, 218
Patterson, Giles J., quoted, 11
"Pax Special," 196-197 .
Peaceful Revolutionist (newspaper), 14
Pennsylvania, 46, 71-73, 138, 142-149
Pennsylvania Railroad, 144
Pennsylvania's Cossacks and the State Police, 146
Pennsylvania State Constabulary, 143, 146
Pennsylvania State Federation of Labor, 74, 143
Peonage, 129
Pepper, George Wharton, 137, 237
Philistinism, 105, 107
Pierce, Bessie L., 210
Pinchot, Gifford, 144, 145, 146, 149
Pittsburgh, Pennsylvania, 71-74
Pittsburgh Coal Company, 147, 148
Plumb Plan, 65
Plummer, C. R., 157
Police Power, The (Freund), 249
Political prisoners, 134, 206, 214
Pollak, Walter H., 221, 261, 262, 263, 269
Pomeroy, Vivian T., 200
Portland (Maine) *News,* 234
Post, Louis F., 38, 60, 61
Pound, Cuthbert, 251, 252
Pound, Roscoe, 95, 199, 262, 270
Powell, Garland W., 204
Powell, Thomas Reed, 105, 112, 262, 264
Practice of free speech, 11-12
Preparedness versus Pacifism (pamphlet), 203
Presbyterian, 64

Press, freedom of the, 7, 15, 20, 39, 40, 45, 68, 84, 86, 93, 126, 137, 166, 246
Professors Astray, 207
Progressivism, 18-19, 20, 25, 31, 110
Prohibition, 25, 103, 108, 181
Propaganda, 176-177
Property, 26
civil rights and, 14-15, 31
Webster, Daniel, quoted on, 14
Protestantism, 94
Protocols of the Elders of Zion, 199
Pulitzer, Ralph, 165
Puritanism, 105, 107

Radicalism, 18, 34, 35, 36
curtailment of, 39, 41, 46, 52, 54, 68-69
farmer, 129
Radin, Max, 253, 263, 264
Railroad Brotherhoods, 115
Railway Labor Board, 159
Railway Review, The, 161
Ralston, Jackson, 90, 92, 95
Randall, John H., Jr., 242
Rand School of Social Science, 66, 67, 169
Rangers, 149-150
Reavis, Rank, 91
Redfield, William C., 178
Reds in America, The, 195, 206
Reed, John, 81
Register, The, 151
Reid, D. P., 45
Religious Society of Friends, 92, 96
Remington, Franklin, 194
Reserve Officer's Association, 191, 196
Richberg, Donald, 238, 258
Roberts, Owen J., 266, 267, 278
Robins, Raymond, 40

Robinson, James Harvey, 175, 206
Robinson, Joseph T., 161
Robinson, Mrs. Margaret, 200
Rockefeller, John D., 147
Rockefeller, John D., Jr., 60
Rocky Mountain Fuel Company, 150
Roe, Gilbert E., 19, 24
Roosevelt, Franklin D., 195, 241, 274, 276, 278, 279-284
Roosevelt, Theodore, 194
Root, E. Talmadge, 199, 200
Root, Elihu, 231
Ross, Edward A., 126, 127, 209
Ross, J. W., 163
Rowell, Chester, 253
Ruthenberg, Charles, 79, 80
Rutledge, Wiley, 284
Ryan, John A., 126, 145, 205, 233
Ryberg, C. E., 42

Sablich, "Flaming Milka," 150
Sabotage, 47, 55
Sacco, Nicola, 99, 108, 112, 150, 164, 165, 170, 216, 264
St. Louis Post Dispatch, 93, 153
Salt Lake Tribune, 65
Sampson, Flem D., 240
Sanders, G. V., 163
Sanford, Justice, 252, 266
Sanger, Margaret, 19, 164, 165, 203
"Save the Union" campaign, 147
Sayre, John Nevin, 126
Scabbard & Blade, 200
Scherf, Louis N., 150
Schlesinger, Arthur M., 202
Schroeder, Theodore, 19, 20, 31-32
Schwab, Charles M., 60
Schwimmer, Rosika, 202, 221-222
Scopes' "Monkey" trial, 112, 132, 163
Seattle general strike (1919), 46, 63, 64, 81

Seattle Post-Intelligencer, 45-46
Security, 22
   quest for, through free speech, 171-183
Sedition, 41-58, 67
Sedition Act (1918), 22, 248
   repeal of, 99
Seditious libel, 13
Sentinels of the Republic, 212
Shakers, 16
Shank, John, 52
Shaw, George Bernard, 87, 206
Sheppard-Towner Maternity Act, 198
Shipstead, Henrik, 238
Shoup, Oliver H., 51
Silver, Abba Hillel, 205
Silvershirts, 281
Sinclair, Upton, 109, 157-158, 209
Slavery, freedom of expression and, 15
Small, Governor (Illinois), 136, 251
Smith, Alfred E., 67, 80, 99, 136, 137
Smith, LeRoy F., 207, 208
Smith, Walter B., 242
Smith Act, 280, 283, 284
Socialist party, 31, 79-80, 87, 180
Socialist Workers party, 280
Socialists, 20, 22, 24, 29, 55, 66, 79, 87, 91, 92, 97, 115, 116-117, 136, 190, 251
Social Justice, 280
Sommer, Frank H., 263
Sons of Liberty, 12
Sons of the American Revolution, 179
Sosnowski, John B., 173
South Carolina, 223, 227
South Dakota, criminal-syndicalism legislation, 42, 44
Spafford, Edward, 204, 215
Spider Web Chart, 192, 193, 196, 198, 232

Spivak, John L., 138, 139
Sprading, Charles T., 34
Springfield Republican, 93
Stearns, Harold, 108
Steele, Walter S., 232
Steel strike (1919), 69-74
Steffens, Lincoln, 19
Stephens, William D., 50
Sterling, Thomas, 68
Sterling bill, 84, 85, 93, 96
Stevenson, Archibald, 39-40, 66, 136, 210
Stewart, Samuel V., 43
Stokes, Rose Pastor, 80
Stone, Harlan Fiske, 80, 188, 194, 196, 260, 262, 267, 278, 279
Stone, Kimbrough, 251
Stone, Warren S., 178
Story of Our American People, The (Horne), 211
Stromberg, Yetta, 245, 269
Stromberg v. *California,* 244, 245
Straight, Mrs. Willard, 168
Strand, Ernest G., 42
Suffrage, woman, 25
Sunday, Billy, 95
Suppression, instruments of, creating the, 38-58
Supreme Court, 80, 172, 210, 222-223, 249-272, 279, 284-285
   freedom of expression and the, 5, 7-8
   Near v. *Minnesota,* 244, 245-246
   Stromberg v. *California,* 244, 245-246
Survey, 72, 85, 160
Sutherland, George, 255, 267, 268
Sweet, Thaddeus C., 87
Syndicalism, criminal, 39, 41-58, 67

Taft, Charles P., 277
Taft, Clinton J., 159
Taft, Henry W., 252

Taft, William Howard, 25, 60, 178, 199, 214, 254-256, 258, 259, 260, 265
Taft-Hartley Act, 283
Taub, Allen, 242
Tennessee, 223
Textbooks, 41, 209, 210, 212
Theory of free speech, 11-22
Thomas, Norman, 155, 220, 235
Thompson, "Big Bill," 203
Thompson, Dorothy, 108
Thurman, Arnold, 263
Tocqueville, Alexis de, quoted, 58
Tönnies, Ferdinand, 6
Topeka Daily Capital, 55
Topeka Daily State, 56
Towne, Charles Hanson, 108
Tracey, John M., 151, 152
Treatise (Cooley), 249, 250
Trilling, Lionel, 242
Tucker, Benjamin, 19
Tugwell, Rexford G., 235
Tulsa (Oklahoma) Daily World, 23
Tumulty, Joseph, 35
Twain, Mark, on freedom of expression, 15

"Un-Americanism," 39-40, 54, 115, 118, 177
Union League Club, 66
Union of Russian Workers, 78-79
Union Theological Seminary, 205
United Front Textile Committee, 153
United Mine Workers, 51, 54, 75, 138-142, 147, 150, 240
United Nations, 280
United States Coal Commission, 144
United States Patriotic Society, 216
United States Steel Corporation, 69, 70
Untermyer, Samuel, 155

Utah, 53-54

Vanzetti, Bartolomeo, 99, 108, 112, 150, 164, 165, 170, 216, 264
Vare interests, 144
Vigilantism, 28, 215, 216
Villard, Oswald Garrison, 118, 134
Vinson, Fred, 284, 285

Wagner Act, 275
Wakefield, Mrs. Jesse, 241
Walker, Jimmy, 234-235
Walker, Mrs. William Sherman, 197, 198, 201
Walsh, Frank P., 95, 186, 252
Walsh, Thomas J., 258
War: Its Causes, Consequences and Cure (Page), 190
Ward, Harry, 126, 207
War Department, U.S., 191, 192
War on Colorado Miners, The (pamphlet), 151
Warren, Charles, 265
Warren, Josiah, 14
Washington (state), 82
    criminal-syndicalism legislation, 44-47
Washington Post, 65
Watch-and-Ward Societies, 107
Webster, Daniel, on property, 14
Weeks, Bartow S., 80
Weeks, John W., 192, 193, 194
Weisbord, Albert, 153, 155, 156
Weiss, Carol, 243
Welch, Francis Ralston, 232
Wells, H. G., 206
West, George P., 50
West, Willis M., 209
Western Federation of Miners, 41, 43, 48
West Virginia, 54, 138-142
West Virginia Federationist, The, 140

WEVD (radio station), 169
Whalen, Grover, 234-236
What Do You Mean—Free Speech? (Pamphlet), 241
Wheeler, Burton K., 43
White, William Allen, 162-163, 176, 199, 202, 214
Whitehead, Alfred North, 3
Whitney, Charlotte Anita, 49-50, 82, 156, 170, 250, 253, 259, 264
Whitney, R. M., 193, 194-195, 198, 205, 206, 211, 218
Wickersham, George W., 88
Wickersham Commission, 159, 236, 265
Wiggins, Mrs. Ella May, 226
Wilkerson, James H., 159-160, 266
Williams, Albert Rhys, 40
Williams, Roger, 246
Williams, Talcott, 209
Wilson, Edmund, 109, 235
Wilson, William B., 72
Wilson, Woodrow, 24, 62, 81, 84, 99, 135, 139, 140
    labor and, 72, 75
    World War I and, 21, 27
Winitsky, Harry, 79, 80
Wisconsin, 57
Wise, John, 246
Wise, Stephen, 126, 199, 205, 233
"Witch-hunting," 21
Wobblies, *see* Industrial Workers of the World
Woll, Matthew, 114, 232
Woltman, Frederick, 148, 139
Woman Patriot, The, 193, 194, 198, 200
Woman suffrage, 25
Women's Christian Temperance Union, 192
Women's International League for Peace and Freedom, 190, 195-196, 198

Women's Patriotic Conference on National Defense, 197
Wood, Leonard, 52
Wood, Will C., 209
Woollcott, Alexander, 108
Woolley, Mary E., 199, 215
Workers' Party, 145, 253
Working Class Union (Oklahoma), 53
World Alliance for International Friendship Through the Churches, 190, 199
World Peace Foundation, 190, 214
World Tomorrow (magazine), 35

World War I, freedom of expression during, 4, 21-22
Wright, Frances, 14
Wright, Frank Lloyd, 113, 114

YMCA, 214
Young, Art, 78
Young, C. C., 49
Young Republicans, 87
Youth Movement in America, The, 195
YWCA, 192, 197, 206

Zechariah, Chafee, 77, 90, 95, 96, 97
Zober, Richard O., 154, 155

About the Author

PAUL L. MURPHY is Professor of History and American Studies at the University of Minnesota. He earned his B.A. at the College of Idaho and his M.A. and Ph.D. from the University of California, Berkeley. Professor Murphy has been on the History faculty of Colorado State University, Ohio State University, Northwestern University, the University of Colorado, and Stanford University. A former Guggenheim Fellow, he is currently Visiting Fulbright Lecturer at the University of Lagos, Nigeria (1971-1972).

Professor Murphy has published articles in scholarly journals and is the author of several books. His most recent book, *The Constitution in Crisis Times, 1918-1969* (1972) was a selection of the Lawyers Literary Club. [2CR]

The Meaning of Freedom of Speech was composed in linotype Caledonia with Caslon Bold display type by The Maple Press Company, York, Pennsylvania. The entire book was printed by offset lithography by LithoCrafters, Inc., Ann Arbor, Michigan.